THE AUTUMN OF THE MIDDLE AGES

JOHAN HUIZINGA

THE AUTUMN
OF THE
MIDDLE AGES

Translated by Rodney J. Payton
and
Ulrich Mammitzsch

THE UNIVERSITY OF CHICAGO PRESS

JOHAN HUIZINGA, born in 1872, became professor of history at the University of Leiden in 1915 and taught there until 1942, when the Nazis closed the university and held him hostage until shortly before his death in 1945. His other books include *Erasmus and the Age of Reformation, Homo Ludens: A Study of the Play Element in Culture,* and *Men and Ideas: History, the Middle Ages, the Renaissance.*

RODNEY PAYTON is professor of Liberal Studies at Western Washington University. He is the author of *A Modern Reader's Guide to Dante's Inferno.* ULRICH MAMMITZSCH (d. 1990) was professor of Liberal Studies at Western Washington University. He is the author of *Evolution of the Garbhadhatu Mandala* and the translator of Dietrich Seckel's *The Buddhist Art of East Asia.*

The University of Chicago Press, Chicago 60637
©1996 by The University of Chicago
All rights reserved. Published 1996
Printed in the United States of America
04 03 02 01 00 99 98 97 96   1 2 3 4 5

ISBN: 0-226-35992-1 (cloth)

This translation is based on the 1921 edition of *Herfsttij der Middeleeuwen.*

Library of Congress Cataloging-in-Publication Data

Huizinga, Johan, 1872–1945.
   [Herfsttij der Middeleeuwen.   English]
   The autumn of the Middle Ages / Johan Huizinga ; translated by
Rodney J. Payton and Ulrich Mammitzsch.
      p.   cm.
   Includes bibliographical references and index.
   1. France—Civilization—1328–1600.   2. Netherlands—
Civilization.   3. Civilization, Medieval.   I. Title.
DC33.2.H83   1996
944'.025—dc20   95-613
                                                                CIP

♾The paper used in this publication meets the minimum requirements of the American National Standard for Information Sciences— Permanence of Paper for Printed Library Materials, ANSI Z39.48-1984.

PIÆ VXORIS ANIMÆ

M. V. H. - S.

CONTENTS

ILLUSTRATIONS FOLLOW PAGE 298

TRANSLATOR'S INTRODUCTION

THE IDEA OF THIS TRANSLATION HAD ITS MOMENT of conception in Karl J. Weintraub's class in History of Culture at the University of Chicago (now more than twenty years ago) when Weintraub commented, with some heat, on the deficiencies of the English translation of *Herfsttij der Middeleeuwen* that we students were using when it was compared to the elegance of the Dutch edition he had on the lectern. The tiny margins of my crumbling paperback are filled with all my efforts to get down the corrections. When I began my own teaching of Huizinga's text, which I had come to treasure, those illegible notes suggested that what I was professing fell far short and an examination of the original showed me that Weintraub's observations were justified. Yet, in spite of the shortcomings of the translation, my students always responded well to Huizinga. Later Professor Weintraub commented to me that it was an indication of the power of its subject and style that Huizinga's book commonly captivated readers in spite of the "very inferior, crippled version"[1] in which it appeared in English.

Therefore when my colleague Ulrich Mammitzsch, now deceased, and I agreed to attempt a new translation there was a certain feeling of being the rescuers of something fine that had been corrupted and undervalued. However, this feeling was somewhat challenged by the fact that Huizinga not only authorized the English translation, but also apparently collaborated with Fritz Hopman in producing it as a variant version of the book. He specifically approved the results in the preface he wrote for the translation.

> This English edition is not a simple translation of the original Dutch (second edition 1921, first 1919), but the result of a work of adaptation, reduction and consolidation under the author's direction. The references, here left out, may be found in full in the original. . . .

> The author wishes to express his sincere thanks to . . .
> Mr. F. Hopman, of Leiden, whose clear insight into the exi-
> gencies of translation rendered the recasting possible, and
> whose endless patience with the wishes of an exacting
> author made the difficult task a work of friendly co-
> operation.[2]

Even given this endorsement by the author, I think that any
studious reader of both the Dutch (or the very accurate German
translation) and the English would conclude that the original is a
much better book. The original is nearly one-third longer and has
many more citations of original material. In the Hopman translation, blocks of text are inexplicably moved around, and sometimes
Hopman's usually good English fails him as when he translates
"mystiek en détail" as "mysticism by retail." It seems that Huizinga ultimately must have thought the original better, as none of
the "adaptation, reduction and consolidation" found its way into
subsequent Dutch printings or foreign translations of the book with
the exception of the revised arrangement of chapters.

The route by which Huizinga arrived at the Hopman translation
can be traced in the *Briefwisseling* (*Correspondence*), if not, entirely,
his motivation for taking it.[3] Huizinga had begun negotiations with
the French publisher Edouard Champion of Paris, who preferred
a shortened version of the book and without the references. This
project fell through, owing to disagreements over the rights of
publication of the French edition in Holland in 1923 (letter 457),
and Huizinga was left with the condensed, but unpublished, French
manuscript. (An accurate French edition was eventually published
by the firm of Payot in 1932, in a translation by Julia Bastin [letter
559].) In 1923, Huizinga was also negotiating with Edward Arnold
and Company about an English edition, and, owing to the fact
that Arnold had no one in their office who could read Dutch, they
reviewed it in the condensed French version. Sir Rennell Rodd, a diplomat, poet, and historian, and Arnold's reviewer, thought the original form of the book would sell only to scholars and preferred it in
its French form, which he thought might have a popular audience
(letter 462) and, although Huizinga protested, he did not do so very
strongly (letter 466). An abridgment on the lines of the French manuscript was ultimately ageed upon (letters 472 and 477) and the Hopman version, called *The Waning of the Middle Ages,* is the result.

All this was taking place while the final arrangements for the German edition were being set. The German edition is precise in all particulars, but the fourteen original Dutch chapters are broken up into twenty-three, which are more even in length. This was Huizinga's own idea, evidently incorporated in the unpublished French translation and eventually carried forward in the English as well (letter 470).

Thus Huizinga clearly preferred a complete translation of *Herfsttij,* although he did think the chapter divisions could be improved. His quarrel with Champion over distribution rights, however, suggests that remuneration was an important issue, as he raised practically no objections to the condensation ultimately produced by Hopman for Arnold and Company. It is possible, too, given that the prospect of a wide market for the book might have had something to do with his thinking, that in obtaining an English edition Huizinga was also looking forward to the American market. Huizinga wrote two books about America, both gently critical.[4] Like his contemporary Freud, Huizinga thought American life to suffer from its lack of social forms; he considered Americans to be materialistic and far, far too hasty in the pursuit of their affairs. He invented a motto for America, "This Here, and Soon," to characterize this haste, which, he thought, all too often, led to superficiality. Perhaps this perception caused him to believe that a simplified and less allusive *Autumn* might succeed best in the American market. The fourteen uneven Dutch chapters became the twenty-three short chapters as in the German edition, much more suitable for daily classroom assignments and for a people with a short attention span. The work of preparing the English translation was given to Fritz Hopman, a student of English literature and journalist, who at one time was chairman of the Maatschappij der Nederlandse Letterkunde (Dutch Literature Society). He was in financial difficulties in 1924, and Huizinga was probably glad to be able to provide him with work.[5]

F. W. N. Hugenholtz's study of the history of the text, *The Fame of a Masterwork,*[6] shows that the first recognition of the book's importance came, not from Huizinga's Dutch colleagues, but in German reviews. The Dutch were inclined to consider *The Autumn of the Middle Ages*[7] far too literary for serious history and mistakenly thought its approach to be old-fashioned rather than realizing that it was truly a revolutionary innovation. *Autumn* was Huizinga's first major work published after he became professor of history at

Leiden, and Leiden was not at that time Holland's "first" university, nor was Huizinga the most famous professor of history. Defensive, in the face of native criticism of the work he might, indeed, have considered the English translation a step to a further revision (the second Dutch edition had appeared in 1921, the Hopman translation came out in 1924). It seems to me, that much of what is left out of the Hopman version are elements which contribute to the "literary," that is to say aesthetic character of the book and this might be a direct response to his Dutch critics.

There is another possible reason for the truncated English version. Probably anyone who reads *Autumn* will notice that it reveals a great deal of the private side of Huizinga himself. In it, the reader sees not only Huizinga's opinions and strong convictions, but glimpses his passions and, I think, his spiritual side as well. Perhaps he realized this and the drawing back so apparent in the original English is an instinctive reaction that he also exhibited in other circumstances.

In his brief autobiography written at the very end of his life[8] Huizinga reveals that he consistently hid his true self even from his colleagues and students. "It is not false modesty when I say that, though I have been known as an early riser since childhood, I never rose quite as early as people believed." The relationship of his work to his private self was frequently misjudged by others. Huizinga almost seems pleased at their confusion.

> Regarding my biography of Erasmus, many people have
> expressed the view that here was a man after my own heart.
> As far as I can tell, nothing could be farther from the truth
> for, much though I admire Erasmus, he inspires me with lit-
> tle sympathy and, as soon as the work was done, I did my
> best to put him out of my mind. I remember a conversation
> in January 1932 with a German colleague who contended
> that *Erasmus* was much more my line of country than the
> *Waning of the Middle Ages* with which, he claimed, I must
> have struggled manfully. I thought about the matter for a
> moment and then I had to smile. In fact, my historical and
> literary studies never struck me as partaking of the nature of
> struggle in any way, nor any of my work as a great chal-
> lenge. Indeed, the whole idea of having to overcome enor-
> mous obstacles was as alien to me as having to compete in a

race, as alien as the spirit of competition whose importance in cultural life I myself have emphasized in my *Homo Ludens*.

When he finds himself on the edge of a deep personal revelation, Huizinga goes so far, and no further.

> . . . In September 1899, I was granted two weeks' extra leave, immediately after beginning of term, to attend the Congress of Orientalists in Rome. I went there with J. P. Vogel, who intended to go on to India, and with André Jolles with whom I had started a close friendship in the autumn of 1896. This friendship was to play a large part in my life for more than 35 years, until 9th October 1933 when it was abruptly cut short—and not by me. I could write a whole book on my relation with Jolles, so full is my mind of him and despite all that has happened—my heart as well.

Huizinga's later works do not reveal the personality of the author as much as *Autumn* does. A prominent sense of the author only again becomes apparent in his great moral essay of the thirties, *In the Shadow of Tomorrow*.[9]

Given Huizinga's importance to historiography, the fact that the English translation is a variant text has not been given enough attention. With the single exception of Weintraub, no one, to my knowledge, has pointed out the critical importance of that fact, even though the introduction might have served as a warning to a professionally critical discipline. Is it possible that English-speaking historians have been discussing this book with their foreign colleagues without realizing that they were reading a significantly different text? If this is so, it is a primary justification for the present translation.

Hopman's work does have the virtue of being graceful. He did have an excellent grasp of English vocabulary, and his rendition is sometimes lovely, but it is not literal and sometimes something more than a literal quality is missing. It is not proper for a translator in the second place to judge too harshly the work of a predecessor, but a reader deserves some indication why one translation should be preferred over another. The most glaring changes in the Hopman from the Dutch second edition are the many omissions of examples drawn from the (in most instances) medieval French sources that Huizinga cites in the original language (although there are a few instances where Hopman includes examples not in the Dutch edition). The present translators felt that the original divisions of the text much more clearly reflected the organization of Huizinga's argument in spite of their rather uneven lengths and Huizinga's second thoughts about the matter. Finally, the Hopman translation omits, as its introduction points out, the documentation. These alterations are restored in this translation.

Much more serious issues are those alterations by Hopman that tend to distort Huizinga's meaning. Hopman is sometimes prone to pull Huizinga's punches. For instance, one of the most significant elements in *Autumn* is its assertions about the proper use of sources, an issue addressed several times. Here is a representative passage in this translation:

> Daily life offered unlimited range for acts of flaming passion and childish imagination. Our medieval historians who prefer to rely as much as possible on official documents because the chronicles are unreliable fall thereby victim to an occasionally dangerous error. The documents tell us little about the difference in tone that separates us from those times; they let us forget the fervent pathos of medieval life. Of all the passions permeating medieval life with their color, only two are mentioned, as a rule by legal documents: greed and quarrelsomeness. Who has not frequently wondered about the nearly incredible violence and stubbornness with which greed, pugnacity, or vindictiveness rise to prominence in the court documents of that period! It is only in the general context of the passions which inflame every sphere of life that these tensions become acceptable and intelligible to us. This is why the authors of the chronicles, no matter how superficial they may be with respect to the actual facts and no matter how often they may err in reporting them, are indispensable if we want to understand that age correctly.

And here is the same passage in Hopman:

> A scientific historian of the Middle Ages, relying first and foremost on official documents, which rarely refer to the

passions, except violence and cupidity, occasionally runs the risk of neglecting the difference of tone between the life of the expiring Middle Ages and that of our own days. Such documents would sometimes make us forget the vehement pathos of medieval life, of which the chroniclers, however defective as to material facts, always keep us in mind.

Not only has Hopman made a strong statement weak, his version misses the nuance of just how passionate Huizinga was about the passions of the Middle Ages.

Similar distortions frequently occur. Here is Hopman's translation of a passage about the profane interest in such things as Mary's marital relationship with Joseph:

> This familiarity with sacred things is, on the one hand, a sign of deep and ingenuous faith; on the other, it entails irreverence whenever mental contact with the infinite fails. Curiosity, ingenuous though it be, leads to profanation.

Here is this translation:

> This fatuous familiarity with God in daily life has to be seen in two ways. On the one hand it testifies to the absolute stability and immediacy of faith, but where this familiarity becomes habitual, it increases the danger that the godless (who are always with us), but also the pious, in moments of insufficient religious tension, continuously profane faith more or less consciously and intentionally.

For the student interested in historiography itself, perhaps the omissions of theoretical statements are the most serious. In the famous discussion of the three routes to the beautiful life in the second chapter, Hopman omits this statement of serious interest to anyone concerned with Huizinga's definitions of culture and civilization and with the movement of his thinking towards the theoretical statement of *Homo Ludens*,[10] which defines the role of play in culture.

> The great divide in the perception of the beauty of life comes much more between the Renaissance and the Modern Period than between the Middle Ages and the Renaissance. The turnabout occurs at the point where art and life begin to diverge. It is the point where art begins to be no longer

in the midst of life, as a noble part of the joy of life itself, but outside of life as something to be highly venerated, as something to turn to in moments of edification or rest. The old dualism separating God and world has thus returned in another form, that of the separation of art and life. Now a line has been drawn right through the enjoyments offered by life. Henceforth they are separated into two halves—one lower, one higher. For medieval man they were all sinful without exception; now they are all considered permissible, but their ethical evaluation differs according to their greater or lesser degree of spirituality.

The things which can make life enjoyable remain the same. They are, now as before, reading, music, fine arts, travel, the enjoyment of nature, sports, fashion, social vanity (knightly orders, honorary offices, gatherings) and the intoxication of the senses. For the majority, the border between the higher and lower levels seems now to be located between the enjoyment of nature and sports. But this border is not firm. Most likely sport will sooner or later again be counted among the higher enjoyments—at least insofar as it is the art of physical strength and courage. For medieval man the border lay, in the best of cases, right after reading; the enjoyment of reading could only be sanctified through striving for virtue or wisdom. For music and the fine arts, it was their service to faith alone which was recognized as being good. Enjoyment *per se* was sinful. The Renaissance had managed to free itself from the rejection of all the joy of life as something sinful, but had not yet found a new way of separating the higher and lower enjoyments of life; the Renaissance wanted an unencumbered enjoyment of all of life. The new distinction is the result of the compromise between the Renaissance and Puritanism that is at the base of modern spiritual attitudes. It amounted to a mutual capitulation in which the one side insisted on saving beauty while the other insisted on the condemnation of sin. Strict Puritanism, just as did the Middle Ages, still condemned as basically sinful and worldly the entire sphere of the beautification of life with an exception being made in cases where such efforts assumed expressly religious forms and sanctified themselves through their use in the service of faith. Only after the Puritan worldview lost its intensity did the Renaissance receptiveness to all the joys of life gain ground again; perhaps even more ground than before because, beginning with the eighteenth century there is a tendency to regard the natural *per se* an element of the ethically good. Anyone attempting to draw the dividing line between the higher and lower enjoyment of life according to the dictates of ethical consciousness would no longer separate art from sensuous enjoyment, the enjoyment of nature from the cult of the body, the elevated from the natural, but would only separate egotism, lies, and vanity from purity.

There are many such issues to which we could point, not in the spirit of demeaning a translation that has served Huizinga well, but in the sense that having done its work and brought the importance of the mind of Huizinga to the attention of the English-speaking world, it is now obsolete and a more critical and deeper look at Huizinga requires access to a version of the work closer to that known by the rest of the world.

This translation was made from the second Dutch edition of 1921. Seen from the vantage point of the second edition, the first has a tentative character that Huizinga eliminated in his revision. Huizinga made further minor revisions in later editions, but the second represents his thinking at its most seminal stage. We compared our work carefully with the German translation of 1924, which, Huizinga notes, follows the second Dutch edition exactly. We have included not only the preface to the Dutch edition, but also the preface that Huizinga wrote for the German translation, for the insight it gives into the title and its comment on the question of translation itself. We have restored the documentation and added a few translators' notes to clarify Huizinga's references to things that might be common knowledge or self-evident to a Dutch reader but not necessarily so to others. This version also includes translations of the citations that Huizinga makes in the original languages. Such translations have become customary in later editions, although they do not appear in the Dutch original we followed. Our translations follow Hopman, but we have made several alterations according to our own judgment.

Ulrich Mammitzsch, my colleague and co-translator, was a noted specialist in Buddhist art and literature, but his formidable erudition extended to great works of all cultures and he was as pleased to discuss Schiller as he was his beloved mandalas. He felt a special affinity for Huizinga, who began his academic life as a student of Eastern culture, and who had a love of literature much like Ulrich's. Mostly, however, Ulrich's dedication to Huizinga was because they were alike in their high-mindedness. As Ulrich Mammitzsch fled the East Zone, not because of political theory, but because he found the Communists to be unethical, so Johan Huizinga was brought to denounce the Nazis from the first principles of civilized behavior. The two minds spoke to one another directly and I will never forget Ulrich's excitement as we read Huizinga's description of the tension in the life of medieval common people, strung between the church and the nobility—a tension which, Ulrich exclaimed, he had seen the last of as a child in rural Germany before the war. He read the book from the inside, so to speak, and I would like to attribute whatever virtues this translation has to his insightful sensitivity.

RODNEY J. PAYTON

PREFACE TO THE FIRST
AND SECOND DUTCH
EDITIONS

IN MOST INSTANCES IT IS THE ORIGIN OF THE NEW
that attracts the attention of the mind to the past. We want to know
how the new ideas and the forms of life that shine in their fullness
during later times came to be. We view past ages primarily in terms
of the promise they hold for those that follow. How eagerly the
Middle Ages have been scrutinized for evidence of the first sprouts
of modern culture, so eagerly that it sometimes must appear as if
the intellectual history of the Middle Ages was nothing but the
advent of the Renaissance. Did we not see everywhere in this age,
which was once regarded as rigid and dead, new growths that all
seemed to point to future perfection? Yet in our search for newly
arising life it is easily forgotten that in history, as in nature, the
processes of death and birth are eternally in step with one another.
Old forms of thought die out while, at the same time and on the
same soil, a new crop begins to bloom.

This book is an attempt to view the time around the fourteenth
and fifteenth centuries, not as announcing the Renaissance, but as
the end of the Middle Ages, as the age of medieval thought in its
last phase of life, as a tree with overripe fruits, fully unfolded and
developed. The luxuriant growth of old compelling forms over the
living core of thought, the drying and rigidifying of a previously
valid store of thought: this is the main content of the following
pages. In writing this text, my eye was trained on the depth of the
evening sky, a sky steeped blood red, desolate with threatening
leaden clouds, full of the false glow of copper. Looking back at
what I have written, the question arises whether, if my eye had
dwelt still longer on the evening sky, the turbid colors may yet
have dissolved into utter clarity. It also seems quite possible that
the image, now that I have given it contours and colors, may yet
have become more gloomy and less serene than I had perceived it

when I started my labors. It can easily happen to one who has his vision trained downward that what he perceives becomes too decrepit and wilted, that too much of the shadow of death has been allowed to fall upon his work.

The point of departure for this work was the attempt to better understand the work of the van Eycks and that of their successors and to understand it within the context of the entire life of that age. The Burgundian community was the frame of reference that I had in mind: it seemed possible to view this community as a civilization in its own right, just like the Italian community of the fourteenth century; the title of the work was first set as *The Century of Burgundy*. But as the scope of this civilization was viewed in a wider perspective, certain limitations had to be abandoned. Just to retain the notion of a postulated unity of Burgundian culture meant that non-Burgundian France had to be given at least as much attention. Thus the place of Burgundy was taken by the dual entities of France and the Netherlands and that in a very different way. While in viewing the dying medieval culture the Dutch element lags behind the French, there are areas where that element has its own significance: in the life of piety and that of art. These are given the opportunity to speak in greater detail.

There is no need to defend the crossing of the fixed geographic boundaries in the tenth chapter so as to call on, next to Ruusbroec and Denis the Carthusian, on Eckhardt, Suso, and Tauler as witnesses. How little my story is justified by the writings I have studied from the fourteenth and fifteenth centuries compared to all those I wanted to read. How much I would have liked to place, next to the evolution of the main types of the different intellectual traditions on which some of the notions of these figures are often based, yet still others. But if I relied among the historiographers on Froissart and Chastellain more than on others, among the poets on Eustache Deschamps, among the theologians on Jean de Gerson and Denis the Carthusian, among the painters on Jan van Eyck—so is this not only the result of the limitation of my material, but even more so the result of the richness of their works and the singularly keen way in which their expressions are the preeminent mirror of the spirit of their age.

It is the forms of life and thought that are used as evidence here. To capture the essential content that rests in the form: is this not the proper task of historical study?

PREFACE TO THE GERMAN TRANSLATION

THE NEED TO BETTER UNDERSTAND THE ART OF THE van Eyck brothers and that of their successors and to view these artists in the context of the life of their time provided the first impetus for this book. But a different, in many respects more comprehensive image emerged during the course of the investigation. It became evident that the fourteenth and fifteenth centuries in France and in the Netherlands in particular are much more suited to give us a sense of the end of the Middle Ages and of the last manifestation of medieval culture than they are to demonstrate to us the awakening Renaissance.

Our minds prefer to concern themselves with "origins" and "beginnings." In most instances the promise that ties one age to its successor appears to be more important than the memories that link it to its predecessor. As a result, the search to find the first sprouts of modern culture in medieval culture was carried out so eagerly and to the point that the term medieval period itself came to be questioned and it appeared as if this epoch was barely something other than the age that ushered in the Renaissance. But dying and becoming keep just as much pace with each other in history as in nature. To trace the vanishing of overripe cultural forms is not less significant—and by no means less fascinating—than to trace the arising of new forms. We do more justice, not only to artists like the van Eycks, but also to [poets such as] Eustache Deschamps, historiographers such as Froissart and Chastellain, theologians such as Jean de Gerson and Denis the Carthusian, and to all representatives of the spirit of this age if we view them not as initiating and heralding what is to come, but rather as completing the forms of an age in its final stage.

The author was, at the time he wrote this book, less aware than now of the danger of comparing historical periods to the seasons of the year; he asks therefore that the title of the book be taken only as a figure of speech that is intended to capture the general mood of the whole.

The translation follows exactly the second revised Dutch edition of 1921 (the first appeared in 1919). If the German tongue still tastes in places the flavor of the Dutch original, we should remind ourselves that a translation in the strict sense of the word is an impossibility even in so closely related languages such as German and Dutch. Why should we be so eager to obliterate fearfully the traces of what is foreign in that which is of foreign origin?

Many have supported this work of translation in a valuable way. We owe a debt of gratitude, next to the translator, primarily to our friends Prof. André Jolles (Leipzig), Prof. W. Vogelsang (Utrecht), and Paul Lehman (Munich). My sincere expression of thanks for his valuable contribution to this work go to Prof. Eugene Lerch, who took it upon himself to translate the French quotations found in the appended section.

Leiden
November 1923

Chapter One

THE PASSIONATE INTENSITY OF LIFE[1]

WHEN THE WORLD WAS HALF A THOUSAND YEARS younger all events had much sharper outlines than now. The distance between sadness and joy, between good and bad fortune, seemed to be much greater than for us; every experience had that degree of directness and absoluteness that joy and sadness still have in the mind of a child. Every event, every deed was defined in given and expressive forms and was in accord with the solemnity of a tight, invariable life style. The great events of human life—birth, marriage, death—by virtue of the sacraments, basked in the radiance of the divine mystery. But even the lesser events—a journey, labor, a visit—were accompanied by a multitude of blessings, ceremonies, sayings, and conventions.

There was less relief available for misfortune and for sickness; they came in a more fearful and more painful way. Sickness contrasted more strongly with health. The cutting cold and the dreaded darkness of winter were more concrete evils. Honor and wealth were enjoyed more fervently and greedily because they contrasted still more than now with lamentable poverty. A fur-lined robe of office, a bright fire in the oven, drink and jest, and a soft bed still possessed that high value for enjoyment that perhaps the English novel, in describing the joy of life, has affirmed over the longest period of time. In short, all things in life had about them something glitteringly and cruelly public. The lepers, shaking their rattles and holding processions, put their deformities openly on display. Every estate, order, and craft could be recognized by its dress. The notables, never appearing without the ostentatious display of their weapons and liveried servants, inspired awe and envy. The administration of justice, the sales of goods, weddings and funerals—all announced themselves through processions, shouts, lamentations and music. The lover carried the emblem of his lady, the member the insignia of his fraternity, the party the colors and coat of arms of its lord.

In their external appearance, too, town and countryside displayed the same contrast and color. The city did not dissipate, as do our cities, into carelessly fashioned, ugly factories and monotonous country homes, but, enclosed by its walls, presented a completely rounded picture that included its innumerable protruding towers. No matter how high and weighty the stone houses of the noblemen or merchants may have been, churches with their proudly rising masses of stone, dominated the city silhouettes.

Just as the contrast between summer and winter was stronger then than in our present lives, so was the difference between light and dark, quiet and noise. The modern city hardly knows pure darkness or true silence anymore, nor does it know the effect of a single small light or that of a lonely distant shout.

From the continuing contrast, from the colorful forms with which every phenomena forced itself on the mind, daily life received the kind of impulses and passionate suggestions that is revealed in the vacillating moods of unrefined exuberance, sudden cruelty, and tender emotions between which the life of the medieval city was suspended.

But one sound always rose above the clamor of busy life and, no matter how much of a tintinnabulation, was never confused with other noises, and, for a moment, lifted everything into an ordered sphere: that of the bells. The bells acted in daily life like concerned good spirits who, with their familiar voices, proclaimed sadness or joy, calm or unrest, assembly or exhortation. People knew them by familiar names: Fat Jacqueline, Bell Roelant; everyone knew their individual tones and instantly recognized their meaning. People never became indifferent to these sounds, no matter how overused they were. During the notorious duel between two burghers of Valenciennes in 1455 that kept the city and the entire court of Burgundy in extraordinary suspense, the great bell sounded as long as the fight lasted, "laquelle fait hideux a oyr"* says Chastellain,[2] "Sonner l'effroy," "faire l'effroy" was what the ringing of the alarm bell was called.[3] How deafening the sound must have been when the bells of all the churches and cloisters of Paris pealed all day, or even all night, because a pope had been

---

* "which is hideous to hear"

elected who was to end the schism or because peace had been arranged between Burgundy and Armagnac.[4]

Processions must have also been deeply moving. During sad times—and these came often—they could occasionally take place day after day even for weeks on end. In 1412, when the fatal conflict between the houses of Orléans and Burgundy had finally led to open civil war, King Charles VI seized the oriflamme so that he and John the Fearless could fight against the Armagnacs, who, by virtue of their alliance with England, had become traitors to their country. Daily processions were ordered to be held in Paris as long as the king was on foreign soil. They continued from the end of May into July and involved ever different groups, orders or guilds, ever different routes and ever different relics: "les plus piteuses processions qui oncques eussent été veues de aage de homme."* All were barefoot with empty stomachs, members of parliament and poor burghers alike; every one who was able carried a candle or a torch. There were always many small children with them. Even the poor country folk from the villages around Paris came running on bare feet. Processions were joined or watched, "en grant pleur, en grant lermes, en grant devocion."† And heavy rain fell almost constantly during the entire period.[5]

Then there were the princely entry processions prepared with all the varied formal skills at the disposal of the main actors. And, with uninterrupted frequency, there were executions. The gruesome fascination and coarse compassion stirred at the place of execution became an important element in the spiritual nourishment of the people. For dealing with vicious robbers and murderers the courts invented terrible punishments: in Brussels a young arsonist and murderer was tied with a chain so that he could move in a circle about a stake surrounded by burning burning bundles of fagots. He introduced himself to the people in moving words as a warning example: "et tellement fit attendrir les coeurs que tout le monde fondoit en larmes de compassion." "Et fut sa fin reccommandée la plus belle que l'on avait oncques vue."[6]‡ During the Burgundian reign of terror in Paris, Messire Nansart du Bois, an

---

* "the most touching processions that had been seen in the memory of men"
† "with great weeping, with many tears, with great devotion."
‡ "and he so touched their hearts that everyone burst into tears and his death was commended as the finest that was ever seen."

Armagnac, was beheaded. Not only did he grant forgiveness to the executioner, who, as was customary, requested it, but he even asked to be kissed by him. "Foison de peuple y avoit, qui quasi tous ploroient à chaudes larmes."[7]* Frequently the sacrificial victims were great lords; in those cases the people had the even greater satisfaction of witnessing stern justice and a more forceful warning about the insecurity of high position than would be conveyed by a painting or a *danse macabre*.[8] The authorities took pains that nothing was lacking in the impression the spectacle made. The nobles took their last walk bedecked in the symbols of their greatness. Jean de Montaigu, grand maitre d'hotel of the king and a victim of the hatred of John the Fearless, travels to the gallows seated high on top of a cart. Two trumpeters precede him. He is dressed in his robes of state, cap, vest, and pants—half white, half red—with golden spurs on his feet. The beheaded body was left hanging on the gallows still wearing those golden spurs. The wealthy canon Nicholas d'Orgemont—who fell victim to the vendetta of the Armagnacs in 1416—was carried through Paris on a garbage cart, clad in a wide purple cloak and cap of the same color to witness the execution of two of his comrades before he was led away to lifelong captivity: "au pain de doleur et à eaue d'angoisse."† The head of Maître Oudart de Bussy, who had turned down a place in parliament, was exhumed by special order of Louis XI and, dressed with a crimson, fur-lined hood, "selon la mode des conseillers de parlement,"‡ was put on display with an attached explanatory poem in the town square of Hesdin. The king himself writes about this case with grim humor.[9]

Rarer than the processions and executions were the sermons given by itinerant preachers who came, from time to time, to stir the people with their words. We, readers of newspapers, can hardly imagine anymore the tremendous impact of the spoken word on naive and ignorant minds. The popular preacher Brother Richard, who may have served Jean d'Arc as father confessor, preached in Paris in 1429 for ten days running. He spoke from five until ten

* "There was a great multitude of people there, almost all of whom wept hot tears."
† "to the bread of adversity, to the water of affliction" (Isaiah 30:20).
‡ "in the style of the members of parliament"

or eleven o'clock in the morning in the Cemetery of the Innocents—where the famous *danse macabre* had been painted—with his
back to the bone chambers where skulls were piled up above the
vaulted walkways to be viewed by the visitors. When he informed
his audience after his tenth sermon that it would have to be his last
since he had not received permission for any more, "les gens grans
et petiz plouroient si piteusement et si fondement, comme s'ilz
veissent porter en terre leurs meilleurs amis, et lui aussi."* When
he finally leaves Paris, the people believe that the next Sunday he
will still preach at St. Denis; a large number, perhaps as many as
six thousand, according to the Burgher of Paris, leave the city on
Saturday evening and spend the night out in the fields in order to
secure good places.[10]

Antoine Fradin, a Franciscan, was also prohibited from preaching in Paris, because he railed against evil government. But this is
precisely what made him so beloved by the people. They guarded
him day and night in the monastery of the Cordeliers; the women
stood watch with their ammunition of ashes and stones ready. People laughed at the proclamation prohibiting the watch: the king
knows nothing about it! When Fradin is finally banned and has to
leave the city, the people give him an escort, "crians et soupirans
moult fort son departement."[11]†

In all cities where the saintly Dominican Vincent Ferrer comes
to preach, the people, the magistrates, the clergy—including bishops and prelates—go out to welcome him, singing his praises. He
travels with a large numbers of supporters, who, every evening
after sunset, go on processions with flagellations and songs. In
every town he is joined by new followers. He has carefully arranged for the food and lodging of all his companions by em-
ploying men of spotless reputation as his quartermasters. Numerous priests from different orders travel with him so that they can
assist him in taking confessions and celebrating mass. A few nota-
ries accompany him to record the legal reconciliations that the holy
preacher manages to arrange wherever he goes. When he preaches,
a wooden frame has to protect him and his entourage against the

---

* "the people, great and small, wept from the bottom of their hearts as if they
were watching their best friends being put into the ground, and so did he."
  † "sobbing and crying loudly at his departure."

throngs who want to kiss his hand or his gown. Work comes to a standstill as long as he speaks. It was a rare occasion when he failed to move his audience to tears, and when he spoke of Judgment Day and the pains of hell or of the sufferings of the Lord, he, just as his audience, broke into such great tears that he had to remain silent, for a time, until the weeping had stopped. The penitents fell to their knees before all the onlookers to tearfully confess their great sins.[12] When the famous Olivier Maillard gave the Lenten sermon at Orléans in 1485, so many people climbed on the roofs of the houses that the roofers submitted claims for sixty-four days of repair work.[13]

All this has the atmosphere of the English-American revivals or of the Salvation Army, but boundlessly extended and much more publicly exposed. There is no reason to suspect that the descriptions of Ferrer's impact are pious exaggerations by his biographers. The sober and dry Monstrelet describes in almost the same manner the impact of the sermons of a certain Brother Thomas—claiming to be a Carmelite, but later found to be an imposter—in northern France and Flanders in 1498. He, too, was escorted into the city by the magistrate while nobles held the reins of his mules; and for his sake many, among them notables whom Monstrelet identifies by name, left home and servants to follow him wherever he went. The prominent burghers erected high pulpits for him and draped them with the most expensive tapestries they could find.

Next to the popular preacher's accounts of the Passion and the Last Things, his attacks on luxury and vanity deeply moved his listeners. The people, Monstrelet writes, were particularly grateful to and fond of Brother Thomas because he attacked ostentation and displays of vanity and especially because he heaped criticism on nobility and clergy. He liked to set small boys (with the promise of indulgences, claims Monstrelet) on those noble ladies who ventured among the congregation wearing their high coiffures, crying "au hennin! au hennin!"[14] so that women during the entire period no longer dared to wear hennins and began to wear hoods like the Beguines.[15] "Mais à l'exemple du lymeçon," says the faithful chronicler, "lequel quand on passe près de luy retrait ses cornes par dedens et quand il ne ot plus riens les reboute dehors, ainsy firent ycelles. Car en assez brief terme après que ledit prescheur se fust départy du pays, elles mesmes recommencèrent comme devant et oublièrent sa doctrine, et reprinrent petit à petit leur viel estat, tel ou plus grant qu'elles avoient accoustumé de porter."[16]*

Brother Richard, as well as Brother Thomas, lit funeral pyres of the vanities, just as Florence was to do in 1497 to such an unprecedented extent, and with such irreplaceable losses for art, at the will of Savonarola. In Paris and Artois, in 1428 and 1429, such actions remained confined to the destruction of playing cards, game boards, dice, hair ornaments, and various baubles that were willingly handed over by men and women. In fifteenth-century France and Italy, these funeral pyres were a frequently repeated expression of the deep piety aroused by the preachers.[17] The turning away from vanity and lust on the part of the remorseful had become embodied in ceremonial form; passionate piety was stylized into solemn communal acts, just as those times tended to turn everything into stylized forms.

We have to transpose ourselves into this impressionability of mind, into this sensitivity to tears and spiritual repentance, into this susceptibility, before we can judge how colorful and intensive life was then.

Scenes of public mourning appeared to be responses to genuine calamities. During the funeral of Charles VII, the people lost their composure when the funeral procession came into view: all court officials "vestus de dueil angoisseux, lesquelz il faisoit moult piteux veoir; et de la grant tristesse et courroux qu'on leur veoit porter pour la mort de leur dit maistre, furent grant pleurs et lamentacions faictes parmy tout ladicte ville."† There were six page boys of the king riding six horses draped entirely in black velvet: "Et Dieu scet le doloreux et piteux dueil qu'ilz faisoient pour leur dit maistre." One of the lads was so saddened that he did not eat nor drink for four days, said the people with great emotion.[18]‡

---

* "Meanwhile, they behaved like snails who pull in their horns when people come near and put them out again when they don't hear anything anymore. After the said preacher had left the neighborhood, they began, in a very short space of time, to behave as before and gradually to resume wearing their old finery as large or larger than they had been."

† "dressed in the deepest mourning, most pitiful to see; and because of the great sorrow and grief they showed at the death of their said master, many tears were shed and lamentations uttered throughout the said town."

‡ "And God knows what doleful and piteous plaints they made, mourning for their master."

But a surplus of tears came not only from great mourning, a vigorous sermon, or the mysteries of faith. Each secular festival also unleashed a flood of tears. An envoy from the King of France to Philip the Good repeatedly breaks into tears during his address. When young John of Coimbra is given his farewell at the Burgundian court, everyone weeps loudly, just as happened on the occasion when the Dauphin was welcomed or during the meeting of the Kings of England and France at Ardres. King Louis XI was observed to shed tears while making his entry into Arras; during his time as Crown Prince at the court of Burgundy, he is described by Chastellain as sobbing or crying on several occasions.[19] Understandably, these accounts are exaggerated: compare them to the "there wasn't a dry eye in the house" of a newspaper report. In his description of the peace congress at Arras in 1435, Jean Germain makes the audience fall to the ground filled with emotions, speechless, sighing, sobbing and crying during the moving addresses by the delegates.[20] This, most likely, did not happen in this manner, but the bishop of Chalons found that it had to be that way. In the exaggeration, one can detect the underlying truth. The same holds true for the floods of tears ascribed to the sensitive minds of the eighteenth century; weeping was both edifying and beautiful. Furthermore, who does not know, even today, the strong emotions, even goose flesh and tears, solemn entry processions can arouse even if the prince who is at the center of all this pomp leaves us indifferent? During those times, such an unmediated emotional state was filled with a half-religious veneration of pomp and greatness and vented itself in genuine tears.

Those who do not comprehend this difference in susceptibility between the fifteenth century and our time may be able to come to appreciate it through a small example from a sphere divorced from that of tears; that is, the sphere of sudden rage. To us, there is hardly a game more peaceful and quiet than chess. La Marche says that during chess games fights break out "et que le plus saige y pert patience."[21]* A conflict between royal princes over a chessboard was still as plausible as a motive in the fifteenth century as in Carolingian romance.

Daily life offered unlimited range for acts of flaming passion and childish imagination. Our medieval historians who prefer to rely

* "and even the wisest would lose his patience."

as much as possible on official documents because the chronicles are unreliable fall thereby victim to an occasionally dangerous error. The documents tell us little about the difference in tone that separates us from those times; they let us forget the fervent pathos of medieval life. Of all the passions permeating medieval life with their color, only two are mentioned, as a rule by legal documents: greed and quarrelsomeness. Who has not frequently wondered about the nearly incredible violence and stubbornness with which greed, pugnacity, or vindictiveness rise to prominence in the court documents of that period! It is only in the general context of the passions that inflame every sphere of life that these tensions become acceptable and intelligible to us. This is why the authors of the chronicles, no matter how superficial they may be with respect to the actual facts and no matter how often they may err in reporting them, are indispensable if we want to understand that age correctly.

In many respects life still wore the color of fairy tales. If the court chroniclers, learned and respected men who knew their princes intimately, were unable to see and describe these distinguished persons other than in terms of archaic and hieratic figures, how great the magic splendor of royalty must have been in the naive imagination of the people. Here is an example of that fairy-tale quality from the historical writings of Chastellain: The young Charles the Bold, still the count of Charolais, has arrived at Sluis of Gorkum, and learns there that his father, the duke, has canceled his pension and all of his benefices. Chastellain now proceeds to describe how the count assembles all his retainers, down to the kitchen boys, and informs them of his misfortunes in a moving address in which he proclaims his respect for his father, his concern for the well-being of his people, and his love for them all. Those who have means of their own he asks to await his fate along with him; those who are poor he sets free to go and, if they should happen to learn that the count's fortune had taken a turn for the better, "return then and you shall find your positions waiting, and you shall be welcomed by me, and I shall reward the patience you have shown for my sake." "Lors oyt-l'on voix lever et larmes espandre et clameur ruer par commun accord: Nous tous, nous tous, monseigneur, vivrons avecques vous et mourrons."* Deeply moved,

* "Then were heard voices and cries and tears flowed and with one accord they shouted: 'We all, we all, my lord, will live and die with you.'"

Charles accepts their offer of fidelity: "Or vivez doncques et souf-frez; et moy je souffreray pour vous, premier que vous ayez faute."* Thereupon the noblemen approach and offer him all their posses-sions, "disant l'un: j'ay mille, l'autre: dix mille, l'autre: j'ay cecy, j'ay cela pour mettre pour vous et pour attendre tout vostre ad-venir."† And everything went on as usual and there was not a single chicken lacking in the kitchen because of all this.[22]

The embellishments of this picture are, of course, Chastellain's. We do not know how far his report stylized what had actually happened. But what really matters is that he sees the prince in the simple forms of the folk ballads. To him, the entire situation is totally dominated by the most primitive emotions of mutual loy-alty, which express themselves with epic simplicity.

While the mechanism of the administration of the state and the state budget had in reality already assumed complicated forms, politics were embodied in the minds of the people in particular, invariable, simple figures. The political references with which the people live are those of the folk song and chivalric romances. Simi-larly, the kings of the period are reduced to a few types, each of which more or less correspond to a motif from song or adventure story: the noble, just prince, the prince betrayed by evil counselors, the prince as avenger of his family's honor, the prince supported by his followers during reverses in his fortune. The subjects of a late medieval state, carrying a heavy burden and being without any voice in the administration of the taxes, lived in constant apprehen-sion that their pennies would be wasted, suspecting that they were not actually spent for the benefit and welfare of the country. This suspicion directed towards the administration of the state was trans-posed into the simplified notion that the king is surrounded by greedy, tricky advisers or that the ostentation and wastefulness of the royal court was to blame for the poor state of the country. Thus political questions were reduced, in the popular mind, to the typical events of a fairy tale. Philip the Good understood what sort of language would be intelligible to the people. During his festivi-

---

* "So stay then and suffer, and I will suffer for you, rather than see you in want."

† "says the one, 'I have a thousand,' the other, 'Ten thousand,' the third, 'I have this or that to put at your service and I am willing to share all that might befall you.'"

ties in The Hague in 1456 he had displayed in a room adjacent to the Knight's Hall precious utensils worth thirty thousand marks in order to impress the Dutch and Frisians who believed that he lacked the funds to take over the Bishopric of Utrecht. Everyone could come there to see the display. Moreover, two boxes containing one hundred thousand golden lions each had been brought from Lille. People were allowed to try to lift them, but tried in vain.[23] Can anyone imagine a more pedagogically skillful mixture of state credit and county-fair amusement?

The lives and deeds of the princes occasionally display a fantastic element that is reminiscent of the Caliph of *Thousand and One Nights*. In the midst of coolly calculated political undertakings, the heroes may occasionally display a daring bravado, or even risk their lives and personal achievements on a whim. Edward III gambled with his own life, that of the Prince of Wales, and the fate of his country by attacking a fleet of Spanish merchant vessels in order to exact vengeance for some acts of piracy.[24] Philip the Good had taken it into his head to marry one of his archers to the daughter of a rich brewer in Lille. When the father resisted and involved the parliament of Paris in the affair, the enraged duke suddenly broke off the important affairs of state that had kept him in Holland and, even though it was the holy season preceding Easter, undertook a dangerous sea voyage from Rotterdam to Sluis to have his own way.[25] Another time in a blinding rage over a quarrel with his son, he ran away from Brussels and lost his way in the forest like a truant schoolboy. When he finally returns, the delicate task of getting him back to his normal routine falls to the knight Phillipe Pot. This adroit courtier finds the right words: "Bonjour monseigneur, bonjour qu'est cecy? Faites-vous du roy Artus maintenant ou de messire Lancelot?"[26]*

How caliph-like it seems to us when the same duke, being told by his physician to have his head shaved, issues an order that all noblemen are to follow his example and orders Peter von Hagenbach to strip the hair from any who fail to comply.[27] Or when the young King Charles VI of France, riding on one horse with a friend in order to witness the entry procession of his own bride, Isabella of Bavaria, was, in the press of the crowd, thrashed by the guards.[28]

* "Good morning, your majesty, good morning; and what is this? Are you playing at King Arthur, now, or is it Sir Lancelot?"

A poet complains that princes promote their jesters or musicians to the position of councilor or minister as indeed happened to Co-quinet the Fool of Burgundy.[29]

Politics are not yet completely in the grip of bureaucracy and protocol; at any moment the prince may abandon them and look elsewhere for guidelines for his administration. Fifteenth-century princes repeatedly consulted visionary ascetics and renowned popular preachers on matters of state. Denis the Carthusian and Vincent Ferrer served as political advisers; the noisy popular preacher Olivier Maillard was privy to the most secret negotiations between princely courts.[30] Because of this, an element of religious tension[31] exists in the highest realms of politics.

At the end of the fourteenth and beginning of the fifteenth centuries, the people, observing the higher realms of princely life and fate, must have, more than ever, thought of it as a bloody romantic sphere filled with dramas of unmitigated tragedy, and the most moving falls from majesty and glory. During the same September month of 1399 when the British Parliament, meeting in Westminster, learned that King Richard II had been defeated and imprisoned by his cousin Lancaster and had resigned the throne, the German electors were gathered in Mainz to depose their king, Wenzel of Luxemburg. The latter was just as vacillating in spirit, incapable of ruling and as moody as his cousin in England, but did not come to as tragic an end as Richard. Wenzel remained for many years King of Bohemia, while Richard's deposition was followed by his mysterious death in prison, which recalled the murder of his grandfather, Edward II, also in prison, seventy years before. Was not the crown a tragic possession, fraught with danger? In a third large kingdom of Christendom a madman, Charles VI, occupied the throne and the country was soon to be ruined by unrestrained factionalism. The jealousy between the houses of Orléans and Burgundy erupted into open hostilities in 1407: Louis of Orléans, the brother of the king, fell victim to vile murderers hired by his cousin the duke of Burgundy, John the Fearless. Twelve years later, vengeance: John the Fearless was treacherously murdered during the solemn meeting on the bridge of Montereau. These two princely murders with their never ending trail of revenge and strife left an undertone of dark hatred in the history of France for a whole century. The popular mind views the misfortunes such as befell France in the light of the great dramatic motifs; it cannot comprehend causes other than personalities and passions.

The Turks appear in the midst of all this and threaten more ominously than before. A few years earlier, 1396, they had destroyed the splendid French army of knights that had recklessly ventured to face them under the same John the Fearless, then still count of Nevers, near Nicopolis. And Christendom was torn apart by the Great Schism, which by now had lasted a quarter of a century. Two individuals called themselves pope, neither one recognized in heartfelt conviction by a number of Western countries. As soon as the Council of Pisa of 1409 had ignominiously failed in its attempt to restore the unity of the church, there would be three who would compete for the papal title. The stubborn Aragonese, Peter von Luna, who hung on in Avignon as Benedict XIII, was known in popular parlance as "The Pope of the Moon." Did this title have the ring of near insanity for simple folks?

In these centuries a good many dethroned kings made the rounds of the princely courts—usually short of money and rich in plans, bathed in the splendor of the mysterious East from which they came: Armenia, Cyprus, and even Constantinople; every one of them a figure from the picture of the Wheel of Fortune (plate 1) from which kings with scepters and crowns came tumbling down. René of Anjou was not one of this number. Though a king without a crown, he lived very well on his wealthy estates in Anjou in Provence. But nobody embodied more clearly the vagaries of princely fortune than this prince from the House of France who had missed the best opportunities time and again, who had reached for the crowns of Hungary, Sicily, and Jerusalem and suffered nothing but defeats, narrow escapes, and long periods of imprisonment. This poet-king without a throne, who delighted in poems of hunting and the art of miniatures, must have been of deep frivolity of mind or he would have been cured by his fate. He had seen almost all of his children die and the daughter who was left to him suffered a fate that in its dark sadness was worse than his own. Margaret of Anjou, full of intelligence, honor, and passion, had, at the age of sixteen married King Henry VI of England, who was weak-minded. The English court was a hell of hatred. Nowhere else had suspicions of royal relatives, charges against powerful servants of the crown, and secretive and judicial murders for the sake of security and partisanship so permeated the political scene as in England. Margaret lived for many years in this atmosphere of persecution and fear before the great family feud between the Lancasters, the house of her husband, and the Yorks, that of her numerous and active cousins, broke out into open, bloody strife. Margaret lost crown and possessions. The changing fortunes of the War of the Roses meant most terrifying dangers and bitter poverty for her. Finally, secure in asylum at the Burgundian court, she gave in her own words to Chastellain, the court chronicler, the moving report of her misfortunes and her aimless wanderings: how she and her young son had been at the mercy of highwaymen, how she had had to beg a Scottish archer for a penny as offering during a mass, "qui demy à dur et à regret luy tira un gros d'Escosse de sa bourse et le luy presta."* The good chronicler, moved by so much suffering, dedicated for her consolation a tract, the *Temple of Bocace*[32]— "Alcun petit traité de fortune, prenant pied sur son inconstance et déceveuse nature."† He believed, in accordance with the standard recipe of those days, that he could not comfort the troubled princess better than with this gloomy gallery of princely misfortunes. Neither of them could know that the worst was yet to come. In 1471 near Tewkesbury, the Lancasters were decisively beaten, Margaret's only son was killed in the battle or murdered shortly thereafter, her husband was secretly killed; she herself spent five years in the Tower, only to be sold by Edward IV to Louis XI, to whom she had to cede the legacy of her father, King René, as a show of gratitude for her liberation.

Hearing of genuine royal children suffering such fates, how could the Burgher of Paris not believe the stories of lost crowns and banishment that vagabonds occasionally told to evoke sympathy and compassion? In 1427 a band of Gypsies appeared in Paris and represented themselves as penitents, "ung duc et ung conte et dix hommes tous à cheval."‡ The rest, 120 people, had to remain outside the city. They claimed to have come from Egypt and said that the Pope had made them do penitence for having left the Chris-

---

* "who, half reluctantly and with regret, took a Scottish groat out of his purse and lent it to her."

† "A certain little treatise on fortune, based on its inconstancy and deceptive nature."

‡ "a duke and a count and ten men, all on horseback."

tian faith. As punishment they had to spend seven years wandering
without ever sleeping in a bed. They said that they had originally
numbered about 1,200, but that their king and queen and all the
others had died on the road. As the only mitigation, they claimed,
the Pope had ordered that each bishop and abbot should give them
ten pounds tournois. The inhabitants of Paris came in huge throngs
to see the strange little band and to have the Gypsy women read
their palms. These managed to move the money from the purses
of the people to their own, "par art magicque ou autrement."[33]*

An aura of adventure and passion surrounded the life of princes,
but it was not only the popular imagination that saw it that way.
Modern man has, as a rule, no idea of the unrestrained extravagance
and inflammability of the medieval heart. Those who only consult
official documents, which are correctly held to contain the most
reliable information for our understanding of history, could fashion
for themselves from this piece of medieval history a picture that
would not be substantially different from a description of ministe-
rial and ambassadorial politics of the eighteenth century. But such
a picture would lack an important element: the crass colors of the
tremendous passions that inspired the people as well as the princes.
There is, no doubt, a passionate element remaining in contemporary politics, but, with the exception of days of turmoil and civil
war, it encounters more checks and obstacles. It is led in hundreds
of ways into fixed channels by the complicated mechanisms of
communal life. During the fifteenth century the immediate emotional affect is still directly expressed in ways that frequently break
through the veneer of utility and calculation. If emotions go hand
in hand with a sense of power, as in the case of princes, the effect is
doubled. Chastellain, in his stilted way, expresses this quite bluntly:
Small wonder, he says, that princes are frequently locked in hostilities with one another, "puisque les princes sont hommes, et leurs
affaires sont haulx et agus, et leurs natures sont subgettes à passions
maintes comme à haine et envie, et sont leurs coeurs vray habitacle
d'icelles des passions à cause de leur gloire en régner."[34]† Does this
not come close to what Burckhardt called "the pathos of rule?"

---

 * "by the art of magic or in other ways."
 † "For princes are men, and their affairs are high and dangerous, and their
natures are subject to many passions such as hatred and envy and their hearts are
veritable dwelling places for these because of their pride in reigning."

Whoever would write a history of the House of Burgundy would have to let the motif of revenge sound through their narrative like a pedal point, as black as a catafalque, advising each one at every turn and in battle giving to each heart its bitter thirst and the taste of broken pride. Certainly, it would be very naive to return to the all too uncomplicated view of its history that the fifteenth century itself had. It will not do, of course, to trace the power struggle from which arose the centuries-long quarrel between France and the Hapsburgs to the blood feud between Orléans and Burgundy, the two branches of the House of Valois. But we should be aware, more than is generally the rule in researching general political and economic causes, that for contemporaries, be they observers or participants in the great legal battles, blood revenge was the essential element that dominated the actions and fates of princes and countries. For them Philip the Good is the foremost of the avengers, "celluy qui pour vengier l'outraige fait sur la personne du duc Jehan soustint la gherre seize ans."[35]* Philip took it upon himself as a sacred duty, "en toute criminelle et mortelle aigreur, il tireroit à la vengeance du mort, si avant que Dieu luy vouldroit permettre; et y mettroit corps et âme, substance et pays tout en l'adventure et en la disposition de fortune, plus réputant oeuvre salutaire et agréable à Dieu de y entendre que de la laisser."† The Dominican who preached the funeral service for the murdered duke caused considerable outrage because he dared to point out the Christian duty of not taking revenge.[36] La Marche spoke as if honor and revenge were both political desires of the lands ruled by the duke: all estates of his lands joined his cry for revenge, he said.[37]

The treaty of Arras in 1435, which was supposed to bring peace between France and Burgundy, begins with penance for the murder at Montereau: a chapel should be dedicated in the church of Noreau where John had first been buried, a requiem should be sung there everyday until the end of time, there should be in the same city a

---

* "he, who to avenge the outrage done to the person of the duke Jean sustained the war for twenty years."

† "in the most violent and deadly rage he would give himself up to revenge the dead, in so far as God would permit him, and he would risk body and soul, possessions and lands, staking everything on the game and on inconstant fortune, because he considered it more salutary and agreeable to God to undertake the task than to leave it."

Carthusian monastery, a cross on the bridge itself where the murder happened, and a mass should be held in the Carthusian church at Dijon where the Burgundian dukes are buried.[38] But these were only a part of all the public penances and debasements demanded by Chancellor Rolin in the name of the duke: churches with chapters not only at Montereau but also at Rome, Ghent, Paris, Santiago de Compostella, and Jerusalem must carve the narrative in stone.[39]

A thirst for revenge dressed in such belabored forms must have dominated the intellect. And what could the people better comprehend of the politics of their princes than these simple, primitive motives of hatred and revenge? The attachment to the prince was childish-impulsive in character; it was a direct feeling of fidelity and community. It was an extension of the strong old emotion that bound the oath-taker to the bailiff and the vassals to their lord. This same emotion blazed into reckless passions during feuds and strife. It was the feeling of party, not of statehood. The later medieval period was the time of the great party conflicts. In Italy, these parties consolidated as early as the thirteenth century, in France and in the Netherlands they popped up everywhere during the fourteenth century. Anyone who studies the history of that period will at times be shocked at the inadequacy of the efforts of modern historians to explain these parties in terms of economic-political causes. Opposing economic interests, held to be basic, are purely mechanical constructions. No one, even with the best of intentions, can find them by reading the sources. This is not an attempt to deny the presence of economic causes in the formation of these party groups, but, dissatisfied with the efforts made to explain them to date, one might well be justified in asking whether a political-psychological view could not offer greater advantages than the economic-political for an explanation of late medieval party conflicts.

What the sources reveal about the rise of the parties is approximately this: in purely feudal times, separate and isolated feuds can be seen everywhere, in which one cannot find any other economic motive than envy by one side of the wealth and possessions of the other. But in addition to the question of material wealth, there is not less importantly that of honor. Family pride and the thirst for vengeance or the passionate loyalty on the part of supporters are, in such cases, primary motivations. To the degree that the power of the state is consolidating and spreading, all these family feuds are polarizing themselves, so to speak, along the lines of regional power and are coagulating into parties that perceive even the cause of their divisions in no other terms than those based on a foundation of solidarity and shared honor. Do we see any more deeply into these causes if we postulate economic conflicts? When an acute contemporary observer declares that no one could discover valid reasons for the hatred between Hoecken and Kabeljauen in Holland,[40] we should not shrug our shoulders in contempt and pretend to be smarter than he is. There is, in fact, no single satisfactory explanation why the Edmonds were Kabeljauisch and the Wassenaers, Hoeckish. The economic contrasts that typify these families are only the products of their position vis-à-vis the prince as followers of this or that party.[41]

How violent the emotions caused by the attachment to the prince could become can be read on any page of medieval history. The author of the miracle play *Little Mary of Nymwegen* shows us how Little Mary's evil aunt, after she and the neighbor ladies work themselves up to the point of exhaustion over the conflict between Arnold and Adolf of Geldern,[42] finally hangs herself because she is upset that the old duke has been freed from captivity. The intent of the author is to warn of the dangers of such partisanship; for that reason he picks an extreme example, a suicide out of partisanship—doubtlessly overdone, but evidence for the party feeling about which the sensitive poet spoke.

There are, however, more comforting examples. The Sheriffs of Abbeville had the bells rung in the middle of the night because a messenger had come from Charles of Charolais with the request to pray for the recovery of his father. The frightened citizens crowded the church, lit hundreds of candles, knelt or lay in tears throughout the night while the bells kept on ringing.[43]

When the people of Paris—in 1429 still favoring the English-Burgundian side[44]—learned that Brother Richard, who had just a short time before moved them with his sermons, was an Armagnac who surreptitiously won over the towns he visited, they cursed him in the name of God and all the saints; and in place of the tin penny bearing the name of Jesus that he had given them, they took up the cross of St. Andrew, the sign of the Burgundian party. People resumed the practice of playing dice against which Brother

Richard had railed so much, "en despit de luy,"* comments the Burgher de Paris.[45]

It would be natural to assume that the schism between Avignon and Rome, since it had no basis in dogma, could not arouse the passions of faith: in any case, not in places far from the centers of those events, where both popes were only known by name, and which were not directly affected by the split. But here too, the schism immediately evoked keen and violent partisanship even to the point of confrontations between believers and nonbelievers. When Bruges changes from the Roman pope to that of Avignon, numerous people leave home and city, profession or benefice, so that they may live in Liege or in another area in conformity to the obedience owed to Urban by their party.[46] Before the battle of Rosebeke in 1382, the leaders of the French troops are in doubt whether the oriflamme, the sacred royal flag only to be used in holy war, can be unfurled in a battle against the Flemish rebels. The decision to do so is made because the Flemish are Urbanites and thus infidels.[47] The French political agent and writer Pierre Salmon, on the occasion of his visit to Utrecht, is unable to find a priest who will let him celebrate Easter, "pour ce qu'ils disoient que je estoie scismatique et que je créoie en Benedic l'antipape,"† so that he, alone in a chapel, has to offer confession as if he were before a priest and heard mass in a Carthusian monastery.[48]

The highly emotional character of partisanship and princely allegiance was still further enhanced by the powerfully suggestive effect of all the party signs, colors, emblems, devices, mottoes, which many times alternated in colorful succession, usually pregnant with murder and mayhem, but occasionally also with humor. In 1380 as many as two thousand persons came out to welcome the young Charles VI to Paris, all dressed alike, half green, half white. Three times between 1411 and 1413, all of Paris suddenly displayed different insignia, purple caps with the cross of St. Andrew, white caps, and then purple again. Even priests and women and children wore them. During the Burgundian reign of terror in Paris in 1411, the Armagnacs were excommunicated every Sunday to the sound of

---

* "in defiance of him."

† "because they said I was a schismatic and believed in Benedict, the antipope."

the church bells. The figures of saints were crowned with the cross of St. Andrew; it was even claimed that a few priests did not want to make the sign of the cross in the straight way the Lord was crucified, but made a slanted version.[49]

The blind passion with which a man supported his party and his lord and, at the same time, pursued his own interests was, in part, an expression of an unmistakable, stone-hard sense of right that medieval man thought proper. It demonstrated an unshakable certainty that every deed justified ultimate retribution. The sense of justice was still three quarters heathen and dominated by a need for vengeance. Though the church sought to soften judicial usage, by pressing for meekness, peace and reconciliation, it failed to change the actual sense of justice. On the contrary, that sense was rendered sterner still by adding to the need for retribution the hatred of sin. All too often sin was, for these agitated minds, whatever their enemy did. The sense of justice had gradually escalated to an extreme tension between the two poles of a barbaric notion of an eye for an eye, a tooth for a tooth and that of a religious abhorrence of sin, while the role of the state, to punish severely, came to be considered more and more an urgent necessity. The sense of insecurity, which in any crisis looks to the power of the state to implement a reign of terror, became chronic in the later Middle Ages. The conception of atonement by transgressors gradually faded into an almost idyllic vestige of an ancient naiveté while the notion that transgressions were both threats to the community and attacks on the majesty of God gained ground. The end of the Middle Ages was an intoxicating time when painful justice and judicial cruelty were in full bloom. People did not doubt for an instant that the criminal deserved his punishment. Intense satisfaction was derived from exemplary deeds of justice performed by the princes themselves. From time to time the authorities waged campaigns of stern justice, sometimes against robbers and petty thieves, sometimes against witches and magicians, sometimes against sodomy.

What strikes us about the judicial cruelty of the later Middle Ages is not the perverse sickness of it, but the dull, animal-like enjoyment, the country fair–like amusement, it provided for the people. The people of Mons paid far too high a price for a robber chief, merely for the pleasure of quartering him, "dont le peuple fust plus joyeulx que si un nouveau corps sainct estoit ressuscité."[50]* During the imprisonment of Maximilian at Bruges in 1488, the rack stands on a high platform in sight of the imprisoned king. The people cannot get enough of the spectacle of magistrates, suspected of treason, undergoing repeated torture. The people delay executions, which the victims themselves request, for the enjoyment of seeing them subjected to even more sufferings.[51]

The unchristian extreme to which this mixture of faith and thirst for revenge led is shown by the prevailing custom in England and France of refusing individuals under the sentence of death not only extreme unction, but also confession. There was no intent to save souls; rather, the intent was to intensify the fear of death by the certainty of the punishments of hell. In vain, Pope Clement V ordered, in 1311, that prisoners condemned to death at least be given the sacrament of penance. The political idealist Philippe de Mézières lobbied repeatedly that this be done, first with Charles V of France, then with Charles VI. But the Chancellor Pierre d'Orgemone, whose "forte cervelle," says Mézières, was more difficult to move than a millstone, resisted, and the wise, peace-loving Charles V declared that the custom was not to be changed in his lifetime. Only after the voice of Jean de Gerson had joined that of Mézières in five considerations against this abuse did a royal edict of February 12, 1397, order that the condemned be granted confession. Pierre de Craon, to whose efforts the decision has to be credited, had a stone cross erected at the gallows in Paris so that the Minorites could assist the condemned there.[52] However, even then the old custom did not disappear from popular usage; as late as shortly after 1500, the bishop of Paris, Etienne Ponchier, found it necessary to reissue the edict of Clement V. In 1427 a robber baron was hanged in Paris; during the execution a respected official, grand treasurer in the service of the regent, vents his hatred of the condemned by preventing the confession that the prisoner had requested. Using abusive language, he follows the condemned up the ladder, hits him with a stick, and attacks the executioner because he has admonished the victim to think of the bliss of his soul. The

---

* "at which the people were more delighted than if a new holy body had been resurrected."

hangman, terrified, hurries his task; the rope breaks, the poor victim falls to the ground, breaks his legs and ribs and must move up the ladder once more.[53]

During medieval times, all those emotions were missing that have made us cautious and tentative in matters of justice: the insight into diminished capacity, the concept of judicial fallibility, the awareness that society has to share in the blame for the guilt of individuals, the question whether an individual ought not be rehabilitated rather than made to suffer. Or, perhaps, better stated: a vague sense of all this is not lacking, but rather concentrates itself, unverbalized, in instant impulses of charity and forgiveness (unconcerned with the issue of guilt) which could suddenly break through the cruel satisfaction over the administration of justice. While we administer a hesitant, toned-down justice, partially filled with a guilty conscience, the Middle Ages knew only two extremes: the full measure of cruel punishment or mercy. In granting mercy the question whether the guilty person deserved mercy for any particular reason was asked much less frequently than now: for any transgression, even the most blatant, full pardon could be granted at any time. In practice, it was not only pure mercy that tipped the scale in favor of acquittal. It is surprising with what equanimity contemporaries report how intervention by respected relatives had secured for a convict "lettres de rémission." Yet most of these letters do not apply to prominent lawbreakers, but to poor common folk who did not have highly placed advocates.[54]

The direct juxtaposition of hard-heartedness and mercy characterizes customs outside the administration of justice. On the one side, frightful harshness towards the wretched and handicapped; on the other, unlimited compassion and the most intimate empathy with the poor, sick, and irrational, which we, in conjunction with cruelty, still know from Russian literature. Satisfaction with an execution was accompanied, and, at least to a certain degree justified, by a strong sense of right. The incredible harshness, the lack of tender sentiment, the cruel mockery, the secret joy behind the pleasure of watching others suffer lacked even this element of justice satisfied. The chronicler Pierre de Fenin closes his report on the end of a band of robbers with the words, "et faisoit-on grant risée, pour ce que c'estoient tous gens de povre estat."[55]*

---

* "and there was a great deal of laughter because they were all poor men."

In Paris in 1425 an "esbatement" was held in which four armored blind men were made to fight for a pig. In the days before they were seen in their battle dress throughout the city, a bagpiper and a man with a huge banner on which the pig is depicted, preceded them.[56]

Velázquez has shown us the touching facial expressions of the female dwarfs who as fools occupied positions of honor at the Spanish court of his time (plate 2). They were prized diversions at the princely courts of the fifteenth century. During the artful *entremets*[57] of the great courts they displayed their skills and their deformities. Madame d'Or, the golden blonde female dwarf of Philip of Burgundy, was well known. She was made to wrestle with the acrobat Hans.[58] To the wedding of Charles the Bold and Margareth of York in 1468 came Madame de Beaugrant, "la naine de Mademoiselle de Bourgogne,"* dressed as a shepherdess, riding around on a golden lion larger than a horse. The Lion could open and close his mouth and sang a song of welcome. The little shepherd girl is given to the young duchess as a gift and is sat on the table.[59] We know of no laments over the lot of these little women, but we do have items from expense accounts that tell us more about them. These accounts report how a duchess had one such little dwarf removed from the house of her parents, how the father or mother came to deliver her, and how they came now and then for a visit and were given a gratuity: "au pere de Belon la folle, qui estoit venu veoir sa fille . . ."† Did the father go home well pleased and highly honored by the court position of his daughter? During the same year a locksmith of Blois delivered two iron necklaces, one "pour attacher Belon la folle et l'autre por mettre au col de la cingesse de Madame la Duchesse."[60]‡

How the mentally ill were treated can be ascertained from a report about the provisions made for Charles VI, who, as king, enjoyed treatment that contrasted favorably with that afforded all others. To bring a wretched mental case to his senses, no better method was conceived than to have him frightened by twelve blackened individuals as if devils had come to take him away.[61]

---

* "the female dwarf of Mademoiselle of Burgundy"
† "to the father of Belon, the fool, who came to visit his daughter . . ."
‡ "to chain up Belon, the fool, and the other to put around the neck of the monkey of her grace, the Duchess."

There is a degree of naiveté in the hard-heartedness of the time that makes our condemnation die on our lips. In the middle of an outbreak of plague that afflicted Paris, the dukes of Burgundy and Orléans called for the installation of a "cour d'amour" to divert the people.[62] During a break in the cruel slaughter of the Armagnacs in 1418, the people of Paris founded the Brotherhood of St. Andrew in the Church of St. Eustatius; every priest and layman carried a wreath of red roses: the church is full of them and smells, "comme s'il fust lavé d'eau rose."[63]* When the witch trials that had descended upon Arras in 1461 like a hellish plague were finally canceled, the burghers celebrated the victory of law with a competition of performances of "folies moralisées"; first prize was a silver fleur-de-lis, fourth prize, two capons: the martyred victims were by this time long dead.[64]

So intense and colorful was life that it could stand the mingling of the smell of blood and roses. Between hellish fears and the most childish jokes, between cruel harshness and sentimental sympathy the people stagger—like a giant with the head of a child, hither and thither. Between the absolute denial of all worldly joys and a frantic yearning for wealth and pleasure, between dark hatred and merry conviviality, they live in extremes.

From the brighter half of their lives little has come down to us: it seems as if the gay mildness and serenity of soul of the fifteenth century have been swallowed into paintings and crystalized in the transparent purity of their lofty music. The laughter of that generation is dead, their untroubled joy and natural zest for life lives only in folk song and farce. This is enough to add to our nostalgia for the lost beauty of other times, a longing for the sunlight of the century of the Van Eycks. But those who really delve into that time must frequently try very hard in order to capture its brighter aspects since, outside the sphere of art, darkness rules. In the dire warnings of the preachers, in the tired sighs of the greatest literature, in the monotonous reports of the chronicles and sources, we hear only the cries of motley sins and the lamentations of misery.

Post-Reformation times no longer saw the cardinal sins of pride, anger, and greed in the purple full-bloodedness and shameless assertiveness with which they walked among the humanity of the fifteenth century. The unlimited arrogance of Burgundy! The

---

* "as if it had been washed in rose water."

whole history of that family, from the deeds of knightly bravado, in which the fast-rising fortunes of the first Philip take root, to the bitter jealousy of John the Fearless and the black lust for revenge in the years after his death, through the long summer of that other magnifico, Philip the Good, to the deranged stubbornness with which the ambitious Charles the Bold met his ruin—is this not a poem of heroic pride? Their lands were the scene of the most intensive lives of the West: Burgundy, as dark with power as with wine, "la colérique Picardie,"* greedy, rich Flanders. These are the same lands in which the splendor of painting, sculpture, and music flower, and where the most violent code of revenge ruled and the most brutal barbarism spread among the aristocracy and burghers.[65]

That age is more conscious of greed than of any other evil. Pride and greed can be placed beside one another as the sins of the old and the new times. Pride is the sin of the feudal and hierarchic period during which possessions and wealth circulate very little. A sense of power is not primarily tied to wealth, it is rather more personal, and power, in order to make itself known, has to manifest itself through imposing displays: a numerous following of faithful retainers, precious adornments, and the impressive appearance of the powerful. The feeling of being more than other men is constantly nourished by feudal and hierarchic thought with living forms: through kneeling obeisance and allegiance, solemn respect and majestic splendor, which, all taken together, make superiority appear as something substantial and sanctioned.

Pride is a symbolic and theological sin; it is rooted deeply in the soil of every conception of life and the world. *Superbia* was the root of all evil: Lucifer's pride was the beginning and cause of all ruin. So Augustine saw it, and it remained so in the minds of those who came after: pride is the source of all sins, they come forth from it as if from their root and stem.[66]

But next to the scripture from which this notion comes, *A superbia initium sumpsit omnis perdito,*[67]† there is another, *Radix omnium malorum est cupiditas.*[68]‡ Following this, one could regard greed as the root of all evil. Because of this, *cupiditas,* which, as such, has

---

* "hot-tempered Picardy"
† Pride gives rise to every evil.
‡ Greed is the root of all evil.

no place in the list of deadly sins, was understood as *avaritia,* as it in fact appears in another reading of the text.[69] And it appears that since about the twelfth century, the conviction had gained credence that it was unrestrained greed that ruined the world and thus replaced pride in the minds of the people as the first and most fatal of sins. The old primacy theology assigns to superbia is drowned out by the steadily rising chorus that blames all the misery of the times to ever-increasing greed. How Dante had cursed it: *la cieca cupidigia!*

But greed lacks the symbolic and theological character of pride; it is the natural and material sin, the purely earthly passion. It is the sin of that period of time in which the circulation of money has changed and loosened the conditions for the deployment of power. Judging human worth becomes an arithmetical process. Now there is much greater leeway for the satisfaction of unrestrained desires and for the accumulation of treasures. And these treasures have not yet that ghostly intangibility that modern credit procedures have bestowed on capital; it is still yellow gold itself that is in the forefront of fantasy. And the utilization of wealth does not yet have that automatic and mechanical character of the routine investment of money: satisfaction still lies in the most drastic extremes of avidity and prodigality. In this extravagance greed enters into marriage with the older pride. Pride was still strong and alive: hierarchic, feudal thought had lost none of its bloom, the lust for pomp and splendor, finery and pageantry was still crimson.

It is precisely this affinity with a primitive pride that bestows on the avidity or greed of the later medieval period its direct, passionate, desperate quality that later times seem to have entirely lost. Protestantism and the Renaissance have given greed an ethical value;, they have legalized it as useful to promote welfare. Its stigma has given way to the degree that the denial of all earthly goods are praised with less conviction. In late medieval times, by contrast, the mind was still able to positively grasp the distinction, not yet lost, between sinful greed versus charity or freely willed poverty.

Throughout the literature and chronicles of the time, from proverb to pious tract, there echoes the bitter hatred of the rich, the complaint over the greed of the great. Sometimes it sounds like a dark anticipation of class struggle, expressed through moral outrage. In this area, we can get a sense of the rich tone of life of this time equally well from documents or narrative sources, but it is the legal documents that reveal the most unabashed greed.

It was possible, in 1436, for the services in one of the best-attended churches in Paris to be suspended for twenty-two days because the bishop refused to reconsecrate the church until he had received a certain number of pennies from two beggars, who had desecrated the church with a bloody stain during a scuffle, and who, being poor, did not have the money. The bishop, Jacques du Chatelier, was considered, "ung homme très pompeux, convoicteux, plus mondain que son estat ne requeroit."* However, in 1441, under his successor, Denys des Moulins, it happened again. This time, for four months, no funerals or processions could be held at the Cemetery of the Innocents, the most famous and sought-after in Paris, because the bishop demanded more for these services than the church could raise. The bishop was called, "homme très pou piteux à quelque personne, s'il ne recevoit argent ou aucun don qui le vaulsist, et pour vray on disoit qu'il avait plus de cinquante procès en Parlement, car de lui n'avoit on rien sans procès."[70]† One would only have to trace in detail the history of one of the "nouveaux riches" of that time, the d'Orgemont family, for example, in all its base stinginess and legal wrangling, in order to understand the tremendous hatred of the people and the scorn that the preachers and poets alike were constantly pouring out against the rich.[71]

The people could not perceive their own fates and the events of their time other than as a continuous succession of economic mishandling, exploitation, war and robbery, inflation, want, and pestilence. The chronic form that war tended to take, the constant threats to the town and the country from all kinds of dangerous riffraff, the eternal threat from a harsh and unreliable administration of justice, and on top of all this, the pressure of the fear of hell and the anxiety about devils and witches, nourished a feeling of general insecurity that tended to paint life's background in dark colors. It

---

* "a very pompous man, grasping, more worldly than his station required."

† "a man who showed very little pity to people, if he did not receive money or another gift which was worthwhile; and it was told for truth that he had more than fifty lawsuits in process, since nothing could be gotten out of him without going to court."

was not only the life of the poor and small that was insecure. In
the lives of the nobility and magistrates too, dramatic turns of fate
and constant dangers became almost the rule. Mathieu d'Escouchy,
a Picard, is one of those chroniclers of which there were so many
in the fifteenth century; his chronicle, simple, exact and impartial,
filled with the conventional veneration for the knightly ideal and
with the traditional moralizing tendency, lets us assume himself to
be an honorable writer who dedicated his talent to accurate historical work. But what a picture of the life of the author of this historical work is shown us by the editor of the original sources![72] Mathieu
d'Escouchy began his professional career as counselor, alderman,
juror, and bailiff [prévôt] of the city of Péronne between 1440 and
1450. From the beginning, we find him in a kind of feud with the
family of the city attorney, Jean Froment, a feud that is carried out
in the courts. Soon the attorney prosecutes d'Escouchy on charges
of forgery and murder, then for "excès et attemptaz." The bailiff,
on his side, threatens the widow of his enemy with an investigation
into the witchcraft of which she is suspected. But the widow succeeds in getting an injunction that forces d'Escouchy to put the
investigation in the hands of the court. The matter comes before
the Parliament of Paris and d'Escouchy ends up in prison for the
first time. Six more times we find him accused and under arrest,
and once a prisoner of war. In every instance these were serious
criminal cases, and more than once he was kept in heavy chains.
The battle of mutual accusations between the families of Froment
and d'Escouchy is interrupted by a violent clash during which the
son of Froment injures d'Escouchy. Both hire assassins to take their
opponent's life. After this long drawn out feud drops out of our
historical horizon, attacks from elsewhere appear. This time the
bailiff is wounded by a monk. New complaints, then, in 1461:
d'Escouchy's move to Nesle apparently under suspicion of wrong-
doing. But this does not hinder him from advancing his career. He
becomes bailiff, alderman, of Ribemont, procurator of the king in
Saint Quentin, and is elevated to the nobility. After new attacks,
incarcerations and penances, we find him again serving in a war.
In 1465 he fights at Montlhéry for the king against Charles the
Bold and is taken prisoner. From a later campaign he returns a
cripple. He marries, but that does not mean the beginning of a
quiet life for him. We find him charged with forging seals, being

taken as a prisoner to Paris, "comme larron et murdrier,"* again in a new feud with a magistrate of Compiégne, made under torture to confess his guilt, prevented from appealing, sentenced, rehabilitated, sentenced anew, until the traces of this life of hatred and persecution finally disappear from the documents.

Such biographies, full of sudden turns, are found whenever we study the lives of individuals identified in the sources of that period. One reads, for instance, the examples collected by Pierre Champion of all those whom Villon considered or named in his will,[73] or in the notes by Tutetey on the diary of the Burgher of Paris. It is always litigations, crimes, conflicts, and persecutions without end that we meet. And we are dealing here with the lives of people randomly brought to light by court, church, or other documents. Chronicles, like that of Jacques du Clercq, which are just a collection of misdeeds may paint too dark a picture of those times. Even the "lettres de rémission," which put daily life before our eyes in such lively precision, point only to the dark side of life, because they deal with nothing but crime. Yet any other probe into randomly chosen material, only confirms our dark vision.

It is an evil world. The fires of hatred and violence burn fiercely. Evil is powerful, the devil covers a darkened earth with his black wings. And soon the end of the world is expected. But mankind does not repent, the church struggles, and the preachers and poets warn and lament in vain.

* "as a robber and murderer"

Chapter Two

THE CRAVING FOR A MORE BEAUTIFUL LIFE

EVERY AGE YEARNS FOR A MORE BEAUTIFUL WORLD. The deeper the desperation and the depression about the confusing present, the more intense that yearning. Towards the end of the Middle Ages the ground tone underlying life is one of bitter despondency. The note of an assertive joy of life and of a strong confidence in an individual's powers, which permeates the history of the Renaissance and that of the age of Enlightenment, is barely audible in the French-Burgundian world of the fifteenth century. Was life really more unhappy then than usual? It may, at times, seem to be the case. Wherever one looks in the sources of that period, in the chronicles, in poetry, in sermons and religious tracts and even official documents—with few exceptions, only the traces of strife, hatred and malevolence, greed and poverty seem to have survived. One may well ask, was this age incapable of enjoying nothing but cruelty, arrogant pride, and intemperance? Is joyfulness and quiet happiness nowhere to be found? To be sure, the age left in its records more traces of its suffering than of its happiness. Its misfortunes became its history. But an instinctive conviction tells us that the sum total of happiness, serene joy, and sweet rest given to man cannot differ very much in one period from that in another. The splendor of late medieval happiness has still not completely vanished; it survives in folk song, in music, in the quiet horizons of landscape paintings and in the sober faces seen in the portraits.

But in the fifteenth century, it is tempting to say, it was not yet customary, it was not in good taste, to loudly praise life and the world. Those given to the serious contemplation of the course of daily events, and who subsequently pronounced judgment on life, were accustomed to dwell on only suffering and despair. They saw time coming to an end and everything earthly inclining to ruin. The optimism that was to rise beginning with the Renaissance, and to fully bloom during the eighteenth century, was still unknown to the French mind of the fifteenth century. Which group is it who are the first to speak, full of hope and satisfaction, about their own times? Not poets, much less religious thinkers; not even statesmen, but rather scholars, the humanists. It is the exultation over rediscovered antique wisdom that first elicits jubilation about the present; this is an intellectual triumph. Ulrich von Hutten's well-known dictum "O saeculum, O literae! Juvat Vivere!" ("O century, O literature! It is a joy to live!") is usually taken in much too wide a sense. It is the enthusiastic man of letters rather than the whole man who is jubilating here. One could easily cite, from the beginning of the sixteenth century, a number of familiar shouts of joy about the splendor of the times, but the facts would make one notice that they are almost exclusively directed towards the regained intellectual world and are by no means dithyrambic expressions of the joy of life in all its fullness. Even the mood of the humanists is tempered by the old, pious turning from the world. Better than from Hutten's too often cited dictum, this can be ascertained from the letters Erasmus wrote around 1517—but no longer from those written only a little later, because the optimism that had prompted this joyous mood soon leaves him.

Erasmus writes, early in 1517, to Wolfgang Fabricius Capito:[1] "I am truly no longer so keen on life, perhaps because I have already lived almost too long as far as I am concerned—I have already begun my 51th year—perhaps because I see in this life nothing so glorious or pleasant as to be worthy of pursuit for someone whom the Christian faith has taught to truly believe that for those who devote their strength to piety a much happier life awaits. Yet now, I could almost fancy becoming young again for a short while if only because I can almost sense that a golden age is about to arise in the near future." He then describes how all the princes of Europe are in agreement and lean towards peace (so dear to him), and continues, "I cannot but hold the firm expectation that there will be in part a new revival and in part a new unfolding not only of law-abiding customs and Christian piety but also of a cleansed and genuine[2] literature and a very beautiful science." Through protection by the princes, needless to say. "We owe it to their pious minds that we witness the awakening and arising of glorious minds—as if in response to a given signal—all pledging to each other the restoration of good literature [*ad restituendas optimas literas*]."

Here we have a pure expression of what the sixteenth century knew of optimism. The basic sentiment of the Renaissance and humanism is actually something entirely different from the unrestrained lust for life that is usually held to be its basic tone. The affirmation of life on the part of Erasmus is shy and a little stiff and, above all, very intellectual. Nevertheless, it is a voice that could not yet be heard, during the fifteenth century, outside of Italy. Intellectuals in France and in the Burgundian provinces around 1400 still prefer to pile their scorn of life and the times on rather thickly and, in a peculiar way (but not without parallel; consider Byronianism), the closer they are to secular life, the darker their mood. Those who express that deep melancholy, so characteristic of that time, most vigorously, are not primarily those have permanently retired from the world into monasteries or scholarship. Mostly they are the chroniclers and the fashionable court poets, given their lack of higher culture and their inability to gain from the joys they perceive any expectations of a turn for the better, who never tire of lamenting the debilities of an aged world and despairing of peace and justice. No one has repeated the lamentation, that all good things have left the world, more interminably than Eustache Deschamps.

> Temps de doleur et de temptacion,
> Aages de plour, d'envie et de tourment,
> Temps de langour et de dampnacion,
> Aages meneur près du definement,
> Temps plains d'orreur qui tout fait faussement,
> Aages menteur, plain d'orgueil et d'envie,
> Temps sanz honeur et sanz vray jugement,
> Aage en tristour qui abrege la vie.[3]*

Dozens of his ballads were composed in this spirit—monotonous, weak variations of the same dull theme. A pronounced melancholy must have dominated the higher estates; why else would

---

* Time of mourning and of temptation, / Age of tears, of envy and of torment, / Time of languor and of damnation, / Age that brings us to the end, / Time full of horror which does all things foolishly, / Lying age, full of pride and envy, / Time without honor and without true judgment, / Age of sadness which shortens life.

the nobility have allowed its favorite poet to repeat these sentiments
with such frequency?

> *Toute léesse deffaut,*
> *Tous cueurs ont prins par assaut*
> *Tristesse et merencolie.*[4]*

Three quarters of a century after Deschamps, Jean Merchinot
still sings in the same key:

> *O miserable et très dolente vie! . . .*
> *La guerre avons, mortalité, famine;*
> *Le froid, le chaud, le jour, le nuit nous mine;*
> *Puces, cirons et tant d'autre vermine*
> *Nous guerroyent. Bref, miserere domine*
> *Noz meschans corps, dont le vivre est très court.*†

He, too, endlessly repeats the bitter conviction that everything in
the world is going badly; justice is mislaid, the powerful plunder
the weak, and the weak, in turn, plunder each other. According to
his own confession, his hypochondria even takes him to the brink
of suicide. He describes himself:

> *Et je, le pouvre escrivain,*
> *Au cueur triste, faible et vain,*
> *Voyant de chascun le dueil,*
> *Soucy me tient en sa main;*
> *Toujours les larmes à l'oeil,*
> *Rien fors mourir je ne vueil.*[5]‡

All the examples of the nobility's mood of life testify to a senti-

---

* All mirth is lost,/All hearts have been taken by storm,/By sadness and melancholy.

† O miserable and most sad life! . . ./There is warfare, death, and famine;/
Cold and heat, day and night make us weak;/Fleas, scabs, and so many other
vermin/Make war on us. In short, have mercy Lord/On our miserable persons,
whose life is very short.

‡ And I poor writer,/With the sad heart, feeble and vain,/When I see everyone
mourning,/Then trouble holds me in her hand,/I always have tears in my eyes,/
For I wish for nothing but to die.

mental need for a dark costume for the soul. Nearly everyone declares that he had seen nothing but misery, that one had to be prepared for something worse and that he would not want to repeat the life he had lived so far. "Moi douloreux homme, né en eclipse de ténèbres en espesses bruynes de lamentation,"* so Chastellain announces himself.[6] "Tant a souffert La Marche"† the court poet and chronicler of Charles the Bold selects as his motto; life has a bitter taste for him and his portrait shows us those morose features that attract our attention in so many pictures of that period.[7]

Is there a life—equally full of earthly arrogant pride and boastful pleasure-seeking and at the same time crowned by so much success—as that of Philip the Good? But even it reveals the despair of the time lurking below its facade. When informed of the death of his one-year-old infant boy he says, "If only God deigned to let me die so young, I would have considered myself fortunate."[8]

Isn't it strange that during this time, in the word "melancholy," the meanings of depression, serious contemplation, and imagination come together? This shows how any serious endeavor of the mind would, of necessity, take it into somber moods. Froissart tells us about Philip van Artevelde, who is musing over a message just received, "quant il eut merancoliet une espasse, il s'avisa que il rescriproit aus commissaires dou roi de France,"‡ etc. Deschamps says about something so ugly that it is beyond all power of imagination, "No painter is so 'merencolieux' that he would be able to paint it."[9]

In the pessimism of all these overburdened, disappointed, and fatigued individuals there is a religious element, but only a very weak one. Their world-weariness certainly echoes the expectation of the approaching end of the world that was poured into minds everywhere by the popular preaching of the revived mendicant orders, with renewed threats and intensified imaginative power. The dark and confusing times, the chronic misery of war were well suited to reinforce these thoughts. There seems to have been, during the last years of the fourteenth century, a popular belief that nobody had been admitted to paradise since the Great Schism be-

---

* "I man of sadness, born in deepest darkness and thick rain of lamentations"
† "So much had La Marche suffered."
‡ "when he had reflected (merancoliet) for a while, he resolved to answer the emissaries of the King of France"

gan.[10] Just turning away from the vain glitter of courtly life made people ready to bid farewell to the world. For all that, the mood of depression as expressed by nearly all princely liegemen and courtiers had hardly any religious substance. At best, religious notions slightly colored the general sense of life's malaise. This penchant for scorning life and the world is a far cry from an essentially religious conviction. The world, says Deschamps, is like a childlike old man; he was innocent in the beginning, then for a long time wise, just, virtuous and brave:

> Or est laches, chetis et molz,
> Vieulx convoiteus et mal parlant;
> Je ne voy que foles et folz . . .
> La fin s'approche, en verité . . .
> Tout va mal . . .[11]*

There is not only weariness with the world, but also an actual dread of life, a fearful shrinking away because of life's inevitable suffering; this is the mental attitude that underlies Buddhism: an irresolute turning away from the effort of everyday life, fear and disgust in anticipation of disease and old age. Blasé individuals shared this dread of life with those who had never succumbed to the temptations of the world because they had always shied away from life.

The poems of Deschamps overflow with miserable aspersions about life. He is fortunate who has no children because small children are nothing but wails and stinks, trouble and worry. They have to be clothed, given shoes, fed, and are always in danger of falling or hurting themselves. They become sick and die, or else they grow up and turn bad; they are put in jail. Nothing but trouble and disappointment, there is no happiness to reward all the worries, efforts, and expenses of their education. There is no greater misfortune than to have deformed children. The poet has no loving words for them; deformed people have black hearts, he has the scripture say. He who is unmarried is fortunate because it is terrible to live with a bad woman and one has to be constantly afraid of losing a

---

* Now he is decaying, pitiful and weak,/Old, covetous and libelous;/I see only fools, men and women both . . ./The end is truly near . . ./Everything is going bad . . .

good one. As well as fleeing from misfortune one must shy away from good fortune. In old age the poet sees nothing but evil and disgust, a miserable physical and mental decay, laughable and calamitous. Old age comes early, for woman at thirty, for men at fifty, and sixty is the normal end of their life span.[12] How far one is here from the pure ideality with which Dante described the dignity of the noble elder in his *Convivio*.[13]

A pious tendency, rarely found in Deschamps, may on occasion elevate reflections on the dread of life, but the basic mood of discouraged failure is always more strongly felt than genuine piety. Serious admonitions to saintliness echo these negative elements more than they reflect a genuine will for sanctification. The irreproachable Jean de Gerson, the Chancellor of the University of Paris, writing a treatise for his sister about the superiority of virginity, cites among his arguments a long list of sufferings and pains bound up with marriage. A husband may turn out to be a drunkard, or be extravagant or miserly. But even if he is a solid and good individual there may be a bad harvest, or epidemic, or shipwrecks may rob him of his worldly possessions. How miserable is pregnancy, how many women die in childbirth! Does a nursing mother ever enjoy undisturbed sleep, what about merriment and joy? Her children may turn out to be malformed or disobedient, her husband may die and the widowed mother be left to face a life of worry and poverty.[14]

Daily reality is viewed in terms of the deepest depression whenever the childlike joy of life or blind hedonism gives way to meditation. Where is that more beautiful world for which every age is bound to yearn?

Those yearning for a better life, at all times, have seen three paths to the distant goal before them. The first of these ordinarily leads away from the world: the path of denial. The more beautiful life seems to be attainable only in the world beyond; it will prove to be a deliverance from all earthly concerns. All the attention wasted on the world delays the promised bliss. This path has been followed in every higher culture. Christianity had impressed this struggle on consciousness, both as the purpose of an individual life and as the basis of culture, to such a degree that it almost entirely prevented people from following the second path for a long time.

The second path was that leading to the improvement and perfection of the world itself. The Middle Ages hardly knew this way.

To them, the world was as good and as bad as it could be; that is, all arrangements, since God had made them, were good: it was man's sinfulness that made the world miserable. For this age, a conscious striving for the improvement or reform of social and political institutions was not the mainspring of thought and deed. To be virtuous in the practice of one's own profession is the only way to benefit the world, and even given this fact, the real goal is still the other life. Moreover, wherever a new social form is actually created, it is seen in principle as a restoration of good old tradition, or as a fight against abuses by virtue of a deliberate delegation of power from the proper authorities. The conscious creation of structures, thought of as truly new, is rare even in the many-faceted legislative work carried out by the French monarchy after Saint Louis. This work was imitated by the dukes of Burgundy in their hereditary territories, but that those labors actually constituted a development of the organization of the state in the direction of more functional forms is a fact of which they were not yet, or barely, aware. They issued ordinances or created offices because this was in tune with their immediate task of promoting the general welfare, not out of a serious vision on their part of a political future.

Nothing contributed so much to the general mood of fearfulness and pessimism about future times than this lack of a firm determination on the part of all to make the world a better and happier place. This world was not included in the promise of better things to come. To those yearning for something better and yet unwilling to bid farewell to the world and all its splendor, nothing was left but despair; nowhere could they see hope or joy anymore. The world would only endure for a short time and only misery remained for those in it.

Once the path of the positive improvement of the world is taken, a new era is born in which the dread of life can give way to courage and hope. This insight waits until the eighteenth century to appear. The Renaissance owes its energetic affirmation of life to different sorts of satisfactions. It is only the eighteenth century that makes the perfectibility of man and society its chief dogma, and the social struggle of the following century lost only the naiveté of its predecessor, not its courage and optimism.

The third path to a better world leads through a land of dreams. It is the most comfortable, but one in which the goal remains at an unchanging distance. If earthly reality is so hopelessly miserable and the denial of the world so difficult, this leaves us to color life with lustrous tones, to live in a dreamland of shining fantasies, and to soften reality in the ecstasy of the ideal. It requires only a simple theme, a single chord, to begin the heart-stirring fugue: a glance at the dreamy bliss of a more beautiful past time suffices, one glimpse of its heroism and its virtue, or just the gay sunshine of life in nature and its enjoyment. All literary culture since antiquity was based on two themes: the heroic and the bucolic. The Middle Ages, the Renaissance, and both the eighteenth and nineteenth centuries managed nothing more than new variations on the old song.

But is this third path to a better life, this fleeing from harsh reality into a beautiful illusion, only a concern of literary culture? Surely it is more than that. Just as the other two paths, it affects the form and content of communal life; and it affects that life the more strongly the more primitive the culture is.

The impact of the three above-mentioned intellectual attitudes on real life itself differs considerably. The most intimate and consistent contact between the labor of life and the ideal goal is found when the idea points to the improvement and perfection of the world itself. In these instances both man's inspirational strength and his confidence flow into material work. Immediate reality is charged with energy. To follow one's life's calling means striving to attain the ideal of a better world. If you wish, here too a blissful dream is the motivating element. To a certain degree, every culture strives towards the creation of a dream world in reality through the transformation of social forms. But while in the other instances we encounter only a mental transformation, the setting up of imaginary perfections in place of the harsh reality one wants to forget, here the object of the dream is reality itself. The idea is to transform reality, to cleanse and improve it. The world appears to be on the good path towards the ideal, if only people would go on working. The ideal form of life seems to be only slightly distant from the life of labor; there is only a minute tension between reality and the dream. Wherever striving for the highest production and cheapest distribution of goods suffices, where the ideal consists of welfare, freedom, and culture, there are comparatively few demands placed on the art of life. There is no longer any need for men to playact the roles of nobleman or hero, wise man or refined courtier.

The first of these three intellectual attitudes, that of world denial, exercises an entirely different influence on real life. Homesickness for eternal bliss renders us indifferent towards the events and forms of earthly existence, desiring only that virtue be generated and maintained in them. The forms of life and society are left as they are, but one strives to permeate them with transcendent morality. This prevents the turning away from the world from having an entirely negative effect on the earthly community as merely denial and abstinence, but allows it to radiate back on society in the form of godly work and practical charity.

But what is the impact of the third attitude on life? Does the yearning for a better life correspond to a dreamed-of ideal? This attitude changes the forms of life into forms of art. But this path does not express its dream of beauty only in artworks as such: it aims at ennobling life itself with beauty and fills communal life with play and forms. Here are found the highest demands on the personal art of living, demands that only an elite can try to meet with an artful life of play.[15] The imitation of heroes and sages is not for everyone; painting life with either heroic or idyllic colors is an expensive pastime and, as a rule, is only partially successful. The struggle to realize the dream of beauty within the forms of society itself has an aristocratic character in its *vitium originis*.

Now we have come to the point from which we intend to view the culture of late medieval times: the point of the beautification of aristocratic life with the forms of the ideal—the artistic light of chivalric romanticism spread over life, with the world costumed in the garb of the round table. The tension between the forms of life and reality is extremely high; the light is false and overdone.

The desire for the beautiful life is generally held to be the most characteristic feature of the Renaissance. Then we witness the greatest harmony in satisfying the thirst for beauty, equally in works of art and in life itself. Art served life and life served art as never before. But here the line between the Middle Ages and the Renaissance is too sharply drawn. The passionate desire to dress life in beauty, the refinement of the art of living, the colorful products of a life lived in imitation of an ideal are much older than the Italian quattrocento. The very motifs of the beautification of life that the Florentines expanded upon are nothing but old medieval forms; Lorenzo de'Medici, even as did Charles the Bold, paid homage to the old knightly ideal as the noble form of life. He even saw in it a model of sorts, its barbarian splendor notwithstanding. Italy discovered new aspects of the beauty of life and gave life a new tone, but the attitude toward life that is usually seen as characteristic of the Renaissance—the striving to transform or even elevate one's own life to a higher level of artistic form—was by no means invented by the Renaissance.

The great divide in the perception of the beauty of life comes much more between the Renaissance and the modern period than between the Middle Ages and the Renaissance. The turnabout occurs at the point where art and life begin to diverge. It is the point where art begins to be no longer in the midst of life, as a noble part of the joy of life itself, but outside of life as something to be highly venerated, as something to turn to in moments of edification or rest. The old dualism separating God and world has thus returned in another form, that of the separation of art and life. Now a line has been drawn right through the enjoyments offered by life. Henceforth they are separated into two halves—one lower, one higher. For medieval man they were all sinful without exception; now they are all considered permissible, but their ethical evaluation differs according to their greater or lesser degree of spirituality.

The things that can make life enjoyable remain the same. They are, now as before, reading, music, fine arts, travel, the enjoyment of nature, sports, fashion, social vanity (knightly orders, honorary offices, gatherings), and the intoxication of the senses. For the majority, the border between the higher and lower levels seems now to be located between the enjoyment of nature and sports. But this border is not firm. Most likely sport will sooner or later again be counted among the higher enjoyments—at least insofar as it is the art of physical strength and courage. For medieval man the border lay, in the best of cases, right after reading; the enjoyment of reading could only be sanctified through striving for virtue or wisdom. For music and the fine arts, it was their service to faith alone that was recognized as being good. Enjoyment *per se* was sinful. The Renaissance had managed to free itself from the rejection of all the joy of life as something sinful, but had not yet found a new way of separating the higher and lower enjoyments of life; the Renaissance wanted an unencumbered enjoyment of all of life. The new distinction is the result of the compromise between the Renaissance and Puritanism that is at the base of modern spiritual attitudes. It amounted to a mutual capitulation in which the one side insisted on saving beauty while the other insisted on the condemnation of sin. Strict Puritanism, just as did the Middle Ages, still condemned as basically sinful and worldly the entire sphere of the beautification of life with an exception being made in cases where such efforts assumed expressly religious forms and sanctified themselves through their use in the service of faith. Only after the Puritan worldview lost its intensity did the Renaissance receptiveness to all the joys of life gain ground again; perhaps even more ground than before, because beginning with the eighteenth century there is a tendency to regard the natural *per se* as an element of the ethically good. Anyone attempting to draw the dividing line between the higher and lower enjoyment of life according to the dictates of ethical consciousness would no longer separate art from sensuous enjoyment, the enjoyment of nature from the cult of the body, the elevated from the natural, but would only separate egotism, lies, and vanity from purity.

Towards the end of the medieval period, even as a new spirit began to stir, there was, in principle, still only the old choice between God and the world: the total rejection of all the splendor and beauty of earthly life or a daring acceptance of it that ran the risk of harming the soul. The beauty of the world became twice as tempting because its sinfulness was recognized; surrendering oneself to it meant, therefore, to enjoy it with unbridled passion. But those who could not do without beauty and yet were unwilling to surrender to the world had no choice but to ennoble beauty. They were able to sanctify the entire sector of art and literature— where admiration constituted the essence of enjoyment—by putting it in the service of faith. And if it was actually the enjoyment of color and line that inspired the connoisseurs of painting and miniatures; the stamp of sinfulness was removed from the enjoyment of these objects because of their sacred subject matter. But what about beauty with a high degree of sinfulness? How could all that, the cult of the body of the knightly sports, courtly life, pride and the avidity for office and honor, and the mesmerizing mystery of love, how could these be made noble and elevated after faith had scorned and condemned them? Here the middle path that led to the land of dreams helped: one dressed everything in the beautiful light of the old fantastic ideals.

The strict cultivation of the beautiful life in the form of a heroic ideal is the characteristic that ties French knightly culture after the twelfth century to the Renaissance. The worship of nature was still too weak to take the beauty of the world in all its nakedness into its service with full conviction as the Greek mind had done: the idea of sin was too powerful for that. Only in so much as people could wrap themselves in the garment of virtue could beauty be brought to culture.

The whole aristocratic life of the later Middle Ages, whether one thinks of France and Burgundy or of Florence, is an attempt to play out a dream. It is always the same dream, that of the old heroes and sages, of knight and maid, of simple and amusing shepherds. France and Burgundy always play the piece in the old style; Florence composes on the set theme a new and more beautiful variation.

Noble and princely life has reached up to its highest possible expression; all the forms of life are equally elevated to the level of mysteries, embellished with color and adornment, masked as virtue. The events of life and the changes of emotion they trigger in us are here framed in beautiful and elevating forms. I well understand that all this is not specifically medieval; it had already arisen in the primitive stages of culture, one can denominate it in chinoiserie and Byzantianism, and it did not die with the Middle Ages, as the Sun King proves.

The stateliness of the court is the arena wherein the aesthetic of the form of life can unfold most fully. It is well known how much importance the Burgundian princes attached to everything that bore on the splendor and stateliness of their courts. Next to military glory, says Chastellain, the courtly ritual is the most important thing demanding attention and its regulation and maintenance are of highest necessity.[16] Olivier de la Marche, the Master of Ceremonies of Charles the Bold, at the instigation of the English king Edward IV, wrote a tract about ritual at the court of Charles, urging this model of ceremony and etiquette as worthy of emulation.[17] The Hapsburgs inherited the beautifully elaborate court life of Burgundy and later exported it to Spain and Austria, at which courts it remained the bulwark of this high artificiality until recently. The court of Burgundy was praised by all as the wealthiest and best ordered.[18] Charles the Bold, above all, known as a man of violent disposition, given to discipline and order but leaving nothing but disorder behind him, had a passion for the most formal forms of life. The old illusion that the prince himself heard the grievances of the poor and powerless and adjudicated them on the spot was dressed by him in a beautiful form. Two or three times a week, after lunch, he had a public audience during which anyone could approach him with petitions. All the noblemen of his house had to be present; none dared to be absent. Carefully ordered according to rank, they were seated on both sides of the passage leading to the high seat of the duke. Kneeling at his feet were the two *maistres des requestes,* the *audiencier,* and a secretary. They read the petitions or dealt with them as instructed by the prince. Behind balustrades placed around the hall were the lower ranking members of the court. On the surface, says Chastellain, it was "un chose magnifique et de grand los,"* but the involuntary spectators were thoroughly bored and he doubted that this method of administering justice was successful. It was, nonetheless, something that he had never seen done by any other prince.[19]

Recreation, too, at the court of Charles the Bold had to take on beautiful forms. "Tournoit toutes ses manières et ses moeurs à sens une part du jour, et avecques jeux et ris entremeslés, se delitoit en beau parler et en amonester ses nobles à vertu, comme un orateur. Et en cestuy regard, plusieurs fois, s'est trouvé assis en un hautdos paré et ses nobles devant luy, là où il leur fit diverses remonstrances selon les divers temps et causes. Et toujours, comme prince et chef sur tous, fut richement et magnifiquement habitué sur tous les autres."[20]† This conscious effort to make an art form of life is actually a perfect realization of the Renaissance, its stiff and naive forms notwithstanding. What Chastellain calls his "haute magnificence de coeur pour estre vu et regardé en singulières choses"‡ is the characteristic quality of Burckhardt's Renaissance man.

The hierarchical arrangements of the courtly household have a Rabelaisian exuberance wherever they involve meals and the kitchen. The courtly table of Charles the Bold, with all the panetiers and carvers and wine pourers and chefs, whose services were regulated with nearly liturgical dignity, resembled the performance

---

* "a magnificent and praiseworthy thing"

† "He was in a habit of devoting a part of his day to serious occupations, and, with games and laughter interspersed, pleased himself with fine speeches and with exhorting his nobles, like an orator, to practice virtue. And in this intention, he was often seen sitting in a chair of state, with his nobles before him, remonstrating with them according to time and circumstances. And always, as the prince and ruler of all, he was richly and magnificently dressed, more so than all the others."

‡ "high magnificence of heart, because he was seen and regarded in extraordinary things"

of a grand and solemn play. The entire court ate in groups of ten in separate rooms, served and attended, as was the duke, with scrupulous observance of rank and standing. Everything was so well regulated that all these groups, after finishing their meal, still had time to greet the duke who was still sitting at his table, "pour luy donner gloire."[21]

In the kitchen (one should try to imagine the heroic kitchen with its seven giant hearths, now all that is left of the ducal palace in Dijon) sits the on-duty chef in an armchair, located between hearth and buffet, from which he is able to overlook the entire room. In his hand he must hold a large wooden spoon "which serves him two purposes: one, to taste soup and sauces; the other to spur the kitchen boys to their duty and, if necessary, to spank them." On rare occasions, as for example, when the first truffles or the first herring are served, the chef himself—holding a torch—may do the honors.

To the stilted courtier who describes all this for us, these are sacred mysteries about which he speaks with respect and in a kind of scholastic scientific manner. When I was a page boy, La Marche says, I was still too young to understand questions of *préséance* and ceremonial.[22] He puts before his readers important questions of precedence and court service in order to answer them on the basis of his mature insights. Why must the cook and not the *écuyer de cuisine* be present at the master's meal? In what manner must the cook come into employment at the court? Who should replace him in case of his absence: the *hateur* or the *potagier*? Here I answer, says the wise man: when a cook is to be employed at the court of a prince, the *maîtres d'hôte,* the *écuyers de cuisine,* and all those employed in the kitchen speak up one by one and by solemn choice made by everyone of them under his oath, the cook takes his position. And to the second question: neither the *hateur* nor the *potagier* may replace him but only an individual chosen by a similar election may substitute for the cook. Why do the panetiers and cupbearers hold the first and second ranks above the meat carvers and cooks? Because their office concerns bread and wine—holy objects glorified by virtue of the sacrament.[23]

One can see in this instance that there is an actual connection between the sphere of faith and that of court etiquette. It does not overstate the case to claim that every means of beautifying and ennobling the forms of life contain a liturgical element that raises the observance of these forms almost to a religious realm. Only this can explain the extraordinary importance people give to all questions of precedence and etiquette, and not only during late medieval times.

Quarrels over royal precedence resulted in the establishment of a regular department of state service in the pre-Romanov days of the Russian empire. Though the western states of medieval times did not create departments, envy about precedence played an important role. It would be easy to gather examples to illustrate this, but here we need only to show how the forms of life were elaborated into beautiful and uplifting games and the wild growth of these games into empty display. Here are just a few examples to demonstrate this. Formal beauty may occasionally completely push practical action aside. Immediately before the battle of Crécy, four French knights reconnoitered the English order of battle. The king, quite impatiently awaiting their report and slowly riding across the field, halts his horse when he sees them returning. They manage to make their way to the presence of the king through the throng of warriors. "What news do you have, messiers?" asks the king. They look at each other without speaking a word because none of them wants to speak ahead of his comrades. And one says to the other, "Sire, you tell it, you speak to the King, I will not speak ahead of you." So they debate a while, back and forth, because no one wants to speak first, "par honneur." Finally, the king orders one of them to report.[24] Practicality had to give way to beautiful form even more so in the case of Messire Gaultier Rallart, *Chevalier du guet* in Paris in 1418. This chief of police never went on his rounds unless he was accompanied by three or four musicians who preceded him. They played so lustily that people said he was practically warning the crooks, "Flee, for I am coming!"[25] This is not an isolated case. There is another case in 1465. The bishop of Evreux, Jean Balure, makes his nightly round in Paris accompanied by clarinets, trumpets and other musical instruments, "qui n'estoit pas acoustumé de faire à gens faisans guet."[26]* The honors due rank and status were strictly observed even at the scaffold: that of the *connétable* de Saint Pol is richly decorated with embroidered lilies, the prayer pillow and the blindfold are of crimson velvet, and the hangman is one who has never hung anyone before—a rather dubious privilege for the condemned.[27]

* "which was not customary for men on watch."

Competition in courtliness and politeness—now characteristically *petit bourgeois*—was extraordinarily strongly developed in the life of the courts of the fifteenth century. It was regarded as a personal and unbearable disgrace not to yield to the higher ranking their proper place. Burgundian dukes gave painfully correct precedence to their royal relations of France. John the Fearless treated his young daughter-in-law, Michelle de France, at all times with exaggerated respect; he called her madame, always knelt before her and offered to serve her constantly—something she was, however, not prepared to tolerate.[28] When Duke Philip the Good learns that his cousin the dauphin, heir to the throne of France, has escaped to Brabant during a conflict with his father the king, he interrupts the siege of Deventer, part of an expedition to bring Frisia under his control, and hurries back to Brussels to welcome his noble guest. The closer the time of their meeting comes, the greater the competition over who will outdo the other in paying homage. Philip is in mortal fear that the dauphin will come out to meet him. He travels posthaste and sends messenger after messenger to make the dauphin wait in place for him. If the dauphin comes to meet him in person, he vows, he'll turn around and travel so far that the dauphin will never find him because the duke will be so ridiculed and shamed that the whole world will never let him forget it. Philip enters Brussels modestly departing from the usual pomp; he hastily dismounts in front of the palace and enters it. He runs forward, then he sees the dauphin who, with the duchess, has left his chamber and who approaches Philip in the courtyard with open arms. Immediately the old duke bares his head, kneels down for a short moment, and runs forward in great haste. The duchess holds on to the dauphin to keep him from taking another step while the dauphin tries in vain to hold the duke on his feet and to keep him from kneeling down. Failing this, he tries to get the duke to stand up. Both weep with emotion, says Chastellain, and all the bystanders weep with them.

For the duration of the stay by this man who, as king, was soon to become the worst enemy of his house, the duke outdoes himself in displays of Chinese servility. He calls himself and his son "de si meschans gens,"* he exposes his sixty-year-old head to the rain, and offers the dauphin all his lands.[29] "Celuy qui se humilie devant

---

* "wretched people"

son plus grand, celuy accroist et multiplie son honneur envers soy-mesme, et de quoy la bonté mesme luy resplend et redonde en face":* with these words Chastellain ends his report about how the Count of Charolais stubbornly refused before a meal to use the same wash basin as Queen Margareth of England and her young son. The noblemen talked about it all day: the case was brought before the old duke, who had two noblemen argue the pros and cons of Charles's attitude. The feudal sense of honor was still alive to the degree that such things were apparently still held to be mean-ingful, beautiful, and edifying. How else are we to understand that refusals to accept precedence could, as a rule, be continued for a quarter of an hour?[30] The longer the refusal, the more impressed the bystanders. Someone entitled to have his hand kissed hides his hand to avoid the honor. The queen of Spain hides her hand in this manner to thwart the young archduke Philip the Beautiful, but the latter, after having waited for a while, unexpectedly seizes her hand and kisses it. The entire Spanish court broke out in laughter on this occasion because the queen was no longer expecting this ges-ture.[31]

All spontaneous displays of tenderness in social relations are care-fully turned into form. It is precisely prescribed which of the ladies at court had to go about holding hands, and even which one or the other had to take the initiative. The invitation, a wave or a call, is a technical term (*hucher*) in the vocabulary of the old court lady who describes Burgundian court etiquette.[32] The formality of pre-venting a departing guest from leaving is carried to the most vexing extremes. The wife of Louis XI is for a few days the guest of Philip of Burgundy; Louis has set a certain day for her return, but the duke refuses to let her go, disregarding the fervent pleas of her attendants and even the queen's own fear of her husband's rage.[33] Goethe said: "There is no external sign of courtesy without a deep ethical cause," but Emerson called courtesy "virtue gone to seed." It is perhaps not justifiable to claim that this ethical cause was still any longer felt during the fifteenth century, but surely the aesthetic value was located somewhere between the honest display of af-fection and barren social form.

---

* "He who humbles himself before someone who is greater than he increases and multiplies his honor himself and the good shines forth and overflows from his face."

It goes without saying that these overelaborated embellishments of life took place above all at the princely courts, where sufficient time and space were available. But that they also permeated the lower spheres of society is proven by the fact that these forms are preserved today precisely among the *petite bourgeoisie* (not to speak of the courts themselves). The customs of urging guests repeatedly to have still another helping of a particular dish, of encouraging them to stay a little longer, of refusing to go ahead of someone, have for the most part disappeared during the last half-century from the etiquette of the higher bourgeoisie. But during the fifteenth century these forms were still in full bloom. Yet while they are most painfully observed, they are the target of biting satire. Above all, it is at church where the stage for beautiful and lengthy displays of civility is found. Most obviously during the *offrande,* because nobody wants to be the first to put his alms on the altar.

> *"Passez." —"Non feray." —"Or avant!*
> *Certes si ferez, ma cousine."*
> *—"Non feray." —"Huchez no voisine,*
> *Qu'elle doit mieux devant offrir."*
> *—"Vous ne le devriez souffrir."*
> *Dist la voisine: "n'appartient*
> *A moy: offrez, qu'à vous ne tient*
> *Que li prestres ne se delivre."*[34]*

Finally after the social superior among them had at last taken the lead, all the time humbly protesting that he did so only to end the stalemate, the quarrel starts over again about who will first kiss *la paix,* the wooden, silver, or ivory plate that had found its way into the mass, following the Agnus Dei, during late medieval times replacing the kiss of peace that had been given mouth to mouth.[35] Because the *paix* was passed from hand to hand among the prominent members of the congregation, who most courteously refused

---

* "Go on." —"I shall not." —"Come forward!/Certainly, you will do so, dear cousin."/—"No, I shall not." —"Call to our neighbor,/That she should offer before you."/—"You should not suffer it."/The neighbor responds; "This is not proper/for me; offer, it is only because of you/That the priest does not continue."

to kiss it first, it became a standard and protracted disturbance of church services.

> *Respondre doit la jeune fame:*
> *—Prenez, je ne prendray pas, dame.*
> *—Si ferez, prenez, douce amie.*
> *—Certes, je ne le prandray mie;*
> *L'en me tendroit pour un sote*
> *—Baillez, damoiselle Masrote.*
> *—Non feray, Jhesucrist m'en gart!*
> *Portez à ma dame Ermagart.*
> *—Dame, prenez. —Saincte Marie,*
> *Portez la paix a la baille.*
> *—Non, mais à la gouverneresse.*[36]*

At last, she accepts it. Even a saintly, world-renouncing man like Franz von Paula considers it his duty to participate in this affectation, and his pious admirers credit this as a sign of true humility, proving that the ethical content had not altogether vanished from these formalities.[37] The importance of these forms, incidentally, is clearly evident in the fact that the precedence that people so civilly forced upon one another in church, was, on the other hand, the cause of volatile and stubborn quarrels.[38] Yielding precedence was a beautiful and praiseworthy denial of a lively noble or bourgeois arrogance.

The entire church visit thus became a kind of minuet, since the quarrel resumed upon leaving the church. Then came the competition to get the higher ranking individuals to walk on the right side, the question of who would cross a plank bridge or enter a narrow alley. Arriving at home, one had to invite the entire company to come inside for a drink—something that Spanish custom still requires—while the invitees, in turn, were obliged to refuse in a most polite manner; whereupon the would-be host had to accompany

---

* The young woman should answer:/—"Take it, I shall not, lady."/—"Yes, do take it, dear friend."/—"Certainly I shall not take it;/People would take me for a fool."/—"Pass it, Miss Marote."/"I shall not, Jesus Christ forbid!/Pass it to the Lady Ermagart."/—"Lady take it." —"Holy Mary,/Take the pax to the bailiff's wife."/—"No, to the governor's wife."

them part of their way: all this again amidst displays of polite refusal by those accompanied.[39]

There is something touching about these beautiful forms, particularly if we remind ourselves that they are the blossoms that arise from the serious struggle with its own arrogance and rage of a race prone to violence and passion. The formal denial of pride frequently fails and, time and again, crass rudeness breaks through the ornate forms. John of Bavaria is a guest in Paris; the luminaries of the city entertain him lavishly but the elector of Liege takes all their money in a game of chance. One of the princes can stand it no longer and cries out: "What the devil kind of a priest is this? How? Shall he take all of our money?" Whereupon John replies, "I am no priest and I don't need your money." And he took the money and tossed it all over the room. "Dont y pluseurs orent grant mervelle de sa grant liberaliteit."[40]* Hue de Lannoy hits someone with an iron glove while the victim is kneeling in accusation before the duke; the Cardinal of Bar calls a priest a liar and a low dog in the presence of the king.[41]

The formal sense of honor is so strong that an affront against etiquette, as is still the case among many Oriental people, wounds like a mortal insult because it causes the beautiful illusion that one's own life is high and pure—something found at the bottom of any unveiled reality—to collapse. To John the Fearless it is a matter of unerasable shame that he has greeted Capeluche, the hangman of Paris, who meets him dressed in full regalia, like a nobleman and touched his hand; only the death of the hangman will redress this outrage.[42] During the state banquet at the coronation of Charles VI in 1380, Philip of Burgundy forces his way to the seat between the king and the duke of Anjou to which he is entitled as the senior of the two; both their entourages approach with shouts and threats to settle the dispute with force, but the king settles it by giving in to the demands of the Burgundian.[43] Amidst the serious life on the campaigns, too, violations of forms are not tolerated. The King of England resents that l'Isle Adam appears before him in a garb of "blanc gris" and looks at him face to face.[44] An English commander sends a peace emissary from the besieged city of Sens to a barber for a shave before receiving him.[45]

The splendid order of the court of Burgundy that was praised

---

* "and many marveled greatly at his liberality."

by contemporaries[46] reveals its true significance only if it is viewed side by side with the confusion customary at the much older French court. Deschamps in a number of ballads decries the misery of court life. His laments mean something more than the usual disapproval of the life of a courtier, about which we will talk later on. Poor food and poor lodgings, constant clamor and confusion, curses and quarrels, envy and mockery: it is a cesspool of sin, a gateway to hell.[47] In spite of the pious veneration of royalty and the proud edifice of grand ceremonies, the decorum of the most significant of events is pitifully lost on more than one occasion. During the funeral of Charles VI at St. Denis in 1422, massive disputes arise between the monks of the abbey and the guild of the salt-weighers (*henouars*) over the state robe and other items of clothing covering the royal corpse; each of the parties insist that it has a claim to them and they engage in a tug-of-war and nearly come to blows. But the duke of Bedford turned the case over to the courts, "et fut le corps enterré!"[48]* The same quarrel is repeated in 1461 during the funeral of Charles VII. Having arrived at the Croix aux Fiens on their way to St. Denis, the salt-weighers, after an exchange of words with the monks of the abbey, refuse to carry the royal corpse any further unless they are paid ten Parisian pounds to which they claim to be entitled. They leave the bier in the middle of the road and the funeral procession is held up for considerable time. The burghers of St. Denis are on the verge of assuming the duties themselves when the *grand écuyer* promises payment out of his own pocket to the *henouars*. Thereupon the procession continues and finally reaches the church at nearly eight o'clock in the evening. Immediately following the funeral a new dispute over the state robe ensues between the monks and the royal *grand écuyer* himself.[49] Similar tumultuous confrontations over the ownership of the utensils of a festive event were a regular part of the festivals, so to speak; disrupting a form had itself become a form.[50]

The general public, which even during the seventeenth century was still a mandatory participant in all the important events of royal life, cause the largest festive occasions, in particular, to frequently lack any semblance of order. During the 1380 coronation banquet the throng of spectators, participants, and servants was so great that the king's waiters, especially hired for the purpose, the

* "and had the body buried!"

connétable and the marshal of Sancerre had to serve the dishes from horseback.[51] When Henry VI of England is crowned king in Paris in 1431, the people crowd into the great hall of the palace at early morning, some to watch, some to pilfer, and some to sneak a bite or two. The lords of parliament, those of the university, the *prévôt des marchands,* and the aldermen are barely able to push their way to the banquet and, when they get there, find that the tables meant for them have been taken by a number of craftsmen. Attempts are made to remove them, "mais quant on en faisoit lever ung ou deux, il s'en asseoit VI ou VIII d'autre costé."[52]* At the coronation of Louis XI in 1461 the Cathedral of Reims is closed early and carefully guarded as a precaution that only as many people be admitted to the church as the choir can safely hold. However, the place near the high altar where the anointment takes place is so crowded that there is hardly any room for the prelate assisting the bishop to move and the princes of the blood on their seats of honor are in acute physical danger.[53]

The church in Paris only reluctantly tolerated the fact that it was (until 1622) the *suffragan* of the Archbishopric of Sens. The archbishop was made to feel in every way that his authority was not appreciated and there was constant reference to the exemption granted by the pope. On February 2, 1492, the archbishop of Sens celebrates a mass in Notre Dame in Paris in the presence of the king. Before the king leaves the church, the archbishop, blessing the crowd, retreats with the priest's cross carried ahead of him. Two of the canons advance with a large number of ecclesiastics, get their hands on the cross and damage it, twist the hand of the man carrying it, and start a tumultuous scene during which the servants of the archbishop have some of their hair pulled out. When the archbishop attempts to end the quarrel, "sans lui mot dire, vinrent prés de lui; Lhuillier [Dean of the cathedral] lui baille du coude dans l'estomac, les autres romprient le chapeau pontifical et les cordons d'icelluy."† The other canon chases the archbishop "disant plusieurs injures en luy mectant le doigt au visage, et prenant son bras tant que dessira son rochet, et n'eust esté que n'eust mis

---

* "but when they had succeeded in making one or two get up, seven or eight sat down on the other side."

† "without saying a word to him, they approached him. Lhuillier elbowed him in the stomach, the others tore up the priest's hat and its ribbons."

sa main au devant, l'eust frappé au visage."* This resulted in a lawsuit that lasted thirteen years.[54]

The passionate and violent mind of the time, hardened and at the same time prone to tears; on the one side despairing of the world, yet on the other reveling in its colorful beauty, could not exist without the strictest formalized behavior. It was essential that the excitement be fixed in a firm frame of standardized forms. Only in this way could life attain a regulated ordering. Thus one's own experiences and those of others were turned into a beautiful, intellectually pleasing presentation; people enjoyed the exaggerated spectacle of suffering and joy under stage lights. The means for a purely spiritual expression was still lacking. Only the aesthetic shaping of emotions allowed that high degree of expression demanded by the times.

This does not mean, of course, that these life forms, above all those relating to the great holy events of birth, marriage, and death, were implemented with such meaning in mind. Customs and ceremonies grow out of primitive beliefs and cults. But the original meaning that constituted their essence has long been lost from consciousness. In its place the forms have been filled with new aesthetic value.

The dressing of sentiment in the garb of a suggestive form reaches its highest development in mourning. There were unlimited possibilities for a splendid exaggeration of sorrow, the counterpart of the hyperbolic expressions of joy during the grandiose court festivities. We do not intend to offer at this point a detailed description of all that somber splendor of black dresses and the lavish display of the funeral ceremonies that accompanied the death of every prince. This is not a characteristic exclusively belonging to the later Middle Ages; monarchies preserve it in our time, and the bourgeois hearse is one of its products. The suggestiveness of the black, used for the clothing not only of the court, but also of the magistrates, the members of the guilds, and ordinary people on the occasion of a princely death, must have been made much stronger by the contrast to the ordinarily rich and varied colors of medieval city life. The funeral pomp displayed over the murdered

---

* "heaping many invectives on him, shaking his finger in the archbishop's face, and grabbing him in such a way by the arm that he tore his vestment; and if the archbishop had not held up his hand, he would have hit him in the face."

John the Fearless was tailored with the most deliberate of intentions for maximum (and in part political) effect. The retinue of warriors accompanying Philip to greet the Kings of England and France displays two thousand black pennons with black standards and banners seven yards long, the fringes of black lace, all embroidered or painted with golden escutcheons. The duke's throne and coach of state have been painted black for the occasion.[55] At a splendid meeting at Troyes, Philip accompanies the Queens of France and England in a velvet mourning garb that trails across the back of his horse and down to the ground.[56] He and his entourage continued to wear black for a considerable period after that.[57]

On occasion an exception in the midst of all that black could enhance the impact: while the entire French court, including the queen, wears black, the king mourns wearing red.[58] And in 1393 the Parisians viewed with consternation the all-white funeral procession for the King of Armenia, Leo of Lusiguan, who had died in exile.[59]

There is no doubt that black mourning dress frequently enclosed a large measure of genuine and passionate grief. Given the medievals' fear of death, strong family attachments, and intense loyalty to their lord, the death of a prince was a truly depressing event. Add to this an injury to the honor of a proud family that made revenge a sacred duty, as was the case with respect to the murder of the duke of Burgundy in 1419, and the expressions of pain and pomp in all their exaggerated forms could well be appropriate to the intensity of the mood. Chastellain deals profusely with the aesthetics of the way the news of the duke's death was transmitted; he invents the long speech, and the weighty and halting style of its dignified rhetoric, with which, at Ghent, the bishop of Tournay gradually prepares the young duke for the terrible news, and he invents the dignified expressions of lament by Philip and his wife, Michelle of France. But we have no reason to doubt the heart of his report: that the news leads to a nervous breakdown on the part of the young duke and that his wife, too, fell into a swoon. The terrible confusion at court, the loud laments in the city—in short, all the intense, unbridled pain with which the news was received—is not to be doubted.[60] Chastellain's report about the expression of pain on the part of Charles the Bold at the passing of Philip in 1467 has elements of truth in it. In this instance the blow was less violent; the old and nearly childish duke had deteriorated for a long time. Relations between the duke and his son had been anything but cordial during the last years. This prompted Chastellain himself to remark that he was astonished to see Charles break down in tears, cry, wring his hands and fall to the ground at the deathbed, "et ne tenoit règle, ne mesure, et tellement qu'il fit chacun s'esmerveiller de sa démesurée douleur."* In the city of Bruges where the duke had died, there too, "estoit pitié de oyr toutes manières de gens crier et plorer et faire leurs diverses lamentaions et regrets."[61]†

It is difficult to tell, from this and similar reports, how far the court style went and how much a noisy display of suffering was considered appropriate and beautiful and how profound the really intense emotions, characteristic of these times, were. There is certainly still a primitive element in it: the loud lament over the dead person that is formalized in the cries of the hired women mourners, that becomes art in the *plourants,* and that bestows something so deeply moving upon grave sculptures, particularly during this period, is a very ancient cultural element.

The combination of primitivity, high sensitivity, and beautiful form can also be sensed in the great fear of conveying the news of a death to a great prince of the Middle Ages. The news of the death of her father is kept from the duchess of Charolais as long as she is pregnant with the future Mary of Burgundy; any news of a death remotely of concern to him is kept from Philip the Good on his sickbed, which means, among other things, that Adolf of Cleve is not permitted to wear mourning dress after the death of his wife. When the duke managed to "get wind" (Chastellain himself uses the term "avoit esté en vent un peu de ceste mort") of the death of his chancellor, Nicolas Rolin, he asked the bishop of Tournay, who had come to see him, whether it was true that the chancellor had died. "Monseigneur," says the bishop, "in truth he may be dead because he is old and broken in body and spirit and will hardly live for long." "Déa!" says the duke, "I don't ask that, I ask whether he is 'mort de mort et trespassé."‡ "Well, monsei-

---

* "and there was neither rule nor measure to his grief, and he astonished everyone with the depths of his sorrow."

† "there was lamentation; all kinds of people weeping and crying and varied shouts of pain and suffering, loudly expressed, could be heard."

‡ "truly dead and gone to the grave."

gneur," the bishop replies, "he has not died, but he is paralyzed on one side and is as good as dead." The duke gets angry, "Vechy merveilles!* Tell me clearly now, whether he is dead." Only then does the bishop admit: "Yes, truly, monseigneur, he has really died."[62] Does not this strange way of conveying the news of a death reveal more of an old superstitious form than mere consideration for a sick person whom all this hesitation could only irritate? All this is part of that sort of thinking that prompted Louis XI never again to wear clothes he had worn when he received any kind of bad news; nor to ride again a horse on which he had been mounted on one of those occasions. Indeed, he even had a section of the Forest of Loches cut down because it was there that he had learned of the death of his newborn son.[63] "M. le chancellier," he writes on May 25, 1483, "je vous mercye des lettres etc. mais je vous pry que m'en envoyés plus par celluy qui les m'a aportées, car je luy ay trouvé le visage terriblement changé depuis que je ne le vitz, et vous prometz par ma foy qu'il m'a fait grant peur; et adieu."[64]†

No matter what old taboo notions may be hidden in the mourning customs, their living cultural value is that they bestow on sorrow a form and turn it into something beautiful and lofty. They bestow a rhythm on pain, transpose real life into the sphere of drama and dress it in the cothurnus.[65] In a primitive culture—I have, for example, the Irish in mind—mourning customs and funeral poetry are still an unbroken whole. Court mourning during Burgundian times can only be understood if viewed in relation to elegy. The displays of mourning demonstrated in beautiful form how totally powerless the affected individual is in the face of suffering. The higher the rank the more heroic the display of pain. The Queen of France had to stay an entire year in the room where she was told of the death of her husband. In the case of princesses, six weeks were the norm. After Madame de Charolais, Isabella de Bourbon, had been told of the death of her father, she did attend the funeral at Couwenberg Castle but thereafter remained for six

---

* "That is humbug!"

† "Monsieur the Chancellor, I thank you for the letters, etc., but I beg you to send no more by him who brought them, for I found his face terribly changed since I last saw him, and I tell you on my honor that he made me much afraid; and farewell."

weeks in her room—all the time lying on her bed, propped up by pillows, but clothed in *barbette,* cap, and overcoat. The room is draped entirely in black. On the floor is a large black sheet in place of a soft carpet, and the antechamber is similarly draped in black. Noble women are confined to bed solely for the death of their husband for six weeks, only ten days for father or mother, but for the rest of the six weeks they remain seated before the bed on a large sheet of black cloth. The death of the eldest brother requires six weeks of confinement to a room, but not to the bed.[66] This makes it clear why, in a time that held this kind of high ceremonial in such honor, one of the most mentioned of the shocking circumstances surrounding the murder of John the Fearless in 1419 was that he was buried dressed only in vest, trousers, and shoes.[67]

The emotion of grief, dressed in beautiful forms and assimilated in this manner, is easily dealt with; the urge to dramatize life leaves room "behind the scene" where nobly embellished pathos can be denied. There is a naive separation between "state" and real life that is revealed in the writings of the old court lady Alienor de Poitiers, who still venerates all these external displays as if they were high mysteries. Following the description of Isabella of Bourbon's magnificent mourning she declares, "Quand Madame estoit en son particulier, elle n'estoit point toujours couchee, ni en une chambre."* The princess receives in this state, but only as a beautiful formality. Alienor adds in a similar vein, "It is proper to wear mourning clothes for two years in memory of a husband if you can't avoid remarriage." Speedy remarriage was frequent, particularly among the highest estates, the princes with the most famous names. The duke of Bedford, Regent of France for the young Henry VI, remarried after only five months.

Next to mourning, confinement during childbirth offered ample opportunities for serious pomp and hierarchical distinctions of ostentation. There, colors have meaning. Green, which was the usual color for the middle-class crib and the *vuurmand*[68] as late as the nineteenth century, was in the fifteenth century the prerogative of queens and princesses. The confinement room of the Queen of France was of green silk (earlier on, it was entirely in white). Even countesses were not permitted to have "la chambre verde." Fabrics,

---

* "When Madame was in private, she by no means always lay in bed nor confined herself to one room."

furs, and the colors of blankets and bedspreads were prescribed. On the dressing table in the room of Isabella of Bourbon, two large candles in silver holders burn continuously because the shutters of the lying-in room are kept closed for fourteen days. Most remarkable however are the stately beds that, like the carriages at the burial of the King of Spain, remain empty. The young mother lies on a couch in front of the fire and the child, Mary of Burgundy, in a cradle in the nursery. In addition, in the confinement room there are two large beds in an artistic ensemble with green drapes. They are made, with covers turned, as if for someone to sleep in them. In the nursery, there are in addition two large bedsteads in green and violet and still another large bed in an antechamber, or *chambre de parement,* that is entirely draped in crimson-colored satin which was donated to John the Fearless by the city of Utrecht; the room was therefore called "la chambre d'Utrecht." During the baptism ceremonies the beds served ceremonial functions.[69]

The aesthetics of formality revealed itself in the everyday look of town and countryside: the strict hierarchy of fabrics, colors, and furs placed the different estates in an eternal frame of reference that both enhanced and protected a sense of their dignity. But the aesthetic of emotional swings was not limited to festive rejoicing and sorrowing on the occasions of birth, marriage, and death, where processions were a function of the necessary ceremonies. Every ethical action was preferably seen in terms of a beautifully embellished form. There is such an element in the admiration for the humility and self-flagellation of a saint, for the repentance of a sinner such as the "moult belle contrition de ses Péchés"* of Agnes Sorel.[70] Every relationship in life is stylized. In contrast to the modern preoccupation with hiding and obscuring intimate relations, medieval man strove to express them as a form and as a spectacle for others. Thus friendship had its elaborated form in the life of the fifteenth century. Side by side with the older brotherhood of blood and the brotherhood of arms, honored by commoners and nobles alike, a form of sentimental friendship, known as "mignon," existed.[71] The princely "mignon" is a formal institution that survived during all of the sixteenth and part of the seventeenth century. The term applies to the relationship between James I of England and Robert Carr and George Villiers; William of Orange

* "most beautiful contrition for her Sins"

at the time of the abdication of Charles V should be seen from this vantage point. "Twelfth Night" can only be understood if we keep this particular form of sentimental friendship in mind while considering the behavior of the duke towards the pretender Cesario. This relationship is a parallel to courtly love. "Sy n'as dame ne mignon," says Chastellain.[72] But any signs that would place it in the tradition of Greek friendship fail to appear. The openness with which mignoncy is treated in an age that was horrified by the *crimen nefandum* silences any suspicion. Bernardino of Siena holds up as models to his Italian compatriots, among whom sodomy was widely spread,[73] France and Germany, where it was unknown. Only princes who are very much hated are on occasion charged with illicit relations with an official favorite, as in the case of Richard II of England with Robert de Vere.[74] Under these circumstances, mignonism is a harmless relationship, which honors those so favored and is freely admitted by them. Commines himself recounts how he had enjoyed the honor of having the distinction of receiving royal favors from Louis XI and how he went about dressed like him.[75] Because it is the clear mark of the relationship, the king always has at his side a *mignon en titre,* wearing the same dress as he, on whom he may lean for support during receptions.[76] Frequently two friends of same age but different rank also dress alike, sleep in the same room, and occasionally even in the same bed.[77] Such inseparable friendship exists between the young Gaston de Foix and his bastard brother, which friendship came to such a tragic end; between Louis of Orléans (then still of Touraine) and Pierre de Craon,[78] between the young duke of Cleve and Jacques de Lalaing. In the same mode, princesses have a trusted female friend, dressed like them and called *mignonne.*[79]

All these beautifully stylized life forms, serving the task of lifting harsh reality into the sphere of noble harmonies, were part of the great art of living without having any direct impact on art itself in the narrow sense of the word. The forms of social etiquette with their friendly appearance of unforced altruism and accommodating recognition of others, the splendor of the court and court etiquette with all its hieratic majesty and seriousness, the gay adornments of marriage and confinement—all this passed in beauty without leaving any traces in art and literature. The means of expression joining them to each other is not art but fashion. Actually, fashion generally is much closer to art than academic aesthetics are willing to admit. As an artificial emphasis on physical beauty and movement, it is intimately linked to one of the arts, i.e. dance, but in other respects the realm of fashion, or better, that of ensemble fitted to an occasion, borders in the fifteenth century much more directly on art than we are inclined to assume. It does so not only because the frequent use of jewels and the use of metals in the fashioning of the garb of warriors added a direct craft element to costumes; fashion shares essential qualities with art itself: style and rhythm are just as indispensable to it as they are to art. During late medieval times, fashion in costume constantly expressed a measure of the style of life that find only a pale reflection even in today's coronation festivities. In daily life the differences in fur and color, cap and bonnet indicated the strict order of the estates, the splendid dignities, states of joy and sadness, and tender relations between friends and lovers.

The aesthetics of all of life's circumstances and life's conditions were elaborated with the greatest possible emphasis. The higher the substance of beauty and ethicality of these relationships, so much the better could they be expressed as a true art. Courtliness and etiquette could only express themselves in life itself, in clothing and jewelry. Mourning, on the other hand, found still another emphatic means of expression in a durable and powerful art form— the tomb monument; the cultural value of mourning was enhanced by its relation to liturgy. But still richer were the aesthetic flowers of the three elements of life: courage, honor, and love.

Chapter Three

~

THE HEROIC DREAM

AT THE END OF THE EIGHTEENTH CENTURY WHEN medieval cultural forms were absorbed as new values of the eighteenth century itself, in other words at the beginning of the Romantic era, the medieval world was seen, first and foremost, as the world of knighthood. The Romantics were inclined to think the term "medieval" simply meant "when knighthood was in flower." More than anything else, they saw in the time the nodding of plumed helmets. As paradoxical as this may sound today, they were in many respects correct. By now, more thorough studies have taught us that chivalry was only a part of the culture of the period and that political and social development took place, for the most part, outside of that form. The period of genuine feudality and the flourishing of knighthood ended during the thirteenth century. What follows is the urban-princely period of the medieval era, during which the dominant factors in state and society are the commercial power of the bourgeoisie and, based on it, the monetary powers of the princes. With the advantage of our hindsight we are accustomed, and justifiably so, to look much more to Ghent and Augsburg, much more to emerging capitalism and the newly arising forms of the state, than to the nobility, whose power, here more so, there less so, was already "broken" everywhere. Historical research itself has been democratized since the days of Romanticism. But those who are accustomed to look at late medieval times under their political-economic aspects cannot help but notice over and over that the sources, particularly the narrative sources, give much more attention to the nobility and their bustle than fits our understanding. This is true not only for later medieval times, but also for the seventeenth century.

The reason for this is the fact that the life form of the nobility still retains its relevance over society long after the nobility as social structure had lost its dominant meaning. The nobility undoubtedly

61

still occupied the first place as a social element in the mind of the fifteenth century, but contemporaries are considered to have placed its importance much too high and that of the bourgeoisie much too low. They failed to realize that the real impetus for social development was located somewhere else than in the life and actions of a warring nobility. This kind of reasoning would blame contemporaries for that mistake and the age of Romanticism for uncritically adopting their view while claiming that modern historical research has unearthed the true facts of late medieval life. This is true as far as political and economic life is concerned. But if we desire to understand cultural life, we have to be aware that the illusion itself retained its value as truth for those who lived it. Even if the noble life forms had been nothing more than the mere surface veneer of life, the task of the historian would still be to understand life in terms of the luster of that finish.

But it was much more than a mere veneer. During medieval times the concept of the division of society into estates permeates all the fibers of theological and political reflections. This concept was by no means limited to the well-known three: clergy, nobility, and third estate. The term estate has not only a greater value, but also a more far-reaching meaning. Generally speaking, any group, any function, any profession was regarded as an estate, which meant that in addition to the division of society into three estates, another such division into twelve estates was possible.[1] Because estate is "state," or "ordo," it contains the notion of an entity willed by God. During the Middle Ages the word estate or "ordre" includes a large number of human groupings that, to our understanding, are rather unalike: the estates that we understand, the professions, stand next to the married state as well as to that of virginity; of the state of sin, *estat de péchié;* of the four *estats de corps et de bouche** at court (panetiers, wine handlers, meat cutters, and kitchen chefs); of the sacerdotal orders (priest, deacon, subdeacon, etc.); of the monastic orders; and of the orders of knights. In medieval thought the term "estate" or "order" is held together in all these cases by an awareness that each of these groups represents a divine institution, that it is an organ of the world edifice that is just as indispensable and just as hierarchically dignified as the heavenly throne and the powers of the angelic ranks.

* estates of body and mouth

In this beautiful image of state and society every estate was assigned a function corresponding, not to its proven utility, but to its degree of holiness or to its splendor. The degeneration of spirituality, the decay of chivalric virtue, could thus be lamented without abandoning even a small part of the ideal image; the sins of men may prevent the realization of the ideal, but the ideal remains the basis and the guide for social thought. The medieval image of society is static, not dynamic.

Chastellain, the court historiographer of Philip the Good and Charles the Bold, whose rich work is here again the best mirror of the thought of the time, sees the society of his day in a wondrous glow. In him we meet a man, born among the meadows of Flanders, who had before his eyes the most splendid unfolding of bourgeois power in the Netherlands, but who was nonetheless so blinded by the external splendor of ostentatious Burgundian life that he regarded knightly courage and knightly virtue as the sources of all the strength within the state.

God created the common people to work, to till the soil, to sustain life through commerce; he created the clergy for works of faith; but he created the nobility to extol virtue, administer justice, and so that the beautiful members of this estate may, through their deeds and customs, be a model for others. Chastellain assigns to the nobility the highest tasks of the state, the protection of the church, the spreading of the faith, the defense of the people against oppression, the supervision of the general welfare, the struggle against violence and tyranny, the stabilization of peace. Their qualities are truth, bravery, integrity, and kindness. The nobility of France, says this pompous panegyrist, meet this ideal standard.[2] We sense in Chastellain's entire work that he actually looked at the events of his time through these rose-colored glasses.

This underestimation of the bourgeoisie resulted from the fact that the stereotype usually associated with the third estate had not been corrected by reality. This stereotype was still as simple and as summary in nature as a calendar picture or a bas-relief depicting the labors of the season: the toiling worker in the field, the industrious craftsman, or the busy merchant. The figure of the powerful patrician who was pushing the nobility from its place, the fact that the nobility constantly renewed itself with the blood and the strength of the bourgeoisie, had as little room in this lapidary type as the figure of the combative guild brother and his ideal of freedom. In the concept of the third estate, the bourgeoisie and the workers remained undifferentiated up until the time of the French Revolution. The figure of the poor farmer or of the indolent and wealthy burgher[3] take turns in dominating the foreground of the picture of the third estate but they do not attain a depiction in accord with their real economic and political functions. A reform program conceived in 1412 by an Augustine monk put forth in all seriousness that every person outside of the nobility should be forced to do manual or field labor or be ordered to leave the country.[4]

This alone explains why someone like Chastellain, whose susceptibility to ethical illusions equals his political naiveté, would assign, next to the lofty qualities of the nobility, only low and slavish qualities to the third estate: "Pour venir au tiers membre qui fait le royaume entier, c'est l'estat des bonnes villes, des marchans et des gens de labeur, des quels ils ne convient faire si longue exposition que des autres, pour cause que de soy il n'est gaires capable de hautes attributions, parce qu'il est au degré servile. [O kevels van Vlaanderen!]"* The virtues of this estate are humility and industry, obedience to their king and a willingness to please their lords.[5]

Is it possible that this total lack of insight into a future of bourgeois liberties and power contributes to the pessimism of Chastellain and kindred spirits whose expectations focused entirely on the nobility?

Even wealthy burghers are still summarily called "villains" by Chastellain.[6] He has not the faintest notion of bourgeoisie honor. Philip the Good habitually abused his powers in order to marry off his "archers," usually members of the lower nobility, or other servants of his house, to wealthy bourgeois widows or daughters. Parents had their daughters marry as early as possible to thwart such advances. One widow is known to have married only two days after her husband's funeral for the same reason.[7] The duke at one time encountered the stubborn resistance of a Lille brewer who refused to let his daughter submit to such a union. The duke had the girl abducted to a safe place whereupon the enraged father

---

* "Coming to the third estate, which completes the kingdom, it is the estate of the good towns, of merchants and of laboring men, of whom it is not becoming to give such a long exposition as of the others, because it is hardly possible to attribute great qualities to them, as they are of servile degree. [O Flemish folk!]"

moved, lock, stock, and barrel, to Tournay, where, outside of the duke's territory, he was able, without impediment, to put the matter before the parliament in Paris. He reaps only pain and sorrow for his efforts and falls ill. The end of the story is highly characteristic of Philip's impulsive character and does not, according to our standards, do him proud.[8] He returns the girl to her mother, who had come to him as a supplicant, but grants her request only after having mocked and humiliated her. Chastellain, usually not afraid to criticize his lord, in this case throws his sympathies entirely on the side of the duke. For the offended father he can only find words such as "ce rebelle brasseur rustique"* and "et encore si meschant vilain."[9]†

Chastellain admits the great financier Jacques Coeur to his *Temple de Bocace,* a kind of hall of honor for the fame and the misfortunes of the nobility, but not without a few words of explanation, in contrast to Gilles de Rais,[10] who is admitted on account of his high birth without much ado in spite of the horrible misdeeds he had committed.[11] Chastellain considers it superfluous to list the names of the burghers who lost their lives in the bitter fighting in the defense of Ghent.[12]

Despite this disdain of the third estate, there is in the ideal of knighthood itself, and in the cultivation of virtue and duties held up to the nobility, an ambiguous element revealing a less arrogant aristocratic attitude towards the people. Side by side with the mockery of peasants, full of hatred and contempt, as we encounter it in the Flemish *Kerelslied* and the *Proverbes del vilain* there exists during the Middle Ages a countercurrent of empathy with poor people and their miserable lot.

> *Si fault de faim perir les innocens*
> *Dont les grans loups font chacun jour ventrée,*
> *Qui amassent a milliers et a cens*
> *Les faulx tresors; c'est le grain, c'est la blée,*
> *Le sang, les os qui ont la terre arée*
> *Des povres gens, dont leur esperit crie*
> *Vengence à Dieu, vé à seignourie . . .*[13]‡

* "this rebellious rustic brewer"
† "and such a naughty villein too."
‡ The innocent must starve;/In this way the big wolves fill their belly every day,/Who by thousands and hundreds/Hoard ill-gotten treasures; it is the grain,

There is always this same note of sorrow: the poor people are visited by wars and drained of their wealth by officialdom, they live in scarcity and misery. Everyone feeds off the peasants while they suffer patiently, "le prince n'en sçait riens,"* and, if they occasionally grumble and denounce the authorities, "povres brebis, povre fol peuple,†" with one word the lord will restore them to calm and reason. In France where the entire country was gradually dragged into the pitiful devastations and uncertainties of the Hundred Years War, one theme of the lament rises to the surface: the peasants are plundered, burned out of their homes, and mistreated at the hands of their own and enemy war parties. They are robbed of their draft animals and are chased from their homes and their lands. The lament, couched in these terms, never ends. It is echoed by the great reform-minded clerics around 1400: by Nicolas de Clémanges in his *Liber de lapsu et reparatione justitiae*,[14] by Gerson in the courageous and moving political sermon that he gave on November 7, 1405, at the palace of the queen in Paris on the theme "vivat rex": "Le pauvre homme n'aura pain à manger, sinon par advanture aucun peu de seigle ou d'orge; sa pauvre femme gerra, et auront quatre au six petits enfans au fouyer, ou au four, qui par advanture sera chauld; demanderont du pain, crieront à la rage de faim. La pauvre mère si n'aura que bouter es dens que un peu de pain ou il y ait du sel. Or, devroit bien suffire cette misere:— viendront ces paillars que chergeront tout . . . tout sera prins, et happé; et querez qui paye."[15]‡ Jean Jouvenel, bishop of Beauvaix, holds up the misery of the people to the estates in bitter laments at Blois in 1433 and at Orléans in 1439.[16] Together with the laments of the other estates about their difficulties, presented in form of a debate, the theme of the people's misery reoccurs in Alain Char-

---

it is the corn,/The blood and the bones with which the soil is tilled/By the poor people, and their spirits cry/To God for vengeance and woe to lordship . . .

   * "the prince knows nothing of this"
   † "poor sheep, poor foolish people"
   ‡ "The poor man will not have bread to eat, except perhaps a handful of rye or barley; his poor wife will lie in and they will have four or six little ones about the hearth or the oven, which perchance will be warm; they will ask for bread, they will scream, mad with hunger. The poor mother will have but a very little salted bread to stuff between their teeth. Now such misery ought to suffice; but no;—the plunderers will come who will seek everything. . . . Everything will be taken and snapped up; and we need not ask who pays."

tier's *Quadriloge invectif*[17] and in Robert Gaguin's *Debat du laboureur, du prestre et du gendarme,*[18] which was inspired by Chartier's work. The chroniclers could not help resuming the topic time and again; their subject matter demanded it.[19] Molinet composed a *Resource du petit peuple.*[20] Meschinot, a serious-minded man, repeats over and over again his warning about the growing devastations of the people.

> *O Dieu voyez du commun l'indigence,*
> *Pourvoyez-y à toute diligence:*
> *Las! par faim, froid, paour et misere tremble.*
> *S'il a peché ou commis négligence*
> *Encontre vous, il demande indulgence.*
> *N'est-ce pitieé des biens que l'on lui emble?*
> *Il n'a plus bled pour porter au molin,*
> *Ou lui oste draps de laine et de lin,*
> *L'eaue, sans plus, lui demeure pour boire.*[21]*

In a volume of complaints handed to the king on the occasion of the assembly of the estates at Tours in 1484, the lament even assumes the character of a political treatise.[22] However, everything remains on the level of a completely stereotyped and negative pity and never becomes a political program. There is still no indication of any well-thought-out ideas of social reform in it, and therefore the same theme will continue to be sung by La Bruyère and by Fénelon until deep into the eighteenth century, and, because there is no reform, the laments of the older Mirabeau, "l'ami des hommes," are little different even though they already sound the note of future resistance.

It was to be expected that those glorifiers of the late medieval ideal of knighthood chimed in with these confessions of pity for the people; this was demanded by the knight's duty to protect the weak. The idea that true nobility is based only on virtue and that, basically, all men are equal also was a part of the ideal of knight-

---

* O God, see the indigence of the common people,/Provide for it with all speed:/Alas! with hunger, cold, fear, and misery they tremble./If they have sinned or have been negligent/Towards you, they pray indulgence./Is it not a pity they have lost their goods?/They have no more corn to take to the mill,/From them their wool and linen are taken,/Water, nothing more, they have left to drink.

hood and was equally stereotyped and theoretical. The historical-cultural significance of both these sentiments may well be over-estimated on occasion. Recognition of the nobility of heart is celebrated as a triumph of the Renaissance. There are plenty of references to the fact that Poggio expresses this idea in his *De nobilitate*. We used to find this old egalitarianism echoed in the revolutionary tenor of John Ball's "when Adam delved and Eve span, where was then the gentleman?" and imagined that noblemen would tremble when they heard this text.

Both ideas were long commonplaces of courtly literature itself just as they were in the salons of the *ancien régime*. The idea of the true nobility of the heart originated with the glorification of courtly love in the poetry of the troubadours. It remains an ethical reflection without any socially active reality.

> *Dont vient a tous souveraine noblesce?*
> *Du gentil cuer, paré de nobles mours.*
> *. . . Nulz n'est villains se du cuer ne lui muet.*[23]*

The idea of equality had been borrowed by the church fathers from Cicero and Seneca. Gregory the Great had left for the approaching medieval age the dictum that "Omnes namque homines natura aequales sumus." This adage had been repeated in the most varied colors and shades without, however, diminishing true inequality, since, to medieval man, the central point of this idea was the imminent equality of death and not a hopelessly distant equality in life. In Eustache Deschamps this idea is expressed in close linkage with the notion of the *danse macabre,* which must have been a source of solace for the injustice of the world during late medieval times. Adam himself addresses his descendants as follows:

> *Enfans, enfans de moy, Adam, venuz,*
> *Qui après Dieu suis peres premerain*
> *Creé de lui, tous estes descenduz*
> *Naturelment de ma coste et d'Evain;*
> *Vo mere fut. Comment est l'un villain*
> *Et l'autre prant le nom de gentillesce*

---

* Whence does sovereign nobility come to one?/From a gentle heart, adorned by noble morals/. . . No one is a villein unless it comes from his heart.

De vous freres? dont vient tele noblesce?
Je ne le sçay, se ce n'est des vertus,
Et les villains de tout vice qui blesce;
Vous estes tous d'une pel revestus.
Quant Dieu me fist de la boe ou je fus,
Homme mortel, faible, pesant et vain,
Eve de moy, il nous crea tous nuz,
Mais l'esperit nous inspira a plain
Perpetuel, puis eusmes soif et faim,
Labour, dolour, et enfans en tristesce;
Pour noz pechiez enfantent a destresce
Toutes femmes; vilment estes conçuz.
Dont vient ce nom: villain, qui les cuers blesce?
Vous estes tous d'une pel revestuz.

Les roys puissans, les contes et les dus,
Li gouverneur du peuple et souverain,
Quant ilz naissent, de quoi sont ilz vestuz?
D'une orde pel.
. . . Prince, pensez, sanz avoir en desdain
Les povres gens, que la mort tient le frain.[24]*

In conformity with this idea, passionate defenders of the ideal of knighthood at times intentionally list the deeds of peasant heroes in order to point out to the nobility "that sometimes those whom they regard as peasants possess the greatest courage."[25]

---

* Children, children, from me, Adam, born,/Who after God am the first father./Created by him, you are descended from me,/Naturally of my rib and of Eve;/She was your mother. How is it that one is a villein/And the other takes the name of gentility,/Of you brothers? Whence comes such nobility?/I do not know, unless it comes from virtues,/And the villains from all vice which wounds:/You are all covered by the same skin./When God made me out of the mud where I lay,/Mortal man, feeble, heavy and vain,/Eve from me, He created us quite nude,/But the imperishable spirit gave us/in abundance; We were hungry and thirsty afterwards,/Labor, pain, and children in sorrow;/For our sins, children are born in pain/by all women; Vilely you are conceived./Whence comes this name: Villein, that wounds the heart?/You are all covered by the same skin./The mighty kings, the counts and the dukes,/The governor of the people and sovereign,/When they are born, with what are they clothed?/By a dirty skin./. . . Prince, remember without disdaining/The poor people, that death holds the reins.

Here is the basis of all of these ideas: the nobility is called to sustain and purify the world by fulfilling the ideal of knighthood. The true life of nobility and the true virtue of nobility are the remedy for evil times: the well-being and tranquility of church and kingdom and the strength of justice depend on it.[26] War entered the world with Cain and Abel and since then has proliferated between the good and the bad. To start it is bad. The very noble and very distinguished state of knighthood is therefore instituted in order to protect, defend, and preserve tranquility for the people upon whom the misery of war is usually visited most painfully.[27] Two things are put in the world by the will of God, we are told in the biography of one of the purest representatives of the late medieval ideal of knighthood, Boucicaut, like two pillars in order to support the order of divine and human laws; without them the world would be nothing but confusion. These two pillars are knighthood and scholarship, "chevalerie et science, qui moult bien conviennent ensemble."[28]* Science, Foy, et Chevalerie are the three lilies of Le Chapel des fleurs de lis of Philippe de Vitri; they represent the three estates. Knighthood is called to protect and guard the other two.[29] The equivalence of knighthood and scholarship, also revealed by the tendency to attach to the doctor's degree the same privileges as to the title of knighthood, demonstrates the high ethical substance of the ideal of knighthood. It places the veneration of higher aspirations and daring next to a higher knowledge and ability. There is a need to see in man a higher potentiality and a need to express this in the fixed forms of two, mutually equal consecrations for higher tasks in life. But of these two, the ideal of knighthood was much more generally and strongly effective, because it combined, together with the ethical element, many aesthetic elements that were intelligible to everyone.

Medieval thought in general is permeated in all regards by elements of faith: in a similar manner the thought of that more limited group that moves in the spheres of the court and the nobility is saturated by the ideal of knighthood. Even notions of faith themselves are incorporated and succumb to the spell of the idea of knighthood: the feat of arms of the Archangel Michael was "la première milicie et prouesse chevaleureuse qui oncques fut mis en

---

* "knighthood and learning which go very well together."

exploict."* The Archangel is the ancestor of knighthood; the "mili-cie terrienne et chevalerie humaine"† is an earthly replication of the host of angels surrounding God's throne.[30]

Does this high expectation respecting the fulfillment of duty by the nobility lead to any more precise definition of the political ideas concerning its duties? One thing is certain: the aspirations for universal peace are based on harmony among the kings, the con-quest of Jerusalem, and the expulsion of the Turks. Philippe de Mézières, never tiring of devising ever new schemes, dreamed of an order of knights that would surpass the old power of the Tem-plars and Hospitaliers. In his *Songe du vieil perelin* he worked out a plan that seemed to guarantee the bliss of the entire world for the foreseeable future. The young King of France—the tract was writ-ten in 1388 when there were still high hopes attached to the hapless Charles VI—will readily make peace with Richard of England, just as young and as innocent of the current quarrels as he. They would have to negotiate personally about this peace, and should tell each other of the wondrous revelations that had foretold the peace to them. They would have to discard all the petty concerns that would raise obstacles if the negotiations were to be trusted to the clergy, legal scholars, or military leaders. The King of France should gen-erously give up a few border towns and castles. Immediately fol-lowing the conclusion of peace, preparations for a crusade should be made. All disputes and feuds should be ended everywhere and the tyrannical administration of the territories be reformed; a gen-eral council should arouse the princes of Christendom to go to war in case sermons were not sufficient to convert the Tartars, Turks, Jews, and Saracens.[31] These far-reaching plans were possibly the subject of conversations during the friendly meetings between Mézières and the young Louis of Orléans in the Celestine monas-tery in Paris. Louis of Orléans himself also entertained such dreams of peace and crusades, though they were tempered by concerns of practical and self-serving politics.[32]

The image of a society sustained by the ideal of knighthood coats the world with a peculiar color. This color peels off rather easily. If one consults the familiar French chroniclers of the fourteenth and

---

* "the first deed of knighthood and chivalrous prowess that was ever achieved."
† "terrestrial knighthood and human chivalry"

fifteenth centuries, such as the keen Froissart, the matter-of-fact Monstrelet and d'Escouchy, the deliberate Chastellain, the courtly Olivier de la Marche, the bombastic Molinet, they all—with the exception of Commines and Thomas Basin—begin with high-sounding declarations that they write for the glorification of knightly virtue and glorious feats of arms.[33] But none of them can stick to it, although Chastellain manages to keep it up longest. While Froissart, himself the author of a hyperromantic knightly epic, *Méliador,* indulges his spirit in the ideal *prouesse* and *grand opertises d'armes,* his journalistic pen continuously writes a record of treason and cruelty, crafty greed and dominance, of a profession of arms that had become entirely devoted to the making of profit. Molinet, disregarding for the moment style and language, constantly forgets his chivalrous intention and reports events clearly and simply; he only occasionally recalls the noble, uplifting task he has set for himself. The knightly tenor is even more superficial in the writings of Monstrelet.

It is as if the spirit of these writers—a superficial spirit, one has to admit—employed the fiction of knighthood as a corrective for the incomprehensibility their own time had for them. It was the only form that allowed for even an imperfect understanding of events. In reality, wars and politics in those days were extremely formless and seemed disconnected. War appeared in most instances as a chronic process of isolated campaigns scattered over large areas, diplomacy as a verbose and deficient instrument that was in one respect dominated by very general traditional ideas and in another by a hopelessly tangled complex of individual petty legal questions. Incapable of discerning in all this a real social development, historiography employed the fiction of the ideal of knighthood and thus traced everything back to a beautiful image of princely honor and knightly virtue, to a pretty game of noble rules that created the illusion of order. If we compare this historical standard to the insight of a historian like Thucydides, we find it to be a rather low vantage point. History becomes a dry report of beautiful or seemingly beautiful feats of arms and ceremonial state occasions. Who, then, given this vantage point, are the proper witnesses of history? The heralds and kings of arms,[34] in Froissart's opinion: they are present at those noble events and are officially called upon to judge them; they are experts in matters of fame and honor, and fame and honor are the motifs of historiography.[35] The statutes of the Golden

Fleece mandated the recording of knightly feats of arms; Lefèvre de Saint Remy, called Toison d'or[36] or the Herald Berry, is the model for king of arms historiographers.

As the ideal of the beautiful life the idea of knighthood has a particular form. In its essence, it is an aesthetic ideal, built out of colorful fantasies and uplifting sentiments. But it aspires to be an ethical ideal: medieval thought could only turn it into an ideal of life by linking it with piety and virtue. Knighthood always fails in that ethical function because it is dragged down by its sinful origin; the core of the ideal is pride elevated into beauty. Chastellain completely understands this when he says, "La gloire des princes pend en orgueil et en haut péril emprendre; toutes principales puissances conviengnent en un point estroit qui se dit orgueil."[37]* Taine says that honor is born from pride—stylized and elevated—the pole of the noble life. While the essential impetus for middle or subordinate social relationships comes from advantage, pride is the great motivating power of the aristocracy: "or parmi les sentiments profonds de l'homme, il n'en est pas qui soit plus proper à se transformer en probité, patriotisme et conscience, car l'homme fier à besoin de son propre respect, et, pour l'obtenir il est tenté de le mériter."[38]† Taine undoubtedly tends to view the aristocracy in too favorable a light. The real history of aristocracies reveals a picture in which pride and unabashed self-aggrandizement go together very well. In spite of all this, Taine's words remain a valid definition of the aristocratic ideal of life. They have a certain kinship with Burckhardt's definition of the Renaissance sense of honor: "This is that enigmatic mixture of conscience and egotism which still is left to modern man after he has lost, whether by his own fault or not, everything else, faith, love, and hope. This sense of honor is compatible with much selfishness and great vices, and is capable of incredible deceites; but likewise, nevertheless, everything noble that has been left in a personality can take this feeling of honor as a point of departure and gain new strength from this source."[39]

---

* "The glory of princes consists in pride and in undertaking exceedingly dangerous things; all princely expressions of power converge in a single point which we call pride."

† "among the profound sentiments of man there is none more apt to be transformed into probity, patriotism and conscience, for a proud man feels the need of self-respect, and to obtain it, he is led to deserve it."

The preoccupation with personal honor and fame—seemingly arising from a high sense of honor at one time and from unrefined pride at another—has been posited by Burckhardt to be the characteristic quality of Renaissance man.[40] In contrast to the particular honor and fame appropriate to a given estate, which still inspired genuinely medieval societies outside Italy, he describes the general-human honor and fame that the Italian mind, strongly influenced by classical antiquity, had aspired to since Dante. It seems to me that this is one of the points where Burckhardt has judged the distance between medieval and Renaissance times and between western Europe and Italy to be too great. That Renaissance love of fame and the preoccupation with honor is at the core of the knightly vision and is of French origin. The honor of a particular estate has broadened into a more general application, has been freed from the feudal sensibilities and fertilized by ideas from classical antiquity. The passionate desire to be praised by posterity is just as well known to the courtly knight of the twelfth century and the unrefined French and German mercenaries of the fourteenth century as it is to the beautiful minds of the Quattrocento. The agreement for the *Combat des Trente* (March 27, 1351) between Robert de Beaumanoir and the English captain Robert Bamborough is concluded by the latter with the words, "and let us so act, that people in times to come will speak of it in halls and palaces, in markets and elsewhere throughout the world."[41] Chastellain, whose esteem for the ideal of knighthood is entirely medieval, nonetheless gives complete expression to the Renaissance spirit when he says,

> *Honneur semont toute noble nature*
> *D'aimer tout ce qui noble est en son estre.*
> *Noblesse aussi y adjoint sa droiture.*[42]*

Elsewhere he states that honor was more precious to Jews and heathens and was observed more carefully among them for its own sake because of the expectation of earthly praise, while Christians, through faith and the Light, are honored in the expectation of heavenly rewards.[43]

---

* Honor urges every noble nature/To love all that is noble in its own essence./ Nobility adds uprightness to it.

Froissart is one of the earliest to recommend bravery, without any religious or direct ethical motivation, for the sake of fame and honor and—being the *enfant terrible* that he is—for the sake of one's career.[44]

The quest for knighthood and honor is inseparably tied to a hero veneration in which medieval and Renaissance elements are intertwined. Knightly life is a life without historical dimensions. It makes little difference whether its heroes are those of the Round Table or those of classical antiquity. Alexander had already been fully incorporated into the ideal world of knighthood by the time when chivalrous romances flourished. The phantasmagoric realm of classical antiquity was not yet separated from that of the Round Table. King René describes in a poem a colorful combination. How he has seen the gravestones of Lancelot, Caesar, David, Hercules, Paris, Troilus, among others, all marked with their particular coat of arms.[45] Knighthood itself was considered to be Roman. "Et bien entretenoit," it is said of Henry IV of England, "la discipline de chevalerie, comme jadis faisoient les Rommains."[46]* The rise of classicism brings some clarity to the historical picture of antiquity. The Portuguese nobleman Vasco de Lucena, who translated Quintus Curtius for Charles the Bold, explains to Charles that he is presenting an authentic Alexander, just as Maerlant had done a century and a half earlier, an Alexander whose story had been stripped of the lies with which all the ordinary histories had disfigured it.[47] But the intent to offer to the king a model worthy of emulation is stronger than ever and few princes are as self-conscious in their desire to equal the ancients through great and splendid deeds as is Charles the Bold. From his youth he had the heroic deeds of Gawain and Lancelot read to him; later, classical antiquity gained the upper hand. There were regularly a few hours of reading in "les haultes histories de Romme"† before going to sleep.[48] Most pleasing to him were the heroes of antiquity: Caesar, Hannibal, and Alexander, "lesques il vouloit ensuyre et contrefaire."[49]‡ All his contemporaries place great emphasis on these deliberate emulations as the impetus for his own deeds, "Il désiroit grand

---

* "and he maintained the discipline of chivalry very well, as did the Romans formerly."
† "lofty stories of Rome"
‡ "whom he wished to follow and imitate."

gloire"—says Commines—"qui estoit ce qui plus le mettoit en ses guerres que nulle autre chose; et eust bien voulu ressembler à ses anciens princes dont il a esté tant parlé après leur mort."[50]* Chastellain saw him put to use for the first time that high feeling for great deeds and beautiful gestures in the ancient style. This occasion was provided when he made his first entry as duke into Mechelen in 1467. He went there to punish a rebellion. The matter was formally investigated and handled by the court. One of the rebels was sentenced to death while others were exiled forever. The scaffold is erected on the town square; the duke takes his seat opposite; the condemned man has already knelt down; the executioner bares his sword; at that moment Charles, who has kept his intentions secret up to this point, calls out: "Stop! Take off his blindfold and let him stand up."

"Et me parcus de lors"—says Chastellain—"que le coeur luy estoit en haut singulier propos pour le temps à venir et pour acquérir gloire et renommée en singulière oeuvre."[51]†

The example of Charles the Bold is quite suitable to convince us that the spirit of the Renaissance and its yearning for the beautiful life of antiquity has its direct roots in the ideal of knighthood. If compared to the Italian virtuoso, there is merely a difference in degrees of literacy and in taste. Charles still reads his classics in translations, and his style of life is still flamboyantly Gothic.

The same inseparability of knightly and Renaissance elements can be found in the cult of the Nine Worthies, "les neuf preux." This group of nine heroes—three pagans, three Jews, three Christians—appears first in chivalric literature: the earliest account is found around 1312 in the "Voeux du paon" by Jacques de Longuyon.[52] The choice of heroes betrays the close linkage with knightly romanticism: Hector, Caesar, Alexander; Joshua, David, Judas Maccabaeus; Arthur, Charlemagne, and Godfrey of Bouillon. Eustache Deschamps adopts this idea from his teacher, Guillaume de Machaut, and devotes numerous poems to it.[53] It is likely that the

---

* "He desired the great glory of fame, which more than anything else led him to undertake his wars; and longed to resemble those ancient princes who have been so much talked of after their death."

† "And then I perceived that he had set his heart on high and singular purposes for the future, and on acquiring glory and renown by extraordinary works."

taste for symmetry that was so characteristic of the late medieval mind accounts for the fact that he added nine brave women to the list of brave men. For this purpose he chose a number of classical figures, some rather peculiar, from Justin and other literary sources. He included Penthesilea, Tomyris, Semiramis, and mangled most of the names considerably. This did not hinder the popularity of the idea and so *preux* and *preuses* can be found in later works, such as *Le Jouvencel*. They are depicted on tapestries, coats of arms are designed for them, and all eighteen lead the procession when Henry VI of England makes his entry into Paris in 1431.[54]

What demonstrates how very much alive these notions remained during the fifteenth century and later is the fact that they became the object of parody. Molinet has fun with nine *preux de gourmandise;*[55] Francis I dresses occasionally *à l'antique* in order to represent one of the *preux*.[56]

But Deschamps has expanded this notion in yet another way than merely by adding female pendants. By adding to the nine a contemporary Frenchman, Bertrand du Guesclin, as the tenth *preux,* he tied the veneration of heroic virtue to the here and now, and thus transposed the *preux* into the sphere of rising French military patriotism.[57] This idea, too, was successful: Louis of Orléans saw to it that the image of the courageous *connétable* was included as the tenth *preux* in the grand hall of Coucy.[58] There were good reasons for the special attention Louis devoted to the memory of du Guesclin; the *connétable* had held him during his baptism and had at that time placed a sword in his hand. The figure of this brave and calculating Breton warrior came to be venerated as a national military hero. It should be noted that during the fifteenth century this veneration did not give first place to Jeanne d'Arc. Any number of military leaders who had fought either side by side with her or against her held a much larger and more honored place in the imagination of their contemporaries than did the peasant girl from Domrémy. People spoke of her without emotion or veneration, and rather as a curiosity. Chastellain, who managed to shift from his Burgundian sentiments to a pathetic French loyalty whenever the occasion demanded, composed a *mystère* on the death of Charles VII in which all the leaders who had fought for him against the English—Dunois, Jean de Bueil, Xaintrailles, la Hire, and a large number of less well known individuals—like a hall of fame for the brave, recite a verse recalling their deeds.[59] They remind one, for a moment at least, of a gallery of Napoleonic generals. But the Maid is not among them.

The Burgundian princes kept in their treasure rooms a number of relics of a romantic sort that were linked to heroes: a sword of St. George, decorated with his coat of arms; a sword that had belonged to "messire Bertram de Claiquin" (du Guesclin); a tooth of the boar of Garin le Loherain; the psalter from which St. Louis studied during childhood.[60] How much the fantastic aspects of knighthood and religion are merging here! One more step, and we have arrived at the collarbone of Livy that was received by Pope Leo X with all solemnity as if it were a relic.[61]

The literary form of late medieval hero veneration is the biography of the perfect knight. Some, like Gilles de Trazegnies, had already become legendary figures; but the most important biographies deal with contemporaries, as, for example, Boucicaut, Jean de Bueil, and Jacques de Lalaing.

Jean le Meingre, usually called *Maréchal* Boucicaut, had served his country during a serious crisis. He was with John the Fearless at Nicopolis in 1396 when the French knightly nobility had carelessly ventured forth to drive the Turks out of Europe and were annihilated by Sultan Bajasid. He was captured again in 1415 at Agincourt and died in captivity six years later. One of his admirers recorded his deeds in 1409, while he was still alive. This account was based on very good information and documentation;[62] however, it is not like a piece of contemporary history, but rather like the depiction of an ideal knight. The reality of a life of sudden reversals disappears under the beautiful gloss of the knightly image. The terrible catastrophe at Nicopolis appears only in muted colors in this *Livre des faicts*. Boucicaut is presented as the type of the simple and pious and yet courtly and well-read knight. The contempt for wealth, mandatory for a true knight, is revealed in the words of Boucicaut's father, who did not intend either to enlarge or to reduce the size of his inherited estate when he said: my children, be honest and brave and you will therefore not lack anything; and if you are worthless it would be a pity to leave you too much.[63] Boucicaut's piety is of a strictly puritan nature. He gets up early and spends about three hours in prayer. No matter how much pressed for time or how busy, he kneels to hear mass twice a day. On Fridays he wears black, on Sundays and holy days he makes a pilgrimage on

foot or has someone read to him from the lives of the saints or from
the histories of "des vaillans trepassez, soit Romains ou autres,"* or
he engages in pious conversation. He is temperate and frugal,
speaks little, and if he does, mostly about God, the saints, the
virtues, or chivalry. He inspires all his servants to be devout and
above reproach and he makes them give up cursing.[64] He is an
active proponent of the noble and chaste service to women; he
honors all women for the sake of one and founds the Ordre de
l'écu verd à la dame blanche for the defense of women that earned
him the praise of Christine de Pisan.[65] In Genoa, where he had
gone in 1401 to run the government for Charles VI, when at one
time he politely bowed to two ladies who had greeted him, his
page boy said, "'Monseigneur, qui sont ces deux femmes à qui
vous avez si grans reverences faictes?'—'Huguenin,' dit-il, 'je ne
scay.' Lors luy dist: 'Monseigneur, elles sont filles communes.'—
'Filles communes,' dist-il, 'Huguenin, j'ayme trop mieulx faire reverence à dix filles communes que avoir failly à une femme de
bien.'"[66]† His motto read, "Ce que vous vouldrez"‡: deliberately
kept mysterious as befits a slogan. Does he have in mind the surrender of his will to the lady to whom he is truly dedicated? Or should
we view it as a generally relaxed attitude towards life such as we
would expect to encounter only in much later times?

The beautiful portrait of the ideal knight was painted in these
colors of piety and restraint, simplicity and loyalty. It is only to be
expected that the real Boucicaut did not conform to this image in
every respect. Violence and greed for gold, the usual concerns for
his estate—these were no strangers even to this noble figure.[67]

But the model knight came also to be seen in an entirely different
hue. The biographic novel about Jean de Bueil, called Le Jouvencel,
was written about half a century later than the life of Boucicaut
and this explains in part the difference in perception. Jean de Bueil
was a captain who had fought under the flag of Jeanne d'Arc, later
participated in the Praguerie uprising (1440) and in the war "du

---

* "the valiant dead —Roman or otherwise."

† "My lord, who are those two women to whom you bowed so low?" "Huguenin," said he, "I do not know." Then he said to him: "My lord, they are
whores." "Whores, you say," said he, "Huguenin, I would rather have saluted
ten whores than to have omitted saluting one respectable woman."

‡ "What you will"

bien public," and died in 1477. While out of favor with the king (about 1465), he had suggested that three of his servants write the story of his life, to be entitled *Le Jouvencel*.[68] In contrast to the life of Boucicaut, where the historical form has a romantic spirit, *Le Jouvencel* reveals, in its invented form, real facts, at least in its first part. It is probably the result of its multiple authorship that the story continues to lose itself in a sugarcoated romanticism. There is found the story of the terrifying campaign of the French marauders in Swiss territory in 1444 and that of the battle of St. Jacob on the Birs, where the peasants of the Basel region met their Thermopylae, stories adorned with the phony embellishments of hackneyed pastorial *Minnelieder*.[69]

In stark contrast, the first part of *Le Jouvencel* offers a simple and genuine picture of the reality of war in those days such as is rarely found anywhere else. Incidentally, these authors, too, do not mention Jeanne d'Arc, who had been a comrade-in-arms of their lord. It is his heroic deeds they glorify. How well he must have told them his war stories. Here we find the announcement of the early stirring of France's military spirit that was later to bring forth the figure of the musketeer, the *grognuard,* and the *poilu*. The attempt to glorify knighthood only betrays itself in the opening passages, where young people are exhorted to become acquainted through this story with a life at arms and are warned against the follies of pride, envy, and greed. Both the pious and the *Minne* elements, so strong in Boucicaut, are absent in the first part of *Le Jouvencel*. What we do encounter here is the misery of war, its deprivations and monotony and the brash courage needed to endure those deprivations and face its dangers. A castellan musters his garrison and counts only fifteen horses, all emaciated nags; most are not shoed. On each horse he puts two men, most of these one-eyed or crippled. To mend the captain's clothing, attempts are made to capture the enemy's laundry. A stolen cow is returned to the enemy captain, upon his request, with all civilities. A description of a nightly patrol across the fields lets us breathe the night air and sense the mighty quiet.[70] *Le Jouvencel* marks the transition from the type of knight to the type of national military man. The hero of the book releases his unfortunate prisoners on condition that they become good Frenchmen. Having attained high honors, he yearns back to that life of adventure and freedom.

Such a realistic knightly figure (which, as already mentioned, is not consistently presented as such to the end of the story) could as yet not be fashioned by Burgundian literature, which was too old-fashioned, too solemn, and too much more a captive of feudal ideas than pure French literature to be ready for such a task. Jacques de Lalaing, compared to Le Jouvencel, is an old-fashioned curiosity, described in terms of the clichés of earlier knight-errants such as Gillon de Trazegnies. The book about the deeds of this venerated Burgundian hero tells more of romantic tournaments than about real war.[71]

The psychology of wartime bravery has perhaps never been expressed, earlier or later, as simply and as truly as in the following words from Le Jouvencel:[72]

> C'est joyeuse chose que la guerre . . . On s'entr'ayme tant à la guerre. Quant on voit sa querelle bonne et son sang bien combatre, la larme en vient à l'ueil. Il vient une doulceur au cueur de loyaulté et de pitié de veoir son amy, qui si vaillamment expose son corps pour faire et accomplir le commandement de nostre createur. Et puis on se dispose d'aller mourir ou vivre avec luy, et pour amour ne l'abandonner point. En cela vient une délectation telle que, qui ne l'a essaiié, il n'est homme qui sceust dire quel bien c'est. Pensez-vous que homme qui face cela craigne la mort? Nennil; car il est tant reconforté il est si ravi, qu'il ne scet où il est. Vraiement il n'a paour de rien.*

This could just as well have come from a modern soldier as from a knight of the fifteenth century. It has nothing to do with the knightly ideal *per se,* but reflects the emotions constituting the background of pure fighting courage itself: the trembling stepping away from narrow egoism into the excitement of facing mortal danger, the deeply touching experience of the bravery of one's comrades,

---

* "It is a joyous thing, is war. . . . You love your comrade so in war. When you see that your quarrel is just and your blood is fighting well, tears come to your eyes. A great sweet feeling of loyalty and of pity fills your heart on seeing your friend so valiantly exposing his body to execute and accomplish the command of our creator. And then you prepare to go and die or live with him, and for love not to abandon him. And out of that, there arises such a delectation, that he who has not tasted it is not fit to say what a delight it is. Do you think that a man who does that fears death? Not at all; for he feels so strengthened, he is so elated, that he does not know where he is. Truly he is afraid of nothing."

the enjoyment of loyalty and self-sacrifice. This primitive ascetic excitement is the basis on which the ideal of knighthood was built into a noble fantasy of male perfection, a close kin of the Greek *kalokagathia,* a purposeful striving for the beautiful life that energetically inspired a number of centuries—but also a mask behind which a world of greed and violence could hide.

Wherever the ideal of knighthood is professed in its purest form, emphasis is placed on the ascetic element. In its first flowering it was paired naturally, or even necessarily, with the monkish ideal in the spiritual orders of knighthood at the time of the Crusades. But as reality time and again gave a cruel lie to the ideal, it sank more and more back into the realm of imagination, where it was able to preserve features of noble asceticism that were rarely evident in the midst of social realities. The knight-errant, as well as the Templar, is poor and free of earthly ties. That ideal of the noble propertyless warrior, says William James, still dominates, "sentimentally if not practically, the military and aristocratic view of life. We glorify the soldier as the man absolutely unencumbered. Owning nothing but his bare life, and willing to toss that up at any moment when the cause commands him, he is the representative of unhampered freedom in ideal directions."[73]

Linking the knightly ideal with the higher elements of religious consciousness, compassion, justice, and fidelity is therefore by no means artificial or superficial. Yet, on the other hand, they are also not that which turns knighthood into the beautiful form of life *kat'exochen* [par excellence]. Neither could knighthood's immediate roots in the manly lust for combat have been elevated if love for women had not been the burning passion that bestowed the warmth of life on that complex of emotion and idea.

The profound ascetic element of courageous self-sacrifice that is characteristic of the knightly ideal is most intimately tied to the erotic base of this view of life and is perhaps merely the ethical transformation of an unsatisfied desire. It is not only in literature and the fine arts that the yearning for love receives its shaping and its stylization. The desire to give love a noble style and noble form finds also a broad arena for its unfolding in the forms of life themselves; in courtly intimacy, social games, jokes and sport. Here, too, love is continuously sublimated and romanticized: in this, life imitates literature, but in the final analysis, it is literature that learns everything from life. The knightly view of love is not based in literature but rather in life. The motif of the knight and his beloved is rooted in the real conditions of life.

The knight and his beloved, the hero for the sake of love, constitute the most primary and unchanging romantic motif that arises and must arise everywhere anew. It is the direct transformation of sensual passion into an ethical or quasi-ethical self-denial. It arises directly from the need, known to every sixteen-year-old male, to display his courage before a woman, to expose himself to dangers and to be strong, to suffer and to shed his blood. The expression and fulfillment of this desire, which seem to be unobtainable, are replaced and elevated[74] to the dream of heroic deeds for love. This immediately posits death as an alternative to fulfillment, and satisfaction is, so to speak, thus guaranteed in either direction.

But the dream of a heroic deed for love, a deed that now fills and infatuates the heart, grows and grows like a luxuriant plant. The initially simple theme has soon spent its force and the mind craves new settings of the same theme. Passion itself imposes stronger colors on the dream of suffering and renunciation. The heroic deed has to consist of freeing or rescuing the woman from even the gravest of danger. A stronger stimulus is thus added to the original motif. At first it is the subject himself who wants to suffer for his woman, but soon this motif is joined by that of the wish to rescue the very object of his desires from suffering. I wonder if at base we can always trace the rescue back to the act of preserving virginity, of fending off another and securing the woman for the rescuer himself? In any event, this is the highest knightly-erotic motif: the young hero who liberates the virgin. Even if the enemy occasionally is an unsuspecting dragon, the sexual element remains just beneath the surface.

Liberating the virgin is the most original romantic motif, forever young. How is it possible that a nowadays outdated explanation of myth saw in this the image of a natural phenomenon while the directness of the thought could be tested daily by everyone![75] Although in literature the motif may be avoided for a time because of excessive repetition, it always comes back again in new forms, as, for instance, in the romance of the cinematic cowboy. There is no doubt that in the individual conception of love outside of literature it has always remained strong.

It is difficult to ascertain to what extent the conception of the hero-lover reveals the masculine or how far the feminine view of love. Is it in the image of willful suffering that a male wishes to see himself, or is it the will of the female that he show himself this way? The former is more likely. In general, the depiction of love as a cultural form expresses the male conception almost exclusively, at least until most recent times. The view of love held by woman always remains hidden and veiled. It is a tender and deep mystery. And it does not even need the romantic elevation into the heroic. Through its character of self-sacrifice and its unbreakable link to motherhood, this view extols itself without heroic fantasy and subservience to the egotistically erotic. Womanly expressions of love are missing from literature not only because literature originated primarily among men, but also because for women, as far as love is concerned, the literary element is much less indispensable.

The figure of the noble savior who willingly suffers for the sake of his beloved is primarily a product of the male imagination, showing man as he wishes to see himself. The tension in his dream of the liberator increases whenever he appears with his true identity hidden and is only recognized after the heroic deed is done. The romantic motif of the hidden identity of the hero is most certainly rooted in the female conception of love. In the ultimate realization of the image of manly strength and courage in the form of the warrior on horseback, female yearning to worship strength and masculine physical pride flow together.

Medieval society cultivated these primitive romantic motifs with boyish insatiability. While the higher literary forms were refined into more ethereal, reserved or spiritual and titillating expressions of desire, the knightly novel repeated, time and again, examples of a fascination that is not always intelligible to us. We frequently are of the opinion that the age should have long outgrown these childish imaginations and take Froissart's *Méliador* or *Perceforest* to be late flowers of the knightly adventure story and anachronisms in their own time. But this is as little the case then as it is in the case of the sensational novels of our own time; however, all this is not pure literature, but, so to speak, applied art. It is the need for models for the erotic imagination that keeps this literature alive and continuously renews it. There is a revival in the middle of the Renaissance in the Amadis novels. If La Noue can still assure us in the latter part of the sixteenth century that the Amadis novels caused an "esprit de vertige" among the same generation that had undergone the tempering of the Renaissance and humanism, how great the romantic receptiveness must have been among the entirely unsophisticated generation of 1400!

The enchantment of the romance of love was not only to be experienced in reading, but also in games and performances. There are two forms in which the game may appear: dramatic representations and sport. The latter form was by far the most important during medieval times. Drama was still, to a great extent, filled with other, pious, subject matter: romantic issues were only exceptions. Medieval sport, on the other hand, and first of all the tournament, was by itself dramatic to a high degree and possessed at the same time a highly erotic ambiance. Sports retain at all times such a dramatic and erotic element; today's rowing or soccer contests contain much more of the emotional qualities of a medieval tournament than athletes and spectators themselves are perhaps conscious of. But while modern sports have returned to a natural, almost Greek simplicity and beauty, medieval, or at least late medieval, tournaments were a sport overladen with embellishments and heavily elaborated, in which the dramatic and romantic element was so deliberately worked out that it virtually came to serve the function of drama itself.

The late Middle Ages is one of the end periods in which the cultural life of the higher circles has become, almost in its entirety, social play. Reality is crass, hard, and cruel; one turns back to the beautiful dream of the knightly ideal and builds the game of life on this foundation. One plays masked as Lancelot. All this is a tremendous self-deception, the glaring unreality of which is only bearable because the lie is denied by faint mockery. The entire knightly culture of the fifteenth century is dominated by a precarious balance between sentimental seriousness and easy derision. All those knightly terms of honor and fidelity and noble *Minne*[76] are handled with perfect seriousness, but the rigid face occasionally relaxes for a moment into a smile. Where else but in Italy could this mood first turn into deliberate parody: in Pulci's *Morgante* and Bonardo's *Orlando Innamorato*. But even then and there, the knightly-romantic sentiment emerges victorious again because, in Ariosto, open mockery gives way to a wondrous transcendence of pain and seriousness. The knightly fantasy has found its most classical expression.

How can we doubt the seriousness of the knightly ideal in French society around 1400? In the noble Boucicaut, the literary type of the model knight, the romantic foundation of the knightly ideal of life is still as strong as anywhere. It is love, he says, which is strongest in making young hearts avid for noble knightly struggles. He himself serves his lady in the old courtly forms: "Toutes servoit, toutes honnoroit pour l'amour d'un. Son parler estoit gracieux, courtois et craintif devant sa dame."[77]*

The contrast between the literary vision of the life of a man like Boucicaut and the bitter reality of his career is almost incomprehensible for us. As a participant and a leader, he was constantly involved in the roughest politics of his time. In 1388 he made his first political journey to the East. He passes the time during that journey by engaging two or three of his comrades-in-arms, Philippe d'Artois, his seneschal, and a certain Creseque, in a poetic defense of the noble true *Minne* that is proper for the perfect knight: *Le livre des cents ballades*.[78] Well, why not? But seven years later, when he served as mentor to the young Count of Nevers (the later John the Fearless) in the ill-conceived knightly adventure of the military campaign against Sultan Bajasid, when he witnessed the terrible catastrophe of Nicopolis where his three fellow poets lost their lives, when the noble youth of France, taken prisoner, were butchered before his very eyes, would not one assume that a serious warrior would have turned cool towards that courtly game and that knightly fancy? It had to teach him, we are inclined to believe, to no longer see the world through colored glasses. But no, his mind remains dedicated to the cult of antique knighthood, as evidenced by his founding of the Ordre de l'écu verd à la dame blanche for the protection of oppressed women. This was his way of taking his position in the artful literary quarrel between the strict and the frivolous ideals of love that in the French court circles of 1400 was an exciting pastime.

The entire presentation of noble love in literature and social life frequently strikes us as intolerably stale and ridiculous. That is the fate of any romantic form that has lost its power as an instrument of passion. In the works of many of the artful poets, passion has vanished from the expensively arranged tournaments; it can only be heard in very rare voices. But the importance of all this, given that it was inferior as literature or art, as a beautification of life or

---

* "he served all, honored all, for the love of one. His speech was graceful, courteous and diffident before his lady."

as an expression of sentiment can only be fathomed if one can again fill the literature itself with living passion. What use is there in reading *Minne* poetry and descriptions of tournaments for facts and historical detail without seeing the gull-like arches of the brows, the dark shining eyes and delicate foreheads, now dust for centuries, but which once were more important than the whole of that literature which remains piled up like rubble?

Only an occasional glimmer allows us to clearly realize exactly the passionate importance of this cultural form. In the poem "Le voeu du Heron," Jean de Beaumont, urged to take his knightly vow of combat, says:

> *Quant sommes ès tavernes, de ces fors vins buvant,*
> *Et ces dames delès qui nous vont regardant,*
> *A ces gorgues polies, ces coliés triant,*
> *Chil oeil vair resplendissent de biauté souriant,*
> *Nature nous semont d'avoir coeur désirant,*
> *. . . Adonc conquerons-nous Yaumont et Agoulant*[79]
> *Et li autre conquierrent Olivier et Rollant.*
> *Mais, quant sommes as camps sus nos destriers courants,*
> *Nos escus à no col et nos lansses bais(s)ans,*
> *Et le froidure grande nous va tout engelant,*
> *Li membres nous effondrent, et derrière et devant,*
> *Et nos ennemies sont envers nous approchant,*
> *Adonc vorrièmes estre en un chélier si grant*
> *Que jamais ne fussions veu tant ne quant.*[80]*

"Helas," Philippe de Croy writes from the headquarters of Charles the Bold near Neuss, "où sont dames pour nous entretenir,

---

* When we are in the tavern, drinking strong wine, / When the ladies pass and look at us, / With those white throats and those tight bodices, / Those sparkling eyes resplendent with smiling beauty, / Nature urges us to have desiring hearts, / . . . Then we could conquer Yaumont and Agoulant / And the others would conquer Olivier and Rollant. / But when we are in camp on our trotting chargers, / Our bucklers round our necks and our lances lowered, / And the great cold freezes us all together, / And our limbs are crushed before and behind, / And our enemies are approaching us, / Then we should wish to be in a cellar so large, / That we might not be seen by any means.

pour nous amonester de bien faire, ne pour nous enchargier em-
prinses, devises, volets ne guimpes!"[81]*

The erotic element of the knightly tournament is most directly
revealed in such customs as the wearing of the beloved's veil or
other garment that carries the fragrance of her hair or of her body.
Caught up in the excitement of combat, women offer one piece of
jewelry after another; when the game is over, they sit there bareheaded with their arms stripped of their sleeves.[82] This becomes a
symbol of keen attraction in the poem from the second half of the
thirteenth century about the three knights and the shirt.[83] A lady
whose husband is not fond of fighting but is otherwise full of noble
gentility sends her chemise to the three knights, who serve her in
Minne. They are to wear it, as battle dress, in the tournament that
her husband is about to hold, without any armor or other protection than helmet and greaves. The first and second knight shy away
from this. The third, who is poor, holds the shirt in his arms
throughout the night and kisses it passionately. He appears in the
tournament wearing the shirt as his battle dress without any armor
underneath it; the shirt becomes torn and soiled with his blood; he
is seriously wounded. His extraordinary bravery is noticed and the
prize is awarded him; the lady gives her heart to him. Now her
beloved asks a favor in return. He sends the bloody shirt back to
her so that she can wear it, bloody and torn, over her dress during
the feast that concludes the tournament. She embraces it tenderly
and attends the feast in her bloodied piece of clothing; most of
those in attendance criticize her, her husband is embarrassed, and
the narrator asks: which of the lovers has done more for the other?

This passionate sphere in which alone the tournament had significance explains why the church fought the custom for such a
long time with such determination. That tournaments actually became the cause of sensational cases of adultery is testified to, for
example, in 1389 by the monk of Saint Denis and, based on his
authority, Jean Juvenal des Ursins.[84] Canon law had long before
prohibited tournaments; originally useful as training for combat, it
was said, they could no longer be tolerated because of numerous
abuses.[85] They drew criticism from the moralists.[86] Petrarch asked
pedantically, where do we read that Cicero and Scipio held tourna-

---

* "Alas, where are women to inspire us, to fire us to bravery, or to charge us
with tokens, insignia, scarves, and veils!"

ments? And the Burgher of Paris shrugged his shoulders. "Prindrent par ne scay quelle folle entreprinse champ de bataille,"* he says about a famous tournament.[87]

The world of the nobility, on the other hand, gives everything related to tournaments and knightly contests an importance that is not even granted to modern sports. It was a very old custom to have a memorial stone placed on the site where a famous duel had been fought. Adam of Bremen knew of one such stone at the border between Holstein and Vargia where a German warrior had once killed the leader of the Vends.[88] During the fifteenth century such memorials were still dedicated in commemoration of famous knightly duels. Near Saint Omer La croix Pélerine remembered the fight between Hautbourdin, the bastard of Saint Pol, with a Spanish knight during the time of the famous Pas d'armes de la Pélerine. Half a century later, Bayard takes time prior to a tournament for a pilgrimage to that cross.[89] The decor and garments that had been used during the Pas d'armes de la Fontaine des Pleurs were dedicated after the tournament to our Beloved Lady of Boulogne and displayed in the church.[90]

Medieval swordplay differs, as already indicated above, from Greek and from modern athletics by its much reduced degree of naturalness. To increase its warlike tone it relies on the excitement of aristocratic pride and aristocratic honor, on its romantic-erotic and artistic splendor. It is overladen with splendor and ornamentation, and overfilled with colorful fantasy. In addition to being play and exercise it is also applied literature. The desires and the dreams of poetic hearts seek a dramatic representation, a staged fulfillment in life itself. Real life was not beautiful enough; it was harsh, cruel, and treacherous. There was little room in courtly and military careers for feelings of courage that arose out of love, but the soul is filled with such sentiments, and people want to experience them and to create a more beautiful life in precious play. The element of genuine courage is most certainly of no less value in a knightly tournament than in a pentathon competition. Its explicitly erotic character was the cause of its bloody intensity. In its motives the tournament is closest to the contests of the Indian epics; in the *Mahâbhârata,* too, fighting over a woman is the central idea.

* "and they went to the battlefield for, I don't know, whatever foolish enterprise."

The fantasy in which the tournament was dressed was that of the Arthur novels, that is, the childish conceptions of the fairy tale: the dream adventure with its shifting of dimensions into giants and dwarfs is joined to the sentimentality of courtly love.

For a *pas d'armes* of the fifteenth century a freely invented romantic circumstance was artificially constructed. It was centered in a novel-like setting given a fitting name: *la fontaine des pleurs, l'arbre Charlemagne.** The fountain is especially constructed.[91] For an entire year an unknown knight on the first of each month will pitch a tent in front of the fountain. Inside the tent a lady (only a painting) sits and holds a unicorn that carries three shields. Any knight touching one of the shields or having them touched by his herald obligates himself to take part in a certain duel. The conditions of this duel are precisely described in the detailed "chapitres" that are at the same time invitations and rules for the tournament.[92] The shields have to be touched while on horseback and for this reason horses are always available for the knights. In another example: at the *Emprise du dragon* four knights wait at a crossroads; no lady may pass this crossroads without having one knight break two lances for her. Otherwise she has to leave a keepsake.[93] Actually, this childish game of forfeits is nothing but a lower form of the usual age-old warrior and *Minne* plays. This relationship is clearly shown by a provision such as the following article from the *Chapitres de la Fontaine des pleurs:* Anyone thrown to the ground during combat has to wear for a whole year a golden bracelet with a lock attached until he finds the lady who has the small key fitting the lock and can free him when he offers his services to her. In another conceit the case is based on a giant who has been captured by a dwarf, complete with a golden tree and a *dame de l'isle celée,*† or on a "noble chevalier esclave et serviteur à la belle géande à la blonde perruque, la plus grande du monde."[94]‡ The anonymity of the knight is a standard feature. He is called *le blanc chevalier, le chevalier mesconnu, le chevalier à la pélerine,*§ or he may even appear as a hero

---

* "the Fountain of Tears, the Tree of Charlemagne"

† "lady of the secret island"

‡ "noble knight, slave and servant of the beautiful giantess with the blonde wig, the greatest in the world."

§ "the white knight," "the unknown knight," "the knight with the cape" from a novel and be called Swan Knight; or he may carry the arms of Lancelot, Tristan, or Palamedes.[95]

In most instances an extra touch of melancholy is spread over the scene: this is already seen in the name *Fontaine des pleurs;* the shields are white, violet and black—all dotted with white tears; they are touched out of compassion for the *Dame de pleurs.* King René appears at the *Emprise du dragon* in the black of mourning—and not without reason!—because he has just bid farewell to his daughter Margareth, who has become Queen of England. The horse is black, draped with a mourning saddlecloth; the lance is black; the shield black and dotted with silver tears.[96] In *l'arbre Charlemagne* the shield is black and violet with gold and black tears. This somber key does not always prevail; in another instance the insatiable lover of beauty King René holds the *Joyesse garde* near Saumur. For forty days he celebrates feasts in the wooden castle "de la joyesse garde" with his wife and daughter and with Jeanne de Laral, who was to become his second wife. The feast is secretly prepared for her. The castle has been put up, painted, and hung with tapestry specifically for that purpose. Everything is red and white. For his *pas d'armes de la bergère* everything is kept in the style of shepherds, the knights and ladies as shepherds and shepherdesses complete with staff and bagpipe. All in gray with touches of gold and silver.[97]

The great game of the beautiful life played as the dream of noble courage and fidelity had another form than that of the tournament. The second form, equally important, was that of the knightly orders. While it may not be easy to show a direct link, no one even casually familiar with the customs of primitive people will have any doubt that the roots of knightly orders, just as those of the tournaments and the chivalric initiations themselves, go back to the sacred customs of a distant past. The ceremony conferring knighthood is an ethically and socially elaborated puberty ritual, granting arms to the young warrior. The staged combat itself is of ancient origin and was once full of sacred meaning. The chivalric orders cannot be separated from the male bands of primitive peoples.

But this link can only be suggested here as an unproven thesis; we are not concerned at this moment with confirming an ethnological hypothesis, but rather with envisioning the ideal value of fully developed knighthood. Who would deny that in all this some of the primitive still survives?

To be sure, the Christian element in the idea is so strong that an explanation founded on purely medieval ecclesiastical and political conditions alone could also be convincing provided one did not realize that universal primitive parallels furnish still more basic explanations.

The first knightly orders, the three great orders of the Holy Land and the three Spanish orders,[98] arose as the purest embodiment of the medieval spirit from a combination of the monastic and knightly ideals at a time when the fight against Islam had become a wondrous reality. They had grown into large political and economic institutions, vast conglomerates of wealth and financial power. Their political usefulness had pushed both their spiritual character and the chivalric play element into the background while their economic success, in turn, had eaten away their political usefulness. As long as the Templars and Hospitalers flourished and were still active in the Holy Land itself the knightly way of life had served a real political function and the knightly orders really were practical organizations serving functions of great significance.

In the fourteenth and fifteenth centuries, however, knightly practice was only an elevated form of life and as a result the element of noble play that was at its very heart had again come to the foreground in the newer chivalric orders. Not that they had become only play. As idea, the orders are still filled with ethical and political aspiration. But this is now illusion and dream, vain scheming. The peculiar idealist Philippe de Mézières saw the remedy for his age in a new knightly order that he called the *Ordre de la Passion*.[99] He wanted all estates included in it. Incidentally, the great chivalric orders of the Crusades had already made use of warriors without noble status. The grand master and the knights should come from the ranks of the nobility, the clergy should provide the patriarch and his suffragans; burghers should become brothers; and rural people and craftsmen servants. The order will thus be a solid amalgamation of the estates for the great struggle against the Turks. There should be four vows. Two are traditional, shared by the monks and the spiritual knights: poverty and obedience. But in place of absolute celibacy Philippe de Mézières put conjugal chastity. He wanted to permit marriage for the practical reason that the oriental climate required it and that it would make the order more desirable. The fourth vow, unknown to earlier orders, is the *summa perfectio,* the highest personal ethical perfection. Here is the colorful picture of a knightly order in which all ideals come together in actions ranging from the making of political plans all the way to the struggle for salvation.

The word *Ordre* mixed a number of meanings without distinguishing among them, encompassing highest holiness as well as the most pragmatic cooperatives. It could mean social status just as well as priestly consecration, or refer to monastic or chivalric orders. That the word "ordre" in the sense of knightly order still retained some spiritual significance is shown by the fact that the word "religion" was used in its place, a usage that normally would perhaps be restricted only to the cloistered orders. Chastellain calls the Golden Fleece *une religion* as if it were a cloistered order and speaks of it with the kind of awe reserved for a holy mystery.[100] Olivier de la Marche speaks of a Portuguese as a "chevalier de la religion de Avys."[101] But there is not only the reverential awe of that pompous Polonius Chastellain to testify to the pious meaning of the Golden Fleece; church attendance and the Mass occupy a dominant position within the entire ritual of the order: the knights sit on the seats of the lords of the cathedral, the memorial services for members who have passed away are conducted in the strictest ecclesiastical style.

Small wonder therefore that membership in a knightly order was felt to be a strong, sacred bond. The knights of the Order of Stars of King John II are obligated, if possible, to abandon membership in all other orders.[102] The duke of Bedford, intending to tie young Philip of Burgundy closer to England, wants to foist the Order of the Garter on him but the Burgundian, fully realizing that this would bind him forever to the English king, finds a way to politely evade the honor.[103] When Charles the Bold accepted the garter and even wore it, Louis XI regarded this as a breach of the treaty of Péronne, which enjoined the duke not to enter into an alliance with England without the king's assent.[104] The English custom of not accepting foreign orders may be regarded as a traditional reminder of the notion that the honor obligates the recipient to remain faithful to the prince who awards it.

That touch of sanctity notwithstanding, we may assume that among the princely circles of the fourteenth and fifteenth centuries there was a feeling that many regarded these artfully contrived new knightly orders as empty pastimes. Why else the endlessly repeated, insistent assurances that all this was in aid of higher, most important purposes? Philip of Burgundy, the noble duke, founded his Toison d'or, says the poet Michault:

> Non point pour jeu ne pour esbatement,
> Mais à la fin que soit attribuée
> Loenge à Dieu trestout premièrement
> Et aux bons gloire et haulte renommée.[105]*

Guillaume Fillastre, too, promises in the preface of his work about the Golden Fleece to explain its importance so that one would realize that the order was not a matter of vanity or a matter of trifling importance. Your father, he addresses Charles the Bold, "n'a pas comme dit est, en vain instituée ycelle ordre."[106]†

It became necessary to emphasize the high intentions of the order if the Golden Fleece were to take the first place Philip's pride craved for it. Since the middle of the fourteenth century, the founding of chivalric orders had become almost a fashion. Every prince simply had to have an order of his own and even noble houses of high status did not want to be left behind. There is Boucicaut with his Ordre de l'écu verd à la dame blanche for the defense of courtly *Minne* and oppressed women. There is King John with his Chevaliers Nostre Dame de la Noble Maison (1351), usually called the Order of the Stars after their insignia. In the noble house at Saint Ouen near Saint Denis they had a *table d'oneur* at which the three bravest princes, the three bravest bannerets,[107] and the three bravest knights had to sit during their festivities. There was further Pierre de Lusignan with his Order of the Sword, which demanded of its members a pure life and put around their necks as witty symbol a golden chain with its links formed in the shape of the letter S, which signified "silence." Amadeus of Savoy founded the Annouciade; Louis de Bourbon the Golden Shield and the Thistle; Enguerrand de Coucy, who had hoped for an imperial crown, the crown reversed; Louis of Orléans the Order of the Porcupine. The Bavarian dukes of Holland-Henegowen had their Order of Antonious,

---

* Not for amusement, nor for recreation,/But for the purpose that praise/Be given to God in the first place,/And glory and high fame to the good.

† "did not, as is said, institute this order for vain purposes."

complete with the T-shaped cross and little bell that attract our attention in numerous portraits.[108]

The founding of such orders was frequently used to celebrate important events, such as happened in the case of Louis Bourbon's return from his term as an English prisoner of war, or, in other cases to make a political point as, for example, with Orléans's *porc-epic,* which turned its quills towards Burgundy. Sometimes the pious character, always significant, very strongly prevailed, as in the founding of an order of St. George in the Franche-Comté when Philibert de Miolans returned from the East with relics of that saint. At times the orders are not much more than ordinary brotherhoods of mutual protection, such as that of the Hazewind, founded by the nobles of the dukedom of Bar in 1416.

The reason for the success of the Golden Fleece, surpassing that of all other newer orders, is the wealth of the Burgundians. The special splendor of the order may have contributed just as much as the fortuitous choice of the symbol itself. Initially the name of the Golden Fleece evoked only the legend of Kolchis. The legend of Jason was generally known; Froissart had it told by a shepherd in a pastorale.[109] But Jason as a hero of legend was suspect; he had broken his vow of fidelity and this theme was bound to trigger unwelcome insinuations concerning the policy of the Burgundians towards France. Alain Chartier put it this way in a poem:

> *A Dieu et aux gens detestables*
> *Est menterie et trahison,*
> *Pour ce n'est point mis à la table*
> *Des preux l'image de Jason,*
> *Qui pour emporter la toison*
> *De Colcos se veult parjurer.*
> *Larrecin ne se peult celer.*[110]*

Jean Germain, the learned bishop of Chalons and chancellor of the order, brought to Philip's attention the fleece that Gideon had spread on the ground and on which the heavenly dew fell. This was an especially good idea because this Fleece of Gideon was one

---

* Detestable to God and to men/Is lying and treason,/For this reason, not placed in the gallery/Of worthies is the image of Jason,/Who to carry off the fleece/of Cholchis was willing to perjure./Larceny cannot remain hidden.

of the most fitting symbols of the fertilization of Mary's womb. The biblical hero thus came to replace the heathen as patron of the Golden Fleece. This enabled Jacques de Clercq to claim that Philip had deliberately refrained from selecting Jason because he had broken his vow of fidelity.[111] A court poet of Charles the Bold called the order "Gedeonis signa."[112] But others, such as the chronicler Theodericus Pauli, continue to speak of the "Vellus Jasonis." Jean Germains's successor as chancellor of the order, Bishop Guillaume Fillastre, went further than his predecessor and discovered four additional fleeces in the Holy Scripture: one of Jacob, one of King Mesa of Moab, one of Job, and one of David.[113] He said that each of these represented a virtue and that he intended to devote a book to each of the six. This was obviously too much of a good thing. Fillastre had the spotted sheep of Jacob serve as symbol of *justitia;*[114] he had simply taken all instances where the Vulgate uses the word "Vellus"—a rather peculiar demonstration of the flexibility of allegory. There is no indication that his idea met with sustained applause.

The pomp and festivities of the Golden Fleece have been described often enough; to mention them here would only add further material to what has been said above in chapter 2 about the pomp of courtly life. One single feature of the order's customs deserves to be cited here because it reveals so clearly the character of a primitive and sacred play. The order counts among its members next to its knights, its officers: the chancellor, the treasurer, the secretary, and, further, the king of arms with his staff of heralds and pursuivants. The latter group, specifically charged with the service of the noble knightly game, are given symbolic names. The king of arms himself has the name Toison d'or, as for example, Jean Lefèvre de Saint Remy and Nicolas of Hames, the latter known from the union of Dutch nobles in 1565. The heralds are given territorial names: Charolais, Zélande. The First of the Pursuivants is named Fusil, after the flint stone in the insignia chain of the order, the emblem of Philip the Good. Others have names with romantic flavor, like Montreal, or of virtues, like Persévérance; or names borrowed from the allegory of the *Roman de la rose,* for example, Humble Requeste, Doulce Pensée, Léal Poursuite. During the great festival such pursuivants were solemnly baptized with these names by the grand master, who sprinkled wine over them.

He also changed their names on the occasion of their elevation to higher rank.[115]

The vows imposed by the chivalric orders are merely a firm collective form of the personal knightly vows to perform some kind of heroic deed. This is perhaps the point where the foundations of the knightly ideal can best be viewed in their interlocking relationships. Those who might be inclined to regard the connection between the act of being dubbed a knight, the tournament, knightly orders, and primitive customs as a mere suggestion will find that the barbaric character of the knightly vow lurks so close to the surface that doubt is no longer possible. We are dealing with genuine survivals, which have parallels in the ancient Indian *vratam,* in the *Nasoräerschaft* of the Jews, and, perhaps most directly, in the practices of the Vikings during their legendary period.

The ethnological problem is not at issue here, but rather the question of what significance the vows had in late medieval spiritual life. Three values are possible. The knightly vows may have a religious-ethical meaning that places them at the same level as clerical vows; their content and meaning can also be of a romantic-erotic sort; and, finally, the vows may have degenerated into a courtly game without any significance other than that of a pastime. Actually, all these existed together at the same time; the idea of the vow vacillates between the highest dedication of life in the service of the most solemn ideal and the most conceited mockery of the elaborate social game that found only amusement in courage, love, and concerns of state. The play element predominates; the vows became, for the most part, embellishments of court festivities. But they always remained tied to the most serious military undertakings: the invasion of France by Edward III, Philip the Good's envisioned crusade.

It is as in the case of the tournaments: as tasteless and as worn as the ready-made romanticism of the *pas d'armes* may appear to us, so too, the vow "of the pheasant," "of the peacock," and "of the egret" seem to be equally vain and insincere, if we are not sensitive to the passion that permeated all this. It is the dream of the more beautiful life just as the festivities and forms of the Florentines of Cosimo, Lorenzo, and Giuliana were this dream. In Italy it attained eternal beauty, but here the dream's magic vanished with those who dreamed it.

The link between the ascetic and the erotic that is at the base of the fantasy of the hero who frees the virgin or sheds his blood for her, the central motif of tournament romanticism, reveals itself in another and perhaps more striking aspect in the knightly vow. In his instructions for his daughter, the knight De la Tour Landry tells us of a peculiar order of noblemen and noblewomen given to the practice of *Minne* that had existed during his days of youth in Poitou and elsewhere. They called themselves "Galois et Galoises" and observed "une ordonnance moult sauvaige,"* the most important element of which was that they had to keep a fire burning in the fireplace and dress themselves warmly in furs and padded hoods during the summer while during the winter they were permitted to wear nothing but a furless coat. They were not allowed any cloak or other protection, hat, gloves or mittens, no matter how freezing the temperature. During winter they scattered green leaves on the floor and hid the chimney behind green branches, and on their bed they had only a thin blanket. This wonderful aberration, so peculiar that the writer is not likely to have invented it, can hardly be regarded as anything but as an ascetic intensification of erotic attraction. Though not perfectly clear in all details, and most likely strongly exaggerated, only minds completely lacking in ethnological knowledge would take all this to be the invention of a chatty old man.[116] The primitive character of the Galois and Galoises is further emphasized by the rule of their order that the husband had to leave his entire house and his wife to the Galois who was his guest in order to go to the Galoise of his visitor; failure to do so meant total disgrace. According to the knight De la Tour Landry, many members of the order had died of cold: "Si doubte moult que ces Galois et Galoises qui moururent en cest etat et en cestes amouretes furent martirs d'amours."[117]†

There are more examples that betray the primitive character of the knightly vows. As, for example, the poem describing the vows that Robert of Artois urged on the King of England, Edward III, and his noblemen in order to start the war against France: "Le voeu de héron." It is a story of little historical value but the spirit of

---

* "a very savage rule of order"
† "and I firmly believe that these Galois and Galoises, who died in this manner, were martyrs of love.

barbarian crudeness that it reveals is well suited to acquaint us with the nature of the knightly vows.

The duke of Salisbury is sitting at the feet of his lady during a feast. When his turn to take a vow has arrived, he asks his beloved to put a finger on his right eye. Even two, she answers and closes the right eye of the knight with two fingers. "Belle, est-il bien clos?" he asks. "Oyl, certainement."* "Well, then," says Salisbury, "then I vow to God the Almighty and his sweet mother, not to open this eye again, no matter what pain and suffering this may cause, until I have lit the flame in France, the country of the enemy, and have fought the men of King Philip:"

> *Or aviegne qu'aviegne, car il n'est autrement.*
> *—Adonc osta son doit la puchelle au cors gent,*
> *Et li iex clos demeure, si que virent la gent.*[118]†

In Froissart we can read of the reality reflected by this literary motif; Froissart tells us that he actually saw English gentlemen who had one eye covered with a piece of cloth so that they could fulfill their vow of seeing with only one eye until they had performed heroic deeds in France.[119]

This primitive crudeness of the "voeu du héron" is still more evident in the vow of Jehan de Faukemont, who will not spare monastery or altar, pregnant woman or child, friends or relatives, in order to serve King Edward. At the end the queen, Philippa of Hennegowen, asks her husband for permission to be also allowed to take a vow.

> *Adonc, dist la roine, je sai bien, que piecha*
> *Que sui grosse d'enfant, que mon corps senti l'a.*
> *Encore n'a il gaires, qu'en mon corps se tourna.*
> *Et je voue et prometh à Dieu qui me créa . . .*
> *Qui la li fruis de moi de mon corps n'istera,*
> *Si m'en arés menée au païs par de-là*
> *Pour avanchier le veu que vo corps voué a;*

---

* "My beauty, is it well closed?" "Yes, certainly."

† Now come what may, for it is not otherwise./—Then the gentle girl took away her finger,/And the eye remained closed, as the people saw.

> *Et s'il en voelh isir, quant besoins n'en sera,*
> *D'un grant coutel d'achier li miens corps s'ochira;*
> *Serai m'asme perdue et li fruis perira!**

This blasphemous vow is met with a chilled silence. The poet only says:

> *Et quant li rois l'entent, moult forment l'en pensa,*
> *Et dist: certainement, nul plues ne vouera.†*

Hair and beard, everywhere bearers of magical power have a special meaning in medieval vows. Benedict XIII, pope of Avignon but actually a prisoner there, swore not to have his beard cut as a sign of his travail until his freedom was restored.[120] When Lumey takes the same vow with respect to taking revenge for the count of Egmont, we encounter one of the last remnants of a custom that had sacred meaning in the distant past.

The meaning of a vow, as a rule, is that someone imposes on himself an austerity as a stimulant to the completion of the vow. In most cases the austerity is linked to food. The first to be taken as knight into his Chevalerie de la Passion by Philippe de Mézières was a Pole who had for nine years not eaten or drunk while sitting down.[121] Bertrand du Guesclin is very hasty with respect to such vows. Once there was a challenge from an English warrior: Bertrand declared that he would only have three wine soups in the name of the Trinity until he had fought the challenger. In another instance he had pledged not to eat meat or take off his clothes until he had taken Montcontour, or even that he would not eat until he had clashed with the English.[122]

Naturally, the nobleman of the fourteenth century was no longer conscious of the magical significance of this fasting. To us, the

---

* Now then, said the queen, I have well known for a long time/That I am with child, my body has felt it;/It has already turned within my body./And I vow, and promise God who created me . . ./That this, my fruit, shall not exit my body,/Until you have taken me into the land over there,/And fulfilled the vow which you have sworn,/And if it is to be born before this has been done,/Then I will kill myself with a big steel knife./My soul will be lost and the fruit will perish.

† And when the king had heard, he thought seriously about it,/And then he said, Now then, there will be no more vows.

underlying motif is very evident from the manifold use of bonds as emblems of a vow. On January 1, 1415, Duke Jean de Bourbon, "desirant eschiver oisiveté, pensant y acquerir bonne renommée et la grâce de la très-belle de qui nous sommes serviteurs,"* takes the vow, together with sixteen other knights and page boys, to wear every Sunday for two years a bond like that of a prisoner on his left leg—the knights' in gold, the pageboys' in silver—until he had found sixteen knights ready to fight the band in a battle on foot "à outrance."[123]† Jacques de Lalaing in 1445 meets a Sicilian knight in Antwerp, Jean de Boniface, who as "chevalier aventureux" has come from the court of Aragon. On his left leg he has an iron, just like slaves used to wear, and, hanging on a golden bracelet, an "emprise" that signifies his readiness to fight.[124] In the novel of the Petit Jehan de Saintré the knight Loiselench wears two golden rings on arm and leg, each on a golden chain, until he finds a knight who "liberates" him from his enterprise.[125] This is what is called "délivrer"; thus the sign is touched when one goes "pour chevalier"; it is torn off if mortal combat is intended. La Curne de Sainte Palaye noticed that, according to Tacitus, the very same custom was found among the ancient Chatten.[126] The bonds worn by the penitent on their pilgrimages or those that pious ascetics put on themselves are related to these "enterprises" of the late medieval knights.

The most famous solemn vow of the fifteenth century, the *Voeux du Faisan,* was taken in 1454 in Lille during a court festival given by Philip the Good in preparation for the crusade. What it still reveals of all this is not much more than a beautiful courtly form. Not that the custom of taking a spontaneous vow during an emergency or moment of strong emotion had lost any of its power. This custom has such deep psychological roots that it is bound neither to education nor faith. The knightly vow as cultural form, however, as a custom elevated to an embellishment of life, reaches its last phase in the splendid extravagances of the Burgundian court.

The theme of the action is still always the unmistakable old theme. Vows are taken during feasts, an oath is made in the name of a bird that is served and later eaten. The Vikings, too, knew the

---

* "with the desire of avoiding idleness, and with the thought, thereby, to obtain honor and the esteem of the very beautiful whose servants we are."
† "to the death."

competition in vows taken during drunken feasts; one of the forms is to touch the wild boar as it is being served.[127] The pheasant of the famous feast at Lille seems to have been alive.[128] The vow was taken in the name of God and his Mother, of ladies and the bird.[129] It is not too daring to assume that the Deity in this instance was not the original recipient of the vow: actually many vows are taken only in the name of the ladies or of birds. There is little variety in the austerities the oath takers imposed upon themselves. Most are related to sleep or food. This knight is not allowed to sleep in a bed on Sundays until he has fought a Saracen, nor may he stay for fourteen consecutive days in the same city. Another may not eat meat on Friday until he has touched the banner of the great Turk; yet another piles ascetic practice on top of ascetic practice: he is not allowed to wear any armor at all, drink wine on Sundays, sleep in a bed, sit at a table, and he has to wear a hair shirt. The manner in which the heroic deed required by the vow is to be carried out is described in precise detail.[130]

How serious is this all? When messire Philippe Pot takes the vow to keep his right arm bare of any armor during the campaign against the Turks, the duke has the following comment added below the vow (which was registered in writing): "Ce n'est pas le plaisir de mon très redoubté seigneur, que messire Phelippe Pot voise en sa compaignie ou saint voyage qu'il a voué, le bras désarmé; mais il est content qu'il voist aveuc lui armé bien et souffisamment ainsi qu'il appartient."[131]* Obviously a vow was still regarded as serious and dangerous. The vow by the duke himself stirs emotions everywhere.[132]

Others take cautiously conditioned vows that testify both to serious intent and to self-satisfaction with a beautiful pretense.[133] On some occasions the vows are addressed to the "much beloved" who is but a pale remnant of herself.[134] A mocking element is not lacking even in the grim *Voeu du héron:* Robert of Artois offers the king, pictured here as not very belligerent, the heron as the most timid of birds. After Edward has taken his vow, all break out in laughter. Jean de Beaumont took the *Voeu du héron* in the words

---

* "It is not the pleasure of my very redoubted lord that Messire Philippe Pot undertakes, in his company, the holy votive journey with his arm bare; but he desires that he should travel with him well and sufficiently armed as is becoming."

already mentioned earlier,[135] which reveal with faint mockery the passionate nature of vows made under the influence of wine and under the eyes of the ladies. According to another story, he loudly took a cynical vow, in the name of the heron, that he would serve that lord from whom he could expect to get the most. Whereupon the English lords laughed.[136] What mood, in spite of all the solemn importance with which the *Voeux du Faisan* were received, must have prevailed at the table when Jennet de Rebreviette took the vow that he, in case he did not receive the favor of his lady before the campaign started, would upon his return from the East marry the first woman or maiden who had 20,000 crowns—"se elle veult."[137]* Yet the same Rebreviette as "pouvre escuier"† ventures forth and fights against the Moors at Ceuta and Granada.

So the exhausted aristocracy laughs at its own ideal. Having dressed and painted their passionate dream of a beautiful life with all their powers of imagination and artfulness and wealth and molded it into a plastic form, they then pondered and realized that life was really not so beautiful—and then laughed.

It was only a vain illusion, that knightly glory, only style and ceremony, a beautiful and insincere play! The real history of the late medieval period, we are told by the researcher who traces the development of the state and of economics in the documents, has little to do with the phony knightly renaissance; it was old varnish that had begun to peel off. The men who made history were by no means dreamers but were very calculating, sober politicians or merchants, be they princes, noblemen, prelates or burghers.

This they certainly were. But the history of culture has just as much to do with dreams of beauty and the illusions of a noble life as with population figures and statistics. A more recent scholar, having studied today's society in terms of the growth of banks and traffic, of political and military conflicts, would be able to state at the end of his studies: "I have noticed very little about music, which obviously had little meaning for this culture."

It seems to be that way if the history of the Middle Ages is described for us from political and economic documents. But it may well be that the knightly ideal, artificial and worn-out as it

* "if she wants."
† "poor squire"

may have been, still continued to exert a more powerful influence on the purely political history of the late Middle Ages than is usually imagined.

The charm of the noble life form is so great that even burghers succumb to it wherever they can. We imagine the Flemish heroes Jacob and Philipp van Artevelde to be true men of the third estate—proud of their bourgeois stature and simplicity. On the contrary: Philipp van Artevelde lived in princely splendor, every day he had musicians perform in front of his lodging, every meal he had served on silver dishes as if he were the count of Flanders. He dressed in purple, red, and "menu vair" like a duke of Brabant or count of Hennegowen. He rode on horseback in the style of a prince, an unfurled banner carried ahead of him to display his coat of arms, a sable with three silver hats.[138] Who appears to be more modern to us than the leading financier of the fifteenth century, Jacques Coeur, the outstanding banker of Charles VII? If we are to believe his biographer, Jacques de Lalaing, this great banker took a lively interest in the old-fashioned knight-errantry of the Hennegowen hero Philipp van Artevelde.[139]

All higher forms of the bourgeois life of modern times are based on imitations of noble life forms. Just as the bread served on a "serviette" (napkin) and the word "serviette" itself have their origin in medieval courtly stateliness,[140] the most bourgeois of the prenuptial pranks are offsprings of the grandiose "entremets" of Lille. In order to fully understand the meaning of the knightly ideal in cultural-historical terms one would have to trace it to Shakespeare's and Moliere's time, or even to the modern gentleman. But in this instance we are concerned with exploring the effect of that ideal on real life during the waning Middle Ages[141] themselves. Could politics and warfare actually be controlled by the knightly idea? Undoubtedly yes, if not by its merits then by its weaknesses. Just as the tragic blunders of today arise from the frenzy of nationalism and cultural arrogance, those of the medieval period arose more than once from chevaleresque notions. Did not the motive for the creation of the new Burgundian state, the gravest mistake France could have committed, rise from a knightly impulse? King John, that knightly maniac, hands the dukedom in 1363 to his young son who had stood with him at Poitiers when the elder son fled. The same holds true for the conscious notion that was intended to justify the later anti-French policy of the Burgundians to their contemporaries: vengeance for Montereau, the defense of knightly honor. I am well aware that all this could also be explained as the results of calculating or even farsighted politics, but this does not keep the contemporaries from regarding the value and lesson of the facts of 1363 as a case of knightly courage that had received princely rewards. The Burgundian state in its rapid unfolding is an edifice of political insight and purposefully sober calculation. But what one may call the Burgundian idea always takes on the forms of the knightly ideal. The nicknames of the dukes—*Sans Peur, Le Hardi, Qui qu'en Hongue,* which was replaced in the case of Philip with *Le Bon*—are all deliberate inventions of court literature so that the prince can be seen in the light of the knightly ideal.[142]

One great political quest was inseparably tied to the knightly ideal: the crusade, Jerusalem! The thought of Jerusalem was constantly before the eyes of all the princes of Europe as the most noble political idea and continued to spur them into action. There was here a peculiar contradiction between practical political interest and political idea. Christendom of the fourteenth and fifteenth centuries faced an Oriental question of the highest urgency: defense against the Turks, who had already taken Adrianopolis (1378) and destroyed the Serbian Empire (1389). Danger loomed in the Balkans. But Europe's first and most imperative political task could not yet be separated from the idea of a crusade. The Turkish question could only be viewed as part of the great holy task that earlier times had failed to accomplish: the liberation of Jerusalem.

This conception put the knightly ideal in the foreground. In this context it could and was bound to have a particularly powerful effect. The religious content of the knightly ideal found its highest expression in this quest, and the liberation of Jerusalem could be nothing but holy and noble knightly work. The limited success in combating the Turks may be explained to a certain degree by the very fact that the religious-knightly ideal was so prominent in shaping the political response to the Orient. The expeditions that required, above all, exact calculation and patient preparation were conceived and implemented under a very high tension that led not to a calm consideration of that which was attainable, but to a romanticizing of the plan: a tension that was bound either to remain fruitless or to become fatal. The catastrophe of Nicopolis in 1396 proved how dangerous it was to mount a serious expedition against a very militant enemy in the old-fashioned style of those knightly jaunts into Prussia or Lithuania where the objective was merely to put to death a few poor heathens. Who was it who designed the plans for the Crusades? Dreamers like Philippe de Mézières, who dedicated his life to them and political fantasizers, one of whom was Philip the Good, all his clever calculations notwithstanding.

The liberation of Jerusalem remained a compelling and vital task for all kings. In 1422, Henry V of England lay dying. The young conqueror of Rouen and Paris was taken away right in the middle of the work with which he had caused France so much misery. The physicians told him that he had less than two hours to live; the confessor and other clerics have come, the seven penitential psalms are read. As the clergymen recite the words "Benigne fac, Domine, in bona voluntate tue Sion, ut aedificentur muri Jerusalem,"[143]* the king makes them stop and, with a loud voice, says that it had been his intention to conquer Jerusalem once peace had been restored in France, "se ce eust été le plaisir de Dieu son createur de la laisser vivre son aage."† Then he lets the reading of the penitential psalms be concluded and dies shortly thereafter.[144]

The Crusades had also for a long time been a pretext for imposing special levies: even Philip the Good had generously availed himself of that opportunity. Yet this could hardly be said to have been only a hypocritical use of the planned crusade for the sake of financial gain.[145] It seems to have been a mixture of serious concerns and of the intent to secure for himself higher fame than that of the Kings of France and England, whose rank was superior to his own, by pursuing this particularly useful and, at the same time, especially knightly plan, to be the savior of Christendom. "Le voyage de Turquie"‡ remained his trump card that he did not play. Chastellain takes pains to stress that the duke was serious about this but that there were important considerations: the times were not ripe, influential people were shaking their heads that the prince intended to undertake such a dangerous campaign given his age; territories and dynasty would both be in peril. While the pope sent him the flag of the cross that was received by Philip in the Hague with all humility and respect in a solemn procession, while vows to take

* "Show favor to Zion and grant her prosperity; rebuild the walls of Jerusalem."
† "if it had pleased God, his creator, to allow him a full span of years."
‡ "the voyage to Turkey"

the journey were made during the festivities in Lille and afterwards, while Joffrey de Toisy reconnoitered the Syrian ports and Jean Chevrot, bishop of Tournay, supervised collections, and Guillaume Fillastre held his entire train in readiness and had already confiscated ships for the campaign, there prevailed, in the midst of all this, a vague premonition that the campaign might not take place in spite of everything.[146] The duke's own vow had a somewhat qualified ring to it; he would venture out if the territories, which God had entrusted to be governed by him, would enjoy peace and security.[147]

Announcing military campaigns, excepting the ideal of the crusade, seemed to have been a popular technique in the clamor for political prestige. These noisily proclaimed campaigns were prepared in great detail, but failed to materialize or had very little consequence, as, for example, the English expedition against Flanders in 1383; or the campaign of Philip the Bold against England in 1387, in which a splendid fleet was assembled and made ready to sail from the port of Sluis; or the campaign of Charles VI against Italy in 1391.

A very special form of knightly fiction used as political propaganda was the repeatedly announced but never accomplished princely duel. I have elsewhere detailed how the quarrels between the states of the fifteenth century were still regarded as quarrels between parties, as personal "querelles."[148] The cause one served was called "la querelle des Bourguignons." What was more natural than that the princes themselves should fight it out just as still proposed in casual political rhetoric? This solution that arose from both a primitive sense of justice and from the knightly imagination actually appeared time and again on the agenda. Reading about the detailed preparations for the princely duels, one wonders if this was only a beautiful game of conscious hypocrisy, again the search for a beautiful life, or whether the knightly adversaries really expected to do battle against each other. There is no doubt that the historians of that period took such challenges just as seriously as the belligerent princes themselves. In 1383 Richard II commissioned his uncle, John of Lancaster, to negotiate peace with the King of France and, as a proper means thereto, a duel between the two kings or between Richard and his three uncles and Charles and his uncles.[149] Monstrelet devotes considerable space, right at the beginning of his chronicle, to the challenge by Louis of Orléans to King Henry

IV of England.[150] To the impetuous and brilliant mind of Orléans, which had scope for fiery devotion, the appreciation of the arts, fantastic ideals of knightly combat and courtly love, side by side with debauchery, cynicism, and the magical arts, such a duel might also have well been a passionate undertaking. The same holds true for the pompous mind of Philip the Good. He, in his turn, provided the most imposing elaboration of the theme backed by all the resources of his wealth and his love of splendor. It was Humphrey of Gloucester whom he challenged in the noble manner in 1425. In the challenge there is clear reference to the motif of *noblesse oblige:* "pour éviter effusion de sang chrestien et la destruction du peuple, dont en mon cuer ay compacion . . . que par mon corps sans plus ceste querelle soit menée à fin, sans y aler avant par voies de guerres dont il convendroit mains gentilz hommes et aultres, tant de vostre ost comme du mien, finer leurs jours piteusement."[151]* All the props for the battle were ready: the costly armor and the splendid garments to be worn by the duke were prepared; work was in progress on the tents, the standards and banners, the coats for the heralds and pursuivants, all displaying in profusion the court of arms of the ducal realm, the tinderbox and the cross of St. Andrew. Philip was in training: "tant en abstinence de sa bouche comme en prenant painne pour luy mettre en alainne."[152] In his park at Hesdin he practiced daily under experienced fencing masters.[153] The bills inform us of the cost of all of this. The expensive tent fashioned for the purpose could be seen in Lille as late as 1460.[154] But the duel never took place.

This did not stop Philip from later issuing a new challenge to the duke of Saxony during their quarrel over Luxembourg. At the feast at Lille when Philip was almost sixty years old, his vow to launch a crusade stated that he would be only too willing to do battle with the great Turk *corps à corps*† if the latter wanted it that way.[155] The stubborn combative spirit of Philip the Good still echoes in a short story by Bandello about how Philip had once been

---

* "to prevent the shedding of the blood of Christians and the destruction of the people on whom my heart has compassion . . . that by my own body this quarrel might be settled, without proceeding by means of wars, which would entail that many noblemen and others, both of your army and of mine, would end their days pitifully."

† "man to man"

kept by great effort on the part of his noblemen from a duel of honor.[156]

This form still survived in the Italy of the high Renaissance. Francesco Gonzaga challenged Cesare Borgia to a duel. With sword and dagger he intended to free Italy from the feared and hated enemy. The duel was averted through the mediation of King Louis XII of France and the case ended with a moving reconciliation.[157] Even Charles V at least twice formally proposed that his quarrels with Francis I be settled by a personal duel, the first time after Francis had returned from captivity and, in the opinion of the Emperor, had broken his word, and then again in 1536.[158]

Duels arranged to settle a point of law, judicial duels, and those that were spontaneous all had a strong survival in custom and thought particularly in Burgundy and in the quarrelsome north of France. Both high and low hailed duels as producing truly decisive results. These concepts, taken by themselves, had little to do with the knightly ideal; they were much older. Knightly culture bestowed on the duel a certain respectability, but duels were also favored outside the circles of nobility. In cases not involving the nobility, duels immediately reveal the full brutality of the age. The knights themselves enjoyed the spectacle much more if their code of honor was not involved in it.

Most remarkable, in this connection, is the concern displayed by noblemen and historians for a judicial duel between two burghers at Valenciennes in 1455.[159] This was a great rarity, since nothing like it had taken place for about a hundred years. The citizens of Valenciennes wanted to see it happen at any cost because to them it meant the maintenance of an old privilege; but the count of Charolais who was in charge of the administration during Philip's absence (in Germany) felt differently and managed to have it postponed month by month while the two litigants, Jacotin Plouvier and Mahuot, were held back like two expensive fighting cocks. As soon as the aging count had returned from his trip to see the Emperor, the decision was made that the battle should take place. Philip was anxious to witness it himself; it was only for this reason that he chose to travel via Valenciennes on his trip from Bruges to Louvain. While knightly spirits like Chastellain and La Marche usually do not provide a realistic account of the festive *pas d'armes* of knights and noblemen in spite of all their efforts to do so, in this instance they record the most clearly seen picture. The crude Fleming whom Chastellain was is revealed here under his enveloping houpelande,[160] which was splendid in gold with a pattern of red squares. No detail of the "moult belle serimonie"* escapes him; his description of the circles of the barriers and benches at the scene is precise.

Each of the poor sacrificial victims has his fencing master at his side. Jacotin as plaintiff appears first, bareheaded with his hair cut short and looking very pale. His entire body has been sewn into a dress of cordovan leather, all just one piece, and he wears nothing underneath. After a few pious obeisances and the welcoming of the duke, who is seated behind a latticed screen, the two combatants are seated opposite one another on two chairs draped in black, and wait until the preparations are completed. The notables in the circle make their comments in subdued voices about the chances of the opponents; nothing escapes them: Mahuot was pale as snow when he kissed the New Testament! Two servants come in and cover the warriors with fat from their necks down to their ankles. In the case of Jacotin the fat is immediately absorbed into the leather, but not in the case of Mahuot; for which of the two is this a favorable sign? Their hands are covered with ashes, they put sugar into their mouths. Then they are given clubs and shields on which there are painted images of saints, which are kissed by the combatants. They hold their shields with the points upward and have in their hands "une bannerolle de devocion," a ribbon with a pious motto.

Mahuot, who is short, opens the duel by scooping up sand with the tip of his shield and flipping it into the eyes of Jacotin. This is followed by intense club fighting that ends with Mahuot's fall; his opponent throws himself on top of Mahuot and rubs sand in his mouth and eyes. But Mahuot manages to get his enemy's finger between his teeth. To free himself, Jacotin presses his thumb into his tormentor's eye and, in spite of Mahuot's cries for mercy, twists his arms behind him and turns Mahuot on his back and proceeds to break his spine. Mahuot, in his death throes, pleads in vain to be allowed to confess; then he cries out, "O monseigneur de Bourgogne, je vou ay si bien servi en vostre guerre de Gand! O monsigneur, pour Dieu, je vous prie mercy, sauvez-moy la vie!"†

---

* "most beautiful ceremony"

† "O, my lord of Burgundy, I have served you well in your war against Ghent! O my lord, for God's sake, I beg for mercy, save my life!"

At this point Chastellain's report breaks off; some pages are missing. From other sources we know how the half-dead Mahuot is hanged by the executioner.

Did Chastellain, after his energetic description of these revolting cruelties end his account with noble knightly contemplations? La Marche did. He tells us about the shame felt by the noblemen after the event for having seen such a thing. Thereupon, this incorrigible court poet continues, God allowed a knightly duel to follow that ended without injuries.

The conflict between the chivalric spirit and reality is most clearly revealed when the knightly ideal attempts to establish its validity in the midst of real war. No matter how much the knightly ideal may have infused fighting courage with form and vigor, as a rule it had a more retarding than promoting effect on the conduct of war because it sacrificed the demands of strategy for those of the beautiful life. Repeatedly the best leaders, on occasion even the kings, exposed themselves to the dangers of a romantic war adventure. Edward III risks his life in a questionable raid on some Spanish naval transports.[161] The knights of King John's Order of Stars have to take an oath that they will not retreat in battle more than four "arpents"; failing that they must either die or surrender, a peculiar rule of the game that, according to Froissart, immediately cost about ninety knights their lives.[162] When Henry V of England in 1415 moved towards the enemy on the eve of the battle of Agincourt, he mistakenly advanced one evening past the village that his officials had designated as his quarters for the night. Now the king, "comme celuy qui gardoit le plus les cérimonies d'honneur très loable,"* had just issued the order that the knights sent out on reconnaissance missions should take off their battle dress so as to spare them the shame of retreating in armor on their way back to camp. Since in this instance he himself had advanced too far in his battle dress he could not turn back, he therefore spent the night at the place he had reached and had his advanced troops move forward accordingly.[163]

During the deliberations over the great French invasion of Flanders in 1382 the knightly spirit continuously resisted the requirements of strategy. "Se nous querons autres chemins que le droit" it is argued against the advice given by Clisson and Coucy to invade

---

* "as the chief guardian of the very laudable ceremonies of honor,"

along unexpected detours, "nous ne monsterons pas que soions
droites gens d'armes."[164]* The same holds for a raid by the French
on the English coast near Dartmouth in 1404. The leader, Guillaume du Châtel, plans to attack the English on their flank because
they have protected themselves on the beach by a trench. But the
Sire de Jaille calls the defenders a troop of peasants; it would be
shameful to avoid meeting such opponents head-on; he urges the
others not to be afraid. These words hit home with Du Châtel: "It
is unknown to the noble heart of a Breton that he be afraid; now
I shall challenge vagrant fortune even though I see death rather
than victory ahead." He adds the vow that he will not beg for
mercy, then goes on the attack. He is killed and his troops are
completely defeated.[165] During the campaign in Flanders there is
constant shuffling for positions in the advance guard; a knight put
in charge of the rear guard stubbornly resists such duties.[166]

The actual application of the knightly ideal to warfare consisted
of agreed-upon *aristies*,[167] be they of two combatants or of groups
of equal numbers. The best-known case is the famous *Combat des
Trente* that was fought in 1351 near Ploërnel in the Bretagne between thirty Frenchmen led by Beaumanoir and a group of Englishmen, Germans, and Bretons. Froissart found it to be extraordinarily beautiful but comments at the end, "Li aucun le tenoient à
proèce, et li aucun à outrage et grant outrecuidance."[168]† A duel
between Guy de la Tremoille and the English nobleman Pierre de
Courtenay in 1386 that was intended to prove the superiority of
either the English or the French was prohibited by the French re-
gents Burgundy and Berry and only stopped at the very last moment.[169] Le Jouvencel shares in this disapproval of such a useless
form of demonstrating bravery. We had already emphasized earlier
how in his case the knight gave way to the commander. When the
duke of Bedford proposes a fight of twelve against twelve, *Le
Jouvencel*'s chronicler has the French leader respond: "There is a
general dictum not to do anything proposed by your enemy. We
are here to drive you out of your positions and that is work
enough." And the challenge is refused. Elsewhere Le Jouvencel had

---

* "If we were to seek another path to the fight . . . we would show that we
are not proper knights."

† "Some held it a prowess, and some held it to be a shame and a great over-
bearing."

one of his officers prohibit such a duel by explaining (he resumes this explanation at the end) that he would never give permission for something like this to happen. These are forbidden things. Those who demand such a duel intend to take something away from their opponent; that is, their honor, and to claim for themselves vainglory, which is of little value, while in the meantime they are negligent in their service to their king and the public good.[170]

This sounds like the voice of the new age. Yet the custom of fighting duels between opposing forces survives until after the Middle Ages. We know of the *Sfida de Barletta,* the fight between Bayard and Sotomaya in 1501; during the Netherlands war we have the fight between Breauté and Lekkerbeetje on the heather near Vught in 1600 and that of Lodewijk van de Kethulle against an Albanesian knight at Deventer in 1591.

In most instances, knightly notions are pushed into the background by considerations of warfare and tactics. But the idea that even battles in open field are nothing but honestly arranged duels for justice always comes to the fore, though it is seldom given its due vis-à-vis the demands of the necessities of war. Heinrich of Trastamara wants to fight it out with the enemy in open field at any price. He voluntarily abandons his advantageous position and loses the battle at Najera (or Navarete). An English contingent proposes to the Scots in 1333 that they come down from their advantageous position onto the plain so that they may fight each other there. Failing to gain access to Calais in order to liberate the town, the French king politely proposes to the English that they should designate a site for battle somewhere else; Willem of Hennegowen goes one step further. He proposes to the French king a three-day armistice so that there would be time to build a bridge that would allow the armies to get close to each other for battle.[171] In all these instances, the knightly offers were declined; strategic interests retained the upper hand, as was the case with Philip the Good, who faced a serious conflict with his knightly honor when he was offered battle three times on the same day but declined to accept.[172]

Yet there remained plenty of opportunities to beautify warfare even in cases where the knightly ideal had to give way to reality. What an aura of pride must have been exuded by the colorful and boastful battle armor itself. On the eve of the battle of Agincourt the armies, encamped opposite each other, stirred up their courage in the darkness with the music of trumpets and trombones. There were serious complaints that the French did not have enough of them "pour eux resjouyr" and therefore remained in a subdued mood.[173]

Towards the end of the fifteenth century mercenaries with large drums based on oriental models made their appearance.[174] The drum with its hypnotic, unmusical effect is a fitting sign of the transition from the chivalric to the modern-military period; it is an element in the mechanization of war. In 1400 the entire beautiful and half-playful suggestion of personal competition for fame and honor is still in full bloom. By means of individualized helmet insignia, weapons, banners, and battle cries combat retains its individual character and an element of sport. Throughout the entire day, a man could hear different individuals raise their cries in a competitive game of arrogant pride.[175] Prior to and after the battle the creation of new knights and the raising of others in rank seal the game: knights are promoted to the rank of banneret by having the tails of their banner cut off.[176] The famous camp of Charles the Bold near Neuss had all the festive splendor of the stateliness of a court: some had their tents "par plaisance" in the form of a castle complete with surrounding galleries and gardens.[177]

The feats of war had to be recorded within the frame of reference provided by knightly notions. Attempts were made to distinguish between battles and mere engagements on technical grounds because each battle had to have its fixed location and name in the annuals of fame. Monstrelet says, "Si fut de ce jour en avant ceste besongne appellée la recontre de Mons en Vimeu. Et ne fu declairée à estre bataille, pour ce que les parties rencontrèrent l'un l'autre aventureusement, et qu'il n'y avoit comme nulles bannières desploiées."[178]* Henry V of England solemnly christens his great victory "pour tant que toutes batailles doivent porter le nom de la prochaine forteresse où elles sont faictes,"† as the battle of Agincourt.[179] Remaining for the night on the battlefield was regarded as the accepted sign of victory.[180]

---

* "From this day on, this encounter was called the struggle of Mons en Vimeu. It was not, however, declared to be a battle because the parties only encountered one another by chance and no flags were displayed."

† "because all battles should take the name of the nearest fortress."

The personal bravery of the prince in battle occasionally has a rather artificial character. Froissart's description of a fight between Edward III and a French nobleman near Calais contains expressions that allow us to assume that they were not bitterly serious, "Là se combati li rois à monsigneur Ustasse moult longuement et messires Ustassc à lui, et tant que il les faisoit moult plaisant veoir."* The Frenchman finally surrenders and the fight is concluded with a supper offered to his prisoner by the king.[181] In the battle of Saint Richier, Philip of Burgundy had somebody else wear his splendid armor because of the danger it attracted, but it was explained that this was done so that he could prove himself better as an ordinary combatant.[182] When the young dukes of Berry and the Bretagne follow Charles the Bold in his "guerre du bien public" they wear, as Commines was told, fake armor of satin with gilded nails.[183]

Everywhere lies shine through the holes in the stately knightly dress. Reality continuously denies the ideal. Therefore it withdraws further and further back into the sphere of literature, festival, and play; only here the illusion of the beautiful knightly life remains. Here one is with the caste among whom such feelings have their only validity.

It is astonishing how instantly the knightly ideal fails whenever it has to assert itself in confrontations with unequals. Whenever the lower classes are confronted, any need for knightly loftiness disappears. Noble Chastellain does not have the least understanding of the stubborn bourgeois honor of the wealthy brewer who does not want to give his daughter to a soldier of the duke and who risks his life and wealth to resist the duke.[184] Froissart reports, without any respect, how Charles VI asks to see the body of Philipp van Artevelde. "Quant on l'eust regardé un espasse on le osta de là et fu pendus à un arbre. Velà le darraine fin de che Phillippe d'Artevelle."[185]† The king was not above kicking the body, "en le traitant de vilain."[186]‡ The most cruel atrocities of the nobility were committed against the burghers of Ghent during the war of 1382. They sent to the city forty grain merchants with their limbs cut

* "Then the king fought for a very long time with Monsigneur Utsasse, and he with him, so that it was a great pleasure to see."

† "When he had looked at it a long time, it was taken from that place and hanged on a tree. This was the last end of Phillippe d'Artevelle."

‡ "in which he treated him like a villain."

off and their eyes gouged out. This did not for a moment lessen Froissart's passion for knighthood.[187] Chastellain, who revels in the heroic deeds of Jacques de Lalaing and the like, mentions without showing any sympathy, that an unknown apprentice from Ghent had dared to attack Lalaing all by himself.[188] La Marche comments somewhat naively about the heroic deeds of a commoner from Ghent that would have been important if they had been accomplished by "un homme de bien."[189]*

Reality pressed the mind in every which way to deny the knightly ideal. Military strategy had long ago abandoned the tournament element; the wars of the fourteenth and fifteenth centuries resorted to stealth and surprise. They were wars of raids and predatory attacks. The English had first introduced the practice of having the knights dismount during battle, and this was adopted by the French.[190] Eustache Deschamps comments mockingly that this was done to keep them from fleeing.[191] It is useful to fight at sea, says Froissart, because there the men cannot run away and vanish.[192] The extraordinary naiveté of the knightly notions as military principles manifests itself in the *Débat des hérauts d'armes de France et d'Angleterre*, a tract from about 1455, in which the supremacy of France or England is contested in the form of a debate. The English herald asked his French counterpart why his king, in contrast to the English king, does not maintain a great fleet. The French herald answers that his king does not need to do that, and , moreover, that the French nobility likes war on land more than that at sea for various reasons, "car il y a danger et perdicion de vie, et Dieu scet quelle pitié quant il fait une tourmente, et si est la malladie de la mer forte à endurer à plusieurs gens. Item, et la dure vie dont il fault vivre, qui n'est pas bien consonante à noblesse."[193]† Though still of only negligible effect, the use of cannons already foreshadowed future changes in warfare. It is like an ironic symbolism that the pride of knight-errantry, "à la mode de bourgogne,"‡ Jacques de Lalaing, was killed by a fiery cannonball.[194]

---

* "a gentleman."

† "because there is danger and loss of life and God knows how awful it is when there is a storm and there is sea sickness that many people find hard to bear. Beyond that, look at the hard life which must be endured and does not become nobility."

‡ "in the style of Burgundy"

The noble-military career had a financial side to it that was often openly admitted. Every page of the histories of late medieval warfare gives us to understand how important prominent prisoners were for the sake of exacting ransom. Froissart does not fail to mention how much the originator of a successful surprise raid gained financially as a result of it.[195] But in addition to the immediate advantages of war, pensions and rents and government posts played a major role in the lives of the knights. Career advancement is publicly acknowledged as a goal. "Je sui uns povres homs qui desire mon avancement,"* says Eustache de Ribeumont. Froissart endlessly explains his *fait diverse* of knightly warfare among others as example of those brave men "qui se désirent à avanchier par armes."[196]†

Deschamps has a ballad in which the knights, pages, and sergeants of the Burgundian court yearn with great anticipation for payday with the refrain

Et quant venra le tresorier?[197]‡

To Chastellain it is natural and fitting that someone striving for earthly fame is stingy and calculating "fort veillant et entendant à grand somme de deniers, soit en pensions, soits en rentes, soit en governemens ou en pratiques."[198] As a matter of fact, the noble Boucicaut himself, who was the model of all knights, seems not to have been entirely free from a certain greed for money.[199] The sober Commines ranks a nobleman according to his stipend as "un gentilhomme de vingt escuz."[200]§

Among the loud voices glorifying knightly warfare there can be heard occasional voices rejecting the knightly ideal. Sometimes they are sober voices, sometimes they are derisive. Noblemen on occasion recognize the dressed-up misery and falsity of such a life of war and tournaments.[201] It does not come as a surprise that Louis XI and Philippe de Commines, two sarcastic minds who had nothing but scorn and contempt for knighthood, found each other. Commines's description of the battle of Montlhéry is entirely mod-

---

* "I am a poor man who desires advancement,"
† "who desire to advance themselves by arms."
‡ And when will the paymaster come?
§ A nobleman of twenty thalers

ern in its sober realism. There are no beautiful heroic deeds, no
invented dramatic events, but only the report of continual advance
and retreat, hesitation and fear, all told with light sarcasm. He
delights in reporting shameful flights with bravery restored when
the moment of danger had passed. He rarely uses the word "honneur" and treats honor almost like a necessary evil. "Mon advis
est que s'il eust voulu s'en aller ceste nuyt, il eust bien faict. . . .
Mais sans doubte là où il avoit de l'honneur, il n'eust point voulu
estre reprins de couardise."* Even where he reports bloody encounters, one searches in vain for the vocabulary of knighthood; he does
not know the words bravery or chivalry.[202]

Does Commines inherit his sober mind from his Zealand
mother, Margretha of Arnemuiden? It appears that in Holland,
the presence of the vain adventurer William IV of Hennegouw
notwithstanding, the knightly spirit died away quite early, while
the Hennegouw with which it was united had always been the true
land of knightly nobility. During the *Combat des Trente* the best
man on the English side was a certain Crokart, formerly a servant
of the Lords of Arkel. He had acquired a large fortune during the
war, estimated to be worth about sixty thousand crowns, and a
stable of thirty horses; he had also acquired considerable fame for
bravery, which had prompted the King of France to offer him a
knighthood and a respectable marriage in the event that he would
become French. This Crokart returned to Holland with his fame
and fortune and held forth in grand style. But the Dutch notables
knew well who he was and ignored him. He finally returned to
the country where knightly fame was more favored.[203]

When Jean de Nevers[204] prepared himself for his journey to Turkey where he was to find Nicopolis, Froissart had the Duke Albert
of Bavaria, the duke of Holland, Zealand, and Hennegouw, say to
his son William, "Guillemme puisque tu as la voulenté de voyagier
et aler en Honguerie et en Turquie et quérir les armes sur gents et
pays qui onques riens ne nous foufirent, ne nul article de raison tu
n'y as d'y aler fors que pour la vayne gloire de ce monde, laisse
Jean de Bourgoigne et nos cousins de France faire leur emprises,

---

* "My opinion is, if he had gone out on this night, he would have been
behaving well . . . but really, when honor came into question he would not have
liked to be accused of cowardice."

et fay la tienne à par toy, et t'en va en Frise et conquiers nostre héritage."[205]*

Of all the lands under the Burgundian duke the nobility of Holland had by far the weakest representation during the Vows of the Cross taken at the festivities in Lille. When after the festivities still more written vows were collected in all territories, twenty-seven came from Artois, fifty-four from Flanders, twenty-seven from Hennegouw, and four from Holland, and even those sound quite conditional and cautious.[206]

But knighthood could hardly have been the life ideal of centuries if it had not contained high values for the development of society, if it had not been socially, ethically, and aesthetically necessary. The power of this ideal had once rested in its beautiful exaggeration. It seems as if the medieval mind in all its bloody passions could only be guided by an ideal that was fixed much too highly: this was done by the church, and was done by the knightly spirit as well. "Without this violence of direction, which men and women have, without a spice of bigot and fanatic, no excitement, no efficiency. We aim above the mark to hit the mark. Every act hath some falsehood of exaggeration in it."[207]

But the more a cultural ideal is filled with the claims to the highest virtues, the greater the disharmony between the life form and reality. Only a time still able to close its eyes to gross reality and receptive to the highest illusion could uphold the knightly ideal with its still half-religious content. The unfolding new culture soon forced the abandonment of the all too lofty aspirations of the old life forms. The knight is transformed into the French *gentilhomme* of the seventeenth century, who, though still maintaining a number of concepts of state and honor, no longer claims to be a warrior for matters of faith or a defender of the weak and oppressed. The place of the type of French nobleman is taken—modified and refined—by the "gentleman," who is derived directly from the type of the old knight. During the successive transformations of the

---

* William, it is your desire to go to Hungary and Turkey and try to fight with people and countries who have never done anything to us and you have no reasonable ground to do this other than vain earthly glory. Let John of Burgundy and our cousins of France go forth on this undertaking and as for you, go to Friesland and conquer our heritage."

ideal the outermost shells, each having become a lie, are peeled away time and again.

The knightly life form was overburdened with ideals of beauty, virtue, and utility. If viewed with a sober sense of reality, as does Commines, all this highly praised chivalry appeared to be as useless and phony as a fabricated, ridiculously anachronistic comedy. The true driving forces that prompted human action and determined the fate of states and communities lay elsewhere. As the social usefulness of the knightly ideal had already become extremely weak, so it was that the ethical aspect, the practice of virtue, which also had been claimed by the knightly ideal, was even weaker. Seen from a truly spiritual point of view, all that noble life was nothing but open sin and vanity. The ideal failed also from a purely aesthetic point of view: even the beauty of that life form could be denied in every respect. Though the knightly ideal may on occasion appear to be desirable to some burghers, a great feeling of fatigue and overindulgence arises among the nobility itself. The beautiful play of courtly life was so colored, so false, so paralyzing. Away from the painfully constructed art of life towards that of secure simplicity and peace!

There were then two ways to preserve the knightly ideal: the one to move towards real, active life and the modern spirit of inquiry, the other that of denial of the world. But the latter, like the Y of Pythagoras,[208] split into two: the main line was that of the genuinely spiritual life, the secondary line kept close to the edge of the world and its pleasures. The yearning for the beautiful life was so strong that even in places where the vanity and degeneration of courtly and combative life were recognized, there still seemed to be a path to a beautiful earthly life, to a sweeter and brighter dream. The old illusion of the pastoral life still radiated its promise of natural bliss with the full glow it had possessed since Theocritus. It seemed to be possible to achieve the great liberation without a struggle through a flight from the hate- and envy-filled scramble for vain honors and vain rank, from oppressive, overburdened luxury and splendor, and from cruel, dangerous war.

The praise of the simple life was a theme that medieval literature had already adopted from antiquity. It is not identical with the pastorale: the two forms are a positive and a negative expression of one and the same emotion. The pastorale describes a positive contrast to courtly life. The negative expression describes a flight from the court, from the praise of the *aurea mediocritas* (the Golden Mean); it denies the aristocratic life ideal, a denial expressed through scholarship, solitary quietude, or work. The motifs are continuously fusing. As early as the twelfth century John of Salisbury and Walter Mapes had written their tracts "de nugis curialium" on the theme of the shortcomings of courtly life. In fourteenth-century France the classic expression of this theme is found in a poem by Philippe de Vitri, bishop of Meaux, who was both a composer and a poet and was praised by Petrarch. In this poem, "Le dit de Franc Gontier,"[209] the fusion with the pastorale is perfect:

> *Soubz feuille vert, sur herbe delitable*
> *Lez ru bruiant et prez clere fontaine*
> *Trouvay fichee une borde portable,*
> *Ilec mengeoit Gontier o dame Helayne*
> *Fromage frais, laict, burre fromaigee,*
> *Craime, matton, pomme, nois, prune, poire,*
> *aulx et oignons, escaillogne froyee*
> *Sur crouste bise, a gros sel, pour mieulx boire.**

After the meal they kiss one another, "et bouche et nez, polie et bien barbue";† thereupon Gontier goes to the forest to chop down a tree while Lady Helayne does the wash.

> *J'oy Gontier en abatant son arbe*
> *Dieu mercier de sa vie seüre;*
> *"Ne scay"—dit-il—"que sont pilliers de marbre,*
> *Pommeaux lusisans, murs vestus de paincture;*
> *Je n'ay paour de traïson tissue*
> *Soubz beau semblant, ne qu'empoisonné soye*
> *En vaisseau d'or. Je n'ay la teste nue*
> *Devant thirant, ne genoil qui s'i ploye.*
> *Verge d'ussier jamais ne me deboute,*

---

* Under green leaves, on delightful grass/Near a noisy brook and a clear fountain/I found a portable hut./There Gontier took his meal with dame Helayne/On fresh cheese, milk, cheese curds,/Cream, cream cheese, apple, nut, plum, pear,/Garlic and onions, chopped shallots/on a brown crust, with coarse salt, the better to drink.

† "mouth as well as nose, to the smooth as well as the bearded."

> *Car jusques la ne m'esprent convoitise,*
> *Ambicion, ne lescherie gloute.*
> *Labour me paist en joieuse franchise;*
> *Moult j'ame Helayne et elle moy sans faille,*
> *Et c'est assez. De tombel n'avons cure."*
> *Lors je dy: "Las! serf de court ne vault maille,*
> *Mais Franc Gontier vault en or jame pure."**

For coming generations this poem remained the classic expression of the ideal of the simple life replete with security and independence, its enjoyment of moderation, good health, work, and natural, uncomplicated love in marriage.

Eustache Deschamps sang the praise of the simple life and rejection of the court in a number of ballads. Among others he presents a faithful imitation of Franc Gontier:

> *En retounant d'un court souveraine*
> *Où j'avoie longuement sejourné,*
> *En un bosquet, dessus une fontaine*
> *Trouvay Robin le franc, enchapelé,*
> *Chapeauls de flours avoit cilz afublé*
> *Dessus son chief, et Marion sa drue . . .*[210]†

He expands the theme by ridiculing military life and knighthood. In simple seriousness he bewails the misery and cruelty of war; there is no estate worse than that of the warrior; the seven cardinal sins are his daily work; greed and the vain quest for fame constitute the essence of war:

---

* I heard Gontier in felling his tree/Thanking God for his security:/"I do not know," said he, "what are pillars of marble,/Shining pommels, walls decorated with paintings;/I have no fear of treason hidden/Under friendly appearances, nor that I shall be poisoned/in a gold cup. I do not bare my head/Before a tyrant, nor bend my knee./No usher's rod ever turns me away,/For no covetousness, ambition, greed/entices me./Work holds me in joyous liberty;/I love Helayne, and she me without fail,/And that is enough. The tomb does not frighten us."/ Then I said, "Alas, a serf of the court is not worth a farthing,/But free Franc Gontier is worth a real gem set in gold."

† Returning from a sovereign's court/Where I had long sojourned,/In a bush, near a fountain,/I found Robin the free, his head crowned,/With chaplets of flowers he had adorned/His head, and Marion, his love . . .

> . . . *Je vueil mener d'or en avant*
> *Estat moien, c'est mon oppinion,*
> *Guerre laissier et vivre en labourant:*
> *guerre mener n'est que dampnacion.*[211]*

Or he mockingly curses those who might want to challenge him, or has a lady expressedly order him not to fight a duel that has been forced on him for her sake.[212]

But mostly the poem is about the theme of the *aurea mediocritas* itself.

> *Je ne requier à Dieu fors qu'il me doint*
> *En ce monde lui server et loer,*
> *Vivre pour moy, cote entiere ou pourpoint,*
> *Aucun cheval pour mon labour porter,*
> *Et qui je puisse mon estat gouverner*
> *Moiennement, en grace, sanz envie,*
> *Sanz trop avoir et sanz pain demander,*
> *Car au jour d'ui est la plus seure vie.*[213]†

Seeking fame and fortune brings nothing but misery. The poor man is satisfied and happy and lives an undisturbed and long life:

> . . . *Un ouvrier et uns povres chartons*
> *Va mauvestuz, deschirez et deschaulz*
> *Mais en ouvrant prant en gré ses travaulz*
> *Et liement fait son euvre fenir.*
> *Par nuit dort bien; pour ce uns telz cueurs loiaulx*
> *Voit quatre roys et leur regne fenir.*[214]‡

---

* . . . I will henceforth live/In a middle station, that is my resolve,/To abandon war and live by labor:/Waging war is but damnation.

† I only ask of God to give me/That in the world I may serve and praise him,/Live for myself, my coat or doublet whole,/One horse to carry my labor./And that I may govern my estate/To no extreme, in grace without envy,/Without having too much, without begging my bread,/For today, this is the safest life.

‡ . . . A working man, a poor teamster/goes ill dressed, torn clothes, ill shod/But laboring he takes pleasure in his work/And merrily finishes it./At night he sleeps well; and therefore such a loyal heart/Sees four kings and their reigns end.

The poet liked the idea that the simple laborer outlived four kings so much that he made repeated use of it.[215]

The editor of Deschamps's poetry, Gaston Raynaud, argues that all the poems with this tendency,[216] usually among the best Deschamps wrote, should be assigned to the late period when he, removed from office, abandoned and disappointed, had gained insight into the vanity of courtly life.[217] This would mean that he had also turned inward, but might it not also be a reaction, an expression of general fatigue? It seems to me that the nobility itself favored and demanded these productions, in the midst of their lives of driving passion and splendor, from a court poet who at other times prostituted his talents to satisfy their crudest need for laughter.

Around 1400 the theme of the disapproval of courtly life is further elaborated within the circle of the earliest French humanists, who were in part identical with the reform party of the great church councils. Pierre d'Ailly himself, a great theologian and church politician, composed, as a companion piece to "Franc Gontier," a picture of the tyrant whose slavish life is filled with anxiety. His brothers-in-spirit used for the purpose of their critiques of courtly life the newly rediscovered form of letters, as in the case of Nicholas de Clémanges[218] and his correspondent Jean de Montreuil.[219] The Milanese Ambrosius de Millis, secretary to the duke of Orléans, belonged to this circle and wrote a literary letter to a Gontier Col in which he has a courtier warn his friend against entering court service.[220] This letter, itself long forgotten, was translated by Alain Chartier, the famous court poet, or was at least published in its translated version with the title *Le Curial* under his name.[221] *Le Curial* was later retranslated into Latin by the humanist Robert Gaguin.[222]

A certain Charles de Rochefort handled the theme in the form of an allegorical poem in the style of the *Roman de la rose*. His *L'abuzé* was ascribed to King René.[223] Jean Meschinot composed poems like those of all his predecessors:

> *La cour est un mer, dort sourt*
> *Vagues d'orgueil, d'envie orages*
> ....
> *Ire esmeut debats et outrages,*
> *que les nefs jettent souvent bas;*

Traison y fait son personnage
nage aultre part pour tes ebats.[224]*

The old theme had not lost its fascination as late as the sixteenth century.[225]

Security, quietude, and independence are the good things of life and for their sake people want to flee the court in order to lead a simple life of work and moderation in the midst of nature. This is the negative side of the ideal. But the positive side is not so much the enjoyment of work and simplicity itself, but the comfort of natural love. The pastoral ideal leads us directly to the forms of erotic culture.

---

* The court is a sea, from which comes / Waves of pride, storms of envy . . . / Wrath stirs up quarrels and outrages, / Which often cause the ships to sink: / Treason has its part here. / Swim elsewhere for your amusement.

Chapter Four

THE FORMS OF LOVE

EVER SINCE THE PROVENÇAL TROUBADOURS OF THE
twelfth century first gave voice to the melody of unsatisfied desire,
the violins of love had sung ever higher until only Dante could
play the instrument purely.

The medieval mind took one of its most important turns when
it developed for the first time an ideal of love with a negative
groundtone. To be sure, antiquity had also sung of the yearning
and pain of love, but did that yearning not merely imply delay and
the titillation of the certainty of fulfillment? And in the love stories
of antiquity that did end sadly, the unavailability of the beloved
was not at issue, but rather a previously satisfied love that was
dramatically ended by death itself, as in the case of Cephalus and
Procris or Pyramus and Thisbe. The feeling of pain in those stories
lay not in erotic frustration, but in the sadness of fate. It is first in
the courtly *Minne* of the troubadours that frustration itself becomes
the vital concern. An intellectual form of erotic thought had been
created that was able to encompass a superabundance of ethical
content, without having, on account of it, to entirely abandon the
connection with the natural love of women. The courtly service of
women that idealized itself by never demanding fulfillment had
arisen from sensual love itself. In *Minne,* love became the field in
which all aesthetic and ethical perfection was allowed to blossom.
The noble lover, according to the theory of courtly *Minne,* was
made virtuous and pure by his love. In lyric poetry the spiritual
element more and more gained the upper hand until, finally, the
effect of love is a state of sacred insight and piety: *La vita nuova.*[1]

This had to be followed by a new turn of direction. In the *dolce
stil nuovo,** Dante and his contemporaries had reached a point be-

* "sweet new style."

126

yond which one cannot pass. Petrarch stands hesitatingly between the ideal of spiritual love and the new inspiration of antiquity. And from Petrarch to Lorenzo de'Medici the love song in Italy returns to the path of natūral sensuality that had permeated the admired models of antiquity. The artificially elaborated system of the courtly *Minne* was abandoned.

In France, and in those lands that were under the spell of the French spirit, a different turn was taken. In those countries the development of erotic thought after the high flowering of the courtly lyric was not as simple. The forms of the old system remain, but they are filled with a new spirit. There, even before the *Vita nuova* had found the true harmonies of a spiritualized passion, the *Roman de la rose* had partially filled the forms of courtly *Minne* with new content. For about two centuries this work by Guillaume de Lorris and Jean Clopinel (or Chopinel),[2] begun before 1240 and completed before 1280, not only completely dominated the forum of aristocratic love, but, because of its wealth of encyclopedic digressions into all sorts of other arenas, was also the treasure house from which educated people drew the most lively elements of their intellectual development. It is impossible to overestimate the importance of the fact that the ruling class of an entire period obtained, in this manner, its view of life and its erudition in the form of an *ars amandi*.* During no other age did the ideal of worldly erudition enter into such intimate union with the love of women than from the twelfth to the fifteenth centuries. All Christian and social virtues, the entire structure of the forms of life, were fitted into the framework of true love by the system of *Minne*. The erotic view of life, either in its older, purely courtly form or in its embodiment in the *Roman de la rose,* can be placed on the same level with its contemporary, scholasticism. Both represent a great effort by the medieval mind to comprehend everything that pertains to life from a single point of view.

The entire struggle to beautify life is concentrated in the colorful presentation of the forms of love. Those who sought beauty in honor and rank, or who endeavored to embellish their lives with splendor and stateliness, in short, those who sought the beauty of life in pride, were constantly reminded of the vanity of these things. In love, however, there appeared to be a purpose and reality for

* "art of love."

all those who had not entirely taken leave of that earthly bliss, which was the enjoyment of beauty itself. In this there was no need to create a beautiful life from noble forms or to emphasize high status. Here dwelled the most profound beauty, the highest bliss itself, which needed only to be given color and form. Every beautiful object, every flower, and every sound could contribute something to the building of love's life form.

The effort to stylize love was more than a vain game. The power of passion itself required that late medieval society transform the life of love into a beautiful play with noble rules. Here above all, if men were not to fall into crude barbarism, there was a need to frame emotions within fixed forms. Among the lower estates it was left to the church to tame unrestrained outbursts, and the church met its task as well as could be managed under the circumstances. The aristocracy, which felt itself to be somewhat independent of the church since it possessed a modicum of culture from outside the ecclesiastical realm, fashioned an obstacle to disorder out of refined eroticism itself; literature, fashion, and the forms of etiquette exercised in this way a normative influence on the life of love.

Or at least, these three created a beautiful illusion within which people could imagine themselves to live, in spite of the fact that even among the upper classes life remained extrordinarily crude. Ordinary behavior had a character of free-spirited insolence that later times have lost. The duke of Burgundy had the bathhouses of Valenciennes put in order for the English envoys expected there "pour eux et pour quiconque avoient de famille, voire bains estorés de tout ce qu'il faut au mestier de Vénus, à prendre par choix et par élection ce que on désiroit mieux, et tout aux frais du duc."[3]* The virtuous behavior of his son, Charles the Bold, was suspected by many to be inappropriate for a prince.[4] Among the mechanical pranks of the pleasure house at Hesdin the bills mention "ung engien pour moullier les dames en marchant par dessoubz."[5]†

Yet this crudity is not simply a failure of the ideal. Even as

---

* "for them and all their retinue, baths provided with everything required for the calling of Venus, to take by choice and by election what they liked best, and all at the expense of the duke."

† "a machine to wet the ladies when they pass under it."

ennobled love had a style of its own, so too did license itself, and a much older one at that. It may be called the epithalamic style. In matters of notions of love, a refined society, such as that of the waning Middle Ages, inherits so many ancient motifs that the erotic styles must compete or merge with one another. The style of courtly *Minne* was confronted by the primitive form of eroticism, with much older roots and an equally vital significance, which glorified the sexual union itself. Although in Christian culture its value was replaced by sacred mystery, eroticism remained as alive as *Minne*.

The entire epithalamic apparatus with its shameless laughter and its phallic symbolism had once been a part of the sacred rites of the wedding festivity itself. The consummation of marriage and the wedding ceremony had once been inseparable: a great mystery that focused on copulation. Then came the church and claimed sanctity and mystery for itself by transposing both the marriage and its consummation into the sacrament of a solemn union. The secondary aspects of the mystery, such as the procession, the song, and the shout of jubilation, were left to the wedding festivities. But, stripped of their sacred power, they were expressed with even more lascivious abandon and the church was never able to tame them. No churchly ethic could repress the exuberant cry of life in the "Hymen, O Hymenäe"! No puritanical mind could banish from custom the shamelessly open character of the wedding night. Even the seventeenth century still knew this open character in its full bloom. Only modern individual sensitivity, which desires to hide in stillness and darkness that which belongs to the two individuals alone, has broken with these public displays.

If we remember that as late as 1641 at the wedding of the young Prince of Orange with Mary of England, the practical jokes rendered the bridegroom, a boy still, nearly incapable of consummating the marriage, we will not be astonished at the frivolous abandon with which princely and noble marriages used to be celebrated around 1400. The obscene grin with which Froissart describes the marriage of Charles VI with Isabella of Bavaria,[6] or the Epithalamium that Deschamps dedicated to Anton of Burgundy are examples for us.[7] The *Cent nouvelles nouvelles* tell us, as something quite ordinary, of a couple who were married during early mass and, after a light meal, immediately went to bed.[8] All the jokes concerning weddings or sex in general were considered suitable for gatherings of ladies. The *Cent nouvelles nouvelles** introduce themselves, even though with some irony, as "glorieuse et édificant euvre,"† as stories "moult plaisants à reconter en toute bonne compagnie."‡ A noble versesmith composed a lascivious ballade at the request of Madame de Bourgogne and all of the ladies and maidens of her court.[9]

It is clear that things such as these were not regarded as violations of the high and rigid ideals of honor and propriety. This is a contradiction that should not be explained by imagining the noble forms and the high degree of prudishness displayed by the Middle Ages in other areas to be hypocritical. Just as little as we can call their shamelessness a saturnalian throwing off of restraints. Still further off the mark is the impression that the epithalamic obscenities are a sign of decadence or aristocratic overrefinement. The double meanings, the indecencies, the lascivious dissimulations are at home in the epithalamic style because they originated there. They become understandable if seen against their ethnological background: as the weakened remnants of the phallic symbolism of primitive culture, as debased mysteries. What once, at a time when the borders between play and seriousness had not been drawn by culture, joined the sacredness of ritual to the exuberance of the joy of life could only be handled, in a Christian society, as titillating mockery and stimulating jest. In direct contradiction to piety and *courteoisie* sexual notions survived in nuptial customs with their vitality intact.

One may, if so inclined, regard the whole comic-erotic genre as wild sprouts from the stem of the epithalamium—the story, the farce, the ditty. The link to the source, however, has long been lost: the literary genre has become independent, the comic effect an end in itself. The comic art remains the same as that of the epithalamium; it depends throughout on a symbolic representation of sexual matters or the depiction of the sexual act in the image of a profession. Almost any craft, any occupation, yielded its form to erotic metaphor, then just as well as now. It is obvious that during the fourteenth and fifteenth centuries, the tournament, the hunt, and music provided the subject matter for this purpose.[10] Both the

* *One Hundred New Stories*
† "honorable and edifying work"
‡ "very suitable to tell in any good company."

treatment of love stories in the form of legal disputes and the *arrestz d'amour* are to be understood from the vantage point of this category of parody. There was still another domain favored to provide a garb for sexual matters; this was the church. The Middle Ages were extraordinarily open in expressing sexual matters in technical ecclesiastical terminology. In the *Cent nouvelles nouvelles,* the use of words such as *bénir* or *confesser* in an indecent sense or the play of words like *saints* or *seins* is untiringly repeated. In refined examples, however, the ecclesiastical-erotic allegory becomes a literary form in itself. The poetic circle around Charles d'Orléans veils the lamentations of love in the forms of monastic asceticism, liturgy, and martyrdom. Echoing the recently successful reform of the Franciscan monastic life around 1400, these poets call themselves *Les amoureux de l'observance.* This is like an ironic byplay to the sacred seriousness of the *dolce stil nuovo.* The desecrating tendency is halfway atoned for by the intensity of the amorous sentiments.

> *Ce sont idi les dix commandemens,*
> *Vray Dieu d'amours . . .* *

So the poet profanes the Ten Commandments, or here, the oath taken on the New Testament:

> *Lors m'appella, et me fist les mains mettre*
> *Sur ung livre, en me faisant promettre*
> *Que feroye loyaument mon devoir*
> *Des points d'amour.*[11]†

Of a dead lover, he says:

> *Et j'ay espoir que brief ou [au] paradis*
> *Des amoureux sera moult hault assis,*
> *Comme martir et très honnoré saint.*‡

---

* These are the ten commandments, / True God of love . . .

† Then call me and command me lay my hands / On a book and order me to swear, / That I will honestly do my duty / In the matters of love.

‡ And I have the hope, that he soon / Will sit high in the Paradise of lovers / As a martyr and highly honored saint.

And of his own dead beloved:

> *J'ay fait l'obseque de ma dame*
> *Dedens le moustier amoureux,*
> *Et le service pour son ame*
> *A chanté Penser doloreux.*
> *Mains sierges de soupirs piteux*
> *Ont esté en son luminaire,*
> *Aussi j'ay fait la tombe faire*
> *De regrets . . .*[12]*

In the candid poem "L'amant rendu cordelier de l'observance d'amour,"† which describes the admittance of a despairing lover into the Monastery of the Martyrs of Love, the entire comic effect promised by the ecclesiastical parody is worked out to the last detail. Does this not indicate that the erotic, time and again and no matter how perversely, is drawn towards reestablishing that contact with the holy that it lost a long time ago?

Eroticism, in order to be culture, had to find at any price a style, a form, which could hold it in bounds, an expression that could veil it. And even where it rejected that form and lowered itself from questionable allegory to realistic and unveiled treatment of sexual activities, eroticism still remained, though unintentionally, stylized. An unsophisticated mind may easily mistake the entire genre for erotic naturalism. This genre, where men never tire and women are always willing, is just as much a romantic fiction as the most noble courtly *Minne*. What other than romanticism is the cowardly neglect of all the natural and social complications of love, the beautiful gloss of undisturbed pleasure as cover for all the false, self-seeking, and tragic elements in sexual activities? Here again we encounter that great cultural motive: the craving for a beautiful life, the need to make life appear more beautiful than it is revealed by reality. Here the life of love is forced into a form that conforms to a fantastic desire but does it now by emphasizing the animal side of humanity. Here is another life ideal: the ideal of chastelessness.

---

* I have celebrated the obsequies of my lady/In the monastery of love,/And the service for her soul/Was sung by Dolorous Thought./Many tapers of pitiful sighs/Have burned in her illumination./Also I had the tomb made/Of regrets . . .
    † "The Lover Made Member of the Order of Love"

Reality is at any time more wretched and cruder than the refined literary ideal of love sees it, but it is also purer and more ethical than it is represented by that shallow eroticism which is usually regarded as naturalistic. Eustache Deschamps, the professional poet, lowers himself in many ballades, in which he has a speaking part, to the most debased transgressions. But he is not the real hero of those indecent scenes, and amongst them we suddenly find a tender poem in which he points out to his daughter the virtues of her dead mother.[13]

As a source of literature and culture the whole epithalamic genre, with all its facets and ramifications, remains of secondary importance. It has as its theme full and complete satisfaction. It is overtly erotic. But that which can serve to shape and adorn life is the covertly erotic, whose theme is the possibility of satisfaction, the promise, the longing, the deprivation, anticipated happiness. Here, the greatest satisfaction is found in that which is unexpressed, disguised by the thin veils of expectation. Because of this, indirect eroticism is much more viable and embraces a much wider sphere of life. And it knows love not only in its major key, or in its laughing mask, but is also capable of transforming the pain of love into beauty and has, therefore, an infinitely higher value for life. It can embrace the ethical elements of faithfulness, of courage, of noble gentility, and being thus bonded with virtues in addition to love, may strive for the ideal.

Completely in agreement with the the general spirit of the later Middle Ages, which desired all thought to be captured in the most detailed images and systems, the *Roman de la rose* succeeded in bestowing on erotic culture in its entirety such a colorful, self-contained, and rich form that it was like a treasury of profane liturgy, doctrine, and legend. The hermaphroditism of the *Roman de la rose,* a work of two authors of vastly different nature and perception, rendered it even more usable as a bible of erotic culture. Texts for the most diverse usages can be found in it.

Guillaume de Lorris, the first poet, paid homage to all the old courtly ideals. The graceful plan and the gay, charming imagination of the work have to be attributed to him. The theme of the dream frequently reoccurs. Early on, the poet sees himself awake on a May morning so that he might hear the nightingale and the lark. His path leads him along a stream to the wall of the mysterious garden of love. On the wall he sees the images of hatred, betrayal, perfidity, rapaciousness, greed, melancholy, false piety, poverty, envy, and age. The anti-courtly qualities. But Dame Oiseuse (laziness), the friend of Déduit (amusement), opens the gate for him. Inside, Liesse (gaiety) leads the dance. The God of Love dances with Beauty in the round dance, and Wealth, Charity, Frankness (Franchise), Courtly Manners (Courteoisie), and Youth take part. While the poet is absorbed in admiration of the Rosebud that he has noticed near the Narcissus Fountain, the God of Love shoots him with his arrows: Beauté, Simplesse, Courteoisie, Compagnie, and Beau-Semblant. The poet declares himself to be the liegeman (*homme lige*) of Love. Amour locks his heart with a key and explains the Commandments of Love, the pains of Love and its comforts (*biens*); these last are Espérance, Doux-Penser, Doux-Parler, and Doux-Regard.

Bel-Accueil, the son of Courteoisie, summons him to the Rose, but at that momemt the guardians of the Rose appear, Danger, Male-Bouche, Peur, and Honte, and drive him away. Now the complications begin. Raison descends from his high tower to plead with the lover; Ami consoles him, and Venus turns all her charms against Chasteté. Franchise and Pitié bring him back to Bel-Accueil, who permits him to kiss the Rose. However, Male-Bouche spreads the alarm, Jalousie comes running, and a strong wall is built around the Rose. Bel-Accueil is imprisoned in a tower. Danger and his servants guard the gates. With the lament of the lover, the work of Guillaume de Lorris comes to an end.

Then, most likely a good time later, Jean de Meun [also known as Jean Clopinel] enters with a much more voluminous sequel. The further course of events—the attack and conquest of the castle of the Rose by Amour and all his allies, that is the courtly virtues assisted by Bien Celer and Faux-Semblant—nearly drowns in a flood of diversions, contemplations, and narrations by means of which the second poet turns the work into a veritable encyclopedia. But most importantly, here speaks a mind so unself-conscious, so coolly skeptical and cynically hardened, such as the Middle Ages rarely produced. And at the same time, a mind with a command of the French language equaled by few. The naive and easy idealism of Guillaume de Lorris is tarnished by the negating spirit of Jean de Meun. De Meun did not believe in ghosts or magicians, in true love or feminine honor, but he had a sense of pathological problems and he put in the mouths of Venus, Nature, and Genius the most daring defense of life's sensual urges.

When Amour fears that he and his army may be defeated, he dispatches Franchise and Doux-Regard to his mother, Venus, who answers his call and comes to him riding her chariot drawn by doves. Told by Amour how things stand, she vows that she will no longer tolerate any woman remaining chaste and urges Amour to take the same oath in respect to men. He does, and the entire army takes the oath with him.

In the meantime, Nature is at her forge, busy with her task of preserving the species in her eternal struggle with Death. She bitterly complains that of all her creatures only humanity disobeys her commandment and refrains from procreation. On her orders, Genius, her priest, after a long confession during which she explains her works to him, joins the army of Love to impose Nature's curse on all those who defy her commandments. Amour dresses Genius in a sacramental gown, with a ring, a staff, and a miter; Venus, laughing loudly, puts a burning candle in his hand

> Qui ne fu pas de cire vierge.*

The excommunication begins with a rejection of virginity, the audacious symbolism of which amounts to a wondrous mysticism. Hell for those who fail to observe the laws of Nature and Love! For the others, the flowering fields where the Son of the Virgin tends his white sheep that graze in eternal bliss on the flowers and plants that bloom there to all eternity.

After Genius has tossed the candle, whose flame sets all the world on fire, into the fortress, the final battle for the tower begins. Venus herself tosses her torch, Honte and Peur flee, and Bel-Accueil allows the lover to pluck the Rose.

Here, anew, the sexual motive is with full consciousness placed in the center of things and dressed in such artificial mystery, indeed, with so much sanctity, that a more pronounced challenge to the Christian ideal of life is not possible. In its perfectly pagan tendency, the *Roman de la rose* may be regarded as a step towards the Renaissance. In its external form, it is seemingly genuinely medi-

---

* "which was not made of virgin wax."

eval. What can be more medieval than the personification of emotional reactions and the circumstances of love taken to their extremes? The figures of the *Roman de la rose,* Bel-Accueil, Doux-Regard, Faux-Semblant, Male-Bouche, Danger, Honte, Peur, are at the same level as the truly medieval representations of the virtues and sins in human form. They are allegories, or something more, half believed in mythologems. Where is the division between these representations and the nymphs, satyrs, and ghosts that awaken to new life in the Renaissance? They are taken from another sphere, but their value to the imagination is the same. The external character of the figures of the *Rose* are occasionally reminiscent of the fantastic flowery figures of Botticelli.

Here the dream of love was depicted in a form that was both artificial and passionate. The detailed allegory satisfied all the needs of the medieval imagination. Without the personifications, the mind would not have been able either to express or to follow the shifts in emotion. The whole colorful fabric and elegant lines of this incomparable puppet show were necessary in order to form a conceptual system of love that people could use to communicate with one another. The figures of Danger, Nouvel Penser, Male-Bouche were used like the handy terms of a scientific psychology. The basic theme carried throughout the poem is in a passionate key since in the place of the pale service to a married woman who was elevated to the clouds by the troubadours as the unreachable object of their longing, there now comes again the most natural erotic motif: the potent attraction of the secret of virginity, symbolized as the Rose, which can only be won by art and endurance.

In theory, love in the *Roman de la rose* remained courtly and noble. The Garden of the Joy of Life is open only to the chosen and only through Love. Whoever wishes to enter must be free of hate, unfaithfulness, perfidy, rapaciousness, greed, envy, old age, and hypocrisy. The positive virtues, however, which must be mustered against all these prove the ideal is no longer ethical as it was in courtly *Minne,* but rather is purely aristocratic. The virtues are: carefreeness, receptability to enjoyment, gaiety of spirit, love, beauty, wealth, gentleness, freedom of spirit (*franchise*), and *Courteoisie.* These are no longer changes in the lover who is ennobled by the reflected glory of the beloved, but are the appropriate means used to win her. And it is no longer the veneration of the woman, misguided as it may have been, which inspires the work, but rather, at least in the case of the second poet, Jean Clopinel, the mocking contempt of her weaknesses, a contempt that has its sources in the sensual nature of this mode of love itself.

But in spite of its strong hold on the minds of the time, the *Roman de la rose* was unable to completely replace the older conception of love. Next to the glorification of flirtation, the idea of pure, knightly, faithful, and self-denying love held its own because it was an essential component of the knightly life ideal. It became a subject of courtly debate, in that colorful circle of abundant, aristocratic life around the French king and his uncles of Berry and Burgundy, which idea of love should have priority in the life of the true nobleman: that of genuine *Courteoisie,* with its yearning faithfulness and service dedicated in honor of a lady, or that of the *Roman de la rose,* where faithfulness was only a means in the service of the hunt for a woman. The noble knight Boucicaut and his comrades had made themselves the advocates of knightly faithfulness during a journey to the East in 1388 and had passed the time in the composition of the *Livre des cent ballades.* The decision between flirtation and faithfulness they left to the *beaux-esprits* of the courts.

The words with which Christine de Pisan entered the fray a few years later sprang from a deeper seriousness. This courageous defender of female honor and female rights turned to the God of Love in a poetic letter that contained the complaint of womankind against all the betrayal and dishonor by the world of men.[14] She rejected with outrage the lessons of the *Roman de la rose.* A few agreed with her, but the work of Jean de Meun continued to have its share of passionate admirers and defenders. In the ensuing literary controversy a number of attackers and defenders had their say. The champions who upheld the *Rose* were of no mean stature. Many wise, scientific, highly learned men—we are assured by the provost of Lille, Jean de Montreuil—held the *Roman de la rose* so highly as to pay it almost divine reverence (*paene ut colerent*) and would rather have rent their shirt than that book!

It is not easy for us to understand the intellectual and emotional conditions that gave rise to this defense. It was not frivolous court pages but earnest high-ranking officials, some even clerics such as the above-mentioned provost of Lille, Jean de Montreuil, secretary to the Dauphin (later duke of Burgundy), who corresponded about this issue with his friends Gontier and Pierre Col in poetic letters written in Latin and who urged others to take up the burden of defending Jean de Meun. What is most peculiar is that this circle that appointed itself defenders of that colorful, abundant medieval work is the same in which the first growth of French humanism was cultivated. Jean de Montreuil is the author of a large number of Ciceronian letters full of humanist attitudes, humanist rhetoric, and humanist vanity. He and his friends Gontier and Pierre Col carry on a correspondence with that earnest, reform-minded theologian Nicolas de Clémanges.

Jean de Montreuil was certainly serious about his literary point of view. The more I study the mysteries of importance and the importance of the mysteries of this deep and famous work of the master Jean de Meun, he wrote to an unknown legal scholar who had attacked the *Rose,* the more I am astonished by your disapproval. —Until his last breath he will defend the book, and there are many who will do the same with their pens, voices, and hands.[15]

In order to prove that this controversy was more than only a part of the great social game of courtly life, I avail myself, finally, of a man who said that when he spoke he did so for the sake of the highest morality and the purest doctrine: the famous theologian and Chancellor of the University of Paris, Jean de Gerson. From his library, on the evening of May 18, 1402, he wrote a tract against the *Roman de la rose.* The tract is an answer to the attack on an earlier treatise by Gerson launched by Pierre Col,[16] and even that had not been the first writing of Gerson on the subject of the *Rose.* The book seemed to him to be a dangerous plague, the source of all immorality; he intended to attack it at every opportunity. Repeatedly he mounted a campaign against the corrupting influence "du vicieux romant de la rose."[17]* If he had a copy of the *Rose*—he said—which was the only one in the world and worth a thousand pounds, he would rather burn it than sell it and turn it over to the public.

Gerson took the form of his argument from his opponent: an allegorical vision. When he awakes one morning, he feels his heart flee from him, "moyennant les plumes et les eles de diverses pensees, d'un lieu en autre jusques à la court saincte de crestienté."† There he meets Justice, Conscience, and Knowledge and hears how

---

* "the slanderous *Roman de la rose.*"

† "on the feathers and wings of my various thoughts, from one place to another, to the holy court of Christianity."

Chasteté accuses Fol amoureux (namely, Jean de Meun) of having banished her and all her disciples from the earth. Her "bonnes gardes" have been represented as the evil figures of the *Rose:* "Honte, Paour, et Dangier le bon portier, qui ne oseroit ne daigneroit ottroyer neïs (pas même) un vilain baisier ou dissolu regard ou ris attraiant ou parole legiere."* Chastity continues to direct a number of charges against Fol amoureux: that he spreads, with the help of the damnable Old Woman,[18] the doctrine "comment toutes jeunes filles doivent vendre leurs corps tost et chierement sans paour et sans vergoigne, et qu'elles ne tiengnent compte de decevoir ou parjurer."† He mocks marriage and the monastic life; he turns all imaginations to carnal desire, and, worst of all, has Venus, Nature, and even lady Raison mingle the notions of Paradise and the Christian mysteries with those of sensual enjoyment.

This is indeed where danger was lurking. The great work with its linking of sensuality, derisive cynicism, and elegant symbolism awakened in the mind a sensuous mysticism that was bound to appear to the serious theologian as an abyss of sinfulness. How daring Gerson's adversary had been in his claims![19] Only the Fol amoureux himself can judge the value of unrestrained passion. Those who do not know it see it only in a mirror and as a dark mystery. That is to say that he borrowed for earthly love the holy word from the letter to the Corinthians so that he could speak of earthly love as the mystic speaks of his ecstasy! He dared to claim that Solomon's high song had been composed to praise Pharaoh's daughter. Those who had denounced the book of the *Rose* had bent their knee before Baal since Nature did not intend that one man would be enough for a woman, and the genius of nature is God. Verily, he even dares to misuse Luke 2:23[20] to prove with the help of the gospel itself that formerly the female sexual organ, the Rose of the novel, had been sacred. And, fully confident in all these blasphemies, he calls on the defenders of this work, on a number of witnesses, and threatens that Gerson himself will fall victim to an irrational love as had happened to other theologians before him.

---

* "Shame, Fear, and Danger [Virtue on Guard], the good porter who would not dare, who would not deign to sanction even an impure kiss or dissolute look, or attractive smile or light speech."

† "how all young girls should sell their bodies early and dearly, without fear and without shame, and that they should make light of deceit and perjury."

The power of the *Roman de la rose* was not broken by Gerson's attack. In 1444 a canon of Liseux, Estienne Legris, offered Jean Lebégue, secretary of the chamber of accounts in Paris, a *Répertoire du la roman de la Rose* that he had written.[21] As late as the end of the fifteenth century Jean Molinet could claim that quotations from the *Rose* were as familiar as common proverbs.[22] He felt called to offer a moralizing commentary on the entire work in which the well at the beginning of the poem becomes the symbol of baptism, the nightingale calling to love becomes the voice of the preacher and theologian, and the Rose, Jesus himself. Clement Marot made a modernized version of the *Rose,* and Ronsard himself still uses allegorical figures such as Belacueil, Fausdanger, etc.[23]

While dignified scholars fought their literary battles, the aristocrats took the controversy as a welcome occasion for staging entertaining festivities and pompous amusements. Boucicaut, who was praised by Christine de Pisan for his defense of the old idea of knightly faithfulness, may have found in her work the inspiration for the founding of his Ordre de l'écu verd à la dame blanche for the defense of unfortunate women. But he could not compete with the Duke of Burgundy, and his order immediately found itself overshadowed by the grandiose inception of the Cour d'amours, which was founded on Feburary 14, 1401, in the Hotel d'Artois in Paris. The Cour d'amours was a splendidly furnished literary salon. Philip the Bold, duke of Burgundy, that crafty old statesman, whom one would not expect to have been interested in such matters, had requested that the king found the Cour d'amours in order to distract people from the epidemic of plague then visited upon Paris, "pour passer partie du tempz plus gracieusement et affin de trouver esveil de nouvelle joye."[24]* The Cour d'amours was based upon the virtues of humility and faithfulness, "à l'onneur, loenge et recommandacion et service de toutes dames et damoiselles." The numerous members were graced with the most glorious titles: both the founders and Charles VI were *Grands conservateurs;* among the *conservateurs* were John the Fearless, his brother Anton of Brabant, and his younger son Philip. There was a Prince d'amour, Pierre de Hauteville from Hennegouw; then there were Ministres, Auditeurs, Chevaliers d'honneur, Conseillers, Chevaliers trésoriers,

---

* "to spend a part of the time more pleasantly and to find new joys arising—to honor, praise, recommend and serve all women and maidens."

Grands Veneurs, Ecuyers d'amour, Maîtres des requêtes, Secré-
taires; in short, the entire apparatus of the court and the government was imitated therein. Princes and prelates could be found in
it, along with burghers and the lower clergy. The functions and
ceremonies were minutely regulated. It was like a Toastmasters'
club. The members were given the task of responding with refrains
in all the existing verse forms: "ballades couronnés ou chapelées,"
chansons, sirventois, complaintes, rondeaux, lais, virelais, etc. Debates were to be carried out, "en forme d'amoureux procès, pour
différentes opinions soustenir."* Ladies would award the prizes,
and it was forbidden to compose verses that dishonored the female
gender.

How truly Burgundian this pompous endeavor, solemn forms
for light amusement. It is striking, and yet understandable, that the
court preserves the strict ideal of noble fidelity. But if we were to
suppose that the nearly seven hundred members of which we know
during the fifteen years we hear of the existence of the society
were all like Boucicaut, honest followers of Christine de Pisan and
therefore enemies of the *Roman de la rose,* we would be in conflict
with the facts. Whatever is known of the behavior of Anton of
Brabant and other high officials of the order renders them unsuitable to be defenders of female honor. One of the members, a certain
Regnault d'Azincourt, is the instigator of a failed attempt to kidnap,
in the grand style, a young merchant widow, using twenty horses
and bringing a priest with him.[25] Another member, the count of
Tonnerre, is guilty of a similar offense. And, just to prove conclu-
sively that the order was nothing but a beautiful social game, the
adversaries of Christine de Pisan, in the literary battle over the
Roman de la rose, themselves were members: Jean de Montreuil and
Gontier and Pierre Col.[26]

The forms of love of that time can be learned from literature,
but we have to try to understand how the forms of love operated
in life itself. A complete system of prescribed forms was available
to fill a young life with aristocratic conventions. How many signs
and symbols of love have later centuries gradually surrendered!
In place of Amour alone there was the entire peculiar personal
mythology of the *Roman de la rose.* Doubtlessly, Bel-Accueil,
Doux-Penser, Faux-Semblant, and the others also lived in the

---

* "in the form of amorous lawsuits to defend different positions."

imagination outside of literary works. There were also the whole range of tender meanings of colors in clothing, in flowers, and in decorations. Color symbolism, which has not yet been entirely forgotten, had a very important place in the life of love in the Middle Ages. Those who could not understand it found a guide in *Le blason des couleurs* that was written around 1458 by the Herald Sizilien, turned into verse in the sixteenth century and ridiculed by Rabelais, not so much because he despised the subject matter, but because he had given some thought to writing about it himself.[27]

When Guillaume de Machaut sees his unknown beloved for the first time, he is delighted that she is wearing a hood of a sky-blue material, trimmed with green parrots, to go with her white dress, because green is the color of new love and blue that of love which is true. Later, when the beautiful time of his poetic love is over, he dreams that her likeness which hangs over his bed has its head turned away and is completely dressed in green, "qui nouvelleté signifie."* He composes a ballade of reproach:

> *En lieu de bleu, dame, vous vestez vert.*[28]†

Rings, veils, all the treasures and little gifts of love have their special functions and their mysterious devices and emblems that frequently degrade into artfully contrived rebuses. The Dauphin went into battle in 1414 with a banner that had on it in gold a "K," a swan (*cygne*), and an "L," which stood for the name of a lady-in-waiting called Cassinelle who served his mother Isabeau.[29] Rabelais, a century later, mocks the "glorieux de court de transporteurs de noms,"‡ who in their mottoes represent *espoir* by a sphere, *peine* by *pennes d'oiseaux,* and *melancholie* by a columbine (*ancholie*).[30] Coquillart speaks of a

> *Mignonne de haulte entreprise*
> *Qui porte des devises à tas.*[31]§

Then there were for keenly infatuated minds games such as *Le*

---

* "signifying novelty."
† Instead of in blue, lady, you dress in green.
‡ "fools of court and changers of names,"
§ A little darling of great courage/who carried bunches of mottos

roi qui ne ment, Le chastel d'amours, Ventes d'amour, and *Jeux à vendre.**
The girl would call out the name of a flower or something else.
The boy had to respond with a rhyme that contained a compliment:

> *Je vous vens la passerose,*
> *—Belle, dire ne vous ose*
> *Comment Amours vers vous me tire,*
> *Si l'apercevez tout sanz dire.*[32]†

The *chastel d'amours* was such a question-and-answer game based
on the figures of the *Roman de la rose:*

> *Du chastel d'Amours vous demant:*
> *Dites le premier fondement!*
> *—Amer loyaument.*
> *Or me nommez le mestre mur*
> *Qui joli le font, fort et seur!*
> *—Celer sagement.*
> *Dites moy qui sont li crenel,*
> *Les fenestres et li carrel!*
> *—Regart atraiant.*
> *Amis, nommez moy le portier!*
> *—Dangier mauparlant.*
> *Qui est la clef qui le puet deffermer?*
> *—Prier courtoisement.*[33]‡

A great part of courtly conversation had been taken up since the
time of the troubadours by questions of the casuistry of love. It
may be regarded as raising nosiness and slander to a literary form.
Mealtime at the court of Louis d'Orléans was enlivened by "beaulx
livres, dits, ballads" and "demandes gracieuses."[34] These last were

---

* "The King Who Does Not Lie," "The Castle of Love," "Sales of Love,"
and "Games for Sale"

† I sell you the hollyhock./—Belle, I dare not tell/How love draws me towards
you/But you know it without a word.

‡ Of the Castle of Love I ask you:/Tell me the first foundation!/—To love
loyally./Now mention the principal wall/Which makes it fine, strong and sure!/
—To conceal wisely./Tell me what are the loopholes,/The windows and the
stones!/—Alluring looks./Friend, mention the porter!/Ill-speaking danger [Virtue
on Guard]./What is the key that can unlock it?/—Courteous request.

preferably put before poets for a decision. A company of ladies and gentlemen came to Machaut with a number of "partures d'amour et de ses aventures."[35]* He had defended, in his *Jugement d'amour,* the thesis that a lady who lost her lover to death should be less pitied than the lover whose beloved is unfaithful. Every love affair was judged in this way, according to strict norms. —"Beau sire, what would you prefer, that evil things were said about your beloved and you found her to be faithful, or that people praised her and you found her to be unfaithful?"— Whereupon the highly formal concept of honor and the strict duty of the lover to guard the public honor of the beloved, required the answer: "Dame, j'aroie plus chier que j'en oïsse bien dire et y trouvasse mal."† If a lady is neglected by her first lover, does she act unfaithfully if she takes a second, who is more forthcoming? May a knight, who has abandoned all hope of ever seeing his lady, who is kept under lock and key by a jealous husband, finally seek a new love? If a knight turning from his beloved to a lady of higher birth, and spurned by the latter, returns to the former, may her honor permit her to forgive him?[36] It is only a small step from this kind of casuistry to dealing with questions of love entirely in a legal format as is done by Martial d'Auvergne in the *Arrestz d'amour.*

All of these conventions of love are known only through the way they are reflected in literature, but they were at home in real life. The code of courtly terms, rules, and forms did not seek only to turn conventions into poems, but also to apply them in aristocratic life or, at least, in conversation. It is, however, difficult to sense the life of that time behind the veil of poetry, because even where real love is described as exactly as possible, the description is made under the influence of the technical apparatus of the readymade illusion of the conventions of love, and presented within the format of the literary stylization. Such is the case in Guillaume de Machaut's fourteenth-century story, overly long and tedious, of the poetic love of the aged poet and a certain Bettina,[37] called *Le livre de voir-dit* ("The Book of the True Event").[38] He must have been nearly sixty years old when Péronelle d'Armentières,[39] about eighteen and of a noble family of Champagne, sent him her first

---

* "graceful games of love and his adventures"

† "Lady, I would prefer to hear her well spoken of and that I should find her bad."

rondel. He was very famous and knew nothing of her. Nevertheless, she offered him her heart and requested that he begin a poetic
correspondence about love with her. The poor poet, sickly, blind
in one eye and troubled by gout, is immediately inflamed. He answers her rondel, and an exchange of letters and poems begins.
Péronelle is proud of this literary connection; at first she makes no
effort to keep it a secret. She insists that the poems tell the whole
truth about their love and that her letters and poems be included
in his account. He fulfills these requests with pleasure: "je feray à
vostre gloire et loenge, chose dont il sera bon mémoire."[40] "Et
mon très-dous cuer," he writes to her, "vous estes courrecié de ce
nous avons si tart commencié? [How could she have started earlier?]
Par Dieu aussi suis-je (with more justification); mais ves-cy le remède; menons si bonne vie que nous porrons, en lieu et en temps,
que nous recompensons le temps que nous avons perdu; et qu'on
parle de nos amours jusques à cent ans cy après, en tout bien et en
tout honneur; car s'il y avoit mal, vous le celeriés à Dieu, se vous
poviés."[41]*

But what was within the bounds of an honorable love in those
days we learn from the narrative passages inserted by Machaut to
string the letters and poems together. The poet receives her painted
portrait, which he has requested, and he venerates it like his god
on earth. He looks forward to their first encounter with great trepi-
dation because of his physical handicaps. His joy knows no bounds
when his young beloved is not horrified by his appearance. She
lies down under a cherry tree to sleep, or pretend to sleep, in his
lap. She grants him greater favors. A pilgrimage to St. Denis and
the Foire du Lendit offers the opportunity to spend a few days
together. By noon of one day, the party is dead tired because of
the throngs and the heat; it is the middle of June. They find shelter
in the overcrowded town with a man who offers them a room
with two beds. In the darkened room, Péronelle's sister-in-law lies
down for a nap. Péronelle and her chambermaid lie down on the

---

* "I shall make, to your glory and praise, something that will be well remembered." "And, my very sweet heart, are you sorry because we have begun so
late? . . . By God, so am I; . . . but here is the remedy: let us enjoy life as much
as circumstances permit, so that we may make up for the time we have lost; and
that people may speak of our love a hundred years hence, and all well and honor-
ably; for if there were evil, you would conceal it from God, if you could."

other bed. She makes the shy poet lie down between them; he lies there still as death for fear of disturbing them. When she awakes, she orders him to embrace her. As the end of their short journey approaches and she becomes aware of his sadness, she permits him to come to her and make his farewells. Though he continues to speak of "onneur" and "onnesté" on this occasion too, his rather blunt account does not make it clear what else she could have denied him. She gives him the small golden key of her honor, her treasure, to guard carefully, but what was left to guard should perhaps be understood as her reputation before her fellowmen.[42]

The poet was not destined to have any more such luck and, lacking any turns of fate, filled the second half of his book with endless tales from mythology. Finally, Péronelle tells him that their relationship must come to an end, probably because of her impending marriage. He, however, decides to remain in love with her and to venerate her. After their deaths, his spirit will ask God to continue to call her beatified soul Toute-belle.

The *Voir-Dit* tells us more about the customs, and also about the emotions, than most of the amorous literature of that time. There is, first, the extraordinary liberties the young girl could take without causing a scandal. Next, there is the naive imperturbability with which everything down to the most intimate acts takes place in the presence of others, be it sister-in-law, lady-in-waiting, or secretary. During the tryst under the cherry tree, the secretary even devises a charming trick: while Péronelle is asleep, he places a green leaf on her mouth and tells Machaut that he should kiss the leaf. When the poet finally dares to do so, the secretary pulls the leaf away so that their lips meet.[43] Equally remarkable is the congruence of amorous and religious duties. The fact that Machaut, as canon of the cathedral of Rheims, was a member of the clergy, should not be taken too seriously. The lower orders of clergy, which sufficed for canonical duties, did not at that time take the vows of celibacy very seriously. Even Petrarch was a canon. That a pilgrimage was chosen for a *rendez-vous* was also not unusual. Amorous adventures while on pilgrimage were very popular. But that pilgrimage carried out by Machaut and Péronelle was done with great seriousness, "très devotement."[44]* At an earlier get-together, they hear mass; he sits behind her:

* "very devoutly."

> . . . *Quant on dist: Agnus dei,*
> *Foy que je doy à Saint Crepais,*
> *Doucement me donna la pais,*
> *entre deux pilers du moustier*
> *Et j'en avoie bien mestier,*
> *Car mes cuers amoureus estoit*
> *Troublés, quant si tost se partoit.*[45]*

The "pais" was a small plate that was passed around to be kissed in place of the "Kiss of Peace" that was given mouth to mouth.[46] In this case, the meaning is that Péronelle offered him her own lips. He awaits her in the garden, reciting his breviary. Upon beginning a novena (a nine-day sequence of certain prayers) he takes a silent vow while entering the church that he will on each of the nine days compose a new poem about love. This does not keep him from speaking of the great devotion with which he prays.[47]

We should not assume that there were frivolous or profane intentions behind all of this. Guillaume de Machaut, all else being said, is an earnest and high-minded poet. We are encountering here the almost incomprehensible way in which, in pre-Tridentine days, the exercise of faith was interwoven with daily life. Soon we will have to say more about this.

The emotion revealed by the letters and the description of this historic love affair is soft, sweetish, and a little sickly. The expression of emotion remains veiled in the narrative flow of words, rationalizing and deliberating, and in the garb of allegorical phantasies and dreams. There is something touching about the deep emotions with which the graying poet describes his own glorious good fortune and the outstanding qualities of Toute-Belle while failing to realize that she is only playing with him and with her own heart.

At almost the same time as Machaut's *Voir-Dit* there appears another work that is in certain ways comparable: *Le livre du chevalier de la Tour Landry pour l'enseignement de ses filles.*[48] It is an aristocratic work just as much as the romance of Machaut and Péronelle d'Armentières, which was played out in the Champagne and in Paris.

---

* . . . When the priest said, Agnus Dei, / Faith I owe to Saint Crepais, / Sweetly she gave me the pax, / Between two pillars of the church. / And I needed it indeed, / For my amorous heart was / Troubled, that we soon had to part.

The Knight de la Tour Landry takes us to Anjou and Poitou. Here, though, there is no aged poet in love, but a somewhat prosaic father who offers reminiscences of his youth, anecdotes and stories "pour mes filles aprandre à roumancier." We would say, to teach them the civilized forms of love. But the instructions are far from being romantic. Rather the examples and admonishments that the careful nobleman holds up to his daughters tend to be warnings against romantic flirtations. Be on guard against silver-tongued people who are always ready with "faux regars longs et pensifs et petits soupirs et de merveilleuses contenances affectées et ont plus de paroles à main que autres gens."[49]* Don't be too accommodating. As a youth he had once been taken by his father to a castle to make the acquaintance of the daughter of the lord of the manor with a view to a prospective engagement. The girl had received him with particular kindness. To find out her true qualities he had spoken with her about all kinds of things. The talk turned to prisoners, and the youth paid the girl a dignified compliment, "'Ma demoiselle, il vaudroit mieulx cheoir à estre vostre prisonnier que à tout plain d'autres, et pense que vostre prison ne seroit pas si dure comme celle des Angloys.' —Se me respondit, qu'elle avoyt vue nagaires cel qu'elle vouldroit bien qu'il feust son prisonnier. Et lors je luy demanday se elle luy feroit male prison, et elle ne dit que nennil dt qu'elle le tandroit ainsi chier comme son propre corps, et je lui dis que celui estoit bien eureux d'avoir si doulce et si noble prison. Que vous dirai-je? Elle avoit assez de langaige et lui sambloit bien, selon ses parolles, qu'elle savoit assez, et si avoit l'ueil bien vif et legier." Upon taking leave she asked him two or three times to come again as if she had already known him for a long time. "Et quant nous fumes partis, mon seigneur de père me dist: Que te samble de celle que tu as veue. Dy m'en ton avis." But her all too ready encouragement had cooled any ardor for a closer acquaintanceship. "Mon seigneur, elle me samble belle et bonne, maiz je ne luy seray jà plus de près que je suis, si vous plaist."† So the engagement did not take place, and the knight later

---

* "false long and pensive looks and little sighs, and wonderful emotional faces, and who have more words at hand than other people."

† "'Mademoiselle, it would be better to fall into your hands as a prisoner than into many another's, and I think your prison would not be so hard as that of the English.' —She replied that she had recently seen one whom she could wish to

naturally found out things that gave him no cause for regret.[50] Similar little bits taken directly from life that would inform us how customs adapted themselves to the ideal are unfortunately exceedingly rare for the centuries with which we are concerned. If only the Knight de la Tour Landry had told us still more about his life! Most of his reminiscences are of a general nature. He desires for his daughters most of all a good marriage. And marriage had little to do with love. He presents a detailed "debat" between himself and his wife about what is permissible in matters of love, "le fait d'amer par amours."* He believes that in certain circumstances a girl may well find honorable love, for example, "en esperance de mariage."† His wife is opposed. It is better for a girl not to fall in love at all, not even with her husband, as it keeps her from true piety. "Car j'ay ouy dire à plusieurs, qui avoient esté amoureuses en leur juenesce, que quant elles estoient à l'eglise, que la pensée et la merencollie[51] leur faisoit plus souvent penser a ces estrois pensiers et dliz de leurs amours que ou (au) service de Dieu,[52] et est l'art d'amours de telle nature que quant l'en (on) est plus au divin office, c'est tant comme le prestre tient nostre seigneur sur l'autel, lors leur venoit plus de menus pensiers."[53]‡ With this deep psychological observation, Machaut and Péronelle would be in agreement. But aside from that, what a difference in perception between the poet and the knight! But how do we reconcile the strictness of the father with the fact that in order to instruct his daughters he repeatedly

---

be her prisoner. And then I asked her, if she would make a bad prison for him, and she said not at all, and that she would hold him as dear as her own person, and I told her that the man would be very fortunate in having such a sweet and noble prison. What can I say? She could talk well enough, and it seemed, to judge from her conversation, that she knew a great deal, and her eyes also had a lively and lightsome expression. . . . And when we had departed my lord my father said to me, 'What do you think of her whom you have seen? Tell me your opinion.' 'Monseigneur, she seems to me all well and good, but I shall never be nearer to her than I am now, if you please.' "

* "to marry for love"

† "in hope of marriage"

‡ "For I have heard many women say who were in love in their youth, that when they were in church, their thoughts and fancies made them dwell more on those nimble imaginations and delights of their love-affairs than on the service of God, and the art of love is of such a nature, that just at the holiest moments of the service, that is to say, when the priest holds our Lord on the altar, the most of these little thoughts will come to them."

uses stories that, given their salacious content, would not be misplaced among those of the *Cent nouvelles nouvelles*?

This loose fit between the beautiful forms of the courtly ideal of love and the reality of engagement and marriage means that the element of play, of conversation, of literary conventions could unfold with little restraint in anything having to do with the refined art of love. There was no room for the ideal of love, for the fiction of faithfulness and sacrifice, in the very material considerations that enter into a marriage, above all an aristocratic marriage. They could only be experienced in the form of beguiling or heart-thrilling play. The tournament provided the game of romantic love its heroic form, the pastoral, the idyllic.

The pastoral in its real significance is something more than a mere literary genre. We are not dealing here with a description of the real life of the shepherd and its simple and natural enjoyments, but rather with its echoed life. The pastoral is an *imitatio*. There is a fiction that in pastoral life the undisturbed naturalness of love finds its essential expression. There is where one can escape, if not in reality, then in dreams. Time and again the pastoral serves as the means to liberate the spirit from the clutch of a highly pressured, dogmatic, and formalized view of love. There is a yearning for deliverance from the oppressive requirements of knightly faithfulness and veneration and from the colorful apparatus of allegory as well as from the crudity, the greed, the social sins, of the life of love in reality. An easy, satisfied, and simple love amidst the innocent enjoyments of nature seems most desirable. That is what appeared to be the lot of Robin and Marion and of Gontier and Helayne; they were the lucky ones, worthy of envy. The much maligned peasant, in his turn, became the ideal.

But the late Middle Ages are still so genuinely aristocratic and vulnerable to beautiful illusions that passion for the life of nature could not yet lead to a vigorous realism except that it be linked in practice to an artful ornamentation of courtly customs. When the aristocracy of the fifteenth century played shepherd and shepherdess the genuine veneration of nature and the admiration of simplicity and work are still very weak. When, three centuries later, Marie-Antoinette milks cows and makes butter in the Trianon, the ideal is already filled with the seriousness of the physiocrats. Nature and work have already become the great sleeping deities of the time, yet aristocratic culture still managed to make a game of it all.

When the intellectual Russian youth around 1870 placed themselves
among the people, to live like peasants for the sake of the peasants,
at that point the ideal became bitterly serious. But then too, it
turned out that its realization was a delusion.

There is a poetic form that represents the middle ground between
the pastoral proper and reality. This is the pastorelle, the short
poem that sings of the opportune adventure between the knight
and the country girl. In these, the overtly erotic found a fresh and
elegant form, which raised it above the obscene and yet still managed to retain all the charm of naturalism. They bring to mind
certain scenes from Guy de Maupassant.

The sentiment is truly pastoral only at the moment when the
lover begins to feel himself to be a shepherd. In this, any contact
with reality vanishes. All the elements of the courtly system of
love are merely transported into a rural setting; a sunny dreamland
engulfs yearning in a mist of flute tunes and bird twitters. It is a
gay sound; even the sorrows of love, yearning, and lamentation,
even the agony of those who are abandoned dissolve in the lovely
sound. In the pastoral, the erotic always finds that indispensable
contact with the joys of nature. Thus, the pastoral became the field
wherein the literary feeling for nature developed. In the beginning
it was not yet concerned with the description of the beauty of
nature, but rather with the immediate enjoyment of sun and summer, shade and fresh water, flowers and birds. The observation of
nature and its description is only a secondary consideration, the
main concern is the dream of love. As a by-product, nature poetry
offers quite a bit of charming realism. The description of life on
the land in a poem such as "Le dit de la pastoure" by Christine de
Pisan creates a new genre.

Once it has taken its place as a courtly ideal, the simple life
becomes a mask. Everything can be put in a country costume. The
imaginative spheres of the pastoral and the knightly romance
merge. Tournaments were held in pastoral dress. King René calls
his the *Pas d'armes de la bergère.*

His contemporaries seem to have seen in this comedy something
really genuine; Chastellain gives René's pastoral vision a place
among the wonders of the world:

> *J'ay un roi de Cécille*
> *Vu devenir berger*

Et sa femme gentille
De se mesme mestier,
Portant la pannetière,
La houlette et chappeau,
Logeans sur la bruyère
Auprès le leur trouppeau.[54]*

In another instance, the pastoral served to dress a slanderous political satire. There is no stranger work of art than the long shepherd poem "Le pastoralet,"[55] in which a partisan of the Burgundians tells in charming guise of the murder of Louis de Orléans so that the misdeed of John the Fearless is excused and all the Burgundian hatred of the Duke of Orléans is vented. Léonet is John's shepherd name, Tristifer that of Orléans; the fantasy of dance and floral decoration is done in a strange manner. Even the battle of Agincourt is done in pastoral guise.[56]

The pastoral element was never missing from court festivities. It was exceptionally suited for the masquerades that as "entremets" provided glamor for festive meals and that were especially suited for political allegories. The picture of the prince as shepherd and the people as his flock had already been presented from another side: from the representation of the original form of the state by the church fathers. The patriarchs had lived as herdsmen; the proper role of authority, for the secular as well as the spiritual, was not to rule, but to guard.

Seigneur, tu es de Dieu bergier;
garde ses bestes loyaument,
Mets les en champ ou en vergier,
Mais ne les perds aucunement,
Pour ta peine auras bon paiement
En bien le gardant, et se non,
A male heure reçus ce nom.[57]†

* I have seen a king of Sicily/Turn shepherd/And his gentle wife/Take to the same trade/Carrying the shepherd's pouch,/The crook and hat,/Dwelling on the heath/Near their flock.

† Seigneur, you are God's shepherd;/Guard his animals loyally,/Lead them to the field or orchard,/But do not lose them by any means,/For your trouble you will be well paid/If you guard them well, and if you do not,/You received this name in an evil hour.

In these verses from Jean Meschinot's "Lunettes des princes" there is no mention of a truly pastoral image. However, as soon as there is an attempt to represent something like this visually, the two notions, the prince as caretaker and the simple shepherd, automatically merge. One *entremet* at a wedding fest in Bruges in 1468 glorified earlier princesses as the "nobles bergieres qui par cy devant ont esté pastoures et gardes des brebis de pardeça."[58]* A play in Valenciennes in 1493 to celebrate the return of Marguerite of Austria from France showed how the country had recovered from its devastations "le tout en bergerie."[59]† We all know the political pastoral in *De Leeuwendalers*.[60] The note of prince as shepherd is also audible in the *Wilhelmus*:[61]

> *Oirlof myn arme schapen*
> *Die syt in groter noot,*
> *Uw herder sal niet slapen,*
> *Al syt gy nu verstroyt.*‡

Even in real war, people played with the notion of the pastoral. Charles the Bold's bombardment of Granson was called "le berger et la bergère."§ When the French mocked the Flemings, calling them shepherds unfit for war, Phillip of Ravenstein showed up on the field with twenty-four nobles dressed as shepherds with crooks and bread baskets.[62]

Even as true knightly devotion set against the ideas of the *Roman de la rose* provided the material for an elegant literary war, so too the pastoral ideal became the subject of such a struggle. Here too, the falsity was too obvious and had to be masked. How little did the hyperbolically contrived, wastefully colored life of the late Middle Ages resemble the ideal of simplicity, freedom, and carefree true love in the midst of nature! The theme of Philippe de Vitri's "Franc Gontier," the type of the simplicity of the Golden Age, was

---

* "noble shepherdesses who formerly tended and guarded the sheep of the country over there [the Netherlands]."

† "all in the style of a pastoral."

‡ Rest to my poor sheep, / Who here in great need, / Your shepherd shall not sleep, / And now that you are scattered, / To God thou shall betake, / Accept his wholesome word, / Live as pious Christians, / Soon it will be done.

§ "the shepherd and the shepherdess"

given endless variations. Everyone claimed to hunger for Franc Gontier's meal in the shade with Lady Helayne, for his menu of cheese, butter, cream, apples, onions, and brown bread, for his lusty wood chopping work, his sense of freedom and lack of care:

> Mon pain est bon; ne faut que nulz me veste;
> L'eaue est saine qu'á boire sui enclin,
> je ne doubte ne tirant ne venin.[63]*

Sometimes the poets temporarily misstep. The same Eustache Deschamps who repeatedly sang the life of Robin and Marion and the praise of natural simplicity and a life filled with work regrets that the court dances to the music of the cornemuse, "cet instrument des hommes bestiaulx."[64]† But it took the much deeper sensitivity and sharp skepticism of François Villon to see through all the falsity of the beautiful dream. There is a merciless mockery in the ballade "Les contrediz Franc Gontier." Cynically, Villon compares the lightheartedness of that ideal countryman with his meal of onions "qui causent fort alaine"‡ and his love under the roses with the comfortable life of the fat priest who has comfort and joy in a well-furnished room with a fire in the fireplace, good wine, and a soft bed. The brown bread and the water of Franc Gontier? "Tous les oyseaulx d'ici en Babiloine"§ would not be able to make Villon suffer such fare even one morning.[65]

Even as did the beautiful dream of the knightly ideal, the other forms in which sex tried to become culture had to be recognized as false and full of lies. Neither the infatuated ideal of noble, chaste, knightly faithfulness, nor the refined lust of the *Roman de la rose,* nor the sweet, comfortable fantasy of the pastoral could hold their own against the storm of life itself. The storm blew from all sides. From the spiritual side came the curse on everything, since sex is the sin that ruins the world. At the bottom of the chalice of the *Roman de la rose,* the moralist sees all the bitter sediment. "Whence," cries Gerson, "whence the bastards, whence the murder

---

* My bread is good; no one needs to clothe me;/The water is healthy, which I desire to drink,/I do not fear either tyrant or poison.

† "that instrument of bestial people."

‡ "which causes strong breath"

§ "All the birds from here to Babylon,"

of children, the abortions, whence the hatred and poisoning in marriage?"[66]

From the side of woman, another charge rings out. All these conventional forms of love are the work of men. Even when it is enjoyed in idealized forms, erotic culture is through and through the product of male self-seeking. What else is the constantly re-peated mocking of marriage and the weaknesses of women, their unfaithfulness and conceit, but a cover for male self-centeredness? To all this defamation I only respond, says Christine de Pisan, that it is not women who wrote these books.[67]

Actually, in the entire erotic as well as the pious literature of the Middle Ages there is hardly a trace of genuine pity for women, for their weakness and the pain and danger that love causes them. Pity had formalized itself into the fiction of the liberation of the virgin that was really only sensual stimulation and self-satisfaction. After the author of the *Quinze joyes de mariage* had listed all the weak-nesses of women in a mutely toned and finely colored satire, he offers to describe the neglect of women,[68] but he does not do it. For the expression of a tender womanly voice, one has to turn to the poetry of Christine herself:

> *Dolce chose est que mariage,*
> *Je le puis bien par moy prouver . . .*[69]*

But how weak the voice of a single woman sounds against the choir of ridicule in which the flat voices of licentiousness and pious morality come together. There is only a small distance between the homiletic contempt of women and the coarse denial of ideal love by prosaic sensuality.

The beautiful play of love as a form of life continued to be played in the knightly style, and in the pastoral, and in the artificial dress of the rose allegory and even though, from all sides, there could be heard the sound of the denial of all these conventions, they retained their value for life and culture until long after the Middle Ages because there are only a few forms in which the ideal of love can dress itself in any age.

---

* Marriage is a sweet thing, / I know that from my own experience . . .

Chapter Five

THE VISION OF DEATH

NO OTHER AGE HAS SO FORCEFULLY AND CONTINU-
ously impressed the idea of death on the whole population as did
the fifteenth century, in which the call of the memento mori* echoes throughout the whole of life. Denis the Carthusian, in the book
he wrote for the guidance of the nobleman, makes the exhortation
that "when he goes to bed, he should imagine not that he is putting
himself to bed, but that others are laying him in his grave."[1] In
earlier times, too, religion had been very serious about reinforcing
the constant preoccupation with death, but the pious tracts of the
early medieval period had only reached those who had already
taken the path that put the world behind them. It was only after
the rise of the popular preachers of the mendicant orders that the
admonitions rose to a threatening chorus that echoed through the
world with the force of a fugue. Towards the end of the medieval
period, the voice of the preachers was joined by a new kind of
pictorial representation that, mostly in the form of woodcuts,
reached all levels of society. These two forceful means of expression, the sermon and the picture, could only express the concept
of death in very simple, direct, and lively images, abrupt and sharp.
The contents of earlier monastic meditations about death were now
condensed into a superficial, primitive, popular, and lapidary image
and in this form held up to the multitudes in sermons and representations. This image of death was able to contain only one of the
large number of conceptions related to death, and that was perishability. It seems as if the late medieval mind could see no other
aspect of death than that of decay.

There were three themes that furnished the melody for the never
ending lament about the end of all earthly glory. First there was the

* "reminder of death"

156

motif that asked, where have all those gone who once filled the earth
with their glory? Then there was the motif of the horrifying sight of
the decomposition of all that had once constituted earthly beauty.
The last was the motif of the *danse macabre* or *Totentanz*, the dance of
death, which whirls away people of any age or profession.

Compared to the two final motifs in their oppressive dread-
fulness, the first, where has all the former splendor gone?, is only
a soft elegiac sigh. It is of ancient vintage and is known throughout
the world of Christianity and Islam. It originated in Greek paganism, the church fathers knew it, and Byron perpetuates it.[2] In
the later Middle Ages it enjoyed a period of unusual popularity. It
can be found in the heavily rhymed hexameters of the Cluniac
monk Bernard of Morlay around 1140:

> *Est ubi gloria nunc Babylonia? nunc ubi dirus*
> *Nabugodonosor, et Darii vigor, illeque Cyrus?*
> *Qualiter orbita viribus inscita (?) praeterierunt,*
> *Fama relinquiter, illaque figitur, hi putruerunt.*
> *Nunc ubi curia, pompaque Julia? Caesar abisti!*
> *Te truculentior, orbe potentior ipse fuisti.*
> ....
> *Nunc ubi Marius atque fabricius inscius auri?*
> *Mors ubi nobilis et memorabilis actio Pauli?*
> *Diva philippica vox ubi coelica nunc Ciceronis?*
> *Pax ubi civibus atque rebellibus ira Catonis?*
> *Nunc ubi Regulus? aut ubi Romulus, aut ubi Remus?*
> *stat rosa pristina nomine, nomina nuda tenemus.*[3]*

It sounds again, this time less pedantically, in verses that retain the
sound of the rhymed hexameters in spite of their shorter structure,

---

* Where is the glory of Babylon? Where is now the terrible/Nebuchadnezzar,
and strong Darius, famous Cyrus?/Like a wheel, left to itself, so they went away;/
Their glory remains in plenty, it is secure—they, however, moulder/Where is
now the Curia Julia, Where the Julian procession? Caesar, you vanished!/And you
were the fiercest in the whole world and the mightiest!/. . ./Where is now Marius
and Fabricius, who were strangers to gold?/Where is the honorable death and
memorable deeds of Paulus?/Where is the heavenly Phillipic voice [Demosthenes],
where that of heavenly Cicero?/Where is Cato's peacefulness for the citizens and
his scorn for the rebels?/Where is now Regulus? Or where Romulus, or where
Remus?/The rose [Rome] of yore is but a name, mere names are left to us.

in the Franciscan verses of the thirteenth century. Jacopone of Todi, the jester of the Lord, is most likely the poet of the verses that appeared under the title "Cur mundis militat sub vana gloria." They include the lines:

> *Dic ubi Salomon, olim tant nobilis*
> *Vel Sampson ubi est, dux invincibilis*
> *Et pulcher Absalon, vultu mirabilis,*
> *Aut dulcis Jonathas, multum amabilis?*
> *Quo Cesar abiit, celsus imperio?*
> *Quo Dives splendidus totus in prandio?*
> *Dic ubi Tullius, clarus eloquio*
> *Vel Aristoteles, summus ingenio?*[4]*

Deschamps sets the same theme in verse several times, Gerson uses it in a sermon; Denis the Carthusian treats it in his tract about the "Four Last Things." Chastellain turns it into a long poem, *Le pas de la mort,* not to mention his other efforts in the same vein.[5] Villon manages to add a new touch, that of gentle sorrow, in the "Ballade des dames du temps jadis" with the refrain:

> *Mais où sont les neiges d'antan?*[6]†

And soon he garnishes it with irony in the ballade about noblemen where, while thinking about the kings, poets, and princes of his time, it occurs to him:

> *Hélas! et le bon roy d'Espaigne*
> *Duquel je ne sçray pas le nom?*[7]‡

The brave courtier Olivier de la Marche would not have dared to make such a joke in his "Parement et triumphe des dames," in

---

* Say, where is Solomon, once so splendid, / Or Sampson, where is he, invincible chief, / And fair Absalom of the wonderful face, / Or sweet Jonathan, the most amiable? / Where has Caesar gone, greatest in power? / Whither the famous rich [Crassus], whose whole soul centered around mealtime? / Say, where is Tullius [Cicero], famous for his speech, / Where is Aristotle, the greatest in genius?

† "But where are the snows of yesterday?"

‡ Alas! And the good king of Spain / Whose name I do not know?

which he thinks about all the dead princesses of his own time in the context of this same theme.

What is left of all human glory and splendor? Memories, a name. But the sadness of this thought was not satisfying enough given the need for a sharp shudder in the face of death. Consequently, the age looks in the mirror of visible terror, and finds there, in the image of the rotting corpse, perishability condensed into a shorter frame of time.

The mind of world-denying medieval man had always liked to dwell amidst dust and worms; in the ecclesiastical tracts about the decay of the world, all the horrifying ideas about decomposition had already been evoked. But the elaboration of details only comes later; it is only towards the end of the fourteenth century that the visual arts take up the motif.[8] A certain degree of skill in realistic expression is required for dealing properly with this motif in sculpture or painting. This power was attained around 1400. At the same time, the motif spread from ecclesiastical to popular literature. Until late in the sixteenth century, gravestones depict the disgustingly varied notion of the naked corpse, with cramped hands and feet, gaping mouth, with worms writhing in the intestines. The mind is over and again invited to dwell on this frightful image. Is it not strange that they dare not take the further step of seeing that decay itself will perish and turn into earth and flowers?

Is it truly pious thinking that entangles itself in this loathing of the purely earthly side of death? Or is it the reaction of an all too intense sensuality that can only awaken itself from its intoxication with life in this manner? Or is it that the dread of life that so strongly permeates the age the mood of disappointment and discouragement of one who has fought and won and now would prefer a complete surrender to that which is transcendent, but somehow is still too close to earthly passion to be able to make that surrender? All these elements of feeling are united in these expressions of the concept of death.

The fear of life: the denial of beauty and joy because suffering and pain are bound up with them. There is an astonishing similarity between the ancient Indian, that is the Buddhist, and the medieval Christian expressions of this sentiment. There, too, is found the incessant preoccupation with disgusting age, sickness, and death, there too, the exaggerated depiction of putrefaction. The naive Indian ascetics even had their own poetic genre, bîbhatsa-rasa, or the sentiment of abhorrence, which was divided into three subdivisions depending on whether the sentiment was caused by disgust, terror, or lust.[9] The Christian monk thought he had put it so well when he pointed to the superficiality of physical beauty. "The beauty of the body is that of skin alone. If people could see what is underneath the skin, as it is said in Boethia that the lynx can do, they would find the sight of woman abhorrent. Her charm consists of slime and blood, of wetness and gall. If anyone considers what is hidden in the nostrils and in the throat and in the belly, he will always think of filth. And if we cannot bring ourselves to touch slime and filth with our fingertips, how can we bring ourselves to embrace the dirt bag itself?[10]

The discouraged refrain of contempt for the world was codified for the later Middle Ages in many tracts, but above all in that of Pope Innocent III, *De contemptu mundi*. It is strange that this powerful statesman, favored by good fortune, holder of the throne of St. Peter, concerned about so many earthly things and interests and actively involved in them, could in his earlier years have been the author of such a scornful view of life. "Concipit mulier cum immunditia et fetore, parit cum tristitia et dolore, nutrit cum angustia et labore, custodit cum instantia et timore."[11] ("Woman conceives in impurity and stench. She gives birth in sorrow and pain. She suckles with strain and effort. She wakes full of dread and fear.") O, those laughing joys of motherhood!—"quis unquam vel unicam diem totam duxit in sua delectatione jucundam . . . quem denique visus vel auditus vel aliquis ictus non offenderit?" ("Who has ever spent a single day totally immersed in pleasure . . . without being hurt by the sight of something, the sound of something or the impact of something?")[12] Is this Christian wisdom or the pouting of a spoiled child?

There is, undoubtedly, in all of this a spirit of tremendous materialism that could not bear the thought of the passing of beauty without despairing of beauty itself. And one should note how (especially in literature, less in the fine arts) female beauty in particular was deplored. Here there is hardly any difference between the religious admonition to think on death and the fleeting nature of earthly things and the regret of an aging courtesan over the decay of beauty that she can no longer offer.

We have first an example in which the edifying admonition is still in the foreground. In the Celestine monastery in Avignon there existed, before the Revolution, a wall painting that tradition ascribed to the artistic founder of the cloister, King René himself. It showed a female corpse, standing upright, wearing an elegant headdress, wrapped in her shroud; worms were devouring her body. The first lines of the inscription read:

> *Une fois sur toute femme belle*
> *Mais par la mort suis devenue telle.*
> *Ma chair estoit très belle, fraische et tendre*
> *Or est-elle toute tournée en cendre.*
> *Mon corps estoit très plaisant et très gent,*
> *Je me souloye souvent vestrir de soye,*
> *Or en droict fault que toute nue je soye.*
> *Forrée estoit de gris et de menu vair,*
> *En grand palais me logeois à mon vueil,*
> *Or suis logiée en ce petit cercueil.*
> *Ma chambre estoit de beaux tapis ornée*
> *Or est d'aragnes ma fosse environée.*[13]*

That these admonitions had their desired effect is proven by the legend that arose later that the royal artist himself, the lover of life and beauty *par excellence,* had looked at his beloved three days after her burial and had then painted her.

The sentiment moves slightly in the direction of sensuality once the warning about perishability is not illustrated by the gruesome corpse of someone else, but when the issue is the bodies of the living, now still beautiful but soon food for the worms. Olivier de la Marche ends his didactic allegorical poem about female clothing, "Le parement et triumphe des dames,"† with death who holds the mirror up to all beauty and conceit:

---

* Once I was beautiful above all women/But by death I became like this,/my flesh was very beautiful, fresh and soft,/Now it has completely turned to ashes./My body was very pleasing and very pretty,/I used frequently to dress in silk,/Now I must justly be quite naked./Clad I was in gray fur and in miniver,/In a great palace I lived as I wished,/Now I am lodged in this little coffin./My room was adorned with fine tapestry,/Now my grave is enveloped by cobwebs.

† "The Ornament and Triumph of the Ladies"

Ces doulx regards, ces yeulz faiz pour plaisance,
Pensez y bien, ilz perdront leur clarté
Nez et sourcilz, la bouche d'eloquence
Se pourrione . . .[14]*

So far this is still an honest memento mori, but it edges imperceptibly into a dispirited, worldly and self-seeking complaint about the disadvantages of old age:

Se vous vivez le droit cours de nature
Dont LX ans est pour ung bien grant nombre,
Vostre beaulté changera en laydure,
Vostre santé en maladie obscure,
Et ne ferez en ce monde que encombre.
Se fille avez, vous luy serez ung umbre,
Celle sera requise et demandée
Et la chascun la mère habandonnée.[15]†

Any pious elevated meaning is very remote when Villon composes his ballades in which "la belle heaulmière," once a famous Parisian courtesan, compares her formerly irresistible charms with the sad decay of her aging body:

Qu'est devenu ce front poly,
Ces cheveulx blons sourcils voultiz,
Grant entroeil le regard joly,
Dont prenoie les plus soubtilz;
Ce beau nez droit, grant ne petiz,
Ces petites joinctes oreilles,
Menton fourchu, cler viz traictiz
Et ces belles levres vermeilles?
. . . .

---

* These sweet looks, these eyes made for pleasure, / Remember, they will lose their luster, / Nose and brows, the eloquent mouth / Will putrefy . . .

† If you live your natural lifetime, / Of which sixty years is a great deal, / your beauty will change into ugliness, / Your health into obscure malady, / And you will be an encumbrance to the earth. / If you have a daughter, you will be a shadow to her, / She will be desired and asked for, / And the mother will be abandoned by all.

Le front ridé, les cheveux gris
Les sourcils cheuz, les yeux estains . . .[16]*

In one of the poetic books of the southern Buddhists there is a song of an old pious nun, Ambapâlî, who has the same past as "la belle heaulmiére." She, too, compares her earlier beauty with disgusting old age, but she is full of gratitude for the demise of useless beauty.[17] But is the distance between this feeling and the preceding as great as it might seem to us?

The vehement disgust over the decomposition of the body explains the great significance that people put on the bodies of some saints, such as that of St. Rosa of Viterbo, which did not decompose. It is one of the most precious glories of Mary that her body was spared earthly decomposition by virtue of its Ascension to heaven.[18] What is speaking in all this is basically a materialistic spirit that cannot shake its preoccupation with the body. The same spirit occasionally reveals itself in the special care with which some bodies were handled. There was a custom of painting the facial features on the corpse of a prominent person immediately after death so that no changes would be noticeable prior to the funeral.[19] The body of a preacher of the apostate sect of the Turlupins who had died in prison prior to the announcement of the verdict upon him, was kept for fourteen days sealed in chalk so that it could be burned along with a living apostate.[20] The practice of taking the bodies of prominent persons, cutting them up, and boiling them until the bones separated from the flesh was widespread. The bones were cleaned and then sent off in a casket for final burial while the flesh and intestines were buried on the spot. In the twelfth and thirteenth centuries, this was quite customary in the case of bishops as well as with a number of kings.[21] In 1299 and again in 1300 the practice was most strictly forbidden by Pope Boniface VIII as a "detestandae feritatis abusus, quem ex quodam more horribili nonnuli fideles improvide prosequuntur."† Nevertheless, in the four-

---

* What has become of this smooth forehead,/Fair hair, curving brows,/Large space between the eyes, pretty looks,/With which I caught the most subtle ones;/ That fine straight nose, neither large nor small,/These tiny ears close to the head,/ The dimpled chin, well-shaped bright face,/And those beautiful vermillion lips?/ . . ./The forehead wrinkled, hair gray,/The brows bare, lackluster eyes . . .

† "abuse of abominable savagery, practised by some of the faithful in a horrible way and inconsiderately."

teenth century there were many papal dispensations that lifted the prohibition and in the fifteenth century the custom was still prized by the English in France. The bodies of Edward of York and Michael de la Pole, count of Suffolk, the most famous Englishmen to die at Agincourt, were handled in this manner.[22] It happened to Henry V himself, and to William Glasdale, who drowned during Joan of Arc's liberation of Orléans, and to a nephew of Sir John Falstaff who fell in the siege of St. Denis in 1435.[23]

In the fourteenth century, the strange word "macabre" appeared, or, as it was originally spelled, "Macabré." "Je fis Macabré la dance,"* says the poet Jean Le Fèvre in 1376. It is a personal name and this might be the much disputed etymology of the word.[24] It is only much later that the adjective is abstracted from "*la danse macabre*" that has acquired for us such a crisp and particular nuance of meaning that with it we can label the entire late medieval vision of death. The motif of death in the form of the "macabre" is primarily found in our times in village cemeteries where one can still sense its echo in verses and figures. By the end of the Middle Ages, this notion had become an important cultural conception. There entered into the realm surrounding the idea of death a new, grippingly fantastic element, a shiver that arose from the gruesomely conscious realm of ghostly fear and cold terror. The all-encompassing religious mechanism immediately turned it into morality by linking it back to the memento mori, but also made use of the entirely gruesome suggestion that the ghostly character of the image brought with it.

Around the *danse macabre* are grouped some related images, which, along with death, are very well suited to frighten and to warn. The depiction of the three dead men and the three living precedes the image of the *danse macabre*.[25] It had already appeared in French literature in the thirteenth century. Three young noblemen suddenly meet three ghastly dead men who point to their own former earthly glory and to the imminent end that awaits the living. The touching figures in the Campo Santo in Pisa are the earliest representation of this theme in formal art; the sculptures on the portal of the Church of the Innocents in Paris where the Duke of Berry had the topic depicted in 1408 are lost. But miniatures and

---

* "I made the Dance Macabre"

woodcuts make this subject a common possession during the fifteenth century and it is also widespread as wall paintings.

The depiction of the three dead men and the three living provides the connection between the repugnant image of decay and the thought, made into an image in the *danse macabre,* that all are equal in death. The development of this subject in the history of art can only be mentioned here in passing. France appears to be the country where the *danse macabre* originates, but how did it come about? Was it actually acted out or was it an image? It is known that the thesis of Emile Mâle that the motifs of the pictorial art of the fifteenth century have their origin in dramatic performances, as a general principle, cannot withstand its critics. But in respect to the *danse macabre,* there might be an exception to the rejection of the thesis, that here the depiction was actually preceded by a performance. In any case, be it earlier or later, the *danse macabre* was actually performed as well as painted and depicted in woodcuts. The duke of Burgundy had it performed in 1449 at his residence in Bruges.[26] If we had any idea of the nature of such a performance, of the colors, the movements, the play of light and shade over the dancers, we would be much better able to understand the strong sense of shock in the minds of the onlookers than we are from the woodcuts of Guyot Marchant and Holbein.

The woodcuts (plate 3) with which the Parisian printer Guyot Marchant illustrated the first edition of the *Danse Macabre* in 1485 were virtually certainly borrowed from the most famous of the *danses macabres,* the 1424 wall painting done in the Hall of Columns in the Cemetery of the Innocents in Paris. The inscriptions beneath the paintings that are preserved in the 1485 edition may perhaps be traced back to the lost poem of Jean Le Fèvre that in turn may have followed a Latin original. Be that as it may, the *danse macabre* in the Cemetery of the Innocents disappeared during the seventeenth century when the hall was torn down. It was the most popular depiction of decay known to the Middle Ages. Day by day, thousands viewed the simple figures at the Cemetery of the Innocents, which served as a strange and macabre meeting place, and read the easily comprehended verses. Each strophe concluded with a well-known proverb. The people found solace in the equality of all in decay and shivered at the prospect of their own end. Nowhere else was ape-like death so much in his own place. Grimly, with the gait of an old, stiff dancing master, he led the pope, the emperor, the nobleman, the day laborer, the monk, the small child, the fool, and all the other professions and estates away. Do the woodcuts of 1485 come anywhere close to the impact of the famous wall paintings? Probably not; the dress of the figures shows that they are not true copies of the painting of 1424. To get a true impression of the *danse macabre* of the Cemetery of the Innocents, one should see those from the church of La Chaise-Dieu,[27] where the ghostly element is further enhanced by the half-finished state of the painting.

The corpse, who reoccurs forty times leading away the living, is actually not Death, but rather a dead man. The verses call the figure *Le Mort* (in the *danse macabre* of women, *La Morte*); it is a dance of the dead, not of Death.[28] Furthermore, there is no skeleton, but a body not yet entirely stripped of its flesh, with its abdomen slit open. Only around 1500 does the figure of the great dancer become the skeleton we know from Holbein. In the meantime, the notion evolves of an unknown deadly *dubbelganger*[29] who personally ends life. "Yo so la Muerte cierta á todas criaturas,"* begins an impressive Spanish *danse macabre* from the end of the fifteenth century.[30] In the older *danse macabre* the untiring dancer is still the living person himself as he will be in the near future, a frightening duplication of his own person, the image that he sees in the mirror. Not, as some would have it, an earlier person of the same rank and status who had died. Here is the point: you, yourself, are in the *danse macabre*, and this is what bestows on it its gruesome powers.

On the fresco that graced the vault of the tomb monument of King René and his Queen Isabella in the Cathedral of Angers, it was actually the king himself who was depicted. One could see a skeleton there (had this earlier been a corpse too?) in a long coat, sitting on a golden throne and kicking away with his feet mitre, crown, orb, and books. The head was resting on a shriveled hand that tried to support a sagging crown.[31]

The original *danse macabre* depicted only men. The intent to tie the admonition of the perishability and conceit of earthly matters to the lesson of social equality naturally moves men, as the holders of social professions and dignities, to the forefront. The *danse macabre* was not only a pious admonition, it was also social satire and

---

* "I am Death, known to all creatures,"

the verses that accompanied it have a faint irony. The same Guyot Marchant published as a continuation of his earlier edition a *danse macabre* of women with verses by Martial d'Auvergne. The unknown engraver of the woodcuts was not up to the standard of the earlier edition; his only contribution was the gruesome figure of a skeleton around whose head a few sparse strands of woman's hair still flutter. In this female version, the sensual theme of beauty that turns into corruption is immediately struck. How could it be otherwise? There were not forty occupations and estates for women. Along with the most noble estates, such as queen, noblewoman, and so forth, there are a few of the spiritual functions or estates such as abbess and nun, and with a few professions such as merchant, baker, etc., the list exhausts itself. Otherwise the list has to view women in the temporary stages of their womanly lives as maiden, beloved, bride, newlywed, and expectant. And so here again, the theme of past or never-achieved joy or beauty sounds yet more shrilly.

One picture was still lacking in the terrifying depiction of the act of dying, and that was of the hour of death itself. The horror of this hour could not be brought to the mind in a more dreadful image than that of the raising of Lazarus. After his resurrection he had known nothing but a sorrowful dread of the death that he had suffered once before. If the righteous must feel such fear, what of the sinner?[32] The vision of the death struggle was the first of the Four Last Things, the "quattour hominum novissima," upon which man was behoven to think: death, final judgment, hell, and heaven. They were, as such, also part of the vision of the beyond. In this instance, in a preliminary way, only the issue of the death of the body itself is raised. Closely related to the theme of the Four Last Things was the *Ars moriendi,* a creation of the fifteenth century that also gained a wide circulation as part of pious thought through printing and the woodcut. It dealt with the five temptations with which the devil snared the dying: doubt of faith, desperation over one's sins, attachment to earthly goods, desperation about one's own sufferings, and finally conceit about one's own virtue. Always an angel appears to fend off Satan's snares with his consolation. The description of the death struggle is an old subject of spiritual literature. One sees the same images reoccur in it over and over again.[33]

In a detailed poem entitled "Le pas de la Mort,"[34] Chastellain has brought all of these motifs together. He begins with a moving narrative that, even given the solemn verbosity characteristic of this author, does not fail to have its effect. His dying beloved calls him to herself and in a broken voice says:

> *Mon amy, regardez ma face.*
> *Voyez que fait dolante mort*
> *Et ne l'oubliez désormais;*
> *C'est celle qu'aimiez si fort;*
> *Et ce corps vostre, vil et ort,*
> *Vous perderez pour un jamais;*
> *Ce sera puant entremais*
> *A la terre et à la vermine;*
> *Dure mort toute beauté fine.**

This induces the poet to compose a Mirror of Death. First, he works out the theme "Where are all the great ones of the earth now?" at far too great a length, his style a little schoolmasterish without any of the easy sadness of Villon. This is followed by something like a first attempt at a *danse macabre,* but without vigor or imagination. At the end he puts in the *Ars moriendi* in verse form. Here is his description of the death struggle:

> *Il n'a membre ne facture*
> *Qui ne sente sa pourreture.*
> *Avant que l'esperit soit hors,*
> *Le coeur qui veult crevier au corps*
> *Haulce et soulière la poitrine*
> *Qui se veult joindre à son eschine.*
> *—La face est tainte et apalie,*
> *Et les yeux treilliés en la teste.*
> *La parolle luy est faillie,*
> *Car la langue au palais se lie.*
> *Le poulx tressault et sy halette.*
> ....

---

* My friend, look at my face, / See what doleful death does, / And henceforth do not forget; / This is she, whom you so loved, / And this body, which is yours, / Will become hateful and filthy to you, forever lost; / It will be a stinking meal / For the earth and for the worms. / Hard death ends all beauty.

Les os desjoindent à tous lez;
Il n'a nerf qu'au rompre ne tende.[35]*

Villon puts all that in half a verse that is much more moving, but one recognizes the common model.[36]

La mort le fait fremir, pallir,
Le nez courber, les vaines tendre,
Le col enfler, la chair mollir,
Joinctes et nerfs croistre et estendre.†

And then again the sensual element that runs through all these terrifying notions:

Corps femenin, qui tant est tendre,
Poly, souef, si precieux,
Te fauldra il ces maulx attendre?
Oy, ou tout vif aller es cieulx.‡

Nowhere else was everything concerning death more completely brought together before the eyes than in the Cemetery of the Innocents in Paris. There one experienced the macabre to the fullest; everything worked together to provide the somber holiness and colorful forms that the late Middle Ages craved so much. The saints to whom the church and churchyard were dedicated, the innocent children who were butchered in place of Christ, evoked with their lamentable martyrdom, the bloody pity in which the age indulged. It is precisely in this century that the veneration of the Holy Children became very popular. But there was more than one *relique* of the boys of Bethlehem there. Louis XI had given to the church

* There is not a limb nor a form/That does not smell of putrefaction./Before the soul is outside,/The heart which wants to burst the body,/Raises and lifts the chest,/Which nearly touches the backbone./—The face is discolored and pale,/And the eyes veiled in the head./Speech fails him,/For the tongue cleaves to the palate./The pulse trembles and he pants./. . ./The bones are disjointed on all sides;/There is not a tendon that does not stretch as to burst.
† Death makes him shudder, pale,/The nose to curve, the veins to swell,/The neck to inflate, the flesh to soften,/Joints and tendons to grow and swell.
‡ O female body, which is so soft,/Smooth, suave, precious,/Do these evils await you?/Yes, or you must go to heaven alive.

that he had dedicated "un Innocent entier"[37] in a great crystal
shrine. People were fond of coming to the churchyard to take their
ease. A bishop of Paris had some earth from the Churchyard of
the Innocents placed in his grave when it happened that he could
not be buried there.[38] The rich and the poor rested there side by
side, but not for long, as the burial ground, which twenty churches
had the right to use, was in so much demand that after a few years
the bodies were exhumed and the tombstones sold. It was said that
there a corpse would decompose down to the bare bones in about
nine days.[39] The skulls and bones were then piled up in the bone
chambers above the Hall of Columns that surrounded the cemetery
on three sides. They lay there in their thousands, open and exposed,
preaching the lesson of the equality of all. Beneath the arcade, the
same lesson could be seen and read in the paintings and verses of
the *danse macabre*. For the construction of the "beaux charniers"*
the noble Boucicaut, among others, had made contributions.[40]
On the portal of the church, the duke of Berry, who wished to
be buried there, had the figures of the three living and the three
dead men sculpted. During the sixteenth century the large statue
of Death was still standing in the cemetery. In the Louvre now,
it is the sole surviving remnant of all that was assembled there
(plate 4).

For the people of the fifteenth century, this place was what the
melancholy palais royal was to the people of 1789. There amid the
continuous burials and exhumations was a promenade and a meeting place. Small shops were found near the bare bones and easy
women under the arcades. There was even an aged female recluse
who lived in the side of the church. Sometimes a mendicant monk
preached in that place that was itself a sermon in the medieval style.
Many times processions of children assembled there; 12,500 says
the Burgher of Paris, all with candles. They marched from the
Innocents to Notre Dame and back. Even festivities were held
there.[41] So much had the dreadful become the familiar.

In the drive to create an unmitigated depiction of death, in which
everything intangible had to be abandoned, only the coarser aspects
of death made it into consciousness. The macabre vision of death
lacked everything elegiac as well as everything tender. And at root,
it is a very earthly, self-preoccupied attitude towards death. It does

* "beautiful bone chambers"

not deal with sadness over the loss of those beloved, but rather with regret about one's own approaching death, which can be seen only as misfortune and terror. There is no thought given to death as consolation, to the end of suffering, eternal rest, the task completed or broken off, no tender memories, no surrender. Nothing of the "divine depth of sorrow." Only once can there be heard a softer sound. In the *danse macabre,* Death addresses the day laborer as follows:

> *Laboureur qui en soing et painne*
> *Avez vescu tout vostre temps,*
> *Morir fault, e'est chose certainne,*
> *Reculler n'y vault ne contens*
> *De mort devez estre contens*
> *Car de grant soussy vous delivre . . .**

But the laborer mourns the life that he had often wished would come to an end.

Martial d'Auvergne in his *danse macabre* of women has the little girl call out to her mother, take care of my doll, my dice, and my beautiful dress! The touching accents of childhood are extraordinarily rare in the literature of the late Middle Ages. There was no room for them in the weighty rigidity of the grand style. Neither churchly or worldly literature really knew the child. When Antoine de la Salle in "Le Reconfort"[42] seeks to comfort a noblewoman over the loss of her little son, he knows no better way to do so than to tell the story of a boy who lost his young life in an even more cruel way; he died as a hostage. He has nothing to offer her to allay her pain other than the lesson of not attaching oneself to anything earthly, but then continues with that story that we know as the fairy tale of the death shroud. The tale of the dead child who comes to its mother and begs her not to cry anymore in order that its shroud might dry. And here is suddenly a much more tender single note than is heard in the memento mori that is sung with a thousand notes. Is it possible that folktale and folk song during all

---

* Laborer, who in care and toil/Have lived all your time,/You must die, that is certain,/No drawing back helps, no struggling./Death should make you happy,/Because it frees you from great sorrow.

those centuries knew all kinds of emotions well that literature hardly knew at all?

Ecclesiastical thought of the late Middle Ages knew only the two extremes: the lament over perishability, over the end of power, glory, and joy, over the decay of beauty, and, on the other hand, jubilation over the saved soul in its state of bliss. Everything in between was unexpressed. In the fixed representation of the *danse macabre* and the gruesome skeleton, the living emotions are ossified.

Chapter Six

<hr/>

THE DEPICTION OF
THE SACRED

THE DEPICTION OF DEATH MAY SERVE AS AN EXAM-
ple of late medieval thought in general, which frequently moves
living thought from the abstract in the direction of the pictorial as
if the whole of intellectual life sought concrete expression, as if
the notion of gold was immediately minted into coin. There is an
unlimited desire to bestow form on everything that is sacred, to
give any religious idea a material shape so that it exists in the
mind like a crisply printed picture. This tendency towards pictorial
expression is constantly in jeopardy of becoming petrified.

The development of external folk piety in late medieval times
cannot be put more succinctly than it is by Jacob Burckhardt in his
Weltgeschichtliche Betrachtungen.

> A powerful religion permeates all the affairs of life and
> lends color to every movement of the spirit, to every ele-
> ment of culture.
>
> In time, of course, those things come to react upon reli-
> gion, and indeed its living core may be stifled by the ideas
> and images it once took into its sphere. The "sanctification
> of all the concerns of life" has its fateful aspect.

And further:

> Now, no religion has ever been quite independent of the
> culture of its people and its time. It is just when religion
> exercises sovereign sway through the agency of literally writ-
> ten scriptures, when all life seems to revolve round that cen-
> tre, "when it is interwoven with life as a whole," that life
> will most infallibly react upon it. Later, these intimate con-
> nections with culture are no longer useful to it, but simply a
> source of danger; nevertheless, a religion will always act in
> this way as long as it is alive.[1]

The life of medieval Christendom is permeated in all aspects by religious images. There is nothing and no action that is not put in its relationship to Christ and faith. Indeed, everything is tuned to a religious understanding of all things in a tremendous outpouring of faith. But in this supernaturalized atmosphere, the religious tension[2] of true transcendence, the stepping away from the material, cannot always occur. If this tension is missing, then everything intended to awaken a consciousness of God rigidifies into terrible banality, being an astonishing this-worldliness in other-worldly terms.[3] Even in a true saint such as Henry Suso,[4] in whom transcendence was probably never absent for a moment, the distance from the sublime to the ridiculous is very short to our no longer medieval sensibilities. He is sublime when, as the knight Boucicaut honored all women for the sake of his earthly mistress, Suso does so for the sake of Mary, or steps aside into the mud for a poor woman. He follows the customs of chivalry and celebrates his bride, Wisdom, on festivals with a wreath and a song. When he hears a *Minnesong* he immediately allegorizes it in terms of Wisdom. But what are we to make of the following? At table Suso cuts his apple into four parts: three parts he eats in the name of the Trinity, the fourth he eats in memory of "the love with which the Heavenly Mother gave the infant Jesus a little apple to eat." And for this reason, he eats that fourth part with its peel, since little boys do not like their apples peeled. A few days after Christmas—at a time when the infant was too young to eat apples—he does not eat the fourth part, but offers it to Mary so that she will give it to her son. Whatever he drinks he takes in five swallows for the sake of the five wounds of the Lord, but since blood and water flowed from Christ's side, he takes the second swallow twice.[5] Here is the "sanctification of all aspects of life" in the most extreme form.

Disregarding for the moment the degree of devotion, and speaking of the liturgical forms within which medieval piety existed, we can see them as examples of the excesses of religious life, provided that this is not done from a dogmatic Protestant position. There had evolved within the church a growth in the number of usages, concepts, and observances that, leaving aside the quality of the ideas that motivated them, terrified the serious theologians. The reforming spirit of the fifteenth century did not turn against these new practices so much because they were unholy or superstitious, but because they overloaded belief itself. The signs of God's ever-

ready mercy had steadily increased in number: next to the sacraments could be found benedictions; relics had become charms; the
power of prayer was formalized in the rosary. The colorful[6] gallery
of saints had acquired even more color and life. And even though
theology clamored for a precise distinction between sacrament and
sacramentalia, what means were there to keep the masses from
basing their faith and hope on the magical and the gaudy? Gerson[7]
met someone in Auxterre who claimed that All Fool's Day, on
which the winter months were commemorated in churches and
monasteries, was just as sacred as the Feast of Mary's Conception.[8]
Nicholas de Clémanges wrote a treatise against establishing any
new festivals. He declared that many of the new ones were of an
entirely apocryphal nature, and he approved of the action of the
Bishop of Auxterre which had abolished most of them.[9] Pierre
d'Ailly in De Reformatione[10] opposes the increase in numbers of
churches, festivals, saints, and days of rest. He deplores the plethora
of pictures and painted objects and the overly tedious minutiae of
the liturgies. He objects to the inclusion of apocryphal writings in
the liturgy of the festivals, the introduction of new hymns and
prayers or other arbitrary innovations and to the all too rigid intensification of vigils, prayers, fasts, and abstentions. There was a
tendency to link every detail of the veneration of the Holy Mother
to a special service. There were special masses, later abolished by
the church, of Mary's piety, of her seven pains, of all festivals of
Mary together, of her sisters Mary Jacoby and Mary Salome, of
the Angel Gabriel, and of all the saints who formed the family tree
of the Lord Jesus.[11] Furthermore, there are too many monastic
orders, says d'Ailly, and this leads to differences of custom, to
divisiveness and to arrogance, to the prideful elevation of one spiritual order above another. First of all he wants to restrict the mendicant orders. Their existence is detrimental to the homes for lepers
and to hospitals and to the miserable poor and truly needy who
have the right and are entitled to beg.[12] He wants to ban the indulgence preachers from the church who soil it with their lies and
expose it to ridicule.[13] Where will the continual founding of new
convents without sufficient funds for their maintenance lead?

It is obvious that Pierre d'Ailly campaigned more against quantitative than against any qualitative evil. In his sermons he does not
specifically question the piety and sanctity of all these things, excepting his criticism of the indulgence sellers, but is more worried

about their unrestrained growth as such. He sees the church suffocating under the burden of trivial details. When Adamus de Ruper
propagated his new Rosicrucian Brotherhood, it, too, met resistance more because of its novelty than its content. His opponents
warned that the people, trusting in the efficacy of such a grand
society given to prayer, would neglect their prescribed penances
and the clergy their breviaries. The parish churches would become
empty if the brotherhood met only in the churches of the Francis-
cans and the Dominicans, and these meetings would lead to partisanship and conspiracies. Finally, the accusation was made that
what the brotherhood offered as grand and miraculous revelations
were mere phantasmagoria, a conglomeration of imagination and
old wives' tales.[14]

A characteristic example of the mechanical way in which sacred
observances tended to multiply in the absence of intervention by
strict authority was the weeklong veneration of the Innocent Children. During the remembrances of the slaying of the children in
Bethlehem on December 28, various semi-pagan solstice practices
merged with mushy sentimentality. The day was thought to be
unlucky. There were many who regarded the day of the week on
which the last Day of Innocents fell to be inauspicious throughout
the year. No work should begin on that day, nor a journey started.
That day of the week was simply called Innocents' Day like the
festival itself. Louis XI observed this custom conscientiously. The
coronation of Edward IV was repeated because it was found to
have taken place the first time on that inauspicious day and René
of Lorraine had to forgo a battle because his mercenaries refused
to fight on the week-anniversary of the day of the children.[15]

Jean de Gerson was prompted by the practice to author a treatise
against superstition in general and this one in particular.[16] He was
one of those who clearly saw the danger to the church posed by
this wild growth of religious ideas. With his keen and somewhat
sober mind he realizes also something of the psychological ground
from which all these things arose. They arise "ex sola hominum
phantasiatione et melancholica imaginatione";* their corrupt imagination results from damage to the brain that can be traced to the
devil's deceit. Thus the devil comes in for his share of the blame.

---

* "They arise from the mere fantasies of men and their melancholy powers of
imagination"

The process is one of ongoing reduction of the infinite to the finite; the miracle is reduced to atoms. To every holy mystery, there attaches itself like a barnacle to a ship, a growth of external elements of faith that desecrate it. The miracle of the Eucharist is permeated with the most sober and material superstitions: that one cannot go blind or suffer a stroke on the day one hears a mass or that one does not age during the time one spends at the service.[17] The church has to be constantly on guard so that God is not brought all too close to earth. It declares heretical the claim that Peter, John, and James had seen the Heavenly Being during the transfiguration just as clearly as they do now in heaven.[18] It is blasphemy for one of the successors of Jeanne d'Arc to claim to have seen God dressed in a long robe and a red overcoat.[19] But can the people be blamed for not being able to make the fine distinctions of theology when the church offers so many colorful images?

Gerson himself did not stay completely away from the evil he fought. He raised his voice against conceited curiosity; that is, that spirit of inquiry that wants to penetrate nature to its last mystery, but he himself dug with immodest zeal into the smallest details of sacred matters. His particular veneration of St. Joseph, for whose festival he assiduously labored, made him eager to know everything about the saint. He dwelled on every detail of the marriage to Mary, their life together, Joseph's abstention, how he came to know about her pregnancy, how old he was. Gerson wanted no part of the caricature that art had made of Joseph: of the old overworked figure depicted by Deschamps and painted by Broederlam (plate 5). He said that Joseph was not yet fifty years old.[20] Elsewhere he permitted himself an observation about the physical constitution of John the Baptist: "semen igitur materiale ex quo corpus compaginandum erat nec durum nimis nec rursus fluidum abundantius fuit."[21]* The famous popular preacher Olivier Maillard used to present to his audience, after his initial remarks, as "une belle question théologale"† inquiries such as whether or not the Virgin must have actively participated in the conception of Christ in order to be called truly the Mother of God or whether Christ's body would have turned to ashes had the Resurrection not

---

* "then the material semen out of which the body was composed was neither too solid nor too fluid."
† "a beautiful theological question"

interfered.[22] The controversy about Mary's Immaculate Conception was met by the Dominicans, contrary to the growing popular
view that felt the need of absolving the Virgin from the beginning
from original sin, by a mixture of biological and embryonic specu-
lations that, today, seem little edifying. Yet, the most zealous theologians were so stubbornly convinced of the importance of their
arguments that they stooped so low as to take the controversy
before the larger public in their sermons.[23] If this was the direction
of the highest churchmen, how could it be other than that everything holy would dissolve into the mundane and the detailed from
which one could only occasionally rise to a consciousness of the
miraculous?

This fatuous familiarity with God in daily life has to be seen in
two ways. On the one hand, it testifies to the absolute stability and
immediacy of faith, but where this familiarity becomes habitual it
increases the danger that the godless (who are always with us), but
also the pious, in moments of insufficient religious tension, will
continuously profane faith more or less consciously and intentionally. In particular, the most tender of all mysteries, the Eucharist,
is threatened in this way. There is certainly no stronger and fervent
emotion of the Catholic faith than the belief in the direct and essential presence of God in the consecrated host. It is an essential element of the religion both in medieval times and now, but in medieval times, given the naive unself-consciousness of unrestrained
speech, it brought about a use of language that, on occasion, seems
profane. A traveler dismounts for a moment and enters a church
"pour veoir Dieu en passant."* Of a priest on a donkey proceeding
on his way with a host it is said, "un Dieu sur un asne."[24]† Of a
woman on her sickbed it is said, "Sy cuidoit transir de la mort et
se fist apporter beau sire Dieux."[25]‡ *Veoir Dieu* was the common
expression if one saw the Host elevated.[26] In all these cases it is not
the use of language itself that is profane, but it becomes profane if
the mind is impious or if words are uttered thoughtlessly. In such
cases what desecration such customary language brings in its wake!
From common usage it is only a small step to mindless familiarities

---

* "to see God in passing."
† "a God on a donkey."
‡ "and she believed she was about to die and had the loving God brought to
her."

such as the saying "Laissez faire à Dieu, qui est homme d'aage.*"[27] Or Froissart's "et li prie à mains jointes, pour si hault homme que Dieu est."[28]† A case that clearly shows how the word "Dieu" used for the host could contaminate the belief in God itself is the following. The bishop of Coutances celebrates a mass in the church of St. Denis. When he elevates the body of the Lord, Hugues Aubriot, the provost of Paris who is walking around the chapel where the mass is being held, is admonished to pray. But Hugues, known as an *esprit fort*‡ answers with a curse that he does not believe in the God of a bishop who lives at the court.[29]

There was not the least intention to mock the sacred in this familiarity, yet the addiction to turning everything holy into pictorial images seems shameless to us. People owned miniatures of Mary similar to the sets of cups called "Hansje in den Kelder."[30] They were small golden figures, highly decorated with precious stones, whose belly could be opened to reveal the Trinity. Such miniatures could be found in the treasury of the dukes of Burgundy.[31] Gerson saw one in the monastery of the Carmelites in Paris. He disapproved, not because of the lack of piety shown by such a crude depiction of the miracle, but because of the heresy of depicting the entire Trinity as the fruit of Mary's womb.[32]

Life was permeated by religion to the degree that the distance between the earthly and the spiritual was in danger of being obliterated at any moment. While on the one hand all of ordinary life was raised to the sphere of the divine, on the other the divine was bound to the mundane in an indissoluble mixture with daily life. Earlier we spoke of the Cemetery of the Innocents in Paris where bones were piled up and exhibited all around the yard. Can one imagine anything more terrible than the life of the nuns walled in the back of the churchyard in this place of horrors? But let us read what contemporaries said about it: "The hermits lived there in a cute little house, walled in to the accompanyment of a beautiful sermon. They received from the king an annual salary of eight pounds in eight installments."[33] This as if we were dealing with ordinary nuns! Where is the religious pathos? Where is it when an

---

* "Let God do it, He is a man of mature years."

† "and begged him with folded hands, because he was as highly placed as God."

‡ "strong spirit"

indulgence is granted for the most ordinary domestic chores such as firing the oven, milking a cow, or scrubbing a pot?[34] At a raffle in Bergen op Zoom in 1518, either "precious prizes" or indulgences could be won.[35] During princely processions into the cities, the precious reliquary shrines, placed on altars, served by prelates and offered to the princes to be kissed in veneration, competed at street corners with sensuous performances, frequently performed in pagan nudity.[36]

The apparent lack of distinction between the religious and worldly spheres is most vividly expressed in the well-known fact that secular melodies may be used—always unchanged—for sacred songs and vice versa. Guillaume Dufay composed his masses to the themes of popular songs such as "Tant je me déduis," "Se la face ay pale," "L'omme armé."* There is a constant interchange between religious and secular terminology. Without objection, expressions for earthly things are borrowed from liturgy and the other way around, too. Above the door to the auditor office in Lille was a verse that reminded everyone that he would eventually have to give account of his gifts to God:

> Lors ouvrira, au son de buysine
> Sa générale et grant chambre des comptes.[37]†

On the other hand, the solemn announcement of a tournament sounds as if it were a festival where indulgences were sold:

> Oez, oez, l'oneur et la louenge
> Et des armes grantdisime pardon.[38]‡

By coincidence in the word "mistère" the concepts contained in both "mysterium" and "ministerium" were blended. This weakened the idea of mystery in everyday language in which everything

---

* "So Much I Enjoy Myself," "If My Face Is Pale," "The Armed Man"

† Then to the sound of the trumpet/God shall open his general and grand accounting office.

‡ Hear ye, Hear ye, the honor and the glory/And the great indulgence conferred by arms.

was called "mistère": the unicorn, the shields, and the doll used in the "Pas d'ames de la Fontaine des pleurs."[39]

As a counterpart to religious symbolism, that is, the interpretation of all earthly things and earthly events as symbols and prefigurations of the divine, the praise of princes is transposed into liturgical metaphor. Whenever the awe of worldly authority seizes medieval man, the language of piety serves as the means of expressing his feelings. The liegemen of the princes of the fifteenth century did not stop short of any profanation. In the court case about the murder of Louis of Orléans the advocate has the ghost of the murdered prince speak to his son, Look at my wounds of which five are particularly cruel and mortal.[40] That is, he makes Christ the image of the murder victim. The bishop of Chalons, in turn, does not shy away from comparing John the Fearless, who was the victim of the avenger of the prince of Orléans, to the lamb of God.[41] Molinet compares Emperor Frederick III, who sent his son Maximillian to marry Mary of Burgundy, to God the Father who had sent his Son to earth, and he spares no pious words to embellish the event. Later when Frederick and Maximillian enter the city of Brussels with the young Philip le Beau, Molinet has the burghers cry with tears in their eyes, "Veez-ci figure de la Trinité, le Père, le Fils et Sainct Esprit."* He offers a wreath of flowers to Mary of Burgundy, a worthy image of our beloved Lady, "except for her virginity."[42]

"Not that I want to deify princes,"[43] says this creature of the courts. Perhaps these are merely hollow phrases rather than deeply felt devotion, but they prove nevertheless the devaluation of holy things by everyday use. How can we blame a poet hired by the court when Gerson himself grants to the princely auditors of his sermons special guardian angels of higher hierarchy and office than those of other men?[44]

In the transfer of religious expressions to the erotic, which we have already mentioned, we are dealing, of course, with something entirely different. In these cases there is an element of deliberate impiety and genuine mockery that is absent in the examples just described. They are related only in that they both arise from fatuous familiarity with the sacred. The authors of the Cent nouvelles nou-

---

* "See here, the image of the Trinity, the Father, the Son and the Holy Ghost."

velles engage in endless plays on words such as "saint" and "seins," and use "dévotion, confesser, bénir"* with obscene meanings. The author of the *Quinze joyes de mariage* chose his title in reference to the joys of Mary.[45] There has already been mention of the idea of love as a pious observance. It is more serious when the defender of the *Roman de la rose* uses sacred terms to refer to "partes corporis inhonesta et pecatta immunda atque turpia."[46]† Here is well demonstrated something of the dangerous contact between the religious and the erotic that the church, with good reason, so feared. There is no more striking example of that contact than the Melun Madonna (plate 6), ascribed to Foucquet, which used to be a diptych and was united with the panel, now in Berlin, which shows the donor, Etienne Chevalier, with St. Stephen (plate 7). Earlier the united work hung in the choir of the Church of Our Lady in Melun. An old tradition, noted in the seventeenth century by Denis Godefroy, a man knowledgeable about medieval times, has it that the features of the Madonna are those of Agnes Sorel,[47] the King's mistress. Chevalier did not hide his passion for her. Even considering all the great qualities of the painting, it is a fashionable doll that we encounter here with a rounded, clean-shaven forehead, widely separated spherical breasts, a high narrow waist, a bizarre and inscrutable facial expression, and surrounded by stiff red and blue angels. All this bestows on the panel a touch of decadent godlessness that is in marked contrast to the vigorous and simple depiction of the donor and his saint on the other side panel. Godefroy saw, on the large blue velvet frame, a series of E's in pearls joined by love knots of gold and silver threads.[48] Does this not reveal a blasphemous nonchalance towards the sacred that could not be outdone by any Renaissance spirit?

The profanation of daily religious practice was almost without bounds. It is said that choristers sang the profane words of the song to whose melodies the service had been set: such songs as "Baisez moi"‡ and "Rouge nez."[49]§ David of Burgundy, the bastard of Philip the Good, made his entry as bishop of Utrecht in the com-

---

* "seins"—bosom; "dévotion"—submission, piety; "bénir"—bless, blessed, pregnant.
  † "dishonorable parts of the body and filthy and hateful sins."
  ‡ "Kiss Me"
  § "Red Nose"

pany of a war party consisting only of noblemen along with his brother, the Bastard of Burgundy, who had accompanied him from Amersfoort. The new bishop was clad in armor "comme seroit un conquéeur de païs, prince séculier,"* says Chastellain with obvious disapproval. In this way he rode to the cathedral and entered it with a procession complete with flags and crosses to pray before the high altar.[50] Let us put this Burgundian arrogance beside the gentle frivolity of Rudolf Agricola's father, the pastor of Baflo, who, on the day he was selected Abbot of Selwert, received the news that his concubine had born him a son, and said, "Today I have twice become a father. May God's blessing be upon it."[51]

Contemporary people regarded the growing disrespect for the church as a recent evil:

> On souloit estre ou temps passé
> En L'église béneignement
> A genoux en humilité
> Delez l'autel moult closement,
> Tout nu le chief piteusement,
> Maiz au jour d'uy, si comme beste,
> On vient à l'autel bien souvent
> Chaperon et chapel en teste.[52]†

On festive days, laments Nicolas of Clémanges, only a few attend mass. They don't stay until it is over and are satisfied with touching the holy water, saluting our Lady by bending their knees once, or kissing the image of a saint. If they happen to see the host elevated, they take pride in this act as if they had done a great deed for Christ. Matins and vespers are read by the priest and his assistants alone.[53] The squire of the village makes the priest wait with his mass until he and his wife have gotten up and dressed.[54]

The most sacred festivals, even Christmas Eve itself, are spent in debauchery with card games, cursing, and blasphemy; if the people are admonished, they point to the example of the nobility and the higher and lower priesthood who behave with impunity.[55]

* "as befits the conqueror of a country, a secular prince."
† Earlier people were/Very pious in church,/On their knees in humility/Close to the altar,/And meekly uncovering their heads,/But at present like beasts/Too often they come to the altar/With hood and hat on their heads.

During vigils there is dancing in the churches themselves to the accompaniment of lascivious songs. Priests set the example by dicing and cursing during their nightly wakes.[56] These are the practices documented by the moralists, who are perhaps always given to taking the darkest view, but the sources more than once confirm this dark image. The city council of Strasbourg every year dispensed eleven hundred liters of wine to those who spent the night of St. Adolf in the cathedral "holding a wake and in prayer."[57] A city councillor complained to Denis the Carthusian that the annual procession of the holy relics provided the occasion for drinking and numerous improprieties. How could this be stopped? The magistrate himself would not be easily persuaded because the procession made money for the city; it attracted people who needed lodging, food, and drink. Above all, it was customary. Denis knew the problem. He knew how shamelessly people acted during processions, by gossiping, laughing, flirting, drinking, and indulging in other uncouth pleasures.[58] His melancholy sigh perfectly fits the procession of the delegation from Ghent carrying the shrine of St. Liéin to the fair at Houthen. In the old days, says Chastellain, the notables were in the habit of carrying the holy body "en grande et haute solempnité et révérence,"* but now it is "une multitude de respaille et de garconnaille mauvaise."† They carry it screaming and howling, singing and dancing, mocking everything in sight, and they are all drunk. Moreover, they are armed and indulge themselves in whatever they wish. Everything is at their mercy given the excuse of their holy burden.[59]

Going to church was an important element of social life. People went there to enjoy dressing up, to show off their rank and prominence and to compete in courtly manners and deportment. As already mentioned,[60] the paten, the "paix," was a constant source of the most irritating competitive courtesy. If a young nobleman enters, the gracious lady stands up and kisses him on the mouth even while the priest elevates the host and the people are on their knees praying.[61] Walking about and talking during mass must have been quite customary.[62] The use of the church as trysting place for young lads and girls was so common that only the moralists were still upset about it. Young men rarely come to church, complains Nico-

* "in great and high solemnity and reverence,"
† "a crowd of rascals and toughs"

las of Clémanges, other than to watch the women who put their elaborate hairstyles and generous décolletés on display there. The virtuous Christine de Pisan rhymes in all innocence:

> *Se souvent vais ou moustier,*
> *C'est tout pour veoir la belle*
> *Fresche comme rose nouvelle.*[63]*

It was not only small trysts for which church afforded the occasion, not merely for handing the beloved the consecrated water, giving her the "paix," lighting a candle for her and kneeling beside her; it did not stop at a few signs and furtive glances.[64] In the churches themselves, even on holy days, prostitutes looked for customers[65] and immoral pictures that corrupted the youth could be bought. No preaching was effective against such evils.[66] Time and again the church and the altar were desecrated by immoral acts.[67]

Pilgrimages, like church services, provided the occasion for pleasure, especially of an amorous nature. Pilgrimages are frequently spoken of as pleasure trips. The Knight de la Tour Landry, who took seriously the instruction of his daughters in good manners, speaks of ladies of leisure who liked to go to tournaments and on pilgrimages. As a warning he cites the example of a woman who went on pilgrimage as an excuse to meet her paramour. "Et pour ce a cy bon exemple comment l'on ne doit pas aler aux sains voiaiges pour nulle folle plaisance."[68]† Nicolas de Clémanges agrees. People go on pilgrimages to distant shrines not so much to fulfill a vow, but to find freedom for straying from the straight and narrow. Pilgrimages are the occasion for all sorts of transgressions. Procuresses are always there to seduce young girls.[69] A common incident in the *Quinze joyes de mariage:* the young wife wishes a little diversion and convinces her husband that the child is ill because she has not completed the pilgrimage she vowed to take during her confinement.[70] The preparations for the wedding of Charles VI with Isabella of Bavaria are launched with a pilgrimage.[71] Small wonder that the serious men of the *devotio moderna* have little use

---

* If I often go to church/it is to see the fair one/fresh as a new rose.

† "and there is here a good example why one should not go on pilgrimage for the sake of silly, worldly lusts."

for pilgrimages. Those who go on many pilgrimages rarely become saints, says Thomas à Kempis, and Frederick van Heilo wrote a special work about the matter, the *Contra peregrinantes.*[72]

In all these sacrileges of the holy through the unabashed intermingling with sinful life there is more naive familiarity with liturgy than open godlessness. Only a culture that is thoroughly permeated with religiosity and that takes faith for granted knows these excesses and degenerations. These people, following the sloppy course of a religious practice half gone to seed, were the same who could suddenly rise to extremes of religious fervor when prodded by the ardent words of one of the mendicant preachers.

Even such a stupid sin as blasphemy only arises from strong faith. Originally a conscious invocation, blasphemy is only the sign of an immediate consciousness, extending to the most trivial things, of the omnipresence of the divine. Only the feeling of truly challenging heaven gives blasphemy its sinful attraction. Only when the oath becomes mechanical and any fear of the fulfillment of the curse has gone does blasphemy slide into the monotonous crudeness of later times. In the late Middle Ages it still had that attraction of daring and arrogance that made it the sport of the nobility. "What?" says the nobleman to the peasant, "You give your soul to the devil and deny God, yet you are not a nobleman?"[73] Deschamps reports that the habit of swearing had descended to people of low estate.

> *Si chétif n'y a qui ne die:*
> *Je renie Dieu et sa mère.*[74]*

People compete in the composition of new and drastic oaths; the most profane man is honored as a master.[75] Deschamps says that originally people everywhere in France swore in Gascon and English and later in Breton and now in Burgundian. He composed two ballads by stringing the most popular curses together, but he gave them a pious meaning in the end. The Burgundian oath was the worst of all, "Je renie Dieu,"[76]† but it was toned down to "Je

---

* There is none so mean but says, /I deny God and His mother.
† "I deny God"

renie de bottes."* Burgundians had the reputation of being master swearers. For the rest, said Gerson, all of France, in spite of her Christianity, suffered more than other countries from this disgusting sin, the cause of pestilence, war, and famine.[77] Even monks swore.[78] Gerson wanted the authorities and estates to help eradicate the evil through strict laws, but light penalties, which could then be rigorously carried out. In 1397 a royal order was actually issued that renewed the old ordinances of 1269 and 1347 against swearing, however not with light and practical penalties, but with such time-honored threats as splitting the lips or cutting out the tongue, penalties that expressed a holy horror of blasphemy. In the register containing the ordinance, there is a note on the margin, "All these oaths are today, 1411, in common use throughout the kingdom without any penalty."[79] Pierre d'Ailly strongly urged the Council of Constance[80] to forcefully combat this evil.

Gerson knows the two extremes between which the sin of blasphemy fluctuates. He has learned from his experience as a confessor that uncorrupted young people, simple and chaste, are tortured by the sharp temptation to deny God and blaspheme. He recommends that they avoid overarduous contemplation of God, since they are not strong enough for that.[81] On the other hand, there are habitual blasphemers like the Burgundians whose deed, abhorrent as it is, does not include perjury since they do not have the intent of taking an oath.[82]

The point where the habit of treating matters of faith lightly becomes irreligiousness cannot be determined with exactitude. Certainly there was in late medieval times a strong tendency to mock piety and the pious. Some prefer to be *esprits forts* and speak jokingly against faith.[83] The popular writers are frivolous and indifferent, as in the story from the *Cent nouvelles nouvelles* where the priest buries his dog in consecrated ground and addresses him as "mon bon chien, a qui Dieu pardoint."† The dog, thereupon, goes "tout droit au paradis des chiens."[84]‡ There is a great resentment of false or mocking piety. Every other word is "papelard."§ The

---

* "I deny boots"
† "My good dog whom God pardons."
‡ "straight to the paradise of dogs."
§ "Heretic."

frequently invoked saying "De jeune angelot vieux diable" or, in solemn Latin meter, "Angelicus juvenis senibus sathanizat in annis"* is for Gerson a thorn in his side. Thus youth is corrupted, he says. A brazen face, scurrilous language and curses, immodest looks and gestures are praised in children. So, he says, What is to be expected of children who play the devil when they get old?[85]

As to the clerics and theologians themselves, Gerson distinguishes between types. One group is composed of ignorant troublemakers, to whom any serious discussion is a burden and religion a fairy tale. Everything they are told about appearances and revelations they reject with loud laughter and great disgust. Another group goes to the opposite extreme and accepts every product of the imagination of deranged people, their dreams and strange ideas as revelation.[86] The populace does not know how to maintain a middle position between two such extremes. They believe prophecies by seers and soothsayers, but if a genuine divine who has frequently had true revelations makes a single error, then the worldly people scorn all those who belong to the clergy, call them imposters and "papelards" and henceforth will no longer listen to any clergyman, considering them all to be malevolent hypocrites.[87]

In most instances of the loudly bemoaned lack of piety we are dealing with the sudden ending of religious tension in a mental life oversaturated with liturgical content and forms. Throughout the entire Middle Ages there are numerous instances of spontaneous unbelief[88] that are not deviations from church teaching based on theological reflection, but merely direct reactions against it. Even though it does not mean much that poets and chroniclers— encountering the enormous sinfulness of their time—exclaimed that no one any longer believed in heaven or hell,[89] in more than one case the latent lack of faith had become conscious and had hardened; it had hardened to the degree that this fact was well known by all and admitted by the unbelievers themselves. "Beaux seigneurs," says Captain Bétisac to his comrades,[90] "je ay regardé à mes besongnes et en ma conscience je tiens grandement Dieu avoir courrouchié, car jà de long temps j'ay erré contre la foy, et ne puis croire qu'il soit riens de la Trinité, ne que le Fils de Dieu se daignast tant abassier que il venist des chieux descendre en corps humain de femme, et croy et dy que, quant nous morons, que il

---

* "the young angel makes an old devil"

n'est riens de âme . . . J'ay tenu celle oppinion depuis que j'eus congnoissance, ct la tenray jusques à la fin."* Hugues Aubriot, provost of Paris, is a fiery enemy of the clergy. He does not believe in the Eucharist and mocks it. He does not celebrate Easter nor go to confession.[91] Jacques du Clercq tells of several noblemen who, in full possession of their senses, refused Extreme Unction.[92] Jean de Montreuil, provost of Lille, writes to one of his learned friends, more in the easy style of an enlightened humanist than as one of the truly pious: "You know our friend Ambrosius de Miliis; you have frequently heard what he thought about religion, faith, Holy Scripture, and all ecclesiastical prescriptions, so that Epicurus would have to be called Catholic in comparison. Well, he is now completely converted. Prior to his conversion he was nonetheless tolerated in the circles of early humanists who were of a fully pious disposition."[93]

On one side of these spontaneous instances of unbelief is the literary paganism of the Renaissance and the educated, a cautious form of Epicureanism, named after Averroës, which flourished in such wide circles as early as the thirteenth century. On the other side are the passionate negations of the ignorant heretics who, whether they be called Turlupins or Brothers of the Free Spirit, crossed the line separating mysticism and pantheism. But these phenomena will be dealt with in a different context later on. For the time being, we have to remain in the sphere of external images of faith and external forms and customs.

For the daily understanding of the mass of people, the existence of a visible image made intellectual proof of faith entirely superfluous. There was no room between what was depicted, and which one met in color and form—that is, depictions of the Trinity, the flames of hell, the catalog of saints—and faith in all this. There was no room for the question, Is this true? All these representations went directly from picture to belief. They existed in the mind fully

---

* "I have attended to my spiritual concerns and, in my conscience, I believe I have greatly angered God, having for a long time already erred against the faith, and I cannot believe a word about the Trinity, nor that the Son of God has humbled Himself to such an extent to come down from heaven into the carnal body of a woman; and I believe and say that when we die there is no such thing as a soul. . . . I have held this opinion ever since I became self-conscious, and I shall hold it to the end."

defined and garbed in all the reality that the church could demand of faith and then some.

But where faith rests on tangible images, it is hardly possible to make qualitative distinctions between the nature and degree of sanctity of the different elements of faith. One picture is as real and commands as much awe as another. That God is to be worshiped and the saints merely venerated is not taught by the picture itself and the difference is lost unless the church constantly warns about the necessary distinction. Nowhere else were pious notions so seriously threatened by the overgrowth of colorful images than in the field of the veneration of saints.

The strict position of the church was simple and elevated enough. Given the belief in the continued existence of personalities after death, the veneration of saints was natural and unquestioned. It was permissible to honor them "per imitationem et reductionem ad Deum."* In the same sense, it was permissible to venerate pictures, relics, holy places, and consecrated objects since, ultimately, all this led to the worship of God himself.[94] The technical distinction between the saints and ordinary people who achieved salvation was established by official canonization. This distinction, although a troublesome formalization, contained nothing that contradicted the spirit of Christianity. The church remained aware that sanctity and bliss were originally of equal value, just as it was aware that canonization was somehow flawed. "It may be assumed," said Gerson, "that infinitely more saints have died, and die everyday, than have been canonized."[95] That pictures were permitted, even though their existence violated the prohibition of such in the second commandment, was justified by the teaching that this prohibition had been necessary prior to the Incarnation because God had been only spirit at that time, but that Christ's coming had canceled that old commandment. Yet, the church desired unconditionally to obey the rest of the second commandment, "Non adorabis ea neque coles."† "We do not adore the images, but honor and adore he who is depicted, God or His saint in whose image it is."[96] Images were only intended to show the simpleminded, who did not know the scriptures, what to believe in.[97]

---

* "as imitations and small reflections of God."
† "You shall neither adore them or serve them."

They were the books of the simpleminded,[98] as we see from this prayer that Villon composed for his mother:

> Femme je suis pourette et ancienne,
> Qui reins ne sçai; oncques lettre ne leuz;
> Au moustier voy dont suis paroissienne
> Paradis paint, où sont harpes et luz,
> Et ung enfer où dampnez sont boulluz:
> L'ung me fait paour, l'autre joye et liesse . . .[99]*

The church was mindful of the fact that to the simple mind just as much opportunity to stray was offered by colorful pictures as by any personal interpretation of scripture. It always treated those gently who lapsed into the worship of images out of ignorance or simplemindedness. "It is enough," says Gerson, "if they intend to do as the church requires."[100]

The question, purely one of history of dogma, whether the church always managed to keep its injunction against direct veneration or even worship of saints, not as intercessors but as the granters of requests, we can leave as it is. We are dealing here, as a question of cultural history, with how far it succeeded in keeping the people from error; that is, what reality, what value for understanding did the saints have in the popular consciousness of the late Middle Ages? To this question only one answer is possible: the saints were such essential, material, and familiar figures of the everyday life of faith that all the common and sensual religious impulses were tied up with them. While the most fervent emotions turned towards Christ and Mary, an entire store of naive and everyday religious feeling crystalized around the veneration of saints. All this helped to keep popular saints in the middle of ordinary life. Popular imagination took hold of them: their figures are as familiar as their attributes. Their gruesome tortures are known as well as their astonishing miracles. They are dressed and endowed like the people themselves. One could meet, everyday, "Messires" St. Roch or St.

---

* Woman I am, poor and old,/Who knows nothing; I never could read;/In the church where I am a parishioner,/I see paradise painted with harps and lutes,/And a hell where the damned are boiled:/The one frightens me, the other brings joy and mirth.

James in the persons of living plague victims or pilgrims. It would be interesting to study how long the dress of saints accorded with the fashions of the day; certainly for the entire fifteenth century. But where is the point at which church art removed them from living popular imagination by dressing them in rhetorical robes? This was not just a case of Renaissance sensitivity to historical costume; as an added element, the popular imagination itself began to abandon them so that they were no longer able to hold their own in popular church art. During the Counter-Reformation, the saints, quite in line with the intent of the church, climbed up several steps and moved out of touch with popular life.

The physical presence that the saints possessed by virtue of their depictions was unusually intensified by the fact that the church permitted and even favored the veneration of their relics. It could not be other than that this clinging to the material had a materializing effect on faith that occasionally led to astonishing extremes. The vigorous faith of the Middle Ages, whenever directed towards relics, was not deterred by fear of secularization or desecration. The people of the mountains of Umbria around the year 1000 tried to kill St. Romuald in order to secure his bones. The monks of Fossanuova where Thomas Aquinas died were so fearful of losing the precious relic that they did not shrink from decapitating, boiling, and preserving the corpse.[101] Before St. Elizabeth of Thuringia was buried, a crowd of devotees cut or tore strips from the winding-sheets of her face and cut off her hair and nails, pieces of her ears and even her nipples.[102] At a solemn feast, Charles VI gave ribs of his ancestor St. Louis to Pierre d'Ailly and to his uncles Berry and Burgundy. He gave a leg to the prelates, who divided it after the meal.[103]

No matter how real and alive the saints seemed to be, only relatively few appear in supernatural experiences. The entire realm of visions, appearances, signs, and ghosts remains separate from the popular imagination about saints, but there are, of course, exceptions. The figures of St. Michael, St. Catherine, and St. Margaret, who appeared to Joan of Arc, come to mind. We could also cite a number of examples from the visionary literature, but as a rule the examples we encounter in these stories were embellished and interpreted, so to speak. When the fourteen holy martyrs, who were so clearly identified by iconography,[104] appear to a young shepherd of Frankenthal near Bamberg in 1446, he does not see them with their proper attributes, but as fourteen identical cherubim. They *tell* him they are the holy martyrs. The popular phantasmagoria is filled with angels and devils, ghosts and white-clad women, but not with saints. Only in exceptional cases do saints play a role in genuine, that is not literary or theologically embellished, superstition. St. Bertulph does at Ghent. Anytime something important is about to happen, he knocks on his coffin in the abby of St. Peter "moult dru et moult fort."* Sometimes the knocking is accompanied by a light earthquake so that the frightened city tries to ward off the unknown danger by large processions.[105] But generally, cold fear attaches itself to vaguely imagined figures rather than to the sharply chiseled images in the church. Just like ghosts, the imagined move about aimlessly, show an indeterminate expression of the horrible in a nebulous gown, or rising from the remote recesses of the brain, show themselves in pure heavenly radiances or in terrifying illusionary forms.

We should not be surprised by all this. It is precisely because the saints had assumed such definite forms and material character that they lacked horror and mystery. Supernatural fear results from unbridled imagination, from the possibility that something new and dreadful could suddenly appear. As soon as the image becomes clearly drawn and defined it arouses a feeling of security and familiarity. The well-known figures of the saints had the reassuring quality of the sight of a policeman in a foreign city. Their veneration, and particularly their depiction, created a neutral zone of comfortably calm faith between the ecstasy of the vision of God and the sweet shudder of the love of Christ on the one hand and the terrifying phantasmagoria, born of the fear of the devil and the frenzy of witchcraft, on the other.

One could even posit that the veneration of saints was a very healthy tempering of the exuberance of the medieval mind, since it was able to deflect many visions of bliss and many fears and reduce them to familiar notions.

By virtue of its perfectly pictorial quality, the veneration of saints belongs to the outward manifestations of religion. It moves along with the stream of everyday thought and occasionally loses its dignity in this stream. The medieval veneration of Joseph is a case in point. It might be looked upon as both a consequence of the pas-

* "very often and very loudly."

sionate veneration of Mary and a backlash against it. This disrespectful interest in the stepfather is the other side of the coin to all the love and glorification showered on the Virgin Mother. The higher Mary rose, the more Joseph became a mere caricature. Fine art had already given him a form dangerously close to that of an uncouth peasant; thus is he depicted on Melchoir Broederlam's diptych at Dijon. But in the fine arts the most profane aspects remain unexpressed. Rather than hold that no mortal could be more highly favored than Joseph, privileged to serve the mother of God and raise her Son, Eustace Deschamps prefers, with naive sobriety, but not godless mockery, to see him as the type of drudging pitiful husband.

> Vous qui servez à femme et à enfans,
> Aiez Joseph toudis en remembrance;
> Femme servit toujours tristes, dolans,
> Et Jhesu Crist garda en son enfance;
> A piè trotoit, son fardel sur sa lance;
> En plusieurs lieux est figuré ainsi,
> Lez un mulet, pour leur faire plaisance,
> Et si n'ot oncq feste en ce monde ci.[106]*

We could accept this if it were intended to console troubled husbands by holding up for them a noble example, though the presentation is lacking dignity. But Deschamps uses Joseph as a virtual warning against taking up the burdens of a family.

> Qu'ot Joseph de povreté
> De dureté
> De maleurté
> Quant Dieux nasquil!
> Maintefois l'a comporté
> Et monté
> Par bonté

---

* You who serve a wife and children/Always keep Joseph in mind;/He served a woman constantly, gloomily and mournfully,/And he guarded Jesus Christ in his infancy;/He went on foot with his bundle on his staff;/In many places he is so pictured,/Next to a mule, for their fair pleasure,/And so he never had any amusement in this world.

Avec sa mère autressi,
Sur sa mule les ravi:
je le vi
paint ainsi;
en Egipte en est alé.

Le bonhomme est painturé
tout lassé
Et troussé
D'un cote et d'un barry.
Un baston au coul posé
Vieil usé
Et rusé.
Feste n'a en ce monde cy,
Mais de lui
Va le cri
C'est Joseph le rassoté.[107]*

This shows how from the familiar image arose an all too familiar conception that threatened any sense of sanctity. Joseph remained a semi-comic figure. Dr. Johannes Eck still had to insist that he not appear in Christmas plays if not in a proper depiction or at least that he not be made to cook the porridge "ne ecclesia Dei irredeatur."[108] Gerson's effort for a proper veneration of Joseph that eventually led to the saint's inclusion in the liturgy in preference to all others was motivated by these undignified excesses.[109] We have already seen, however, how Gerson's seriousmindedness did not keep him from immodest curiosity about things that seem to be inevitably linked to Joseph's marriage. Sober minds (and Gerson, despite his predilection for mysticism, was in many respects a sober mind) were often led by contemplations of Mary's marriage to considerations of an earthly sort. The Knight de la Tour Landry, also a typically sober and correct fellow, sees it in this light: "Dieux voulst que elle espousast le saint homme Joseph, qui estoit vieulx

---

* What poverty Joseph suffered/And hardship/And misery,/When God was born!/Many a time he has carried him/And lifted him up out of kindness./Together with his mother/On his mule/He led them/Into Egypt./I saw him/Painted thus./The good man is painted/Quite exhausted/and dressed/In a frock and a striped garment;/Leaning on his stick/Old, spent,/And broken./No earthly joy had he,/But of him/Goes the cry/It is Joseph the fool.

et preudomme; car Dieu voust naistre soubz umbre de mariage pour
obéir à la loy qui lors couroit, *pour exchever les paroles du monde.*"[110]*
An unpublished work of the fifteenth century presents the mystic
marriage of the soul with the heavenly bridegroom in the customary
terms of a bourgeois courtship. Jesus, the Bridegroom, tells God the
Father: "S'il te plaist, jeme marriray et auray grant foueson d'enfants et
de famille."† The Father objects to his son's choice, a black Ethiopian.
Here the passage from the Song of Songs is echoed: "Nigra sum
sed formosa."‡ Such a union would be a misalliance and dishonor the
family. The angel serving as intermediary puts in a good word for
the bride: "Combien que ceste fille soit noire, neanmoins elle est gracieuse, et a belle composicion de corps et de membres et est bien habille
pour porter fouezon d'enfans."§ The father responds: "Mon cher fils
m'a dit qu'elle est noir et brunete. Certes je vueil que son espouse soit
jeune, courtoise, joyle, gracieuse et belle et qu'elle ait beaux membres."** The angel then praises her face and all her limbs, which are
the virtues of her soul. The father declares himself bested and tells his
son:

> *Prens la, car elle est plaisant*
> *Pour bien amer son doulx amant;*
> *Or prens de nois biens largement*
> *Et luy en donne habondamment.*[111]††

There is no doubt of the seriously devout intent of this work. It is
only one example of how unbridled imagination leads to triviality.
    Every saint, by the possession of a distinct and vivid outward

---

    * "God wished that she should marry that saintly man Joseph, who was old
and upright, for God wished to be born in wedlock, to comply with the current
legal requirements, *to avoid gossip.*"
    † "If it pleases you, I shall marry and shall have a large bevy of children and
relations."
    ‡ "I am black, but comely" [Song of Songs 1:5].
    § "Even though this maiden is black, nonetheless, she is graceful and has a
beautiful body and limbs and is well suited to bear many children."
    ** "My beloved son has said to me that she is black and brown. Certainly, I
desire that my son's bride should be young, courteous, pretty, graceful, and beautiful, and should have beautiful limbs."
    †† Take her, for she is pleasing,/fit to love her sweet bridegroom;/Now take
plenty of our possessions,/And give them to her in abundance.

shape, had his own marked personality,[112] quite different from the angels, who, with the exception of the three great archangels, were never given personalized images. The personality of each saint was strongly accentuated by the special function that each one had. People turned to one saint for a certain emergency and to another for recovery from a certain disease. Frequently a detail of the saint's legend or an attribute of a depiction was the source of the specialization, as in the case of St. Apollonia, who had her teeth pulled during her martyrdom and was thus appealed to in case of toothache. Once the functions of saints became so specialized, it was inevitable that their veneration became somewhat mechanical. When the cure of plague was attributed to St. Roch, it was inevitable that too much stress was laid on his part in the healing and that the chain of thought required by sound doctrine, namely that the saint worked his healing by interceding with God, was in danger of being left out altogether. This was notably the case in regard to the fourteen holy martyrs (sometimes five, eight, ten, or fifteen) whose veneration was especially important towards the end of the medieval period. St. Barbara and St. Christopher are the most frequently depicted of this group. According to popular tradition, God had granted to the fourteen the power of warding off any imminent danger through the mere invocation of their name.

> Ilz sont cinq sains, en la genealogie,
> Et cinq sainctes, à qui Dieu octria
> Benignement a la fin de leur vie,
> Que quiconques de cuer les requerra,
> En tous perilz, que Dieu essaucera
> Leur prieres, pour quelconque mesaise.
> Saiges est doc qui ces cinq servira,
> Jorges, Denis, Christofle, Giles et Blaise.[113]*

In the popular imagination, any notion of the purely interceding function was bound to be entirely lost by virtue of this delegation of

---

* There are five saints in the genealogy, / And five female saints to whom God has granted / Benignantly at the end of their lives, / That who ever invokes their help with all his heart / In all dangers, that God will hear / Their intercedence in all disorders whatever. / He is wise who serves these five, / George, Denis, Christopher, Giles, and Blaise.

omnipotent and spontaneous effect. The holy martyrs had become prefects of the Deity. Various missals of the late medieval period that contain the office of the fourteen holy martyrs clearly express the binding character of their intercession: "Deus qui electos sanctos tuos Georgium etc. etc. specialibus privilegiis prae cunctis aliis decorasti, ut omnes, qui in necessitatibus suis eorum implorant auxilium, secundum promissionem tuae gratiae petitionis suae salutarem consequantur effectum."[114]* After the Council of Trent, the church abolished the mass of the Holy Martyrs because of the danger that faith would attach itself to them as to a talisman. In fact, it was already the case that a daily viewing of the image of St. Christopher was considered sufficient for protection against any fatality.[115]

As to the reason that these fourteen were turned into a welfare company, it should be noted that their depictions all had sensational attributes that stimulated the imagination. St. Achatius had a crown of thorns, St. Giles was accompanied by a hind, St. George by a dragon, St. Blaise was in a den with wild beasts, St. Christopher was a giant, St. Cyriac had the devil in chains. St. Denis was carrying his own head under his arm, St. Erasmus was in his gruesome torture being disemboweled on the rack, St. Eustace was with a stag carrying a cross between his antlers, St. Pantaleon was depicted as a physician with a lion, St. Vitus in a cauldron, St. Barbara in her tower, St. Catherine with her wheel and sword, St. Margaret with a dragon.[116] It cannot be ruled out that the special attention given these fourteen arose from the characteristics of their images.

A number of different saints were linked with specific diseases, such as St. Anthony with various festering skin diseases, St. Maur with gout, St. Sebastian, St. Roch, St. Giles, St. Christopher, St. Valentine, St. Adrian with plague. Here we find yet another cause of the degeneration of popular religion: the disease was named after the saint, St. Anthony's fire, "mal de St. Maur," and many others. The saint was therefore from the very beginning in the forefront of the mind of those who thought about the disease. Those

---

* "O God, who hath distinguished Thy chosen saints, George, etc., etc., with special privileges before all others, that all those who in their need invoke their help shall obtain the salutary fulfillment of their prayer, according to the promise of Thy grace."

thoughts were charged with violent swings of emotion, with fear and disgust. This is particularly true with respect to the plague. The saints linked to the plague were most eagerly venerated during the fifteenth century: with services in the churches, through processions, brotherhoods, as virtual spiritual health insurance. How easily the strong awareness of God's wrath, rekindled by each epidemic, could be deflected against the saint who took over as cause. The disease was not caused by God's unfathomable justice, but by the wrath of the saint who sent the illness and demanded propitiation. If he cured the disease, why should he have not caused it in the first place? This constituted a heathen transposition of faith from the religious-ethical to the magical sphere. The church could have been held responsible for this only to the extent that it did not take sufficiently into account that its pure teaching would become clouded in ignorant minds.

The testimony for the presence of this notion among the people is so large that it rules out any doubt that among the circles of the ignorant the saints were occasionally really regarded as having caused the disease. "Que Saint Antoine me arde"* is a common curse. "Saint Antoine arde le tripot," "Saint Antoine arde la monture!"[117]† are curses in which the saint functions entirely as an evil fire-demon.

> Saint Anthoine me vent trop chier Son mal,
> le feu ou corps me boute.‡

Deschamps has a beggar say about his skin disease. And he barks at a sufferer from gout: if you cannot walk, you at least save the road fee.

> Saint Mor ne te fera fremir.[118]§

Robert Gaguin, who did not attack the veneration of saints *per se* in a poem of ridicule, "De validorum per Francium mendi-

---

* "May Saint Anthony burn me"
† "Saint Anthony burn the brothel, Saint Anthony burn that horse!"
‡ "Saint Anthony sells me his evil all too dear, /He stokes the fire in my body."
§ "Saint Maur will not make you tremble."

cantium varia astucia," describes beggars as follows: "This one falls to earth while spitting stinking saliva and he rants that this is a miracle worked by St. John. Others are visited with pustules by St. Fiacrius. And you, O Damianius, keep me from passing water. St. Anthony makes their joints burn with miserable fire. St. Pius turns them into cripples and paralyses their limbs."[119]

Erasmus ridicules the same popular belief when he has Theotimus respond to the question by Philecous whether saints are worse in heaven or on earth: "Yes, the saints who reign in heaven should not be insulted. When they were alive who was more gentle than Cornelius, who more good natured than Anthony, more patient than John the Baptist? But what terrible diseases they send now if they are not, as you have heard, venerated properly."[120] Rabelais claims that popular preachers themselves told the congregations that St. Sebastian was the originator of the plague and St. Eutropius of dropsy (because of the phonetic similarity with *ydeopique*).[121] Henry Estienne also mentions such belief.[122]

The emotional and intellectual content of the veneration of saints had been defined to such a large extent by the colors and forms of the images that the direct aesthetic perception continuously threatened to cancel out the religious notion. Between the sight of the radiance of the gold, the scrupulously faithful description of the material of their clothing, the pious look of the eyes, and the living reality of the saints in the popular consciousness, there was hardly any room left for considering what the church permitted and what it prohibited as offerings of veneration and devotion to these splendid beings. The saints lived in the minds of the people as gods. It is not surprising that this danger to popular piety was feared in the concerned circles of the Windesheimers, who were seeking to maintain a proper faith; but it is also noticeable when the same idea strikes the mind of a superficial and banal court poet such as Eustace Deschamps, since he, in all his limitations, is such an excellent mirror of the intellectual life of his times.

> *Ne faictes pas les dieux d'argent*
> *D'or, de fust, de pierre ou d'arain,*
> *Qui font ydolatrer la gent . . .*
> *Car l'ouvrage est forme plaisant;*
> *Leur painture dont je me plain*
> *La beauté de l'or reluisant,*

THE DEPICTION OF THE SACRED 201

Font croire à maint peuple incertain
que ce soient dieu pour certain,
Et servent par pensées foles
Telz ymages qui font caroles
Es moustiers où trop en mettons;
C'est tres mal fait: a brief paroles,
Telz simulacres n'aourons.

. . . .

Prince, un Dieu croions seulement
Et aourons parfaictement
Aux champs, partout, car c'est raisons,
Non pas fautz dieux, fer n'ayment,
Pierres qui n'ont entendement:
Telz simulacres n'aourons.[123]*

Should we not regard the clamor for the veneration of angels as a conscious reaction against the veneration of saints? Living faith had crystalized too firmly in the veneration of saints; a need arose for a more fluid understanding of veneration and ideas about protection. These could attach themselves to the barely envisioned images of angels and could thus again become unmediated religious experience. It is again Gerson—this conscientious zealot for purity of faith—who repeatedly recommends the veneration of guardian angels.[124] But there arises again the dangerous preoccupation with details that could only damage the pious substance of this veneration. The "studiositas theologorum," says Gerson, raises a number of questions with respect to angels: whether they ever leave us, whether they know in advance if we will be elected or dammed, whether Christ or Mary had a guardian angel, and whether the Antichrist will have one. Whether our good angel can speak to our soul without the images of the imagination, whether they spur us

---

* Do not make gods of silver,/Of gold, of wood, of stone, or of bronze,/ That lead the people to idolatry . . ./Because the work has a pleasant shape;/ Their coloring of which I complain,/The beauty of shining gold,/Make many ignorant people believe/That these are God for certain,/And they serve by foolish thoughts/Such images as stand about/In churches where they place too many of them;/That is very ill done; in short,/Let us not adore such counterfeits./. . ./ Prince, let us believe in one God/And adore him to perfection/In the fields, everywhere, for this is right,/No false gods, of iron or stone,/Stones which have no understanding:/Let us not adore such counterfeits.

to do good just as the devil spurs us to do evil, whether they can see our thoughts. How numerous the questions are. These *studiositas,* Gerson concludes, belong to the theologians, but *curiositas* should be far removed from all those who should attend more to devotion than to subtle speculation.[125]

The Reformation, a century later, found the veneration of saints nearly defenseless at a time when it did not attack belief in witches and devils as such. It did not even attempt to do so because it itself was still caught up in that belief. Was not this caused by the fact that the veneration of saints had become *caput mortuum,* that everything in the veneration of saints had been expressed so completely in image, legend, and prayer that it was no longer sustained by gripping awe? The veneration of saints no longer had any roots in something unformed or unexpressed—roots in which demonic thought was strongly anchored. And when the Counter-Reformation cultivated anew a purified veneration of saints, it had to work on the mind with the gardener's knife of a more strict discipline so as to prune the all too luxuriant growth of the popular imagination.

Chapter Seven

THE PIOUS PERSONALITY

THE PEOPLE USUALLY LIVED IN THE LACKADAISICAL corruption of an entirely externalized religion. Their firm belief engendered both fear and delight, but the ordinary religious form did not involve the unsophisticated in any questions or spiritual struggles such as Protestantism was destined to do. A comfortable lack of religious awe and the complacencies of everyday life alternated with periods of the most intense displays of the passionate piety that spasmodically seized the people. The continuous contrast between the strong and weak states of religious tension cannot be explained by dividing the herd into two groups, the pious and children of the world, as if a part of the people consistently led lives of strict religiosity while others were only externally devout. Our perception of late medieval northern Dutch and lower German pietism could easily lead us to such mistaken conclusions. To be sure, pietist circles separated themselves from secular life in the *devotio moderna* of the Fraterhouses and the Windesheim convents and among them sustained religious tension became normal, but as pious people *par excellence* they formed a contrast to the large majority. France and the southern Netherlands, on the other hand, hardly experienced this phenomenon in the form of a movement at all. Yet here too, the emotions that were the basis of the *devotio moderna* had the same effect as in the calm lands along the Yssel. In the south, such a formal separation from secular life never occurred; passionate devotion remained a part of general religious life, but peaked, from time to time, in more intense and shorter outbursts. In our own time the same difference in temperament separates the Latin peoples from their northern neighbors; those in the south accept contradictions more readily. They feel less need to go the whole way and find it easier to combine the easy skeptical attitude of daily life with the high emotional stirrings of blessed moments.

The low esteem in which the clergy was held, which throughout the Middle Ages parallels the high veneration of the priestly estate, may be explained in part as the result of the worldly behavior of the higher clergy and the considerable loss in status of the lower clergy, or as the result of old pagan instincts. The mind of the people, only incompletely Christianized, had never quite lost its disgust for men who were not allowed to fight and had to be chaste. Knightly pride, rooted in courage and love, just like the crude mind of the people, rejected the spiritual. The corruption of the clergy contributed its share. For centuries the higher and lower estates alike had reveled in the figure of the unchaste monk and debauched fat clergyman. A latent hatred of the clergy had always existed. The more a preacher railed against the sins of his estate, the greater his appeal to the people.[1] As soon as a preacher attacks the clergy, we are told by Bernardinus of Siena, the audience is prone to forget everything else; there is no better way to keep the service lively at times when the congregation tends to get sleepy or uncomfortable because they are too warm or too cold. Instantly all those in attendance become wide-awake and in good spirits.[2] While, on the one hand, the dramatic religious movement caused by the itinerant popular preachers of the fourteenth and fifteenth centuries originated in the revival of the mendicant orders, on the the other hand, these same mendicants became the objects of ridicule because of their dissolute lifestyle. The unworthy priest of popular literature who, like a lowly servant, reads mass for three grooten or who serves as father confessor on a regular retainer, "pour absoudre du tout,"* is usually a mendicant monk.[3] Molinet, who is otherwise very pious in every respect, expresses the facile mockery directed at the mendicant orders in a New Year's wish:

> *Prions Dieu que les Jacobins*
> *Puissent manger les Augustins*
> *Et les Carmes soient pendus*
> *Des cordes des Frères Menus.*[4]†

* "in order to absolve everyone"

† We pray God that the Jacobins/Might eat the Augustinians/And that the Carmelites might be hung/With the cords of the Friars Minor.

The dogmatic conception of poverty that was incorporated in the mendicant orders was no longer intellectually satisfying. The formal symbolism of poverty as a spiritual idea had been replaced by the issue of real social misery. The new insight occurs towards the end of the fourteenth century in England, where, earlier than in other countries, eyes were opened to an appreciation of the economic factors in life. The author of that strangely dreamy and misty poem *The Vision Concerning Piers Plowman* is the first to focus on the troubles of the hardworking masses and, filled with hatred of the mendicants, of the idle, the wasteful, the phony cripples, of the *validi mendicantes,* who were the bane of the Middle Ages, to praise the sacred nature of ordinary labor. But even in the highest theological circles, some, such as Pierre d'Ailly, do not shy away from contrasting the *vere pauperes,* the truly poor, with the mendicant orders. There is no doubt that the serious approach to faith taken by the *devotio moderna* puts its adherents somewhat in contrast to the mendicant orders.

All we hear of day-to-day religious life shows abrupt alternations of nearly diametrically opposed extremes. The ridicule heaped on priests and monks and the hatred felt for them are merely the opposite side of a general and profound attachment and veneration. A naive perception of religious duties gives way just as quickly to an excess of devotion. In 1437, upon the return of the French king to his capital, there was a solemn service for the repose of the soul of the duke of Armagnac,[5] whose murder had begun the sad period of years just endured. The people flock to witness the occasion, but there is disappointment because no alms are distributed. The Burgher of Paris casually reports that nearly four thousand of those in attendance would not have gone if they had known that nothing was to be given out. "Et le maudirent qui avant prièrent pour lui."[6]* But these are the same Parisians who shed floods of tears at the numerous processions and squirm at the words of itinerant preachers. Ghillebert de Lannoy, when in Rotterdam, saw a riot calmed by a priest who held up the Corpus Domine.[7]

The great contradictions and the strong shifts in religious tension are as well revealed in the lives of the educated as they are in the lives of the ignorant masses. Religious illumination comes time and

---

* "and they who had earlier prayed for him now cursed him."

again with the force of a sudden blow. It is always a watered-down repetition of the experience of St. Francis when he took the words of the gospels to be direct orders. A knight heard the reading of the baptismal formula for perhaps the twentieth time, but suddenly realized the full sanctity and wonderful utility of the words and resolved to turn the Devil away, without making the sign of the cross, merely by remembering his own baptism.[8] —Le Jouvencel witnesses a duel. The parties stand ready to swear the justice of their cause on the Host. Suddenly the knight realizes the absolute necessity that one of the oaths must be false, that one of the two must of necessity be damned, and says, Don't swear. Fight for a stake of five hundred schillings, but don't take an oath.[9]

The piety of the upper crust, with their heavy load of excessive ostentation and pleasure seeking, has, for that reason, something of a forced quality, like that found in the piety of the people. Charles V of France is wont to abandon a hunt just as it reaches its most exciting moment in order to attend a mass.[10] The young Anne of Burgundy, the bride of Bedford, the English regent in conquered France, angers the Burgher of Paris on one occasion by splashing excrement on a procession during one of her wild outings on horseback. On another occasion, however, she leaves the gay festivities of the court at midnight in order to hear matins with Celestine nuns. Her early death was caused by an illness she contracted during a visit to the poor sick in the Hotel Dieu.[11]

The contrast between piety and sinfulness are found in their puzzling extremes in the person of Louis d'Orléans, who, among the prominent servants of luxury and indulgence, was the most overindulged and passionate man in the world. He had even taken up witchcraft and refused to recant.[12] This same Orléans is, nonetheless, so devout that he has a cell in the regular dormitory of the Celestines where he participates in the cloistered life, hears matins at midnight and, on occasion, mass five or six times a day.[13] There is a cruel mixture of religion and crime in the life of Gilles de Rais, who, in the middle of his murder of children at Machecoul, sponsored a service in honor of the Blessed Innocents for the bliss of his soul. He was astonished when his judges accused him of heresy. Many join piety with less bloody sins; there are many examples of devout worldliness: the barbaric Gaston Phébus, Count of Foix; the frivolous King René; the refined Charles d'Orléans. John of Bavaria, most feared and most ambitious, pays a visit in disguise to Lidwina van Schiedam, to consult about the state of his soul.[14] Jean Coustain, the traitorous servant of Philip the Good, a godless man who hardly ever attended mass and never gave alms, when in the hands of his executioner gave himself to God in a passionate plea voiced in his coarse Burgundian dialect.[15]

Philip the Good, himself, is one of the most striking examples of the intertwining of piety and worldliness. This man of extravagant festivities and numerous bastards, of political calculation, of tremendous pride and rage, is an earnest pietist. He remains on his knees long after mass is over. For four days a week, and during all the vigils of Our Lady and the apostles, he fasts on bread and water. Sometimes he does not eat anything until four in the afternoon. He gives many alms, always secretly.[16] After the surprise attack on Luxembourg he remained so long after mass immersed in his breviary and, after that, in special prayers of thanksgiving, that his entourage, waiting on horseback because the battle was not over, became impatient: the duke, they insisted, could easily make up saying his Our Fathers at another time. Warned that delay was dangerous, the duke responded merely, "Si Dieu m'a donné victoire, il la me gardera."[17]*

We should not see hypocrisy or conceited bigotry in all this, but rather a state of tension between two spiritual poles that is no longer possible for the modern mind. For them, it is possible because of the perfect dualism between the sinful world and the Kingdom of God. In the medieval mind, all the higher, purer feelings were absorbed by religion so that the natural and sensuous drives were bound to be consciously rejected and allowed to sink to the level of sinful worldliness. Two views of life took shape side by side in the medieval mind: the piously ascetic view that pulled all ethical conceptions into itself and the worldly mentality, completely left to the devil, that took revenge with ever greater abandon. If one of the two dominates, then one encounters either saints or dissolute sinners. As a rule, they remain in balance, although the scales oscillate violently. One sees passionate human beings come into view whose fully blooming sinfulness makes their overflowing pity break out all the more vehemently.

When we observe how medieval poets compose the most pious songs of praise alongside all kinds of profane and obscene pieces,

---

* "If God wants to give me the victory, He will keep it for me."

as do so many poets, such as Deschamps, Antoine de la Salle, and Jean Molinet, then we have even less cause to attribute these productions to hypothetical periods of worldliness and introspection as we do in the case of modern poets. The contradiction, no matter how incomprehensible to us, must be accepted.

There occur bizarre blends of the love of ostentation and strong devotion. The unrestrained desire to decorate and depict all aspects of life and thought with colorful embellishments and forms is not limited to the overburdening of religion with paintings, the work of the goldsmith, and sculpture. Even spiritual life itself is occasionally embellished because of the hunger for color and glamor. Brother Thomas complains bitterly of all the luxury and ostentation, but the platform from which he speaks has been draped by the people with the most splendid tapestries that could be found.[18] Philipe de Mézières is the perfect type of the splendor-loving pietist. He decided the most minute details of the clothing for the Order of the Passion that he intended to found. The object of his dream resembles a festival of color. The knights should wear red, green, scarlet, or azure depending on their rank; the Grand Master, white. White was also the color of the ceremonial dress. The cross should be red, the belts of leather or silk with horn buckles and ornaments of gilded brass. Boots were to be black and capes red. The dress of the brothers, servants, priests, and women were also described.[19] Nothing came of the order; Philippe de Mézières remained all his life the great dreamer of crusades and maker of plans. But in the cloister of the Celestines in Paris he found the place that could satisfy him; as strict as the order was, so the church and cloister sparkled with gold and precious stones, a mausoleum for princes and princesses.[20] Christine de Pisan regarded this church as beauty perfected. Mézières spent some time there as a lay brother, took part in the strict life of the cloister, but remained at the same time in contact with the great lords and artistic minds of his time; a mundane artistic counterpart to Gerard Groote.[21] His princely friend Orléans was also attracted to this place, where he found the moments of reflection that punctuated his debauched life, and there too, he found his early grave. It is certainly no accident that those two lovers of splendor Louis d'Orléans and his uncle Philip the Bold of Burgundy chose as the places to indulge their love of art the houses of the strictest cloistered orders, where the contrast between the lives of the monks and the splendor of the decorations could be felt most strongly: Orléans in those of the Celestines, Burgundy in those of the Carthusians at Champmol near Dijon.

Old King René discovered a hermit while on a hunt near Angers: a priest who had given up his sinecure and lived on black bread and berries. The king was moved by his virtue and had a hut and small chapel built for him. For himself, he made a garden and built a modest garden house, which he decorated with paintings and allegories. He frequently went to "son cher ermitage de Reculée"* to converse with his artists and scholars.[22] Is this medieval, is it Renaissance, or is it not eighteenth century?

A duke of Savoy becomes a hermit with a gilded belt, red cap, golden cross, and good wine.[23]

It is only a step from that devotional splendor to expressions of hyperbolic humility, which in turn are themselves full-fledged extravagance. Olivier de la Marche retained from his boyhood memories the arrival of King Jacques de Bourbon of Naples, who, under the influence of the saintly Colette, had renounced the world. The king, shabbily dressed, was carried in a cart, "telle sans aultre difference que les civieres en quoy l'on porte les fiens et les ordures communement." Behind came an elegant courtly escort. "Et ouys racompter et dire"—says La Marche, full of admiration—"que en toutes les villes où il venoit, il faisoit semblables entrées par humilité."[24]†

Such picturesque self-deprecation is not found in the prescriptions, recommended by many holy examples, for funerals, which are expected to be fitting representations of the deceased's unworthiness. The holy Pierre Thomas, bosom friend and spiritual teacher of Philippe de Mézières, feeling his approaching death, had himself put in a sack, a rope put around his neck and placed on the ground. This was his imitation, much exaggerated, of St. Francis, who had himself put on the ground as he lay dying. Bury me, said Pierre Thomas, in the entrance to the choir, if possible, so that everyone will have to step on my body, even goats and dogs.[25] Mézières, his admiring disciple, takes his turn at outdoing his master in fantastic humility. A heavy iron chain is to be put around

* "his dear hermitage of Reculée"
† "not differing from the barrows in which dung and ordure are usually carried . . . and I have heard it recounted and said . . . that in all towns where he came, he made similar entries out of humility."

his neck during his last hours. As soon as he has given up the ghost, he is to be dragged by his feet, naked, to the choir. There he is to be left until his burial with his arms spread in the form of a cross, tied with three ropes to a board that is to take the place of an expensively ornamented coffin upon which someone might have been tempted to paint his vain worldly motto, "se Dieu l'eust tant hay qu'il fust mors ès cours des princes de ce monde."* The board, covered with two ells of canvas or coarse black linen, is to be dragged in the same manner to the burial pit into which the naked body of the poor pilgrim is to be thrown as it is. A small grave marker is to be erected. Only his good friend in God, Martin, and the executors of his last will are to be notified of his death.

It is almost self-evident that a mind given so much to protocol and ceremony and the ever fashioning of new plans with greater and greater details would leave many testaments. There is no mention, in the later documents, of the provisions of 1392 and when he died in 1405 he was given an ordinary funeral, dressed in the garb of his beloved Celestine order; there were two tomb inscriptions, which most likely were composed by him.[26]

To the ideal of holiness, one could almost say to the romanticism of holiness, the fifteenth century did not yet contribute anything that heralded the new age. Even the Renaissance did not change the ideal of holiness. Unaffected by the strong currents guiding culture into new paths, the ideal of holiness remained, both before and after the great crisis of the Reformation, what it always was. The saint is as timeless as the mystic. The types of saints in the Counter-Reformation are the same as those of the later Middle Ages, and these do not differ in any special way from those of the earlier Middle Ages. There are, in the one or the other period, some who are great activists, saints of the fiery word or the passionately inspired deed: including, on the one hand, such as Ignatius Loyola, Francis Xavier, and Karl Borromeus; on the other, Bernardine of Sienna, Vincent Ferrer, and John of Capistrano. These are joined by the mystics who find rapture in contemplation, similar to the types of saints found in Islam and Buddhism, Aloysius Gonzaga in the sixteenth century; Francis de Paola, Colette, and Peter of Luxembourg in the fourteenth and fifteenth centuries. Between

---

* "if God had hated him so much that he let him die at the court of princes of this world."

these two types are all those who share something of both extremes; as a matter of fact, they may on occasion even combine these extreme characteristics in their highest degree.

It might even be possible to place the romanticism of saintliness on an equal footing with the romanticism of knighthood; both arise from a need to realize certain aspects of an ideal life form in the life of an individual or in literature. It is remarkable that the romanticism of holiness has at all times taken much more delight in the fantastically exciting extremes of abstinence and humility than in great elevating deeds of religious culture. Holiness is not attained by churchly social service, no matter how great, but rather through wondrous piety. The great energetic figures only gain a holy reputation when their deeds are bathed in the glow of the supernatural. This rules out Nicholas of Cusa, but not his fellow spirit, Denis the Carthusian.[27]

In this context, it is of greatest interest for us to observe how the circles of refined splendor, those circles that venerated the knightly ideal and continued to do so after the Middle Ages were over, dealt with the ideal of holiness. Though their contacts with this ideal form were not so numerous, they did occur. The princely circles managed a few times to produce a saint. One of these is Charles de Blois. On his mother's side he sprang from the house of Valois and, through his marriage with the heir of the Bretagne, Jeanne de Penthièvre, became involved in a dispute about succession that took the greater part of his life. Under the terms of his marriage contract, he was obligated to adopt the coat of arms and battle cry of the dukedom. He found himself confronted by another pretender, Jean de Montfort, and the ensuing conflict over the Bretagne coincided with the beginning of the Hundred Years War. The defense of Montfort's claim was one of the complications that prompted Edward III to come to France. The count of Blois accepted battle like a true knight and fought as well as the best leaders of his time. Taken prisoner in 1347, just prior to the siege of Calais, he was held in England until 1356. He resumed the fight for the dukedom in 1362 and was killed in 1364 near Aurai while fighting bravely at the side of Bertrand du Guesclin and Beaumanoir.

This war hero, whose life differed in none of its external features from those of so many princely pretenders and leaders of his time, had led a life of strict austerity since the days of his youth. When he was a boy, his father had kept him away from edifying books because such books would be inappropriate for someone of his calling. He slept on straw on the ground next to the bed of his wife, and a hair shirt was found under his armor at the time of his death in battle. He took confession each evening before going to bed, because, as he said, no Christian should go to sleep with his sins unforgiven. During his captivity in London, he was wont to visit cemeteries and, on his knees, recite the *De profundis*. The Breton page whom he asked to recite the responses refused, arguing that these locations were the burial grounds of those who had killed his parents and friends and had burned their houses.

After his liberation, he intends to walk barefoot from La Roche-Derrien, where he began his imprisonment, to Tréguier, the site of a shrine of St. Ives, the patron of the Bretagne, whose biography he had written while a captive. The people hear about his plans and strew his path with straw and blankets. The count of Blois, however, takes a different route and ends up with feet so sore that he cannot walk for fifteen weeks.[28] Immediately following his death, his princely relatives, among them his brother-in-law, Louis of Anjou, attempt to have him canonized. The proceedings, which resulted in beatification, took place in Angers in the year 1371.

The strange thing, if we can rely on Froissart, is that this same Charles de Blois had a bastard. "Là fu occis en bon couvenant li dis messires Charles de Blois, le viaire sus ses ennemis, et uns siens filz bastars qui s'appeloit messires Jehans de Blois, et pluiseur aultre chevalier et escuier de Bretagne."[29]* Are we to reject this as an evident falsehood?[30] Or should we assume that the combination of pity and sensuality that was present in figures such as Louis d'Orléans and Philip the Good was even more noticeably present in the count de Blois?

Such a question does not arise about the life of another nobleman of that time, Pierre of Luxembourg. This scion of the house of the Dukes of Luxembourg, which during the fourteenth century held such a respectable place in the German empire as well as in the courts of France and Burgundy, is a fitting example of what William James calls "the under-witted saint,"[31] whose narrow mind can only exist in a fearfully closed-in little world of pious thinking.

---

* "There was killed in good style the aforesaid Lord Charles of Blois, with his face to the enemy, and a bastard son of his called Jehans de Blois, and several other knights and squires of Brittany."

He was born in 1369, not long before his father was killed in the fighting near Baesweiler (1371) between Brabant and Geldern. His spiritual history takes us back again to the cloister of the Celestines in Paris, where the eight-year-old boy came in contact with Philippe de Mézières. He was already overburdened with church offices as a mere boy, first with different cathedral sinecures, and then, at the age of fifteen, with the Bishopric of Metz and still later with a cardinalship. He died in 1387, not yet eighteen, and Avignon immediately went to work to secure his canonization. The most important authorities were pressed into service for this task: The King of France issued the petition and it was supported by the cathedral chapter of Paris and by the University of Paris. During the proceedings of 1389 the greatest notables of France appeared as witnesses: Pierre's brother André of Luxembourg, Louis of Bourbon, and Enguerrand de Coucy. Owing to the negligence of the Avignon pope, sainthood was not bestowed (beatitude was proclaimed in 1527), but the veneration justified by the petition had been recognized long before this and developed without interference. At the spot in Avignon where the body was buried and where daily the most remarkable miracles were reported, the king founded a Celestine monastery in imitation of the monastery in Paris that was the preferred sanctuary of the princely circles in those days. The dukes of Orléans, Berry and Burgundy, came to lay the first stones for the king.[32] Pierre Salmon tells us how he heard mass in the chapel of the holy one a few years later.[33]

There is something pitiful about the image of the princely ascetic who died so young, conveyed by the witnesses during the proceedings about his canonization. Peter of Luxembourg was an unusually tall boy, sickly, who even as a child knew nothing but the seriousness of a fearful and strict faith. He reproached his little brother who had laughed, because while it was written that Our Lord had cried, it was not recorded that he ever laughed. "Douls, courtois et debonnaire," Froissart calls him, "vierge de son corps, moult large aumosnier. Le plus du jour et de la nuit il estoit en orisons. En toute sa vye il n'y ot fors humilité."[34]* Initially his aristocratic elders attempted to make him give up his world-renouncing plans.

---

* "Sweet, courteous and debonair . . . virgin as to body, a great giver of alms. The greater part of the day and the night he spent in prayer. And in all his life there was nothing but humility."

When he spoke about his desire to become an itinerant priest, he was told, you are much too tall; everyone would instantly recognize you and you wouldn't be able to stand the cold. How could you preach in favor of a crusade? For a moment we hear the groundtone of that small, rigid mind: "Je vous bien," says Peter, "qu'on me veut faire venir de bonne voye à la malvaise: certes, certes, si je m'y mets, je feray tant que tout le monde parlera de moy."* Sire, responds Master Jean de Marche, his confessor, there is no one who wants you to do evil, only good.

It is evident that the noble relatives begin to feel admiration and pride about the case once the ascetic inclinations of the youngster prove to be irrevocable. A saint, and such a young saint, of their kind and dwelling among them! Try to imagine the poor sickly youth weighed down by the burden of church offices, living in the midst of the extravagant splendor and arrogance of the court life of Berry and Burgundy, himself covered with dirt and parasites and always concerned with his small miserable sins. Confession itself became a bad habit with him. Every day he recorded his sins on a piece of paper and, when prevented from doing so on a journey, he made up for it by long hours spent recording sins after the travels were completed. He was observed writing at night and checking his list by candlelight. He would get up in darkness to take confession from one of his chaplains. Sometimes he knocked in vain at the door of their chambers; they pretended to be deaf. If admitted, he would read his sins from his note sheets. These confessions increased from two or three times a week to twice a day as he approached the end. During his final days his confessor was not allowed to leave his side. He finally died of consumption and having asked to be buried like a pauper, a whole box full of pieces of paper was found on which the sins of his little life had been recorded day by day.[35]

There is yet another case that provides evidence illuminating the relationship between court circles and saintliness: the stay of Saint Francis of Paola at the court of Louis XI. The particular type of piousness of the king is so well known that there is no need to describe it in detail at this point. Louis, "qui achetoit la grace de

---

* "I see well . . . that you want to lead me from the right road to the bad; but assuredly, if once I enter on it, I shall do so much that the whole world will talk of me."

Dieu et de la Vierge Marie á plus grans deniers que oncques ne fist roy,"[36]* shows all the qualities of the most overt and complacent fetishism. His veneration for relics and passion for pilgrimages and processions seems to lack any of the higher impulses and any shadow of awed restraint. He treats sacred objects as if they were expensive home remedies. The cross of St. Laud that was kept in Angers had to be brought to Nantes for no other purpose than to have an oath taken on it.[37] An oath on the cross of St. Laud counted more to Louis than any other oath. When the *connétable* of Saint Pol is called into the presence of the king and asks the king to swear to his safety on the cross of St Laud, the king responds, any oath but that one.[38] When his end, which he feared above all other things, approaches, the most precious relics are sent to him from everywhere. The pope sends him, among other things, the *corporale* of St. Peter himself; even the Great Turk offers a collection of relics that were still in Constantinople. On the buffet next to the king's sickbed is the sacred Ampoule itself, which had been brought from Reims, from whence it had never been removed before. Some said that the king wanted to test the efficacy of the container of ointment by having his whole body salved.[39] Such religious impulses are usually found only in the history of the Merovingians.

It is hardly possible to draw a line between Louis's passion for collecting exotic animals such as reindeer and elands and his passion for precious relics. He corresponds with Lorenzo de'Medici about the ring of Saint Zanobi, a local Florentine saint, and about an "agnus dei," the plant-like growth also known as "agnus scythicus," which was regarded as an exotic rarity.[40] In the strange household in the castle of Plessis lès Tours during Louis's last days one could find pious intercessors and musicians wandering about together. "At this time the king had a large number of musicians come with their strings and wood-winds. He provided quarters for them in Saint-Cosme near Tours. Some 120 of them gathered there, among them many shepherds from around Poitou. Sometimes they played in front of the royal apartments, but without seeing the king. The king was not only to enjoy the aforementioned instruments in order to pass the time, they were also intended to keep him awake. He also summoned a large number of bigots,

---

* "who bought the grace of God and of the Virgin Mary for more money than ever king did"

both male and female, and devotees, hermits and saintly people, to come and pray to God without interruption that the king might not die, but go on living."[41]

Even Saint Francis of Paola, the Calabrian hermit, who managed to outdo the humility of the Minorites by founding the Minims, became, in a literal sense, the object of Louis's collecting mania. During his final illness, the king summoned the saint with the expressed intent that the prayers of the saint might prolong his life.[42] After several messages to the King of Naples had not borne fruit, the king, through diplomatically intervening with the pope, managed to secure the arrival, very much against Francis's will, of the miracle man. A noble entourage accompanied the monk from Italy.[43] —But when he arrived, Louis was not convinced of his authenticity, "because he had been cheated by several persons operating under the pretense of saintliness." Following suggestions from his personal physician, he had the holy man kept under surveillance and had his virtue tested in a variety of ways.[44] The saint passed all tests with distinction. His asceticism was of the most barbaric kind, reminiscent of the practices of his countrymen of the tenth century, St. Niles and St. Romauld. He flees at the sight of a woman. He has not touched a coin since he was a boy. He usually sleeps standing up or leaning on something; he never has his hair cut or his beard shaved. He never eats meat and is served only roots.[45] The king is still personally engaged during his last month in writing to secure proper food for his strange holy man: "Monsieur de Genas, je vous prie de m'envoyer des citrons et des oranges douces et des poires muscadelles et des pastenargues, et c'est pour le saint homme qui ne mange ny chair ny poisson: et vous me ferés ung fort grant plaisir."[46]* He never refers to him other than as "le saint homme," so that Commines, who met the saint on several occasions, does not seem to have known his name.[47] But he was also called "le saint homme" by those who ridiculed the arrival of this weird guest or did not believe in his holiness, such as, for instance, the king's physician, Jacques Coitier.[48] Commines couches his reports in terms of sober reservations. "Il est encores vif," he concludes, "par quoy se pourrait bien changer ou en my-

---

* "Monsieur de Genas, I beg you to send me lemons and sweet oranges, and muscatel pears, and parsnips, and it is for the holy man who eats neither flesh nor fish; and you will do me a very great favor."

eulx ou in pis, par quoy me tays, pour se que plusieurs se moc-
quoient de la venue de ce hermite, qu'ilz appelloient 'sainct
homme.' "* However, Commines himself testifies that no one had
seen "de si saincte vie, ne où il semblast myeulx que le Sainct
Esperit parlast par sa bouche."† And the learned theologians of
Paris, Jan Standonck and Jean Quintin, who had been dispatched
to talk to the saintly man about founding a convent of Minims in
Paris, were most profoundly moved and returned to Paris cured
of their prejudices.[49]

The interest the dukes of Burgundy take in the saints of their
time is less self-seeking than that displayed by Louis XI in Saint
Francis of Paola. It is noticeable that more than one of the great
visionaries and ascetics regularly appears as intermediary or adviser
in political matters. This is the case with St. Colette, the blessed
Denis of Ryckel and the Carthusian. Colette was treated by the
house of Burgundy with particular distinction; Philip the Good and
his mother, Margarita of Bavaria, knew her personally and sought
her advice.[50] She negotiated complicated matters between the
houses of France, Savoy, and Burgundy. Charles the Bold, Mary
and Maximilian, and Margaret of Austria repeatedly pressed for
her canonization. More important yet is the role played by Denis
the Carthusian in the public life of his time. He, too, was in repeated contact with the house of Burgundy and acted as adviser to
Philip the Good. Along with Cardinal Nicholas of Cusa, whom
he had accompanied on his famous journey throughout the German
empire, he was received, in 1451, by the duke in Brussels. Denis,
who is constantly depressed by the feeling that things are going
badly for the church and Christendom and that the great calamity
is imminent, asks in a vision, Lord, will the Turks reach Rome?
He reminds the duke of the crusade.[51] The "inclytus devotus ac
optimus princeps et dux,"‡ to whom he dedicates his tract on the
princely life, cannot be anyone other than Philip. Charles the Bold
joins Denis in his efforts to found a Carthusian house at Hertogen-

---

* "He is still alive . . . so that he may well change, for the better or for the
worst, so that I shall be silent, as many mocked at the arrival of this hermit,
whom they called 'holy man.' "

† "of such saintly life, nor one in whom the Holy Spirit seemed more to speak
through his mouth."

‡ "famous pious man and greatest prince and duke,"

bosch in honor of St. Sophia of Constantinople, whom the duke understandably regards as a saint whereas she is really the figure of eternal wisdom.[52] Duke Arnold of Geldern asks Denis for advice about his quarrel with his son Adolf.[53]

Not only princes, but also numerous noblemen, clerics, and burghers came for advice to his cell at Roermond; he was constantly busy resolving innumerable difficulties, doubts and questions of conscience.

Denis the Carthusian is the perfect type of the powerful religious enthusiast produced by the waning Middle Ages. His life was incredibly energetic; he combined the ecstasies of the great mystics, the wildest asceticism, the continuous visions and revelations of a spiritual seer with a vast activity as a theological writer and practical spiritual adviser. He was as close to the great mystics as he was to the practical Windesheimers such as Brugman, for whom he writes his famous guide for the Christian life,[54] or to Nicholas of Cusa or even to the witch hunters or those who enthusiastically labored for the abolition of clerical abuses.[55] His energies must have been inexhaustible. His writings fill forty-five quarto volumes. It is as if through him the entire stream of medieval theology flows once again. "Qui Dionysium legit, nihil non legit"* was said by the theologians of the sixteenth century. Responding to a request from an old lay brother, Willem, he writes about the mutual recognition of souls in the hereafter with the same touch with which he handles the most profound questions of a philosophical nature. He promises Brother Willem that he will write as simply as possible and says that Willem can translate it into Dutch.[56] Everything his great predecessors had thought, he expresses in an endless flood of simply expressed thoughts. It has all the characteristics of a late work: summarizing, concluding, breaking no new ground. The quotations from Bernard of Clairvaux or Hugo of Saint Victor sparkle like jewels on the simple unicolor garment of Denis's prose. All of his works were written, proofread, improved, indexed, and illuminated by himself until at the end of his life he ended his writing with a well-chosen quotation: "Ad securae taciturnitatis portum me transferre intendo,—I will go now to the haven of secure taciturnity."[57]

He knew no rest. Daily he recited nearly all the Psalms; at least

* "He who reads Dionysius, has read everything."

half are necessary, he declares. During every activity, dressing and undressing, he prays. After midnight mass, when others go to rest, he remains awake. He is strong and tall and his body can withstand everything. I have an iron head and a copper stomach, he says. Without disgust, indeed by preference, he enjoys spoiled food, such as wormy butter, cherries partially consumed by snails; these kinds of parasites have no deadly poisons, he says, one can eat them with confidence. He hangs oversalted herrings out until they rot; I would rather eat food that stinks than that which is too salty.[58]

He accomplishes the entire mental work of the deepest philosophical speculation and definition, not in the context of an even-tempered and undisturbed scholarly life, but with a mind subject to the constant upheavals of receptiveness to every dramatic stirring of the supernatural. As a boy he got up by the light of the moon because he thought it was time to go to school.[59] He stutters; he is called "Taterbek" by a devil whom he tried to exorcise. He sees that the room of the dying Lady of Vlodrop is full of devils; they knock his stick out of his hand. No one has experienced the dread of the "Four Last Things" to the extent he has. The violent attacks of the devil upon the dying is a repeated subject of his sermons. He constantly communicates with the deceased. Have spirits often appeared to him? asks one of the brothers. O, hundreds and hundreds of times, he answers. He sees his father in Purgatory and resists the impulse to free him. He is constantly confronted by apparitions, revelations, and visions, but is reluctant to speak about them. He is ashamed of the ecstasies he experiences as a result of external stimuli: above all music, which sometimes seizes him in the midst of a noble gathering listening to his wisdom and exhortations. Among the honorary names of the great theologians, his is Doctor Ecstaticus.

We should not think that such a great figure as Denis the Carthusian was spared the sort of suspicions and ridicule heaped on the strange miracle man of Louis XI. He, too, had to wage a constant battle against the denunciations and mockeries of the world. In the mentality of the fifteenth century we already see the stirrings of resentment and rejection of the highest expressions of medieval faith; stirrings that exist side by side with unrestrained devotion and enthusiasm.

Chapter Eight

RELIGIOUS EXCITATION
AND RELIGIOUS FANTASY

FROM THE TIME IN THE TWELFTH CENTURY WHEN the lyrical mysticism of Bernard of Clairvaux had begun the fugue of flowering emotion over the passion of Christ, the medieval mind came in ever increasing measure to be filled with devout empathy with the story of his passion; consciousness was entirely permeated and saturated with Christ and the Cross. In earliest childhood the image of the Crucifixion was planted in tender minds in such large and somber dimensions that it overshadowed all other emotion with its dark mood. When still a child, Jean de Gerson was told by his father, who was standing in front of a wall with his arms outspread, "Look, my boy, here is how your God, who created and saved you, was crucified and died." The image remained etched in his memory even in old age, and he blessed his pious father for it on the day of his father's death, which fell on the feast of the Exaltation of the Cross.[1] Colette, when a child four years of age, heard her mother weep and sigh during her daily prayers as she vicariously suffered the mockery, the beatings, and the martyrdom of the Passion. The memory of these prayers became fixed in her oversensitive mind with such intensity that she experienced daily throughout her whole life a most intense tightening and pain in her heart at the hour of the Crucifixion. She suffered more than any woman in childbirth during the times she was reading about the sufferings of the Lord.[2] A preacher might occasionally stand silently in front of his congregation, in the position of the crucified Lord, for a quarter of an hour.[3]

The mind was filled with Christ to such a degree that the Christological note immediately began to sound whenever any act or thought showed even the slightest congruence with the life or suffering of the Lord. A poor nun who carries firewood to the kitchen imagines that she is carrying the Cross. The notion of carrying wood by itself is enough to bathe the activity in the bright glow of the highest act of love. A blind woman, washing her laundry, imagines the washtub and washroom to be the manger and the stable.[4] The profaning overflow of princely homage into religious ideas, such as the comparison of Louis XI with Jesus or of the Emperor and his son and grandson with the Trinity,[5] was equally the result of that overabundance of devotional content.

The fifteenth century displays this strong religious emotion in a dual form. On the one side it reveals itself in those vehement moments when an itinerant preacher periodically seizes a whole crowd with his words, igniting all that spiritual fuel like dry tinder. This is the spasmodic expression of that Christological emotion: passionate, intense, but highly transitory. The other aspect is shown by a few individuals who lead their sensitivity into a path of eternal quietude and normalize it into a new life form, that of introspectiveness. This is the pietistic circle of those who, fully conscious of being innovators, call themselves the Modern Devotees, that is contemporary people of piety. As a formal movement the *devotio moderna* is restricted to the northern Netherlands and lower Germany, but the spirit that gave rise to it also existed in France.

Little remains to us of the forceful impact of the sermon on spiritual culture. We know what tremendous influence preachers had,[6] but it is not granted to us to relive the actual excitement they generated. The written versions of sermons do not touch our hearts; how could they? The people of the time had already become indifferent to the written versions. Many who heard Vincent Ferrer and then read his sermons, says his biographer, assure us that they are barely a shadow of what they experienced when they heard them out of his own mouth.[7] No wonder. What we have in the printed sermons of Vincent Ferrer or Olivier Maillard[8] is barely more than the basic material used by their eloquence, stripped of all oratorical heat and apparently formal in their divisions into sections, first, seventh, etc. We know that the people were always moved by the gripping account of the terror of hell, by the thundering threats of the punishment of sin, and by all the lyrical outpourings about the Passion story and God's love. We know the devices employed by the preachers; no effect was too crude, no change from laughter to tears too abrupt, no intemperate raising of the voice too crass.[9] But we really have to guess about the kinds of excitement they generated on the basis of always identical reports about quarrels between cities over who would have the favor of the next sermon and over the ostentation, usually reserved for princes, lavished by the officials and the people on the procession welcoming the preacher into the city; and about how the preacher would occasionally have to interrupt his sermon because of the weeping of the crowd. During a sermon by Vincent Ferrer, a man and a woman under sentence of death were led past the site. Vincent asked that the execution be delayed, hid the pair beneath his pulpit for the duration, and preached about their sins. After the sermon, nothing was found beneath the pulpit but a few bones. The people believed nothing but that the words of the saintly man had burnt the sinners and at the same time saved them.[10]

The tense emotions of the masses as they listened to the words of the preacher always evaporated without a chance of becoming a part of the written tradition, but the "introspectiveness" of the modern devotion we know much better. In every pietist circle, religion not only supplies the form of life, but also the forms of its socialization: the cozy spiritual intercourse in quiet intimacy between simple men and women whose vast heaven covered a tiny world over which sweeps the mighty rustle of eternity. The friends of Thomas à Kempis admire his ignorance of mundane things; a prior of Windesheim is given the complimentary nickname Jan I-Don't-Know. They have no use for the world unless it is simplified; they purify it by excluding evil.[11] Within this narrow sphere, they live in the joy of a sensitive mutual fondness. They keep one another in constant view so that all the signs of blessedness can be detected; visits are their delight,[12] hence their special inclination towards biographical description to which we owe our detailed knowledge of their spiritual state.

In the regulated form in the Netherlands, the *devotio moderna* created a strong conventional form for the pious life. Devotees were recognized by their calm, measured motions, their stooped way of walking, some by the broad smile on their face or their new clothes that were intentionally patched. Not least of all, there were their copious tears: "Devotio est quaedam cordis teneritudo, qua quis in pias faciliter resolvitur lacrimas." — Devotion is a certain tenderness of the heart that allows an individual to easily dissolve in tears. One has to ask God for the "daily baptism of tears," they are the wings of prayer or, in the words of St. Bernard, the wine of angels. One should surrender to the bliss of praiseworthy tears, should be ready for them, and encourage them, throughout the year, but especially during Lent, so that one will be able to say with the Psalmist, "Fuerunt mihi lacrimae meae panes die ac nocte." Sometimes tears come so readily that we pray with sighs and wailing ("ita ut suspiriose ac cum rugitu oremus"), but if they do not come of themselves, one should not squeeze them out too hard, but be satisfied with the tears of the heart. In the presence of others, the signs of an unusual spiritual devotion should be avoided.[13]

Vincent Ferrer shed so many tears every time he celebrated mass that nearly all those present wept with him and occasionally produced a wailing like that over a death. Weeping was such a joy to him that he was reluctant to withhold his tears.[14]

In France the new pietism did not experience such a strange forcing into a particular form such as that of the Dutch Fraterhouses or Windesheim Congregations. Related spirits in France either remained in the secular world or joined existing orders where the new pietism did then gradually lead to the implementation of a stricter observance. In France, the phenomenon is not widely known among bourgeois circles. This may have accounted for the fact that French piety had a more passionate, spasmodic character than its Dutch counterpart. It resorted more readily to exaggerated forms but also evaporated more easily. Towards the end of the Middle Ages, visitors from more southern regions to the northern Netherlands notice on more than one occasion the serious and general piety that they observe to be a special characteristic of the people of this country.[15]

Dutch devotees abandoned the contact with intensive mysticism that had been characteristic of the initial stages of their life form and along with that abandonment they managed to keep dangerous and fantastic heretical deviations in check. Dutch modern devotion was obedient and orthodox, practical, decent and occasionally even sensible. In contrast, French devotion seems to have oscillated much more widely, touching time and again on the more extravagant phenomena of faith.

When the Groningen Dominican Mattheus Grabow went to Constance to present to the council all the complaints of the mendicant orders against the new Brothers of the Common Life and, if possible, to get them condemned, it was in the great leader of conservative church politics, Jean de Gerson himself, that the disciples of Gerard Groote found their defender. Gerson was completely competent to judge whether this was an expression of genuine piety and a permitted form of organization, since the distinction between genuine piety and exaggerated expressions of faith was one of those points to which he was constantly attentive. Gerson had a cautious, conscientious, academic mind, honest, pure, and of good will. He had a cautious concern for good form that frequently betrayed the fact that his fine mind had risen from its humble origin to its truly aristocratic reputation. Moreover, he was a psychologist and had a sense of style. As we know, sense of style and orthodoxy are most intimately related. Small wonder that the contemporary expressions of the life of faith repeatedly aroused his suspicion and concern. It is strange that the types of piety of which he disapproved as exaggerated and dangerous strongly remind us of the modern devotion that he defended. But this is understandable. His French sheep lacked a secure sheepfold, a discipline and organization that would hold all those zealous believers within the borders of what the church could tolerate.

Gerson saw the dangers of popular devotion everywhere. He considered it a mistake to take mysticism into the street.[16] The world, he says, is in the last period shortly before the end and, like a demented old man, is victimized by all kinds of fantasies, visions, and illusions, which make many individuals stray from the truth.[17] Lacking proper guidance, many succumb to all too strict fasts, all too extended vigils, and superfluous tears with which they cloud their brains. They turn a deaf ear to admonitions for moderation. Let them be on guard, because they can easily fall victim to the Devil's delusions. A short time ago, he had visited a wife and mother in Arras who, against the wishes of her husband, engaged in total fasts that lasted two to four days, for which she was greatly admired. Gerson had talked with her, had thoroughly tested her, and found that her abstinence was arrogant and stubborn because she ate with insatiable voracity when such fasts ended. As a reason for her self-inflicted austerities, she stated nothing other than that she was unworthy to eat bread. Her external appearance already betrayed her approaching insanity.[18] Another woman, an epileptic, whose corns twinged whenever a soul went to hell, who read sins from foreheads, and who claimed that she saved three souls a day, confessed under threat of torture that she only behaved this way because it was her means of making a living.[19]

Gerson did not value very highly the visions and revelations of recent times that were available to the reading public everywhere. He even rejected those of famous saints such as Bridget of Sweden and Catherine of Siena.[20] He had heard so many revelations that he had been robbed of his trust in them. Many declared that it had been revealed to them that they would become pope; a learned man had even described it with his own hand and had supported it with various proofs. Yet another had been convinced, in succession, that he would become pope, still later, that he would become the Antichrist, or at least his forerunner, and had for this reason entertained the idea of committing suicide so that Christendom would be spared such an evil.[21] Nothing is so dangerous, says Gerson, as ignorant devotion. If the pious poor hear that Mary's spirit exulted in God, they try to exult too and, sometimes in love, sometimes in fear, imagine all kinds of things to happen. They see all kinds of visions that they cannot distinguish from the truth and that they take for miracles and proof of their excellent devotion.[22] This, however, is exactly what the modern devotion prescribed: "He who is intent upon making himself, by this path, with all his heart and by all his efforts, equal in spirit to the sufferings of the Lord, should strive to make himself humble and fearful. And if he is in danger, he should join this danger to the danger of Christ and be ready to share it with him."[23]

The contemplative life is fraught with great dangers, says Gerson; many have become melancholy or mentally ill because of it.[24] He knows how easily overlong fasts can lead to madness or hallucinations; he also knows of the role of fasts in magic.[25] Now, where is the man with such a keen eye for the psychological element in the expressions of faith to draw the boundary between what is holy and permissible and what should be rejected? He himself sensed that the question of orthodoxy alone did not suffice; as a trained theologian it was easy enough to pronounce judgement whenever there was evident departure from dogma. There remained, however, those cases that were outside the pale of dogma, where an ethical evaluation of the expressions of faith had to be his guide and where his sense of appropriateness and good taste had to prompt his judgment. There is no virtue more lost from sight in these miserable times of the schism than that of "discretio," says Gerson.[26]

While to Jean de Gerson the criterion of dogma was no longer the only one to tip the scale in distinguishing between false and true piety, so much the more are we today inclined to judge types of religious intensity not only by the yardstick of their orthodoxy or heresy, but according to their psychological nature. Dogmatic distinctions were not seen by the people of that time themselves. They received from the heretical Brother Thomas just as much edification as they did from the saintly Vincent Ferrer; they denounced St. Colette and her successor as swindlers and hypocrites.[27] Colette displays all those characteristics that James called the theopathic state,[28] which is rooted in the soil of a most painful supersensitivity. She cannot stand the sight of fire or tolerate its heat. Candles are the only exception. She has an exaggerated fear of flies, slugs, ants, stench, or impurity. She feels the same sickening disgust for sexuality that was in later times displayed by St. Aloysius Gonzaga. She prefers to have only virgins in her congregation, loathes married saints, and regrets that her mother took her father in a second marriage.[29] This passion for purest virginity was praised by the church as uplifting and worthy of emulation. Virginity was harmless as long as it proclaimed itself in the form of a personal disgust for anything sexual. But this same feeling became dangerous, both to the church and to the individual proclaiming his adherence to it, in another form: whenever virginity no longer, like a snail, pulled in its feelers so as to lock itself securely into a sphere of purity of its own, but rather desired this preoccupation with chastity to be applied to the church and the social lives of others. The church had to deny this striving for purity time and again whenever it assumed revolutionary forms and expressed itself in vehement attacks on the impurity of priests or the debauchery of monks, because the medieval church knew that it was not in her power to turn away these evils. Jean de Varennes paid for his insistence in the miserable prison in which he was locked by the bishop of Reims. This Jean de Varennes was a learned theologian and a famous preacher who seemed to be in line for a bishopric or even a cardinal's hat while he was serving at the papal court of Avignon as chaplain to the young cardinal of Luxembourg. But all this had come to an end when he abruptly renounced all his benefices, with the exception of a sinecure at Notre Dame at Reims, renounced his rank and returned from Avignon to his native region where he began to lead a saintly life and to preach in Saint Lié. "Et avoit moult grant hantise e poeuple qui le venoient vier de tous pays pour la simple vie très-noble et moult honneste qui il menoit."* People thought that he would become pope; he was called "le saint homme de S. Lié."† Many tried to kiss his hand and touch his gown because of his miraculous powers. Some considered him to be a messenger of God or even a divine being; all of France spoke of nothing else.[30]

But not everyone believed in the sincerity of his intentions; there were those who spoke of the "fou de S. Lié"‡ or suspected him of using these sensational means for the purpose of gaining the high clerical offices that had escaped him so far. Jean de Varennes, as many earlier individuals, allows us to see how a passion for sexual purity is transposed into revolutionary ways of thought. It is as if he reduces all the complaints about the degeneration of the church to one and the same evil: unchastity. He preaches, red-hot in his outrage, protests, and complaints, against the church authorities, most of all against the archbishop of Reims. "Au loup, au loup,"§ he shouts to the masses, and they understand only too well who is meant by the "wolf" and eagerly shout back, "Hahay, aus leus, mes bones gens, aus leus." But it seems that Jean de Varennes did not have all the courage of his convictions. In his defense from prison he claims that he had never said that he meant the archbishop; he was only quoting the proverb "qui est tigneus, il ne doit pas oster son chaperon" ("he who has head sores should not take off his cap").[31] No matter how far he may have actually gone, what his audience had heard in the sermon was the old teaching that had so often threatened to disrupt the life of the church: the sacraments of a priest living an unchaste life are invalid. The host he celebrates is nothing but bread, baptism and absolution are worthless if done by him. In the case of Jean de Varennes this was only part of a more extremist program of chastity: priests should not be allowed to live even with a nun or an old woman; twenty-two or twenty-three sins are connected with marriage; adulterers should be punished according to the old covenant; Christ himself would have stoned the woman taken in adultery if he had been

---

* "And he was much visited by people who came to see him from all countries on account of the simple, very noble and most honest life he led."

† "Saint of St. Lié"

‡ "fool of St. Lié"

§ "After the wolf, after the wolf!"

certain of her guilt; there was no chaste woman in all of France; no bastard could do good or be blessed.[32]

The church always had to defend itself out of its sense of self-preservation against this insistent form of disgust over unchastity. Once doubts were to be raised about the efficacy of the sacraments dispensed by unworthy priests, the entire life of the church would be shaken to its foundations. Gerson put Jean de Varennes on the same level as Jan Hus, someone with originally good intentions led astray by zealousness.[33]

On the other hand, the church was usually very indulgent in another area, tolerating highly sensuous depictions of the love of God. But the conscientious chancellor of the University of Paris saw danger here, too, and warned against it.

He knew this danger from his great psychological experience and in various aspects, dogmatic as well as ethical. "One day would not be sufficient for me," he said, "if I had to count all the many crazed acts of those in love, of those who have lost their senses: amantium, immo et amentium."[34] Indeed, he knew from experience, "Amor spiriritualis facile labitur in nudum carnalum amorem" ("Spiritual love easily turns into purely carnal love").[35] Who else but himself could Gerson have meant when he speaks of a man known to him once who had, out of praiseworthy devotion, cultivated a trusting friendship in the Lord with a spiritual sister: "In the beginning there was no fire of a carnal nature, but gradually a love grew from the regular meetings that was no longer rooted in God, so that he could no longer resist visiting her or thinking of her in her absence. Still, he suspected nothing sinful, no devilish deceit, until a more prolonged absence caused him to gain an insight into the danger and God turned him away from it just in time."[36] From then on, he was "un homme averti" and benefited from it. His entire work, "De diversis diaboli tentationibus,"[37] is a keen analysis of a state of mind comparable to that of the Dutch modern devotees. Above all, it is the "dulcedo Dei," the "sweetness" of the Windesheimers that Gerson distrusted. The Devil, he says, sometimes offers man an immeasurable and wondrous sweetness (dulcedo) of a kind like devotion and resembling it, so that one makes that enjoyment and sweetness (suavitas) his sole goal and only loves and follows God in order to attain that enjoyment.[38] Elsewhere[39] he says of the same dulcedo dei: Many have been defeated by the all too intense cultivation of such feelings; they have turned to the ravings of their heart as if they were embracing God, and have been miserably mistaken. This excess leads to all kinds of useless effort. Some try to attain that state of complete insensitivity and passivity in which all their acts are the result of the will of God, or that mystic realization of and union with God wherein He is no longer conceived of as a being or truth or goodness. —This was also the basis of Gerson's critique of Ruusbroec,[40] in whose naiveté he did not believe. He criticizes Ruusbroec's notion of the "Ornament of the Spiritual Wedding," which implies that the perfect soul viewing God does not only view Him by means of the clarity that is the divine essence, but by means of the fact that this soul is God, Himself.[41]

The sense of the destruction of individuality that the mystics of all times have enjoyed could not be admitted by a defender of the moderate, old-fashioned Bernardinian mysticism such as Gerson. A visionary had told him that her spirit had been destroyed in a real act of destruction while viewing God, and had then been created anew. "How do you know that?" he asked her. She herself had felt it, was her answer. The logical absurdity of this explanation is triumphant proof, to the intellectual chancellor, of how reprehensible such a feeling is.[42] It was dangerous to express such emotions intellectually; the church could only tolerate them in the form of images such as the one that had the heart of Catherine of Siena transformed into the heart of Christ. But Marguerite Porete of Hennegouw, a member of the Brothers of the Free Spirit, who had also felt her soul to be destroyed in God, was burnt at the stake in Paris in 1310.[43]

The great danger posed by the feeling of annihilation of self was the conclusion reached by Indian as well as Christian mystics that the perfect, viewing and loving soul is no longer capable of sinning. Immersed in God, it no longer has a will of its own; what remains is only the divine will and if there should exist any carnal inclinations there can be no sin in them.[44] Innumerable poor and ignorant persons have been mislead by such teachings into a life of the most terrible excesses, as illustrated, for example, by the sects of the Bégards, the Brothers of the Free Spirit, and the Turlupins. Whenever Gerson spoke about the dangers of the mad love of God,[45] he remembers the warning examples of those sects.[46] But nearly identical emotions are found among the devotees. The Windesheimer Hendrik van Herp accuses his own spiritual relatives of spiritual adultery.[47] There were in this sphere of thought devilish traps, producing the most perverse godlessness. Gerson tells of a respected man who had confessed to a Carthusian that he would not be barred from the love of God by a mortal sin, and he specifically named unchastity, that rather it inflamed him to praise and to desire the divine sweetness the more intensely.[48]

The church was on guard as soon as the stirrings of mysticism were transformed into clearly formulated convictions or found social applications. As long as the results were mere passionate fantasies of a symbolic nature, the church permitted even the most exuberant of them. Johannes Brugman was allowed to apply all the characteristics of a drunkard to the Incarnation of Christ, a drunkard who forgets himself, sees no danger, does not get angry when mocked, gives everything away. "O, and was he not drunk when love forced him to come from the highest heaven into this lowest valley of the world?" He walks around heaven and serves the prophets from well-filled jugs, "and they drank until they burst and then David with his harp jumped before the table as if he were the fool of my Lord."[49]

Not only the grotesque Brugman, but also the pure Ruusbroec liked to picture the love of God in the guise of drunkenness. Next to drunkenness there is the image of hunger. They may both be an allusion to the biblical "que edunt me, adhuc esurient, et qui bibunt me, adhuc sitient,"[50] which, uttered by Sapientia, was taken to be the word of the Lord. The metaphor of the human spirit constantly visited by an eternal hunger for God was put in this manner: "An eternal hunger begins here which is never satisfied. This is an internal longing and desire of the loving power and of the created spirit for an uncreated good. . . . These are the poorest people alive because they are greedy and voracious and they are possessed by greed. No matter how much they eat and drink, they never become satiated by it, because this kind of hunger is eternal. . . . And if God were to grant to these unfortunates, all the gifts of the saints save the gift of Himself, the gaping greed of the spirit would yet remain hungry and unsatisfied." But just as the guise of drunkenness, that of hunger is subject to a reversal.

> Christ's hunger is great beyond measure; he devours us all to the ground, because he is a greedy indulger and his hunger is insatiable. He devours the marrow from our

bones. Yet we do not begrudge it and we will begrudge it
less the better we taste him. No matter what he eats of us
he cannot become satiated for he is greedy and his hunger is
beyond measure. Although we are poor, he pays no mind
to it and has no wish to leave anything to us. First he prepares his food and burns all our sins and infirmities in love;
when we are cleansed and roasted in love he yawns greedily
to swallow all this. . . . If we could see the greedy lust
which Christ has for our bliss, we would not be able to
stop flying into his mouth. And if Jesus devours us entirely,
he gives us, in turn, himself; and he gives us the spiritual
hunger and thirst to partake of Him with eternal lust. He
gives us spiritual hunger and to our heartfelt love his own
body as food. And if we eat this body and, within us, enjoy
it with deep devotion, from it will flow his glorious hot
blood into our nature and into all our veins. . . . Look, thus
we will always eat and be eaten, and rise and fall with love,
and this is our life in eternity.[51]

One small step more and we have gone once again from the
highest mysticism to a flat symbolism. "You will eat him," says
Jean Berthelemy speaking of Communion in *Le livre de crainte
amoureuse,* "roasted in fire, well cooked, but not burnt. Just as the
Easter lamb was well cooked and roasted between two fires of
wood or coal, so was sweet Jesus tied on Good Friday on the spit
of the worthy cross and, between the two fires of very painful
death and suffering and that of all consuming love and *Minne* which
he bore for our souls and for our bliss, he was roasted and slowly
cooked in order to save us."[52]
The metaphors of drunkenness and hunger by themselves contradict the view that the feeling of religious bliss had to be symbolized erotically.[53] The influx of the divine influence was felt just like
drinking or becoming satiated. A female devotee feels flooded by
the blood of Jesus Christ and faints.[54] The blood fantasy that was
continually invigorated by the belief in transubstantiation expresses
itself in the most intoxicating extremes of red-hot emotion. The
wounds of Jesus, says Bonaventura, are the blood red flowers of
our sweet and blooming paradise, above which the soul, like a
butterfly, has to fly, drinking first from one flower and then from
another. Through the wound in his side, the soul has to penetrate

to His heart itself. At the same time, His blood flows in the brooks of paradise. All the warm, red blood has flowed through Suso's mouth into his heart and soul.[55] Catherine of Siena is one of the saints who have drunk from the blood flowing from the wound in Christ's side, just as it was granted to others to taste the milk from Mary's breast, as, for instance, St. Bernard, Henry Suso, and Alain de la Roche.

Alain de la Roche, in Latin Alanus de Rupe, called Van der Klip by his Dutch friends, may be regarded as one of the most noticeable types of the French, more extreme devotion, and of the ultra-concrete fantasies of faith of late medieval times. Born around 1428 in the Bretagne, he was active as a Dominican primarily in the north of France and in the Netherlands. He died in 1475 in Zwolle among the Brethren of the Common Life, with whom he maintained lively relations. His main task was agitation for the use of the rosary; for this purpose, he founded a worldwide prayer brotherhood for which he prescribed the fixed system of Hail Marys alternating with Our Fathers. In the printed works of this visionary, mainly sermons and descriptions of his visions,[56] we notice the strongly sexual element of his fantasy, but at the same time the absence of any note of a glowing passion which could justify his sexual emotions. The sensual expression of the all dissolving love of God has here become mere *procédé*. It contains nothing of the overflowing fervor which elevates the fantasies about hunger, thirst, blood, and love of the great mystics. His meditations about every part of Mary's body, which he recommends, his exact description of how he had repeatedly been refreshed by Mary's milk, in his systematic symbolism in which he identifies each word of the Lord's Prayer as the bridal bed of one of the virtues, all this reveals a spirit on the decline, the decay of the strongly colored piety of the late medieval period into the form of a flower past its prime.

The sexual element also has a place in the satanic fantasies. Alain de la Roche sees the monsters of sin with disgusting genitals from which a fiery and sulphur-like cloud is emitted that darkens the earth with its smoke. He sees the *meretrix apostasiae** who devours the apostates, vomits them up and devours them again, kisses and

---

* "prostitute of apostasy"

cuddles them like a mother, and from her womb gives birth to them over and over again.[57]

This is the dark side of the "sweetness" of the devotees. As an inevitable complement to the sweet heavenly fantasy, the mind harbored a black cesspool of hellish notions that were expressed in the fiery language of earthly sensuality. It is not so strange that there are connections between the sedate circles of the Windesheimers and the darkest product of the Middle Ages in their final years: the witch-hunting madness that had by then grown into that fatally concluding system of theological zeal and judicial severity. Alanus de Rupe is a link in the chain. He was the teacher of his fellow Dominican, Jacob Sprenger, who not only coauthored the *Hammer of Witches*[58] with Heinrich Institoris, but was also the promoter in Germany of Alanus's Brotherhood of the Rosary.

Chapter Nine

THE DECLINE
OF SYMBOLISM

RELIGIOUS EMOTIONS ALWAYS TENDED TO TRANS-
form themselves into lively images. The mentality of the time believed it had come to understand a mystery once it had placed it
before its eyes. Therefore, this need to worship the inexpressible
through visible signs resulted in the constant creation of new images. In the fourteenth century, the image of the cross and the lamb
were not any longer sufficient to contain the overflowing love of
Jesus; added to them was the veneration of the name of Jesus itself,
and, for some, the new image threatened to become dominant.
Henry Suso had the name of Jesus tattooed over his heart and
compared it to the picture of the beloved that a lover has sewn into
his clothing. He sent handkerchiefs with the sweet name embroidered on them to his spiritual children.[1] Bernardino of Siena, concluding his powerful sermon, lit two candles and displayed a tablet
a yard square on which the name of Jesus, in blue on gold and
surrounded with an aurora, could be seen. "The people who filled
the church, fell to their knees sobbing and crying over the love
of Jesus."[2] Many other Francescans and preachers of other orders
imitated the practice. Denis the Carthusian was depicted holding
such a tablet raised in his hands. The sun-like rays around the crest
on the arms of Geneva are derived from this form of veneration.[3]
The practice appeared suspect to the church authorities; there was
talk of superstition and idolatry and riots for and against the custom
occurred. Bernardino was invited to appear before the Curia, and
Pope Martin V prohibited the practice.[4] However, the urge to worship the Lord in a visible sign soon found a different and sanctioned
form: the monstrance,[5] which displaced the Host itself as an object
of veneration. Replacing the form of a tower, which it had at the
time of its first appearance in the fourteenth century, the monstrance took the shape of the radiant sun, the symbol of divine
love. Again, the church had reservations; at first the use of the

monstrance was restricted to the week of the Festival of the Sacraments.

The excess of elements into which the declining Middle Ages
dissolved almost everything would have resulted in nothing but a
wild phantasmagoria had it not been for the fact that almost every
image could find a place in the huge, all encompassing mental
system of symbolism.

There was no great truth of which the medieval mind was more
certain than those words from the Corinthians, "Videmus nunc
per speculum in aenigmate, tunc autem facie ad faciem" ("For now
we see through a glass darkly; but then face to face"). They never
forgot that everything would be absurd if it exhausted its meaning
in its immediate function and form of manifestation, and that all
things extend in an important way into the world beyond. That
insight is still familiar to us as an inarticulate feeling in those moments when the sound of rain on leaves or the light of a lamp on
a table penetrates momentarily into a deeper level of perception
than that serving practical thought and action. It may surface in
the form of a sickening obsession to the effect that all things seem
to be pregnant with a threatening personal intent or with an enigma
that we must solve but cannot. It may also, more frequently, fill
us with that calm and strengthening certainty that our own life
shares in the mysterious meaning of the world. The more that
feeling condenses into awe of the One from which all things flow,
the more readily it will move from the clear certainty of isolated
moments to a lasting, ever present feeling or even to an articulated
conviction. "By cultivating the continuous sense of our connection
with the power that made things as they are, we are tempered more
towardly for their reception. The outward face of nature need not
alter, but the expressions of meaning in it alter. It was dead and is
alive again. It is like the difference between looking on a person
without love, or upon the same person with love. . . . When we
see all things in God, and refer all things to him, we read in common matters superior expressions of meaning."[6]

This is the emotional foundation from which symbolism arises.
In God, nothing empty or meaningless exists. "Nihil vacuum
neque sine signo apud Deum."[7] As soon as the idea of God was
conceptualized, everything originating in Him and finding meaning
in Him also crystalized into thoughts articulated in words. And
thus comes into being that noble and lofty idea of the world as a

great symbolic nexus—a cathedral of ideas, the highest rhythmic and polyphonic expression of all that can be thought.

The symbolic mode of thought is independent of and of equal value to the genetic mode. The latter, perceiving the world as development, was not as alien to the medieval mind as is often depicted. But the arising of one thing from another was only seen in the naive figure of direct procreation or in a branching off and, by logical deduction, applied to the things of the mind. One could see it in the structure of genealogies, of the branches of trees: an "arbor e origine iuris et legnum" ordered everything, as far as the law was concerned, into the image of a tree and its widely spreading branches. In this deductive application, evolutionary thought retained a somewhat formalized, arbitrary, and barren quality.

Viewed from the standpoint of causal thinking, symbolism represents an intellectual shortcut. Thought attempts to find the connection between things, not by tracing the hidden turns of their causal ties, but rather by suddenly jumping over these causal connections. The connection is not a link between cause and effect, but one of meaning and purpose. The conviction that such a link exists may come into existence whenever two things share an essential quality that relates to something of general value. Or, in other words, any association on the basis of any identity may be directly transformed into an awareness of an essential and mystic connection. From a psychological vantage point this may appear to us as a very meager intellectual function. From an ethnological viewpoint we can see that it is also very primitive. Primitiveness of thought reveals itself in its weak ability to perceive the boundaries between things; it attempts to incorporate into the idea of a particular thing all that which constitutes by its very presence any kind of connection based on similarity or membership in a particular category. The symbolizing function is most intimately related to this.

But symbolism loses any semblance of arbitrariness and immaturity as soon as we realize that it is inseparably linked to that worldview that was known as realism during medieval times and that we, somewhat less fittingly, call Platonic idealism.

The symbolic postulation of identity on the basis of shared characteristics is only meaningful if the qualities shared by the symbol and the thing symbolized are regarded as being truly essential. White and red roses bloom among thorns. The medieval mind

immediately sees in this fact symbolic significance: virgins and martyrs shine in glory among those who persecute them. How is this
postulate of identity achieved? By virtue of the identity of the qualities: beauty, tenderness, purity. The blood red tint of the roses is
also that of the virgin and the martyr. But this connectedness is
only truly meaningful and full of mystic significance if the linkage,
the quality, the essence between the two constituents of the particular symbolism are shared by each of them. In other words, where
red and white are regarded not as mere labels for physical differences on a quantitative basis, but as real entities, as realities themselves. Our intellect is still capable of seeing things in this way at
any time[8] if we can momentarily capture the wisdom of primitive
man, the child, the poet, or the mystic. For all these, the natural
essence of things is locked up in their general quality. This characteristic is their being, the nucleus of their essence. Beauty, tenderness, whiteness by being essences are identities: everything white
is beautiful, tender, and everything that is white has to be connected, has to have the same basis to its existence, has to have the
same importance before God. —This is why, in medieval thought,
an inseparable link exists between symbolism and realism (in the
medieval sense of the word).

We should not be too concerned, here, with the quarrel over
"universals." To be sure, the realism proclaimed by the *universalia
ante res,* which ascribed essence and preexistence to general terms,
did not dominate medieval thought. There were also nominalists:
the *universalia post rem* had its defenders. However, the thesis is not
too daring that radical nominalism has never been something else
other than a countercurrent, a reaction, an opposition, and that the
younger, more moderate nominalism only accommodated certain
philosophical reservations about an extreme realism, but placed no
obstacle in the path of the inherent-realistic thought of medieval
intellectual culture in general.[9]

Inherent to the entire culture. Because what matters is not primarily that dispute among keen-minded theologians, but the ideas
that completely dominate the life of fantasy and thought as it is
expressed in art, ethics, and daily life. They are all extremely realistic, not because high theology had been educated in a long tradition
of neo-Platonism, but because realism, independent of philosophy,
is the primitive mode of thought. To the primitive mind, everything that is capable of being named immediately assumes an es-

sence, be it a quality, a form, or something else. They project themselves automatically on the heavens. Their essence may almost always (but not necessarily always) be personified; the dance of anthropomorphic terms may begin at any moment.

All realism in the medieval sense is ultimately anthropomorphism. If the thought that ascribes an independent essence to an idea wishes to make it visible, there is no other way except through personification. Here is the locus where symbolism and realism turn into allegory. An allegory is symbolism projected on a superficial power of imagination; it is the intentional expression and, with it, also the exhausting of a symbol; the transposition of a passionate cry into a grammatically correct sentence. Goethe describes the contrast as follows: "Allegory changes manifestation into a term, the term into an image, but does so in such a way that the term can always be kept linked to the image and preserved in it. The term is completely captured in the image and expressed by it. Symbolism changes the manifestation into an idea, the idea into an image and does so in such a manner that the idea remains forever effective and unreachable and, though spoken of in all languages, inexpressible."[10]

Allegory has the potential of being reduced to a pedantic commonplace and, at the same time, of reducing an idea to an image. The manner by which allegory entered medieval thought, namely as a literary product of late antiquity, in the allegorical productions of Martianus Capella and Prudentius, increased its pedantic and senile character. However, it would be wrong to believe that medieval allegory and personification lack authenticity and vitality. If it lacked these, why did medieval culture cultivate allegory so consistently and with such dedication?

Taken together, these three ways of thought—realism, symbolism, and personification—illuminated the medieval mind like a flood of light. Psychology is prone to deal with symbolism in its entirety in terms of the association of ideas. Historians of culture, however, have to view that form of thought with greater reverence. The value for life of a symbolic interpretation of all of existence was incalculable. Symbolism created an image of the world more strictly unified by stronger connections than causal-scientific thought is capable of. It embraces in its strong arms all of nature and all of history. In both, it creates an indissoluble order of rank, an architectural structure, a hierarchical subordination. Since in any symbolic context one thing has to be higher and another lower, things of equal value cannot be symbols of each other, but, together, can only point to a third that is higher than they. There is ample room in symbolic thought for an immeasurable variety of relationships among things, since anything with its individual qualities can be the symbol of yet other things, and may, with one and the same quality, signify quite various other things, since the highest things are symbolized by thousands of lower things. Nothing is too low to signify the highest of things and to point to it for the purpose of its glorification. The walnut signifies Christ; the seed kernel is the divine nature, the outer shell His human nature, and the woody membrane in between is the cross. All things offer support and stability to the mind as it climbs to the eternal; all things lift each other to the heights. Symbolic thought causes the continuous transfusion of the feeling for God's majesty and for eternity into everything that can be perceived and thought. It never allows the fire of the mystic life to be extinguished. It permeates the idea of anything with heightened aesthetic and ethical value. Just try to imagine the enjoyment of seeing every jewel sparkle with the splendor of its symbolic value, of the moment when the identity of roses with virginity is more than just poetic Sunday dress, the time when identification points to the essence of both. It is a true polyphony of thought. In a completely thought-out symbolism, each element reverberates in a harmonious musical chord of symbols. Symbolic thinking yields to that intoxication of thought, leads to that pre-intellectual obscuring of the definition of things, that muting of rational thought, which lifts the intensity of the feeling for life to its very peak.

All realms of thought are joined in this harmonious connectedness. The facts of the Old Testament have meaning, they prefigure those of the New Testament. Profane history reflects them both. In any thinking, just as in a kaleidoscope, a beautiful symmetric figure takes shape from the chaotic mass of particles. Every symbol, by virtue of the fact that all of them are ultimately aligned around the central miracle of the Eucharist, attains a super-value, a much stronger degree of reality, and at this level signification is no longer symbolic, it is identity; The Host is Christ. And the priest who eats it becomes the tomb of the Lord because of his act. The derived symbol partakes in the reality of the highest mystery, every act of signification becomes a mystic one-being.[11]

Through symbolism it becomes possible both to honor and enjoy the world, which, by itself, is damnable, and to ennoble the
earthly enterprise, since every profession has its relationship to the
highest and holiest. The labor of the craftsman is the eternal generation and incarnation of the word and the alliance between God and
the soul.[12] Even between earthly and divine love the threads of
symbolic contact run to and fro. The strong religious individual-
ism, that is the cultivation of one's own soul to attain virtue and
bliss, found its wholesome counterweight in realism and symbolism that separated one's own suffering and one's own virtue from
the particular character of the individual personality and elevated
both into the sphere of universals.

The ethical value of symbolic thought is inseparable from its
formative value. Symbolic formulation is like music added to the
text of logically formulated doctrinal statements that would sound
stiff and insufficient without the music. "En ce temps où la speculation est encour toute scolaire, les concepts définis sont facilement
en désaccord avec les intuitions profondes."[13]* Symbolism opened
the entire wealth of religious notions to art, which could express
them with rich sound and in full color and, at the same time,
bestow on them both an obscure and a soaring quality that allowed
art to become the vehicle for the most profound intuitions on their
way to the understanding of the inexpressible.

The waning[14] Middle Ages display this entire world of thought
in its last flourishing. The world was perfectly pictured through
that all encompassing symbolism, and the individual symbols
turned into petrified flowers. From the time of antiquity, symbolism had a tendency to become purely mechanical. Once established
as a principle of thought, symbolism arises not only from poetic
imagination and enthusiasm, but attaches itself to the intellectual
function like a parasitic plant and degenerates into pure habit and
a disease of thought. Whole perspectives of symbolic contact arise,
particularly when the symbolic contact comes from a mere correspondence in number. Symbolizing becomes simply the use of
arithmetical tables. The twelve months are supposed to signify the
twelve apostles, the four seasons the Evangelists, and the entire
year is then bound to mean Christ.[15]

---

* "In those times when speculation has become completely abstract, defined
concepts are easily in disaccord with profound intuitions."

Conglomerates of systems based on the number seven take shape. The Seven Cardinal Virtues correspond to the seven requests of the Lord's Prayer, the Seven Gifts of the Holy Spirit, The Seven Praises of Bliss, and the Seven Penitential Psalms. These, in turn are related to the Seven Moments of the Passion and the Seven Sacraments. Every individual unit of the sevens corresponds again as contrast or cure for the Seven Cardinal Sins, which are represented by seven animals that are followed by seven diseases.[16] For a true healer of souls and moralist such as Gerson, from whom the above examples are taken, the practical ethical value of the symbolic relations predominates. For a visionary such as Alain de la Roche, it is the aesthetic element in the relationship that is most important.[17] He has to establish a system depending on the numbers ten and fifteen because the prayer cycle of the Brotherhood of the Rosary, which commanded his zealous support, comprises 150 aves interrupted by fifteen paters. The fifteen paters are the fifteen moments of the Passion, the 150 aves are the Psalms. But they mean much more. Multiplying the eleven heavenly spheres plus the four elements by the ten categories: *substantia, qualitas, quantitas,* etc. yields the 150 *habitudines naturales;* the same *habitudines naturales* one obtains by multiplying the Ten Commandments by the fifteen virtues. The three theological, the four cardinal, the seven capital virtues amount to fourteen, "restant duae: religio et poenitentia," which means that there is one too many, but Temperantia, the Cardinal Virtue, corresponds to Abstinentia,[18] the Capital Virtue, which means that fifteen are left. Each of these virtues is a queen who has her bridal bed in one of the segments of the Lord's Prayer. Each of the words of the ave means one of the Fifteen Perfections of Mary and at the same time a precious stone on the *rupis angelica,* which is Mary herself; every word drives away a sin or the animal symbolizing it. They are also branches of a tree laden with fruit in which all the saints are sitting, and the steps of a stair. For example, the word ave signifies Mary's innocence and a diamond. It drives away pride, which, in turn, is symbolized by a lion. The word Mary means her wisdom and a carbuncle; it drives away envy, symbolized by a black dog. In his vision, Alain sees the disgusting figures of the sin-symbolizing animals and the shining colors of the precious stones. The stones' miraculous powers, long famous, give rise, in turn, to new symbolic associations. The sardonyx is black, red, and white just as Mary was black in her humility, red in her pain, and white in her glory and mercy. Used as a seal, wax will not stick to this stone. This signifies the virtue of honorability, it drives away unchastity and causes people to be honorable and chaste. The pearl is the word *gratia* and also Mary's own mercy. It is generated inside a seashell from a heavenly dew "sine admixtione cuiuscunque seminis propagationis." Mary herself is this shell; in this instance the symbolism is slightly shifted because one would expect that Mary would be the pearl if one were to follow the pattern of the other precious stones. The kaleidoscopic nature of symbolism is also strikingly expressed here: the words "created from heavenly dew" also call to mind, albeit not made explicit, the other trope of the virgin birth, the fleece on which Gideon prayed that the holy sign might descend.

The symbolizing mode of thought had been almost entirely spent. Finding symbols and allegories had become mere play, a superficial fantasizing on a simple association of ideas. A symbol retains an emotional value only by virtue of the holiness of the thing it symbolizes; as soon as symbolizing shifts from the purely religious realm to one exclusively moral, its hopeless degeneration is exposed. Froissart, in an elaborate poem "Le orloge amoureus," manages to connect all the qualities of love to the different parts of a clockwork.[19] Chastellain and Molinet compete in political symbolism. In the three estates the characteristic qualities of Mary are represented; the seven Electors of the Holy Roman Empire, three spiritual and four secular, represent the three Theological and the four Cardinal Virtues; the five cities, St. Omer, Aire, Lille, Douai, and Valenciennes, that remained loyal to Burgundy in 1477 become the Five Wise Virgins.[20] Actually, this is a reverse symbolism; the lower does not point to the higher, but rather the higher to the lower, since, in the mind of the inventor, the earthly things that he intends to glorify with some heavenly ornamentation are foremost. The *Donatus moralisatus seu per allegoriam traductus,* occasionally ascribed to Gerson, blended Latin grammar with theological symbolism: the noun is man, pronouns show that he is a sinner. At the lowest level of signification is a poem such as "Le parement et triumphe des dames," by Olivier de la Marche, in which the entire female toilette is compared to virtues and outstanding qualities. The old courtier's worthy sermon is punctuated by an occasional facetious wink of the eye. The slipper signifies humility:

De la pantouffle ne vous vient que santé
Et tout prouffil sans griefve maladie,
Pour luy donner tiltre d'auctorité
Je luy donne le nom d'humilité. *

In this way shoes become caution and industry; stockings endurance; the garter resolution; the shirt honorability; and the corset chastity.[21]

But even in their most listless expressions, symbolism and allegory retained for the medieval mind much more lively emotional value than we might realize. The function of symbolic equations and personalized figures was so fully developed that any thought would almost automatically be transposed into a "personage," that is into a character. Any idea was regarded as an entity, any quality as substance, and as entity it was immediately personified by the intelligence that conceived it. Denis the Carthusian saw the church in his visions in just as personal a shape as it had when it was presented onstage at the court festivity at Lille. In one of his revelations, he envisions the future *Reformatio* that church sought brought about by the fathers of the Council and by Denis's brother-in-spirit, Nicholas of Cusa: the church to come in its future purity. He envisions the spiritual beauty of that purified church as a marvelous and very precious garment, of indescribable physical beauty in its artistic blend of colors and figures. In another instance, he sees the church oppressed: ugly, mangy, bloodless, poor, weak, and downtrodden. The Lord says to Denis, Hark to your mother, my bride, the Holy Church, and Denis hears an inner voice as if it emanates from the figure of the church, "quasi ex persona ecclesiae."[22] In this, the idea is so bound up with the image that it is hardly felt to be necessary to trace back from the image to the idea, or that the allegory be explained in all its details. Only the theme need be given, no matter how imperfectly. The colorful garment is completely adequate for conveying the ideal of spiritual perfection; this is the dissolution of a concept into an image; a phenomena that is familiar to us from moments when ideas dissolve into music.

---

* The slipper only gives us health/And all profit without serious illness,/To give it a title to authority/I give it the name of humility.

We should remind ourselves at this point of the allegorical figures from the *Roman de la rose*. When we encounter the names
Bel-Accueil, Doulce Mercy, Humble Requeste, it is only with dif-
ficulty that we think of something tangible. But for the people of
the time they were realities clothed in living form and imbued with
passion. They are perfectly comparable to Roman divinities that
were also derived from abstractions, such as Pavor, Pallor, and
Concordia, etc. What Usener says about them is almost perfectly
applicable to medieval allegorical figures: "The conception confronted the soul with sensual force and exercised such power that
the word that designated it could be considered a divine individual,
in spite of all the adjectival mobility that it had left at its disposal."[23]
Otherwise the *Roman de la rose* would have been unreadable. Doux-
Penser, Honte, Souvenirs, and the others lived in the heads of the
declining Middle Ages as semi-divine beings. In the case of one of
the *Rose* figures an even further concretization took place: Danger,
originally the menace threatening the suitor during the courtship,
became, in the jargon of love, the betrayed husband.

Repeatedly allegories are employed to express ideas particularly
important to an argument. The bishop of Chalons, intent upon
issuing a very serious warning over political activities to Philip the
Good, presents the remonstrance which he gave on St. Andrew's
Day in the castle of Hesdin, to the duke, the duchess, and the
entourage, in the form of an allegory. He has *Haultesse de Signourie*,
who first resided in the Empire, later at the French and finally at
the Burgundian court, sitting and wailing inconsolably about the
fact that she was threatened in Burgundy by "Uncaring of
Princes," "Weakness of Councils," "Envy of Servants," "Extor-
tion of Subjects." He has these confronted by other personalities
such as "Alertness of Princes," and so forth, who have to expel the
unfaithful servants of the court.[24] Every quality has been rendered
independent and personified. This was obviously the way to make
an impression, something that we will find understandable if we
realize that allegory still served a very vital function in the thought
of those times.

The Burgher of Paris is a conventional fellow rarely given to the
enjoyment of cleverly turned phrases or mental games. Yet, when
approaching the most terrible events he has to describe, the Burgundian murders that permeated Paris in June 1418 with the same
stench of blood smelled in September 1792, he resorts to allegory:[25]

"Lors se leva la deesse de Discorde, qui estoit en la tour de Mauconseil, et esveilla Ire la forccnée et Convoitise et Enragerie et Vengence, et prindrent armes de toutes manières et bouterent hors d'avec eulx Raison, Justice, Memoire de Dieu et Atrempance moult honteusement."* This continues in the same vein, alternating with direct descriptions of the atrocities. "Et en mains que on yroit cent pas de terre depuis que mors estoient, ne leur demouroit que leurs brayes, et estoient en tas comme porcs ou millieu de la boe . . .";† torrents of rain wash the wounds clean. Why are allegories employed at this juncture? Because the author wants to rise to a higher intellectual level than that of the description of everyday events in the other parts of his diary. He has a need to see these terrible events rising out of something other than mere personal intentions, and allegory serves him as a means to express the tragic sentiment.

How much of the function of personifying and allegorizing was still alive in late medieval times is demonstrated exactly in those places where it irritates us the most. In the *tableau-vivant,* where conventional figures are draped in nonessential garb, thus telling people that this is only play, we, too, are still somewhat able to enjoy allegory. But during the fifteenth century holy, as well as allegorical, figures went about in everyday garb, and new personifications could be added at any moment to serve any ideas one wanted to express. When Charles de Rochefort in "L'abuzé en court" wants to tell about the *Moralité* of the careless youth who had strayed from the path because of his experiences at court, he pulls out of his sleeve a number of new allegories in the style of the *Roman de la rose.* All of them, beginning with Fol cuidier and Fol bombance, are completely lacking in lifelike qualities to our taste. Towards the end, when Pauvreté and Maladie drag the youth to the hospital, they appear, in the miniatures that illustrate the poem, as noblemen of the time; even Le Temps requires no beard or scythe but appears dressed in regular vest and pants. The personifications appear too primitive to us because of the naive rigidity

---

* "Then arose the goddess of Discord, who lived in the tower of Evil Counsel, and Rage and Vengeance, and they took up arms of all sorts and cast out Reason, Justice, Remembrance of God, and Moderation most shamefully."

† "And since the time they were dead was the short time a man needs to go a hundred paces, they had only their pants on, and they lay in heaps like swine, covered with filth."

of the illustrations; everything tender and moving that is felt by the age itself in the conception of the figures is thereby lost to us. But in the commonplace nature of the piece is the sign of its vitality. Olivier de la Marche was not embarrassed at all by the fact that the twelve Virtues, performing an *estrement* during a court festival in Lille in 1454, begin to dance, "en guise de mommerie et à faire bonne chiere, pour la feste plus joyeusement parfournier,"* after their poem had been read.[26] —In our understanding, human characteristics can still be somewhat linked, albeit unintentionally, to virtues and emotions, but the medieval mind does not hesitate to turn ideas into persons, even in cases where we fail to see anthropomorphic links. Lent, as a personified figure, taking to the field against the army of Carnival is not a creation of Brueghel's mad imagination; the poem "Bataille de Karesme et de charnage," in which the cheese fights against the roach, the sausage against the eel, originated as early as the end of the thirteenth century and was already imitated by 1330 by the Spanish poet Juan Ruiz.[27] Lent appears in proverbs, too: "Quaresme fait ses flans la nuit de pasques" ("During Easter week, Lent bakes his cakes"). Elsewhere the formative process goes still farther; in some northern German churches a doll was suspended in the choir of the church and called "Lent." Wednesday before Easter these *hungerdocks* were cut down during mass.[28]

Was there any difference between the reality of the holy figures and the purely symbolic? The former were confirmed by the church, had a historical character of their own, and had been shaped into images of wood and stone. On the other hand, the latter had points of contact with the life of one's own soul and with free fantasy. One may in all seriousness consider that Fortune and Faux-Semblant were just as alive as St. Barbara and St. Christopher. Let us not forget that one figure rose from free fantasy outside of any dogmatic sanction and acquired a greater reality than any saint and survived them all: Death.

There is actually no essential contrast between the allegory of the Middle Ages and the mythology of the Renaissance. In the first place, the figures of mythology are companions to free allegories

---

* "in the fashion of mummers, and to raise the mood in order to arouse the greatest enjoyment."

during a good part of the Middle Ages; Venus plays her part in poems that are purely medieval. Second, free allegory is still in full bloom until well into the sixteenth century and beyond. During the fourteenth century, a virtual contest between allegory and mythology took place. In the poems of Froissart next to Doux-Semblant, Jonece, Plaisance, Refus, Danger, Escondit, Franchise there appears a strange collection of mythologems sometimes disfigured beyond recognition: Atropos, Clothos, Lachesis, Telephus, Idrophus, Neptisphoras! As far as the wealth of their forms is concerned, the gods and goddesses still come out on the short end if compared to the personages of the *Roman de la rose;* they remain hollow and shadowlike. Or, in cases where they have the scene all to themselves, they become extremely baroque and unclassical, as in the "Epistre d'Othéa" of Christine de Pisan. This relationship is reversed with the arrival of the Renaissance. Gradually the Olympians and the nymphs come to replace the Rose and the symbols in importance. From the treasures of antiquity, the classical figures obtained a wealth of style and sentiment, a poetic beauty, and, above all, a sense of unity with nature, in the face of which once lively allegory faded and wasted away.

Symbolism, with its handmaid allegory, had become a mere mental game; the meaningful had became meaningless. Symbolic thought prevented the development of causal-genetic thinking. This is not to say that symbolism precluded it; the natural-genetic connection of things has its place alongside the symbolic connection, but it remained unimportant as long as interest had not shifted away from symbolism and turned towards the natural development of things. One clarifying example: for the relationship between spiritual and worldly authority, the medieval world had settled on two symbolic comparisons: one was that of the two heavenly bodies, the one that God had placed above the other at the time of the creation; the other was that of the two swords that the disciples had with them when Christ was arrested. To the medieval mind, these symbols were by no means merely clever comparisons; they established the basis of the relationships between authorities that were not allowed to shed this mystic linkage. These images have the same conceptual value Peter has as the rock of the church. The force of the symbol gets in the way of examining the historical development of both powers. When Dante recognizes secular authority to be necessary and decisive in *De monarchia,* he first must destroy the power of the symbol by questioning its applicability in order to clear the path for the historical investigation.

A comment by Luther attacks the evil of arbitrary, haphazard allegory in theology. He is speaking of the great masters of medieval theology, of Denis the Carthusian, of Guilielmus Durandus, the author of the "Rationale divinorum officiorum," of Bonaventura and Gerson, when he exclaims, "Allegorical studies are the work of idle people. Or do you think it would be difficult to spin an allegory about any given matter? Who is so poor in mind that he could not try his hand at allegory?"[29]

Symbolism was a poor means of expressing those connections that we know to be essential at times when they rise to consciousness as we listen to music—"Videmus nunc per speculum in aenigmate." There was an awareness of looking at an enigma yet here were attempts to distinguish the images in the mirror, to explain images through images, and to hold up mirrors to mirrors. The whole world was capsulated in independent figures; it was a time of overripeness and the falling of blossoms. Thought had become too dependent on figures; the visual tendency, so very characteristic of the waning Middle Ages, was now overpowering. Everything that could be thought had become plastic and pictorial. The conception of the world had reached the quietude of a cathedral in the moonlight in which thought was allowed to rest.

Chapter Ten

THE FAILURE
OF IMAGINATION

SYMBOLISM WAS VERY NEARLY THE LIFE'S BREATH OF medieval thought. The habit of seeing all things in their meaningful interrelationships and their relationship to the eternal both muted the boundaries between things and kept the world of thought alive with radiant, glowing color. Once, however, the symbolizing function has disappeared or become merely mechanical, the grand edifice of God-willed dependencies becomes a necropolis. A systematic idealism that everywhere presupposes a relationship between things as a result of their assumed essential general characteristics leads to a rigid and barren cataloguing in which the division and subdivision of terms, carried out purely deductively, is all too convenient. Ideas can be made to fit into the vault of the world edifice so readily. However, with the exception of the rules of abstract logic, there is no corrective that could ever point to an error in classification, so that the mind is deceived as to the value of its conclusions and the infallibility of the system itself is overestimated. All terms, precise and imprecise, stand like stars in the firmament and in order to come to know the nature of a thing one does not inquire into its internal construction or into the long shadow of its historical development, but looks towards the heavens where it shines as an idea.

The habit of always extending things towards the ideal along an imaginary line is shown continuously in the medieval treatment of political, social, and ethical disputes. Even what is most mundane and common must be viewed in a universal context. For example, there was an ongoing controversy at the University of Paris as to whether any kind of payment should be asked for the degree of licentiate. Pierre d'Ailly himself took the floor to oppose the fee in opposition to the chancellor of the university. Instead of debating whether the demand was historically justified or debating its validity according to the legal code, d'Ailly framed his argument entirely in a scholastic manner: based on the text "Radix omnium malorum cupiditas," d'Ailly took on the task of proving three things: that to demand the payment constituted simony; that it went against natural and divine law; and that it was a heresy.[1] In order to criticize specific excesses that had disgraced a certain procession, Denis the Carthusian puts together everything concerning the procession from its beginning: as things happened under the old law, etc.[2] without dealing with the issues themselves. This is the reason for the tedious and disappointing nature of almost any medieval proof; it points immediately to the sky above and loses itself from the very beginning in cases from Holy Scripture and in moral generalities.

This perfect idealism reveals itself everywhere. Every mode of life, every social estate or occupation found itself circumscribed by a religious-ethical ideal according to which everyone has to reform himself to meet the requirements of his profession in order to serve the Lord properly.[3] The emphasis given by Denis the Carthusian to the sanctity of the earthly profession has been interpreted as a sign of the new times, something characteristic of the Reformation. In the tract *De vita et regimine, episcoporum, archidiaconorum,* etc., which he ultimately summarized, for his friend Brugman, in two volumes collectively entitled *De doctrina et regulis vital christianorium,* he held up to every profession the ideal of the sanctifying fulfillment of duty; to the bishop, the prelate, the archdeacon, the canon, the pastor, the disciple, the prince, the nobleman, the knight, the merchants, the married, the widows, the young maidens, the brothers in the monasteries.[4] But there is something truly medieval about just this separation of each estate into something independent, and the detailed description and teaching of duties has about it only abstract and general qualities and does not touch the real character of the profession.

This universal tracing back to the general is a quality that, under the label "typism," Lamprecht[5] singled out as the very special characteristic feature of the medieval mind. But this feature is a mental consequence, a need, that arises from deeply rooted idealism. It is not so much an inability to see things in their own individuality as much as it is the deliberate desire to indicate the relationship of things to the highest point of reference, to their ethical ideality and their general significance. It was precisely the impersonal element that was sought out in everything; the value of anything was taken to be its value as a normal and model case. This lack of interest in a thing's individuality and uniqueness, to a certain degree intentional, is a universalizing habit of thought characteristic of a low degree of intellectual development.

The medieval mind busied itself to the highest degree with dissecting the entire world and all of life into independent ideas, only to arrange these ideas into numerous large feudal relationships or intellectual hierarchies. Thus the medieval mind was able to separate every concept from the context to which it belonged and see it in its essential independent existence. When Bishop Fulco of Toulouse was rebuked for giving alms to an Albigensian woman, he answered, "I do not give it to the heretic, but to the poor woman." And the French Queen Margareta of Scotland, who had kissed the sleeping poet Alain Chartier on the mouth, excused her behavior, "Je n'ay pas baisé l'homme mais la précieuse bouche de laquelle sont yssuz et sortis tant de bons mots et vertueuses paroles."[6]* A saying had it, "Haereticare potero, sed haereticus non ero."[7]† Does all this—in these examples from the realm of ordinary thought—correspond to what in the highest speculation of theology was meant to distinguish between God's *voluntas antecedens,*‡ desiring the salvation of all, and his *voluntas consequens,*§ which extends salvation only to the elect?[8]

It all became an insomniac's gnawing mulling over of all things unrestrained by the causal connections seen in reality; a virtually automatic analysis that finally amounted to nothing more than an endless exercise in numbering. No arena was more tempting for such elaborations than that of virtues and sins. Every sin has its fixed number of causes, its derivatives, its daughters, and its harmful effects. Twelve errors, said Denis, cheat the sinner: he deceives himself, he surrenders to the devil, he takes his own life, he rejects his wealth (his virtue), he sells himself for nothing (while he himself has been bought with the blood of Christ), he turns away from his most faithful lover, he thinks he is resisting the Almighty, he serves the devil, he acquires absence of peace, he opens for himself access to hell, he blocks his path to heaven, and he follows that to hell.

---

* "I did not kiss the man, but the precious mouth whence have issued and gone forth so many good words and virtuous sayings."

† "It may be that I err in my faith, but I will not be a heretic."

‡ "antecedent will"

§ "consequent will"

Each one of these errors is illustrated, depicted, and, in a way, defined with passages of scripture, images, and details. It is so defined that it acquires the decided certainty and independence of a figure on a church portal. Then the same sequence is given anew with a deeper meaning: the seriousness of a sin has to be measured from seven standpoints: from the standpoint of God, from that of the sinner, the content, circumstances, purpose, from the standpoint of the nature of sin itself, and from that of its consequences. Several of these points are, in turn, again subdivided into eight or fourteen others; for example, the second into fourteen: the sin is heavier or lighter depending on the received benefits, on knowledge, earlier virtues, the office, the consecration, the ability to offer resistance, faith, age. There are six weaknesses of the spirit that make one prone to sin.[9] This process can be compared to Buddhism: there too, we find this kind of systematic morality that is designed to provide guidance for the exercise of virtue.

This anatomizing of sin could easily have weakened the feeling of guilt that it was supposed to strengthen, deflecting it into acts of squeezing the classifications for all they were worth, if it had not at the same time stimulated the imagination of sin and the notion of punishment. No human can perfectly grasp or completely understand the enormity of sin in his present life.[10] All moral conceptions are made to carry an intolerably heavy burden by directly linking them over and over again to the majesty of God. Every sin, no matter how trivial, affects the entire universe. Just as Buddhist literature, encountering the great deed of a bodhisattva, hears the applause of the heavenly beings in the form of rains of flowers, shining light, and gentle earthquakes, Denis—in his more somber mood—hears how all the blessed and the just, the heavenly spheres, all the elements, and even unintelligent beings and soulless objects shout the condemnation of the unjust.[11] His attempt to sharpen the fear of sin, death, justice, and hell in a most painful manner by offering detailed descriptions and dreadful images does not fall short of a terrifying effect, perhaps precisely because of the nonpoetic way his mind worked. Dante touched the darkness and cruelty of hell with beauty: Farinata and Ugolino are heroic in their corruption and Lucifer, flapping his wings, impresses us with his majesty. The monk Denis remains totally unpoetic in spite of his mystic intensity. He presents hell to us exclusively in terms of highest dread and misery. Pain and suffering are described in acid colors that the sinner should make every effort to imagine as realistically as possible. "Let us always keep before our mind's eye," says Denis, "an overheated and glowing stove and inside a naked man, supine, who will never be released from such pain. Does not his pain appear unbearable to us for even a single moment? How lost he appears to us! Just imagine how he is writhing in the stove, how he screams, cries, lives, what dread he suffers, what sufferings pierce him, particularly when he realizes his unbearable pain will never end!"[12]

The question may occur to us, how those who kept these images of hell before them could have burnt people alive on earth. Denis presents the heat of the fire, the gruesome cold, the disgusting worms, the stench, hunger, thirst, the chains and the darkness and the unspeakable filth of hell. The endless echo of wailing and screaming, the sight of the devil—all this spreads like a suffocating nightmarish shroud over the soul and senses of the readers. But even more cutting is the dread of the cerebral pain, of repentance, fear, the empty feeling of infinite deprivation and condemnation, of the unspeakable hatred of God and the envy of the bliss enjoyed by his chosen. In the minds of the damned there is nothing but confusion, compulsion, and a consciousness filled with error and delusions, blindness and frenzy. The knowledge that all this will remain so for all times and all eternity raises the awareness to a height of dizzy terror.[13]

There is no need to substantiate the fact that the fear of eternal pain, either as a sudden "divine dread" or as a gnawing and pro-longed sickness, is frequently cited as motivation for a life of quiet contemplation and devotion.[14] Everything was geared to this end. A tract about the four last things, death, judgment, hell, and eternal life, perhaps borrowed from the one authored by Denis, provided the customary reading at mealtime for the guests of the Winde-sheim convent.[15] Truly a bitter seasoning! But such spicy means served to motivate people to continuously seek ethical perfection. Medieval man resembles somebody who has been treated for too long with strong medicines, now he will react only to the most potent stimulants. In order to let the praiseworthy quality of a particular virtue shine in its fullest glory, nothing but the most extreme examples would do for the medieval mind. In these exam-ples, less extreme notions of ethics would already have been suffi-cient to turn virtue into its own caricature. For patience we are offered the example of St. Giles who, wounded by an arrow, asked God that his wound never heal as long as he lived; for temperance, the example of those saints who mixed ashes with their food; for chastity, the model of those who took a woman to bed with them to test their fortitude or that of the pitiful fantasies of virgins who, in order to escape their virtue's enemies, grew a beard or thick body hair. The attraction of the example can be vested just as well in the extreme youth of the saint: St. Nicholas refusing his mother's milk on high holy days. For steadfastness, Gerson recommends St. Quiricus—a martyr aged three years or even only nine months—who refused to be consoled by the prefect and was tossed into the abyss.[16]

The need to experience the glory of virtue in such strong potions is again linked to the all dominating idealism. To view virtue as an idea pulled, so to speak, the ground of everyday life from under its appreciation; its beauty was seen in the utmost perfection of its independent existence and not in the daily round of failure and new beginnings.

Medieval realism (that is, hyperidealism) has to be regarded as a primitive mode of thought, all the impact of Christianized neo-Platonism notwithstanding. We are dealing with the attitude of primitive man (but for the medievals freely sublimated by philosophy), who assigns essence and being to all abstract matters. While we may be justified in regarding the hyperbolic veneration of virtue as a product of high religion, in its counterpart—the contempt of the world—we clearly recognize the link that ties medieval thought to the thought forms of a distant past. I have in mind the fact that the tract *De contemptu mundi** cannot avoid placing too much weight on the evil of everything material. There is no greater motivation to despise the world than disgust over bodily functions; that is, secretion and procreation. This is the most pitiful part of medieval ethics: the disgust over man as "formatus de spurcissimo spermate, conceptus in puritu carnis sanguine menstruo nutritus, qui fertur esse tam detestabilis et immundus, ut ex ejus contactu fruges non germinent, arescant arbusta . . . et si canes inde comederint, in rabiem efferantur."† What else is this sensuality bent into its oppo-

* *On Contempt of the World*

† "made from the dirtiest semen, conceived in the titillation of the flesh, nourished with menstrual blood so that it will so as loathsome and impure that fruit

site but a remnant of primitive realism in which savages fear magic substances in excrements and in everything accompanying conception and birth. There is a straight and rather short line that links the magic fear, which prompted primitive peoples to turn away from women and the most female of their female functions, to the ascetic hatred and cursing of women that disfigures Christian literature since Tertullian and Jerome.

Everything is thought of as having substance. This is nowhere expressed as clearly as in the teaching of the *thesaurus ecclesiae*[17] about the treasure of supererogation (*operum superogationum*) of Christ and all the saints.[18] Even though the concept of such a treasury and the notion that all the faithful as members of the *corpus mysticum Christi*—the church—partake of this treasury is very old, the teaching that these good works constitute an inexhaustible store that can be distributed by the church and particularly by the pope appeared only during the thirteenth century. Alexander of Hales is the first who uses the *thesaurus* in that technical sense of the word that it has retained ever since.[19] The teaching met resistance until it finally found its complete description and explanation in the bull *Unigenitis* of Pope Clement VI in 1343. The treasury is treated in this bull just like a capital account that Christ entrusted to Peter and his disciples. It not only increases day by day, but the more people are made to follow the right path through its application, the larger the treasury of merits becomes.[20]

If good works were so substantial, sins, perhaps even more intensely, could be so regarded. Even though the church emphatically taught that sin was neither an entity nor a thing,[21] it was inevitable that ignorant minds came to be convinced—given the technique of forgiving sin on the part of the church, in conjunction with the colorful presentation and the elaborate systematization of sin—that sin was a substance (just as it is viewed in the *Artharva-Veda*). The perception of sin as an infectious substance could only be reinforced when Denis—even though he intended these examples only as metaphors—calls sin a fever, a cold and corrupted humor, and the like.[22] That the law, not so timidly concerned with dogmatic purity, reflects such perception is shown by the fact that English jurists employed the idea that a felony involved the corruption of the

---

will not grow and plants will wither when touched by it . . . if dogs eat it, they will go mad."

blood.[23] The blood of the savior, too, was subjected to the same hypersubstantial view: it was a real substance; one drop would have been sufficient to save the world, but we are given it in abundance, says St. Bernard, and St. Thomas Aquinas waxes poetic:

> *Pie Pelicane, Jesu domine,*
> *me immundum munda tuo sanguine*
> *cuius una stilla salvum facere*
> *Totum mundum quit ab omni scelere.*[24]*

In Denis the Carthusian we observe a desperate struggle to define the conceptions of eternal life in spatial terms. The eternal light is of immeasurable dignity; to enjoy God within oneself is infinite perfection; the Redeemer was necessarily of infinite majesty and effectiveness (*efficacia*); sin is of infinite enormity because it is a transgression against infinite holiness; for this reason the act of atonement requires a subject with infinite ability.[25] The negative space-adjective "infinite" here has in every instance the function of making conceivable the importance, the potential of the holy. In order to convey to his reader a sense of eternity, Denis employs an image: imagine a sand hill as large as the universe. Every hundred thousand years a grain of sand is removed from the hill. It will be leveled, but even after such an incomprehensible length of time, the punishment of hell will not have been shortened, nor will it be any closer to its end than it was when the first grain of sand was removed. Nonetheless, it would greatly console the damned if they knew that they would be liberated as soon as the mountain disappeared.[26]

If the attempt is made to express the joys of heaven or the majesty of God in a similar manner, all that happens is that the idea itself is presented in ever higher pitched clamor. The expression of the joys of heaven remain extremely primitive. Human language is unable to evoke a vision of bliss equally drastic as the one it conceives of terror. One has only to delve deeply into the low dens of mankind to find raw material for the description of ugliness and misery; but to describe the highest bliss would require one to strain one's neck trying to look to the heavens. Denis exhausts himself

---

* Pious Pelican, Lord Jesus,/Cleanse me, an impure one, by your blood,/O which one drop can save/the whole world from iniquity.

in desperate superlatives; that is, in a purely mathematical reinforcement of the idea of bliss, without, however, rendering it clearer or more profound. "Trinitas super substantialis, superadoranda et superbona . . . dirige nos ad superlucidam tui ipsius contemplationem." God is, "supermisericordissimus, superdignissimus, superamabilissimus, supersplendidissimus, superomnipotens et supersapiens, supergloriosissimus."[27]*

But of what use is it to pile up superlatives, or qualitative visions of height, width, immeasurability, and inexhaustability? These are mere images, exercises in reducing the idea of infinity to images born of the finite world. This leads inevitably to a weakening and externalization of the concept of eternity. Eternity is not immeasurable time. Every sensation, once expressed, loses its directness; every quality ascribed to God takes something away from his majesty.

At this point begins the gigantic struggle to climb with the help of the powers of the human mind to the absolute imagelessness of the deity: a struggle that remains everywhere and everytime the same and is not tied to any particular culture or era. "There is about mystical utterances an eternal unanimity which ought to make a critic stop and think, and which brings it about that the mystical classics have, as has been said, neither birthday nor native land."[28] —The props of the imagination cannot be immediately dispensed with. One by one the shortcomings of the means of expression become evident. The concrete embodiments of the idea and the colorful garb of symbolism are the first to go. Once this has happened, there is no longer any mention of blood or atonement, of the Eucharist, of Father, Son, and Holy Ghost. There is almost no mention of Christ in Eckhart's mysticism and just as little of the church and the sacraments. But still the expressions for the mystic vision of being, for truth, for the deity remain tied to natural concepts, those of light and expansion. Later, these turn into negatives, into silence, emptiness, darkness. Thereupon, the shortcomings of these terms, devoid of form and content, is realized, and the attempt is made to remove their deficiencies by continuously cou-

* "Trinity super-substantial, super-adorable and super-good . . . lead us to the super-bright contemplation of Thyself." [The Lord is] "super-merciful, super-dignified, super-kind, super-radiant, super-omnipotent and super-wise, superglorious."

pling them with their opposites. Ultimately, there is nothing left but pure negation: the deity that is recognized in the Nothingness of what exists, because it stands above all, is called by the mystics, Nothing. This is what Scotus Eriugena[29] does, and Angelus Silesius when he says:

> God is a pure Nothing, unperturbed by Now and Here.
> The more you try to grasp him, the more he is lost to you.[30]

This progression of the viewing mind, by stages, to the abandonment of all concepts did not, of course, take place in this strict sequence. Most mystic statements show all the phases synchronically, mixed and blended with one another. They already existed in India, were already fully developed in Pseudo-Dionysius the Areopagite, who is the source of all Christian mysticism, and are revived in the German mysticism of the fourteenth century.

The following passage from the revelation of Denis the Carthusian may serve as an example.[31] He is talking to God, who is angry: "At this answer the friar, turning inward, saw himself transposed into a sphere of infinite light and most sweet. In a tremendous silence he called out with a secret voice that did not sound outside of himself to the most secret and truly hidden, incomprehensible God: 'O Thou, super-loveable God, Thou Thyself art the light and the sphere of light in which Thy chosen ones go sweetly to their rest, to regain their strength, find peaceful slumber and true sleep. Thou art like an ever-level, immeasurable desert in which the truly pious spirit—entirely purified by special love, enlightened from above and vibrantly inflamed—roams without becoming lost and becomes lost without roaming, succumbs in bliss and recovers without having been weakened.' " In this passage there is first the image of light—still positive—followed by that of sleep, then the desert, and finally by the opposites that cancel one another.

The image of the desert, the horizontal notion of space, alternates with the vertical notion of the abyss. The latter was a tremendous store of mystic formulations. The expression of the absence of any particular qualities of the deity, in Eckhart's words, "the mannerless and formless abyss of the silent, empty deity," unites the infinite horizontal and vertical extensions to create a sensation of vertigo. It is said of Pascal that he constantly envisioned an abyss at his side; such a sensation is here reduced to a standard mystic expression. In these visions of the abyss and the silence, the most vibrant descriptions of the indescribable mystic experience are reached. Susa jubilantly exclaims, "Wol uf dar, herz und sin und muot, in daz grundlos abgründ aller lieplichen dingen!"[32]* Master Eckhart, in his breathless fixation, says,

"Dirre funke (the mystic nucleus of the individual being) . . . engnüeget an vater noch an sune noch an heiligem geiste noch an den drin personen, als verre als iecliîchiu bestêt in ir eigenschaft. Ich spriche wêrliîche, daz diseme selben liehte niht begnüeget an der einberkeit der fruhtberliîchen art gotliîcher nâtûre. Ich wil noch mê sprechen, daz noch wunderliîcher lûtet: ich spriche biî guoter wârheit, daz disem liehte niht genüeget an dem einveltigen stillestânden gotliîchen wesenne, daz weder giît noch ennimet, mêr: ez wil wizzen, wannen diz wesen har kome, ez wil in den einveltigen grunt, in die stillen wüeste, dâ nie unterscheit in geluogete weder vater noch sun noch heiligeist; in dem innegen, da nieman heime ist, da benüeget ez inme liehte, unt da ist ez einiger dan in ime selber; want dirre grunt ist ein einvetic stille, diu in ir selber unbegeglich ist. Only in this way will the soul come completely to blessedness, "daz sie sich wirfet in die wüesten gotheit, dâ noch werc noch bilde enist, daz si sich da verliese unde versenke in die wüestenunge."[33]†

Tauler says, "In this, the beatified and purified spirit plunges into the divine darkness, into calm silence and an incomprehensible

---

* "Well be, heart and mind and soul in the bottomless abyss of all lovely things."

† "This spark . . . is not satisfied either with the Father nor with the Son nor yet with the Holy Ghost, nor with the Trinity itself, in so far as each one exists in its own being. Indeed, I affirm: this light is not even satisfied when the divine nature is born in him as a generative fruit. I will say one thing more that will sound even stranger: I maintain in all seriousness that this light is also not satisfied with the unified divine being, resting in itself, which neither gives nor receives: rather, it will know whence this being comes; it wants to enter the simple ground, the silent desert; into which never anything distinct has ever been seen; not-Father, not-Son, not–Holy Ghost; in the innermost where no one is at home, only there is this light satisfied, and it belongs to it more fervently than to itself. Because this ground is a simple (bare of all particulars) silence which rests in itself" . . . "entering into the empty deity, where there is neither work nor image; that it can lose itself there and immerse itself into the wilderness."

and inexpressible union. In this immersion is lost all notion of equal and unequal; in this abyss the spirit loses itself and knows nothing of God nor of itself nor of equal and unequal nor of utility . . . because it is joined to God's unity and has lost all ability to separate."[34]

Ruusbroec uses all these means of expressing the mystic experience even more realistically than the Germans:

> *Roept dan alle met openre herten:*
> *O gheweldich slont!*
> *Al sonder mont,*
> *Voere ons in dinen afgront:*
> *Ende make ons dine minne cont.**

The enjoyment of the bliss of the union with God "is wild and chaotic, like losing oneself since there is neither guidance, nor way, nor path, nor statutes, nor measure." "We shall be de-elevated, de-immersed, de-widened, de-lengthened (the cancelation of all notions of space), losing ourselves in an eternal state, which knows no return."[35] The enjoyment of bliss is such "that God and all saints and elevated men who experience it are devoured into an undefinable state that is one of not-knowing and of eternal immersion."[36] God gives the fullness of bliss to all alike, "but those who receive it are not alike, and yet there is something for everyone." That is, in the union with God, they cannot hold themselves against the wealth of bliss offered to them. "But after being lost in the darkness of the desert, there is nothing left. There is neither giving nor receiving, but simple pure being. In it, God and all those united with him are immersed and lost and they shall never more find Him in this formless mode of being."[37]

All negations have been united in the following passage:

> Thereupon follows the seventh step (of love), the noblest, the highest that can be experienced in time and eternity.
> It comes at the moment when we find within ourselves a groundless not-knowing that is beyond all confessing and knowing; when we die and lose ourselves in an eternal

---

* Let them shout with open heart:/O tremendous abyss!/Entirely without mouth,/Lead us into your abyss/And make known thy love to us.

namelessness beyond all those names that we bestow on God or on creatures; when we see, then find within our- selves, an eternal state of not-doing beyond any desire for practicing virtues, and where no one is able to assert his indi- vidual desire, and when, beyond all blessed spirits, we find a bottomless bliss where we are all one and are the same one that is bliss itself in its own selfhood, and when we see all the blessed spirits, their being immersed, departed and lost, into their supra-existence, into an unknown formless darkness.[38]

In this simple, artless blissfulness all difference of creatures is dissolved. "They take leave of themselves. losing themselves in a bottomless state of groundless ignorance; there all clarity is re- turned to darkness and the three personages give way to the essen- tial unity."[39]

Always there is the futile effort to do away with all images, to express "our empty state which is mere formlessness"—which only God can grant. "He rids us of all images and pulls us back to our origin. There we find nothing but a wild, void, unformed emptiness forever corresponding with eternity."[40]

In these quotations from Ruusbroec the two last mentioned ele- ments of description are exhausted: light transforming itself into darkness and pure negation, the abandonment of all positive knowledge. The practice of calling the innermost secret essence of God his darkness originates with the Pseudo-Areopagite. His namesake, admirer, and commentator, Denis the Carthusian, elab- orates on this expression. "And the most unexcelled, immeasur- able, invisible fullness of Your eternal light is called darkness in which, as it is said, You dwell, who makes darkness his refuge. And the divine darkness itself is veiled from all light and hidden from all sight because of the indescribable, impenetrable splendor of its own clarity."[41] Darkness is not knowing, the ending of every concept. "The more the spirit approaches Your super-shining di- vine light, the more Your unapproachability and incomprehensibil- ity become apparent and as soon as the spirit has entered into this darkness all names and all thought soon succumb entirely [*omne mox nomen omnisque cognitio prorsus deficient*]. But this will be granted the spirit: to see You, to see that you are entirely invisible. The clearer the spirit sees this, the clearer it will see you. We ask to become like this super-light darkness, O Blessed Trinity, and to see You by virtue of invisibility and not-knowing and to recognize that You are above all seeing and knowing. You appear to those above who have overcome and left behind all that which can be perceived and comprehended and everything that is created, including themselves. They enter into the darkness in which you truly are."[42]

Just as light becomes darkness, the highest life changes itself into death. Once the soul has understood, says Master Eckhart, that no creature can enter God's kingdom, then the soul will go its own way and no longer seek God. "Und allhie so stirbit si iren eigenen hohsten tot. In disem tot verleuset di sele alle begerung und alle bild und alle vestentnüzz und alle form und wirt beraubt aller wesen. Und dez seit sicher als got lebt: als wenik mag di sele, di also geistlich tot ist, einik weis oder einik bild vorgetragen einigen menschen. Wann diser geist ist tot und is begraben in der gotheit."* Soul, if you cannot drown yourself in this bottomless sea of the Diety, you cannot confess this divine death.[43]

Denis says elsewhere that viewing God through negations is more perfect than doing so through affirmations. "Because if I say, God is kindness, essence [*essentia*]), life, I seem to hint at what God is as if that which He is had anything in common with creation or resembled it to any degree. It is certain that He is incomprehensible and unknown, unfathomable and inexpressible, and is separated from everything he creates by an immeasurable and totally incomparable difference and uniqueness."[44] He calls the unifying wisdom (*sapientia unitiva*) unreasonable, meaningless, and foolish.[45]

How similarly and yet how differently these sounds echo from ancient India.

> The disciple came to the master and said, "Teach me the
> Brahma, O Honored One! But the master remained silent.
> When the other repeated for the second and third time,
> "Teach me the Brahma, O Honored One!," the master said,

---

* "And here it dies its highest death. In this death the soul loses all craving and all images and all power of comprehension and all form and is deprived of all being. And you can be sure as God lives: as little as a dead man, who is physically dead, can move, as little can a soul, which is spiritually dead like that, reveal any mode or any image to any man. Because this spirit is dead and buried in the Deity."

"I'll teach you, but you won't understand it. This âtman [the self] is quiet."[46]

The Gods wanted to know âtman from Prajâpati. They lived with him for thirty-two years as Brahma students. Then he taught them that the little man one sees in another's eye or the reflection in the water is the self. Then looking after them as they departed, he said to himself, There they go without having comprehended the self. After another thirty-two years he revealed to Indra, in response to his objections, that he who walks in a dream, he is âtman. And after once more the same interval, "That which, when man has fallen asleep, is immersed, has come entirely to rest, is no longer seen in any dream,—that is the self." "But he, the âtman is neither this nor that."[47]

The entire sequence of opposing negations is now exhausted to explain the self's nature.

Like someone who, embraced by a beloved woman, is not conscious of what is external or internal, thus the spirit, embraced by the self, which is cognition, is not conscious of what is external or what is internal. That is the form of its being: craving satisfied, he himself is his craving, being without craving, and divorced from suffering. Then father is not-father, mother is not-mother, world is not-world . . .[48]

Had the power of images been overcome? Not a single thought can be expressed without image or metaphor. When we speak of the incomprehensible essence of things, every word is image. The mind is not satisfied with speaking only in negation of that which is highest and most fervently desired, and the poet has to come to the rescue whenever the wise man with his definitions and terms reaches an impasse. From the snowy peaks of his formal visions, the sweet lyrical mind of Suso always found the way back to the flowery fantasies of the older mysticism of St. Bernard. In the midst of the ecstasy of the highest contemplation, all the color and form of allegory return. Suso sees his betrothed, Eternal Wisdom: "si swepte hoh ob ime in einem gewültigen throne (Heaven): sie luhte als der morgensterne, und schein als diu splindiu sunne; ire krone waz ewikeit, ihr wat seliket, ihr wort süzzkeit, ihr umbfang alles lustes gnuhsamkeit: si waz verr und nahe, hoh und neider; si waz gegenwürtig und doch verborgen; si liess mit ir umbgan, und moht si noch nieman begriffen."[49]*

There were still other ways back from the lonely heights of an individual, solitary, formless, and imageless mysticism. Those heights could be reached only by exhausting the mystery of the sacraments and liturgy; only if one had completely exhausted the symbolic aesthetic miracle of the dogmas and sacraments could one shake off the forms of images and ascend to the nonconceptual vision of the mystics. But the mind was incapable of enjoying its clarity at any time and as often as it desired; clarity was restricted to moments of unusual grace and short duration. Moreover, the church was always waiting below with its wise and economic system of mysteries. In its liturgy the church had concentrated the contact of the mind with the divine into the experience of definite moments and had imposed on the mystery form and color. That is why ritual always survived unbridled mysticism: it saved energy. With equanimity the church tolerated aesthetic mysticism's wild flowers of the imagination, but it feared true, radical mysticism, which put to the flames everything on which the church was built: its harmonious symbolism, its dogmas and sacraments.

"Unitive wisdom is unreasonable, meaningless and foolish." The path of the mystic leads to the infinite and to unconsciousness. By denying any connection between the Deity and anything created, transcendence is destroyed. The bridge back to life is burnt. "Alle creatûre sint ein lûter niht. Ich sprich niht, daz sie kleine sîn oder iht sîn, sie sind ein lûter niht. Swaz niht wesens hât daz ist niht. Alle creatûre hânt kein wesen, wan ir wesen swebet an der gegenwertigkeit gotes."[50]†

Intensive mysticism means a return to a pre-intellectual spiritual life. All intellectualism is lost in it, is overcome and rendered superfluous. But if, all this notwithstanding, mysticism has borne rich fruit for culture, this is the result of the fact that mysticism always

---

* "She soared high above him in a clouded sky; she was bright as the morning star and shone like the radiant sun; her crown was eternity, her dress was bliss, her words sweetness, her embrace satisfied all lust; she was far and near, high and low; she was present and yet hidden; she could be approached, but no one could hold her."

† "All creatures are a pure nothing. I don't say they are small or they are something, they are a pure nothing. What has no being, that is nothing. All creatures have no being, because their being soars in the presence of God."

proceeds through preparatory stages and only gradually discards the forms of custom and culture. Its fruits for civilization are born in its first stages below the upper limit of vegetation. This is where the orchard of ethical perfection blossoms as the required preparation for anyone who wishes to achieve the vision: peace and gentility of mind, the suppression of desire, the virtues of simplicity, moderation, industriousness, seriousness, and fervor. This was the case in India and the same thing is true here: the initial impact of mysticism is moral and practical, consisting above all in the practice of practical charity. All the great mystics have lavishly praised practicality. Master Eckhart himself ranked Martha above Mary[51] and said that one should even abandon the ecstasy of Paul if one could help a pauper with a bowl of soup. The history of mysticism, beginning with Eckhart and continuing with his disciple Tauler, points more and more in the direction of dignifying the practical element. Ruusbroec, too, praises quiet unassuming work, and Denis the Carthusian represents in person the union of a practical sense of daily religious life and the most intense individual mysticism. In the Netherlands began that movement in which these concomitant elements of mysticism—moralism, pietism, charity, industriousness—became the main focus. This meant that from the intense mysticism of the remote moments of a few flow the extensive mysticism of the everyday life of the many, the ongoing communal fervor of modern devotees, in place of lonely and rare ecstasy. The sober mysticism, one is tempted to say.

In the Fraterhouses and the monasteries of the Windesheim Congregation, we find, constantly poured over quiet daily work, the radiance of religious fervor that was constantly present in the mind of the congregation. The flexible lyrical and the unrestrained striving elements have both been abandoned and, together with them, has evaporated the danger of faith gone wrong. The brothers and sisters are perfectly orthodox and conservative. It was mysticism *en detail:* one had not been struck by lightning, one had only received a little spark, and experienced in the small, quiet, unassuming circle the transport of ecstasy in the form of intimate spiritual communion, the exchange of letters and self-contemplation. Emotional and spiritual life was cultivated like a greenhouse plant; there was much narrow puritanism, much moral exercise, a stifling of laughter and of basic human drives, and much pietist simplemindedness.

But the most powerful and beautiful work of that period, the

Imitatio Christi, arose in those circles. Here we meet the man, no theologian, no humanist, no philosopher, no poet, and actually also no mystic, who wrote the book destined to become for centuries a source of solace. Thomas à Kempis, quiet, introverted, full of tenderness for the miracle of the mass and with a most narrow perception of divine guidance, knew nothing about the outrage over church administration or secular life, such as inspired the preachers, or of the multifaceted ambitions of a Gerson, Denis, or Nicholas of Cusa, or of the wild fantasies of a John Brugman or of the colorful symbolism of an Alain de la Roche. He looked only for the element of quietude in all things and found it "in angello cum li bello": "O quam salubre quam iucundum et suave est sedere in solitudine et tacere ei loqui cum Deo!" ("O how wholesome, how pleasant and sweet it is to sit in solitude and to be silent and speak with God!").[52] And his book, of simple wisdom for living and dying, addressed to resigned minds, became a book for all the ages. In this book all neo-Platonic mysticism has been abandoned. Its only basis is the voice of the beloved Bernard of Clairvaux. It does not present any development of philosophical thought, it only contains a number of the most simple ideas grouped in the form of sayings around a central point. Every one of them is couched in short, straightforward sentences; there is no subordination and hardly any correlation of ideas. There is none of the lyric resonance of a Henry Suso or the tense sparkle of a Ruusbroec. Ringing with the sound of parallel sentences and weak assonances, the *Imitatio* would appear to be prose, if it were not for that monotonous rhythm that makes it resemble the ocean on a soft rainy evening or the autumnal sigh of the wind. There is something miraculous about the effect of the *Imitatio*. The thinker does not captivate us with his power or élan, as for example, Augustine, or by flowering prose, as St. Bernard, nor with the depth or fullness of his thought. Everything is even and melancholy, everything is kept in a minor key. There is only peace, calm, a quiet, resigned expectation, and solace. "Taedet me vitae temporalis" ("Earthly life is a burden to me"), Thomas says somewhere else.[53] And yet, the words of this man, removed from the world, are able to strengthen us for life in this world as are those of no other. There is something this book for the tired of all ages shares with the expressions of intense mysticism: here too, the power of images is overcome as far as possible and the colorful garb of glittering symbols is discarded. For this very reason, the *Imitatio* is not limited to one cultural epoch; like ecstatic contemplations of the All-One, it departs from all culture and belongs to no culture in particular. This explains its two thousand editions as well as the different suppositions concerning its author and its time of composition that fall into a range of three hundred years. Thomas did not speak that "Ama nesciri" ("I love to remain unknown") in vain.

Chapter Eleven

THE FORMS OF THOUGHT
IN PRACTICE

TO UNDERSTAND MEDIEVAL THOUGHT IN ITS TOTAL
unity, it is necessary to study the fixed forms of thought not only
as they occur in the conceptions of faith and in the realms of higher
speculation, but also as they are found in everyday wisdom and
mundane practices, since medieval thought was dominated by the
same large patterns in both its higher and more common expressions. While in matters of faith and contemplation the question is
always open as to how far the forms of thought are the result or
the echo of a long written tradition going far back to Greek and
Jewish, or even Egyptian and Babylonian, roots, common forms
of life as we encounter them in their naive and spontaneous expressions are unencumbered by the weight of neo-Platonism and the
like.

In his daily life medieval man thought in the same forms as in
his theology. The foundation is furnished in both instances by that
architectural idealism which the scholastics call realism: the need
to separate each insight and conceive of it as an individual entity
and then to link the entities into hierarchical units and to continuously erect temples and cathedrals with them, like a child playing
with building blocks.

Everything that had won for itself a secure place in life, that was
melded into the forms of life, was taken to be ordained by God's
plan for the world. This applied to the most ordinary customs and
usages as well as the highest of things. This is clearly evident, for
example, in the perception of the rules of court etiquette revealed
in the descriptions of the courts by Olivier de la Marche and Alienor de Poitiers. Old Alienor regards those rules as wise laws that
were at one time implemented in the courts of kings by judicious
choice and that are to be observed for all times to come. She speaks
of them as if they were the wisdom of the centuries: "et alors j'ouy

dire aux anciens qui sçavoient . . ."* She sees the times degenerating. For about ten years, a few ladies in Flanders have placed the maternity bed before the fire, "de quoy l'on s'est bien mocqué";† this has never been done before; where will it lead? "Mais un chacun fait à cette heure à guise; par quoy est à doubter que tout ira mal."[1]‡

La Marche asks himself and his readers important questions with respect to the rational cause of all these ceremonial things: why does the "fruitier" have "le mestier de la cire" in his department? The answer is that the wax is sucked by the bees from the same flowers from which come the fruit: "pourquoy on a ordonné trés bien ceste chose."[2]§ This strong medieval tendency to create an organ for each function is nothing but the result of that way of thinking which ascribed independence to any quality, and which saw each one as a separate idea. The King of England had an official under his *magna sergenteria*** whose office it was to hold the head of the king whenever he crossed the channel and became seasick. In 1442 this position was held by a certain John Baker, who passed it on to his two daughters.[3]

The habit of giving names to all things, even those that are inanimate, should be regarded in the same light. This is a faint whiff of primitive anthropomorphism that occurs even today in military life, itself in many respects a return to a primitive form of life, when cannons are given names. That urge was much stronger during medieval times. Just as the swords in the knightly novels, the bombards of the wars of the fourteenth and fifteenth centuries had their names: "le Chien d'Orléans," "la Gringade," "la Bourgeoisie," "de Dulle Griete." A remnant of this practice remains in that individual diamonds still have names. Several of the jewels of Charles the Bold were named: "le sancy," "les trois frères," "la hote," "la balle de Flandres." That ships in our time have retained their names, but houses and church bells have not, may be due to the fact that a ship changes its location and has to be recognizable

---

* "and then I have heard it said by the ancients who knew . . ."

† "at which the people mocked a good deal"

‡ "But at present everyone does what he pleases: because of which we may well be afraid that all will go badly."

§ "fruitmaster . . . wax department . . . so that this matter is very well ordained thus."

** "grand sergeanty"

at any time, but also in part because a ship retains more of a personal quality than a house; a feeling that is expressed by speakers of English who use the pronoun "she" when referring to a ship. The personal perception of inanimate objects was much more prominent during medieval times; then everything was given a name: the cells in a prison just as well as every house and every clock.[4]

Medieval men sought, as they put it, the "morality," the hidden lesson in everything, the essential ethical significance. Every historical or literary incident has the potential to crystalize into a parable, into a moral example, into evidential proof; every statement could become a dictum, a text, or a saying. Just like the holy symbolic links between the Old and the New Testaments, moral links come into being that make it possible to immediately hold up to any event the mirror of a model, an exemplary type from the Bible, history, or literature. To prompt someone to forgiveness, confront him with biblical cases of forgiveness. To warn of the dangers of marriage, string together all instances of the unfortunate marriages of antiquity. John the Fearless, in order to excuse the murder of Orléans, compares himself to Joab and his victim to Absalom, and claims to have been better than Joab because the king had not expressedly prohibited murder. "Ainssy avoit le bon duc Jehan attrait ce fait à moralité."[5]* This is a broad and naive application of the principles of jurisprudence that only now is beginning to be seen in modern legal practice as a residue of an obsolete way of thinking.

Every serious attempt to arrive at proof will be grounded in a text as the point of support and departure. The twelve propositions for and against revoking obedience to the Avignon pope with which the matter of the schism was debated during the national Council of Paris in 1406 were all based on a scriptural passage.[6] A worldly orator will begin, just like a preacher, with his text.[7]

There is no more striking example of all the features mentioned above than the notorious plea by Master Jean Petit with which he attempted to justify the assassination of Louis d'Orléans at the instigation of the duke of Burgundy.

More than three months had passed since the brother of the king had been cut down one evening by the hired assassins for whom

* "Thus had good duke John drawn the moral inference of the case."

John the Fearless had secured lodging in a house in the Rue Vieille
du Temple just prior to the event. The Burgundian initially expressed great sorrow during the funeral service, but as soon as he
saw that the investigation would lead to the hôtel d'Artois where
he had the murderers hidden, he conferred with his uncle Berry
and confessed to him that he had ordered the murder to be carried
out because he had succumbed to the instigations of the Devil. He
thereupon fled from Paris to Flanders. At Ghent he proclaimed his
first justification for his crime and returned to Paris relying on
the hatred directed by everyone towards Orléans and on his own
popularity with the Parisians, who, in fact, did gladly welcome
him back. In Amiens, the duke had consulted with two men who
had distinguished themselves as orators during the 1406 church
assembly in Paris: Master Jean Petit and Pierre aux Boeufs. They
were given the task of sprucing up the plea given at Ghent, which
had been written by Simon de Saulx, so that it could be presented at
Paris before the princes and nobles and ensure that they be dutifully
impressed and the duke's actions justified.

Therewith, Master Jean Petit, biblical scholar, preacher, and
poet, appears on March 8, 1408, in the Hôtel de Saint Pol in Paris
before a most exhalted audience, among whom the Dauphin, the
King of Naples, the dukes of Berry and Bretagne are the front
rank. He begins with appropriate humility, I, wretch that I am,
am neither theologian nor jurist, "une très grande paour me fiert
au cuer, voire si grand, que mon engin et ma mémoire s'en fuit,
et ce peu de sens que je cuidoie avoir, m'a jà du tout laissé."*
He then proceeds to elaborate, in a highly restrained style, on a
masterpiece of dark political malice that his mind had erected on
the text "Radix omnium malorum cupiditas." The entire plea is
artfully illustrated with scholastic distinctions and secondary texts;
it is illustrated by examples from scripture and history. From the
colorful details with which the defense describes the perfidy of the
slain Orléans, the plea acquires a devilish liveliness and romantic
tension. It opens with a list of the twelve obligations binding the
duke of Burgundy to favor, love, and avenge the King of France.
Commending himself to the aid of God, the Virgin, and St. John

---

* "I have a great deal of fear in my heart, truly fear so great that my spirit and
my memory have fled, and, that to make it worse, the little understanding I had,
has completely left me."

the Evangelist, Petit begins to detail his evidence for the defense, which is divided into major and minor proofs and a conclusion. At the head of them all he states his text: "Radix omnium malorum cupiditas." Two practical applications are derived from it: greed generates apostates, it creates traitors. The evils of apostasy and treason are divided and subdivided and then demonstrated by the use of three examples: Lucifer, Absalom, and Athalia[8] are conjured up in the minds of the audience as the types of traitors. This is followed by eight truths that justify the murder of tyrants: he who conspires against the king deserves death and damnation, the more so the higher his position; anyone is free to kill him. "Je prouve ceste verité par douze raison en 'honneur des douze apostres":* three pronouncements from doctors of the church, three from philosophers, three from jurists, and three from Holy Scripture. The plea continues in this manner until the eight truths are covered. A quotation from "De casibus virorum illustrium" by "le philosophe moral Boccace" is given in proof that the tyrant may be killed from ambush. The eight truths produce eight "correlaria" to which a ninth is added that hints at all the dark events in which slander and suspicion had assigned Orléans a gruesome part. All the old suspicions that had followed the ambitious and reckless prince since the days of his youth are again fanned to a state of red heat, how he, in 1392, had been the deliberate instigator of the fateful "bal des ardents" during which his brother, the young king, had barely escaped the fiery death of his companions, who, disguised as ruffians, had come in contact with a carelessly held torch.[9] Orléans's conversations with the "magician" Philippe de Mézières in the monastery of the Celestines furnished material for all kind of insinuations about plans for murder and poisonings. His generally known predilection for magic gives rise to the most lively horror stories: for example, Orléans was said to have gone, one Sunday morning, to La Tour Montjay on the Marne in the company of an apostate monk, a page, and a servant; the monk made two brown and green clad devils named Heremas and Estramain appear. In a hellish ceremony they consecrated a sword, a dagger, and a ring, whereupon the travelers took down a hanged man from the gallows at Montfaucon, and so forth. Master Jean even manages to extract

---

* "I shall prove this truth by twelve reasons in honor of the twelve apostles."

some dark meanings from the meaningless ramblings of the mad king.[10]

After things have been raised in this way to the general-ethical level by putting them into the light of biblical patterns and moral dictums, thus artfully feeding the fires of disgust and horror, there bursts forth in the minor proofs, which step by step follow the structure of the major proofs, the flood of direct accusations. All the passionate party hatred at the disposal of a mind unleashed is used to attack the memory of the murder victim.

Jean Petit held the floor for four hours. After he had finished, his client, the duke of Burgundy, said, "Je vous avoue."* The text of the justification was presented to the duke and his closest relatives in four precious volumes, bound in pressed leather, decorated with gold, and illustrated with miniatures. One copy is still preserved in Vienna. A printed version of the tract could also be purchased.[11]

The need to elevate any event of life into a moral model, to raise all sentences to maxims, whereby they became something substantial and unassailable, in short, that process of crystalizing thought, finds its most general and natural expression in the proverb. The proverb had a very lively function in medieval thinking. Hundreds were in general use, almost all of them deft and hitting the mark. The wisdom shown in proverbs is at times conventional, occasionally beneficial and profound; the tone is frequently ironic, the mood mostly kind and always resigned. The proverb never preaches opposition, always only surrender. With a smile or a sigh, it allows the egoist to triumph, lets the hypocrite go scot-free. "Les grans poissons mangent les plus petis." "Les mal vestus assiet on dos ou vent." "Nul n'est chaste si ne besongne." Many sound cynical. "L'homme est bon tant qu'il craint sa peau." "Au besoing on s'aide du diable." But beneath them all resides a gentle spirit that does not desire to be judgmental. "Il n'est si ferré qui ne glice."† The lamentations of the moralists over human sinfulness and corruption are confronted by the smiling understanding of folk

---

* "I avouch you."

† "The big fishes eat the smaller." "The badly dressed are placed with their back to the wind." "None is chaste if it's not necessary . . ." "Men are good so long as it saves their skin." "At need we let the devil help us." . . . "There is no horse so well shod that he never slips."

wisdom. In the proverb, the wisdom and morality of all times and spheres are condensed into a single image. On some occasions the tone of the proverbs is nearly evangelical, but they also sometimes are almost paganly naive. A people with many proverbs in living use leaves matters of dispute, motivation, and argumentation to the theologians and philosophers; the proverbs settle every argument by reference to a judgment that hits the nail right on the head. They scorn weighty arguments and avoid much confusion. The proverb cuts through knotty problems; once a proverb is applied, the matter is settled. This ability to crystalize ideas has significant advantages for culture.

It is surprising how many proverbs were familiar in late medieval times.[12] In their common utility they conform so much to the intellectual content of literature that the authors of those days make generous use of them. For example, poems in which every stanza ends with a proverb are very popular. After a scandalous incident, a slanderous poem, written in this form by an unknown author, is directed against the *prévôt* of Paris, Hugues Aubriot.[13] Other examples are Alain Chartier's "Ballade de Fougères,"[14] Molinet in a number of different pieces from his "Faictz et Dictz,"[15] Coquillart's "Complaincte de Eco,"[16] and Villon's ballade that is entirely made up of proverbs.[17] Robert Gaguins's "Le passe temps d'oysiveté"[18] belongs to this category. With few exceptions, all its 171 stanzas end with a suitable proverb. Or, do these proverb-like moral dictums (of which only a few can be found in collections of proverbs familiar to me) spring from Gaguin's own poetic mind? If this should be the case, it only would provide stronger proof of the vital function allotted to proverbs in late medieval thought. In this instance we would be able to prove that, linked to a poem, they arose consciously from the mind of an individual poet to provide well-rounded, fixed, generally understandable judgments.

Even sermons do not shun putting proverbs side by side with sacred texts, and they both mingle together in debates during church or state assemblies. Gerson, Jean de Varennes, Jean Petit, Guillaume Fillastre, Olivier Maillard employ the most common proverbs in their sermons in support of their arguments: "Qui de tout se tait, de tout a paix," "Chef bien peigné porte mal bacinet." "D'aultrui cuir large courroye." "Selon seigneur mesnie duite." "De tel juge tel jugement." "Qui commun sert, nul ne l'en paye."

"Qui est tigneux, il ne doit pas oster son chaperon."[19]* There is even a link between the proverb and the *Imitatio Christi,* which, in form, is based on collections, or "rapiaria," of wisdom of various kinds and origins.

There are, in the waning Middle Ages, many authors whose powers of judgment do not really rise above the level of the proverbs they employ so consistently. A chronicler from the late fourteenth century, Geoffroi de Paris, laces his rhymed chronicle with proverbs expressing the moral lessons of the events he records.[20] In the use of this technique he is wiser than Froissart and Le Jouvencel, whose homemade dictums frequently sound like half-baked proverbs: "Enssi aviennent li fait d'armes: on piert une fois et l'autre fois gaagn'on." "Or n'est-il riens dont on ne se tanne." "On dit, et vray est, que il n'est chose plus certaine que la mort."[21]†

Another crystalized form of thought similar to the proverb is the motto, a favorite object of careful cultivation during late medieval times. Mottoes are not, as are proverbs, wisdom generally applied, but are entirely personal adages. The motto was raised to the status of a kind of insignia for the person who possessed it, attached with golden letters to his own life to serve as a lesson that, by virtue of its formal repetition, resulting from the fact that it was attached to all pieces of clothing and personal objects, was expected to provide support for himself and others and to suggest ideas to both. The sentiment of the motto, in most instances, is one of surrender, just as in the case of proverbs, or one of expectation, occasionally with the touch of an unarticulated element to render the motto mysterious: "Quand sera ce? "Tost ou tard vienne" "Va oultre" "Autre fois mieulx." "Plus deuil que joye."‡ The great majority of them refer to love: "Aultre naray." "Vostre plaisir."

---

* "He who is silent about all things is troubled by nothing." "A well-groomed head wears the helmet badly." "You cut wide belts from the skin of your neighbor." "As the lord, so the servant." "As the judge, so the judgment." "He who serves the common weal is paid by none for his trouble." "Those who have head sores should not take off their hats."

† "That's the way it is with fighting, sometimes you win, sometimes you lose." "Now, there is nothing which people won't eventually get tired of." "People say, and it's true, that there is nothing more certain than death."

‡ "When will it be?" "Soon or late it may come." "Onward." "Better next time." "More sorrow than joy."

"Souvienne vous" "Plus que toutes."* These are knightly mottoes displayed on saddle blankets and armor. On rings we find some of a more intimate nature: "Mon cuer avez." "Je le desire." "Pour toujours" "Tout pour vous."†

Emblems complement mottoes. They either illustrate the mottoes in tangible form or are loosely connected with them, like the knotty staff joined to the motto "Je l'envie," and the porcupine with "Cominus et enimus" of Louis d'Orléans, and the plane with "Ic houd" of his enemy John the Fearless, or the flint and steel of Philip the Good.[22] Motto and emblem have their home in the heraldic sphere of thought. To medieval man, the coat of arms is more than a genealogical hobby. A man's arms assume a significance like that of a totem.[23] Lions, lilies, and crosses become symbols in which an entire complex of pride and aspiration, fidelity and sense of community are expressed in an independent, indivisible image.

The need to isolate every case as an independently existing entity, to see it as an idea, expresses itself as the strong medieval inclination towards casuistry: another result of the far-reaching idealism. To every question, there is an ideal solution; this ideal solution is arrived at as soon as one has recognized the correct relationship between the case at hand and the eternal truths. This relationship is to be deduced by the application of formal rules to the facts. Not only questions of ethics and law are answered in this way; the casuistic view also dominates a number of other spheres of life. Wherever style and form are the main concern, wherever the element of play comes to the forefront in a cultural form, casuistry is triumphant. This is true, first and foremost, in matters of ceremony and etiquette. Here the casuistic view has its proper place; here it is an adequate form of thought for the questions raised because they involve only a sequence of cases that are determined by honored precedence and formal rules. The same is true for the similar "games" of the coat of arms and the hunt. As mentioned earlier,[24] the conception of love as a beautiful social game of stylish forms and rules gave rise to the need for an elaborate casuistry.

Finally, all kinds of casuistry were attached to the customs of war. The strong influence of the chivalric idea on the entire notion of war gave to the latter an element of play. Issues such as legal

---

* "I shall have no other." "Your pleasure." "Remember." "More than all."
† "You have my heart." "I desire it." "Forever." "All for you."

claims to booty, the opening of hostilities, the adherence to a word of honor were joined to that category of rules that governed the tournament and the amusements of the hunt. The need to limit the application of force by laws and rules arose not as much from an instinct for international law, as from chivalric conceptions of honor and style of life. Only by a conscientious casuistry and the formulation of strictly formal rules was it possible to bring the conduct of war somewhat into harmony with the honor of the knightly estate.

The beginnings of international law are therefore mixed with the rules of the game involving the use of weapons. In 1352, Geoffroy de Charny put a number of casuistic questions before King John II of France for his decision in his capacity as Grand Master of the Order of the Star, which he had just founded: twenty of the questions concern the "jouste," twenty-one concern the tournament, and ninety-three, war.[25] Twenty-five years later, Honoré Bonet, prior of Selonart in the Provence and doctor of canon law, dedicated to the young Charles VI his *Arbre des batailles,* a tract about martial law, which, according to later editions, still had practical value in the latter part of the sixteenth century.[26] The tract contains a mixture of questions, some of which are of greatest significance for international law while others are of trifling value and only concerned with the rules of the game. Is it permissible to wage war against the infidel without compelling reason? Bonet answers most emphatically: No, not even for the purpose of converting them. Is a prince allowed to refuse passage through his territory to another prince? Does the sacred protection (much violated) that the plowman and his ox enjoy against the force of war extend to his asses and servants?[27] Is a clergyman obligated to help his father or his bishop? Is someone who has lost his borrowed armor during battle obligated to return it? Is it permissible to do battle on holy days? Which is better, to do battle on an empty stomach or after a meal?[28] To all these questions the prior has answers based on biblical passages, canonical law, and the commentaries.

The most important points of the rules of war were those involving the taking of prisoners. The ransom of a noble prisoner was among the most tempting prospects of battle for nobleman and mercenary alike. Here was an unlimited field for casuistic rules. Here too, international law and chivalric "point d'honneur" are scrambled. Are Frenchmen permitted to make, on English soil, captives of poor merchants, farmers, and herdsmen because a state of war exists with England? Under what circumstances is it permissible to escape from captivity? What is the value of a safe conduct?[29] In the biographical novel *Le Jouvencel* such cases are dealt with in terms of practical experiences. A dispute between two captains over a prisoner is brought before the commander: "I first grabbed him," says the one, "first by the arm and his right hand and ripped off his glove." "But," says the other, "he gave me his right hand and his word first." Both actions established claims to the precious possession, the prisoner, but the latter is recognized as having precedent. To whom belongs a prisoner who escapes and is recaptured? The solution is this: If the case happens in the area of the battle, the prisoner belongs to the new captor, if outside the battlefield, he remains the property of the original owner. Is a prisoner who has given his word allowed to run away if his captor puts him in chains in spite of his having given his word not to run away? What if the captor had neglected to have him give his word?[30]

The medieval inclination to overestimate the independent value of a thing or a case results, aside from the casuistic way of thinking, in another consequence. We are familiar with François Villon's grand satiric poem "The Testament," in which he bequeathed all his possessions to friends and enemies. There are several such poetic testaments; for example, that of "Barbeau's Mule" by Henri Baude.[31] The testament is a handy form, but it is only intelligible if we keep in mind that medieval men were accustomed to disposing in a will of even the most trivial of their possessions separately and in great detail. A poor woman bequeaths her Sunday dress and her bonnet to her parish; her bed to her godchild, a fur to her nurse, her everyday dress to a pauper, and four pounds *turnoise,* which constitutes her only wealth, together with yet another dress and bonnet to the Minorites.[32] Is this not a very trivial example of the frame of mind that postulated every case of virtue to be an eternal example and that saw in every fashion a divine ordinance? The adhesion of the mind to the particularity and value of each single thing is what dominates the mind of the collector and the miser like a disease.

All the features listed above may be summarized under the term formalism. The inherent conception of the transcendent reality of things means that every notion is defined by fixed borders, that it stands isolated in a plastic form, and that this form is all important. Mortal and venial sins can be distinguished according to fixed rules. The sense of justice is unshakable; it need not sway for a moment: as the old legal dictum has it, the deed judges the man. In judging a deed, the formal content is always the main point. Long ago, in the primitive law of ancient Germanic times, that formalism was so strong that the dispensations of justice did not take into account whether intent or negligence was involved: the deed was the deed and brought in its wake its punishment. A deed left undone, or a crime merely attempted, went unpunished.[33] Even in much more recent times, an accidental lapse during the recitation of the oath formula could still lead to the loss of legal rights: an oath is an oath and is very sacred. Economic interests meant the end of that formalism. The foreign merchant who had only an imperfect command of the local language could not be exposed to this risk without raising the possibility that commerce might be impeded. It is only to be expected that in the laws of the cities, the "Vare," the danger of losing one's rights in this way was eliminated; initially as a special privilege and ultimately as a general rule. However, the vestiges of a far-reaching formalism in legal matters remain quite numerous in later medieval times.

The extreme sensitivity to anything touching external honor is a phenomenon rooted in formalistic thought. In 1445 a certain Jan van Domburg had fled into a church in Middelburg in order to seek asylum because of a charge of murder against him. As was the custom, the place of refuge was surrounded on all sides. His sister, a nun, was observed repeatedly urging him to be killed fighting rather than force his family to endure the shame of having him fall into the hand of his executioners. When this finally happened, the Domburg maiden claimed his body so that at least he could be given a dignified burial.[34] For tournaments the saddle blanket of a nobleman's horse was customarily decorated with his coat of arms. Olivier de la Marche finds this rather improper because the horse, "une beste irraisonnable," might stumble and the arms be dragged in the dirt. The entire family would be dishonored.[35] Shortly after the duke of Burgundy had paid a visit to the Chastel en Porcien, a nobleman in a fit of madness attempted suicide there. The event causes indescribable horror, "et n'en savoit-

on comment porter la honte après se grant joye demenée."* Although it was well known that the act was caused by madness,
the unfortunate perpetrator was banned from the chateau after his
recovery, "et ahonty à tous jours."[36]†

A telling example of the plastic way in which the need to rehabil-
itate violated honor was met is provided by the following case. In
1478 a certain Laurent Guernier was erroneously hanged in Paris.
He had received a pardon for his crime, but he was not informed
in time. This was discovered after a year, and his body was given
an honorable funeral at the request of his brother. The bier was
preceded by the four town criers replete with their rattles, the coat
of arms of the dead man on their chests. Surrounding the bier were
four candle bearers and eight torchbearers. All wore mourning
clothes and displayed the same coat of arms. The funeral party
proceeded through Paris from the Porte Saint Denis to the Porte
Saint Antoine. From there, the body was transported to its birth-
place in Provins. One of the criers shouted repeatedly, "Bonnes
gens, dictes voz patenostres pour l'âme de feu Laurent Guernier,
en son vivant demourant à Provins qu'on a nouvellement trouvé
mort soubz ung chesne."[37]‡

The great strength of the principle of blood revenge, which particularly thrived in such prosperous and highly cultured regions as
northern France and the southern Netherlands, is also linked to the
formalistic nature of thought.[38] The motivation in such cases of
revenge is frequently not fiery rage or relentless hatred, but rather
that the honor of the offended family has to be given its due by
the shedding of blood. Sometimes, a decision is made not to kill
someone and instead the attempt is made to wound him in the
thighs, arms, or face. Special care is taken not to be burdened with
the responsibility of having had one's opponent die in a state of
sin. Du Clercq tells of a case where people who wanted to murder
their sister-in-law took pains to bring along a priest.[39]

The formal character of atonement and revenge, in its turn, cre-

---

* "and people did not know how one could bear the shame after the great joy
that had been displayed."

† "banned for all his days."

‡ "Good people, say your paternosters for the soul of the late Laurent Guernier, in his life an inhabitant of Provins, who was lately found dead under an oak
tree."

ates the situation wherein injustice is corrected by symbolic punishments or exercises of penance. In all the great reconciliations of the fifteenth century strong emphasis is placed on the symbolic element: the demolition of the houses that are reminders of the transgression, the donation of memorial crosses, the walling shut of gates, not to mention public ceremonies of penance and the funding of masses for the souls of the departed or chapels. This happened as part of the suit brought by the house of Orléans against John the Fearless; the peace of Arras in 1435; the penance of rebellious Bruges in 1437; and the even more severe penance given to Ghent in 1453, where the entire population dressed entirely in black, without belts, with bare heads and feet and, led by the main perpetrators, who wore nothing but their shirts in a heavy downpour, marched in procession to plead with the duke in unison for forgiveness.[40] During the reconciliation with his brother in 1469, Louis XI first demands the ring with which the bishop of Lisieux had installed the prince as duke of Normandy and then, at Rouen, has the ring broken on an anvil in the presence of notables.[41]

The generally prevailing formalism is also at the base of that faith in the effect of the spoken word which reveals itself in primitive cultures in all its fullness and still survives in late medieval times in the form of formulas of blessing, of magic, and of condemnation. A solemn appeal still has something of the quality of a wish in a fairy tale. When intense pleas fail to move Philip the Good to grant clemency to a condemned man, the task is given to Isabella of Bourbon, Philip's beloved daughter-in-law, with the hope that he will not be able to turn her down, because, says she, "I have never asked you for anything important."[42] And the plan works.— The same spirit is also revealed in Gerson's expressed surprise that morals have not improved in spite of all the preaching: I don't know what I can say, sermons are given all the time, but always in vain.[43]

Those qualities that frequently give the mind of the later Middle Ages its hollow and superficial character are directly spawned by general formalism. First is the unusual simplification of motivation. Given the hierarchical order of the system of classification, and taking as the point of departure the plastic independence of any notion and the need to explain any connection on the basis of a generally valid truth, the causal mental function works like a telephone switchboard: all kinds of connections may occur at any time, but always only of two numbers at a time. Only isolated features of any condition or any connection are seen and these features are greatly exaggerated and variously embellished; the picture of an experience always shows the few and heavy lines of a primitive woodcut. One motif always suffices as an explanation with a predilection for the most general, the most direct, or the crudest. For the Burgundians, the motive for the murder of the duke of Orléans can be only one thing: the king has asked the duke of Burgundy to avenge the adulterous affair of the queen with Orléans.[44] A pure question of the style of a formal letter is enough explanation in the minds of contemporaries for the great uprising at Ghent.[45]

The medieval mind loves to generalize a case. Olivier de la Marche concludes from a single case of English impartiality in earlier times that the English were virtuous in those days and that, for that very reason, they would be able to conquer France.[46] The tremendous exaggeration that results directly from the fact that cases are seen as too highly colored and too isolated is further strengthened by virtue of there always being for every case ready parallels from Holy Scripture that elevate the case into a sphere of higher consequence. When, for example, in 1404 a procession of Parisian students is disrupted and two of the students are injured while another has his coat ripped to shreds, the outraged chancellor is placated by a suggestive connection, "les enfants, les jolis escoliers comme agneaux innocens,"* whereupon he immediately compares the case to the slaughter of the Innocents in Bethlehem.[47]

Where for every case an explanation is so easily at hand and where this explanation, once it has been accepted, is firmly believed, an unusual potential for mistaken judgments prevails. If we have to assume, with Nietzsche, that "to do without mistaken judgments would make life impossible," then the vigorous life that attracts our attention in earlier times has to be credited in part to these very mistaken judgments. Any age demanding an extraordinary mobilization of all its strength demands that mistaken judgments come in a higher degree to the assistance of the nerves. Medieval men may be said to have lived continuously in such an intellectual crisis; they were unable, even for a moment, to do without the crudest of mistaken judgments that, under the influence of partisanship, reached an unparalleled degree of viciousness. The

---

* "the children, the pretty scholars, like innocent lambs"

Burgundian attitude towards the great enmity with Orléans demonstrates this. The numerical proportions of the dead of both sides
were distorted by the victors to a ridiculous degree: Chastellain has
five noblemen killed in the battle of Gavere on the side of the
princes as compared to twenty or thirty thousand on the side of
the Ghent rebels.[48] It is one of Commines's most modern characteristics that he does not indulge in these exaggerations.[49]

What are we to make of the peculiar rashness that is continuously
revealed in the superficiality, inexactness, and credulity of the waning Middle Ages? It is almost as if they had not even the slightest
need for real thought, as if the passage of fleeting and dream-like
images provided sufficient nourishment for their minds. Purely
outward circumstances, superficially described: that is the hallmark
of scribes such as Froissart and Monstrelet. How did the endlessly
indecisive battles and sieges over which Froissart wasted his talent
manage to rivet his attention? Side by side with determined parti-
sans, we find among the chroniclers men whose political sympathies cannot be determined at all, for example, Froissart and Pierre
de Fenin, because their talents are exhausted to such a large degree
in narrating the minutiae of external events. They do not distinguish the important from the unimportant. Monstrelet was present
at the conversation between the duke of Burgundy and his captive
Jeanne d'Arc, but does not recall what they talked about.[50] This
inexactness, even with respect to events that were important to
themselves, knows no bounds. Thomas Basin, who supervised the
process of rehabilitating Jeanne d'Arc, says in his chronicle that
she was born in Vaucouleurs. He has her brought by Baudricourt
himself, whom he identifies as the lord rather than the captain of
the city of Tours, and miscalculates the date of her first meeting
with the Dauphin by three months.[51] Olivier de la Marche, the
jewel among all the courtiers, errs consistently in matters of descent
and relationship in the ducal family and even is mistaken about the
date (in 1468) of the marriage of Charles the Bold and Margareth
of York. He had himself participated in the festivities of the event,
but dates them after the siege of Neuss in 1475.[52] Even Commines
is not free of such confusions: he repeatedly multiplies any given
span of years by two, and repeats his tale of the death of Adolph
of Gelder three times.[53]

The lack of an ability to make critical distinctions and the degree
of credulity are so clearly manifest on each page of medieval litera-

ture that it is unnecessary to cite examples. Naturally there are large gradations depending on the level of education of particular individuals. Among the people of Burgundy that peculiar form of barbaric credulity still dominated that never really believed in the death of an imposing ruler; this credulity was alive with respect to Charles the Bold so that as late as ten years after the battle of Nancy, people would still lend money on the terms that it would be repaid when the duke would return. Basin sees in this nothing but foolishness, as does Molinet; he mentions it among his "Mervilles du monde:"

> J'ay veu chose incongneue:
> Ung mort ressusciter,
> Et sur sa revenue
> Par milliers achapter.
> L'ung dit: il est en vie,
> L'autre: ce n'est que vent.
> Tous bons cueurs sans envie
> Le regrettent souvent.[54]*

However, given the influence of strong passion and the all too ready power of imagination, belief in the reality of imagined facts easily took root among the people. Given the disposition of the mind to think in terms of strongly isolated conceptions, the mere presence of an idea in the mind soon led to the assumption of its credibility. Once an idea had begun to bounce about in the brain with a particular name or form, it likely would be taken into the system of moral and religious images and automatically come to share their high credibility.

While on the one hand, ideas, by virtue of their sharp definition, their hierarchical connections, and their frequently anthropomorphic character, are particularly fixed and immobile, there is, on the other hand, the danger that in the vivid form of the idea its content would be lost. Eustache Deschamps dedicated a long allegorical and satirical didactic poem, "Le Miroir de Mariage,"[55] to the disad-

---

* I have seen an unknown thing:/A dead man revived,/And on his return/ Buy for thousands./The one says: He is alive,/The other: It is but wind./All good hearts, void of envy/regret his loss often.

vantages of marriage. One of its major characters is Franc Vouloir,* spurred on by Folie and Désir to marriage, but prevented from doing so by Repertoire de science.

What meaning does the poet intend to confer on the abstraction Franc Vouloir? In one sense he is the gay freedom of the bachelor, but at other times, free will in the philosophical sense. The imagination of the poet is so strongly absorbed by the personification of Franc Vouloir, in its own right, that he does not feel any need to clearly define the idea of his figure, but allows him to move from one extreme to another.

The same poem illustrates in another way how an idea, once elaborated, becomes amorphous or evaporates entirely. The tone of the poem echoes the familiar philistine and basically sensuous ridicule of the weakness and virtue of women; an amusement throughout the Middle Ages. To our sensibilities, the pious praises of a spiritual marriage and of the contemplative life itself, which Repertoire de science serves up to his friend Franc Vouloir in the latter part of the poem, are a crass dissonance with that tone.[56] But it is equally strange to us that the poet occasionally puts high truths in the mouths of Folie and Désir, truths that we would expect to come from the other side of the dispute.[57]

Here, as is frequently the case in the expressions of the Middle Ages, we are faced with the question: Did the poet take what he praised seriously? Just as we could have asked: Did Jean Petit and his Burgundian patrons believe all the gruesome details with which they soiled the memory of Orléans? Did the princes and noblemen really take all the bizarre fantasies and comedies with which they embellished their knightly schemes and vows seriously? It is extremely difficult, in matters of medieval thought, to clearly separate seriousness from play, the honest conviction from that mental disposition that the English call "pretending," which is the disposition of a child at play that also occupies such an important place in primitive cultures,[58] and that is expressed less through *geveinsdheid* ("make-believe") than through *aacnstellerij* ("act as if").

This blending of seriousness and play is characteristic of several areas. Above all, it is war into which people like to inject a comic element. The ridicule directed by the besieged upon their enemies is something they are sometimes made to pay for dearly. The peo-

* Free Will

ple of Meaux put an ass on their wall to torment Henry V of England; the people of Condé declare that they are not yet able to surrender because they were still baking their Easter cakes; in Montereau the burghers standing on the walls dust off their helmets after the cannons of the besiegers fire.[59] In the same vein, the camp of Charles the Bold at Neuss was set up like a vast country fair; the noblemen have, "par plaisance," their tents built in the form of castles complete with galleries and gardens. All kinds of amusements are provided.[60]

There is one area where the addition of ridicule to the most serious matters seems garish: the dark arena of the belief in devils and witches. Although the fantasies about devils were directly rooted in the deep fear that nourished this belief, the naive imagination nevertheless rendered such figures so childishly colorful and so familiar to everyone that they sometimes lost their terrifying aspect. It is not only in literature that the Devil appears as a comic figure; even in the gruesome seriousness of the witchcraft trials Satan's company is frequently fashioned in the manner of Hieronymus Bosch and the hellish smell of sulfur blends with the fluff of the farce. The devils who, under their captains Tahu and Gorgias, threw a cloister of nuns into disorder have names "assez consonnans aux noms de mondains habits, instruments et jeux du temps présent, comme Pantoufle, Courtaulx et Mornifle."[61]*

The fifteenth century is more than any other the century of the persecution of witches. At the very moment with which we customarily conclude the Middle Ages and delight in the flourishing of humanism, the systematic elaboration of the witch craze, that terrible outgrowth of medieval thought is revealed by the *Malleus maleficarum* and the *Bulle summis desiderantes* (1487 and 1484). No humanism, no Reformation prevents this madness. Does not the humanist Jean Bodin, even after 1550, in his *Demonomie* give the most learned and substantial nourishment to this persecution mania? The new times and the new knowledge did not immediately reject the cruelties of the witch-hunts. Oddly, the more temperate pronouncements about witchcraft that were proclaimed by the Gelder physician Johannes Wier were already widely suggested during the fifteenth century.

---

* "agreeing with the names of common articles of clothing, instruments and games of the present time such as Pantoufle, Courtaulx and Mornifle."

The attitude of the late medieval mind towards superstition, that is witchcraft and magic, is quite vacillatory and fluid. The age is not quite as helplessly given to all this witchcraft madness as one is tempted to conclude given its general credulity and lack of critical thinking. There are many expressions of doubt and of rational thought. Time and again evil erupts from a new cauldron of demonic mania and succeeds in surviving for a long time. Magic and witches were at home in special regions, for the most part mountainous areas: Savoy, Switzerland, Lorraine, and Scotland. But epidemic eruptions occur outside of those areas. Around 1400 even the French court was a hotbed of sorcery. A preacher warns the court nobility that care must be taken lest the phrase "vieilles sorcières" gradually come to be "nobles sorciers."[62] Particularly the atmosphere of the circles around Louis d'Orléans was charged with the devilish arts; the charges and suspicions raised by Jean Petit did not, in this respect, lack all justification. Orléans's friend and adviser, the aged Philippe de Mézières himself, suspected by the Burgundians to be the mysterious instigator of all those misdeeds, reports that he had learned magic from a Spaniard some time ago and how much effort it had cost him to forget this evil knowledge. As late as ten or twelve years after he had left Spain, "à sa volenté ne povoit pas bien extirper de son cuer les dessusdits signes et l'effect d'iceulx contra Dieu,"* until he was finally saved through confession and resistance with the help of God's mercy, "de ceste grand folie, qui est à l'âme crestienne anemie."[63] Masters of witchcraft were preferably sought in remote regions; a man desirous of conversing with the devil and unable to find anyone to teach him this art is told to go to "Ecosse la sauvage."[64]†

Orléans had his own masters of witchcraft and necromancers. He had one of them, whose skill did not satisfy him, burnt at the stake.[65] Admonished to check whether in the opinion of the scholars his superstitious practices were permissible, he responded, "Why should I consult them? I am well aware that they would counsel against it and yet I am absolutely determined to keep acting and believing as before, and I will not give it up."[66] Gerson links

---

* "He could not voluntarily extirpate from his mind the aforesaid signs and their effect against God . . . from this great folly, which is an enemy to the Christian soul."

† "wild Scotland."

these stubbornly sinful practices to Orléans's sudden death; he disapproves of the attempts to cure the mad king with the help of magic; one practitioner had already died in the flames for his lack of success.[67]

One special magical practice in particular is repeatedly mentioned as having been current at princely courts; this practice, called *invultare* in Latin and *envoûtement* in French, is the attempt, known all over the world, to destroy one's enemies by having a baptised wax figure, or another image, cursed in his name, or melted or pierced. Philip VI of France is said to have had such an image of himself, which had come into his possession, thrown into the fire with the words, "We will see who is the more powerful, the devil to ruin me or God to save me."[68] —The Burgundian dukes, too, were persecuted in this manner. "N'ay-je devers moy"—complains Charolais bitterly—"les bouts de cire baptisés dyaboliquement et pleins d'abominables mystères contre moy et autres?"[69]* Philip the Good, who, in contrast to his royal nephew, represents in many ways a more conservative view of life, such as in his preference for chivalry and splendor, in his crusade plans, in the old-fashioned literary forms that he protected, seems to have been leaning to a more enlightened opinion in manners of superstition than the French court, particularly Louis XI himself. Philip puts no store in the inauspicious day of the Innocent Children that repeats itself every week; he does not seek information about the future from astrologers and fortune-tellers, "car en toutes choses se monstra homme de lealle entière foy envers Dieu, sans enquerir riens de ses secrets,"† says Chastellain, who shares the same position.[70] Through the duke's intervention the terrible persecution of witches and magicians in Arras in 1461, one of the great epidemics of the witch craze, came to an end.

The terrible delusion of which the persecution of witches is in part the result was contributed to by the fact that the concepts of magic and heresy had become confused. In general, everything emotionally linked to the disgust, fear, and hatred of intolerable

---

* "Do I not have before me the candle stubs, baptised by devilish means and full of abominable mysteries against me and the others?"

† "because in all things he showed himself to be a man of correct and complete trust in God, without having any need to know His secrets."

transgressions, even such things outside of the direct realm of faith, was expressed by the term heresy. Monstrelet, for example, calls the sadistic crimes of Gilles de Rais simply "hérésie."[71] The common word for magic in fifteenth-century France was *vauderie*, which had lost its particular link with the Waldensians. In the "*Vauderie d'Arras*," we can trace both the terrifyingly sick delusion that was shortly to hatch the *Malleus maleficarum*[72] and the general doubt, among common people and nobles alike, as to the reality of all the misdeeds that were uncovered. One of the inquisitors claimed that one-third of Christianity was soiled by *vauderie*. His trust in God led him to the terrifying conclusion that anyone accused of sorcery would of necessity be guilty. God would not allow someone not a magician to be accused of such practices. "Et quand on arguoit contre lui, fuissent clercqs ou aultres, disoit qu'on debvroit prendre iceulx comme suspects d'estre vauldois."* If someone insists that some of the apparitions are the products of imagination, this inquisitor calls him suspicious. The inquisitor even claimed that he could tell if someone was involved in *vauderie* merely by looking at him. The man went mad in his later years, but the witches and magicians had been burnt at the stake in the meantime.

The city of Arras acquired such an evil reputation as a result of these persecutions that its merchants were refused lodging or credit out of fear that, on the next day, they might be accused of witchcraft and lose all their possessions to confiscation. All this notwithstanding, says Jacques du Clercq, outside of Arras not one in a thousand believed in the truth of all this: "onques on n'avoit veu es marches de par decha tels cas advenu."† When the victims are forced to recant their evil deeds prior to their execution, the people of Arras themselves have their doubts. A poem, full of hatred for the prosecutors, accuses them of having started it all out of greed; the bishop himself calls it a conspiracy, "une chose controuvée par aulcunes mauvaises personnes."[73]‡ The duke of Burgundy asks the faculty of Louvain for advice, and several of its representatives declare that *vauderie* is not real, that it is a mere illusion. There-

---

* "And when someone argued with him, be it a cleric or a lay person, he said that that one ought to be seized as suspected of the Waldensian heresy.

† "such things were never before heard of happening in these countries."

‡ "a matter conjured by a few bad subjects."

upon Philip sends his king of arms, Toison d'or, to the city and thenceforth there were no more victims and those still under investigation were treated more gently.

Finally, the witch trials of Arras were entirely annulled. The city celebrated the occasion with a joyful feast and edifying moral plays.[74]

The view that the delusions of the witches themselves, their rides through the sky and their sabbath orgies, were nothing but figments of their own imagination is a position that had already been advanced during the fifteenth century by several individuals. But this did not mean that the role of the Devil has been dropped from the agenda, because it is he who creates this fateful illusion in the first place; it is an error, but one which originates with Satan. This is still the position of Johannes Wier in the sixteenth century. Martin Lefranc, prior of the Church of Lausanne, the poet of the great "Le Champion des dames," which he dedicated in 1440 to Philip the Good, expressed the following enlightened position on witchcraft:

> Il n'est vielle tant estou(r)dye,
> Qui fist de ces choses la mendre
> Mais pour la faire ou ardre ou pendre,
> L'ennemy de nature humaine,
> Qui trop de faulx engins scet tendre,
> Les sens faussement lui demaine.
> Il n'est ne baston ne bastonne
> Sur quoy puist personne voler,
> Mais quant le diable leur estonne
> La teste, elles cuident aler
> En quelque place pour galer
> Et accomplir leur volonté.
> De Romme on les orra parler,
> Et sy n'y auront já esté.
> ....
> Les dyables sont tous en abisme,
> —Dist Franc-Vouloir—enchaienniez
> Et n'auront turquoise ni lime
> Dont soient já desprisonnez.
> Comment dont aux cristiennez
> Viennent ilz faire tant de ruzes

> *Et tant de cas désordonnez?*
> *Entendre ne sçay tes habuzes.**

And, at another place in the same poem:

> *Je ne croiray tant que je vive*
> *que femme corporellement*
> *Voit par l'air comme merle ou grive,*
> *—Dit le Champion prestement.—*
> *Saint Augustine dit plainement*
> *C'est illusion et fantosme;*
> *Et ne le croient aultrement*
> *Gregoire, Ambroise ne Jherosme.*
> *Quant la pourelle est en sa couche,*
> *Pour y dormir et reposer,*
> *L'ennemi qui point ne se couche*
> *Se vient encoste allé poser.*
> *Lors illusions composer*
> *Lui scet sy tres soubtillement,*
> *Qu'elle croit faire ou proposer*
> *Ce qu'elle songe seulement.*
> *Force la vielle songera*
> *Que sur un chat ou sur un chien*
> *A l'assemblée s'en ira;*
> *Mais certes il n'en sera rien:*
> *Et sy n'est baston ne mesrien*
> *Qui le peut ung pas enlever.*[75]†

---

* There is no aged woman so stupid/Who has been guilty of committing the least of these deeds,/But in order to have them burned or hanged,/The enemy confuses human nature./He who knows how to set so many traps,/To make the mind malicious./There are neither sticks nor rods/On which a human could fly,/But when the devil has confused/Their mind, they believe that they fly/Somewhere to indulge in pleasure/And to accomplish their lust./Then they can be heard to speak of Rome,/Though they have never been there./. . ./The devils are all in hell,/Tied up—says Franc-Vouloir—/And they will never get pliers or files/To get rid of their chains./How, then, should they be able to come/And play so many tricks on the Christian Children/And to indulge in so many lascivious adventures?/I can't understand your silliness.

† As long as I live, I shall not believe/That a woman can bodily/Travel through the air like blackbird or thrush,/—Said the Champion forthwith.—/Saint Augustine says plainly/That it is an illusion and fantasy,/And others think it is nothing,/Also Gregory, Ambroise and Jerome./When the poor woman lies in

Froissart considers the case of the Gascon nobleman and his demon companion, Horton, whom he describes so masterfully, to be an "erreur."[76] Gerson displays a tendency to take his evaluation of devilish illusion one step further and seek a natural explanation for all kinds of superstitious phenomena. Many of them, he says, arise simply from the human imagination and melancholy delusions, and these, in turn, are based in most instances on some corruption of the power of imagination that itself can be caused by damage to the brain. Such a view seems enlightened enough; even as that which holds that pagan vestiges and poetic inventions play a part in superstition. But even though Gerson admits that many alleged devilish deeds can be attributed to natural causes, he too ultimately gives credit to the Devil; that internal damage to the brain is itself the result of devilish illusion.[77]

Outside the frightful sphere of the persecution of witches, the church countered superstition with effective and suitable means. The preacher Brother Richard has "Madagoires" (mandrakes, mandragora, alraun) brought to be burned, "que maintes sotes gens gardoient en lieux repos, et avoient si grant foy en celle ordure, que pour vray ilz creoient fermement, que tant comme ilz l'avoient, mais qu'il fust bien nettement en beaux drapeaulx de soie ou de lin enveloppé, que jamais jour de leur vie ne seroient pouvres."[78]*—Burghers who had their palm read by a band of gypsies are excommunicated, and a procession is held to ward off that evil which could come from godlessness.[79]

A tract by Denis the Carthusian shows clearly where the border between faith and superstition was drawn, on which basis church doctrine attempted to reject some ideas and to purify others by imparting to them a truly religious content. Amulets, acts of conjuration, blessings, and so forth, says Denis, do not by themselves have the power to cause an effect. In this, they differ from the

---

her bed,/In order to sleep and rest there,/The enemy who never lies down to sleep/Comes and remains by her side./Then to call up illusions/Before her he can so subtly,/That she thinks she does or proposes to do/What she only dreams./Perhaps the gammer will dream/That on a cat or a dog/She will go to the meeting;/But certainly nothing will happen;/And there is neither a stick nor a beam/That could lift her a step.

* "which many ignorant people keep in a quiet place, and they have such great faith in this manure, that they truly strongly believe that as long as they keep it beautifully draped in silk or in linen, they will never be poor."

words of the sacrament, which, when recited with the correct intentions, do have an undeniable effect because God has, so to speak, tied his power to these words. Benedictions, however, are only to be regarded as humble requests, are only to be uttered with the appropriate pious formulation, and are only based on faith in God. If they usually have an effect, this is the case either because God imparts to them, if properly done, that effect or because, in cases where they are done differently—if, for instance, the Sign of the Cross is made improperly—their effect, should they actually be effective in spite of everything, is a delusion of the Devil. But the Devil's works are not miracles, because the devils know the secret powers of nature; the effect is therefore a natural one just as the premonitions of birds, etc., are based on natural causes. —Denis concedes that in folk practices all those blessings, amulets, and the like appear to have an evident worth, but he denies their value and voices the opinion that clerics should rather prohibit all such things.[80]

Generally speaking, the attitude towards anything that appeared to be supernatural may be characterized as vacillating between rational, natural explanations, spontaneous pious affirmation, and the distrust of the tricks of the Devil and devilish deceit. The dictum "Omnia quae visibiliter fiunt in hoc mundo, possunt fieri per daemones" ("Everything that appears visible in this world could be caused by the Devil"), affirmed by the authority of St. Augustine and St. Thomas Aquinas, caused uncertainty among the pious. The cases in which a miserable hysteria drove the burghers into a short-lived frenzy only to be unmasked after it had run its course are not counted among the rarer of occasions.[81]

Chapter Twelve

ART IN LIFE[1]

FRENCH-BURGUNDIAN CULTURE OF LATE MEDIEVAL times is best known to the present age through its fine art, most notably its painting. Our perception of the time is dominated by the brothers Van Eyck, Rogier van der Weyden, Memling, and the sculptor Sluter. This has not always been the case. Some fifty years ago or even somewhat earlier, the average educated person knew those times primarily through their history. This knowledge was not, certainly, as a rule acquired directly from Monstrelet and Chastellain, but rather from De Barante's *Histoire des Ducs de Bourgogne,* which is based on those two authors. And is it not the case, that over and beyond De Barante, it was mostly Victor Hugo's *Notre Dame de Paris* that embodied the image most people had of that period?[2]

The image that came from these sources was grim and somber. The chroniclers themselves, and those who dealt with the subject during the Romantic period of the nineteenth century, allowed the dark and repulsive aspects of late medieval times to emerge: its bloody cruelty, its arrogance and its greed, its lust for revenge and its misery. The lighter colors in this depiction come from the splendidly bloated vanity of the famous court festivities that were replete with the sparkle of worn allegories and unbearable luxury.

And now? Now that age basks in our perception in the lofty, dignified seriousness and the deep peace of the Van Eycks and Memling; that world half a millennium ago appears to us to be permeated by a splendid light of simple gaiety, by a treasure of spiritual depth. The formerly wild and dark image has been transformed into one of peace and serenity. It seems as if all the evidence we have, in addition to the fine arts of that period, testifies to the presence of beauty and wisdom: the music of Dufay and his disciples, the words of Ruusbroec and Thomas à Kempis. Even in those places where the cruelty and misery of those times still reverberates loudly, in the history of Jeanne d'Arc and the poetry of Villon, we perceive nothing but loftiness and empathy.

What is the reason for this profoundly deep difference between the two images of this time, the one reflected in art and the other derived from history and literature? Is it a characteristic of that particular age that there was a great gulf between the different spheres and forms of life? Was the sphere of life from which the pure and spiritual art of the painters arose different and better than that of the princes, nobles, and litterateurs? Is it possible that the painters, along with Ruusbroec, the Windesheimers, and the folk song, belonged to a peaceful limbo on the outskirts of a glaring hell? Or is it a common phenomenon that the fine arts leave a brighter image of an age than the words of poets and historians?

The answer to the last question is absolutely affirmative. As a matter of fact, the image we have fashioned for ourselves of all earlier cultures has become more cheerful since we have turned from reading to seeing, and since our historical sense organ has become increasingly visual. The fine arts, the primary source for our perception of the past, do not openly lament. The bitter after-taste produced by the pain of the ages evaporates in the fine arts. Once articulated in words, the lamentations over the suffering of the world always retain their tone of immediate grief and dissatisfaction, touching us always with sadness and pity; while suffering expressed through the means of the fine arts at once slips into the elegiac and serenely peaceful.

Those who think that an age can be comprehended in its entire reality through art leave a general error in historical criticism uncorrected. In respect to Burgundian times in particular, there is, moreover, the danger of a specific error of perception: the failure to correctly assess the relationship between the fine arts and the literary expressions of culture.

The observer is drawn into this mistake if he does not take into account that he begins by taking a very different position towards art than he does towards literature because of the difference in their state of preservation. The literature of the late medieval period, with a few individual exceptions, is known to us nearly completely. We know it in its highest and lowest forms, in all its categories and styles, ranging from the most lofty to the most ordinary, from the most theoretical to the most concrete. The entire life of the age is reflected and expressed in its literature. Further, the written tradition is not exhausted by literature alone; the entire corpus of official papers and documents is at our disposal to complete our information. The fine arts, in contrast, which already, by virtue of their particular nature, reflect the life of the age less directly and comprehensively, are only available to us in fragments. Only very few remnants survive outside of church art. All of the secular fine arts, most of the applied arts, are nearly completely missing; most lacking are those forms in which the changing facets of the connection between the production of art and the life of the community is revealed. What the limited treasury of altarpieces and tomb monuments teach us about this connection is far from enough; the image offered by art remains isolated outside our knowledge of the robust life of that age. For comprehending the function of the fine arts in life, the admiring study of the surviving masterpieces does not suffice: that which has been lost also demands our attention.

Art was still an integral part of life during that age. Life was shaped by strong forms and held together and measured by the sacraments of the church, the annual sequence of festivals, and the divisions of the day. The labors and joys of life all had their fixed forms: religion, knighthood, and courtly *Minne* provided the most important of these forms. Art had the task of embellishing the forms in which life was lived with beauty. What was sought was not art itself, but the beautiful life. In contrast to later ages, one did not step outside a more or less indifferent daily routine in order to enjoy art in solitary contemplation for the sake of solace or edification; rather, art was used to intensify the splendor of life itself. It is the destiny of art to vibrate in concert with the high points of life, be it in the highest flights of piety or in the proudest enjoyment of earthly moments. During the Middle Ages art was not yet perceived as beauty *per se*. It was for the most part applied art, even in cases where we would consider the works to be their own reason for being. That is to say, for the Middle Ages, the reason for desiring a given work of art rested in its purpose, rested in the fact that artworks are the servants of any one of the forms of life. In cases where, disregarding any practical uses, the pure ideal of beauty guides the creating artist himself, this happens to a large part subconsciously. The first sprouts of a love for art for its own sake appear as a wild growth on the production of art: princes and noblemen piled up objects of art until they became collections; this rendered them useless: they were then enjoyed as curiosities, as precious parts of the princely treasury. The actual sense of art that arises during the Renaissance has this foundation.

In the appreciation of the great works of art of the fifteenth century, particularly of altarpieces and tomb art, contemporaries went far beyond aesthetic considerations. Their importance and purpose outweighed their beauty by far. They had to be beautiful because the object was sacred or its purpose lofty. The purpose was always more or less practical in nature. Altarpieces have a twofold significance: ceremonially displayed during high festivals, they serve the purposes of elevating the piety of the congregation and keeping the memory of the pious donors alive. We know that the altarpiece of the *Adoration of the Lamb* by Hubert and Jan van Eyck (plates 8, 9) was only rarely opened. Whenever the administrators of the cities of the Netherlands ordered plaques illustrating famous judgments or legal acts to decorate the law courts in the town halls, for example the *Judgment of Cambyses* by Gerard David in Bruges (plate 10), or the *Judgment of the Emperor Otto* by Dirk Bouts at Louvain (plate 11), or the lost paintings from Brussels by Rogier van der Weyden, the purpose was to keep before the eyes of the judges a solemn and vibrant reminder of their duty. —Just how sensitive the reactions to the content of the depictions decorating the walls were is shown by the following instance. In 1384, a meeting was called in Lelinghem that, it was hoped, would lead to an armistice between France and England. The duke of Berry had the barren walls of the old chapel in which the princely emissaries were to meet decorated with tapestries depicting the battles of antiquity. But when John of Gaunt, the duke of Lancaster, saw them upon entering the chapel, he demanded their removal: those aspiring to make peace should not have war and destruction depicted before them. In their place other tapestries were hung depicting the implements of the Passion of Christ.[3]

The portrait is inseparably tied to its practical significance and, even in our own day, has retained its moral value as a family possession, because the feelings about life, the love of parents and family pride, which it serves, are much less used up than the forms of social life to which the legal scenes belong. Portraits also had the additional function of making those to be engaged to be married known to one another. Among the emissaries whom Philip the Good sent to Portugal in 1428 to find a bride for him was Jan van Eyck, who was to paint the portrait of the princess. Sometimes the fiction is maintained that the bridegroom had fallen in love with the unknown bride merely by looking at the portrait, as, for example, in the case of the courtship of Richard II of England with the six-year-old Isabella of France.[4] There are even occasional claims that a choice had been made by comparing different portraits. When the young Charles VI of France has to take a wife and the choice falls among the daughters of the dukes of Bavaria, Austria, and Lorraine, an excellent painter is dispatched to paint portraits of all three candidates. The king is shown the pictures and chooses the fourteen-year-old Isabella of Bavaria, because he finds her by far the prettiest.[5]

Nowhere else is the purpose of a work of art so predominantly practical as in the case of tomb monuments, which confronted sculpture in that age with its highest task. But the practical function of art was not restricted to sculpture alone. The intense desire for a visible image of the deceased had to be satisfied even during the funeral. On occasion, the deceased was represented by a living individual. During the funeral of Bertrand du Guesclin at St. Denis, four mounted knights in armor appeared in the church, "representans la personne du mort quand il vivoit."[6]* A bill from the year 1375 mentions a funeral ceremony in the house of Polignac, "cinq sols à Blaise pour avoir fait le chevalier mort à la sepulture."[7]† For royal funerals, a leather puppet fully dressed in princely regalia is most often used; the goal is always a near resemblance.[8] It appears on some occasions that more than one such image would be present in a procession. The emotions of the people were focused on the sight of those images.[9] The death mask, which made its appearance in France during the fifteenth century, probably originated in the fashioning of these funeral puppets.

A work almost always has a particular end, a particular purpose connected with daily life. This obscures the boundary between the fine arts and the crafts, or better, this boundary is not yet drawn. Neither does a boundary yet exist with regard to the person of the artist himself. Among the group of highly individual masters in the service of the courts of Flanders, Berry, and Burgundy, the creation of individual paintings by the artists alternates freely with the tasks of illuminating handwritten manuscripts and polychrom-

---

* "representing the dead man when he was alive."
† "Five sols to Blaise for representing the dead knight at the funeral."

PLATE 1. *Wheel of Fortune.* Codex miniature. Biblioteca Nazionale, Florence, Italy. Courtesy of Alinari/Art Resource, New York.

PLATE 2. Velázquez, Diego Rodriguez de Silva. *The Maids of Honor.*
Prado, Madrid.

Occurrunt alo pereundi mille figure. Mors oz minº penc ꝙ mꝛa moꝛt is habet
Vado moꝛi preful: baculum.   Vado moꝛi miles: belli cert ami
fãdalia. mittram. Nolens fiue   ne victoꝛ. Moꝛtem non didici
volens defero: vado moꝛi.   vincere: vado moꝛi.

Le moꝛt
Que vous tires la tefte arriere
Archeuefque: tire vous pꝛes.
Aues vous peur quon ne voº fiere
Ne doubtez vous ventres apꝛes.
Nett pas toufiours la moꝛt epꝛes
Tout hôme: et le fuit cofte a cofte.
Rendꝛe conuient debtes. et pꝛetz,
Vne fois fault compter a lofte.

Larcheuefque
Las: ie ne fcay ou regarder
Tât fuis par moꝛt a grant deftroit
Ou fuiray ie pour moy aider:
Certes qui bien la congnoiftroit
Hoꝛs de raifon iamais niftroit:
Plus ne gerray en chambꝛe paite.
Moꝛir me conuient ceft le dꝛoit.
Quât faire fault ceft grât côtraite.

Le moꝛt
Vous qui entre les grans barons
Aues eu renom cheualier:
Obliez trompettes. clarons.
Et me fuiues fans fommellier.
Les dames folies reueillier:
En faifant danfer longue piece.
A autre danfe fault vefilier
Ce que lun fait lautre depiece.

Le cheualier
Oꝛ ay ie efte autorife
En pleufeurs fais: et bien fame.
Des grans. et des petis pꝛife.
Auec ce des dames ame.
Ne oneques ne fus diffame
A la court de feigneur notable:
Mais a ce cop fuis tout pafme
Deffoubz le ciel na rien eftable.

PLATE 3. Marchand, Guyot. *Danse Macabre.* 1486. Bibliothèque Nationale, Paris. Courtesy of Giraudon/Art Resource, New York.

PLATE 4. French School. Figure of Death from the Cemetery of the Innocents, Paris. 16th century. Louvre, Paris. Courtesy of Giraudon/Art Resource, New York.

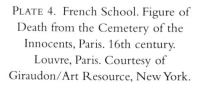

PLATE 5. Broederlam, Melchior. *The Flight into Egypt*. Musée de Beaux-Arts, Dijon.

PLATE 6. Foucquet, Jean. *Melun Madonna*. Koninklijk Museum, Antwerp.

PLATE 7. Foucquet, Jean. *Etienne Chevalier with St. Stephen.*
Gemaeldegalerie, Staatliche Museen, Berlin. Courtesy of Foto
Marburg/Art Resource, New York.

PLATE 8. Van Eyck, Jan. Ghent Altarpiece, closed. 1432. Cathedral St. Bavo, Ghent.
Courtesy of Giraudon/Art Resource, New York.

PLATE 9. Van Eyck, Jan. Ghent Altarpiece, open. 1432. Cathedral St. Bavo, Ghent.
Courtesy of Giraudon/Art Resource, New York.

PLATE 10. David, Gerard. *Judgement of Cambyses.* Municipal Museum, Bruges. Courtesy of Alinari/Art Resource, New York.

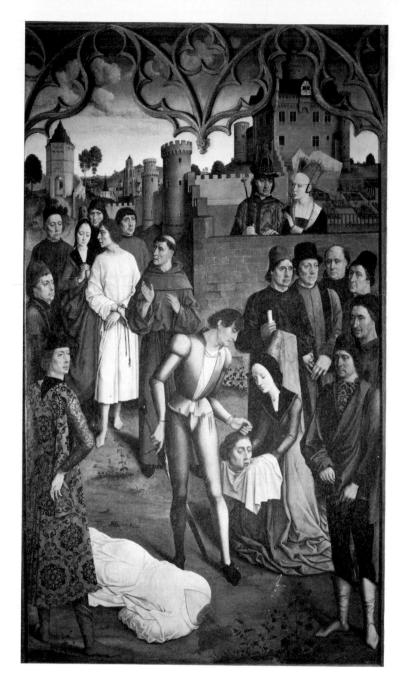

PLATE 11. Bouts, Dirk. *Judgement of the Emperor Otto* (Scene 1).
Musée Royaux, Brussels.

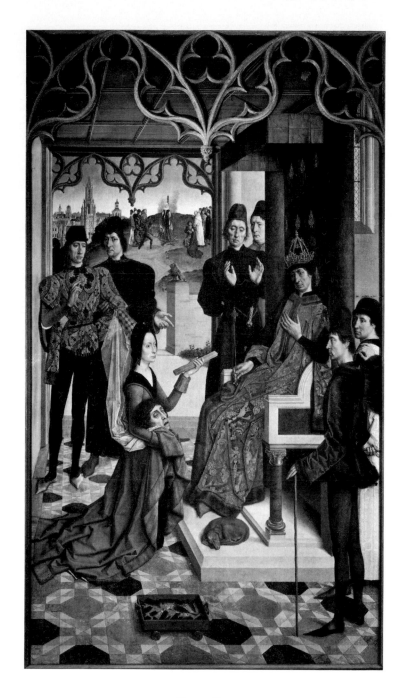

(Scene 2)

PLATE 12. Breughel, Pieter the Elder. The Old Port of Naples. Palazzo
Doria, Rome. Courtesy of Alinari/Art Resource, New York.

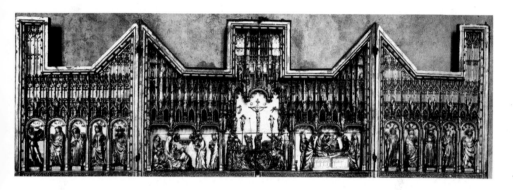

PLATE 13. Baerze, Jacques de. *Retable of the Crucifixion*. Musée des
Beaux-Arts, Dijon.

PLATE 14. Van der Weyden, Rogier. *Last Judgement Altarpiece* (open).
Hotel-Dieu, Beaune, France. Courtesy of Giraudon/Art Resource,
New York.

PLATE 15. Van Eyck, Jan. *Autun Altarpiece.* Louvre, Paris. Cliché des Musées Nationaux, Paris.

PLATE 16. Van Eyck, Jan. *Autun Altarpiece:* detail of landscape in background.
Louvre, Paris. Cliché des Musées Nationaux, Paris.

PLATE 17. Van der Weyden, Rogier. *Altarpiece of the Seven Sacraments.*
Koninklijk Museum, Antwerp.

PLATE 18. Juan de la Huerta/Antoine le Moiturier. *Tomb of John the Fearless.* Musée des Beaux-Arts, Dijon.

PLATE 19. Claus Sluter/Claus de Werve. *Tomb of Philip the Bold.* Musée de Beaux-Arts, Dijon.

PLATE 20. Sluter, Claus. Moses from *The Well of Moses*. 1395–1404.
Chartreuse de Champmol, Dijon. Courtesy of Giraudon/Art
Resource, New York.

PLATE 21. Van Eyck, Jan. *Wedding Portrait (Giovanni Arnolfini and Cenami Arnolfini)*. Reproduced by courtesy of the Trustees, The National Gallery, London.

PLATE 22. Van der Weyden, Rogier. *Bladelin Altarpiece.*
Gemaeldegalerie, Staatliche Museen, Berlin. Courtesy of Giraudon/
Art Resource, New York.

PLATE 23. Van Eyck, Jan. *St. Jerome in His Study.* c. 1435. Oil on linen
paper on oak, 20.6 cm. x 13.3 cm. Accession no. 25.4. Photograph
©The Detroit Institute of Arts, 1995. City of Detroit Purchase.

PLATE 24. Van Eyck, Jan. *Margaretha
van Eyck*. Municipal Museum,
Bruges. Courtesy of Foto
Marburg/Art Resource, New York.

PLATE 25. Van Eyck, Jan. *Baudoin de
Lannoy*. Gemaeldegalerie, Staatliche
Museen, Berlin. Courtesy of Foto
Marburg/Art Resource, New York.

PLATE 26. Van Eyck, Jan. *Madonna of Canon van der Paele.* Municipal
Museum, Bruges. Foto Marburg/Art Resource, New York.

PLATE 27. Van Eyck, Jan. *Giovanni Arnolfini*. Gemaeldegalerie, Staatlich Museen, Berlin. Courtesy of Foto Marburg/Art Resource, New York.

PLATE 28. Van Eyck, Jan. *Leal Souvenier.* Reproduced by courtesy of the Trustees, National Gallery, London.

PLATE 29 (opposite). Van Eyck, Jan. *Annunciation*. Andrew W. Mellon Collection, © 1994 Board of Trustees, National Gallery of Art, Washington, D.C.

PLATE 30. De Witte, Emmanuel. *The Fishmonger's Stall*. Courtesy of Museum Boymans-van Beuningen, Rotterdam.

PLATE 31. Sint Jans, Geertgen tot. *Nativity.* Reproduced by courtesy
of the Trustees, The National Gallery, London.

PLATE 32. Limburg Brothers.
September (Grape Harvest). Calendar page from
the manuscript *Très Riches Heures du Duc de
Berry.* Musée Conde, Chantilly. Courtesy of
Giraudon/Art Resource,
New York.

PLATE 33. Limburg Brothers. *March.*
Calendar page from *Très Riches Heures du Duc
de Berry.* Musée Conde, Chantilly. Courtesy of
Giraudon/Art Resource, New York.

PLATE 34. Limburg Brothers. *December.*
Calendar page from *Très Riches Heures du Duc
de Berry.* Musée Conde, Chantilly. Courtesy
of Giraudon/Art Resource, New York.

PLATE 35. Limburg Brothers. *February.*
Calendar page from *Très Riches Heures du Duc
de Berry.* Musée Conde, Chantilly. Courtesy
of Giraudon/Art Resource, New York.

PLATE 36. Campin, Robert (Master of Flémalle).
Annunciation (right panel). All rights reserved.
The Metropolitan Museum of Art.

PLATE 37. Van Eyck, Hubert and Jan. *The Three Marys at the Open Sepulchre.* Museum Boymans-van Beuningen, Rotterdam.

PLATE 38. Limburg Brothers. *Purification*. From *Très Riches Heures du Duc de Berry*. Musée Conde, Chantilly. Courtesy of Giraudon/Art Resource, New York.

PLATE 39. Limburg Brothers. *Visitation*. From *Très Riches Heures du Duc de Berry*. Musée Conde, Chantilly. Courtesy of Giraudon/ Art Resource, New York.

PLATE 40. Breughel, Pieter the Elder. *The Battle between Carnival and Lent.*
Courtesy of Kunsthistorisches Museum, Vienna.

PLATE 41. Rembrandt Harmensz van Rijn. *The Beggars.* Courtesy
Foto Marburg/Art Resource, New York.

PLATE 42. Murillo, Bartolomé. *Beggar Boy.* Louvre, Paris. Cliché des Musées Nationaux–Paris.

PLATE 43. Steinlen, Theophile. *Flower Sellers on the Boulevard*. Musée
de la Ville de Paris, Musée Carnavalet, Paris.

PLATE 44. Northern Netherlands School: *Lysbeth van Durenvoode.*
Rijksmuseum, Amsterdam.

PLATE 45. Master of the Bonner Diptych: *Love Magic*. Museum der Bildenden Künste, Leipzig.

ing sculptures. They also have to lend their hands to painting coats of arms on shields and banners and designing tournament costumes and official robes. Melchoir Broederlam, initially painter to Louis of Male, the count of Flanders, subsequently to Louis's son-in-law, the first duke of Burgundy, decorated five carved chairs for the house of the count. He repaired and painted the rare mechanical contraptions in Hesdin Castle that sprayed the guests with water or powder. He worked on the duchess's carriage. Still later, he supervised the sumptuous decorations of the fleet that was assembled by the duke of Burgundy in 1387 in the port of Sluis for an expedition against England that never took place. Court painters were always employed during princely weddings and funerals. In the workshops of Jan van Eyck statues were painted and he himself fashioned a kind of world map for Duke Philip on which cities and countries could be seen minutely and clearly painted. Hugo van der Goes painted advertisements for indulgences. Gerard David is reputed to have painted scenic decorations on the railings or shutters of the room in the *Broodhuis** in Bruges wherein Maximillian was incarcerated in 1488 so as to make the stay of the royal prisoner more pleasant.

Of the many works from the hands of the great and not so great artists only a fraction of a rather special kind have been preserved. These are primarily tomb monuments, altarpieces, portraits, and miniatures. With the exception of portraits, only very little survives of secular painting. Of the ornamental arts and crafts, we have a number of specific categories: church utensils, clerical vestments, some furniture. How much would our insight into the character of the art of the fifteenth century be improved if we could place the bathing scenes of Jan van Eyck or Rogier van der Weyden or the hunting scenes side by side with the many pietàs and madonnas. We are hardly able to form any understanding of the entire field of the applied arts. To do so, we would have to see the ecclesiastical paraments and the stately robes of the court, bedecked with precious stones and bells, all together. We would have to be able to see the splendidly decorated ships of which the miniatures convey only a highly deficient, mechanical notion. There are only a few things whose beauty aroused so much enthusiasm in Froissart as that of ships.[10] The banners, richly decorated with coats of arms,

* "Breadhouse"

fluttering from the tops of the mast, were sometimes so long that they touched the water. In the paintings of ships by Peter Breughel these unusually long and broad streamers can still be seen (plate 12). The ship of Philip the Bold, on which Melchior Broederlam worked in 1387 at Sluis, was covered with blue and gold; large coats of arms graced the pavilion of the aftercastle. The sails were strewn with marguerites, the initials of the ducal couple and their slogan, "Il me tarde." Noblemen vied with one another to see whose ship was most expensively decorated for the expedition to England. Painters are well off, says Froissart,[11] they are able to demand any price, and there are never enough of them. He claims that many ships had the masts covered with gold leaf. Guy de la Trémoïlle, in particular, spared no expense: He spent more than two thousand pounds for gilding. "L'on ne se povoit de chose adviser pour luy jolyer, ne deviser, que le seigneur de la Trimouille ne le feist faire en ses nefs. Et tout ce paioient les povres gens parmy France . . ."*

This taste for splendid extravagance would undoubtedly catch our attention forcefully if we could see the lost secular decorative arts. The surviving works of art most decidedly do share that tendency towards extravagance, but since we value this quality in art least, we pay less attention to it. We only seek to enjoy the profound beauty of any given work. Everything that is mere splendor and pomp has lost its attraction for us. For contemporaries, however, this very pomp and splendor was of tremendous importance.

French-Burgundian culture of the waning Middle Ages counts among those cultures in which beauty is replaced by splendor. Late medieval art reflects the spirit of the late Middle Ages faithfully, a spirit that had run its course. What we had posited as one of the most important characteristics of late medieval thought, the depiction of everything that could be thought down to the smallest detail, the oversaturation of the mind with an endless system of formal representation, this, too, constitutes the essence of the art of that time. Art, too, tries to leave nothing unformed, unpresented, or undecorated. The flamboyant Gothic is like an endless organ postlude; it breaks down all forms by this self-analyzing

---

* "One could not even conceive a way to make the ship prettier which the lord de la Trémoïlle did not have done. And all this paid for by the poor people of France."

process; every detail finds its continuous elaboration, each line its counterline. It is an unrestrainedly wild overgrowth of the idea by the form; ornate detail attacks every surface and line. That *horror vacui,* which may perhaps be identified as a characteristic of end periods of intellectual development, dominates in this art.

This all means that the boundaries between splendor and beauty become less distinct. Embellishment and ornamentation no longer serve the glorification of the naturally beautiful, but rather overgrow and thus threaten to choke it. The farther the departure from purely pictorial art, the more unrestrained the wild overgrowth of formal ornamentation covering content. There is little opportunity for sculpture to engage in this wild growth of forms as long as it creates freestanding figures: the statues of the Moses Fountain and the "plourants"[12] of the tombstones compete, in their strict, simple, naturalness, with Donatello. But as soon as the task of the art of sculpture is of a decorative nature or falls into the realm of painting and, bound by the reduced dimensions of the relief, reproduces entire scenes, sculpture, too, overindulges in restless, overloaded displays. Those who see the carvings by Jacques de Baerze at the tabernacle in Dijon next to the paintings of Broederlam will notice the disharmony between them (plate 13). In painting, wherever it is purely representational, simplicity and quietude dominate; carving, by its very nature decorative, treats the shaping of figures ornamentally, and one perceives the phenomenon of forms crowding each other out as something that supplants the quietude of the painted object. The difference between painting and tapestries is of the same kind. The art of weaving, even in cases where it assumes a task of a purely representational nature, by virtue of its set technique, stands closer to ornamentation and is unable to extricate itself from the exaggerated need for embellishment. Tapestries are overcrowded with figures and colors and remain apparently archaic in form.[13] Departing still further from the pure fine arts, we encounter clothing. Clothing, too, belongs undeniably to art, but it is part of its very purpose that allure and ostentation predominate over beauty itself. Moreover, personal vanity pulls the art of clothing into the sphere of passion and sensuousness where the qualities that comprise the essence of high art, balance and harmony, come second.

An extravagance like that found in the style of dress between 1350 and 1480 has not been experienced in later ages, at least not in such a general and sustained way. Certainly there have been extravagant fashions in later times, such as the dress of the mercenaries around 1520 and aristocratic French costume in 1660, but the unrestrained exaggeration and overprofusion so characteristic of French-Burgundian dress for a century has no parallel. In their dress we are privileged to observe what the sense of beauty of that age, left to its own undisturbed impulses, would accomplish. A court costume is overburdened with hundreds of precious stones and all its proportions are exaggerated to a ridiculous degree; the headdress of women assumes the sugarloaf form of the hennin; natural hair is hidden or removed at the temples and from the area of the forehead at the hairline, so that the curiously vaulted foreheads that were considered beautiful were prominently displayed. The décolletage began abruptly. Male garments, however, displayed still more numerous extravagances; most striking of all, the elongated toes of the shoes, the *poulaines*, which the knights at Nicopolis[14] had to cut off in order to be able to flee, the narrow waists, the balloon-like puffed-up sleeves that rose at the shoulders, the houpelandes dangling to the feet, and the short jackets that barely covered the hips, the tall caps or hats narrowing at the tips or shaped like a cylinder, the bonnets wondrously draped around the head reminiscent of a cock's comb or a flickering flame. The more festive the more extravagant, since all this beauty was equated with splendor, stateliness, *estat*.[15] The mourning dress that Philip the Good wears after the murder of his father while receiving the King of England is so long that it trails from the tall horse he is riding all the way to the ground.[16]

All this wasteful splendor reaches its climax in the festivities of the court. Everyone remembers the descriptions of the Burgundian court festivities, such as the banquet at Lille in 1454, where the guests took their vows to participate in the crusade against the Turks while the pheasants were being served, or the wedding feast of Charles the Bold and Margareth of York at Bruges in 1468.[17] We cannot imagine a greater distance than that which exists between the consecrated atmosphere of the Ghent and Louvain altars and these expressions of barbaric princely ostentation. The descriptions of all those *estremets* with pastry from within which musicians performed, the overly ornate ships and castles, the monkeys, whales, giants, and dwarfs, and all the worn allegory belonging to them force us to see them as unusually insipid performances.

However, isn't the distance we perceive between the two extremes of church art and the art of the court festivities easily exaggerated in more than one respect? First of all, we have to be clear
about the function that the festivity served in society. It still had
the purpose that it had among primitive peoples; that is, to be the
sovereign expression of the culture, to be the form in which the
highest joy of life was expressed by the community, and to express
the sense of that community. During times of great social renewal,
such as at the time of the French Revolution, festivities sometimes
regain that important social and aesthetic function.

Modern man is in a position to seek individually the confirma-
tion of his view of life and the purest enjoyment of his *joie de vivre*
during any moment of leisure in self-chosen relaxations. But an
age in which the spiritual luxuries are still poorly distributed and
less accessible requires for the purpose of renewal a communal act:
the festival. The greater the contrast with the misery of daily life,
the more indispensable the festival and the stronger the means required to bestow splendor on life by virtue of the ecstasy of beauty
and enjoyment that lights up the darkness of reality. The fifteenth
century was an age of great emotional depression and thorough
pessimism. We have already mentioned earlier the permanent pressure from injustice and violence, hell and damnation, pestilence,
fire and hunger, Satan and the witches, under which the century
lived. Mankind in its wretchedness needed more than the daily
repeated promise of heavenly bliss and God's watchful care and
benevolence: from time to time a glorious, solemn, and communal
affirmation of the beauty of life was required. The enjoyment of
life in its primary forms—play, love, drink, dance, and song—does
not suffice. Life has to be ennobled through beauty, to be stylized
in a social expression of the joy of life. For the individual, relief
through the reading of books, listening to music, seeing art, or
enjoying nature was still out of reach; books were too expensive,
nature too dangerous, and art was no more than a small part of
the festival.

The folk festival had only song and dance for its original sources
of beauty. For the beauty of color and form folk festivals based
themselves on church festivals, which had both in abundance, and
usually took place immediately after a church festival. The separation of the urban festival from the church form, and its establishment of a decor of its own, took place throughout the entire fif-

teenth century through the labor of the rhetoricians. Prior to this time, the princely courts had been in a position both to arrange a purely secular festival with an attendant display of art and to bestow on the festival a splendor of its own. But display and splendor are not sufficient for festivals; nothing is as indispensable for them as style.

The church festival possessed style because of its liturgy. In a beautiful communal social gesture the church festivals always managed to give moving expression to a lofty idea. The sacred dignity and noble stateliness of the ceremonies were not destroyed even by the most extreme overgrowth of festive details, which bordered on the burlesque. But from where were court festivals to obtain style? On which conception was it to be based? —The answer could be none other than the chivalric ideal, because the entire life of the court was based on it. Was the chivalric ideal tied to a style, to a liturgy, so to speak? Indeed; everything related to the act of bestowing knighthood, the rules of orders, tournaments, *préséance, hommage,* and service, the entire game of the kings at arms, heralds, coats of arms, constituted the style. To the degree the court festival was based on those elements, it most decidedly possessed in the eyes of contemporaries a greatly elevated style. Strong sensitivity to the stylish festive air of the ceremonial procedure frequently comes naturally to modern man, independent of all the awe with which all matters aristocratic or monarchic are seen. How much more so it must have been for those who were still captivated by the delusion of that chivalric ideal whenever they encountered the pompous display of costumes with their long trains and glittering colors!

But court festivals aspired to more. They wanted to present the dream of the heroic life in its extreme form. This is where the style failed. The entire apparatus of knightly fancy and splendor was no longer filled with real life. Everything had become much too literary, a sickly renaissance, an empty convention. The inner decay of the form of life remained hidden under the overload of glamour and etiquette. The chivalric idea of the fifteenth century revels in a romanticism that is hollow and worn throughout. And that was the source from which the court festival was supposed to derive the inspiration for its performances and presentations. How could it create a style from such a styleless, undisciplined, and stale literature as that of chivalric romanticism in its decay?

The aesthetic value of the *entremets* should be seen in this light: They were applied literature. Actually, this was the only way this literature could be made bearable, since in the *entremets* the fleeting, superficial shapes of all the colorful literary dream figures had to make room for the necessity of the material representation.

The heavy barbarian seriousness evident in all this fits well into the Burgundian court, which seemed to have lost the lighter and more harmonious French spirit through its contact with the North. All the tremendous display is taken solemnly and seriously. The great festivity of the duke at Lille was both the end and the climax of a number of banquets given by the court nobility in competition with each other. All this had started quite simply and with little expense; the number of guests and the luxury of the menus and *entremets* was gradually increased. By being offered a wreath by his host, a guest was designated to take his turn as successor; in this manner the knights were followed by the great lords and the great lords by the princes, all this with steadily increasing expense and stateliness, until it was finally the turn of the duke himself. But Philip intended to hold more than a splendid feast; he intended to collect vows for the crusade against the Turks for the reconquest of Constantinople, which had fallen a year earlier. This was the officially proclaimed goal of the duke's life. To prepare for the feast, he appointed a commission with the knight of the Fleece, Jean de Lannoy, as its leader. Olivier de la Marche, too, was a member. Whenever he comes to this issue in his memoirs he becomes very solemn: "Pour ce que grandes et honnorables oeuvres désirent loingtaine renomée et perpétuelle mémoire."* These are the words with which he begins to reminisce about those great events.[18] The first councillors, who were closest to the duke, regularly attended the deliberations: even Chancellor Rolin and Antoine de Croy, the First Chamberlain, were consulted before agreement was reached where "les cérémonies et les mistères" should be held.

All these beautiful events have been described so often that there is no need to do so here. Some had even crossed the channel to witness the spectacle. Joining the guests were innumerable noble onlookers, the majority of whom were masked. First the guests took a stroll to admire the splendid stationary displays; then came

* "Because great and honorable achievements deserve a lasting renown and perpetual remembrance."

the performances with living persons and *tableaux vivants*. Olivier himself played the leading role of Sainte Eglise when she entered during the most important scene inside a tower placed on the back of an elephant led by a giant Turk. The tables were given the most marvelous decorations: a manned carrack[19] with full sails, a meadow with trees, a spring, rocks, and a picture of St. Andreas, Lusignan Castle with the fairy Melusine, a windmill and a bird-shooting scene, a forest with moving wild animals, and, finally, the church with an organ and singers that, alternating with the twenty-eight-man orchestra that was sitting in a pie, offered musical performances.

What matters here is the degree of taste or tastelessness that is found in all this. The subject matter itself is nothing but a loose mixture of mythological, allegorical, and moralizing images, but what about the execution? There is no doubt that the effect was largely sought through extravagance. The Tower of Gorkum that served as ostentatious table decoration during a 1468 wedding celebration was forty-six feet tall.[20] La Marche reports about a whale fashioned for the same occasion: "Et certes ce fut un moult bel entremectz, car il y avoit dedans plus de quarante personnes."[21]* As to the miracles of mechanical gadgetry, such as the living birds that fly out of the mouth of the dragon with whom Hercules does battle and other such astonishing contraptions, it is difficult to associate them with any notion of art. The comic element is only poorly represented in them. From inside the Gorkum tower, wild boars play trumpets, goats perform a motet, wolves play the flute, four large asses perform as singers—and do so before Charles the Bold, who was a connoisseur of music of some stature.

I do not wish to cast doubt that, in spite of everything, there were found among all the displays of the festival, particularly among the sculptural pieces, a good many genuine works of art alongside the predominantly silly ostentation. We should remember that the people who delighted in this gargantuan splendor and wasted serious thought on it were the same people who commissioned the works of Jan van Eyck and Rogier van der Weyden. The duke himself was their patron, as was Rolin, the donor of the altars of Beaune (plate 14) and Autun (plates 15, 16), and Jean

---

* "And this certainly was a very fine entremet for there were more than forty persons in it."

Chevrot, who was the patron of Rogier's *Seven Sacraments* (plate 17), and many others, such as Lannoy. It is even more significant that the creators of these and similar ostentations were these very same painters. Though it happens that we have no definite information about Jan van Eyck or Rogier, we do know it to be a fact that others, Colard Marmion, Simon Marmion, and Jacques Daret, for example, often had a hand in such festivals. For the festival in 1468, the date of which was unexpectedly moved up, the entire guild of painters was mobilized to assure completion; in great haste journeymen from Ghent, Brussels, Louvain, Thirlemont, Bergen, Quesnoy, Valenciennes, Douai, Cambrai, Arras, Lille, Ypres, Courtray, and Oudenarde were dispatched to Bruges.[22] What was produced by their hands cannot have been completely ugly. One would readily exchange many a mediocre altarpiece for the thirty fully equipped ships, complete with the coats of arms of the ducal lords, of the banquet of 1468, the sixty women in different regional costumes[23] holding fruit baskets and bird cages, and the windmills and bird catchers.

Even at the risk of sacrilege, it is tempting to go one step further and assert that on occasion we have to keep in mind this lost art of table decoration, now completely vanished, in order to better understand Claus Sluter[24] and others like him.

Among the other arts, that of funeral sculpture served a clearly practical function. The task facing the sculptors charged with creating the tomb monuments for the Burgundian dukes was not one of imaginative beauty, but was rather concerned with glorifying princely grandeur. Their task was much more strictly limited and more precisely prescribed than that of the painters, who in commissioned works were allowed to give much freer reign to their creative urges and who could paint whatever they wanted when not working on a commission. The sculptor of that age probably did little work outside of his commissions and the motifs of his work were limited in number and tied to a strong tradition. Sculptors were then much more tightly dependent on the dukes than the painters. The two great Dutch artists who were enticed out of their country by the magnet of French artistic life were totally monopolized by the duke of Burgundy. Sluter lived in a house in Dijon assigned and furnished for him by the duke.[25] He lived there like a great lord, but at the same time like an employee of the court. The court rank "varlet de chambre de monsegneur le duc de bourgogne,"* which Sluter shared with his cousin Claes van de Werve and Jan van Eyck, had an authoritative meaning for the sculptors. Claes van de Werve, who continued Sluter's work, became one of the tragic victims of art in the service of the court: kept in Dijon year in and out in order to complete the tomb monument of John the Fearless (plates 18, 19), a task for which there were never funds available, his splendidly promising career wasted away in futile waiting and he died having never been able to finish his task.

This relationship of servitude, however, runs contrary to the fact that it is in the nature of the art of sculpture always to approach a certain peak of simplicity and freedom, primarily because of the limited nature of its means, its material, and its subject matter. We call this peak of simplicity and freedom classicism. It is reached as soon as one of the great masters, even be it only one, regardless of time and place, guides the chisel. No matter what the task the age intends to force upon the art of sculpture, the human figure and its clothing allow for only a few variations in their depiction in wood and stone. The differences between the Roman portrait sculpture of the Imperial period, Goujon and Colombe in the sixteenth century, and Houdon and Pajou in the eighteenth are much smaller than in any other field of art.

The art of Sluter, and those like him, shares in the eternal nature of the art of sculpture. And yet . . . we don't perceive Sluter's works as they really were and were intended to be. As soon as one visualizes the Moses Fountain, just in the manner it delighted its contemporaries at the time when the papal legate (1418) granted absolution to anyone who visited it with pious intentions—one realizes why we dared to mention Sluter's art and that of the *entremets* in one breath.

The Moses Fountain is known only as a fragment (plate 20). The first duke of Burgundy wished to see the fountain, surmounted by an image of the Mount of Calvary, put into the yard of the Carthusians in his beloved Champmol. The main part of the work is comprised of the figure of the crucified Christ with Mary, John, and the Magdalen placed at the foot of the cross. The work had already vanished, for the most part, prior to the Revolution, which so irretrievably disfigured the Champmol. Below the central part,

* "chamberlain of the duke of Burgundy"

and surrounding the base that is held up around the edge by angels, stand the six figures from the Old Testament who prophesied the death of the Messiah: Moses, David, Isaiah, Jeremiah, Daniel, and Zachariah, each with an attached banderole on which the prophetic texts can be read. The entire depiction has to the highest degree the character of a performance. This is not so much because of the fact that the *tableaux vivants* or "personnages," which during processions and banquets usually had figures with such banderoles attached to them, or that the Messiah prophecies from the Old Testament were the most important subjects of such representations, as because of the fact that this depiction has an unusually strong verbal effect about it. The words of the inscriptions have an emphasized place of importance. We only reach a full understanding of the work if we completely absorb the sacred import of those texts.[26] "Immolabit enum universa multitudo filiorum Israel ad vesperam," reads Moses's dictum. "Foderunt manus meas et pedes meos, dinumeraverunt omnia ossa mea," is the citation from the Psalms of David. "Sicut ovis ad occisionem ducetur et quasi agnus coram tondente se obmutescet et non aperiet os suum," from Isaiah. "O vos omnes qui transitis per viam, attendite et videte si est dolor sicut dolor meus," Jeremiah. "Post hebdomades sexaginta duas occidetur Christus," Daniel. "Appenderunt mercedem meam triginta argenteos," Zachariah. So reads the lament, rising in six voices around the base of the cross. This is the essential feature of the work. And the connection between the figures and the text is stressed with such emphasis, there is something so compelling in the gesture of one figure and the face of another, that the entire group is almost in danger of losing the ataraxia that is the privilege of all great sculpture. The viewer is addressed almost too directly. Sluter knew, as few artists have, how to express the sanctity of his subject matter. But, from the point of view of pure art, this weight of sanctity constitutes something overdone. Compared with Michelangelo's tomb figures, Sluter's prophets are too expressive, too personal. We would perhaps consider this criticism to be doubly meritorious if more than only the head and torso of the main figure of Christ in his rigid majesty had been preserved. All we can see is how the angels, those wondrously poetic angels who in their naive grace are so infinitely more angelic than the angels of Van Eyck, direct the devotion of the prophets to the scene above them.

The strongly representative character of the Calvary of Champ-

mol is based, however, on something other than its purely sculptural qualities; that is, on the splendor in which the entire work
was cast. It should be imagined as if it were painted in polychrome
by Jean Maelweel and gilded by Hermann of Cologne.[27] Not a
single colorful or dramatic effect had been left out. The prophets
in their golden coats were standing on green pedestals; Moses and
Zachariah in red robes, their coats lined in blue; David entirely in
blue with golden stars; Jeremiah in dark blue; Jessiah, the saddest
of them all, in brocade. Golden suns and initials filled the empty
areas. Add to all this the coats of arms! The proud coats of arms
of the ducal region gleamed not only on the shaft of the base below
the prophets, but even on the crosspiece of the great, entirely gilded
cross—on its extensions shaped like capitals had been placed the
coats of arms of Burgundy and Flanders! This, perhaps more than
the gilded copper pair of glasses, supplied by Hannequin de Hacht
for the nose of Jeremiah, testifies to the spirit that gave rise to this
grand ducal work of art.

The dependence of this work on its princely sponsors contributes
to a somewhat tragic and elevated element because of the greatness
by means of which the artist manages to evade the restrictions of
his commission. The representation of the "Plourants" around the
sarcophagus had become obligatory in Burgundian funeral art long
ago.[28] Its aim was not a creative expression of pain in all its depths,
but rather only a very realistic depiction of a part of the actual
procession that had accompanied the body to the grave and with
all the dignitaries readily recognizable. How skillfully Sluter and his
assistants managed to turn this motif into a profound and dignified
depiction of grief, into a funeral march in stone!

But this may perhaps be overstating the assumption of disharmony between sponsor and artist. It is not entirely certain that it
was not Sluter himself who found the pair of glasses on Jeremiah
to be a great idea. Taste and tastelessness were, so to speak, not
separated in the minds of that age; the genuine appreciation of art
and the infatuation with pomp and curiosities had not yet parted
company. The naive imagination was still able to enjoy without
embarrassment that which was bizarre as if it were beautiful. A
collection such as that in the Green Vault in Dresden displays the
separated *caput mortuum* that had once been a whole with the
princely art collections. In Hesdin Castle, which was both a treasure
house of art and a pleasure garden filled with those mechanical

amusements, *engins d'esbatement,* Caxton came across a room decorated with paintings depicting the story of Jason, the hero of the
Golden Fleece. For the sake of greater effect, lightning, thunder,
snow, and rain making implements were attached in imitation of
Medea's magic tricks.[29]

Imagination was also freely indulged in creating the performances, the *personnages,* which were placed on street corners during
princely entry processions. During the 1389 entry into Paris of
Isabella of Bavaria as wife of Charles VI, a white stag with gilded
antlers and a crown around its neck[30] was placed among the holy
scenes. The stag rested on a *lit de justice* and moved his eyes, antlers,
feet, and, to conclude, raised a sword. During the same procession
an angel "par engins bien faits"* descended from the tower of
Notre Dame, entered through a gap in the blue taffeta canopy
covering the entire bridge just at the moment the queen passed by,
placed a crown on her head and disappeared in the same way it
had arrived "comme s'il s'en fust retourné de soy mesmes au
ciel."[31]† Philip the Good is presented with a similarly descending
maiden[32] during an entry into Ghent, as is Charles VII in Reims in
1484.[33] We are hard put to imagine anything more silly than a
so-called pantomime horse moved by a man inside, but during the
fifteenth century this was apparently not the case. In any event, Le
Fèvre de Saint Remy reports, without a trace of ridicule, about a
performance by four trumpeters and twelve noblemen "sur che-
vaulx de artifice," "saillans et poursaillians tellement que belle
chose estoit à veoir."[34]‡

The separation of all that bizarre decoration, which has vanished
without a trace, from the individual works of art that have been
preserved, a separation that our appreciation of art demands and
that has been aided by the all destroying passage of time, hardly
existed for contemporaries. The artistic life of the Burgundian age
was still entirely determined by the forms of social life. Art served.
It had primarily a social function; this was primarily to display
splendor and to emphasize the importance of the individual, not
the artist but rather the donor. This is not contradicted by the fact

---

* "by an ingenious mechanism"
† "as if he had returned to heaven of his own accord."
‡ "on an artificial horse, sallying forth and caracoling in such a way that it was
a fine thing to see."

that in church art, pompous splendor serves to direct pious thoughts upward and that the donor, out of a pious impulse, puts his own figure in the foreground. On the other hand, the art of secular painting is not always as luxuriant and arrogant as would be suitable for bloated courtly life. Too much is missing of the entire environment in which art existed for a clear understanding of the manner in which art and life touched and dissolved in each other. Moreover, our knowledge of this art itself is much too fragmentary for that purpose. It is not court and church alone that comprise the life of that age.

This is the reason for the special importance of the few works of art in which something of the life outside those two spheres finds its expression. One of these works radiates in its own peerless delight: the portrait of the Arnolfini *Marriage* (plate 21). It represents the art of the fifteenth century in its purest form and allows us to come closest to the enigmatic personality of the painter Jan van Eyck. Painting the portrait did not require that he reproduce the splendid majesty of God nor sense the haughtiness of the nobleman: he painted his friends on the occasion of their wedding. Was the subject of the painting really Jean Arnoulphin, as he was called in Flanders, the merchant from Lucca? This face, which Jan van Eyck painted twice,[35] is not at all Italian. But the title of the painting as *Hernoul le fin avec sa femme dedens une chambre,* in the 1516[36] inventory of paintings belonging to Margaret of Austria, provides strong support for the assumption that he is Arnolfini. In that case, the painting should not actually be called a "bourgeois portrait," since Arnolfini was a highly placed individual who repeatedly served as adviser to the ducal government in important matters. Be that as it may, the man depicted here was a friend of Jan van Eyck. This is shown by the delicately phrased inscription above the mirror with which the painter has signed his work: "Johannes de Eyck fuit his, 1434." Jan van Eyck was here. Just a short time ago. The deep silence of the chamber still reverberates with the sound of his voice. The intimate tenderness and the calm peace, which we are to meet again only in Rembrandt, are encased in this work as if it were, so to speak, Jan's own heart. All of a sudden, that evening during the Middle Ages is brought back to us, an evening we know of, but so often seek in vain in literature, in history, and in the life of faith of that age: the happy, noble, pure, and simple medieval age of folk song and church music. How far they are, that loud laughter and unrestrained passion!

At this moment perhaps we can see in our imagination Jan van Eyck, who stood outside the tension-filled, vibrant life of his time, a simple man, a dreamer who went through life with his head bowed, looking inside himself. Caution!—or this will turn out like an art-historical novel about how the duke's "varlet de chambre" served his high lord reluctantly, how his companions, full of pain, had to deny their high art so that they could join the work of staging courtly festivities and equipping fleets!

There is nothing in our possession that could justify any such notion. The art of the Van Eycks', which we so admire, stood right in the middle of the courtly life that is so repugnant to us. The little we know of the life of those painters makes them appear to be men of the great world. The duke of Berry is on the best of terms with his painters. Froissart met him in intimate conversation with André Beauneveu in his marvelous castle at Mehun sur Yevre.[37] The three brothers from Limburg, the great illustrators, delight the duke at New Year with a surprise: a newly illustrated manuscript, "un livre contrefait" consisting "d'un piéce de bois blanc paincte en semblance d'un livre, où il n'a nulz feuillets ne riens escript."[38]* There is no doubt that Jan van Eyck moved in courtly circles. The secret diplomatic missions entrusted to him by Philip the Good required knowledge of the world. He was regarded in his century as a literary man who read the classics and studied geometry. His modest motto has a touch of the bizarre: "Als ik kan"—"As I can"—disguised in Greek letters.

If not warned by these and similar facts, we may be easily inclined to see the art of the Van Eycks as occupying a different place than it does in the life of the fifteenth century. In our view, there were in that time two spheres of life that were strictly separated. On the one side, the culture of the court, the nobility, and the wealthy burghers: boastful, craving honor and wealth, riotously colored, glowing with passion; on the other side, the quiet, uniformly gray sphere of the *devotio moderna:* the serious men and the submissive wives of the middle class who sought spiritual support

---

* "a false book . . . of a block of white wood painted to look like a book, in which there were no leaves and nothing was written."

in the Fraterhouses and from the Windesheimers. This is also the sphere of Ruusbroec and of St. Colette. This is the sphere to which, according to our sentiments, the art of the Van Eycks with its pious quiet mysticism belongs. Yet it is more likely to be at home in the other sphere. The modern *dévotés* rejected the great art that unfolded during their age. They resisted polyphonic music and even organs,[39] while the splendor-loving Burgundians Bishop David of Utrecht and Charles the Bold himself had the foremost composers as their masters of music, such men as Obrecht in Utrecht, Busnois for the duke, who even took him with him to his camp near Neuss. The *Ordinarius* of Windesheim prohibited any embellished songs, and Thomas à Kempis states: "If you cannot sing like the lark and the nightingale, sing like the raven and the frogs in the pond. They sing as God has given them to sing."[40] It is only natural that they commented less on painting, but they desired their books to be simple and not to be illustrated.[41] It is very likely that they would have regarded even a work like the *Adoration of the Lamb* (plates 8, 9) as an expression of unmitigated pride.

But was the separation of the two spheres really drawn as sharply as it appears to us? We have already spoken of that earlier. There are numerous points where the court circles and the circles of the strict God-fearing men and women contact one another. St. Colette and Denis the Carthusian have dealings with the dukes; Margareth of York, the second wife of Charles the Bold, takes a lively interest in the "reformed" monasteries of Belgium. Beatrix of Ravenstein, one of the most prominent individuals at the Burgundian court, wears the hair shirt under her robes of state. "Vestue de drap d'or et de royaux atournemens a luy duisans, et feignant estre la plus mondaine des autres, livrant ascout à toutes paroles perdues, comme maintes font, et monstrant de dehors de pareil usages avecques les lascives et huiseuses, portoit journellement la haire sur sa chair nue, jeunoit en pain et en eau mainte journée par fiction couverte, et son mary absent couchoit en la paille de on lit mainte nuyt."[42]* The act of turning inwardly, which had become the per-

---

* "Dressed in gold cloth and royal ornaments, befitting her estate, and appearing to be the most worldly of them all, giving an ear to those empty words (as one does) and displaying the outward nature of the most careless and conceited, she wore day after day the hair shirt on her naked skin, fasted secretly on bread and water and, when her husband was absent, slept in the straw of her bed."

manent mode of life for the modern devotees, is also known to the haughty, even if only as a sporadic and faint echo of the sumptuous style of life. When Philip the Good departed for Regensburg after the great feast at Lille in order to negotiate with the emperor, several noblemen and women of the court joined the order "qui menèrent moult belle et saincte vie."[43] * —The chroniclers who describe with such broad detail all the pomp and stateliness cannot help but repeat time and again a turning away from "pompes et beubans."† Even Olivier de la Marche ponders after the feast at Lille about "les oultraigeux excés et la grant despense qui pour la cause de ces banquetz ont esté faictz."‡ He saw no "entendement de vertu" in it, with the exception of the *estremets* in which the church appeared, but another sage at the court made it clear to him why things had to be as they were.[44] Louis XI retained his hatred of everything that smacked of luxury, a hatred he had acquired during his stay at the court of Burgundy.[45]

The artists worked in and for circles quite different than those of the Modern Devotion. Even though the roots of the flourishing of painting as well as those of the renewal of faith can be found in urban communal life, the art of the Van Eycks and their successors cannot be called bourgeois. The court and the nobility had taken possession of art. We actually owe the advance of the art of miniatures to that full artistic refinement that is characteristic of the work of the Limburg brothers and the Hours of Turin primarily to princely sponsorship. The fact of the matter is that the wealthy bourgeoisie of the large Belgian cities aspired to a noble form of life. The difference between the art of the southern Netherlands and France, on the one hand, and the little that we can call art in the northern Netherlands of the fifteenth century, on the other, is best understood as a difference in milieu: there the sumptuous mature life of Bruges, Ghent, and Brussels, in constant contact with the court; here a remote country town such as Haarlem, in every respect much more like the quiet towns of the Yssel that were home to the *devotio moderna*. If we may call the works of Dirk Bouts "Haarlemism" (what works of his we possess were created in

---

* "in order to live a beautiful and pious life."

† "pomp and pride."

‡ "the outrageous excess and the great waste that was made for the purpose of that banquet."

the south, which had attracted him also), it is the simple, astringent, reserved qualities of his art that are genuinely bourgeois in contrast to the aristocratic conceits, the pompous elegance, pride, and glitter of the southern masters. The Haarlem school does indeed approach bourgeois seriousness.

The sponsors of the great paintings, as far as we know them, were nearly exclusively representatives of the great capitals of the age. They were the princes themselves, the high officials of the courts, and the great parvenus, so numerous during the Burgundian period and who took the court as their guiding model to the same degree as did the other sponsors of art. Burgundian power rests in particular on the ability to put the power of money into service and to create new powers of capital for the nobility through donations and favoritism. Those circles indulging in the displays of the Golden Fleece and in the ostentation of festivities and tournaments move in the form of life of the chivalric ideal. On that movingly pious painting of the *Seven Sacraments* (plate 17) in the museum at Antwerp, the coat of arms of the bishop of Tournay, Jean Chevrot, points to him as the most likely donor of the painting. He, next to Rolin, was the closest adviser of the duke,[46] an eager servant in matters concerning the Golden Fleece and the grand project for the crusade. The type of the great capitalist of the time is Pieter Bladelyn, whose pious figure is known to us from the triptych that graces the altar of the church in his town of Middelburg in Flanders (plate 22). He had climbed from the position of tax collector in his native Bruges to that of general ducal treasurer. Through frugality and strict control, he had improved governmental finances. He became treasurer of the Golden Fleece and was admitted to the order; in 1440 he was employed on the important mission to ransom Charles of Orléans from English captivity; he was scheduled to participate in the campaign against the Turks as financial administrator. His contemporaries were amazed over his wealth. He used it for the construction of dikes, and the founding of the new town of Middelburg.[47]

Jodocus Vydt, who is shown on the Ghent altar as donor, and the prelate Van de Paele also were among the great capitalists of their time. The De Croys and the Lannoys are noble *nouveaux riches*. Contemporaries were shocked over the rise of Nicolas Rolin, the chancellor who, "venu de petit lieu,"* as jurist, became a financier and diplomat employed in the positions of highest service. The great Burgundian treaties between 1419 and 1435 were his work. "Soloit tout gouverner tout seul et à part uy manier et porter tout, fust de guerre, fust de paix, fust en fait de finances."[48]† He managed, by methods not entirely above reproach, to accumulate incredible wealth, which he used for numerous donations. In spite of this, his greed and arrogance were spoken of with the greatest hatred. The spirit of piety that drove him to make his donations was widely mistrusted. Rolin, kneeling so piously in the painting (now in the Louvre) by Jan van Eyck that he commissioned to be painted for his hometown of Autun (plate 15) and, yet again, just as piously, in the painting by Rogier van der Weyden, donated to the hospital in Beaune (plate 14), was known for his exclusive concern with earthly matters. "He harvested the earth," says Chastellain, "as if life on earth was eternal. This led his mind astray because he was unwilling to impose barriers or limitations even though his advanced age held his approaching end up to his eyes." Jacques du Clercq comments, "Le dit chancellier fust reputé ung des sages hommes du royaume à parler temporellement: car au regard de l'espirituel je m'en tais."[49]‡

Are we to suspect the presence of a hypocritical nature behind the countenance of the donor of *La vierge,* Chancellor Rolin? We have already spoken[50] of the puzzling congruence of secular sins such as pride, greed, and unchastity with serious piety and strong faith present in such characters as Philip of Burgundy and Louis d'Orléans. Rolin should perhaps also be counted among these ethical types of his time. The nature of such individuals from centuries past is not easily fathomed.

The painting of the fifteenth century is located in the sphere where the extremes of the mystical and the crudely earthy easily touch one another. The faith that speaks here is so overt that no earthly depiction is too sensuous or too extreme for it. Van Eyck

---

* "came from the humble people,"

† "He used to govern everything quite alone and manage and bear the burden of all business by himself, be it of war, be it of peace, be it of matters of finance."

‡ "Said chancellor was reputed among the sages of the realm, to speak temporally; for as to spiritual matters, I shall be silent."

is capable of draping his angels and divine figures in the heavy ponderousness of stiff robes dripping with gold and precious stones; to point upwards he does not yet need the fluttering tips of garments and fidgety legs of the Baroque.

Though that faith is entirely direct and stark, it is by no means primitive on account of this. To label the painters of the fifteenth century primitive means running the risk of a misunderstanding. In this context, primitive can only mean coming first, in as far as an older painting is known to us; primitive is therefore only a purely chronological label. But there is a general inclination to tie to this label the notion that the mind of these artists was primitive. This is quite incorrect. The spirit of that art is that of faith itself, just as already has been described: the utmost in the use of the creative imagination to work through and elaborate all that which belongs to faith.

At one time the divine figures had been seen, stiff and rigid, in the infinite distance. This was followed by the pathos of inner emotions and had bloomed, accompanied by songs and a flood of tears, in the mysticism of the twelfth century, most of all with St. Bernard. The Deity had been beseeched with sobbing emotion. To better empathize with divine suffering, all the forms and colors that the imagination drew from earthly life had been forced on Christ and the saints. A stream of rich human images had poured through heaven and divided into innumerable small branches. Gradually everything holy was depicted in ever more refined elaboration down to the most minute detail. With his ardent arms, man had pulled heaven to earth.

Initially, and for a long time, the word had been superior in its formative powers to sculpted and painted creations. At a time when sculpture still retained much of the mechanical quality of the older images and was limited both by its materials and its compass, literature was already beginning to describe all the positions of the body and all the emotions of the drama at the cross down to the smallest fact. The *Meditationes vitae Christi,* already credited to Bonaventura by 1400,[51] became the model of this pathetic naturalism that presented such life-like details of the scenes of the nativity and childhood, of the deposition from the cross and the lament over the body, that there was precise information about how Joseph of Arimathea had climbed the ladder and how he had to press down on the hand of the Lord in order to pull out the nail.

But in the meantime, pictorial technique had also advanced: fine art not only caught up, but went ahead. In the art of the Van Eycks the representation of the sacred objects in painting had reached a degree of detail and naturalism that, taken strictly in an art-historical sense, could perhaps be called a beginning, but that, in terms of cultural history, represents a conclusion. The utmost tension in the earthly depiction of the divine had thus been reached; the mystic content of the conception was ready to evaporate from the pictures and leave behind only the infatuation with the colorful forms.

Accordingly, the naturalism of the Van Eycks, which is usually regarded in art history as an element announcing the arrival of the Renaissance, should rather be regarded as the complete unfolding of the medieval spirit. It contains the same natural presentation of the saints that we could observe in respect to all matters relating to the veneration of saints in the sermons of John Brugman, in the elaborated contemplations of Gerson, and in the descriptions of the pains of hell by Denis the Carthusian.

Time and again, the form threatens to overgrow the content and keep it from rejuvenating itself. The art of Van Eyck is, in content, still entirely medieval. No new ideas are expressed by it. This art constitutes an ultimate, a terminal point. The medieval system of concepts had been built to heaven. All that was left was to paint and decorate it.

The contemporaries of the Van Eycks were clearly aware of two things in their admiration of the great paintings: first, of the proper representation of the subject matter, and second, of the incredible skill, the fabulous perfection of the details and the absolute faithfulness to nature. On the one hand there is an appreciation that is located more in the sphere of piety than in the arena of aesthetic sensitivity; on the other hand there is a naive astonishment that, in our opinion, does not rise to the level of aesthetic sensitivity. A Genoese writer around 1450, Bartolomeo Fazio, is the first whose art-historical contemplations of the works of Jan van Eyck, some of which are now lost, are known to us. He praises the beauty and dignity of a Mary figure, the hair of the angel Gabriel, "which even surpassed genuine hair," the sacred strictness of the asceticism radiating from the face of John the Baptist, the manner in which a Jerome really "lives." He also admires the perspective in *St. Jerome in his Study* (plate 23): the sunbeam entering through a gap; the mirror image of a bathing woman; the drops of sweat on the body of another; the burning lamp; the landscape with wanderers and mountains, forests, villages, and castles; the endless distances of the horizon; and, once more, the mirror.[52] His manner of expression reveals only astonishment. He drifts comfortably on with the flow of unrestrained imagination; he does not raise questions about the degree of beauty found in the entire picture. This is still an entirely medieval evaluation of a medieval work.

After Renaissance conceptions of beauty had asserted themselves a century later, this overly detailed execution of the independent details is held to be the fundamental error of Flemish art. If Francesceo de Holanda, the Portuguese painter who claims that his meditations on art are conversations with Michelangelo, is really reproducing the opinions of the powerful master, Michelangelo said that:

> Flemish painting is more pleasing to all the pious than Italian painting. The latter never evokes tears while the former makes them weep copiously. This is by no means a result of the power and merits of that art, but has to be credited entirely to the great sensitivity of pious Flemish painting that exactly agrees with the taste of women, particularly the elderly and the very young ones, and also with that of monks, nuns and all refined people who are not sensitive to true harmony. Painting in Flanders is done primarily to reproduce deceptively the external appearance of things, mostly objects that arouse our enthusiastic approval or are beyond reproach such as saints or prophets. But as a rule, they paint a landscape with many figures in it. And though the eye is pleased by all this, there is in reality, neither art nor reason in it, no "symmetria," no proportions, no choice, no greatness. Put simply, this painting is without power or splendor; it intends to perfectly reproduce many things simultaneously when a single one of these things would merit enough importance for the painter to devote all his powers to it.

The label "pious" here means all those of medieval spirit. In the eyes of the grand master, the old beauty became a concern of the little and the weak. But not all agreed. To Dürer and Quinten

Metsys and to Jan van Scorel, who is reputed to have kissed *The Lamb of God* (plate 9), this old art is by no means dead. But in this instance Michelangelo precisely represents the Renaissance. His charges against Flemish art are exactly against the essential features of the late medieval mind: the vehement sentimentality, the inclination to regard every detail as an independent entity, to be totally absorbed by the variety and color of the seen object. The new Renaissance perception of art and life resists this. This new perception is, as always, only accessible to us at the expense of temporarily turning a blind eye on past beauty or truth.

An awareness of a conscious aesthetic appreciation and a verbal expression for it developed rather late. Admirers of art during the fifteenth century have at their disposal only the manner of expression we could expect of a burgher, caught in the instance of astonishment, for whom the very idea of artistic beauty has not yet dawned. Whenever the beauty of art penetrates his mind with its radiance and thrills him, he immediately converts the emotion either into a sense of being filled with God or into an awareness of the joy of life.

Denis the Carthusian wrote a treatise *De venustate mundi et pulchritudine Dei*.[53] The title already tells us that true beauty is only for God to know; the world can only be *venustus:* pretty, lovely. The beauties of created things, he says, are only the outpouring of the highest beauty; a creation is deemed beautiful only insofar as it shares in the beauty of divinity and, by virtue of this fact, comes somewhat to resemble the highest.[54] On the basis of this far-ranging and elevated aesthetic theory, for which Denis relies on the Pseudo-Areopagite, Augustine, Hugo of St. Victor, and Alexander of Hales,[55] a pure analysis of all beauty could have been built. But the mind of the fifteenth century fails completely to meet the challenge. Denis even borrows his examples of earthly beauty, a leaf, the sea and its changing colors, the restless sea, from the fine minds of his twelfth-century predecessors, Richard and Hugo, members of the monastery of St. Victor. Whenever he is intent on an analysis of beauty itself, he remains entirely on the surface. Herbs are beautiful because they are green, stones because they sparkle, the human body, as well as the dromedary and the camel, because it is suited to its purpose. The world is beautiful because it is long and wide, the heavenly bodies because they are round and bright. In mountains we admire size; in rivers, length; in fields and forests, expanse; and in the earth itself, its unmeasurable quantity.

Medieval thought always traces the idea of beauty back to the concepts of perfection, proportion, and splendor. "Nam ad pulchritudinem," says Thomas Aquinas, "tria requiruntur. Primo quidem integritas sive perfectio: quae enim diminuta sunt, hoc ipso turpis sunt. Et debita proportio sive consonantia. Et iterum claritas: unde quae habent colorem nitidum, pulchra esse dicuntur."[56]* Denis attempts to apply a similar yardstick. The results are somewhat clumsy; applied aesthetics are always a miserable matter. No wonder that the mind is incapable of dwelling on earthly beauty when tackling such an abstraction as the notion of beauty itself. Denis always veers to unseen beauty whenever he undertakes to describe the beautiful: to the beauty of the angels and the empyrean; or he seeks to find it in abstract things: the beauty of life is the conduct of life under the guidance and command of divine law, freed from the ugliness of sin. He does not speak of the beauty of art, not to mention that of music, which he could be most likely expected to have become aware of as having an aesthetic value in its own right.

Once, the same Denis had entered the Church of St. John in 'sHertogenbosch while the organ was playing and the sweet melody had immediately transported him and his melting heart into a sustained ecstasy.[57] The sensation of beauty was instantly turned to religion. It is likely that it did not occur to him that in the beauty of music or of the fine arts there was something else to be admired than the holy *per se*.

Denis was one of those who opposed the introduction of modern polyphonic music into the church. The breaking of the voice into parts (*fractio vocis*) seems like the sign of a broken soul, he says, repeating an older authority; it is comparable to curled hair on a man or to pleated garments on a woman, sheer vanity. Some, who had practiced such polyphonic song had confided to him that it involved arrogance and a certain lasciviousness of mind (*lascivia anima*). He admits that there are pious individuals who are inspired

---

* "Three things are required for beauty . . . First, integrity or completeness, because what is unfinished is repugnant. Next, proportion or consonance is required. And finally, clarity, since we call beautiful whatever has a pure color."

by melodies to the most intensive contemplation and devotion. This explains why the church went so far as to permit organs. But when the artful music serves to please the ear and delight those who are present, particularly the women, it is decidedly objectionable.[58]

This makes it evident that the medieval mind, whenever it intends to convey the nature of musical emotions, still has no other means of expression at its disposal than the vocabulary used for the sinful stirrings of the emotions, of pride, and a certain degree of lasciviousness.

Much was being written about musical aesthetics. As a rule, these tracts were based on the musical theories of antiquity, which were no longer understood; in the final analysis they tell us little about how the beauty of music was really enjoyed. Whenever they come to the point of expressing what it was that was actually found to be beautiful about music, the texts become vague and strongly resemble those dealing with the admiration of painting. In one place it is the heavenly joy that is appreciated in music, in another it is the text painting.[59] All this helped to make musical emotions appear to be related in essence to heavenly enjoyment; a depiction of sacred entities was not at stake as it was in painting, but only a shadow of the joys of heaven themselves. When good old Molinet, who apparently loved music himself, tells us that Charles the Bold, who was known as a great lover of music, passed the time in his camp near Neuss with literature and especially with music, it is not only his rhetorical bent that causes him to jubilate: "Car musique est la résonnance des cieux, la voix des anges, la joie de paradis, l'espoir de l'air, l'organe de l'église, le chant des oyselets, la récréacion de tous cueurs tristes et désolés, la persécution et enchassement des diables."[60]* The ecstatic element in the enjoyment of music was, of course, well known: "The power of harmonies," Pierre d'Ailly tells us, "raptures the human soul so much to itself that it is not only elevated above other passions and cares, but even above itself."[61]

As in painting, the striking imitation of things was greatly admired, but the danger of seeking beauty through imitation was

---

* "Because music is the resonance of the heavens, the voice of the angels, the joy of paradise, the hope of the air, the organ of the Church, the song of the little birds, the recreation of all gloomy and despairing hearts, the persecution and the driving away of the devils."

much greater for music. Music had already made most eager use of this means of expression for a long time. The caccia (from which the English word "catch" used for a canon comes), originally representing a hunt, is the best-known example. Olivier de la Marche says that he had heard in such a piece the yelping of dogs, the baying of hounds, and the blaring of trumpets as if one were in the forest.[62] At the beginning of the sixteenth century the inventions of Jannequin, a student of Josquin de Prés, present hunts, the tumult of the battle of Marigiano, the market cries of Paris, "le caquet des femmes,"* and the singing of birds in musical form.

The theoretical analysis of beauty is deficient, the means of expressing admiration superficial. Analysis does not go much further than to substitute for an explanation of beauty the terms of measure, gracefulness, order, greatness, and utility; above all, the terms splendor and light are used. For an explanation of spiritual beauty, Denis traces all these terms back to the notion of light: reason is a light; wisdom, science, and skill are nothing but light-like rays that illuminate the mind with their clarity.[63]

If we were to study the sense of beauty of that age, not in its definition of the idea of beauty or in what is said in a state of emotions about a painting or about music, but rather in its spontaneous expressions of gay enthusiasm for beauty, we would notice that these expressions are almost always drawn to sensations of light and splendor and to the sense of a lively movement.

Froissart was rarely under the influence of the beauty of things, he was much too busy with his endless tales, but there is one spectacle that never fails to inspire him to utter words of joyful rapture: ships on water with fluttering flags and pennants on which colorful coats of arms glisten in the sun. Or the play of the rays of the sun on helmets, armor, lance tips, the flags, and banners of an approaching troop of mounted knights.[64] Eustache Deschamps admired the beauty of turning windmills and of the sun in a dewdrop; La Marche remarked how beautifully the sunlight glittered on the blond hair of a group of German and Bohemian knights.[65] —Linked to this admiration for everything that glitters is the decoration of costumes, which during the fifteenth century still depended primarily on the application of an overabundant number of precious stones. It is only later that these are replaced by ties

---

* "The chattering of women,"

and bows. To further enhance the splendor by their tinkling, small bells or coins were worn. La Hire wears a red coat covered in its entirety with large silver cowbells. Captain Salazar appears in an entry procession in 1465 accompanied by twenty armored riders whose horses are all hung with large silver bells; on the saddlecloth of his own horse, attached to each of the figures with which it is decorated, is a large gilded silver bell. During the entry of Louis XI into Paris in 1461, the horses of Charolais, Croy, St. Pol, and many others, have numerous large bells attached to their saddlecloths; the mount of Charolais carried on its back a large bell suspended between four posts. Charles the Bold appeared for a tournament in a festive robe covered with an abundance of tinkling Rhenish guilders; English noblemen wore robes with golden nobles on them.[66] During the wedding of the count of Geneva at Chambéry in 1434, gentlemen and ladies all dressed in white covered with *or clinquant* perform a dance. The gentlemen also wore broad belts with many little bells attached to them.[67]

The same naive enjoyment of anything that attracted great attention is again noticeable in the sense of colors that prevailed at the time. To determine this sense exactly would require an extensive statistical investigation that would have to include the color scale of the fine arts as well as the art of costume and ornament. As far as clothing is concerned, this investigation would have to be based on the numerous descriptions rather than on the few preserved remnants of actual material. I only present a few preliminary impressions gathered from descriptions of tournaments and entry processions. We have to deal here with ceremonial and official dress that display, of course, an entirely different style than that which dominates daily attire. Ordinary clothing employs quite a lot of gray, black, and purple.[68] In festive and official dress we notice, first of all, how red dominates. No one would expect anything different from that age. Entry processions were frequently mounted entirely in red.[69] Along with red, white has a significant place as a uniform color for festivities. In the coordination of colors any combination was tolerated: red-blue and blue-purple do occur. In a festive performance described by La Marche, a girl appeared in violet silk on a palfrey[70] with a blue-silk saddle blanket, accompanied by three men in cinnabar red and pages in green silk.[71] A preference for darkly glowing and muted combinations is unmistakable.

It is remarkable that black and violet are more popular for clothing than green and blue, while yellow and brown are almost entirely missing. Black, above all black velvet, undoubtedly represents the proud, somber splendor that the time loved, with its
arrogant distance from the gay wealth of color found everywhere.
Philip the Good, after having passed the days of his youth, always
wore black and had his entourage and horses in the same color.[72]
The favorite colors of King René, even more eager for distinction
and refinement, were gray-white-black.[73]

The rare presence of blue and green should not, incidentally, be
entirely regarded as a direct expression of the sense of color. More
than the other colors, blue and green held symbolic significance
and these meanings were so specific that they nearly rendered both
colors unsuitable for regular clothing. Both were the colors of love:
green symbolized the state of being in love, blue faithfulness.[74] Or,
better put, these two were in a very special way the colors of love,
but the other colors could also serve in the symbolism of love.
Deschamps says of a group of suitors:

> *Li uns se vest pour li de vert,*
> *L'autre de bleu, l'autre de blanc,*
> *L'autre s'en vest vermeil com sanc,*
> *Et cilz qui plus la veult avoir*
> *Pour son grant dueil s'en vest de noir.*[75]*

But green was especially the color of young, hopeful Minne:

> *Il te fauldra de vert vestir,*
> *C'est la livrée aux amoureulx.*[76]†

It was therefore especially appropriate that knight-errants be
dressed in green.[77] A lover showed his faithfulness by wearing blue;
for this reason, Christine de Pisan has the lady answer her suitor
when he indicates his blue garment:

---

* Some dress themselves for her in green, / The other blue, another in white, /
Another in vermillion like blood, / And he who desires her most / Because of his
great sorrow dresses in black.

† You will have to dress in green, / It is the livery of those in love.

Au bleu vestir ne tient mie le fait,
N'a devises porter, d'amer sa dame,
Mais au servir de loyal cuer parfait
Elle sans plus, et la garder, de blasme
. . . Là gist l'amour, non pas au bleu porter,
Mais puet estre que plusieurs le meffait
De faulseté cuident couvrir soubz lame
Par bleu porter. . . .[78]*

This may perhaps explain why the color blue, if used with hypo-critical intent, could also signify infidelity and why it, in a reverse leap of logic, signified not only the unfaithful individual but also the victim of unfaithfulness. In Holland, the blue *Huik*[79] signified the adulteress, and the *côté bleue* is the dress of the cuckold:

Que cils qui m'a de cote vleue armé
Et fait monstrer au doy, soit occis.[80]†

Again, the above may be what lies behind the general use of blue as the color of folly—the blue boat is the vehicle of fools.[81]

The fact that yellow and brown remained in the background may be explained by an aversion to their quality; that is, the unre-flected sense of color gave them a negative symbolic meaning. In other words, yellow and brown were disliked because they were held to be ugly and, for that reason, were given an inauspicious meaning. A man trapped in an unhappy marriage would say:

Sur toute couleur j'ayme la tennée
Pour ce que je l'ayme m'en suys habillée,
Et touts les aultres ay mis en obly.
Hellas! mes amours ne sont ycy.‡

---

* To wear mottoes of love for one's lady,/or to wear blue is no proof,/But to serve her with a perfectly loyal heart/And no others, and to keep her from blame/. . . Love lies in that, not in wearing blue,/But it may be that many think/To cover the offense of falsehood under a tombstone/By wearing blue. . . .

† That he, who dresses me in the blue coat/And causes people to point their fingers at me, will be killed!

‡ Of all colors I love brown best,/And because I love it, I dress in it,/I have forgotten all other colors./Alas! What I love is not here.

Or in another ditty:

> Gris et tannée puis bien porter
> Car ennuyé suis d'espérance.[82]*

Incidentally, gray, in contrast to brown, appears frequently in festive dress; as a color of sadness it possessed perhaps a more elegiac nuance than brown.

By this time, yellow already signified enmity. Henry of Württemberg and his entourage, all dressed in yellow, passed before the duke of Burgundy "et fut le duc adverty que c'estoit contre luy."[83]†

From the middle of the century on, the use of black and white seems temporarily to be in decline while that of blue and green is on the rise (but this is only a preliminary impression that is in need of further supporting evidence). During the sixteenth century, it will be noticed that the most daring combinations of color in dress, already mentioned above, have for the largest part disappeared, just at the same time as art is attempting to circumvent the naive contrast of primary colors. For the artists of the Burgundian regions the sense of the harmony of colors does not come from Italy. Gerard David, who stiffly continues to work precisely in the style of the older school, does display, in comparison to his predecessors, a refinement of his sense of color that demonstrates that this sense is related in its development to the general shaping of the mind. Here we encounter a field where investigations into the history of art and culture still have much to expect of each other.

---

* I may well wear gray and tan/For I have no longer any hope.

† "and the duke was informed that it was meant for him."/[Note 15] furthermore, she did not have a formal hairdo like other ladies who were of royal standing.

Chapter Thirteen

IMAGE AND WORD

EACH ATTEMPT MADE TO DATE TO CLEARLY SEPA-
rate the Middle Ages and the Renaissance has resulted in an apparent pushing of the boundaries ever further back. People saw in the
distant Middle Ages forms and movements that already appeared
to bear the stamp of the age to come, and the term "Renaissance,"
to make it include all these phenomena, has been stretched to the
point that it has lost all its dynamic powers.[1] All this holds true on
the opposite side. Those who take in the spirit of the Renaissance
without preconceived notions find more "medieval" elements in it
than theory would seem to permit. Ariosto, Rabelais, Margarete
of Navarre, Castiglione, just as are all of the fine arts with respect
to form and content, are full of medieval elements. And yet to us,
the contrast continues to exist: Middle Ages and Renaissance are
expressions in which we sense the basic differences in the nature
of an age just as clearly as the difference between apple and straw-
berry, while at the same time it remains virtually impossible to
describe this difference in greater detail.

But it is necessary to retrace the term Renaissance (which, in
contrast to the term Middle Ages, does not, *a priori,* have a restricted reference to a period of time) as much as possible to its
original meaning. It is clearly objectionable to count, as Fierens
Gevaert[2] and others do, Sluter and the Van Eycks among Renaissance painters. These artists have an entirely medieval taste about
them. They are also medieval in matters of form and content. In
content, because their art has shed nothing of the old and embraced
nothing of the new as far as subject matter, ideas, and meaning are
concerned. In form, because their conscientious realism and their
desire to depict everything as corporeally as possible is, above all,
the perfect product of a genuinely medieval spirit. Then, this is
how we observed this spirit working in religious thought and cre-
ativity, in the thought forms of everyday life and everywhere else.

The tendency towards this elaborate realism is abandoned by the Renaissance during the period of its full development in the Cinquecento, while the Quattrocento still shares it with the North.

For all practical purposes, this new spirit does not find its expression in the fine arts and in the literature of the fifteenth century in France and Burgundy, whatever else of the new beauty may appear there. Art and literature still serve a spirit that was on the verge of losing its bloom; they belong to the system of medieval thought and its ultimate perfection. They have no other task than that of providing perfect depictions and embellishments of concepts that have been long thought through. The mind seems to be exhausted, the spirit awaits new inspiration.

Now, in periods where the depictions of beauty are limited to nothing other than exact descriptions and the pure expression of intellectual material that is already clarified and worked through, the pictorial arts are of more profound value than literature. This, of course, is not the judgment of contemporaries. To them, the idea, even if no longer flourishing, still retains so much of its convincing and significant qualities that it is loved and admired particularly in its embellished literary form. All those poems echoing the melody of the fifteenth century, which appear to our sensitivities to be so hopelessly monotonous and superficial, were praised much more enthusiastically than any painting was ever praised. The profound emotional value of the pictorial arts had not yet dawned on the contemporaries, or at least not to the degree that they were able to express it.

The fact that to us by far the largest part of that literature has lost any fragrance and luster while we are moved, possibly more profoundly than were contemporaries, by the fine arts, may be explained by the profound difference in the effect of art and word. But it would be all too convenient and, at the same time, all too incomprehensible if we were to look for the difference in the quality of the talents and to assume that the poets, excepting Villon and Charles d'Orléans, had been nothing but conventional empty heads, in contrast to the painters, who were all geniuses.

Where two do the same thing, it is not necessarily the same. If the painter limits himself to the simple reproduction in line and color of an external reality, there is always found behind all that purely formal imitation an ultimate remainder that is left unsaid and that cannot be spoken of. However, if the poet aspires to nothing higher than a mere linguistic expression of a visible or already comprehended reality, he exhausts with his words the treasure of the unspoken. Granted, there is the possibility of adding a new unexpressed beauty by virtue of rhythm and sound, but if these elements, too, are weak, the effect of the poem only lasts as long as the idea itself captivates the listener. Contemporaries still react to an idea with a number of living associations because the idea is interwoven with their lives and they regard it as new and blooming in the splendor of the new words found for it.

But if the idea does not any longer captivate us for its own sake, the poem can remain effective only through its form. The form is incomparably important and may even be so new and alive that questions concerning the content of the idea are rarely raised. In the literature of the fifteenth century a new beauty of forms is already beginning to blossom. But by far the most poetry is still in old forms. Rhythm and sound are of weak quality. Under these circumstances literature, devoid of new ideas and new forms, remains an endless series of postludes on worn-out themes. Those poets have no future.

For the painter of such a period of intellectual history, the day comes later, because he lives on the treasure of the unspoken and it is the wealth of this treasure that determines the most profound and most lasting effect of all art. Look at the portraits by Van Eyck. Here we have the sharply cut, distant face of his wife (plate 24). There the rigid, morose, aristocratic head of Baudouin de Lannoy (plate 25). And there, again, the frightening, mysterious facial expression of the Canon van de Paele, the sickly, relaxed pose of the Berlin Arnolfini (plate 27), the Egyptian-mysterious quality of *Leal Souvenier* (plate 28). Hidden deep in all these is the miracle of the personality explored to its innermost reaches. In this we encounter the most profound characterization possible: we are allowed to see it, but it cannot be put into words. Even if Van Eyck had simultaneously also been the greatest poet of his century, the secret that reveals itself in the pictures would not have opened itself to him in words.

The lack of congruence in the attitude and spirit of art and literature of the fifteenth century rests most profoundly on this fact. But once the difference is correctly understood, a comparison of literary and pictorial expression in certain examples and in particular details nonetheless reveals again much greater congruence than one initially may have assumed. If the work of the Van Eycks and their successors is selected as the most representative expression in art, what literary works would have to be juxtaposed with them for a proper comparison? Those dealing with the same subject matter do not come first, but rather those that rise from the same sources, are the products of the same sphere of life. This sphere, as we have earlier indicated, is those of the extravagant princely court and the wealthy, ostentatious bourgeoisie. The literature that is at the same level as the art of Jan Van Eyck is courtly, or at least aristocratic, is written in French, and is read and admired by the same circles that place their orders with the great painters.

On the surface it appears as if we are faced with a great contrast that makes any comparison nearly meaningless: the subject matter of painting is overwhelmingly religious, that of French-Burgundian literature overwhelmingly secular. But our view does not extend far enough in both directions: in the fine arts, the secular element at one time occupied a much larger place than the remnants lead us to assume; and in literature worldly genres tend to attract much too much of our attention. The forms of expression of major concern in literary history are the *Minnelied,* the sequels of the *Roman de la rose,* the later versions of the chivalric novel, the rising novella, satire, and historiography. In painting, the profound seriousness of the altar pictures and the portrait come first to mind. In literature we are first reminded of the lustful leer of the erotic satires and the monotonous terrors of the chronicles. It almost seems as if the fifteenth century painted its virtues but described its sins. But even on the literary side such a view is too limited: not only did pious books still occupy the larger amount of space in the well-stocked libraries of the Burgundian dukes, but the pious, edifying, and moralizing element continued to make its claims even in secular literature and even among the displays of the greatest frivolity.

Let us return once more to the premise that the effects produced by the art and literature of the fifteenth century are strongly mismatched. The literature, with the exception of only a few poets, fatigues and bores us. It is all endlessly elaborated allegories in which not a single figure offers anything new or individually its own and which, in content, present nothing other than the long-established ethical thought of past centuries, which has often gone stale. Over and again the same themes: the sleeping hero in an orchard has a vision of a symbolic lady, the morning stroll early in the month of May, the quarrel between the lady and her lover or between two female friends or any other combination about a point of the casuistry of love. Hopeless superficiality, a style ornamented with fool's gold, sugar-sweet romanticism, worn-out fantasy, sober moralizing: we sigh and ask ourselves over and over again, Are these really the contemporaries of Jan van Eyck? Could he really have admired all this? —Most likely, yes. This is not any stranger than seeing Bach making do with the work of a petit bourgeoisie rhyme-smith inspired by a rheumatic parochial dogmatism.

Contemporaries who see the works of art being born accept them without distinction into their life dream. They do not appreciate them on the basis of objective aesthetic perfection, but on the basis of the resounding reverberation within them of the sacredness or passionate vitality of their subject matter. Only when the old life dream is dreamed out with the passing of time, and sacredness and passion have vanished like the scent of a rose, only then, by virtue of its means of expression, that is, its style, structure, and its harmony, does the purely artistic effect of a work of art begin. These elements may actually be the same in both the fine arts and literature, but they may, nonetheless, generate an entirely different artistic evaluation.

Literature and art of the fifteenth century possess both parts of that general characteristic that we have already spoken of as being essential for the medieval mind: the full elaboration of all details, the tendency not to leave any thought unexpressed, no matter what idea urges itself on the mind, so that eventually everything could be turned into images as distinctly visible and conceptualized as possible. Erasmus tells us that he had once listened, in Paris, to a clergyman preach about the prodigal son for forty days running and had, in this way, filled the entire Lenten period. The preacher described the son's journey away from home and back again, how he had once in a lodge eaten tongue pâté for lunch, at another time had passed a water mill, had gambled and had stopped at a vegetarian kitchen. The preacher labored to squeeze the words of the prophets and evangelists for all they were worth to make them fit all his freely invented chatter. "Because of this, he seemed God-like to the inexperienced crowd and the important fat notables alike."[3]

We propose now to demonstrate this characteristically unrestrained elaboration by an analysis of two paintings by Jan van

Eyck. First, *The Madonna of Chancellor Rolin,* now in the Louvre (plates 15, 16).

The scrupulous exactness with which the material of the dresses, the marble of the floor tiles and of the columns, the sparkle of the windowpane and the mass book of the chancellor are treated would be called pedantic in any artist other than Van Eyck. In one detail, the exaggerated execution has a truly irritating effect, that is, in the adornment of the capitals on which, in a corner, as if put into brackets, are depicted the expulsion from paradise, the sacrifice of Cain and Abel, the exit from the Ark of Noah, and Ham's sin. But this ardor for elaborating detail only reaches its climax outside of the open hall that encloses the main figures. Here we find opening, as a wide vista through the colonnades, the most marvelous perspective Van Eyck ever painted. We quote Durand-Gréville's description:[4]

> If one, tempted by curiosity, is careless enough to get too close, one is lost; one is captured for the entire time the effort of a sustained attention may last; as in a dream one sees ornament after ornament, the crown of the Virgin, the art of the goldsmith; one sees, figure by figure, the groups that, without rendering them overweight, fill the capitals of the columns; blossom by blossom, leaf by leaf in the profusion of the ground; the surprised eye discovers, between the head of the divine child and the Virgin, a city replete with gables and beautiful church steeples, a large church with numerous buttresses, a spacious square cut into two parts in its whole width by a staircase, and on the square come, walk, run, innumerable brush stokes that signify an equal number of living figures; our eye is attracted to a bridge formed like the back of a donkey (dropping off on both ends) that is crowded with groups of peoples thronging and crossing each other's paths; our eye follows the bends of a river where microscopically small barks travel; in the middle of the river is an island, smaller than the finger nail of a child, on which rises a stately castle complete with numerous bell towers and surrounded by trees; to the left, our eye scans a river embankment lined by trees and crowded with people on a stroll; moving still farther, it transcends one by one the round peaks of green hills, comes to rest for a

moment on the distant line of snow-capped mountains and then loses itself in the infinity of a faintly blue sky where surging clouds are fading into oblivion.

And O, Wonder!: in all this, contrary to the claims of Michelangelo's pupil, unity and harmony are not lost. "Et quand le jour tombe, une minute avant que la voix des gardiens ne vienne mettre fin á votre contemplation, voyez comme le chef d'oeuvre se transfigure dans la douceur du crépuscule; comme son ciel devient encore plus profond; comme la scène principale, dont les couleurs se sont évanouies, se plonge dans l'infini mystère de l'Harmonie et de l'Unité . . ."[5]*

Another painting particularly suited for the study of the technique of infinite detailing is the *Annunciation,* now in the Hermitage in St. Petersburg (plate 29). At the time the triptych, of which this work constitutes the right wing, actually existed as a whole, what a miraculous creation it must have been. It seems as if Van Eyck intended to demonstrate the complete virtuosity, shrinking away from nothing, of a master who can do anything, and dares everything. None of his works are simultaneously more primitive, more hieratic, and more contrived. The angel does not enter with his message into the intimacy of a dwelling chamber (the scene that the entire genre of domestic painting took as its point of departure), but, as was prescribed by the code of forms of the older art, into a church. Both figures lack in pose and facial expression the gentle sensitivity displayed in the depiction of the Annunciation on the outer side of the altar in Ghent. The angel greets Mary with a formal nod, not, as in Ghent, with a lily; he does not wear a small diadem, but is depicted with scepter and a splendid crown; and he has a rigid Aegean-smile on his face. In the glowing splendor of the colors of his garments, the luster of the pearls, the gold and precious stones, he excels all the other angelic figures painted by Van Eyck. The dress is green and gold, the brocade coat dark red and gold, and his wings are decked with peacock feathers. Mary's book, the pillow on the chair, everything is again detailed with the

---

* "And as the day ends, one minute before the voice of the curator breaks into your contemplation, the eye sees how the masterpiece transforms itself in the softness of twilight; how the sky becomes still darker; how the main scene, whose colors are faded, submerges in the eternal mystery of harmony and unity . . ."

greatest of care. In the church building the details are fitted with anecdotal elaborations. The tiles show the signs of the zodiac, of which five are visible, and in addition three scenes from the story of Samson and one from the life of David. The back of the church, between its vaults, is decorated with images of Isaac and Jacob in the form of medallions; Christ on a globe accompanied by two Seraphim can be seen in the uppermost part of a glass window; and, next to it, in wall paintings, are the scenes of the finding of Moses and the reception of the tablets of the law. All is explained by clearly readable inscriptions. Only in the compartments of the ceiling do the decorations, still hinted at even there, become unclear to the eye.

And again the miracle that in such an amassing of elaborate details, just as in the case of the *Madonna* of Rolin, the unity of key and mood is not lost! In that case there is the gaiety of bright daylight that pulls the eye across the main scene into the great distance; in this case the most mysterious darkness of the high vaulted church veils the entire scene in such a mist of sobriety and *mysterium* that it is difficult for the eye to detect all the anecdotal details.

This is the effect of the "unbridled elaboration"[6] in painting! The painter, this painter, was able to vent his most unbounded lust for detail (or, should we say, to meet the annoying orders of an ignorant, but pious donor?) in an area less than half a square meter in size without tiring us any more than a glance at the lively throngs of reality would do. Because one glance is all we are given; the dimension alone already exercises a limiting force and entering into the beauty and the distinct qualities of everything depicted takes place without the expense of much intellectual effort; many perfections are not even noticed, or if they are, immediately vanish from consciousness and are totally immersed in the effect of color or perspective.

If we postulate that the literature of the fifteenth century (that is, of *belle littérature,* since folk art does not enter into this context) shared the general quality of the "endless expression of detail," this happens in an entirely different sense. Not in the sense of a minutely detailed, spider web–like realism that delights in the surface appearance of things. This is not yet the way this quality expresses itself in literature. Descriptions of nature and persons still rely on the simple means of medieval poetry; the individual objects participating in generating the mood of the poet are mentioned but not described: the substantive dominates the adjective. Only the main qualities of objects, as, for example, their colors (their sounds), are given. The unrestrained elaboration of details in the literary imagination is more quantitative than qualitative in nature; it consists in piling up very many individual objects rather than in analyzing their qualities in detail. The poet does not understand the art of omission. He does not know the empty spot; he lacks the sense for appreciating the effect of that which is left unexpressed. This applies to the thoughts expressed by him as well as to the images he conjures up. Even the thoughts evoked by the object are linked as completely as possible. All of poetry is just as overcrowded with details as is painting. But why is it that in literature such overabundance of details leaves a so much less harmonious impression?

This may be explained up to a point by the fact that the relationship between primary and secondary concerns is exactly the reverse in poetry than it is in painting. In painting, the difference between the main concern, that is, the adequate expression of the object, and secondary concerns is small. In painting everything is essential. To us the perfect harmony of painting can lie in a single detail.

In the paintings of the fifteenth century is it, above all, the profound piety and thus the competent expression of the subject matter that we admire first? Take the example of the Ghent Altarpiece! (Plates 8, 9.) How little is our attention drawn to the large figures of God, Mary, and John the Baptist! In the main scene, our eye shifts time and again away from the lamb, the center of the picture, to the throng of worshipers on the sides and the nature scene in the background. The eye continues to be drawn to the margin: to Adam and Eve and to the portraits of the donors. And if, at least in the Annunciation scene, the most moving magic charm rests in the figure of the angel and the Virgin, that is, in the expressive pious element, we delight, even in this instance, almost more intensively in the copper kettle and the view of the sunny street. In these details, which were only a secondary concern for the artist, the mystery of everyday things blossoms in its quiet glow. Here we sense the direct emotional stirring about the miraculous quality of all things. There is—other than that we approach *The Lamb of God* with a preconceived religious conception—no difference between the art-emotion in viewing the sacred depiction of the worship of the Eucharist and the emotion we feel seeing the *Fishmonger's Stall* (plate 30) by Emmanuel de Witte in the Rotterdam Museum.

It is exactly in the details that the artist has complete freedom. Strict conventions are imposed in matters of the depiction of the main concern of the painting, the depiction of the sacred subject matter. Every church painting has its iconographic code from which no deviation is tolerated. But the artist has an unlimited field left to him where he can freely unfold his creative urges. In the garments, the props, and the background he is able to do, without encumbrances and outside guidance, what is the essential task of a painter: to paint. Here he can reproduce, unrestrained by any convention, what he sees and how he sees it. The solid, rigid edifice of the holy picture carries the wealth of his details like a shining treasure, just like a woman with a flower on her dress.

In the poetry of the fifteenth century, this relationship is, in a certain sense, precisely reversed. The poet has a free hand with respect to the main issue: he may, if he is able, find a new idea, but detail and background are to the highest degree subject to the force of convention. There exists for nearly every detail a normed form of expression, a stencil, which they were reluctant to abandon. Everything, flowers, the enjoyment of nature, sadness and joy, has its fixed form of expression that the poet can somewhat polish and color, without creating it anew.

He polishes and colors his subject matter endlessly because the wholesome restriction imposed on the painter by the surface he has to fill is lacking; the surface confronting the poet is always infinite. The limitation of subject matter is unknown to him. Because of this very freedom, he has to be a greater mind than the painter if he wants to accomplish something exceptional. Even the average painter will give joy to later generations; the average poet, however, sinks into oblivion.

To demonstrate the effect of "unbridled elaboration" using a work of the fifteenth century, it would be necessary to go straight to such a work in its entirety (and they are long!). But since this is not possible, a few samples will have to do.

Alain Chartier was regarded as the greatest poet of his time. He was compared to Petrarch, and Clément Marot still counts him among the best. The brief anecdote I mentioned earlier may be taken as proof of his popularity.[7] By the standards of his time he could be put at the level of one of the greatest painters. The beginning of his poem *Le livre des quatre dames,* a conversation among four noble women whose lovers had fought at Agincourt, provides for us, as the rules required, the landscape that is the background of the picture.[8] This landscape should be compared to the well-known landscape of the Ghent Altarpiece: the wondrous flowery meadow with scrupulously executed vegetation, with the church steeples rising behind shady hilltops, an example of the most unbridled elaboration.

The poet ventures out into the spring morning to dispel his prolonged melancholy.

> *Pour oblier melencolie,*
> *Et pour faire chiere plus lie,*
> *Ung doulx matin aux champs issy,*
> *Au premier jour qu'amours ralie*
> *Les cueurs en la saison jolie . . .**

All this is purely conventional and no rhythmic or formal beauty lifts it above the most ordinary mediocrity. Now follows the description of the spring morning:

> *Tout autour oiseaulx voletoient,*
> *Et si très-doulcement chantoient,*
> *Qu'il n'est cueur qui n'en fust joyeulx.*
> *Et en chantant en l'air montoient,*
> *Et puis l'un l'autre surmontoient*
> *A l'estrivée à qui mieulx mieulx.*
> *Le temps n'estoit mie nueux,*
> *De bleu estoient vestuz les cieux,*
> *Et le beau soleil cler luisoit.†*

---

* To forget melancholy, / And to cheer myself, / One sweet morning I went into the fields, / On the first day on which love joins / Hearts in the beautiful season . . .

† All around birds were flying, / And they sang so very sweetly, / That there is no heart that would not be gladdened by it. / And while singing they rose up in the air, / And then passed and repassed one another / Vying with each other as to which should rise the highest. / The weather was not cloudy at all. / The heavens were clad in blue, / And the beautiful sun was shining brightly.

The simple acknowledgment of the glories of the season and the location would have had a very good effect, if only the poet had known how to restrain himself. There is a real charm in the very simplicity of this nature poem, but it lacks any strong form. The narrative continues in its measured clip; after a closer description of the songs of the birds there follows:

> Les arbres regarday flourir,
> Et lièvres et connins courir.
> Du printempts tout s'esjouyssoit.
> Là sembloit amour seignourir.
> Nul n'y peult vieillir ne mourir,
> Ce me semble, tant qu'il y soit.
> Des erbes ung flair doulx issoit,
> Que l'air sery adoulcissoit,
> Et en bruiant par la valee
> Ung petit ruisselet passoit,
> Qui les pays amoitissoit,
> Dont l'eau ne e'estoit pas salee.
> Là buvoient les oysillons,
> Après ce que des grisillons,
> Des mouschettes et papillons
> Ilz avoient pris leur pasture.
> Lasniers, aoutours, esmerillons
> Vy, et mouches, aux aguillons,
> Qui de beau miel paveillons
> Firent aux arbres par mesure.
> De l'autre part fut la closture
> D'ung pré gracieux, où nature
> Sema les fleurs sur la verdure,
> blanches, jaunes, rouges et perses.
> D'arbres flouriz fut la ceinture,
> Aussi blancs que se neige pure
> Les couvroit ce sembloit paincture,
> Tant y eut de couleurs diverses.*

* I saw the trees blossom, / And hares and rabbits run. / Everything rejoiced at the Spring. / Amour seemed to hold sway there. / None could age or die, / It seemed to me, so long as he was there. / From the grass rose a sweet smell, / Which the clear air made sweeter still, / And purling through the valley, / A little brook passed / Moistening the lands / Of which the water was not salty. / There drank the little

A brook rushes over pebbles; fish are swimming in it; a small forest spreads its branches like green curtains above the banks. There is another list of birds: ducks, doves, egrets, and pheasants are nesting yonder.

What, compared to the painting, constitutes in the poem the different effect of the detailed elaboration of the natural scenery? What, in other words, is the effect of one and the same inspiration merely expressed by different means? It is that the painter is compelled by the character of his art to adhere to simple faithfulness to nature while the poem loses itself in formless superficiality and the listing of conventional motifs.

In this instance, poetry is not as close to painting as is prose. The latter is less tied to particular motifs. It intends, at times, to put greater emphasis on the conscientious depiction of perceived reality and executes this with the help of freer means. In this way, perhaps, prose, better than poetry, demonstrates the more profound relationships between literature and the fine arts.

The basic characteristic of the late medieval mind is its predominantly visual nature. This characteristic is closely related to the atrophy of the mind. Thought takes place exclusively through visual conceptions. Everything that is expressed is couched in visual terms. The absolute lack of intellectual content in the allegorical recitations and poems was bearable because satisfaction was attained through the visual realization alone. The tendency to express directly the external aspects of things found a stronger and more perfect means of expression through pictorial rather than literary means. In the same way, it was able to express itself more forcefully in prose than in poetry. This is the reason why the prose of the fifteenth century constitutes in several respects the middle term between painting and poetry. All three have the unrestrained elaboration of details in common, but in painting and prose this leads to a direct realism unknown in poetry, which is left without anything better at its disposal to replace it.

---

birds/After they had fed upon crickets,/Little flies and butterflies./I saw there lanners, hawks, and merlins,/And flies with a sting/Who made pavilions of fine honey/In the trees by measure./In another part was the enclosure/Of a charming meadow, where nature/Strewed flowers on the verdure/White, yellow, red, and violet./It was encircled by blossoming trees/As white as if pure snow/Covered them, it looked like a painting,/So many various colors there were.

There is one author above all in whose work we notice the same crystal-clear view of the external manifestations as in Van Eyck: Georges Chastellain. He was Flemish, from the Aalst region. Though he calls himself "léal François," "François de naissance,"* it appears that Flemish was his mother tongue. La Marche calls him, "natif flameng, toutesfois mettant par escript en langaige franchois."† He himself pointed with modest pride to his Flemish characteristics of unrefined rusticity; he speaks of "sa brute langue," calls himself, "homme flandrin, homme de palus bestiaux, ygnorant, bloisant de langue, gras de bouche et de palat et tout enfangié d'autres povretés corporelles à la nature de la terre."[9]‡ He owes the all too heavy cothurnism[10] of his stilted prose to that people's manner as well as the grave "grandiloquence" that makes him more or less unpalatable to French readers. His ornate style has something of an elephantine clumsiness about it; a contemporary rightly calls him "cette grosse cloche si hault sonnant."[11]§ But we may perhaps credit his Flemish nature for the keen observations of his style and his vivid colorfulness. Both remind us repeatedly of modern Belgian authors.

An unmistakable kinship exists between Chastellain and Jan van Eyck—and at the same time a difference of artistic level. The less valued qualities of Van Eyck correspond, under the most favorable circumstances, to the best in Chastellain and it means a lot to be the equal of Jan van Eyck at his least. I am thinking, for example, of the singing angels on the Ghent Altarpiece. The heavy garments, all dark red and gold with sparkling gems, the overly emphasized, distorted face, the somewhat pedantic ornaments of the music stand all are the painterly equivalent of the dazzling bombast of the literary Burgundian court style. But while in painting this rhetorical element occupies a subordinate position, it becomes the major concern in Chastellain's prose. His keen observations and his lively realism drown, in most instances, in a flood of overly beautifully elaborated phrases and in a clamor of decorative words.

---

* "a loyal Frenchman . . . French by birth,"

† "Flemish born, though writing in French."

‡ "his coarse speech . . . a Flemish man, a man of the cattle-breeding marshes, rude, ignorant, stammering of tongue, greasy of mouth and of palate and quite bemired with other physical defects, proper to the nature of the land."

§ "this fat bell with the loud sound."

But whenever Chastellain describes an event that particularly captivates his Flemish spirit, an entirely direct, plastic earthiness enters into his narrative, all ceremonial elements notwithstanding, which makes it extraordinarily suitable for its task. His repertoire of ideas is no larger than that of his contemporaries; the counterfeit coin of religious, ethical, and knightly convictions that had been passed around for some time function with him for ideas. The conception is entirely superficial, but its depiction is crisp and lively.

His portrayal of Philip the Good nearly approaches the directness of a Van Eyck.[12] With the deliberateness of a chronicler who is a novelist at heart, he tells in particular detail of a quarrel between the duke and his son Charles early in the year 1457. Nowhere else does his strongly visual perception of things come so sharply into focus. All the external circumstances surrounding the event are presented with perfect clarity. It is mandatory that a few lengthy passages of this narrative be presented now.

At issue is a position at the court of the young count of Charolais. The duke, in spite of an earlier promise, intended to give the position to one of the Croys who enjoyed great favor with him; Charles, who disliked seeing these favors go their way, opposed them.

> Le duc donques par un lundy qui estoit le jour Saint-Anthoine,[13] après sa messe, aiant bien désir que sa maison demorast paisible et sans discention entre ses serviteurs, et que son fils aussi fist par son conseil et plaisir, après que jà avoit dit une grant part de ses heurs et que la cappelle estoit vuide de gens, il appela son fils à venir vers luy et lui dist doucement: "Charles, de l'estrif qui est entre les sires de Sempy et de Hémeries pour le lieu de chambrelen, je vueil que vous y mettez cès et que le sire de Sempy obtiengne le lieu vacant." Adont dist le conte: "Monseigneur, vous m'avez baillié une fois vostre ordonnance en laquelle le sire de Sempy n'est point, et monseigneur, s'il vous plaist, je vous prie que ceste-là je la puisse garder." —"Déa, ce dit le duc lors, ne vous chailliez des ordonnances, c'est à moy à croistre et à diminuer, je vueil que le sire de Sempy y soit mis." —"Hahan! ce dist le conte (car ainsi jurait tousjours), monseigneur, je vous prie, pardonnez-moy, car je ne le

pourroye faire, je me tiens a ce que vous m'avez ordonné.
Ce a fait le seigneur de Croy qui m'a brassé cecy, je le vois
bien." —"Comment, ce dist le duc, me désobéyrez-vous?
ne ferez-vous pas ce que je vueil?" —"Monseigneur, je vous
obéyray volentiers, mais je ne feray point cela." Et le duc,
à ces mots, enfelly de ire, respondit: Hà! garsson, déso-
béyras-tu à ma volenté? va hoys de mes yeux," et le sang,
avecques les paroles, lui tira à coeur, et devint pâle et puis à
coup enflambé et si espoentable en son vis, comme je l'oys
recorder au clerc de la chappelle qui seul estoit emprès luy,
qui hideur estoit à le regarder . . .*

Is this not filled with vigor? The soft opening phrases, the rising
rage during the brief exchange of words, the hesitating speech of
the son in which one can already hear the speech of the Charles
the Bold he is to be.

The way the duke looks at his son so terrifies the duchess (whose
presence has not been mentioned until this point) that she, pushing
her son in front of her, hastily tries to flee the wrath of her husband,
silently making her way from the oratory[14] through the chapel.
But she has to turn various corners before she reaches the door and

---

* "The duke then, on a Monday, which was Saint Anthony's day after mass,
being very desirous that his house should remain peaceful and without dissentions
between his servants and that his son, too, should do his will and pleasure, after
he had already said a great part of his hours, and the chapel was empty of people,
called his son to come to him and said to him gently: 'Charles, the quarrel that
is going on between the lords of Sempy and of Hémeries, about this place of
chamberlain, I wish that you put a stop to it, and that the lord of Sempy obtain
the vacancy.' Then said the count: 'Monseigneur, you once gave me your orders
in which the lord of Sempy is not mentioned, and monseigneur, if you please, I
pray you, that I may keep to them.' —'Déa,' this said the duke then, 'do not
trouble yourself about orders, it belongs to me to raise and to lower, I wish that
the lord of Sempy be placed there.'—'Hahan!' this said the count (for he always
swore like that), 'Monseigneur, I beg you, forgive me, for I could not do it, I
abide by what you have ordered me. This was done by my lord of Croy, who
played me this trick, I can see that.'—'How,' this said the duke, 'will you disobey
me? will you not do what I wish?' —'Monseigneur, I shall gladly obey you, but
I shall not do this.' And the duke, at these words, chocking with anger, replied:
'Há! boy, will you disobey my will? Go out of my sight,' and the blood with
these words rushing to his heart, he turned pale and then all at once flushed and
there came such a horrible expression on his face, as I heard from the clerk of the
chapel, who was alone with him, that it was hideous to look at him . . ."

the scribe has the key: "Caron, ouvrenous,"* says the duchess, but
the scribe falls down at her feet and pleads that her son first ask
for forgiveness before they leave the chapel. She turns to Charles to
plead in all earnesty, but he answers arrogantly and loudly: "Déa,
madame, monseigneur m'a deffendu ses yeux et est indigné sur
moy, par quoy, après avoir eu celle deffense, je ne m'y retourneray
point si tost ains m'en yray a la garde de Dieu, je ne sçray où."†
Suddenly the voice of the duke, who had remained seated on his
prie-Dieu,[15] exhausted with rage, was heard . . . and the duchess
cries out in mortal fear to the scribe : "Mon amy, tost tost ouvrez-
nous, il nous convient partir ou nous sommes morts."‡

Philip is now under the spell of the hot blood of the Valois:
having returned to his chambers, the old duke falls into a kind of
youthful frenzy. Towards evening he secretly rides out of Brussels,
alone and insufficiently protected. "Les jours pour celle heurre
d'alors estoient courts, et estoit jà basse vesprée quant ce prince
droit-cy monta à cheval, et ne demandoit riens autre fors estre
emmy les champs seul et à par luy. Sy porta ainsy l'anventure que
ce propre jour-là, après un long et âpre gel, il faisoit un releng, et
par une longue épaisse bruyne, qui avoit couru tout ce jour là,
vesprée tourna en pluie bien menue, mais très-mouillant et laquelle
destrempoit les terres et romoit glasces avecques vent qui s'y en-
trebouta."§ Doesn't this sound like a Camille Lemonnier?[16]

Then follows the description of the nocturnal wanderings
through fields and forests in which the most lively naturalism and
a moralizing rhetoric filled with a strange sense of its own importance enter into a peculiar mixture. The duke wanders about tired
and hungry. His cries are unanswered. He is lured by a river that

* "Caron, open the door for us,"
† "Faith, madam, monseigneur has forbidden me to come into his sight and
is indignant at me, so that, after this prohibition, I shall not return to him so
soon, but under God's care, I shall go away, I do not know where."
‡ "My friend, now, now, open the door for us so that we may leave, or we
are dead."
§ "The days were short at that time, and it was already evening when that
prince here mounted his horse, and asked nothing but to be alone out in the fields.
It so happened that on that day after a long and sharp frost it had begun to thaw,
and because of a lasting thick fog that had been about all day, in the evening a
fine but very penetrating rain began to fall, which soaked the fields and broke the
ice, as did the wind that joined in."

looks to him like a path, but his horse shys away just in time. He falls off his horse and injures himself. He listens in vain for the crowing of a rooster or the barking of a dog that could lead him back to human habitations. Finally he sees a light shining and tries to get near it; he loses sight of it, finds it again, and finally is able to reach it. "Mais plus l'approchoit, plus sambloit hideuse chose et espoentable, car feu partoit d'une mote d'en plus de mille lieux, avecques grosse fumière, dont nul ne pensast à celle heure fors que ce fust ou purgatoire d'aucune âme ou autre illusion de l'ennemy . . ."* He abruptly halts his horse. But then he recalls that charcoal makers burn their coal deep in the woods. This was indeed such a charcoal fire. But there was no house or cottage anywhere near. Only after having wandered for a while more is he led by the barking of a dog to the hut of a poor man where he finds rest and food.

Similarly characteristic passages from the work of Chastellain are the descriptions of a duel between two burghers at Valenciennes, of the nocturnal fight between the Frisian delegation in Haag and the Burgundian noblemen whom they disturb in their nightly rest by playing catch in an upper room in their wooden shoes, of the riot in 1467 in Ghent when Charles's first visit as duke coincides with the fair in Houthen from which the people return with the shrine of St. Lieven.[17]

Time and again we see, by virtue of unintended trifling details, how clearly the author really perceives all these external things. The duke, confronted with the riot, faces "multitude de faces en bacinets enrouillés et dont les dedans estoient grignans barbes de vilain, mordans lèvres."† The rogue who forces his way to the side of the duke at the window wears an iron glove with a black finish. He bangs it on the windowsill to compel silence.[18]

This ability to narrate in crisp, simple words that which is perceived, precisely and directly, corresponds in literature to that which in painting is accomplished, with a perfect power of expres-

---

* "But the more he approached it, the more it seemed a hideous and frightful thing, for fire came out of a mound in more than a thousand places with thick smoke, and, at that hour, anyone would think that it was the purgatory of some soul or some other illusion of the devil."

† "a multitude of faces in rusty helmets, framing the grinning beards of villains, biting their lips."

sion, by the tremendous visual sharpness of a Van Eyck. In literature that realism is usually interfered with by conventional forms.
It is retarded in its expression and remains an exception in the midst
of a mountain of dry rhetoric while shining in painting like the
blossoms on an apple tree.

In this regard, painting is far ahead of literature in its means of
expression. In reproducing the effects of light painting already has
an astonishing virtuosity. Above all, the miniaturist strove to capture the glow of a moment. In painting, this talent is seen to have
first come to its full development in the *Nativity* (plate 31) by Geertgen tot Sint Jans. The illuminators had already tried to capture the
play of the light of the torches on the armor of the soldiers during
the capture of Christ. The strange master who illuminated King
René's *Cuer d'amours espris* succeeded in depicting a radiant sunrise
and the most mysterious effects of dusk. The master of the *Heures
d' Ailly* already dares to try his hand on the sun breaking through
the clouds after a storm.[19]

Literature had only primitive means at its disposal for the specific
reproduction of light effects. There is, to be sure, a high sensitivity
to the play of bright light, as mentioned above. There is even an
awareness of beauty as being first of all, a matter of shining elegance. All the writers and poets of the fifteenth century like to
mention the glow of sunlight, candles, and weapons. But they do
not go beyond simple acknowledgment; there is as yet no literary
procedure for the description of such things.

We have to look elsewhere if we desire to find a literary equivalent for the effect of light in painting. In literature, the momentary
expression is primarily achieved by a lively application of direct
speech. There is hardly another literature that so consistently reproduces speech directly. This practice leads to tiresome abuse. Froissart and his fellow spirits even dress explanations of political conditions in the form of questions and answers. The endless dialogues,
in their ceremonial key and with their hollow sound, occasionally
heighten rather than interrupt monotony. But the writers do frequently succeed in creating the illusion of directness and spontane-
ity completely convincingly by the use of this technique. Froissart,
above all, is a master of lively dialogue.

"Lors il entendi les nouvelles que leur ville estoit prise." (The
whole speech is shouted.) "'Et de quel gens?' demande-il. Re-
spondirent ceulx qui à luy parloient: 'Ce sont Bretons!' — 'Ha,'

dist-il, 'Bretons sont mal gent, ils pilleront et ardront la ville et puis partiront.' [The shouting continues] 'Et quel cry crient-ils?' dist le chevalier. —'Certes, sire, ils crient La Trimouille!' "*

Froissart employs the device of always having the partner in the dialogue repeat in amazement the last word of the speaker so that a certain element of haste is created. —"'Monseigneur, Gaston est mort.' —'Mort?' dist le conte. —'Certes, mort est-il pour vray monseigneur.'"† And elsewhere: "Si luy demanda, en cause d'amours et de lignaige, conseil. —'Conseil, respondi l'archevesque, 'certes, beaux nieps, c'est trop tard. Vous voulés clore l'estable quant le cheval est perdu.' "20‡

Poetry too, makes generous use of this stylistic device. In a short rhyme sequence the question and answer may alternate twice:

> Mort, je me plaing. —De qui? —De toy.
> —Que t'ay je fait? —Ma dame as pris.
> —C'est vérité. —Dy moy pour quoy.
> Il me plaisoit. —Tu as mespris.21§

In this example the technique of repeated breaks in the dialogue is no longer a means, but rather an end: it is a virtuosity. The poet Jean Meschinot knew how to take this artistic device to its extreme. In a ballade in which poor France remonstrates with her king (Louis XI) about his guilt, the speaker changes in each of the thirty lines three or four times. We have to admit that the effect of the poem as political satire does not suffer from this peculiar form. The first segment reads as follows:

* "Then he heard the news that their town was taken. 'And by what people?' he asks. Those with whom he was speaking answered, 'They are Bretons!' 'Ha,' says he, 'Bretons are bad people, they will pillage and burn and afterwards depart.' 'And what war-cry do they cry?' said the knight. 'Sure my lord, they cry La Trimouille!' "

† "My lord, Gaston is dead." "Dead?" said the count. "Indeed, he is dead in sooth, my lord."

‡ "So he asked for counsel in matters of love and lineage. The archbishop answered, 'Counsel, sure, good nephew, it is too late for that. You want to shut the stable when the horse is lost.' "

§ Death, I complain. —Of whom? —Of you./—What have I done to you? —You have taken my lady./—That is true. —Tell me why?/—It pleased me. —You mistook.

Sire . . . —Que veux? —Entendez . . . —Quoy? —Mon
   cas.
—Or dy. —Je suys . . . —Qui? —La destruicte France!
—Par qui? —Par vous. —Comment? —En tous estats.
—Tu mens. —Non fais. —Que le dit? —Ma souffrance.
—Que souffres tu? —Meschief. —Quel? —A oultrance.
—Je n'en croy rien. —Bien y pert. —N'en dy plus!
—Las! si feray. —Tu perds temps. —Quelz abus!
—Qu'ay-je mal fait? —Contre paix. —Et comment?
—Guerroyant . . . —Qui? —Vos amys et congnus.
—Parle plus beau. —Je ne puis, bonnement.[22]*

There is another example of superficial naturalism in the literature of the time. Though Froissart is concerned with the description
of heroic knightly deeds, what he describes almost against his will,
one is tempted to say, is the prosaic reality of war. Just as Commines, who had his fill of chivalry, Froissart well describes the
atmosphere of fatigue, the futile pursuits, the random movements,
and the restlessness of a camp at night. He is a master at describing
hesitation and waiting.[23]

In his simple and precise reproduction of the external conditions
of an event, he does on occasion even attain an almost tragic power,
as, for example, in the report of the death of young Gaston Phébus,
who had been stabbed by his father in a rage.[24] —The work is so
photographically exact that in his words the quality of the narrator
to whom he owed his endless *faits divers* can be detected. Everything he tells us about his traveling companion, the knight Espaing,
for example, is told very well, indeed.

Whenever literature is at work, simply observing and without
the encumbrance of convention, it is comparable to painting, even
if it does not attain its level.

We should not look for the literary descriptions that come closest

---

* Sire . . . —What do you want? —Listen . . . —To what —To my case./
—Speak out. —I am . . . —Who? —Devastated France!/—By whom? —By
you. —How? —In all estates./—You lie. —I do not. —Who says so? —My
sufferings./—What do you suffer? —Misery. —Which? —The extremity of misery./—I do not believe a word of it. —Evidently. —Do not say any more about
it!/—Alas! I must. —You waste time. —What a shame!/—What ill have I done?
—Against peace. —And how?/—By making war . . . —With whom? —With
your friends and kinsmen./—Speak more pleasingly. —I cannot, in truth.

to painting among the descriptions of nature precisely because we are concerned with the unself-conscious observation of an individual event about which we are told. Nature descriptions in the fifteenth century are not as yet based on direct unself-conscious observation. Events are related because they appear to be important. Their external circumstances are reported just as a film sensitive to light makes a record. A conscious literary procedure does not yet exist. A description of nature, however, which in painting is merely a secondary appendage, that is, presents itself totally unself-consciously, appears in literature to be a conscious artistic device. Being of a purely secondary character, descriptions of nature in painting could, by virtue of this fact, retain their purity and simplicity. Since the background was not important to the subject matter of the painting itself and played no part in its hieratic style, the painters of the fifteenth century were able to put into their landscapes a degree of harmonious naturalness that was still prohibited in the strict disposition of the subject matter constituting the main concern. An exact parallel to this phenomenon is offered by Egyptian art: it abandons the code of forms when modeling the miniature figure of a slave because the figure of a slave is of no significance. The formal code usually requires that the human figure be distorted, but figures created outside the code of forms may, therefore, on occasion share in the simple natural faithfulness of animal figures.

The weaker the relationship between the landscape and the main subject matter to be depicted, the stronger the harmonious and natural qualities of the painting as a whole. Behind the reckless, bizarre, and pompous veneration of the kings in the *Très-riches heures de Chantilly*[25] appears the view of Bourges in all the atmospheric and rhythmic perfection of its dreamlike softness.

In literature, nature descriptions are still entirely dressed in the garb of the pastorale. We have already drawn attention to the argument at court over the pros and cons of the simple rustic life. Just as in those days when Rousseau had his way, it was in good taste to declare that one was tired of the vanity of courtly life and to affect a wise flight from court replete with dark bread and the carefree love of Robin and Marion. This was a sentimental reaction to the full-blooded splendor and proud egotism of reality, not totally lacking in genuine sentiment, yet in its major components merely a literary attitude.

The love of nature belonged to this attitude. Its poetic expression is conventional. Nature was a necessary element in the grand social game of courtly-erotic culture. The terms for the beauty of flowers and the songs of birds were intentionally cultivated in the customary forms that every player understood. The description of nature in literature is thus at an entirely different level than that in painting.

Disregarding for a moment pastorales and the opening stanzas of poems with their obligatory motif of spring mornings, one rarely senses a desire for descriptions of nature. Though occasionally a few such descriptions may appear in literature, as for example, in the work of Chastellain when he describes the beginning of spring thaw (and it is precisely this sort of unintentional description that is by far the most suggestive), it is pastorale poetry that remains the most likely place to locate the rising literary feeling for nature. Next to the pages from Alain Chartier, which we quoted above, to illustrate the effects of elaborate details in general, we could place the poem "Regnault et Jehanneton," in which the kingly shepherd René dresses his love for Jeanne de Laval. Here too, we find no coherent vision of a piece of nature, no unity such as the painter could bestow on his landscape through color and light, but only an unhurried enumeration of details. First the singing of birds, one after the other, the insects, the frogs, followed by the ploughing peasants:

> Et d'autre part, les paisans au labour
> Si chantent hault, voire sans nul séjour,
>   Resjoyssant
> Leurs beufs, lesquelx vont tout-bel charruant
> La terre grasse, qui le bon froment rent;
> Et en ce point ilz les vont rescriant,
>   Selon leur nom:
> A l'un fauveau et l'autre Grison,
> Brunet, Blanchet, Blondeau ou Compaignon;
> Puis les touchent tel foiz de l'aiguillon
>   pour avancer.[26]*

---

* And on the other side the peasants sing at their work/So loudly, truly unceasing, rejoicing./Their oxen, stoutly plow/The fertile earth, which brings forth good food;/And they call them by their names:/One, "Fauveau," another, "Grison,"/"Brunet," "Blanchet," Blondeau" or Compaignon";/They often poke them with their pointed stick,/To make them go forward.

Admittedly, there is a certain freshness in all this and a happy tone, but it should be compared with the calendar depictions of the breviaries. King René presents us with all the ingredients for a good description of nature, a palette of colors, so to speak, but nothing else. Moreover, in describing the coming of dusk, his effort to express a certain mood is unmistakable. The other birds are silent, but the quail still cries, partridges scurry to their nests, deer and rabbits emerge. The sun just a moment ago was still brightening the top of a tower, then the air turns cold, owls and bats begin to make their fluttering sounds, and the bell of the chapel sounds the Ave.

The calendar leaves of the *Très-riches heures* provide an opportunity to compare the same motif in the fine arts and in literature. The splendid castles that fill in the background in the works of the Limburg brothers are well known. The poetic works of Eustace Deschamps may be cited as their literary counterparts. In a number of seven short poems he sings the praises of different northern French castles: Beauté, which was later to provide shelter for Agnes Sorel, Bièvre, Cachan, Clermont, Nieppe, Noroy, and Coucy.[27] Deschamps would have to be a poet with much more powerful wings if he were to achieve the same effect as the Limburg brothers managed to convey in these most tender and delicate expressions of the art of miniatures. On the September leaf (plate 32), the castle of Saumur rises behind the grape harvesting scene as in a dream: the tops of towers with their high wind vanes, the finials, the lily ornaments of the spires, the twenty slender chimneys, all that blossoms like a bed of wild white flowers in the dark blue air. Or take the majestic broad somberness of the princely Lusignan on the March leaf (plate 33), the gloomy towers of Vincennes rising threateningly above the dried foliage of the December forest (plate 34).[28]

Did the poet, or at least this poet, possess equivalent means of expression for evoking such images? Of course not. The description of the architectural forms of a castle, such as in the poem on Bièvre castle could not have any effect. As a matter of fact, all he has to offer is a listing of the enjoyments offered by the castle. Naturally, the painter, being outside the castle, looks at it, while the poet, being inside, looks out:

Son filz ainsné, daulphin de Viennois,
Donna le nom à ce lieu de Beauté.
Et c'est bien drois, car moult est delectables:
L'en y oit bien le rossignol chanter;
Marne l'ensaint, les haulz bois profitables
Du noble parc puet l'en veoir branler . . .
Les prez sont pres, les jardins deduisables,
Les beaus preaulx, fontenis bel et cler,
Vignes aussi et les terres arables,
*Moulins tournans, beaus plains à regarder.**

How different this effect from that of the miniatures! Yet in spite of everything, painting and poem share both procedure and subject matter: they list what is visible (and in the poem what is audible). The view of the painter, however, is firmly focused on a particular and limited complex: in his listing he has to present unity, limitation, and coherence. Paul van Limburg may put all the details of winter in his February picture (plate 35): the peasants warming themselves over a fire in the foreground, the laundry hung for drying, the crows on a snowy ground, the sheepfold, the beehives, the barrel, and the cart; all this and the entire country background with the quiet village and the lonely house on the hill. Yet the calm unity of the painting remains perfect. But the poet's view keeps moving aimlessly; it finds no point of rest. He does not know how to limit himself and does not convey a unified vision.

The form is overrun by the content. In literature, form and content are both old; in painting, however, content is old while the form is new. In painting, there is much more expression in form than in content. The painter is able to put his entire unarticulated wisdom into the form: the idea, the mood, the psychology can be reproduced without the trouble of putting all this into words. The period is predominantly visually oriented. This explains why the pictorial expression is so superior to the literary: a literature whose perception is primarily visual fails.

* His eldest son, the dauphin of Viennois, / Gave this spot the name of Beauty. / And justly, for it is very delectable: / One hears the nightingale sing there; / The river Marne surrounds it, the lofty pleasant woods / Of the noble park may be seen swaying on the wind . . . / Meadows are near, pleasure gardens, / The fine lawns, beautiful and clear fountains, / Vineyards and arable lands, / Turning mills, plains beautiful to view.

The poetry of the fifteenth century seems to live on almost no new ideas. A general impotence to invent new forms prevails; all that is left is to rework or modernize the old subject matter. There is a pause in all thought; the mind, having completed the medieval edifice, is tired and hesitates. Emptiness and barrenness everywhere. One despairs of the world; everything regresses; a strong depression of the soul alone predominates. Deschamps sighs:

> *Helas! on dit que je ne fais mès rien,*
> *Qui jadis fis mainte chose nouvelle;*
> *La raison est que je n'ay pas merrien*
> *Dont je fisse chose bonne ne belle.*[29]*

To us, nothing seems to provide stronger proof of stagnation and decay than the fact that the old rhymed chivalric novels and other poems were rendered in overly long equivalent prose. Yet in spite of everything, this "de-rhyming" of the fifteenth century augurs a transition to a new spirit. As late as the thirteenth century everything could be put into rhymes, including matters concerning medicine, and natural history, just as ancient Indian literature applied the verse form to all academic pursuits. The fixed form signified that the oral presentation is the intended form of communication. This is not a personal, emotional, expressive presentation, but a mechanical recitation since in more primitive literary epochs verses are virtually sung to a fixed and monotonous melody. The new need for prose reveals a drive for expression, an ascendancy of the more modern practice of reading over the old form of oral presentation. This is also linked to the division of the subject matter into smaller chapters with summarizing titles that becomes generally accepted during the fifteenth century while earlier books were less structured. Prose was confronted with relatively higher demands than poetry; in the old rhymed forms everything is still accepted as before; prose, in contrast, is the art form.

But the higher quality of prose in general is found in its formal elements. It is just as little filled with new ideas as poetry. Froissart

---

* Alas! it is said that I no longer make anything./I who formerly made many new things;/The reason is that I have no subject matter/Of which to make good or fine things.

is the perfect type of a mind that does not think in words but simply depicts. He rarely has ideas, but only images of facts. He knows only a few ethical motifs and emotions: fidelity, honor, greed, courage, and all these only in their simplest form. He applies no theology, no allegory, no mythology; if hard-pressed, some morality; he only narrates, correctly, effortlessly, totally matter-of-factly, but is lacking in content and he never grips our emotions except with the mechanical superficiality of the way reality is reproduced in the cinema. His contemplations are of an unparalleled banality; everything is boring, nothing is more certain than death, sometimes, though, one may win or lose. Particular notions are accompanied with automatic certainty by the same set judgments: for example, whenever he speaks of the Germans he maintains that they treat their prisoners badly and that they are particularly greedy.[30]

Even Froissart's frequently cited clever *bons mots* lose, if read in context, much of their impact. For example, it is frequently considered to be an astute characterization of the first duke of Burgundy, calculating and persistent Philip the Bold, when Froissart calls him "sage, froid et imaginatif, et qui sur ses besognes veoit au loin."* But Froissart applies this label to everyone![31] Even the well-known "Ainsi ot messire Jehan de Blois femme et guerre qui trop luy cousta,"[32]† if taken in context, does not actually make the point one reads into it.

One element is totally missing in Froissart: rhetoric. And, it is precisely rhetoric that hid from his contemporaries the lack of new ideas. They may be said to have reveled in the splendor of an artfully embellished style: Ideas are regarded as new because of their stately appearance. All terms wear brocaded garments. Terms of honor and duty wear the colorful costume of the chivalric illusion. The sense of nature is clothed in the costume of the pastorale, and love is mostly restricted by the allegory of the *Roman de la rose*. Not a single thought is allowed to stand naked and free. Thoughts are rarely allowed to move other than in the measured steps of endless processions.

---

* "wise, cool and imaginative, and farsighted in business."

† "so Jean de Blois acquired the wife and the war which was to cost him so much."

The rhetorical-ornamental element is also not lacking in the fine arts. There are innumerable parts in particular paintings that can be called painted rhetoric. As, for example, St. George on Van Eyck's *Madonna of the Canon Van de Paele,* who recommends the donor to the Virgin. How clearly the artist tried to make the golden armor and splendid helmet of St. George antique. How weakly rhetorical is his gesture. The work of Paul van Limburg also displays this consciously rhetorical element in the overloaded bizarre splendor, an unmistakable effort at an exotic, theatrical expression, with which the three kings make their appearance.

The poetry of the fifteenth century puts forth its most advantageous side as long as it does not attempt to express profound ideas and is freed also from the task of doing this beautifully. It is at its best when it evokes, only for a moment, an image, a mood. Its effect depends on its formal elements: the image, the tone, the rhythm. This is why this poetry fails in large-scale, long-winded artful works where rhythmic and tonal qualities are subordinate. However, this poetry is fresh in those genres where form is the main concern: the rondeau, the ballade, which build on a simple light idea and derive their power from image, tone, and rhythm. These are the simple and directly creative qualities of the folk song; whenever the art song gets closest to the folk song it exudes its greatest charm.

During the fourteenth century a reversal occurs in the relationship between lyrical poetry and music. During the older periods poems, even nonlyrical ones, were inseparably tied to musical presentations. It is even assumed that the *chansons de geste,* those sequences of ten or twelve syllables (just as the Indian sloka), were also sung in the same manner. The normal type of the medieval poet is the one who has written the poem and composed its accompanying music as well. This holds true in the fourteenth century for a figure such as Guillaume de Machaut. It is he who establishes both the most common lyrical forms of his times, ballade, rondel, etc., and the form of the *débat.* Machaut's rondels and ballades are characterized by great simplicity, little color, and light intellectual content. These are advantageous features because in this instance the poem comprises only half of the work of art. The song with music is the better the less colorful and expressive it is, as, for example the simple rondel:

Au departir de vous mon cuer vous lais
Et je m'en vois dolans et esplourés.
Pour vous servir, sans retraire jamais,
Au departir de vous mon cuer vous lais.
Et par m'ame, je n'arai bien ne pais
Jusqu'au retour, einsi desconfortés.
Au departir de vous mon cuer vous lais.
Et je m'en vois dolans et esploures.[33]*

Deschamps is no longer the composer of the music for his ballades. He is therefore much more colorful and restless than Machaut, and for the same reason frequently more interesting though of lesser poetic style. It goes without saying that the fleeting, light poem that almost lacks any content and is meant to be accompanied by a certain tune does not die out even though the poets are no longer the composers of the melodies. The rondel retains its style, as is shown by the following by Jean Meschinot:

M'aimerez-vous bien,
Dictes, par vostre ame?
Mais que je vous ame
Plus que nulle rien,
M'aimerez-vous bien?
Dieu mit tant de bien
En vous, que c'est basme;
Pour ce je me clame
Vostre. Mais combien
M'aimerez-vous bien?[34]†

* On parting from you I leave you my heart./And I go away lamenting and weeping/That it may serve you without ever being retracted./On parting from you I leave you my heart/And by my soul, I shall indeed have nothing good nor peace,/Till my return, being thus discomforted./On parting from you I leave you my heart/And I go away lamenting and weeping.

† Will you love me indeed,/Tell me, by your soul?/If I love you/More than anything,/Will you love me indeed?/God put so much goodness/In you that it is balm./Therefore I proclaim myself/Yours. But how much/Will you love me indeed?

The clean, simple talent of Christine de Pisan is particularly
suited for these fleeting effects. She had the same facility in compos-
ing verses as all her contemporaries: with little variation in form
and idea, smooth and colorless, calm and quiet, accompanied by a
soft jesting melancholy. These are truly literary poems. They are
entirely courtly in thought and tone. They remind us of the ivory
plaques of the fourteenth century that repeat, over and over, in
purely conventional depictions the same motifs: a hunting scene,
an event from *Tristan and Isolde* or from the *Roman de la rose*, graceful, cool, and charming. Where Christine in her gentle refinement
finds also the tone of the folk song, the result is sometimes something totally pure. A reunion, for example:

> *Tu soies le très bien venu,*
> *M'amour, or m'embrace et me baise*
> *Et comment t'es tu maintenu*
> *Puis ton depart? Sain et bien aise*
> *As tu esté tousjours? Ça vien*
> *Costé moy, te sié et me conte*
> *Comment t'a esté, mal ou bien,*
> *Car de ce vueil savoir le compte.*
>
> *—Ma dame, a qui je suis tenu*
> *Plus que aultre, a nul n'en desplaise,*
> *Sachés que desir m'a tenu*
> *Si court qu'oncques n'oz tel mesaise,*
> *Ne plaisir ne prenoie en rien*
> *Loings de vous. Amours, qui cuers dompte,*
> *Me disoit: "Loyauté me tien,*
> *Car de ce vueil savoir le compte."*
>
> *—Dont m'as tu ton serment tenu,*
> *Bon gré t'en sçray par saint Nicaise;*
> *Et puis que sain es revenu*
> *Joye arons assez; or t'apaise*
> *Et me dis se scez de combien*
> *Le mal qu'en as eu a plus monte*
> *Que cil qu'a souffert le cuer mien,*
> *Car de ce vueil savoir le compte.*
>
> *—Plus mal que vous, si com retien,*
> *Ay eu, mais dites sanz mesconte,*

Quans baisiers en aray je bien?
Car de ce vueil savoir le compte.[35]*

Or a lover's longing:

Il a au jour d'ui un mois
Que mon ami s'en ala.
Mon cuer remaint morne et cois,
Il a au jour d'ui un mois.

"A Dieu, me dit, je m'en vois";
Ne puis a moy ne parla,
Il a au jour d'ui un mois.[36]†

A surrender:

"Mon ami, ne plourez plus;
Car tant me faittes pitié
Que mon cuer se rent conclus
A vostre doulce amistié.
Reprenez autre maniere;
Pour Dieu, plus ne vous doulez,
Et me faittes bonne chiere:
Je vueil quanque vous voulez."‡

* You are most welcome,/My love; now embrace me and kiss me,/And how have you been/Since your departure? Healthy and at ease/Have you always been? Here come/Beside me, sit down and tell me/How you have been, ill or well,/For of this I want to have an account./—My lady, to whom I am bound/More than any other, may it displease no one,/Know that desire so seized me/That I never had such discomfort,/Nor did I take pleasure in anything/Far from you. Amour, who tames hearts,/Said to me, "Remain faithful to me,/For of this I want to have an account."/—So you kept your oath to me./I thank you much for it by Saint Nicaise;/And as you came back safe and sound,/We shall have joy enough; now be at ease/And tell me if you know by how much/The grief you had from it exceeds/That which my heart has suffered,/For of this I want to have an account./—More grief than you, as I think I had,/But you, tell me accurately/How many kisses shall I have for it?/For of this I want to have an account.

† It is a month today/Since my lover departed./My heart remains gloomy and silent,/It is a month today./"Good-bye," he said, "I am going";/Since then he has not spoken to me,/It is a month today.

‡ Friend, weep no more;/For I am so touched with pity/That my heart gives itself up/To your sweet friendship./Change your manner;/For God's sake, be sad no longer,/And show me a cheerful face:/I desire whatever you wish.

The tender, spontaneous femininity of these songs, lacking the masculine-weighty fantastic reflections and the colorful dress of the figures from the *Roman de la rose,* makes them palatable to us. All they offer to us is a single, just felt emotion; the theme has just touched the heart and is then immediately turned into an image without requiring any help from an idea to accomplish this. This poetry has that quality that is characteristic of music and poetry of all periods in which the inspiration is based exclusively on the simple vision of a moment: the theme is pure and strong, the song opens with clear and firm notes, like the song of a blackbird, but the poet or composer has already spent himself after the stanza; the mood vanishes, the execution is trapped in the quagmire of weak rhetoric. We meet with the same disappointment that almost all poets of the fifteenth century have for us.

Here is an example from Christine's ballades:

> *Quant chacun s'en revient de l'ost*
> *Pou quoy demeures tu derriere?*
> *Et si scez que m'amour entiere*
> *T'ay baillée en garde et depost.*[37]*

We would now expect an accomplished medieval-French Leonore ballade. But the poetess has nothing else to say but this opening. Another two short unimportant stanzas put an end to the matter.

But how fresh is the opening of Froissart's "Le debat dou cheval et dou levrier":

> *Froissart d'Escoce revenoit*
> *Sus un cheval cui gris estoit,*
> *Un blanc levrier menoit en lasse.*
> *"Las," dist le levrier, "Je me lasse,*
> *Grisel, quant nous reposerons?*
> *Il est heure que nous mongons."*[38]†

---

* When everybody comes back from the army/Why do you stay behind?/You know that I pledged you/My loyal love to protect and keep.

† Froissart came back from Scotland/On a horse which was gray./He led a white greyhound on a leash./"Alas," said the greyhound, "I am tired,/Grisel, when shall we rest?/It is time we were feeding."

This tone is, however, not carried through; the poem collapses immediately. The theme is only sensed, not thought. The themes are, however, at times splendidly suggestive. In Pierre Michault's "Danse aux aveugles" we see mankind engaged in the eternal dance around the throne of love, good fortune, and death.[39] But the execution is below standard from the very beginning. An "Exclamacion des os Sainct Innocent," by an unknown poet, opens with the shout of the bones in the bone houses of the famous cemetery:

> *Les os sommes de povres trepassez.*
> *Cy amassez par monceaulx compassez.*
> *Rompus, cassez, sans reigle ne compas . . .*[40]*

As the opening of the most somber lament of death, these lines are well suited; but all of this leads to nothing other than a *memento mori* of the most ordinary kind.

These are all preliminary sketches suitable for pictorial works. For the painter, such a single vision already contains the subject matter for a fully elaborated picture, but for the poet, it remains insufficient.

Does all this mean that the power of painting in the fifteenth century excels that of literature in every respect? No. There are always areas in which literature has richer and more immediate means of expression at its disposal than do the fine arts. Ridicule, above all, is one such area. The fine arts, whenever they lower themselves to the level of caricature, are able to express the comic sentiment only to a small degree. Visually expressed, the comic element tends to become serious. Only in cases where the admixture of the comic element in the complexity of life is very small, where it is only seasoning and not the dominant taste, are works of fine art able to keep pace with the spoken or written word. Genre painting contains the comic element at its weakest.

Here the fine arts are still completely on their own ground. The unbridled elaboration of detail that we already ascribed to the painting of the fifteenth century shades imperceptibly into the leisurely narration of trivia until it becomes genre. With the Master of Flémalle detail becomes "genre." His carpenter Joseph sits and makes

---

* We are the bones of the poor dead,/Here heaped up in measured mounds,/ Broken, fractured, without rule or order . . .

mousetraps (plate 36); the character of genre is present in all the details. The step from the purely painterly vision to that of genre is taken when Van Eyck leaves a window shade open or paints a sideboard or a fireplace in the manner of the Master of Flémalle.

But even in the case of genre, words have a dimension in which they surpass depiction; they are capable of explicitly expressing states of mind. In our discussion of Deschamps's descriptions of the beauty of castles, we stated that they had actually failed and were infinitely far behind that of which miniature art was capable. But we should compare the ballade in which Deschamps describes, as in a genre picture, how he lay ill in his shabby castle of Fismes.[41] The owls, crows, starlings, and sparrows who nest in the tower keep him awake:

> *C'est une estrange melodie*
> *Qui ne semble pas grant deduit*
> *A gens qui sont en maladie.*
> *Premiers les corbes font sçavoir*
> *Pour certain si tost qu'il est jour:*
> *De fort crier font loeur pouoir*
> *Le gros, le gresle, sanz sejour;*
> *Mieulx vauldroit le son d'un tabour*
> *Que telz cris de divers oyseaulx,*
> *Puis vient la proie; vaches, veaulx,*
> *Crians, muyans, et trop vuit,*
> *Joint du moustier la sonnerie,*
> *Qui tout l'entendement destruit*
> *A gens qui sont en maladie.**

Towards evening the owls come and scare the patient with their lamenting cries that make him think of death:

* It is a strange melody/Which is not a great amusement/To people who are ill./First the ravens let us know/For certain as soon as it is day:/They cry aloud with all their might,/The fat and the thin bird, without interruption./Even the sound of a drum would be better/Than the cries of various birds,/Then come the cattle; cows, calves,/Bellowing, lowing, all this is noxious,/When one has an empty brain,/The bells of the church join in,/Which destroys the reason altogether/Of people who are ill.

C'est froit hostel et mal reduit
*A gens qui sont en maladie.**

As soon as even a glimmer of a comic element or even only a
more leisurely way of narrating begins to appear, the method of
stringing lists of things together is no longer so tiring. Lively lists
of bourgeoisie customs, long, leisurely descriptions of the female
toilet break the monotony. In his long allegorical poem *Le espinette
amoureuse,* Froissart suddenly enchants us with a listing of about
sixty children's games that he used to play as a little boy in Valenciennes.[42] The literary service of the devil of gluttony has already
begun. The abundant feasts of Zola, Huysmans, and Anatole
France have their prototypes in medieval times. How appetizingly
Froissart describes the *bon vivants* from Brussels who crowd around
fat Duke Wenzel at the battle of Bäsweiler; they have their servants
with them, each with a large wine flask tied to the saddle, bread
and cheese, smoked salmon, trouts and eel paste, all neatly wrapped
in small napkins; they considerably confuse the order of battle.[43]
As a result of its proclivity for genre-like qualities, the literature
of that time is capable of turning even the most sober subject into
verse. Deschamps is able to plead for money in verse without lowering his accustomed poetic standards; in a series of ballades he begs
for an official robe that had been promised to him, for firewood, a
horse, and back pay that is due him.[44]
From this it is only a small step from genre types to the bizarre
and burlesque or, if you want, to the art of Breughel. In this form
of the comic, painting is still the equal of literature. The Breughel-
like element is already completely present in the art of the fourteenth century. It is there in Melchior Broedelam's *Flight into Egypt*
(plate 5), in Dijon; in the three sleeping soldiers in the *Marys at the
Sepulchre* that is ascribed to Hubert van Eyck (plate 37). No one is
as forceful with intentionally bizarre elements as is Paul van Limburg. A spectator in *The Purification of the Virgin* wears a crooked
magician's hat a meter high with fathom-long sleeves (plate 38).
There is the burlesque in the baptismal fount, which is decorated
with three grotesque masks with their tongues out. In the background of the *Visitation* a hero in a tower does battle with a snail

---

* It is a cold hostel and ill refuge/For people who are ill.

and another man pushes a wheelbarrow holding a pig playing a bagpipe (plate 39).[45]

The literature of the fifteenth century is bizarre on almost every one of its pages; its artificial style and the strangely fantastic costumes of its allegories testify to this fact. Motifs, through which Breughel's unleashed fantasy was later to vent its fury, as for example the quarrel between Lent and Carnival, the struggle between meat and fish, were already popular in the literature of the fifteenth century (plate 40). Breughelish to a high degree is Deschamps's keen vision in which he has the troops, gathering in Sluis for a campaign against England, appear to the guard as an army of rats and mice.

> "Avant, avant! tirez-vous ça.
> Je voy merveille, ce me semble."
> —"Et quoy, guette, que vois-tu là?"
> "Je voy dix mille rats ensemble
> Et mainte souris qui s'assemble
> Dessus la rive de la mer . . ."*

In another instance he is sitting at a table at court, mournful and unfocused, when suddenly he notices how the courtiers are eating: one chews like a pig, that one nibbles like a mouse, this uses his teeth like a saw, that one distorts his face, the beard of the other whips up and down. "While they ate, they looked like devils."[46]

Whenever literature describes the life of ordinary people, it automatically resorts to that deft realism mixed with humor that was so to blossom in the fine arts. Chastellain's description of the poor peasant who gives shelter to the lost duke of Burgundy is like a work by Breughel.[47] Pastorales, in their description of eating, dancing, and wooing shepherds, are time and again drawn from their basic sentimental and romantic theme towards a fresh naturalism of slightly comic effect. We count among this an interest in worn-out clothing that had already begun to stir in both the literature and art of the fifteenth century. The calendar miniatures emphasize with great enjoyment the threadbare knees of the mowers in the wheat

---

* "Forward, forward! turn there./I see a marvel, it seems to me."/—"And what, watchman, do you see there?"/"I see ten thousand rats assembled/And a multitude of mice collecting/On the seashore . . . "

or paint the rags of beggars receiving alms. In all this we have the point of origin of that line that, via Rembrandt's sketches (plate 41) and Murillo's begging youths (plate 42), leads to the street people of Steinlen (plate 43).

But at the same time, one is struck by the great difference between the pictorial and the literary. While the fine arts already perceive the picturesque qualities of a beggar, that is, are sensitive to the magic of form, literature, for the time being, is only concerned with the beggar's significance, whether it laments, praises, or condemns him. In the condemnations, in particular, are the archetypes of the realistic literary depictions of poverty. Beggars had become terribly troublesome towards the end of the medieval period. Their pitiful hordes took shelter in the churches and disrupted church services with their cries and noisy carryings on. Among them were to be found many evil people, *validi mendicantes*. In 1428 the cathedral chapter of Notre Dame in Paris attempted in vain to restrict them to the church doors; only later were they at least pushed from the choir into the nave of the church.[48] Deschamps never tires of making his hatred of these miserable people known; he regards them all as hypocrites and cheaters. Beat and drive them from the churches, he shouts, hang or burn them![49] The road traveled from here to the modern literary description of misery seems to be much longer than that which the fine arts had to traverse. In painting, a new element entered all on its own; in literature, in contrast, a newly matured social sensitivity had first to create entirely new forms of expression.

Wherever the comic element, be it either weaker or stronger, coarser or more subtle, was already provided by the appearance of the subject matter itself, as in the case of genre or burlesque, the fine arts were able to keep pace with the word. But there were spheres of humor that were quite inaccessible to pictorial expression, where neither color nor line were able to express anything. In all places where the comic element is intended to provoke healthy laughter: in the comedy, farce, burlesque, the joke, in short, in all the forms of the crudely comic, literature rules unchallenged. A very particular spirit is heard in that rich treasure of late medieval culture.

Even where ridicule sounds its most exquisite notes and waxes about the most serious things in life, about love and one's own suffering, in the realm of the faint smile literature is master. The affected, smoothed-over, and worn forms of eroticism undergo refinement and purification by the admixture of irony.

Outside eroticism, irony is still awkward and naive. French authors around 1400 occasionally were careful to warn their readers when they spoke ironically. Deschamps praises the good times; everything is going perfectly, everywhere peace and justice reign:

> L'en me demande chascun jour
> Qu'il me semble du temps que voy,
> Et je respons: c'est tout honour,
> Loyauté, verité et foy,
> Largesce, prouesce et arroy,
> Charité et biens qui s'advance
> Pour le commun; mais, par ma loy,
> Je ne di pas quanque je pense.*

In another place at the end of a ballade with the same tendency he says: "Tous ces poins a rebours retien."[50]† Yet another has the refrain: "C'est grant pechiez d'anisy blasmer le monde":‡

> Prince, s'il est par tout generalment
> comme je say, toute vertu habonde;
> Mais tel m'orroit qui diroit: "Il se ment" . . .[51]§

A *bel esprit* from the second half of the fifteenth century entitles his epigram: "Soubz une meschante paincture faicte de mauvaises couleurs et du plus meschant peinctre du monde, par manière d'yronnie par maître Jehan Robertet."[52]**

But how subtle irony becomes as soon as it deals with love. In these instances irony blends with gentle melancholy, with the sub-

---

* People ask me every day/What I think of the present times,/And I answer, it is all honor,/Loyalty, truth and faith,/Liberality, heroism and order,/Largesse and kindness that will advance/The common good; but by my faith,/I do not say what I think.

† "Take all these points the other way about."

‡ "It is a great sin to reproach the world in this manner."

§ Prince, if it is generally everywhere/As I know, all virtue abounds;/But many a man hearing me will say, "He lies . . ."

** "under a bad picture done in bad colors and by the most paltry painter in the world, in an ironical manner by master Jean Robertet."

dued tenderness with which the eroticism of the fifteenth century puts something new into the old forms. The hard heart melts with a sob. A note sounds that had not before been heard in earthly love: *de profundis.**

This is self-mockery, the figure of the "amant remis et renié"† that Villon embraces; these are the muted small songs of disillusionment sung by Charles d'Orléans, the smile through tears: "Je riz en pleurs,"‡ which was not only of Villon's invention. An old biblical adage, "risus dolore miscebitur et extrema gaudii luctus occupat,"[53]§ revived in a new application, acquired a bitter and refined emotional meaning. Alain Chartier, the slick court poet, knows this motif as well as Villon, the vagabond. Earlier than both, it is already found in Othe de Granson.[54] The following examples are from Alain Chartier.

> *Je n'ay bouche qui puisse rire,*
> *Que les yeulx ne la desmentissent:*
> *Car le cueur l'en vouldroit desdire*
> *Par les lermes qui des yeulx issent.***

Or of a disconsolate lover:

> *De faire chiere s'efforcoit*
> *Et menoit une joye fainte,*
> *Et à chanter con cueur forçoit*
> *Non pas pour plaisir, mais pour crainte,*
> *Car tousjours ung relaiz de plainte*
> *S'enlassoit au ton de sa voix,*
> *Et revenoit à son attainte*
> *Comme l'oysel au chant du bois.*[55]††

* "out of the depths."

† "lover who has been turned away"

‡ "I laugh through tears"

§ "Even in laughter the heart may be sorrowful; and the end of mirth is heaviness."

** I don't have a mouth which could laugh,/Without my eyes belying it:/For the heart would deny it/By the tears issuing from the eyes.

†† He constrained himself to be cheerful/And showed a feigned joy,/And forced his heart to sing/Not from pleasure, but from fear,/For ever a reminder of complaint/Entwined itself with the tone of his voice,/And he returned to his suffering/As the Ousel returns to his song in the wood.

At the end of a poem, the poet, in the style of a vagabond song, denies his suffering:

> C'est livret voult dicter et faire escripre
> Pour passer temps sans courage villain
> Ung simple clerc que l'en appelle Alain,
> Qui parle ainsi d'amours pour oyr dire.[56]*

Or, in a detailed imaginative scene at the end of King René's endless *Cuer d'amours espris,* the chamberlain, holding a candle, checks to see if the king has lost his heart, but cannot discover any hole in his side:

> Sy me dist tout en soubzriant
> Que je dormisse seulement
> Et que n'avoye nullement
> Pour ce mal garde de morir.[57]†

The old conventional forms had acquired a new freshness by the new sentiment. No one has taken the customary personification of sentiments as far as Charles d'Orléans. He views his own heart as a separate being:

> Je suys celluy au cueur vestu de noir . . .[58]‡

The older lyric, even the *dolce stil nuova,* had taken personification with sacred seriousness, but in the poems of Charles d'Orléans the line between seriousness and mockery can no longer be drawn; he exaggerates personification without losing the subtle feeling in the process:

> Un jour à mon cueur devisoye
> Qui en secret à moy parloit,

* This book meant to speak and to describe/To pass the time without vulgar mood/A simple clerk called Alain/Who speaks of love by hearsay.

† So he told me smiling/That I should sleep/And be not at all afraid/That I should die of this evil.

‡ I am the one whose heart is draped in black . . .

Et en parlant lui demandoye
Se point d'espargne fait avoit
D'aucuns biens quant Amours servoit:
Il me dist que très voulentiers
La vérité m'en compteroit,
Mais qu'eust visité ses papiers.

Quant ce m'eut dit, It print sa voye
Et d'avecques moy se partoit.
Après entrer je le véoye
En ung comptouer qu'il avoit:
Là, de ça et de là queroit,
En cherchant plusieurs vieulx caïers
Car le vray monstrer me vouloit,
Mais qu'eust visitez ses papiers . . .[59]*

In the above passage, the comic element predominates, in that which follows, it is seriousness:

Ne hurtez plus à l'uis de ma pensée,
Soing et Soucy, sans tant vous travailler;
Car elle dort et ne veult s'esveiller,
Toute la nuit en peine a despensée.

En dangier est, se s'elle n'est bien pansée;
Cessez, cessez, laissez la sommeiller;
Ne hurtez plus à l'uis de ma pensée,
Soing et Soucy, sans tant vous travailler . . .[60]†

---

* "One day I was talking with my heart/Which secretly spoke to me,/And in talking I asked it/If it had saved/Any goods while serving Amour:/It said quite willingly/It would tell me the truth about it,/As soon as it had consulted its papers./Having told me this it went away/And from me departed./Then I saw it enter/In an accounts office it had:/There it rummaged here and there,/In looking for several old writing books,/For it would show me the truth,/As soon as it had consulted its papers . . ."

† Do not knock at the door of my mind anymore,/Anxiety and Care, do not trouble yourselves;/For it sleeps and does not want to wake,/It has passed all night in torment./It will be in danger, if not well nursed;/Stop, stop, let it slumber;/Do not knock at the door of my mind anymore,/Anxiety and Care, do not trouble yourselves.

Disguising the lovers in churchly forms not only serves ob-
scenely graphic language and crude irreverence as in the *Cent nouvelles nouvelles,* it also provides the most tender, nearly elegiac, love
poem produced by the fifteenth century with its form: "L'amant
rendu cordelier à l'observance d'amours." By the mixture with the
seasoning of blasphemy, so favored by the mind of the fifteenth century, softly sad eroticism acquired an even more pronounced taste.

The motif of the lovers as members of a spiritual order had
already given rise, in the circle of Charles d'Orléans, to a poetic
brotherhood that called itself *les amoureux de l'observance.* But was
it really Martial d'Auvergne who elaborated this motif into this
moving poem that towers so much above his other work?

The wretched and disappointed lover renounces the world in the
strange monastery where only distressed lovers, *les amoureux martyrs,* are accepted. In a calm dialogue with the prior he tells the
gentle story of his unrequited love and is admonished to forget it.
Beneath the medieval-satirical dress here is fully formed the mood
of a Watteau and of the Pierrot cult, only without moonlight.[61]
Did she not have the habit, asks the prior, of casting a loving glance
in your direction or saying in passing a "Dieu gart?"* It never went
that far, answers the lover; but at night I stood for three hours at
her door and looked up at the eaves:

> *Et puis, quant je oyoye les verrières*
> *De la maison qui cliquetoient,*
> *Lors me sembloit que mes priéres*
> *Exaussées d'elle sy estoient.†*

"Were you sure that she noticed you?" asks the prior.

> *Se m'aist Dieu, j'estoye tant ravis,*
> *Que ne savoye mon sens ne estre,*
> *Car, sans parler, m'estoit advis*
> *Que le vent ventoit sa fenestre*
> *Et que m'avoit bien peu congnoistre,*
> *En disant bas: "Doint bonne nuyt,"*

---

* "God protect you."
† And then, when I heard the window/Of the house clatter,/Then it seemed
to me that my prayers/Had been heard by her.

Et Dieu scet se j'estoye grant maistre
Après cela toute la nuyt.[62]*

He slept wonderfully in this bliss:

Tellement estoie restauré
Que, sans tourner ne travailler,
Ja faisoie un somme doré,
Sans point la nuyt me resveiller,
Et puis, avant que m'abiller,
Pour en rendre à Amours louanges,
Baisoie troys fois mon orillier,
En riant à par moy aux anges.†

During his solemn acceptance into the order, his lady, who had scorned him, faints, and a small golden heart enameled with tears, which he had given her as a gift, falls out of her dress:

Les aultres, pour leur mal couvrir
A force leurs cueurs retenoient,
Passans temps a clorre et rouvrir
Les heures qu'en leurs mains tenoient,
Dont souvent les feuillès tournoient
En signe de devocion;
Mais les deulz et pleurs que menoient
Monstroient bien leur affection.‡

When the prior finally gets around to enumerating his new duties and warns him never to listen to the nightingale, never to slumber

---

* So help me God, I was so ravished,/That I was scarcely conscious,/For, without being told, it seemed to me/that the wind moved her window/And she could well have recognized me,/Perhaps saying softly: "Good night, then,"/And God knows I felt like a great master/After this all night.

† I felt so refreshed/That, without turning or tossing,/I enjoyed golden slumber,/Without waking up all night,/And then, before dressing,/To praise Amour for it,/I kissed my pillow thrice,/While laughing to myself at the angels.

‡ The others, to hide their affliction/Controlled their hearts by force,/Passing the time closing and opening/The breviaries they held in their hands,/Of which they turned the leaves/As a sign of devotion;/But by their sorrow and tears they/Clearly showed their emotion.

under "eglantiers et aubespines," and, above all, never to look into the eyes of women, then the poem laments on the theme of *doux yeux* in an endless melody with ever varying stanzas:

> *Doux yeulx qui tousjours vont et viennent;*
> *Doulx yeulx eschauffans le plisson,*
> *De ceulx qui amoureux deviennent . . .*

> *Doux yeulx a cler esperlissans,*
> *Qui dient: C'est fait quant tu vouldras,*
> *A ceulx qu'ils sentent bien puissans . . .*[63]*

During the fifteenth century all the conventional forms of eroticism are, imperceptibly, permeated with this gentle, subdued note of relaxed melancholy. The old satire of cynical derision of women is thus suddenly pierced by an entirely different mood: in the *Quinze joyes de mariage* the earlier imbecile reviling of women is tempered by a note of quiet disillusionment and depression. This imparts to it the sadness of a modern novel about marriage; the ideas are shallow and hastily expressed; the conversations, in their tenderness, do not reflect malicious intent.

In matters of the means of expression for love, literature had the schooling of centuries behind it. Its masters were such diverse spirits as Plato and Ovid, the troubadours and the minstrels, Dante and Jean de Meun. The fine arts, in contrast, were still unusually primitive in this arena and remained so for a long time. Only during the eighteenth century does the artistic representation of love catch up with the literary description in matters of refinement and wealth of expression. The painting of the fifteenth century is still incapable of being frivolous and sentimental. It is still denied the expression of the roguish element. The picture of the maiden Lysbet van Durenvoode, by an unknown master before 1430 (plate 44), shows a figure of such strict dignity that she was once described as the figure of the donor of a devotional picture, but the text on the banderole she holds in her hand reads: "Mi verdriet lange te hopen,

---

* Sweet eyes that move back and forth;/Sweet eyes enwarming the skin,/Of those who fall in love. . ./Sweet eyes of pearly clearness,/That say: I am ready when you please,/to those who feel those eyes powerfully . . .

Wie is hi die syn hert hout open?"* This art knows both chaste and obscene elements. It does not yet possess the means to express the intermediate stages. It says little about the life of love and does so in naive and innocent forms. We do have, of course, to remind ourselves anew that most art of this sort that existed has been lost. It would be of extraordinary interest to us if we could compare the sort of nudity painted by Van Eyck in his *Bath of Women* or that by Rogier where two young men peep laughingly through a chink (both pictures are described by Fazio) with that of Van Eyck's Adam and Eve in the Ghent Altarpiece. Incidentally, the erotic element is not altogether lacking in Adam and Eve; the artist undoubtedly followed the conventional code of female beauty with respect to the small breasts that are placed too high, the long slender arms, the protruding belly. But how naively all this is done; he has neither the ability nor the slightest desire to titillate the senses.—Charm, however, is said to be the essential element of the *Little Love Magic* that is labeled "from the school of Jan van Eyck,"[64] a room in which a girl, naked as is proper for magic, attempts to force the appearance of her beloved by sorcery (plate 45). Nudity is presented in this instance in that same unpretentious concupiscence that we encounter in the nude pictures by Cranach.

It was not prudishness that so limited the role of depiction in eroticism. The late Middle Ages display a peculiar contrast between a strongly developed sense of modesty and a surprising lack of restraint. For the latter we need not cite any examples; it shows itself everywhere. The sense of modesty, on the other hand, can be seen, for example, in the fact that the victims in the worst scenes of murder or pillage are shown in their shirts or underwear. The Burgher of Paris is never so disgusted as when this rule is violated: "Et ne volut pas convoitise que on leur laissast neis leurs brayes, pour tant qu'ilz vaulsissent 4 deniers, qui estoit un des plus grans cruaultés et inhumanité chrestienne à aultre de quoy on peut parler."[65]† In the report of the cruelty of the Bastard of Vauru[66] to a poor woman he is disgusted that the knavish villain cut her dress

---

* "I am weary of hoping so long. Where is he who holds his heart open?"

† "And it can't be laid to greed that they left them only in their pants since they were worth only four deniers—which was terribly gruesome and one of the greatest Christian inhumanities against one's neighbor that it is possible to imagine."

off slightly below the waist far more than he is about the cruelties inflicted upon the other victims.[67] —Given the prevailing sense of modesty, it is even more remarkable that the female nude, still little used in art, was given such free reign in the *tableau vivant*. No entry procession lacked the presentation, *personnages,* of naked goddesses or nymphs, as those Dürer saw during Charles V's entry into Antwerp in 1520[68] and who prompted Hans Makart's erroneous assumption that the women had been part of the procession. The presentations were performed on small stages at certain locations, sometimes even in water, as for example, the sirens who swam by the bridge over the river Leie "toutes nues et échevelées ainsi comme on les peint,"* during the entry of Philip the Good into Ghent in 1457.[69] The Judgment of Paris was the most popular subject of such performances. —They should be understood as nothing more than manifestations of a naive popular sensuality rather than of a Greek sense of beauty or of a trivial lack of modesty. Jean de Roye describes the sirens, placed not too far from the figure of the crucified one between the thieves, with the following words: "Et sy avoit encores trois bien belles filles, faisans personnages de seraines toutes nues, et leur veoit on le beau tetin droit, separé, rond et dur, qui estoit chose bien plaisant, et disoient de petiz motetz et bergeretes; et près d'eulx jouoient plusieurs bas instrumens qui rendoient de grandes melodies."[70]† Molinet reports with what delight the people viewed the *Judgement of Paris* during the 1494 entry of Philip the Beautiful into Antwerp: "mais le hourd ou les gens donnoient le plus affectueux regard fut sur l'histoire des trois déesses, qui l'on véoit au nud et de femmes vives."[71]‡ Just consider how great is the distance from any pure sense of beauty that is shown in Lille in 1468 when the performance of that scene during the entry of Charles the Bold was parodied by a fat Venus, an emaciated Juno, a hunchbacked Minerva, all wearing golden crowns on their heads.[72] The presentation of nudity remained the fashion until late in the sixteenth century. During the entry of the

---

* "completely nude and with disheveled hair as they are painted"

† "And there were also three very handsome girls, representing quite naked sirens, and one saw their beautiful erected, separate, round and hard breasts, which was a very pleasant sight, and they recited little motets and bergerettes; and near them several deep-toned instruments were playing fine melodies."

‡ "but the stand at which the people looked with the greatest pleasure was the history of the three goddesses represented nude by living women."

duke of the Bretagne into Reims in 1532, a naked Ceres with a Bacchus[73] could be seen, and even William of Orange, on his entry into Brussels on September 18, 1578, was still treated to the sight of an Andromeda, "a maiden in chains, as naked as she was born from her Mother's womb; she seemed a marble statue." So comments Johan Baptista Houwaert, who had arranged the tableaux.[74]

The backwardness of pictorial expression compared to literature is, incidentally, not limited to the comic, the sentimental, and the erotic. Pictorial expression reaches a limit whenever it is no longer supported by the predominantly visual orientation that we had been inclined to regard as the reason for the superiority of painting over literature in general. Whenever something more than a directly clear image of the natural world was needed, painting fails step by step and it becomes suddenly very evident how well founded Michelangelo's charge was: this art seeks to depict many things simultaneously in perfection; while a single one of them would be important enough to devote all energies to it.

Let us return to a painting by Jan van Eyck. His art is unsurpassed as long as it works close-up, microscopically, so to say: in the facial features, for example, or the material of the garments and the jewels. The absolutely keen observation suffices in these cases. But as soon as the perceived reality has to be made part of a different equation, so to speak, as is the case in the presentation of buildings and landscapes, one becomes aware of some weaknesses, in spite of the intrinsic charm exuded by the early perspective. For example, there can be a certain lack of cohesion, a somewhat deficient disposition. The more the depiction is conditioned by intentional composition, and the more a pictorial form has to be created in order to do justice to the particular subject matter of a painting, the more evident the failure becomes.

No one will deny the claim that in the illustrated breviaries, the calendar pages are superior to those with depictions of stories from the Holy Scriptures. In the case of the former, direct perception and its narrative reproduction sufficed. But for the composition of an important action, or of a presentation with movement and many persons, a feeling for rhythmic construction and cohesion is required above all. Giotto had once possessed it and Michelangelo was to correctly handle it again. But the characteristic of the art of the fifteenth century was its many-faceted quality. Only where this many-faceted quality itself becomes cohesiveness is that effect of a high degree of harmony attained as in the *Adoration of the Lamb*. There we actually find rhythm, an incomparably strong rhythm, the triumphant rhythm of all those groups converging on the center. But this rhythm is, so to speak, derived from purely mathematical coordination, from the multifacetedness itself. Van Eyck avoids the difficulties of composition by depicting only scenes of strict quietude; he achieves a static but not a dynamic harmony.

This, above all, marks the great distance between Rogier van der Weyden and Van Eyck. Rogier limits himself so that he may find rhythm; he does not always attain it, but he is always aspiring to it.

There was an old, strict tradition of depiction with respect to the most important themes of the Holy Scripture. The painter was no longer required to find for himself the arrangement of his painting.[75] Some of these *sujets* came close to a rhythmic structure of their own. In scenes like that of a pietà, a deposition, the adoration of the shepherds, rhythm comes naturally. Just recall such works as the *Pietà* by Rogier van der Weyden in Madrid, those of the Avignon school in the Louvre and in Brussels, those of Petrus Christus, Geertgen tot Sint Jans, the *Belles heures d'Ailly*.[76]

But wherever the scene becomes livelier, such as the mockery of Christ, the carrying of the cross, the adoration of the Kings, difficulties of composition mount and a certain unrest, an insufficient cohesion of visual conception, results. In cases where the iconographic norms of the church leave the artist to his own devices, he finds himself in a rather helpless position. The judicial scenes to which Dirk Bouts and Gerard David still gave a certain ceremonial arrangement were already rather weak as far as composition is concerned. Composition becomes awkward and clumsy in the *Martyrdom of St. Erasmus* in Louvan, and in that of *St. Hippolytus*, who is quartered by horses, in Bruges, the flawed structure is positively repugnant.

Whenever never before seen fantasies are to be depicted, the art of the fifteenth century veers into the ridiculous. Great painting was protected against this by its strict *sujets;* but the art of book illustration did not have the luxury of avoiding the depiction of all the mythological and allegorical fantasies made available by literature. The illustration of the *Epitre d'Othéa à Hector*,[77] a detailed mythological fantasy probably by Christine de Pisan, provides a good example. Here we have the most awkward cases. The Greek gods have large wings attached to the backs of their ermine coats or Burgundian robes of state; the entire design as expression misses the mark: Minos; Saturn, who devours his children; Midas, who distributes the prizes, all are fashioned equally naively, yet whenever the illustrator was allowed to delight in the background with a small shepherd and his sheep, or a little hill with a gallows and a wheel, he displays his usual skill.[78] But this is where the positive power of these artists has its limits. In the final analysis, they are just about as limited as the poets in their freely creative formative work.

The imagination had been led into a dead-end street by allegorical presentation. An image cannot be freely fashioned because it has to completely comprise the thought, and the thought is restrained in its flight by the image. Imagination had become accustomed to transposing thought as soberly as possible, and without a sense of style, to the picture. *Temperantia* wears a clockwork on her head to indicate her nature. The illustrator of the *Epitre d'Othéa* simply uses a small wall clock for this purpose, which he also places on the wall of Philip the Good.[79] If a keen and naturally observant mind like Chastellain paints allegorical figures from his own experience they turn out to be extraordinarily affected. For example, he envisions four ladies who accuse him in his *Exposition sur vérité mal prise,* which he wrote to justify himself in the wake of his daring political poem *Le dit de Vérité.*[80] These ladies are called Indignation, Reprobation, Accusation, and Vindication. We cite his description of the second:[81]

Ceste dame droit-cy se monstroit avoir les conditions
seures, raisons moult aguës et mordantes; grignoit les dens
et mâchoit ses lèvres: niquoit de la teste souvent; et monstrant signe d'estre arguëresse, sauteloit sur ses pieds et tournoit l'un costé puis çà l'autre costé puis là; portoit manière
d'impatience et de contradiction: le droit oeil avoit clos et
l'autre ouvert; avoit un sacq plein de livres devant lui, dont
les uns mit en son escours comme chéris, les autres jetta au
loin par despit; deschira papiers et feuilles; quayers jetta au
loin par despit; deschira papiers et feuilles; quayers jetta au
feu félonnement; rioit sur les uns et les baisoit, sur les autres
cracha par vilennie et les foula des pieds; avoit une plume en
sa main, pleine d'encre, de laquelle roioit maintes ecritures
notables . . . d'une esponge aussy noircissoit aucunes
ymages, autres esgratinoit aux ongles . . . et les tierces

> rasoit toutes au net et les planoit comme pour les mettres
> hors de mémoire; et se monstroit dure et felle ennemie à
> beaucoup de gens de bien, plus volontairement que par
> raison.*

But in another passage he observes how Lady *Paix* spreads her
coat, raises it into the air, and how the coat then divides into four
other ladies: *Paix de coeur, Paix de bouche, Paix de semblant, Paix de
vrax effet.*[82]† In yet another of his allegories, female figures appear
called "Pesanteur de tes Pays, Diverse condition et qualité de tes
divers peuples, L'envie et haine des François et des voisines nations,"‡ as if political editorials could be allegorized.[83] That all these
figures were not envisioned, but invented, is demonstrated, on top
of all this, by the fact that they display their names on banderoles;
he does not fashion these figures directly from his living imagination, but presents them as in painting or a performance.

In *La mort du duc Philippe, mystère par manière de lamentation* he sees
his duke as a flask filled with precious ointment that is suspended on
a thread from the sky; the earth has nourished the flask on its
breast.[84] Molinet sees how Christ as the pelican (a customary image) not only feeds his young with his blood but also washes the
mirror of death with it.[85]

The inspiration of beauty is lost here: a playful and false joke,
an exhausted spirit awaits new fertilization. In the dream motif,
consistently used as the framework of an action, we rarely sense

---

* "This dame here is said to have acrid conditions and very tart and biting
reasons; she ground her teeth and bit her lips; often nodded her head; and indicated
by gesture that she was arguing, jumped on her feet and turned to this side and
to that; she proved to be impatient and inclined to contradict; the right eye was
closed and the other open; she had a bag full of books before her, of which she
put some into her girdle, as if they were dear to her, the others she thew away
spitefully; she tore up papers and leaves; she threw writing books into the fire
furiously; she smiled on some and kissed them; she spat on others out of meanness
and trod them underfoot; she had a pen in her hand, full of ink, with which she
crossed out many important writings . . . ; also with a sponge she blackened some
pictures, she scratched out others with her nails, and others she erased wholly and
smoothed them as if to have them forgotten; and showed herself a hard and fell
enemy to many respectable people, more arbitrarily than reasonably."

† "Peace of Heart, Peace of Mouth, Seeming Peace, Peace of True Effect."

‡ "Importance of your Lands, Various qualities and conditions of your several
peoples, The Envy and Hatred of Frenchmen and of Neighboring Nations"

genuine dream elements such as occur so movingly in Dante and Shakespeare. Not even the illusion that the poet has really experienced his conception as a vision is always maintained: Chastellain calls himself "l'inventeur ou le fantasieur de ceste vision."[86]*

On the barren field of allegorical depiction only mockery can grow new blossoms. As soon as an allegory is seasoned with humor, it still manages to produce a certain effect. Deschamps asks the physician how Virtues and Law are faring:

> *Phisicien, comment fait Droit?*
> *—Sur m'ame, il est en petit point . . .*
> *—Que fait Raison? . . .*
> *Perdu a son entendement,*
> *Elle parle mais faiblement,*
> *Et Justice est toute ydiote . . .*[87]†

The different types of fantasy are scrambled together without any sense of style. There is no more bizarre product than a political pamphlet in the garb of the pastorale. The unknown poet, who calls himself Burarius, has in "Le pastoralet" described all the slander heaped by the Burgundians on the party of Orléans and has done it in the tone of a pastorale. He makes Orléans, John the Fearless, and their entire proud and grim entourage into gentle shepherds. The coats of the shepherds have either fleur-de-lis or lions rampant on them. There are "bergiers à long jupel." These are the clergy.[88] The shepherd, Tristifer-Orléans, takes bread and cheese away from the others, also their apples, nuts, and flutes; he takes the bells from the sheep. He threatens those who resist with his big shepherd's staff until he himself is slain with one. Occasionally the poet almost forgets his somber theme and indulges in the sweetest pastorale only to interrupt this fantasy in a strange way with bitter political slander.[89]

Molinet mixes all the motifs of faith, war, coats of arms, and love in a proclamation from the Creator to all true lovers:

---

* "the inventor and conjuror of this vision"

† Physician, what about Law?/—By my soul, he is poorly . . ./—How does Reason? . . ./She is out of her mind,/She speaks but feebly,/And Justice has become an idiot . . .

Nous Dieu d'amours, créateur, roy de gloire
Salut à tous vrays amans d'humble affaire
Comme il soit vray depuis la victoire
De nostre filz sur le mont de Calvaire
Plusieurs souldars par peu de congnoissance
*De noz armes, font au dyable allyance . . .**

Then the proper coat of arms is described for them: a shield of silver, the upper part of gold with five wounds; the Church Militant is granted the right to recruit and take into service all those who want to rally to the arms:

Mais qu'en pleurs et en larmes,
De cueur contrict et foy sans abuser.[90]†

The devices employed by Molinet to gain the praise of his contemporaries as an inspired rhetorician and poet appear to us like the last degenerative stage of a form of expression shortly before its demise. He engages in the most tasteless wordplay: "Et ainsi demoura l'escluse en paix qui lui fut incluse, car la guerre fut d'elle excluse plus solitaire que rencluse."[91]‡ In the introduction to his moralized prose version of the *Roman de la rose,* he plays with his name Molinet: "Et affin que je ne perde le froment de ma labeur, et que la farine que en sera molue puisse avoir fleur salutaire, j'ay intencion, se Dieu m'en donne la grace, de tourner et convertir soubz mes rudes meulles le vicieux au vertueux, le corporel en l'espirituel, la mondanité en divinité, et souverainement de la moraliser. Et par ainsi nous tirerons le miel hors de la dure pierre, et las rose vermeille hors des poignans espines, où nous trouverons grain et graine, fruict, fleur et feuille, très souefve odeur, odorant verdure, verdoyant floriture, florissant norriture, nourrissant fruict et fruc-

---

* We God of Love, creator, king of glory/All hail to all true lovers in their humility!/As it is true that since the victory/Of our son on Mount Calvary/Several soldiers through lack of knowledge/Of our arms, make an alliance with the devil . . .

† Who now in sobbing and in tears,/With a contrite heart and faithful without deceit.

‡ "And so Sluys remained in peace that was included with her, for war was excluded from her, lonelier than a recluse."

tifiant pasture."[92]* How much this looks like the end of an age—how threadbare and spent! But this is precisely what the contemporary admired as something new; medieval poetry actually didn't know the play on words, it played more with images, as does Olivier de la Marche, who was Molinet's kindred spirit and admirer:

> *Là prins fièvre de souvenance*
> *Et catherre de desplaisir,*
> *Une migraine de souffrance,*
> *Colicque d'une impascience,*
> *Mal de dens non a soustenir,*
> *Mon cueur ne porroit plus souffrir*
> *Les regretz de ma destinee*
> *Par douleur non accoustumée.*[93]†

Meschinot is just as much a slave to the feeble allegory as La Marche; the eyeglasses of his "Lunettes des princes" are Prudence and Justice; Force is the frame, Temperance the nail that holds everything together. Raison hands the poet the pair of glasses together with directions for their use. Sent by heaven, Raison enters his mind in order to hold a feast there, but finds everything spoiled by Despair, which leaves nothing there "pour disner bonne-ment."[94]‡

Everything seems degenerated and decayed. And yet, we have already entered an age when the new spirit of the Renaissance is at large in the land. Its great new inspiration, the pure new form—where do we find it?

---

* "And lest I lose the wheat of my labor, and that the flour into which it will be ground may have wholesome blossom, I intend, if God gives me grace for it, to turn and convert under my rough millstones the vicious into the virtuous, the corporeal into the spiritual, the worldly into the divine, and, above all, to moralize it. And in this way we shall gather honey from the hard stone and the vermeil rose from sharp thorns, where we shall find grains and seed, fruit, flower and leaf, very sweet fragrance, sweet-smelling verdure, verdant florescence, flourishing nurture, nourishing fruit and fruitful pasture."

† Then I am gripped with the fever of thought/And the catarrh of displeasure,/ A migraine of sorrow,/Colic of impatience,/Unbearable toothache./My heart could no longer take it,/The regrets of my fate/Through unaccustomed sorrow.

‡ "to eat his fill."

Chapter Fourteen

The Coming of the New Form

THE RELATIONSHIP BETWEEN RISING HUMANISM AND
the dying spirit of the Middle Ages is much more complicated
than we are inclined to imagine. To us, who see the two cultural
complexes very sharply separated, it appears as if the receptiveness
to the eternal youth of antiquity and the denial of the entire worn-
out apparatus of the medieval expression of thought had come, like
a sudden revelation, to everyone at once. As if the spirit, mortally
tired of allegory and the flamboyant style, had suddenly understood: not this, but that! As if the golden harmony of classical
antiquity had suddenly stood before their eyes like a long-awaited
liberation, and as if they had embraced antiquity with the joy of
someone who had finally found his salvation.

But this was not the case. In the middle of the garden of medieval
thought, between the luxuriantly growing old seeds, classicism
grew gradually. At the beginning it is only a formal element of the
imagination. Only later does it become a great new inspiration of
the soul. And even then, the spirit and forms of expression that
we are accustomed to regard as the old, medieval ones do not die
on the vine.

In order to recognize this more clearly, it would be useful to
observe the approach of the Renaissance in greater detail than can
be done here. This scrutiny should focus, not on Italy but on
France, the country that had provided the most fertile soil for everything that comprised the splendid wealth of genuinely medieval
culture. Viewing the Italian Quattrocento in its glorious contrast
to late medieval life anywhere else, we gain an overall impression
of balance, gaiety, and freedom, pure and sonorous. Taken together, these qualities are regarded to be the Renaissance, and perhaps taken for the signature of the new spirit. In the meantime,
thanks to the unavoidable one-sidedness without which no historical judgment can be reached, it is forgotten that in the Italy of the

Quattrocento, too, the firm foundation of cultural life still remained genuinely medieval, that in the minds of the Renaissance itself medieval features are much more deeply impressed than is generally realized. But in the general perception it is the tone of the Renaissance that dominates.

However, a general look at the French-Burgundian world of the fifteenth century gives the primary impression of a fundamentally somber mood, a barbarian splendor, bizarre and overloaded forms, an imagination that had become threadbare—all the signs of the medieval spirit in its last gasps. In this instance it is easily forgotten that, here too, the Renaissance was approaching from all sides; but here it had not yet become dominant, and had not yet transformed the underlying groundtone.

The remarkable thing in all this is that the new arrives as form before it really becomes a new spirit.

The new classical forms arise in the middle of the old notions and relationships of life. Humanism got its start by nothing more dramatic than that a learned circle took more care than usual to observe a pure Latin and classical sentence structure. Such a circle flourished around 1400 in France; it was comprised of a few clerics and magistrates: Jean de Montreuil, canon of Lille and royal secretary; Nicolas de Clémanges, the famous literary leader; the reform-minded cleric Gontier Col; Ambrosius Miliis, princely private secretary (as was the first named).[1] They write beautiful and proud humanist letters to one another, which are in no way inferior to later products of the genre, neither in the hollow generality of the thought, in the deliberate importance, in the forced structure of the sentences and the unclear expression, nor in the delight in learned play. Jean de Montreuil gets excited over the question whether "orreolum" and "schedula" were to be written with or without an "h" and over the use of "k" in Latin words. "If you do not come to my assistance, worthy teacher and brother," he writes to Clémanges,[2] "I will lose my good name and deserve death now that I have noticed that in my last letter to my Lord and Father, the Bishop of Cambray, overly hasty and casual as the pen is wont to be, I put in the place of the comparative case 'proprior,' the word 'proximore.' Do correct it or our critics will write denunciatory tracts about it."[3] It is clear that these letters are designed to be learned literary exercises for the public. Also genuinely humanistic are his attacks on his friend Ambrosius, who had charged Cicero with self-contradiction and who had ranked Ovid above Virgil.[4]

In one of his letters Montreuil provides a leisurely description of the cloister of Charlieu near Senlis. It is very noticeable how he suddenly becomes more readable as soon as he simply narrates, in medieval style, what can be seen there. How the sparrows in the refectory share the meal, so that one may entertain doubts whether the king had instituted the benefice for the monks or for the birds; how a little wren acts as if he were the abbot, how the donkey of the gardener asks the letter writer to keep him in mind in his epistle. All this sounds fresh and attractive, but not specifically humanist.[5] But let us not forget that we had already met the same Jean de Montreuil and Gontier Col as passionate defenders of the *Roman de la rose* and as members of the *Cours d'amours* of 1401. Does this not demonstrate how external an element of life this early humanism was? It is only a reinforced effect of medieval school erudition and is little different from the revival of the classical Latin tradition that can be observed in Alcuin and his fellow spirits during the time of Charlemagne and later in the French schools of the twelfth century.

Though this first French humanism spends its force in the small circle of men who had nourished it without finding a direct successor, it is nonetheless already linked to the large international intellectual movement. Jean de Montreuil and his kindred spirits already see in Petrarch their shining model. They repeatedly mention Coluccio Salutati, the Florentine Chancellor who in the middle of the fourteenth century had introduced the new Latin rhetoric into the language of state documents.[6] However, in France, Petrarch, if we may say so, is still embraced with the medieval spirit. He had been a personal friend of some of the leading minds of an earlier generation, the poet Philippe de Vitri; the philosopher and politician Nicolas Oresme, who had educated the dauphin (Charles V). Philippe de Mézières also seems to have known Petrarch. These men are no humanists even though the ideas of Oresme contained much that is new. If it is true, as Paulin Paris[7] assumed, that Machaut's Peronne d'Armentières was influenced in her desire for a poetic conduct of courtship not only by the example of Heloise, but also by Laura, *Le voir-dit* would constitute a remarkable testimony to the fact that a work in which we are prone to sense above all the arrival of modern ideas could, nonetheless, inspire a medieval work.

But are we not, as a rule, already predisposed to see Petrarch and Boccaccio too exclusively from their modern side? We regard them as the first innovators and do so with justification. But it would be wrong to assume that, being the first humanists, they would actually no longer properly fit into the fourteenth century. Their entire work, no matter how much of a new breath may permeate it, stands on the culture of their age. Beyond that, it should be noted that Petrarch and Boccaccio were known outside of Italy during the waning Middle Ages not because of their vernacular writings, which were to make them immortal, but through their Latin works. Petrarch was, to his contemporaries, primarily an Erasmus *avant la lettre,* a many-talented and tasteful author of treatises about ethics and life, a great writer of letters, the romanticist of antiquity with his "Liber de viris illustribus" and "Rerum memorandum libri IV." The subjects he dealt with, *De contemptu mundi, De otio religiosorum, De vita solitaria,* are completely in the tradition of medieval thought. His glorification of the heroes of antiquity is much closer to the veneration of the *neuf preux*[8] than one might assume. It is far from peculiar that there were contacts between Petrarch and Geert Groote or that Jean de Varennes, the fanatic of Saint-Lié,[9] invokes Petrarch's authority to defend himself against suspicions of heresy[10] and that he borrows from Petrarch the text for a new prayer: "tota caeca christianitas." How much Petrarch meant to his century is expressed by Jean de Montreuil in the following words: "devotissimus, catholicus ac celeberrimus philosophus moralis."[11] Denis the Carthusian was still in a position to borrow from Petrarch a lament over that truly medieval idea, the loss of the Holy Sepulchre; "but since the style of Franciscus is rhetorical and difficult, I will cite the meaning of his words rather than their form."[12]

Petrarch had given particular impetus to those classic literary expressions of the first French humanists by his derisive statement that there were no rhetoricians and poets outside Italy. The *bels esprits* in France would not take this lying down. Nicolas de Clémanges and Jean de Montreuil raise a lively protest against such a claim.[13]

Boccaccio's influence was similar to that of Petrarch albeit in a more limited field. He was not venerated as the author of the *Decameron* but as "le docteur de patience en adversité," the author of *Libri de casibus virorum illustrium* and *De claris mulieribus.* Boccaccio had staked out for himself the role of a kind of impresario of Fortuna with these strange collections of works about the vagrancies of human fate. Chastellain sees him in this light.[14] He entitles a rather bizarre treatise about all sorts of tragic individual fates of his time *Le Temple de Bocace,* in which the spirits of the "noble historien" is evoked to console Margareth of England over her misfortune. The claim that Boccaccio was insufficiently or mistakenly seen by the still too medieval Burgundians is without merit. They grasped his strongly medieval side, which we run the risk of forgetting entirely.

It is not so much a difference in effort or mood that distinguishes rising humanism in France from that in Italy, but rather a nuance in taste and erudition. The imitation of antiquity does not come as easily to the French as it does to those born under the skies of Tuscany or in the shadow of the Colosseum even though the learned authors early acquired a facile command of the classical-Latin style of letters. The secular authors are, however, still inexperienced in the fine points of mythology and history. Machaut, who was no scholar and has to be regarded as secular poet in spite of all his spiritual dignity, hopelessly confuses the names of the seven sages. Chastellain mistakes Pelleus with Pelias; La Marche, Proteus with Pirithous. The poet of the "Pastoralet" speaks of "le bon roy scypion d'afrique."* The authors of *Le Jouvencel* derive "politique" from πολυς and an allegedly Greek "icos, gardien," "qui est à dire gardien de pluralité."[15]†

Nonetheless, the classical vision does, time and again, break through their medieval allegorical form. A poet such as that of the ragged pastorale "Le pastoralet" suddenly bestows a hint of the splendor of the Quattrocento on his description of the god Silvanus and in a prayer to Pan only to return abruptly to the well traveled paths of the old ways.[16] Just as Van Eyck sometimes presents the forms of classical architecture within his purely medieval compositions, authors attempt to incorporate still purely formal and ornamental classical features. The chroniclers test their strength with speeches on matters of state and war, *contiones,* in the style of Livy, or they mention wondrous signs, *prodigia,* because Livy did the same.[17] The clumsier this application of classical forms, the more

---

* "the good king Scipio of Africa."
† "that is to say, guardian of the multitude."

instructive the material for studying the transition from the Middle Ages to the Renaissance. The bishop of Châlons, Jean Germain, attempts to describe the peace conference at Arras in 1435 in the forceful marked style of the Romans. His intent is to attain a Livian effect by using short sentences and descriptions of vivid clarity. But the result is a caricature of ancient prose, just as bloated as it is naive, drawn like the little figures of a calendar page from a breviary, but failing in style.[18] Antiquity is still seen in extraordinarily alien terms. On the occasion of the funeral services for Charles the Bold in Nancy, the young duke of Lorraine, who defeated him, appears dressed in mourning, "à l'antique," to pay his last respects to the body of his enemy; that is, he wears a long golden beard stretching down to his belt. In this way he represents one of the nine *preux* and celebrates his own triumph. In this masquerade he prays for a quarter of an hour.[19]

In the minds of the French around 1400, the terms *rhétorique, orateur, poésie* were congruous with the idea of antiquity. To them they meant the enviable perfection of antiquity, above all a form artfully elaborated. All these poets of the fifteenth century (a few even earlier), whenever they follow their feelings and actually have something to say, compose flowing, simple, frequently powerful, and occasionally tender poems. But if they intend these poems to be particularly beautiful, they draw on mythology, use pretentious Latinizing expressions and call themselves "Rhetoricien." Christine de Pisan expressedly distinguishes a mythological poem from her usual work as "balade pouétique."[20] When Eustache Deschamps sends his works to his fellow artist and admirer Chaucer, he resorts to the most impalatable, quasi-classical mishmash:

> *O Socrates plains de philosophie,*
> *Seneque en meurs et Anglux en pratique,*
> *Ovides grans en ta poeterie,*
> *Bries en parler, saiges en rethorique*
> *Aigles tres haulz, qui par ta théorique*
> *Enlumines le regne d'Eneas.*
> *L'Isle aux Geans, ceuls de Bruth, et qui as*
> *Semé les fleurs et panté le rosier,*
> *Aux ignorans de la langue pandras,*
> *Grant translateur, noble Geffroy Chaucier!*

....

A toy pour ce de la fontaine Helye
Requier avoir un buvraige autentique,
Dont la doys est du tout en ta baillie.
Pour rafrener d'elle ma soif ethique,
Qui en Gaule seray paralitique
Jusques a ce que tu m'abuveras.[21]*

Here we have the beginning of that *manière* that was soon to evolve into the ridiculous Latinization of the noble French language on which Villon and Rabelais were to heap their scorn.[22] This style is found over and over in poetic correspondence, in dedications and speeches, in short, whenever something is expected to be particularly beautiful. Chastellain speaks of "Vostre très-humble et obéissante serve et ancelle, la ville de Gand," "la viscéral intime douleur et tribulation";† La Marche of "nostre francigéne locution et langue vernacule";‡ Molinet of "abreuvé de la doulce et melliflue liqueur procedant de la fontaine caballine," "ce vertueux duc scipionique," "gens de muliébre courage."[23]§

These ideals of a refined *rhetorique* are not only the ideals of a pure literary expression, they are at the same time the ideals of the highest literary communication. All of humanism, just as the poetry of the troubadoirs had been, is a social game, a kind of conversation, a striving for a higher form of life. Even the conversation of the learned men of the sixteenth and seventeenth centuries by no means denies this fact. In this respect, France occupies the middle ground between Italy and the Netherlands. In Italy, where lan-

---

* O Socrates full of philosophy, / Seneca in morals and Englishman in practice, / Great Ovid in your poetry, / Brief of speech, well-versed in rhetoric, / Exalted eagle who by your erudition / Has illuminated the reign of Aeneas. / The island of the giants, and that of Brut, and those who have / Sown flowers and planted the eglantine, / For the ignorant of the language, you will pour your self forth, / Great translator, noble Geoffrey Chaucer!/. . ./From you therefore out of the fountain of Heyle / I ask to have an authentic draught, / Of which the conduit is entirely in your power / To slake my ethical thirst, / I who in Gaul shall be paralyzed / Till you shall give me to drink.

† "your very humble and obedient slave and servant, the city of Ghent," "the intestinal inward sorrow and tribulation."

‡ "our French-born locution and vernacular tongue."

§ "having drunk from the sweet and mellifluous liquor proceeding from the Hippocrene fountain," "this virtuous scripionic duke," "people of womanly courage."

guage and thought still had the least distance between themselves and genuine, authentic antiquity, humanistic forms could readily be accepted into the highest life of the people. The Italian language can hardly be said to have been violated by a somewhat stronger Latinized form of expression. The humanist club spirit readily matched the customs of society. The Italian humanists represented the gradual development of Italian folk culture and, because of that, the first type of modern man. In the Burgundian regions, however, the spirit and form of society were still so medieval that the effort towards a renewed and purified expression could initially be embodied in perfectly old-fashioned form in the "Chambers of Rhetoricians." As cooperatives they are but a continuation of the medieval brotherhood, and the spirit they emanate is, for the time being, new only with respect to the entirely external formal aspect. Modern culture is first inaugurated in them by the biblical humanism of Erasmus.

France, with the exception of the northern provinces, does not know the old-fashioned apparatus of the "Chambers of Rhetoricians," but its *noble rhetoriciens* do not yet resemble the Italian humanists either. They, too, still retain much of the spirit and form of the medieval age. It may be claimed without exaggeration, that the French authors and poets of the fifteenth century who best manage to steer clear of classicism are closer to the modern development of literature than those who pay homage to Latinism and oratorical form. The modern authors, such as Villon, Coquillart, Henri Baude, as well as Charles d'Orléans and the author of "L'amant rendu cordelier," are those whose minds are unencumbered by all this, even if still dressed in medieval form. In poetry and prose, at least, the classicistic aspiration proves to have a retarding influence. The pompous spokesmen of the heavily draped Burgundian ideal, such as Chastellain, La Marche, Molinet, are the old-fashioned minds of French literature. But even they, once they manage to free themselves here and there from their artfully embellished ideal and compose or write as it comes from the heart and goes straight to the heart, without much ado, they become readable and, at the same time, appear to be more modern.

A second-rate poet, Jean Robertet (1420–90), secretary to three dukes of Bourbon and three French kings, regarded Georges Chastellain, the Flemish Burgundian, as the peak of the most noble poetic art. This admiration gave rise to a literary correspondence that is offered here as an illustration of the above comments. To make the acquaintance of Chastellain, Robertet relied on the services of a certain Montferrant who lived in Bruges as governor of a young Bourbon who had been raised at the court of his uncle the duke of Burgundy. He sent to Montferrant, in addition to a bombastic hymn of praise for the aging court chronicler and poet, two letters addressed to Chastellain: one in French and one in Latin. When Chastellain did not immediately accept the proposal for a literary correspondence, Montferrant fashioned a laborious encouragement according to the old recipe: *les Douze Dames de Rhétorique* had appeared to him. They were called *Science, Eloquence, Gravité de Sens, Profondité,* etc. Chastellain succumbed to this temptation. The letters of the three are arranged around the *Douze Dames de Rhétorique.*[24] It was, however, not long before Chastellain had his fill and discontinued the exchange of letters.

Robertet uses quasi-modern Latinism in its silliest form. He describes a cold: "J'ay esté en aucun temps en la case nostre en repos, durant une partie de la brumale froidure."[25]* The hyperbolic expressions in which Robertet couches his admiration are just as simpleminded. After he had finally received his poetic letter from Chastellain (which, in fact, was much better than his own poetry), he wrote to Montferrant:

> *Frappé en l'oeil d'une clarté terrible*
> *Attaint au coeur d'éloquence incrédible,*
> *A humain sens difficile à produire,*
> *Tout offusquié de lumière incendible*
> *Outre percant de ray presqu'impossible*
> *Sur obscur corps qui jamais ne peut luire,*
> *Ravi, abstrait me trouve en mon déduire,*
> *En extase corps gisant à la terre,*
> *Foible esperit perplex à voye enquerre*
> *Pour trouver lieu et oportune yssue*
> *Du pas estroit où je suis mis en serre,*
> *Pris à la rets qu'amour vraye a tissue.*†

---

* "I have for some time rested in our house during a part of this foggy coldness."

† Struck in the eye by a terrible brightness/Touched in the heart by incredible eloquence,/Difficult for the human mind to produce,/Quite obscured by incendiary light/Penetrating with almost unbearable rays/To a dark body that can never

And continues in prose: "Où est l'oeil capable de tel objet visible, l'oreille pour ouyr le haut son argentin et tintinabule d'or?"* And what, he asks of Montferrant, "amy des dieux immortels et chéri des hommes, haut pis Ulixien, plein de melliflue faconde," about that? "N'est-ce resplendeur équale au curre Phoebus?"† "Is it not more than Orpheus's lyre, la tube d'Amphion, la Mercuriale fleute qui endormyt Argus?"‡ etc. [26]

With this extreme display of bloated authorial humility, these three poets, adhering faithfully to the medieval prescription, keep step. But not these three alone; all their contemporaries still honor this form. La Marche hopes that there may be some use for his memoirs as modest flowers in a wreath, and compares his work to the ruminations of a stag. Molinet invites all "orateurs" to trim all that is superfluous from his work. Even Commines expresses the hope that the archbishop of Vienna to whom he sends his efforts may perhaps have occasion to include them in a Latin work. [27]

The poetic correspondence between Robertet, Chastellain, and Montferrat demonstrates that the golden luster of the new classicism is only attached to a picture that is really medieval. And this Robertet, we should remind ourselves, has spent some time in Italy, "en Ytalie, sur qui les respections du ciel influent aorné parler, et vers qui tyrent toutes douceurs élémentaires pour lá fondre harmonie." [28]§ But he apparently did not bring home much of the harmony of the Quattrocento. To his mind, the excellence of Italy consisted only in the "aorné parler," in the purely external cultivation of an artificial style.

The only thing that renders this impression of delicately embellished antiquating dubious for a moment is a touch of irony that occasionally surfaces unmistakably amid the affected outpourings

---

shine,/Ravished, distraught, I find myself in my contemplation,/My body in ecstasy lying on the ground,/My feeble spirit is at a loss to go in quest of a path/ In order to find a place and opportune exit/From the narrow pass where I am hemmed in,/Caught in the toils which true love has netted.

* "where is the eye that could see such a visible object, where is the ear to hear the high silver tone and golden tintinnabulations?"

† "friend of the immortal gods, beloved of men, high Ulyssean breast, full of mellifluous eloquence . . . is this not splendor equal to the car of Phoebus?"

‡ "the reed of Amphion, the Mercurial flute, which caused Argus to fall sleep?"

§ "in Italy, on which the kind influences of heaven bring beautiful speech, and towards which all elemental sweetness is drawn, there to dissolve into harmony."

of the heart. Your Robertet, the ladies of rhetoric tell Montfer-rant,[29]—"il est exemple de Tullian art, et forme de subtilité Téren-cienne . . . qui succié a de nos seins notre plus intériore substance par faveur; qui, outre la grâce donnée en propre terroir, se est allé rendre en pays gourmant pour réfection nouvelle (that is, Italian), là ou enfans parlent en aubes à leurs mères, frians d'escole en doc-trine sur permission de eage."* Chastellain terminated the corre-spondence because he was tired of it; the gate had long been open for *Dame Vanité,* he was now locking it. "Robertet m'a surfondu de sa nuée, et dont les perles, qui en celle se congréent comme grésil, me font resplendir mes vestements; mais qu'en est mieux au corps obscur dessoubs, lorsque ma robe decoit les voyans?"† If Robertet were to continue in this manner, Chastellain would throw them into the fire unread. In the event that he wants to speak unaffectedly, as is proper among friends, George would not with-draw his affection.

The fact that under the classical gown still dwells a medieval mind is less obvious in cases where the humanist uses only Latin. In those cases the imperfect notion of the spirit of antiquity does not betray itself by a clumsy treatment; then the scholar can imitate without encumbrance and imitate quite effectively. A humanist such as Robert Gaguin (1433–1501) appears to us in his letters and speeches to be already almost as modern as Erasmus, who owed his early fame to him; it was Gaguin who published in his compen-dium of French history the first academic work of history in France (1495),[30] a letter by Erasmus who thus came to see some of his writing in print for the first time. Even if Gaguin knew as little Greek as Petrarch,[31] he is, for this reason, no less a genuine human-ist. We see at the same time, however, how the old spirit still lives in him. He still uses his rhetorical skills in Latin for the old medieval subjects such as a diatribe against marriage[32] or disapproval of life at court, by retranslating Alain Chartier's *Curial* back into Latin.

---

* "is an example of Ciceronian art and a kind of Terence-like subtlety . . . he, who was favored to absorb from our breasts our innermost substance; who, going beyond the grace granted by his own soil, to new refreshment in the land of good taste (Italy) has gone, there, where children in morning songs speak to their mothers, eager for school and widely learned beyond their years."

† "Robertet has rained on me from his cloud, he, whose pearls gather in this cloud like hail, has made my garment shine; but what of the dark body under-neath, if my dress deceives the clear sighted?"

Or, in this instance in a French poem, he treats the social value of the estates in the frequently used form of a debate, "Le debat du laboureur, du prestre et du gendarme." In his French poems, Gaguin, who had a perfect command of the Latin style, did not indulge in any of the rhetorical embellishments; there were no Latinized forms, no hyperbolic phrases, no mythology. As a French poet he stands squarely on the side of those who preserve in their medieval form their naturalness and, with it, their readability. For him, the humanist form is hardly anything other than a gown that he can casually don; it may fit him well, but he moves more freely without that splendiferousness. The Renaissance is only loosely tied to the French spirit of the fifteenth century.

We are accustomed to regard the appearance of pagan-sounding expression as an unmistakable criterion for the beginning of the Renaissance. But every student of medieval literature knows that this literary paganism was by no means limited to the sphere of the Renaissance. When humanists call God "princips superum" and Mary "genetrix tonantis," they do not commit a sacrilege. This purely external transposing of the persons of the Christian faith into the names of pagan mythology is very old[33] and means little or nothing for the content of religious sentiment. The arch-poet of the twelfth century unconcernably rhymes in his confession:

> *Vita vetus displicet, mores placent novi;*
> *Homo videt faciem, sed cor patet Iovi.**

When Deschamps speaks of "Jupiter venu de Paradis,"[34]† he does not intend any godlessness; as little as does Villon in the touching ballade he made for his mother when, in order to pray, he calls Our Dear Lady "haulte Déesse."[35]‡

A certain heathen coloration also belongs to the pastorale; there it was safe to have the pagan deities appear. In "Le pastoralet," the Celestine monastery in Paris is called "temple au haulz bois pour le diex prier."[36]§ But nobody was led astray by such innocent pa-

---

* The old life displeased, the new morals are fallen;/Mankind sees the face, yet the heart is open to honest Jupiter.
† "Jupiter come from Paradise,"
‡ "High Goddess."
§ "the temple in the high woods where people pray to the gods."

ganism. On top of all this, the poet also declared "se pour estrangier ma muse je parle des dieux des païens, sy sont les pastours crestiens et moy."[37]* Molinet, too, shifts responsibility for having Mars and Minerva appear in a dream poem to "Raison et entendement," who say to him: "Tu le dois faire non pas pour adjouter foy aux dieux et déesses, mais pour ce que Nostre Seigneur seul inspire les gens ainsi qu'il lui plaist, et souventes fois par divers inspirations."[38]†

Much of the literary paganism of the fully developed Renaissance should not be taken more seriously than these expressions. However, if a feel for recognizing pagan faith as such, particularly pagan sacrifices, announces itself, it is of deeper significance for the advance of the new spirit. This sentiment may surface even among those as deeply rooted in the Middle Ages as Chastellain:

> *Des dieux jadis les nations gentiles*
> *Quirent l'amour par humbles sacrifices,*
> *Lesquels, posé que ne fussent utiles,*
> *Furent nientmoins rendables et fertiles*
> *De maint grant fruit et de haulx bénéfices,*
> *Monstrans par fait que d'amour les offices*
> *Et d'honneur humble, impartis où qu'ils soient*
> *Pour percer ciel et enfer suffisoient.*[39]‡

The sound of the Renaissance may suddenly ring out in the midst of medieval life. During a *pas d'armes* in Arras in 1446, Philippe de Ternant, contrary to the then prevailing custom, appears without a "bannerole de devocion," a banner with a pious saying or figure. "Laquelle chose je ne prise point,"§ comments La Marche on this infamy. But still more infamous is the motto worn by Ternant:

---

* "If, to lend my Muse some strangeness, I speak of the pagan gods, the shepherds and myself are Christians all the same."

† "Reason and Understanding" . . . "You should do it, not to instill faith in gods and goddesses, but because our Lord alone inspires people as it pleases Him and frequently by differing means."

‡ Formerly the gentile nations of the gods, / Sought love by humble sacrifices, / Which, taken for granted that they were useless, / Were nevertheless profitable and prolific, / Of much important fruit and high benefits, / Which shows by facts that offices of love / And of humble homage, rendered wherever they were, / Were sufficient to pierce heaven and hell.

§ "Which I by no means approve."

"Je souhaite que avoir puisse de mes desirs assouvissance et jamais aultre bien n'eusse."[40]* This could well have been the motto of the most free-thinking libertines of the sixteenth century.

Individuals did not have to go to classic literature for a source for this real paganism. They could find it in their own medieval treasury, the *Roman de la rose*. The paganism was found in the erotic cultural forms. Here Venus and the God of Love had, for a long time, their hiding place where they received something more than purely rhetorical veneration. Jean de Meun embodies the great pagan. For innumerable readers since the thirteenth century, the school of paganism had not been his merging of the names of the gods of antiquity with those of Jesus and Mary, but the fact that he offered in a most daring fashion earthly lust permeated with the Christian notion of bliss. It is difficult to imagine a greater blasphemy than the words from Genesis: "Then the Lord regretted that he had made man on the earth," put, with a reversed meaning, into the mouth of Mother Nature, who, in his poem, functions perfectly as a demiurge: Nature regretted having created human beings because they do not pay attention to the commandment to procreate:

> *Si m'aïst Diex li crucefis,*
> *Moult me repens dont homme fis*[41]†

It is amazing that the church that was overzealously on guard against small dogmatic deviations of a speculative nature, and reacted to them with such vehemence, allowed the teaching of this breviary for the aristocracy to continue to grow luxuriously in the mind without putting any impediments in its way.

The new form and the new spirit do not correspond to each other. Just as the thoughts of the coming age were expressed in a medieval garb, the most medieval ideas were presented in sapphic meters with a whole train of mythological figures. Classicism and the modern spirit are two entirely different entities. Literary classicism is a child born aged. Antiquity hardly held more significance for the renewal of *la belle littérature* than the arrows of Philotectes. The case is entirely different in the fine arts and scientific thinking:

---

* "I wish I could have satisfied all my desires and never had any other good."
† So help me God who was crucified:/I much repent that I made man.

for both, antique purity of presentation and expression, antique multifaceted interests, antique control of one's own life and insight into man, meant much more than a mere crutch on which to lean. In the fine arts, the overcoming of superfluity, exaggeration, twistedness, of the grimace and of the flamboyantly curved, was all the work of antiquity. In the domain of thought, it was still more indispensable and fertile. But in the literary domain classicism was more an impediment than a prerequsite to an unfolding simplicity and harmony.

Those few in the France of the fifteenth century who adopt humanistic forms do not yet ring in the Renaissance because their sentiments and orientation are still medieval. The Renaissance only arrives when the "tone of life" is changing, when the ebb tide of the deadly denial of life has given way to a new flood and a stiff, fresh breeze is blowing; it arrives only when the joyful insight (or was it an illusion?) has ripened that all the glories of the ancient world, of which for so long men had seen themselves the reflection, could be reclaimed.

NOTES

Translator's Introduction

1. As Professor Weintraub characterizes it in his *Visions of Culture* (Chicago: The University of Chicago Press, 1966), p. 212.

2. Johan Huizinga, *The Waning of the Middle Ages,* trans. F. Hopman (Garden City, N.Y.: Doubleday and Company, Inc., 1954).

3. ———, 1989. *Briefwisseling I 1894–1924* (Veen: Tjeenkwillink).

4. ———, 1972. *America: A Dutch Historian's Vision, from Afar and Near,* trans. and ed. Herbert H. Rowen (New York: Harper & Row). This volume contains both *Man and the Masses in America* and *Life and Thought in America.*

5. Pesch, A. J. van, 1932. "Levensbericht van F. J. Hopman," in *Handelingen en Levensberichten van de Maatschappij der Nederlandsche Letterkunde* (Leiden: E. J. Brill), pp. 177–92.

6. In *Johan Huizinga 1872–1972. Papers delivered to the Johan Huizinga Conference Groningen 11–15 December 1972,* eds. W. H. R. Coops *et. al.* (The Hague: Martinus Nijhoff, 1973), pp. 91–103.

7. As we have translated the book's title. We refer to the Hopman translation as *Waning.*

8. Available in English as *My Path to History,* in *Dutch Civilization in the Seventeenth Century and Other Essays,* ed. Pieter Geyl and F. W. N. Hugenholtz, trans. Arnold J. Pomerans (New York: Frederick Unger Publishing Co., 1968), pp. 244–76. This translation, too, leaves much to be desired.

9. *In the Shadow of Tomorrow,* trans. J. H. Huizinga (New York: W. W. Norton & Company, Inc. n.d.).

10. *Homo Ludens: A Study of the Play-Element in Culture* (Boston: The Beacon Press, 1955).

Chapter 1

1. [Trans. (Throughout, all translators' comments will be preceded by this abbreviation in brackets)] Huizinga's title is *'s Levens felheid,* literally, *Life's Facets,* and the *fel* carries the sense of something that affects the senses strongly. Perhaps there is a bit of the idea of tension between states of mind or emotion, *spanning,* as the span of a bridge, as well. The implication is that medieval life, lived in such suspended tension between sharply, even crassly, contrasting states, strongly affected people's senses. This is the beginning of a subtle, but forceful development of metaphor that is an important part of Huizinga's narrative technique.

2. Oeuvres de Georges Chastellain, ed. Kervyn de Lettenhove, Bruxelles 1863–66; 8 vols., III, p. 44.

3. Chastellain, II, p. 267; Mémoires d'Olivier de la Marche, ed. Beaune et d'Arbaumont (Soc. de l'historie de France), 1883–88; 4 vols., II, p. 248.

4. Journal d'un bourgeois de Paris, ed. A. Tuetey (Publ. de la soc. de l'historie de Paris, Doc. no. III), 1881, pp. 5, 56.

5. Journal d'un bourgeois, pp. 20–24. See Journal de Jean de Roye, dite Chronique scandaleuse, ed. B. de Mandrot (Soc. de l'historie de France), 1894–96, 2 vols., I, p. 330.

6. Chastellain, III, p. 461; see V, p. 403.

7. Jean Juvenal des Ursins, Chronique, ed. Michaud et Poujoulat, Nouvelle collection des mémoires, II, 1412, p. 474.

8. [Trans.] The image of the life of people as a dance to death: frequently painted and depicted in poetry. See below, chap. 5.

9. See Journal d'un bourgeois, pp. 6, 70; Jean Molinet, Chronique, ed. Buchon (Coll. de chron. nat.), 1827–28, 5 vols., II, p. 23; Lettres de Louis XI, ed. Vaesen, Charavay, de Mandrot (Soc. de l'hist. de France), 1883–1909, 11 vols., 20. Apr. 1477, VI, p. 158; Chronique scandaleuse, II, p. 47; Chronique scandaleuse, Interpolations, II, p. 364.

10. Journal d'un bourgeois, p. 234–37.

11. Chron. scand., II, p. 70, 72.

12. Vita auct. Petro Ranzano O. P. (1455), Acta sanctorum Apr. t. I, pp. 494ff.

13. J. Soyer, Notes pour servir à l'histoire littéraire. Du succes de la prédication de frère Olivier Maillart à Orléans en 1485, Bulletin de la société archéologique et historique de l'Orléanais, t. XVIII, 1919, according to Revue historique, t. 131, p. 351.

14. [Trans.] Hennin. A style of coiffure in the shape of a cone rising very high from which veils were suspended.

15. [Trans.] A mystical order for lay women that performed good works and was given to publicly reading the Bible aloud in French. Not officially sanctioned by the church. See: Barbara Tuchmann, The Distant Mirror. Alfred A. Knopf, New York, 1978, p. 317.

16. Enguerrand de Monstrelet, Chroniques, ed. Douët d'Arcq. (Soc. de l'hist. de France) 1857–62, 6 vols., IV, pp. 302–6.

17. Wadding, Annales Minorum, X, p. 72; K. Hefele, Der h. Bernhardin von Siena und die franziskanische wanderpredigt in Italien. Freiburg 1912, S. 47, 80.

18. Chron. scand., I, p. 22, 1461; Jean Chartier, Hist. de Charles VII, ed. N. Godefroy, 1661, p. 320.

19. Chastellain, III, pp. 36, 98, 124, 125, 210, 238, 239, 247, 474; Jacques du Clercq, Mémoires (1448–1467), ed. de Reiffenberg, Bruxelles 1823, 4 vols., IV, p. 40, II, p. 280, 355, III, p. 100; Juvenal des Ursins, pp. 405, 407, 420; Molinet, III, pp. 36, 314.

20. Jean Germain, Liber de virtutibus Philippi ducis Burgundiae, ed. Kervyn de Lettenhove, Chron. rel. à l'hist. de la Belg. sous la dom. des ducs de Bourg. (Coll. des chron. belges), 1876, II, p. 50.

21. La Marche, I, p. 61.

22. Chastellain, IV, pp. 333f.

23. Chastellain, III, p. 92.

24. Jean Froissart, Chroniques, ed. S. Luce et G. Raynaud (Soc. de l'hist. de France), 1869–1899, 11 vols. (only up to 1385), IV, pp. 89–93.

25. Chastellain, III, pp. 85ff.

26. Chastellain, III, p. 279.

27. La Marche, II, p. 421.

28. Juvenal des Ursins, p. 379.

29. Martin Le Franc, Le Champion des dames, See G. Doutrepont, La littérature francaise à la cour des ducs de Bourgogne (Bibl. de XVe siecle t. VIII), Paris, Champion, 1909, p. 304.

30. Acta sanctorum Apr. t. I, p. 496; A. Renaudet, Préréforme et humanisme à Paris 1494–1517, Paris, Champion, 1916, p. 163.

31. [Trans.] *Spanning*. See note 1.

32. Chastellain, IV, pp. 300f., VII, p. 75; see Thomas Basin, De rebus gestis Caroli VII. et Lud. XI. historiarum libri XII, ed. Quicherat (Soc. de l'hist. de France), 1855–1859, 4 vols., I, p. 158.

33. Journal d'un bourgeois, p. 219.

34. Chastellain III, p. 30.

35. La Marche, I, p. 89.

36. Chastellain, I, pp. 82, 79; Monstrelet, III, p. 361.

37. La Marche, I, p. 201.

38. On the Treaty of Arras see among others La Marche, I, p. 207.

39. Chastellain, I, p. 196.

40. Basin, III, p. 74, [Trans.] 40 [Trans.] *Hoecken and Kabeljauen:* The names of two political parties that formed during the complicated struggle for succession in Holland, Zeeland, and Hainaut. In standard interpretations the Kabeljauen (codfish) were the party of the ascending burghers while the Hoecken (hooks) were the declining nobles who hoped to snare the wealth of the burghers. Huizinga repeatedly cautions against accepting such simple economic explanations.

41. That a perception like this by no means rules out a recognition of economic factors, not to mention the charge that it was formulated as a protest against the economic explanation of history, can be demonstrated by the following quotation from Jaures: "Mais il n'y a pas seulement dans l'histoire des luttes de classes, il y a aussi des luttes de partis. J'entends qu'en dehors des affinités ou des antagonismes économiques il se forme des groupements de passions, des intérêts d'orgueil, de domination, qui se disputent la surface de l'histoire et qui déterminent de tres vastes ébranlements." Histoire de la révolution francaise, IV, p. 1458.

42. [Trans.] *Arnold and Adolf of Geldern:* Arnold had secured the dukedom by ceding much of the power of the position to a council of nobles and leading burghers that led his wife and son Adolf to conspire against him. Arnold, in retaliation, sold the succession to Charles the Bold, who became Duke of Gelder upon Arnold's death. When Charles was killed, Adolf was released from prison. He mounted a campaign to regain the dukedom, but was killed at the siege of Tournai.

43. Chastellain, IV, p. 201; see my Studie uit de voorgeschiedenis van ons nationaal besef, in De Gids 1912, I.

44. [Trans.] In the Hundred Years War (1337–1453). The struggle between

England and France over territory and dynastic issues which waxed and waned during nearly the whole period covered by Huizinga's study. Though the *Autumn of the Middle Ages* is a cultural history of France and Burgundy at the time of the war, Huizinga does not narrate the events of that war, although an alert reader will be able to detect many of them. In part, Huizinga assumes basic familiarity with this history on the part of his readers, but the omission is also a deliberate break with the narrative historical tradition. The reader might be well served by reading a good encyclopedia article on both the Hundred Years War and the history of Burgundy.

45. Journal d'un bourgeois, p. 242; see Monstrelet, IV, p. 341d.

46. Jan van Dixmude, ed. Lambin, Ypres 1839, p. 283.

47. Froissart, ed. Luce, XI, p. 52.

48. Mémoires de Pierre le Fruictier dit Salmon, Buchon 3ᵉ suppl. de Froissart, XV, p. 22.

49. Chronique du Religieux de Saint Denis, ed. Bellaguet (Coll. des documents inédits) 1839–1852, 6 vols., I, p. 34; Juvenal des Ursins, pp. 342, 467–471; Journal d'un bourgeois, pp. 12, 31, 44. [Trans.] A St. Andrew's cross is a cross in the shape of an "X." It was an insignium of the Burgundian party, hence pro-English. It is still a part of the Union Jack.

50. Molinet, III, p. 487.

51. Molinet, III, pp. 226, 241, 283–287; La Marche, III, pp. 289, 302.

52. Clementis V constitutiones. lib. V. tit. 9, c. l.; Joannis Gersonii, Opera omnia, ed. L. Ellies Dupin, ed. II, Hagae Comitis 1728, 5 vols., II, p. 427; Ordonnances des rois de France, t. VIII, p. 122; N. Jorga, Philippe de Mézières et la croisade au XIVe siècle (Bibl. de l'ecole des hautes études, fasc. 110), 1896, p. 438; Religieux de S. Denis, II, p. 533.

53. Journal d'un bourgeois, pp. 223, 229.

54. Jacques du Clercq, IV, p. 265. Petit-Dutaillis, Documents nouveaux sur les moeurs populaires et le droit de venegeance das les Pays-Bas au XVe siecle (Bibl. du XVe Siecle), Paris, Champion, 1908, pp. 7, 21.

55. Pierre de Fenin (Petitot, Coll. de mém. VII), p. 593; see his story of the fool who was beaten to death, p. 619.

56. Journal d'un bourgeois, p. 204.

57. [Trans.] *entremets*. Although the word comes to mean side dishes, Huizinga uses it in an older sense meaning elaborate entertainments held between the courses of aristocratic banquets. See chap. 12 for descriptions of some of these *entremets*.

58. Jean Lefèvre de Saint-Remy, Chronique, ed. F. Morand (Soc. de l'hist. de France), 1876, 2 vols., II, p. 168; Laborde, Les ducs de Bourgogne, Etudes sur les lettres, les arts, et l'industrie pendant le XVe siecle, Paris 1849–1853, 3 vols., II, p. 208.

59. La Marche, III, p. 135; Laborde, II, p. 325.

60. Laborde, III, pp. 355, 398. Le Moyen-age, XX, 1907, pp. 193–201.

61. Juvenal des Ursins, pp. 438, 1405. See, however, Rel. de. S. Denis, III, p. 349.

62. Piaget, Romania, XX, p. 417 en XXXI, 1902, pp. 597–603.

63. Journal d'un bourgeois, p. 95.

64. Jacques de Clercq, III, p. 262.

65. Jacques du Clercq passim; Petit Dutaillis, Documents etc., p. 131.

66. Hugo of St. Victor, De fructibus carnia et spiritus, Migne CLXXVI, p. 997.

67. Tobit 4:14. ([Trans.] In English Bibles, Tobit 4:13.)

68. I Timothy 6:10.

69. Petrus Damiani, Epist. lib. I, 15, Migne CXLIV, p. 234, id. Contra philargyriam ib. CXLV, p. 533; Pseudo-Bernardus, Liber de modo bene vivendi 44, 45, Migne CLXXXLV, p. 1266.

70. Journal d'un bourgeois, pp. 325, 343, 357; in the note on the citations from the parliamentary records.

71. L. Mirot, Les d'Orgemont, leur origine, leur fortune, etc. (Bibl. du XVe siecle), Paris, 1913; P. Champion, Francois Villon, Sa vie et son temps (Bibl. du XVe siècle), Paris, 1913, II, pp. 230f.

72. Mathieu d'Escouchy, Chronique, ed. G. du Fresne de Beaucourt (Soc. de l'hist. de France), 1863–1864, 3 vols., I, p. iv–xxiii.

73. P. Champion, François Villon, sa vie et son temps (Bibl. du XVe siècle), Paris, 1913, 2 vols.

Chapter 2

1. Allen, no. 541, Antwerpen, 26 February 1516/17; see no. 542, no. 566, no. 862, no. 967.

2. *Germanae,* which, in this particular instance, cannot be translated as "German."

3. Eustache Deschamps, Oeuvres complètes, ed. De Queux de Saint Hilaire et G. Raynaud (Soc. des anciens textes français) 1878–1903, 11 vols., no. 31 (I, p. 113, see nos. 85, 126, 152, 162, 176, 248, 366, 375, 386, 400, 933, 936, 1195, 1196, 1207, 1213, 1239, 1240, etc.; Chastellain, I pp. 9, 27, IV pp. 5, 56, VI pp. 206, 208, 219, 295; Alain Chartier, Oeuvres, ed. A. Duchesne, Paris 1617, p. 262; Alanus de Rupe, Sermo, II, p. 313 (B. Alanus redivivus, ed J. A. Coppenstein, Naples, 1642).

4. Deschamps, no. 562 (IV, p. 18).

5. A. de la Borderie, Jean Meschinot, sa vie et ses oeuvres (Bibl. de l'Ecole des chartes), LVI, 1895, pp. 277, 280, 305, 310, 312, 622, etc.

6. Chastellain, I, p. 10 Prologue; see Complainte de fortune, VIII, p. 334.

7. La Marche, I p. 186, IV p. 89; H. Stein, Etude sur Olivier de la Marche, historien, poete et diplomate (Mém. couronnés etc., de l'Acad royale de Belg. t. XLIX), Bruxelles 1888, frontispiece.

8. Monstrelet, IV, p. 430.

9. Froissart, ed. Luce, X, p. 275; Deschamps no. 810 (IV, p. 327); see Les Quinze joyes de mariage (Paris, Marpon et Flammarion), p. 64 (quinte joye); Le livre messire Geoffroi de Charney, Romania, XXXVI, 1897, p. 399.

10. Joannis de Varennis responsiones ad capitula accusationum etc. §17, by Gerson, Opera, I, p. 920.

11. Deschamps, no. 95 (I, p. 203).

12. Deschamps, Le miroir de mariage, IX, pp. 25, 69, 81, no. 1004 (V, p. 259), further II pp. 8, 183–188, III pp. 39, 373, VII p. 3, IX p. 209, etc.

13. Convivio lib., IV, cap. 27, 28.

14. Discours de l'excellence de virginité, Gerson, Opera III, p. 382; see Dionysius Cartusianus, De vanitate mundi, Opera omnia, cura et labore monachorum sacr. ord. Cart., Monstrolii-Tornaci 1896–1913, 41, vol. XXXIX, p. 472.

15. [Trans.] *Levensspel.* Life game. An important element in Huizinga's thinking about how culture arises. The forms of life, of which chivalry is one, arise through *play,* which, as Huizinga explains in the later *Homo Ludens,* is neither unconscious (people always know when they are "playing" at being a knight or shepherd) nor nonseriousness. See below, note 65.

16. Chastellain, V, p. 364.

17. La Marche, IV, p. cxiv.—The old Dutch translation of his Estat de la maison du duc Charles de Bourgogne by Matthaeus, Analecta, I, pp. 357–494.

18. Christine de Pisan, Oeuvres poétiques, ed. M. Roy (Soc. des anciens texts français), 1886–1896, 3 vols., I, p. 251, no. 38; Leo von Rozmitals Reise, ed. Schmeller (Bibl. des lit. Vereins zu Stuttgart, t. VII), 1844, pp. 24, 149.

19. La Marche, IV, pp. 4ff.; Chastellain, V, p. 370.

20. Chastellain, V, p. 368.

21. La Marche, IV, Estat de la maison, pp. 34ff.

22. La Marche, I, p. 277.

23. La Marche, IV, Estat de la maison, pp. 34, 51, 20, 31.

24. Froissart, ed. Luce, III, p. 172.

25. Journal d'un bourgeois, §218, p. 105.

26. Chronique scandaleuse, I, p. 53.

27. Molinet, I, p. 184; Basin, II, p. 376.

28. Alienor de Poitiers, Les honneurs de la cour, ed. La Curne de Sainte Palaye, Mémoires sur l'ancienne chevalerie, 1781, II, p. 201.

29. Chastellain, III pp. 196–212, 290, 292, 308, IV pp. 412–414, 428; Alienor de Poitiers, pp. 209, 212.

30. Alienor de Poitiers, p. 210; Chastellain, IV, p. 312; Juvenal des Ursins, p. 405; La Marche, I, p. 278, Froissart, ed. Luce, I, pp. 16, 22, etc.

31. Molinet, V, pp. 194, 192.

32. Alienor de Poitiers, p. 190; Deschamps, IX, p. 109.

33. Chastellain, V, p. 27–33.

34. Only on your account must the priest wait. Deschamps, IX, Le miroir de mariage, pp. 109–110.

35. There are more examples of such "paix" in Laborde, II, nos. 43, 45, 75, 126, 140, 5293. The English term, now rare, is "osculatory." The plate frequently had a figure of Christ or the Virgin painted on it.

36. Deschamps, IX, Le miroir de mariage, p. 300, see VIII, p. 156 ballade no. 1462; Molinet, V, p. 195; Les cent nouvelles nouvelles, ed. Th. Wright, II, p. 123; see Les Quinze joyes de mariage, p. 185.

37. Canonization procedure at Tours, Acta Sanctorum Apr. t. I, p. 152.

38. Such quarrels over rank among Dutch nobles, which were already pointed out by W. Moll, Kerkgeschiedenis van Nederland voor de hervorming (Utrecht 1864–69), 2 Teile (5 Stücke), II, 3, p. 284, are described in greater detail by H. Obreen, Bydragen voor Vaderlandsche Geschiedenis en Oudheidkunde, X⁴, p. 308.

39. Deschamps, IX, pp. 111–114.

40. Jean de Stavelot, Chronique ed. Borgnet (Coll. des chron. belges) 1861, p. 96.

41. Pierre de Fenin, p. 607; Journal d'un bourgeois, p. 9.

42. According to Jevenal des Ursins, p. 543, and Thomas Basin, I. p. 31. The Journal d'un bourgeois gives another cause for the death sentence, as does Le Livre des trahisons, ed. Kervyn de Lettenhove (Chron. rel. à hist. de Belg. sous les ducs de Bourg.), II, p. 138.

43. Rel. de S. Denis, I, p. 30; Juvenal des Ursins, p. 341.

44. Pierre de Fenin, p. 606; Monstrelet, IV, p. 9.

45. Pierre de Fenin. p. 604.

46. Christine de Pisan, I, p. 251, no. 38; Chastellain, V, p. 364ff.; Rozmitals Reise, pp. 24, 149.

47. Deschamps, I, nos. 80, 114, 118, II, nos. 256, 266, IV, nos. 800, 803, V, nos. 1018, 1024, 1029, VII, nos. 253, X, nos. 13, 14.

48. Anonymous report from the fifteenth century in Journal de l'inst. hist., IV. p. 353; see Juvenal des Ursins, p. 569; Rel. de S. Denis, VI, p. 492.

49. Jean Chartier, Hist. de Charles VII, ed. D. Godefroy 1661, p. 318.

50. Entry of the Dauphin as duke of Brittany into Rennes 1532, in Th. Godefroy, Le cérémonial françois 1649, p. 619.

51. Rel. de S. Denis, I, p. 32.

52. Journal d'un bourgeois, p. 277.

53. Thomas Basin, II, p. 9.

54. A. Renaudet, Préréforme et humanisme a Paris, p. 11. Based on the documents of the trial.

55. De Laborde, Les ducs de Bourgogne, I, p. 172, 177.

56. Livre des trahisons, p. 156.

57. Chastellain, I, p. 188.

58. Alienor de Poitiers, Les honneurs de la cour, p. 254.

59. Rel. de S. Denis, II, p. 114.

60. Chastellain, I p. 49, V p. 240; see La Marche, I, p. 201; Monstrelet, III, p. 358; Lefèvre de S. Remy, I, p. 380.

61. Chastellain, V, p. 228; see IV, p. 210.

62. Chastellain, III, p. 296; IV, p. 213, 216.

63. Chronique scandaleuse, interpol., II, p. 332.

64. Lettres de Louis XI, X, p. 110.

65. [Trans.] In this sentence is the kernel of Huizinga's theory of the role of play in culture that was later to be elaborated in *Homo Ludens*. Mourning customs are "play" in the sense that they enable us to deal with an otherwise crushing reality. To Huizinga, such forms are never unconsciously performed; the player always recognizes the game just as the actor in his thick-soled *corthurni* never confuses himself with the role he is playing.

The theatrical metaphor is important. See below, chapter 13, p. 342.

66. Alienor de Poitiers, Les honneurs de la cour, pp. 254–256.

67. Lefèvre de S. Remy, II, p. 11; Pierre de Fenin, pp. 599, 605; Monstrelet, III, p. 347; Theod. Pauli, De rebus actis sub ducibus Burgundiae compendium, ed Kervyn de Lettenhove (Chron. rel. à l'hist. de Belg. sous dom. des ducs de Bourg. t. III), p. 267.

68. [Trans.] *vuurmand*. A kind of cabinet warmed by coals and used to dry an infant's linens and blankets. For this information we are indebted to Helen Roozen of Mt. Vernon, Washington, and her sister Jeanne Roozen of Heemstede, Holland.

69. Alienor de Poitiers, pp. 217–245; Laborde, II, p. 267, Inventory of 1420.

70. Successor to Monstrelet, 1449 (Chastellain, V, p. 367).

71. See Petit Dutaillis, Documents nouveaux sur les moeurs populaires, etc., p. 14; La Curne de S. Palaye, Mémoires sur l'ancienne chevalerie, I, p. 272.

72. Chastellain. Le Pas de la mort, VI, p. 61.

73. Hefele, Der h. Bernhardin v. Siena etc. p. 42. On the prosecution of sodomy in France, Jacques du Clercq, II, pp. 272, 282, 337, 338, 350, III, p. 15.

74. Thomas Walsingham, Historia Anglicana, II, 148 (Rolls series ed. H. T. Riley, 1864). In the case of Henry II of France, the guilty nature of the mignons is not to be doubted, but this happens at the end of the sixteenth century.

75. Philippe de Commines, Mémoires, ed. B. de Mandrot (Coll. de textes pour servir a l'enseignement de l'histoire) 1901–1913, 2 vols., I, p. 316.

76. La Marche, II, p. 425; Molinet, II, pp. 29, 280; Chastellain, IV, p. 41.

77. Les cent nouvelles, II, p. 61; Froissart, ed. Kervyn, XI, p. 93.

78. Froissart, ed. Kervyn, ib. XIV, p. 318; Le livre des faits de Jacques de Lalaing, p. 29, 247 (Chastellain, VIII); La Marche, I, p. 268; L'hystoire du petit Jehan de Saintré, chap. 47.

79. Chastellain, IV, p. 237.

Chapter 3

1. Deschamps, II, p. 226.

2. Chastellain, Le miroir des nobles hommes en France, VI, p. 204. Exposition sur vérité mal prise, VI, p. 416. L'entrée du roys Loys en nouveau règne, VII, p. 10.

3. Froissart, ed. Kervyn, XIII, p. 22; Jean Germain, Liber de virtutibus ducis Burg., p. 109; Molinet, I p. 83, III p. 100.

4. Monstrelet, II, p. 241.

5. Chastellain, VII, pp. 13–16.

6. Chastellain, III, p. 82; IV, p. 170; V, pp. 279, 309.

7. Jacques du Clercq, II, p. 245, see p. 339.

8. See above p. 11.

9. Chastellain, III, pp. 82–89.

10. [Trans.] *Gilles de Rais:* Baron of Rais who fought bravely on the side of Jeanne d'Arc and who was made marshal of France in 1429. Falling upon hard times, he turned to magic and alchemy, for which he attempted to atone by holy acts. At the same time he pursued a secret life of kidnapping, pederasty, sodomy, and murder. His frightful acts are described in horrific detail in Huysmans's 1891 novel *Là Bas,* which Huizinga read as a young man. Some sources identify Gilles de Rais with the figure of Bluebeard, but Gilles's crimes were committed against young boys. Michelet calls him "bête d'extermination."

11. Chastellain, VIII, pp. 90 ff.

12. Chastellain, II, p. 345.

13. Deschamps, no. 113, I, p. 230.

14. Nicholas de Clémanges, Opera, ed. Lydius, Leiden 1613, p. 48. cap. IX.

15. In the Latin translation of Gerson, Opera, IV, p. 583–622; the French text is from 1824, the cited text by D. H. Carnahan, The Ad Deum vadit of Jean Gerson, University of Illinois studies in language and literature 1917, III, no. 1, p. 13. See Denifle et Chatelain, Chartularium Univ. Paris. IV, no. 1819.

16. In H. Denifle, La guerre de cent Ans et la désolation des eglises etc. en France, Paris 1897–99, 2 vols., I, pp. 497–513.

17. Alain Chartier, Oeuvres, ed. Duchesne, p. 402.

18. Rob. Gaguini Epistole et orationes, ed. L. Thuasne (Bibl. litt. de la Renaissance), Paris 1903, 2 vols., II pp. 321, 350.

19. Froissart, ed. Kervyn, XII, p. 4, Le livre des trahisons, pp. 19, 26; Chastellain, I p. xxx, III p. 325, V pp. 260, 275, 325, VII, pp. 466–480; Thomas Basin, passim, especially I, pp. 44, 56, 59, 115; see La complainte du povre commun et des povres laboureurs de France (Monstrelet, VI, p. 176–190).

20. Les Faicts de Dictz de messire Jehan Molinet, Paris, Jehan Petit, 1537, f. 87 vso.

21. Ballade 19, in A. de la Borderie, Jean Meschinot, sa vie et ses oeuvres (Bibl. de l'école des chartes), LVI, 1895, p. 296; see Les lunettes des princes, ibid., pp. 607, 613.

22. Masselin, Journal des Etats Généraux de France tenus à Tours en 1484, ed. A. Bernier (Coll. des documents inédits), p. 672.

23. Deschamps, VI, no. 1140, p. 67. The link between the idea of equality and the "nobility of the heart" is the point of the words of Ghismonda to her father Tancred in the first novella of the fourth day in Boccaccio's Decameron.

24. Deschamps, VI, p. 124, no. 1176.

25. Molinet, II, p. 104–107; Jean le Maire de Belges, Les chansons de Namur 1507.

26. Chastellain, Le miroir des nobles hommes de France, VI, pp. 203, 211, 214.

27. Le Jouvencel, ed. C. Favre et L. Lecestre (Soc. de l'hist. de France) 1887–89, 2 vols., I, p. 13.

28. Livre des faicts du mareschal de Boucicaut, Petitot, Coll de mém., VI, p. 375.

29. Philippe de Vitri, Le chapel des fleurs de lis (1335), ed. A. Piaget, Romania XXVII, 1898, pp. 8off.

30. Molinet, I, p. 16–17.

31. N. Jorga, Philippe de Mézières, p. 469.

32. Jorga, Mézières, p. 506.

33. Froissart, ed. Luce, I, pp. 2–3; Monstrelet, I, p. 2; d'Escouchy, I, p. 1; Chastellain, I prologue, II p. 116, VI p. 266; La Marche, I, p. 187; Molinet, I p. 17, II p. 54.

34. [Trans.] Heralds and Kings of Arms: Heralds were originally royal messengers, but not, however, trumpeters. The position evolved into that of those in charge of tournaments and the regulations concerning coats of arms. Kings of Arms were the chief heralds of particular chivalric orders. See Charles MacKinnon of Dunakin, Heraldry.

35. Lefèvre de S. Remy, II, p. 249; Froissart, ed Luce, I, p. 1; see Le débat des hérauts d'armes de France et d'Angleterre, ed. L. Pannier et P. Meyer (Soc. des anciens textes français), 1887, p. 1.

36. [Trans.] *Lefèvre de S. Remy,* Toison d'or, King of Arms of the Order of the Golden Fleece.

37. Chastellain, V, p. 443.

38. Les origines de la France contemporaine, La révolution, I, p. 190.

39. Die Kultur der Renaissance in Italien, X, II, p. 155.

40. Burckhardt, Die Kulture, X, I, p. 152–165.

41. Froissart, ed. Luce, IV, p. 112; where the name Bamborough, called as well Bembro or Brembo, is mangled into Brandebourch.

42. Le dit de vérité, Chastellain, VI, p. 221.

43. Le livre de la paix, Chastellain, VIII, p. 367.

44. Froissart, ed Luce, I, p. 3.

45. Le cuer d'amours épris, Oeuvres du roi René, ed. De Quatrebarbes, Angers 1845, 4 vols., III, p. 112.

46. Lefèvre de S. Remy, II, p. 68.

47. Doutrepont, p. 183.

48. La Marche, II, p. 216, 334.

49. Ph. Wielant, Antiquités de Flandre, ed. De Smet (Corp. chron. Flandriae, IV), p. 56.

50. Commines, I, p. 390, see the anecdote in Doutrepont, p. 185.

51. Chastellain, V, p. 316–319.

52. P. Meyer, Bull. de la soc. des anc. textes français, p. 45–54.

53. Deschamps, nos. 12, 93, 207, 239, 362, 403, 432, 652, I pp. 86, 199, II p. 29, X pp. xxxv, xxviff.

54. Journal d'un bourgeois, p. 274. In the middle of the sixteenth century John Coke still knew them as The nyne worthyes, The debate between the Heraldes, ed. L. Pannier et P. Meyer, Le débat des hérauts d'armes, p. 108, §171, while Cervantes called them "todos los nueve de la fama"; Don Quijote, I, 5.

55. Molinet, Faictz et Dictz, f. 151 v.

56. La Curne de Sainte Palaye, II, p. 88.

57. Deschamps, nos. 206, 239, II pp. 27, 69, no. 312, II p. 324, Le lay du très bon connestable B. du Guesclin.

58. S. Luce, La France pendant la querre de cent ans, p. 231: Du Guesclin, dixième preux.

59. Chastellain, La mort du roy charles VII, VI, p. 440.

60. Laborde, II, p. 242, no. 4091; 138, no. 242; see also p. 146, no. 3343; p. 260, no. 4220; p. 266, no. 4253. The psalter was acquired during the War of the Spanish Succession by Joan van den Berg, the *Kommissar der Generalstaaten* in Belgium, and is today in the University of Leiden library.

61. Burckhardt, *Die Kultur der Renaissance in Italien,* X, I, p. 246.

62. Le livre des faicts du maréchal Boucicaut, ed. Petitot, Coll. de mémoires, I. serie, VI, VII.

63. Le livre des faicts, VI, p. 379.

64. Le livre des faicts, VII, pp. 214, 185, 200–201.

65. Chr. de Pisan, Le débât des deux amants, Oeuvres poétiques, II, p. 96.

66. Antoine de la Salle, La salade, chap. 3, Paris, M. le Noir, 1521, f. 4 vso.

67. Le livre des cent ballades, ed. G. Raynaud (Soc. des anciens textes français), p. lv.

68. Ed. C. Favre and L. Lecestre (Soc. de l'hist. de France), 1887–89.

69. [Trans.] *Minnelieder:* Songs composed by the knightly class of practitioners of the northern versions of courtly love.

70. Le Jouvencel, I, p. 25.

71. Le livre des faits du bon chevalier Messire Jacques de Lalaing, ed. Kervyn de Lettenhove, in Chastellain, Oeuvres, VIII.

72. Le Jouvencel, II, p. 20.

73. W. James, The varieties of religious experience. Gifford lectures 1901–1902. London 1903, p. 318.

74. [Trans.] *Opgeheven* (German, *aufgehoben*) has the connotation of canceling and then raising up into a higher synthesis. Here the sensual passion is spiritualized into the heroic dream.

75. [Trans.] This obscure passage is probably a reflection of Huizinga's early studies in philology. He apparently refers to a theory suggested by Max Müller that traced the origin of all myth back to celestial phenomena such as the rising and setting of the sun. Huizinga's suggestion that a much more natural explanation lies in the sexual drive of young men is a rejection of complexity in favor of common sense and is a counterpoint to his rejection of the too facile simplifications of economic determinism. See Richard M. Dorson (ed.), *Pagan Customs and Savage Myths* (Chicago: University of Chicago Press, 1968).

76. [Trans.] Huizinga uses the term for love *Min* (German, *Minne*) to refer to the elevated love of the practice of courtly love. Occasionally, he uses *Min* to specify the heavenly love of God. In this translation, we have used *Minne* only where the reference is to courtly love.

77. Le livre des faicts, p. 398

78. Ed. G. Raynaud, Société des anciens textes français, 1905.

79. Two heros from the Romance of Aspremont.

80. Les voeux du héron vs. 354–371, ed. Soc des bibliophiles de Mons, no. 8, 1839.

81. Letter of the Count of Chimay to Chastellain, Oeuvres, VIII, p. 266.

82. Perceforest, in Quatrebarbes, Oeuvres de roi René, II, p. xciv.

83. Des trois chevaliers et del chainse, in Jacques de Baisieux, ed. Scheler, Trouvères belges, I, 1876, p. 162.

84. Rel. de S. Denis, I, p. 594ff.; Juvenal des Ursins, p. 379.

85. Among others forbidden by the Lateran Synod of 1215; again by Pope Nicholas II, 1279; see Raynaldus, Annales ecclesiastici, III (= Baronius XXII), 1279, xvi–xx; Dionysii Cartusiani Opera, I, XXXVI, p. 206.

86. Deschamps, I p. 222, no. 108; p. 223, no. 109.

87. Journal d'un bourgeois de Paris, pp. 59, 56.

88. Adam v. Bremen, Gesta Hammaburg. eccl. pontificum, lib., II, cap. 1.

89. La Marche, II, pp. 119, 144; d'Escouchy, I, p. 245.

90. Chastellain, VIII, p. 238.

91. La Marche, I, p. 292.

92. Le livre des faits de Jacques de Lalaing, in Chastellain, VIII, pp. 188ff.

93. Oeuvres du roi René, I, p. lxxv.
94. La Marche, III, p. 123; Molinet, V, p. 18.
95. La Marche, II, pp. 118, 121, 122, 133, 341; Chastellain, I p. 256, VIII pp. 217, 246.
96. La Marche, II p. 173, I p. 285; Oeuvres du roi René, I, p. lxxv.
97. Oeuvres du roi René, I, pp. lxxxvi, 57.
98. [Trans.] *Knightly orders*. Huizinga probably means as the three orders of the Holy Land the Templars, the Knights of Saint John the Baptist (*Hospitallers*), and the Teutonic Knights. The three Spanish orders are the Order of Santiago, the Knights of Calatrava, and perhaps the Knights of Christ, although these last were Portuguese.
99. N. Jorga, Phil. de Mézières, p. 348.
100. Chastellain, II, p. 7; IV, p. 233, cf. 269; VI, p. 154.
101. La Marche, I, p. 109.
102. Statuten des ordens, in Luc d'Achéry, Spicilegium, III, p. 730.
103. Chastellain, II, p. 10.
104. Chronique scandaleuse, I, p. 236.
105. Le songe de la thoison d'or, in Doutrepont, p. 154.
106. Fillastre, Le premier volume de la toison d'or, Paris 1515, fol. 2.
107. [Trans.] *Bannerets:* Knights who had distinguished themselves and been promoted to the command of a section of knights.
108. Boucicaut, I, p. 504; Jorga, Ph. de Mézières, pp. 83, 463[8]; Romania, XXVI, pp. 395[1], 396[1]; Deschamps, XI, p. 28; Oeuvres du roi René, I, p. xi; Monstrelet, V, p. 449.
109. Froissart, Poésies, ed. A Scheler (Acad. royale de Belgique), 1870–72, 3 vols., II, p. 341.
110. Alain Chartier, La ballade de Fougères, p. 718.
111. La Marche, IV, p. 164; Jacques du Clercq, II, p. 6.
112. Liber Karoleidos vs. 88 (Chron. rel. a l'hist de Belg. sous la dom. des ducs de Bourg), III.
113. Gen. 30, 32; 4 Kings, 3, 4; Job 31:20; Psalm 71:6.
114. Guillaume Fillastre, Le second volume de la toison d'or, Paris, Franc. Regnault, 1516, fol. 1, 2.
115. La Marche, III p. 201, IV p. 67; Lefèvre de S. Remy, II, p. 292; the ceremonial of such a christening is in Humphrey of Glocester's Herald Nicholas Upton, De officio militari, ed. E. Bysshe (Bissaeus), London 1654, lib. I, c. XI, p. 19.
116. Presumably Deschamps is hinting at this order in the envoi of the ballade on the love order of the leaves (as opposed to that of the Flowers), no. 767, IV, p. 262; see 763: "Royne sur fleurs en vertu demourant, Galoys, Dannoy, Mornay, Pierre ensement De tremoille . . . vont . . . vostre bien qui est grant etc."
117. Le livre du chevalier de la Tour Landry, ed. A. de Montaiglon (Bibl. elzevirenne), Paris, 1854, p. 241ff.
118. Voeu du héron, ed. Soc. des bibl. de Mons, p. 17.
119. Froissart, ed. Luce, I, p. 124.
120. Rel. de S. Denis, III, p. 72. Harald Harfagri took a vow not to cut his

hair until he had conquered all of Norway. Haraldar saga Harfagra, cap. 4; see Voluspa 33.

121. Jorga, Ph. de Mézières, p. 76.

122. Claude Menard, Hist. de Bertrand du Guesclin, pp. 39, 55, 410, 488, La Curne, I, p. 240. Luther still speaks of the superstitious vows by the soldiers of his time, Tischreden, Weimarer Ausg. II, no. 2753 b, p. 632–33.

123. Douet d'Arcq, Choix de pièces inédites rel. au règne de Charles VI. (Soc. de l'hist. de France, 1863), I, p. 370.

124. Le livre des faits, chaps. XVIff., in Chastellain, VIII, p. 70.

125. Le petit Jehan de Saintré, chap. 48.

126. Germania, chap. 31; La Curne, I, p. 236.

127. Heimskringla, Olafssaga Tryggvasonar, chap. 35; Weinhold, Altnordisches Leben, p. 462.

128. La Marche, II, p. 366.

129. La Marche, II, p. 381–387.

130. La Marche, loc. cit.; d'Escouchy, II, pp. 166, 218.

131. d'Escouchy, II, p. 189.

132. Doutrepont, p. 513.

133. Doutrepont, pp. 110, 112.

134. Chastellain, III, p. 376.

135. See above p. 87.

136. Chronique de Berne (Molinier no. 3103), in Kervyn, Froissart, II, p. 531.

137. d'Escouchy, II, p. 220.

138. Froissart, ed. Luce, X, pp. 240, 243.

139. Le livre des faits, Chastellain, VIII, pp. 158–161.

140. La Marche, IV, Estat de la Maison, pp. 34, 47.

141. [Trans.] "Waning" here translates laatste.

142. See my essay, "Uit de voorgeschiedenis van ons nationaal desef," de Gils, 1912, I.

143. Psalms 50:19; in the King James and Revised eds., 51:18; and in the Vulgate, 51:20.

144. Monstrelet, IV, p. 112; Pierre de Fenin, p. 363; Lefèvre de S. Remy, II, p. 63; Chastellain, I, p. 331.

145. See J. D. Hintzen, De Kruistochtplannen van Philip den Goede, Dissertation: University of Leiden, 1918.

146. Chastellain, III, pp. 6, 10, 34, 77, 118, 119, 178, 334; IV, pp. 125, 128, 171, 431, 437, 451, 470; V, p. 49.

147. La Marche, II, p. 382.

148. De Gids, 1912, I, Uit de voorgeschiedenis van ons nationaal besef.

149. Rymer, Foedera III, pars 3, p. 158 = VII, p. 407.

150. Monstrelet, I, pp. 43ff.

151. Monstrelet, IV, p. 219.

152. Pierre de Fenin, p. 626–27; Monstrelet, IV, p. 244; Liber de virtutibus, p. 27.

153. Lefèvre de S. Remy, II, p. 107.

154. Laborde, I, pp. 201ff.

155. La Marche, II, pp. 27, 382.

156. Bandello, I, Nov. 39; Filippo duca di Burgogna si mette fuor di proposito a grandissimo periglio.

157. F. von Bezold, Aus dem Briefwechsel der Markgräfin Isabella von Este-Gonzaga, Archiv f. Kulturgesch., VIII, p. 396.

158. Papiers de Granvelle, I, pp. 360ff.; Geschichte Karls V, II, p. 641; Fueter, Geschichte des europäischen staatensystems 1492–1559, p. 307. See from Erasmus to Nicolaus Beraldus, 25 May 1522, Dedication of De Ratione conscribendi epistolas, Leidener Ausg., I, p. 344.

159. Chastellain, III, pp. 38–49; La Marche, II, pp. 406ff.; d'Escouchy, II, pp. 300ff.; Corp. chron. Flandr., III, p. 525; Petit Dutaillis, Documents nouveaux, pp. 113, 137. —For an apparently safe form of judicial duel see Deschamps, IX, p. 21.

160. [Trans.] houpelande: A tunic with a long skirt (OED).

161. Froissart, ed. Luce, IV, pp. 89–94.

162. Froissart, IV, pp. 127–28.

163. Lefèvre de S. Remy, I, p. 241.

164. Froissart, ed. Luce, XI, p. 3.

165. Rel. de S. Denis, III, p. 175.

166. Froissart, ed. Luce, XI, pp. 24ff.; VI, p. 156.

167. [Trans.] Aristies: A useful term for which there does not seem to be an English equivalent. A knight or group of knights who fight in circumstances to which they and their opponents have agreed in advance; a pitched battle.

168. Froissart, ed. Luce, IV, p. 110. 115. Other similar combats for instance, Molinier, Sources, IV, no. 3707; Molinet, IV, p. 294.

169. Rel. de S. Denis, I, p. 392.

170. Le Jouvencel, I, p. 209; II, pp. 99, 103.

171. Froissart, ed. Luce, I, p. 65; IV, p. 49; II, p. 32.

172. Chastellain, II, p. 140.

173. Monstrelet, III, p. 101; Lefèvre de S. Remy, I, p. 247.

174. Molinet, II, pp. 36, 48; III, pp. 98, 453; IV, p. 372.

175. Froissart, ed. Luce, III, p. 187; XI, p. 22.

176. Chastellain, II, 374.

177. Molinet, I, p. 65.

178. Monstrelet, IV, p. 65.

179. Monstrelet, III, p. 111; Lefèvre de S. Remy, I, p. 259.

180. Basin, III, p. 57.

181. Froissart, ed. Luce, IV, p. 80.

182. Chastellain, I, p. 260; La Marche, I, p. 89.

183. Commines, I, p. 55.

184. Chastellain, III, pp. 82ff.

185. Froissart, ed. Luce, IX, p. 220; XI, p. 202.

186. Ms. Chronik von Oudenarde, in Rel de S. Denis, I, p. 229[1]. [Trans.] The king was fourteen years old.

187. Froissart, ed. Luce, XI, p. 58.

188. Chastellain, II, p. 259.

189. La Marche, II, p. 324.

190. Chastellain, I, p. 28; Commines, I, p. 31; see Petit Dutaillis in Lavisse, Histoire de France, IV², p. 33.

191. Deschamps, IX, p. 80; see vs. 2228, 2295; XI, p. 173.

192. Froissart, ed. Luce, II, p. 37.

193. Le débat des hérauts d'armes, §86, 87, p. 33

194. Livre des faits, Chastellain, VIII, p. 252².

195. Froissart, ed Kervyn, XI, p. 24.

196. Froissart, ed. Luce, IV, p. 83, ed. Kervyn, XI, p. 24.

197. Deschamps, IV, no. 785, p. 289.

198. Chastellain, V, p. 217.

199. Le songe véritable, Mém. de la soc. de l'hist. de Paris, t. XVII, p. 325, in Raynaud, Les cent ballades, p. iv.

200. Commines, I, p. 295.

201. Livres messires Geoffroy de Charny, Romania XXVI.

202. Commines, I, pp. 36-42, 86, 164.

203. Froissart, ed. Luce, IV, p. 70, 302; see ed. Kervyn de Lettenhove, Bruxelles 1869-1877, 26 vols., V, p. 513.

204. [Trans.] *Jean de Nevers:* The name of John the Fearless before he became duke of Burgundy. Nevers was one of the territories of the dukes of Burgundy in central France.

205. Froissart, ed. Kervyn, XV, p. 227.

206. Doutrepont, p. 112.

207. Emerson, Nature, ed. Routledge, 1881, 230-31.

208. [Trans.] *The Y of Pythagoras:* An image of the course of the afterlife that Plato elevates to a myth in book 10 of *Republic.* Huizinga uses it simply as the image of a path which splits, one of the branches itself having two branches.

209. Piaget, Romania, XXVII, 1898, p. 63.

210. Deschamps, no. 315, III, p. 1.

211. Deschamps, I, p. 161 no. 65; see I, p. 78 no. 7, p. 175 no. 75.

212. Deschamps, nos. 1287, 1288, 1289; VII, p. 33; see no. 178, I, p. 313.

213. Deschamps, no. 240, II, p. 71; see no. 196, II, p. 15.

214. Deschamps, no. 184, I, p. 320.

215. Deschamps, no. 1124, no. 307; VI, p. 41; II, p. 213, Lai de franchise.

216. See further Deschamps, nos. 199, 200, 201, 258, 291, 970, 973, 1017, 1018, 1021, 1201, 1258.

217. Deschamps, XI, p. 94.

218. N. de Clémanges, Opera, ed. 1613, Epistolae no. 14, p. 57; no. 18, p. 72; no. 104, p. 296.

219. Joh. de Monasteriolo, Epistolae, Martène et Durand, Ampl. Collectio, II, c. 1398.

220. Joh. de Monasteriolo, Epistolae, c. 1459.

221. Alain Chartier, Oeuvres, ed. Duchesne, 1617, p. 391.

222. See Roberti Gaguini Epistole et orationes, ed. Thuasne (Paris: E. Bouillon, 1903), I, p. 37; II, p. 202.

223. Oeuvres du roi René, ed. Quatrebarbes, IV, p. 73; see Thuasne, Gaguini, II, p. 204.

224. Meschinot, ed. 1522, f. 94, in La Borderie, Bibl. de l'Ecole des Chartes, LVI, 1895, p. 313.

225. See Thuasne, Gaguini, II, p. 205.

Chapter 4

1. [Trans.] *La vita nuova. The New Life*—Dante's masterpiece of courtly love poetry.

2. As the newest [1914] translator of the Roman de la rose, E. Langlois, renders the name.

3. Chastellain, IV, p. 165.

4. Basin, II, p. 224.

5. La Marche, II, p. 350.

6. [Trans.] "And if they passed that night together in great delight, one can well believe it." In Tuchmann, *Mirror,* p. 420.

7. Froissart, IX, pp. 223–236; Deschamps, VII, no. 1282.

8. Cent nouvelles nouvelles, ed. Wright, II, p. 15; see I, p. 277; II, pp. 20, 168, and so forth, and the Quinze joyes de mariage, passim.

9. Petit de Julleville, Jean Regnier, balli d'Auxerre, Revue d'hist. litt. de la France, 1895, p. 157, in Doutrepont, p. 383; see Deschamps, VIII, p. 43.

10. Deschamps, VI, p. 112, no. 1169, La leçon de musique.

11. Charles d'Orléans, Poésies complètes, Paris 1874, 2 vols., I, pp. 12, 42.

12. Charles d'Orléans, I, p. 88.

13. Deschamps, VI, p 82, no. 1151; see also V, p. 132, no. 926; IX, p. 94, c. 31; VI, p. 138, no. 1184; XI, p. 18, no. 1438; XI, pp. 269, 286[1].

14. Christine de Pisan, l'Epistre au dieu d'amours, Oeuvres poétiques, ed. M. Roy, II, p. 1.

15. Joh. de Monasteriolo, Epistolae, Martène et Durand, Amplissima. collectio, II col., p. 1409, 1421, 1422.

16. Piaget, Chronologie des épistres sur le Roman de la rose, Etudes romanes dédiées à Gaston Paris, Paris, 1891, p. 119.

17. Gerson, Opera, III, p. 597; Gerson, Considérations sur St. Joseph, III, p. 866; Sermo contra luxuriem, III, pp. 923, 925, 930, 968.

18. [Trans.] *Old Woman:* Another allegorical figure of the *Roman de la rose.*

19. After Gerson.—The ms. letter of Pierre Col in the Bibl. nationale mss français 1563, f. 183, was not accessible to me.

20. [Trans.] "As it is written in the law of the Lord, Every male that openeth the womb shall be called holy to the Lord."

21. Bibl. de l'école des chartes, LX, 1899, p. 569.

22. E. Langlois, Le roman de la rose (Société des anciens textes français), 1914, T.I., Introduction, p. 36.

23. Ronsard, Amours, no. CLXI.

24. A. Piaget, La cour amoureuse dite de Charles VI, Romania, XX p. 417, XXXI p. 599, Doutrepont, p. 367.

25. Leroux de Lincy, Tentative de rapt etc. en 1405, Bibl. de l'école de chartes, 2. serie, III, 1846, p. 316.

26. Piaget, Romania, XX, p. 447.

27. Oeuvres de Rabelais, ed. Abel Lefranc c.s. I., Gargantua chap. 9, p. 96.

28. Guillaume de Machaut, Le livre du voir-dit, ed. p. P. Paris (Société des bibliophiles françois), 1875, pp. 82, 213, 214, 240, 299, 309, 347, 351.

29. Juvenal des Ursins, p. 496.

30. Rabelais, Gargantua, chap. 9

31. Coquillart, Droits nouveaux, I, p. 111.

32. Christine de Pisan, I, p. 187ff.

33. E. Hoepffner, Frage- und Antwortspiele in der franz. Literatur des 14 Jahrh., Zeitschrift f. roman. Philogie, XXXIII, 1909, pp. 695, 703.

34. Christine de Pisan, Le dit de la rose, 75, Oeuvres poétiques, II, p. 31.

35. Machaut, Remède de fortune, 3879ff. Oeuvres, ed. Hoepffner (Soc. des anc. textes français), 1908-11, 2 vols., II, p. 142.

36. Christine de Pisan, Le livre des trois jugements, Oeuvres poétiques, II, p. 111.

37. [Trans.] Bettina. Bettina von Arnim was a young woman who carried on a correspondence with the older Goethe. The Briefwechsel Goethes mit einem Kinde was published in 1835.

38. Le livre du voir-dit. The hypothesis that there is no reality to the history of this affair (following Hanf, Zeitschrift für roman. Philogie, XXII, p. 145) lacks any proof.

39. A castle near Château Thierry.

40. Voir-Dit, lettre, II, p. 20.

41. Voir-Dit, lettre, XXVII, p. 203.

42. Voir-Dit, pp. 20, 96, 146, 154, 162.

43. The kiss separated by a leaf reoccurs: see Le grand garde derrière str. 6, W. G. C. Byvanck, Un poete inconnu de la société de François Villon, Paris, Champion, 1891, p. 27. Compare the figure of speech: "he held no leaf in front of his mouth."

44. Voir-Dit, pp. 143, 144.

45. Voir-Dit, p. 110.

46. See above, p. 48.

47. Voir-Dit, pp. 98, 70.

48. Le livre du chevalier de la Tour Landry, ed. A. de Montaiglon (Bibl. elzevirienne), 1854.

49. p. 245.

50. p. 28.

51. See above, p. 32.

52. The sentence is completely illogical (pensée . . . fait penser . . . à pensiers); they seize upon one, but nowhere so often as in church.

53. pp. 249, 252-254.

54. Recollections des merveilles, Chastellain, VII, p. 200; see the description of the Joutes de Saint Inglevert, mentioned by Kervyn, Froissart, XIV, p. 406.

55. Le pastoralet, ed. Kervyn de Lettenhove (Chron. rel. à l'hist. de Belg. sous la dom. des ducs de Bourg.), II, p. 573. For this mixture of pastoral form and political purpose, the poet finds his parallel in no less a man than Ariosto, whose single pastoral composition was dedicated to the defense of his patron, Cardinal

Ippolito d'Este, on the occasion of the plot by Albertino Boschetti (1506). The case of the cardinal was hardly better than that of John the Fearless, and the support of Ariosto hardly more sympathetic than that of the unknown Burgundian. See G. Bertoni, L'Orlando furioso e la rinascenza a Ferrara, Modena, 1919, pp. 42, 247.

56. P. 215[1].

57. Meschinot, Les Lunettes des princes, in La Borderie (Bibl. de l'Ec. des chartes, LVI, 1895), p. 606.

58. La Marche, III, p. 135; see Molinet, Recollection des merveilles, about the imprisonment of Maximillian at Bruges; "Les moutons detenterent En son parc le bergier," Faictz et dictz, f. 208 vso.

59. Molinet, IV, p. 389.

60. [Trans.] Leewendalers. A one-act play by Vondel.

61. [Trans.] The Dutch national anthem.

62. Molinet, I, pp. 190, 194; III, p. 138; see Juvenal des Ursins. p. 382.

63. Deschamps, II, p. 213, Lay de franchise, see Chr. de Pisan, Le dit de al Pastoure, Le pastoralet, Roi René, Regnant et Jehanneton, Martial d'Auvergne, vigilles du roi Charles VII, etc., etc.

64. Deschamps, no. 923, see XI, p. 322.

65. Villon, ed. Longnon, p. 83.

66. Gerson, Opera, III, p. 302.

67. L'epistre au dieu d'amours, II, p. 14.

68. Quinze joyes de mariage, p. 222.

69. Oeuvres poétiques, I, p. 237, no. 26.

Chapter 5

1. Directorium vitae nobilium, Dionysii opera, t. XXXVII, p. 550; t. XXXVIII, p. 358

2. Don Juan, c. 11, 76–80, see C. H. Becker, Ubi sunt qui ante in mundo fuere. Essays dedicated to Ernst Kuhn 11 February 1916, pp. 87–105.

3. Bernardi Morlanensis, De contemptu mundi, ed. Th. Wright, the Anglo-Latin satirical poets and epigrammatists of the twelfth century (Rerum Britannicarum medii aevi scriptores), London, 1872, 2 vols., II, p. 37.

4. Earlier ascribed to Bernhard of Clairvaux, held by a few to be by Walter Mapes; see H. L. Daniel, Thesaurus hymnologicus, Lipsiae 1841–1856, IV, p. 288.

5. Deschamps, III, nos. 330, 345, 368, 399; Gerson, Sermo III de defunctis, Opera, III, p. 1568; Dion. Cart., De quatuor hominim novissimis, Opera, t. XLI, p. 511; Chastellain, VI, p. 52.

6. Villon, ed. Longnon, p. 33.

7. Villon, ed. Longnon, p. 34.

8. Emile Mâle, L'art religieux à la fin du moyen-âge, Paris 1908, p. 376.

9. See my work De Vidûshaka in het Indisch tooneel, Groningen 1897, p. 77.

10. Odo of Cluny, Collationum lib. III, Migne t. CXXXIII, p. 556.

11. Innocentius III, De contemptu mundi sive de miseria conditionis humanae libri tres, Migne t. CCXVII, p. 702.

12. Innocentius III, p. 713.

13. Oeuvres de roi René, ed. Quatrebarbes I, p. ci. After the fifth and the eighth lines there appears to be a verse missing. Possibly to rhyme with "menu vair" should be "mangé des vers" or something similar.

14. Olivier de la Marche, Le parement et triumphe des dames, Paris, Michel le Noir, 1520, at the end.

15. La Marche, Le parement et triumphe des dames, at the end.

16. Villon, Testament, vs. 453ff., ed. Longnon, p. 39.

17. H. Kern, Het Lied van Ambapâlî uit de Therîgâthâ, Versl. en Meded. der Koninkl. Akad. van Wetenschappen te Amsterdam 5, III, p. 153, 1917.

18. Molinet, Faictz et dictz, fo. 4, fo. 42 v.

19. Procedure concerning the beatification of Peter of Luxembourg, 1390, Acta sanctorum Julii, I, p. 562. Compare the regular renewal of the wax in which the bodies of the English kings and their relatives are wrapped, Rymer, Foedera VII, 361, 433 = III³, 140, 168, etc.

20. Les Grandes chroniques de France, ed. Paulin Paris 1836–1838, 6 vols., VI, p. 334.

21. See the detailed study of Dietrich Schäfer, Mittelalterlicher Brauch bei de Überführung von Leichen. Sitzungsberichte der preussischen Akademie der Wissenschaften, 1920, pp. 478–498.

22. Lefèvre de S. Remy, I, p. 200, wherein one must read Suffolk for Oxford.

23. Juvenal des Ursins, p. 567; Journal d'un bourgeois, pp. 237, 307, 671.

24. See also the extensive literature on the theme, G. Huet, Notes d'histoire littéraire, III, Le moyen âge, XX, 1918, p. 148.

25. See the above cited Emile Mâle, L'art religieux à la fin du moyen-âge, II, 2. La Mort.

26. Laborde, II, 1, 393.

27. A few reproductions by Mâle, L'art religieux à la fin du moyen-âge, and in the Gazette des beaux arts 1918, avril–juin, p. 167.

28. Through the researches of Huet, Notes de l'hist. littéraire, it is clearly seen that a round dance of the dead was the primitive source to which Goethe returned in his Totentanz.

29. [Trans.] dubbeldanger: German Doppelgänger.

30. Earlier and incorrectly thought to be older (1350). See G. Ticknor, Geschichte der schönen Literatur in Spanien (original in English), I p. 77, II p. 598; Grobers Grundrisz, II¹ p. 1180, II² p. 428.

31. Oeuvres du roi René, I, p. clii.

32. Chastellain, Le pas de la mort, VI, p. 59.

33. See Innocentius III, De contemptu mundi, II, c. 42; Dion. Cart., De quatuor hominum novissimis, t. XLI, p. 496.

34. Chastellain, Oeuvres, VI, p. 49.

35. Loc. cit., p. 60.

36. Villon, Testament, XLI, vs. 321–28, ed. Longnon, p. 33.

37. Champion, Villon, I, p. 303.

38. Mâle, L'art religieux . . . , p. 389.

39. Leroux de Lincy, Livre des légendes, p. 95.

40. Le livre des faits, etc., II, p. 184.

41. Journal d'un bourgeois, I, pp. 233-234, 392, 276. See further Champion, Villon, I, p. 306.

42. A. de la Salle, Le reconfort de Madame du Fresne, ed. J Nève, Paris 1903.

Chapter 6

1. J. Burckhardt, Weltgeschichtliche Betrachtungen, 1905, p. 97, 147.

2. [Trans.] *Spanning*. See chap. 1, n. 1

3. [Trans.] *This-worldliness in other-worldly terms:* That is, to envision the after-life or the divine merely as an exaggerated version of this life; a habit of thought which demeans the transcendent by lowering it to the material. For a later, fuller use of this terminology, see Arthur O. Lovejoy, *The Great Chain of Being*. Boston: Harvard University Press, 1964.

4. [Trans.] *Suso:* 1300-1366. A follower of the great German mystic Meister Eckhart. He was an accomplished ascetic as well as a renowned preacher.

5. Heinrich Seuse, Leben, ed. Bihlmeyer, Deutsche Schriften, 1907, pp. 24, 25.

6. [Trans.] *bonte:* German *buntes,* colorful. An adjective very often used by Huizinga in *Autumn*. The translator's temptation to replace it with synonyms should be resisted since the "colorful" aspect of such as the images of saints is precisely why they are "this-worldly." Huizinga would have remembered Mephistopheles' temptation of the student in *Faust:* "Grey, my friend, is all of theory, and green is life's golden tree" (I, 2, 2039).

7. [Trans.] *Gerson:* 1363-1429. A student of Pierre d'Ailly and succeeded him as Chancellor of the University of Paris. An enemy of scholastic speculation and a nominalist, he was also a delicate mystic. Of very humble origin, he rose to his position through strength of mind. He was very prominent in the attempts to heal the Great Schism. One feels that Huizinga admired him greatly.

8. Gerson, Opera, III, p. 309.

9. Nic. de Clémanges, De novis festivitatibus non instituendis, Opera, ed. Lydius Lugd. Bat. 1613, pp. 151, 159.

10. In Gerson, Opera, II, p. 911.

11. Acta sanctorum, Apr. t. III, p. 149.

12. Ac aliis vere pauperibus et miserabilibus indigentibus, quibus convenit jus et verus titulus mendicandi.

13. Qui ecclesiam suis mendaciis maculant et eam irrisibilem reddunt.

14. Alanus Redivivus, ed. J. Coppenstein, 1642, p. 77.

15. Commines, I, p. 310; Chastellain, V, p. 27; Le Jouvencel, I, p. 82; Jean Lud, in Deutsche Geschichtsblätter, XV, p. 248; Journal d'un bourgeois, p. 384; Paston Letters, II, p. 18; J, H. Ramsay, Lancaster and York, II, p. 275; Play of Sir John Oldcastle, II, p. 2 and others.

16. Contra superstitionem praesertim Innocentum, Opera, I, p. 203.

17. Gerson, Quaedam argumentatio adversus eos qui publice volunt dogmatizare etc. Opera, II, pp. 521-522.

18. Johannis de Varennis Responsiones etc., Gerson, I, p. 909.

19. Journal d'un bourgeois, p. 259. For "une hucque vermeille par dessoubz," which is impossible, read "par dessus."

20. Gerson, Considérations sur Saint Joseph, III, pp. 842-68, Josephina, IV,

p. 753; Sermo de natalitate beatae Mariae Virginis, III, p. 1351; Further IV, p. 729, 731, 732, 735, 736.

21. Gerson, De distinctione verarum visionum a falsis, Opera, I, p. 50.

22. C. Schmidt, Der Prediger Olivier Maillard, Zeitschrift f. hist. Theologie, 1856, p. 501.

23. See Thuasne, Rob. Gaguini, Ep. Or., I, pp. 72ff.

24. Les cent nouvelles nouvelles, ed. Wright, II, pp. 75ff., 12ff.

25. Le livre du chevalier de la Tour Landry, ed. de Montaiglon, p. 56.

26. Loc. cit., p. 257: "Se elles ouyssent sonner la messe ou a veoir Dieu."

27. Leroux de Lincy, Le livre des Proverbes français, Paris, 1859, 2 vols., I, p. 21.

28. Froissart, ed. Luce, V, p. 24.

29. "Cum juramento asseruit non credere in Deum dicti episcopi," Rel. de S. Denis, I, p. 102.

30. [Trans.] Hansje in den Kelder. Hans in the cellar. A rare antique drinking dish in which through a clever mechanism a little figure pops up when the dish is filled. The dish was used to toast an expectant mother. We are indebted to Willemina Rathonyi-Reuz of the Canadian Association for the Advancement of Netherlandic Studies for this information.

31. Laborde, II, p. 264, no. 4238, Inventory of 1420; ib. II, p. 10, no. 77. Inventory of Charles the Bold, who well might be the source of this specimen.

32. Gerson, Opera, III, p. 947.

33. Journal d'un bourgeois, p. 366².

34. A Dutch letter of indulgence from the fourteenth century, ed. J. Verdam, Ned. Archief voor Kerkgesch. 1900, pp. 117–22.

35. A. Eekhof, De questierders van den aflaat in de Noordelijke Nederl., 's Gravenhagem 1909, p. 12.

36. Chastellain, I, pp. 187–89; entry of Henry V and Philip of Burgundy into Paris 1420; II, p. 16: Entry of the latter into Ghent 1430.

37. Doutrepont, p. 379.

38. Deschamps, III, p. 89, no. 357; le roi René, Traicté de la forme de devise d'un tournoy, Oeuvres, II, p. 9.

39. Olivier de la Marche, II, p. 202.

40. Monstrelet, I, p. 285, cf. 306.

41. Liber de virtutibus Philippe ducis Burgundiae, pp. 13, 16 (Chron. rel. à l'hist de Belgique sous la dom. des ducs de Bourg., II).

42. Molinet, II pp. 84–94, III p. 98; Faictz et Dictz, f. 47, see I, p. 240, and also Chastellain, III pp. 209, 260, IV p. 48, V p. 301, VII p.1ff.

43. Molinet, III, p. 109.

44. Gerson, Oratio ad regem Franciae, Opera, IV, p. 662.

45. Quinze joyes de Mariage, p. XIII.

46. Gerson, Opera, III, p. 299.

47. [Trans.] Agnes Sorel 1422–50. The first "official" mistress of a King of France, she served Charles VII. He gave her the castle of Beauté, where she died after childbirth and profound repentance.

48. Friedländer, Jahrb. d. K. Preuss. Kunstsammlungen, XVII, 1896, p. 206.

49. Wetzer und Welte, Kirchenlexicon, see Musik, col. 2040; see Erasmus, Christiani Matrimonii Institutio, Opera (ed. Lugd. Bat.), V, col. 718c: "Nunc

sonis neqissimis aptantur verba sacra, nihilo magis decore, quam si thaidis orna-
tum addas Catoni. Interdum nec verba silentur impudica cantorum licentia."
[Trans.: "Nowadays the most frivolous tunes are given holy words, which is no
better than if one put the jewelry of Thais on Cato. And given the whore-like
shamelessness of the singers, the (secular) words are not even held back."]

50. Chastellain, III, p. 155.

51. H. van den Velden, Rod. Agricola, een nederlandsch Humanist der 15
eeuw, I, dl., Leiden 1911, p. 44.

52. Deschamps, X, no. 33, p. lxi, in the next to the last line we find "l'ostel,"
which, of course, makes no sense.

53. Nic. de Clémanges, De novis celebritatibus non instituendis, Opera, ed.
Lydius, 1613, p. 143.

54. Le livre du chevalier de la Tour Landry, pp. 66, 70.

55. Gerson, sermo de nativitate Domini, Opera, III, pp. 946, 947.

56. Nicolas de Clémanges, De novis celebritatibus non instituendis, p. 147.

57. O. Winckelmann, Zur Kulturgeschichte des Strassburger Münsters,
Zeitschr. f. d. Geschichte des Oberrheins, N. F. XXII, 2.

58. Dionysius Cartusianus, De modo agendi processiones etc., Opera,
XXXVI, pp. 198ff.

59. Chastellain, V, pp. 253ff.

60. See above, p. 48.

61. Michel Menot, Sermones, f. 144 vso., in Champion, Villon, I, p. 202.

62. Le livre du chevalier de la Tour Landry, p. 65; Olivier de la Marche, II,
p. 89; L'amant rendu cordelier, p. 25, huitain 68; Rel. de S. Denis, I, p. 102.

63. Christine de Pisan, Oeuvres poétiques, I, p. 172, see p. 60, l'epistre au
dieu d'Amours, II, 3; Deschamps V p. 51 no. 871, II p. 185 vs 75; See above, p.
147.

64. L'amant rendu cordelier, p. 25.

65. Menot, Sermones, p. 202.

66. Gerson, Expostulatio . . . adversus corruptionem juventutis per lascivas
imagines et alia hujus modi, Opera, III, p. 291; cf. De parvulis Christum trahendis,
ib. p. 281; Contra tentationem blasphemiae, ib. p. 246.

67. Le livre du chevalier de la Tour Landry, pp. 80, 81; see Machaut, Livre
du voir-dit, pp. 143ff.

68. Tour Landry, pp. 55, 63, 73, 79.

69. Nicolas de Clémanges, De novis celebritatibus . . ., p. 145.

70. Quinze joyes de mariage, p. 127; see pp. 19, 29, 124.

71. Froissart, ed. Luce et Raynaud, XI, pp. 225ff.

72. Chron. Montis S. Agnetis, p. 341; J. C. Pool, Frederik v. Heilo en aijne
schriften, Amsterdam 1866, p. 126; see Hendrik Mande in W. Moll, Joh. Brugman
en het godsdienstig leven onzer vaderen in de 15ᵉ eeuw, 1854, 2 vols., I, p. 264.

73. Gerson, Centilogium de impulsibus, Opera, III, p. 154.

74. Deschamps, IV, p. 322 no. 807; see I, p. 272 no. 146: "si n'y a Si meschant
qui encor ne die Je regni Dieu. . ."

75. Gerson, Adversus lascivas imagines, Opera, III, p. 292; Sermo de nativatate
Domini, III, p. 946.

76. Deschamps, I, pp. 271ff. nos. 145, 146, p. 217 no. 105; see II, p. lvi, and Gerson, III, p. 85.

77. Gerson, Considérations sur le peché de blasphème, Opera, III, p. 889.

78. Regulae morales, Opera, III, p. 85.

79. Ordonnances des rois de France, t. VIII, p. 130; Rel. de S. Denis, II, p. 533.

80. P. d'Ailly, De reformatione, cap. 6, de reform. laicorum, in Gerson, Opera II, p. 914.

81. Gerson, Contra foedam tentationem blasphemiae, Opera, III, p. 243.

82. Gerson, Regulae morales, Opera, III, p. 85.

83. Gerson, Contra foedam tentationem blasphemiae, Opera, III, p. 246: hi qui audacter contra fidem loquuntur in forma joci etc.

84. Cent nouvelles nouvelles, II, p. 205.

85. Gerson, Sermo de S. Nicolao, Opera, III, p. 1577; De parvulis ad Christum trahendis ib. p. 279. Against this same saying also Dionysius Cart., Inter Jesum et puerum dialogus, art. 2, Opera, t. XXXVIII, p. 190.

86. Gerson, De distinctione verarum visionum a falsis, Opera, I, p. 45.

87. Ibid., p. 58.

88. Petrus Damiani, Opera, XII, 29; Migne, P. L., 145, p. 283; see for the twelfth and thirteenth centuries Hauck, Kirchengeschichte Deutschlands, IV, pp. 81, 898.

89. Deschamps, VI, p. 109, no. 1167, id., no. 1222; Commines, I, p. 449.

90. Froissart, ed. Kervyn, XIV, p. 67.

91. Rel. de S. Denis, I, pp. 102, 104; Jean Juvenal des Ursins, p. 346.

92. Jacques du Clercq, II, pp. 277, 340; IV, p. 59; see Molinet IV, p. 390, Rel. de S. Denis, I, p. 643.

93. Joh. de Monasteriolo, Epistolae, II, p. 1415; see ep. 75, 76, p. 1456 of Ambr. de Miliis to Gontier Col, in which he complains about Jean de Montreuil.

94. Gerson, Sermo III in Sancti Ludovici, Opera, III, p. 1451.

95. Gerson, Contra impugnantes ordinem carthusiensium, Opera, II, p. 713.

96. Gerson, De decem praceptis, Opera, I, p. 245.

97. Gerson, Sermo de nativ. Domini, Opera, III, p. 947.

98. Nic. de Clémanges, De novis celebr. etc., p. 151.

99. Villon, Testament, vs. 893ff., ed Longnon, p. 57.

100. Gerson, Sermo de nativitate Domine, Opera, III, p. 947; Regulae morales, ib. p. 86; Liber de vita spirituali animae, ib. p. 66.

101. Hist. translationis corporis sanctissimi ecclesiae doctoris divi Thom. de Aq., 1368, auct. fr. Raymundo Hugonis O. P., Acta sanctorum Martii, I, p. 725.

102. Report of the papal commissioner Bishop Conrad of Hildesheim and Abbot Hermann of Georgenthal about the testimony concerning St. Elisabeth of Marburg in January 1235, given in Historisches Jahrbuch der Görres-Gesellschaft, XXVIII, p. 887.

103. Rel. de S. Denis, II, p. 37.

104. See below p. 198.

105. Chastellain, III, p. 407; IV, p. 216.

106. Deschamps, I, p. 277, no. 150.

107. Deschamps, II, p. 348, no. 314.

108. From Johann Ecks's Pfarrbuch for U. L. Frau in Ingolstadt, in Archiv für Kulturgesch., VIII, p. 103.

109. Joseph Seitz, Die Verehrung des heil. Joseph in ihrer gesch. Entwicklung, etc., Freiburg, Herder, 1908.

110. Le livre du chevalier de la Tour Landry, p. 212.

111. B. Nat. Ms. fr. 1875, in Ch. Oulmont, Le verger, le temple et la cellule, essai sur la sensualité dans les oeuvres de mystique religieuse, Paris 1912, pp. 284ff.

112. See the passages about the images of saints in E. Mâle, L'art religieux à la fin du moyen-âge, chap. IV.

113. Deschamps, I, p. 114, no. 32; VI, p. 243, no. 1237.

114. Bambergisches Missale from 1490, in Uhrig, Die 14 hl. Nothelfer (XIV. Auxiliatores), Theol. Quartalschrift, LXX, 1888, p. 72; see an Utrecht Missal from 1514 and a Dominican Missal of 1550, in Acta sanctorum Aprilis, t. III, p. 149.

115. Erasmus, Ratio seu methodus compendio pervendi ad veram theologiam, ed. Basel, 1520, p. 171. ([Trans.] Added in the German translation: see Moriae Encomium, cap. 40; Colloquia, Militaria, LB I 642.)

116. In the just cited ballade of Deschamps we also find Martha, who destroyed the Tarasque at Tarascon. [Trans.] That is, St. Martha, who destroyed a monster called the Tarasque at the town of Tarascon in southern France.

117. Oeuvres de Coquillart, ed. Ch. d'Héricault (Bibl. elzevirenne), 1857, II, p. 281.

118. Deschamps, no. 1230, VI, p. 232.

119. Rob. Gaguini, Epistole et orationes, ed. Thuasne, II, p. 176.

120. Colloquia, Exequiae Seraphicae, ed. Elzev., p. 620. [Trans.] The German translation adds: I, c. 869 B, see Ep. 447, line 426, Allen II, p. 303, and cites the Colloquia as Leidener Ausg.

121. Gargantua, chap. 45.

122. Apologie pour Hérodote, chap. 38, ed. Ristelhuber, 1879, II, p. 324.

123. Deschamps, VIII, p. 201, no. 1489.

124. Gerson, de Angelis, Opera, III, p. 1481; De praeceptis decalogi, I, p. 431; Oratio ad bonum angelum suum, III, p. 511; Tractatus VIII super Magnificat, IV, p. 370; see III, pp. 137, 553, 739.

125. Gerson, Opera, IV, p. 389.

Chapter 7

1. Monstrelet, IV, p. 304.

2. Bernh. of Siena, Opera, I, p. 100, in Hefele, Der h. Bernhardin von Siena . . ., p. 36.

3. Les cent nouvelles nouvelles, II, p. 157; Les quinze joyes de mariage, pp. 111, 215.

4. Molinet, Faictz et dictz, f. 188 vso.

5. [Trans.] duke of Armagnac: A title of Louis d'Orléans.

6. Journal d'un bourgeois, p. 336, see p. 242, no. 514.

7. Ghillebert de Lannoy, Oeuvres, ed. Ch. Potvin, Louvain, 1878, p. 163.

8. Les cent nouvelles nouvelles, II, p. 101.

9. Le Jouvencel, II, p. 107.

10. Songe de viel pelerin, bij Jorga, Phi. de Mézières, p. 423[6].

11. Journal d'un bourgeois, pp. 214, 289[2].

12. Gerson, Opera, I, p. 206.

13. Jorga, Phil. de Mézières, p. 506.

14. W. Moll, Johannes Brugman, II, p. 125.

15. Chastellain, IV, p. 263–65.

16. Chastellain, II, p. 300; VII, p. 222. Jean Germain, Liber de virtutibus, p. 10 (The less severe fasting exercise mentioned here may belong to a different time); Jean Jouffroy, De Philippo duce oratio (Chron. rel. à l'hist de Belg. sous la dom. des ducs de Bourg., III), p. 118.

17. La Marche, II, p. 40.

18. Monstrelet, IV, p. 302.

19. Jorga, Phil. de Mézières, p. 350.

20. See Jorga, Phil. de Mézières, p. 444; Champion, Villon, I, p. 17.

21. [Trans.] Gerard Groote: 1340–84. Mystic and popular preacher who founded both the Brethren of the Common Life and the Windesheim Convent (although the latter did not come into existence until after his death). Some modern opinion is that it is he rather than Thomas à Kempis who was the author of the Imitatio Christi.

22. Oeuvres du roi René, ed. Quatrebarbes, I, p. cx.

23. Monstrelet, V, p. 112.

24. La Marche, I, p. 194.

25. Acta sanctorum Jan., t. II, p. 1018.

26. Jorga, Phil. de Mézières, pp. 509, 512.

27. It is not important in this connection whether the church had clarified the question of recommending persons for sainthood or only for beatification.

28. André Du Chesne, Hist. de la maison de Chastillon sur Marne, Paris 1621, Preuves, pp. 126–31, Extraict de l'enqueste faite pour la canonization de Charles de Blois, pp. 223, 234.

29. Froissart, ed. Luce, VI, p. 168.

30. The grounds on which Dom Plaine, Revue des questions historiques, XI, p. 41, objects to Froissart's testimony do not seem cogent enough to me.

31. W. James, The varieties of religious experience, pp. 370f.

32. Ordonnances des rois de France, t. VIII, p. 398, Nov. 1400, 426, 18 March 1401.

33. Mémoires de Pierre Salmon, ed. Buchon, Coll. de chron. nationales, 3e Supplément de Froissart, XV, p. 49.

34. Froissart, ed. Kervyn, XIII, p. 40.

35. Acta sanctorum Julii, t. I, p. 486–628. Prof. Wensinck has brought to my attention that the custom of keeping a daily list of sins is a very old saintly tradition already described by Johannes Climacus (c. 600), Scala Paradisi, ed. Raderus, Paris 1633, p. 65; that it is also known in Islam, by Ghazâlî, and that it is still recommended by Ignatius of Loyola in the Exercitia spiritualia.

36. La Marche, I, p. 180.

37. Lettres de Louis XI, t. VI, p. 514, cf. V, p. 86, X, p. 65.

38. Commines, I, p. 291.

39. Commines, II, pp. 67, 68.

40. Commines, II, p. 57; Lettres X, p. 16; IX, p. 260. At times, there was such an *agnus scythicus* in the Colouia Museum at Haarlem.

41. Chron. scan., II, p. 122.

42. Commines, II, pp. 55, 77.

43. Acta sanctorum Apr. t., I, p. 115.—Lettres de Louis XI, X, pp. 76, 90.

44. Sed volens caute atque astute agere propterea quod a pluribus fuisset sub umbra sanctitatis deceptus, decrevit variis modis experiri virtutem servi Dei, Acta sanctorum, Apr., t. I, p. 115.

45. Acta sanctorum, Apr., t. I, p. 108; Commines, II, p. 55.

46. Lettres, X, pp. 124, 29. June 1483.

47. Lettres, X, p. 4 *passim;* Commines, II, p. 54.

48. Commines, II, p. 56; Acta sanctorum, Apr., t. I, p. 115.

49. A. Renaudet, Préréforme et humanisme à Paris, p. 172.

50. Doutrepont, p. 226.

51. Vita Dionysii auct. Theod. Loer, Dion. Opera, I, p. xliiff., id. De vita et regimine principum, t. XXXVII, p. 497.

52. Opera, t. XLI, p. 621; D. A. Mougel, Denys le chartreux, sa vie etc.; Montreuil, 1896, p. 63.

53. Opera, t. XLI, p. 617; Vita, I, p. xxxi; Mougel, p. 51; Bijdragen en mededeelingen van het historisch genootschap te Utrecht, XVIII, p. 331d.

54. Opera, t. XXXIX, p. 496; Mougel, p. 54; Moll, Johannes Brugman, I, p. 74; Kerkgesch., II 2, p. 124; K. Krogh-Tonning, Der letzte Scholastiker, Freiburg 1904, p. 175.

55. Mougel, p. 58.

56. De mutua cogitione, Opera, t. XXXVI, p. 178.

57. Vita, Opera, t. I, p. xxiv, xxxviii.

58. Vita, Opera, t. I, p. XXVI.

59. De munificentia Dei beneficiis Dei, Opera, t. XXXIV, art. 26, p. 319.

Chapter 8

1. Gerson, Tractatus VIII super Magnificat, Opera, IV, p. 386.

2. Acta sanctorum Martii, t. I, p. 561, see pp. 540, 601.

3. Hefele, Der h. Bernhardin von Siena . . ., p. 79.

4. Moll, Johannes Brugman, II, pp. 74, 86.

5. See above, p. 181.

6. See above, p. 4.

7. Acta sanctorum Apr, t. I, p. 195. —The picture which Hefele (Der h. Bernhardin von Siena . . .) gives of the preachers in Italy is in many regards accurate for French-speaking countries.

8. Opus quadragesimale Sancti Vincentii, 1482, and Oliverii Maillardi Sermones dominicales etc., Paris, Jean Petit, 1515. In the first edition (see p. 316, note 2) I stated that I had not found the work of these two in the Netherlands. Dr. C. van Slee and Miss M. E. Kronenberg were kind enough to point out to me that the DeVente Athenaeum Library owns both.

9. Life of S. Petrus Thomasius, Carmeliter, in Philippe de Mézières, Acta sanctorum Jan., t. II, p. 997; also Dionysius Cartusianus over Brugman's style of

preaching: De vita et regimine episcoporum, nobilium, etc., etc., vol. 37ff.; Inter Jesum et puerum dialogus, vol. 38.

10. Acta sanctorum Apr., t. I, p. 513.

11. James, Varieties of Religious Experience, p. 348: "For sensitiveness and narrowness, when they occur together, as they often do, require above all things a simplified world to dwell in"; cf. p. 353[1].

12. Moll, Brugman, I, p. 52.

13. Dion. Cart. De quotidiano baptimate lacrimarum, t. XXIX, p. 84; De oratione, t. XLI, p. 31–55; Expositio hymni Audi conditor, t. XXXV, p. 34.

14. Acta sanctorum Apr., t. I, pp. 485, 494.

15. Chastellain, III p. 119; Antonio de Beatis (1517), L. Pastor, Die Reise des Kardinals Luigi d'Aragona, Freiburg 1905, p. 51[3], 52; Polydorus Vergilius, Anglicae historiae libri XXVI, Basileae, 1546, p. 15.

16. Gerson, Epistola contra libellum Johannis de Schonhavia, Opera, I, p. 79.

17. Gerson, De distinctione verarum visionum a falsis, Opera, I, p. 44.

18. Ibid., p. 48.

19. Gerson, De examinatione doctrinarum, Opera, I, p. 19.

20. Ibid., p. 16, 17.

21. Gerson, De distinctione etc., I, p. 44.

22. Gerson, Tractatus II super Magnificat, Opera, IV, p. 248.

23. Sixty-five useful articles on the Passion of our Lord, Moll, Brugman, II, p. 75.

24. Gerson, De monte contemplationis, Opera, III, p. 562.

25. Gerson, De distinctione etc., Opera, I, p. 49.

26. Ibid.

27. Acta sanctorum Martii, t. I, p. 562.

28. James, Varieties of religious experience, p. 343.

29. Acta sanctorum, Martii, t. 1, p. 552ff.

30. Froissart, ed. Kervyn, XV, p. 132; Rel. de S. Denis, II, p. 124; Johannis de Varennis, Responsiones ad capita accusationum in Gerson, Opera, I, pp. 925, 926.

31. Responsiones, Opera, I, p. 936.

32. Ibid., p. 910ff.

33. Gerson, De probatione spirituum, Opera, I, p. 41.

34. Gerson, Epistola contra libellum Joh. de Schonhavia (polemics over Ruusbroec), Opera, I, p. 82.

35. Gerson, Sermo contra luxuriem, Opera, III, p. 924.

36. Gerson, De distinctione etc., Opera, I, p. 55.

37. Opera, III, pp. 589ff.

38. Ibid., p. 593.

39. Gerson, De consolatione theologiae, Opera, I, p. 174.

40. [Trans.] Ruusbroec: 1293–1381. Dutch mystic, the teacher of Groote. Unlike many other mystics, Ruusbroec did not teach the the soul was extinguished in God at the highest ecstasy, but that it retained its identity.

41. Gerson, Epistola . . . super tertia parte libri Johannis Ruysbroeck, De ornatu nupt. spir., Opera, I, pp. 59, 67 passim.

42. Gerson, Epistola contra libellum Joh. de Schonhavia, Opera, I, p. 82.

43. The same feeling in a modern person: "I committed myself to Him in the profoundest belief that my individuality was going to be destroyed, that he would take all from me, and that I was willing." James, Varieties of religious experience, p. 223.

44. Gerson, De distinctione etc., Opera, I, p. 55; De libris caute legendis, Opera, I, p. 114.

45. [Trans.] *the mad love of God:* Huizinga here uses the poetic form for love, *min.*

46. Gerson, De examinatione doctrinarum, Opera, I, p. 19; De distinctione, I, p. 55; De libris caute legendis, I, p. 114; Epistola super Joh. Ruysbroeck De ornatu, I, p. 62; De consolatione theologiae, I, p. 174; De susceptione humanitatis Christi, I, p. 455; De nuptiis Christi et ecclesiae, II, p. 370; De triplici theologia, III, p. 869.

47. Moll, Johannes Brugman, I, p. 57.

48. Gerson, De distinctione etc., I, p. 55.

49. Moll, Brugman, I, pp. 234, 314.

50. Ecclesiasticus 24: 29 [the English languages bibles: 24:21]; see Meister Eckhart, Predigten no. 43, p. 146, par. 26.

51. Ruusbroec, Die Spieghel der ewigher salicheit, cap. 7, Die chierheit der gheesteleker brulocht, l. II c 53, Werken, ed. David en Snellaert (Maatsch. der Vlaemsche bibliophilen) 1860², 1868, III pp. 156–59, VI p. 132.

52. After the ms. in Oulmont, Le verger, le temple, et la cellule, p. 277.

53. See the refutation of this opinion by James, Varieties of Religious Experience, pp. 10¹, 191 276.

54. Moll, Brugman, II, p. 84.

55. Oulmont, Le verger, le temple, et la cellule, pp. 204, 210.

56. B. Alanus redivivus, ed. J. A. Coppenstein, Neapel 1642, pp. 29, 31, 105, 108, 116 *passim.*

57. Alanus redivivus, pp. 209, 218.

58. [Trans.] *The Hammer of Witches:* The most astonishing work of pathological religious fanaticism to come out of the Middle Ages; it prescribes techniques for the trials of accused witches that assure a guilty verdict, yet the authors clearly believe in the validity of their approach. It is available in a modern edition. H. Kramer and J. Sprenger, *The Malleus Maleficarum.* trans. M. Summers (New York: Dover Publications, 1971). The translator, Montague Summers, was a famous eccentric and his editorial comments in favor of the persecution of witches can be ignored.

Chapter 9

1. Seuse, Leben, chap. 4, 45. Deutsche Schriften, S. 15, 154; Acta sanctorum Jan. t. II, p. 656.

2. Hefele, Der h. Bernhardin von Siena . . ., p. 167; see p. 259, "Über den Namen Jesus," B's defense of the custom.

3. Eug. Demole, Le soleil comme cimier des armes de Geneve, note in Revue historique, CXXIII, p. 450.

4. Rod. Hospinianus, De templis etc., ed. II a, Turgi, 1603, p. 213.

5. [Trans.] *Monstrance:* A container for holding the Host after it is consecrated.

6. James, Varieties of religious experience, pp. 474, 475.

7. Irenaeus, Adversus haereses libri V, l. IV c. 21^3.

8. Concerning the necessity of such realism see James, Varieties of religious experience, p. 56.

9. [Trans.] *Universals, Realism, Nominalism:* These complex issues are much too involved to be adequately handled by a brief note. However, the position of the church was that there existed in the world (perhaps in the mind of God) universals of which all particulars are imperfect examples. That is to say, that beauty existed as such (*ante rem*) fully apparent to God. Man, on the other hand, only experiences particular expressions of beauty (in nature or art, for instance). Necessarily, since man is fallen, man's experience of beauty is incomplete. Nevertheless, since man's experience of beauty is truly a part of universal beauty, God and man are tied together in a shared reality. The church is the mediator between God and man in this reality. This realist mentality logically gives credence to symbolic thought, since in it any particular entity refers to the universal of which it is a reflection. The nominalists, on the other hand, held that our only knowledge is of particulars and that we generalize from our knowledge of particulars to create a universal. After (*post rem*) we have seen enough particular examples of beauty, we form a general idea of beauty. The problem with this, from the point of view of a centralized church, is that God and man do not necessarily share the same reality and the church is not necessarily the only means by which a person can attain salvation. Huizinga's claim is that the nominalists still believe in universals, although for them they are created by human thought rather than existing *a priori*. Since universals exist, symbolic modes of thought have attraction and value for the nominalist as well as the realist. For an elegant explanation of these issues see Steven Ozment, *The Age of Reform 1250–1550.* New Haven: Yale University Press, 1980.

10. Goethe, Sprüche in Prosa, nos. 742, 743.

11. St. Bernard, Libellus ad quendam sacerdotem, in Dion. Cart., De vita et regimine curatorum, t. XXXVII, p. 222.

12. Bonaventura, De reductione artium ad theologiam, Opera, ed. Paris, 1871, t. VII, p. 502.

13. P. Rousselot, Pour l'historie de probleme de l'amour (Bäumker und von Hertling, Beitr zur Gesch. der Philosophie in Mittelalter, VI, 6), Münster 1908.

14. [Trans.] *Eindigende* (German *Ausgehenden*): The use of this term here and in similar places somewhat justifies the use of the title *Waning of the Middle Ages* in the previous translation of the work.

15. Sicard, Mitrale sive de officiis ecclesiasticis summa, Migne, t. CCXIII, c. 232.

16. Gerson, Compendium Theologiae, Opera, I, pp. 234, 303f., 325; Meditatio super septimo psalmo poenitentiali, IV, p. 26.

17. Alanus redivivus, passim.

18. On page 12 Fortitudo is equated with Abstinentia, however on page 201 it is Temperantia that falls into the place. There are still other variations.

19. Froissart, Poésies, ed. Scheler, I, p. 53.

20. Chastellain, Traité par forme d'allégorie mystique sur l'entrée du roy Loys en nouveau règne, Oeuvres, VII, p. 1; Molinet, II, p. 71, III, p. 112.

21. See Coquillart, Les droits nouveaux, ed. d'Héricault, I, p. 72.

22. Opera, I, p. xliv ff.

23. H. Usener, Götternamen, Versuch zu einer Lehre von der religïsen Begriffsbildung, Bonn 1896, p. 73.

24. J. Mangeart, Catalogue des mss. de la bibl. de Valenciennes, 1860, p. 687.

25. Journal d'un bourgeois, p. 96.

26. La Marche, II, p. 378.

27. Histoire littéraire de la France (XIVe siecle), t. XXIV, 1862, p. 541; Grôbers Grundriss, II, 1, p. 877, II, 2, p. 406; see les Cent nouvelles nouvelles, II, p. 183, Rabelais, Pantagruel, 1, IV, chap. 29.

28. H. Grotefend, Korrespondenzblatt des Gesamtvereins etc., 67, 1919, p. 124, Dock = doll.

29. De captivitate babylonica ecclesiae praeludium, Weimarer Ausgabe, VI, p. 562.

Chapter 10

1. Petri de Alliaco, Tractatus I, adversus cancellarium Parisiensem, in Gerson, Opera, I, p. 723.

2. Dion. Cart., Opera, t. XXXVI, p. 200.

3. Dion. Cart. Revelatio II, Opera, I, p. xiv.

4. Dion. Cart., Opera, t. XXXVII, XXXVIII, XXXIX, p. 496.

5. [Trans.] *Lamprecht:* Along with Burckhardt, whose great *Kultur der Renaissance in Italien* has important interactions with *Autumn,* Lamprecht was a significant figure in the development of historiography preceding Huizinga. For a full treatment of Burckhardt, Lamprecht, and others see Karl J. Weintraub, *Visions of Culture.* Chicago: The University of Chicago Press, 1969.

6. Alain Chartier, Oeuvres, p. xi.

7. Gerson, Opera, I, p. 17.

8. Dion. Cart., Opera, t. XVIII, p. 433.

9. Dion. Cart., Opera, XXXIX, p. 18 ff., De vitiis et virtutibus, p. 363; De gravitate et enormitate peccati, ibid., t. XXIX, p. 50.

10. Dion. Cart., Opera, XXXIX, p. 37.

11. Ibid. p. 56.

12. Dion Cart., De quatuor hominum novissimis, Opera, t. XLI, p. 545.

13. Dion. Cart., De quatuor hominum novissimis, t. XLI, pp. 489ff.

14. Moll, Brugman, I, pp. 20, 23, 28.

15. Moll, Brugman, I., p. 320[1].

16. The example of St. Aegidius, Germanus, Quiricus in Gerson, De via imitativa, III, p. 777; see Contra gulam sermo, ibid., p. 909.—Olivier Maillard, Serm. de sanctis fol. 8a.

17. [Trans.] *thesaurus ecclesiae.* the treasury of the church. The doctrine that Christ's sacrifice on the cross and the works of the saints are a source of merit (grace) from which all can draw. Here it is explained in a modern handbook:

The lives of the saints were immensely fruitful. By their constant attention to the interior voice of God, and by their obedience to His will and
to His Church, they became dear to Him; they knew that the best way to
serve Him lay in their service to others, and thus they offered their lives
as a supplication and a reparation for all those still laden with the burden
of the punishment due to their sins. Through their good works they grew
continuously in the love of God, but their expiation greatly exceeded that
which was required for their own shortcomings. Recognizing their desire
to share their spiritual wealth with others, the Church uses this overflow
of the merits of her saints—joined to the infinite merit of Christ Himself—as an offering to God by which the balance of reparation due to His
justice may be paid by their sacrificial love (N. G. M. Van Doornik, S.
Jelsma, and A. Van de Lisdonk, *A Handbook of the Catholic Faith,* ed. John
Greenwood, New York: Image Books, 1956, pp. 290–91).

18. Innocentius III, De contemptu mundi l. I, c. 1, Migne, t. CCXVII,
pp. 702ff.

19. Wetzer und Welte, Kirchenlexikon, XI, 1601, Freiburg im Breisgau,
Herder, 1882–1903.

20. Extravag. commun. lib. V, tit. IX, cap. 2—"Quanto plures ex eius appli-
catione trahuntur ad iustitiam, tanto magis accrescit ipsorum cumulus mer-
itorum."

21. Bonaventura, In secundum librum sententiarum, dist. 41, art. 1, qu. 2;
ibid. 30, 2, 1, 34; in quart. lib. sent. d. 34, a. 1, qu. 2, Breviloquii pars II, Opera,
ed. Paris, 1871, t. III, pp. 577a, 335, 438, VI, p. 327b, VII, p. 271ab.

22. Dion. Cart., De vitiis et virtutibus, Opera, t. XXXIX, p. 20.

23. McKechnie, William Sharp, Magna Carta, p. 401, Glasgow, J. Maclehose
and Sons, 1905.

24. From the hymn "Adore te devoto." The same thought is in the earlier
mentioned Bull Unigenitus. See Marlow, Faustus: "See, where Christ's blood
streams in the firmament! One drop of blood will save me."

25. Dion. Cart., Dialogion de fide cath., Opera, t. XVIII, p. 366.

26. Dion. Cart., Dialogion de fide cath., t. XLI, p. 489.

27. Dion. Cart., De laudibus sanctae et individuae trinitatis, t. XXXV, p. 137;
de laud glor. Virg. Mariae and passim. He borrowed the use of the super-terms
from Dionysius Areopagita.

28. James, Varieties of religious experience, p. 419.

29. Joannis Scoti, De divisione naturae, i. III c. 19, Migne, Patr. latina, t.
CXXII, p. 681.

30. Angelus Silesius, Cherubinischer Wandersmann, I, 25, Halle a. S., M.
Niemeyer, 1895.

31. Opera, I, p. xliv.

32. Seuse, Leben, cap. 3, ed. K. Bihlmeyer, Deutsche Schriften, Stuttgard
1907, p. 14. See cap. 5, p. 21, l. 3 and below.

33. Meister Eckhart, Predigten, nos. 60 and 76, ed. F. Pfeiffer, Deutsche Mystiker des XIV. Jahrh., Leipzig 1857, II, p. 193, ll. 34ff.; p. 242, ll. 2ff.

34. Tauler, Predigten, no. 28, ed. F. Vettor Deutsche Texte des Mittelalters, XI), Berlin 1910, p. 117, ll. 30ff.

35. Ruusbroec, Dat boec van seven sloten, cap. 19, Werken, ed. David, IV, pp. 106–8.

36. Ruusbroec, Dat boec van den rike de ghelieven, cap. 43, ed. David, IV, p. 264.

37. Ibid., cap. 35, p. 246.

38. Ruusbroec, Van seven trappen in den graet der gheesteliker minnen, cap. 14, ed. David, IV, p. 53. For *ontfonken* I read *ontsonken*.

39. Ruusbroec, Boec vna der hoechster waerheit, ed. David, p. 263; see Spieghel der ewigher salicheit, cap. 25, p. 231.

40. Spieghel der ewigher salicheit, cap. 19, p. 144, cap. 23, p. 227.

41. II, Par. 6, 1: Dominus pollicitus est, ut habitaret in caligine. Ps 17, 13: Et posuit tenebras latibulum suum. [Trans. Huizinga's references are to the Vulgate (Latin) Bible. In English Bibles this would be II Chronicles 6:1: The Lord has said that he would dwell in thick darkness. Psalm 18:11: He made darkness his secret place.]

42. Dion. Cart., De laudibus sanctae et individuae trinijtatis per modum horarum, Opera, t. XXXV, pp. 137–38, id. XLI, p. 263 etc.; see De passione dni salvatoris dialogus, t. XXXV, p. 274: "ingrediendo caliginem hoc est ad supersplendidissimae ac prorsus incomprehensibilis Deitatis praefatam notitiam pertingendo per omnem negationem ab ea."

43. Jostes, Meister Eckhart und seine Jünger, 1895, p. 95.

44. Dion. Cart., De contemplatione, lib. III, art. 5, Opera, t. XLI, p. 259.

45. Dion. Cart., De contemplatione, t. XLI, p. 269, after Dion. Areop.

46. Cankara ad Brahmasûtram, 3, 2, 17.

47. Chandogya-upanishad, 8.

48. Brhadâranyaka-upanishad, 4, 3, 21, 22.

49. Seuse, Leben, cap. 4, p. 14.

50. Eckhart, Predigten, no. 40, p. 136, par. 23.

51. Eckhart, Predigten, no. 9, pp. 47ff.

52. Thomas à Kempis, Soliloquium animae, Opera omnia, ed. M. J. Pohl, Freiburg 1902–10, 7 vols., I, p. 230.

53. Thomas à Kempis, Soliloquium animae, p. 222.

Chapter 11

1. Alienor de Poitiers, Les honneurs de la cour, pp. 184, 189, 242, 266.

2. Olivier de la Marche, L'estat de la maison etc., t. IV, p. 56; see similar questions above, p. 44.

3. J. H. Round, The king's serjeants and officers of state with their coronation services, London 1911, p. 41.

4. [Trans.] For instance, the cell of Maximillian in Bruges was called the "Broodhuis." See p. 299.

5. Le livre des trahisons, p. 27

6. Rel. de S. Denis, III, p. 464ff.; Juvenal des Ursins, p. 440; Noël Valois, La France et le grand schisme d'occident, Paris, 1896–1902, 4 vols., III, p. 433.

7. Juvenal des Ursins, p. 342.

8. [Trans.] *Athalia:* A Jewish figure who slew all the male heirs to the throne so that she might gain the sucession. II Kings 22–23.

9. [Trans.] *bal des ardents:* At a masquerade ball given by the queen (Isabella of Bavaria) to celebrate the wedding of one of her ladies, Charles VI (thirteen years old!) and a group of his playmates dressed themselves as "wood savages" in costumes made of wax and hemp. Knowing that these costumes were dangerously flammable, the king gave orders that no flames were to be allowed in the ballroom, but Louis d'Orléans entered with his retinue carrying torches. Louis himself held the torch that set the revelers aflame. The king was saved by the duchess de Berry (herself only fifteen), who put out his fire with her dress. All save one of the king's companions died. See Tuchmann, *Mirror.*

10. [Trans.] Charles VI was a victim of frequent spells of insanity, during which he relentlessly persecuted the queen.

11. Monstrelet, I, pp. 177–42; Coville, Le véritable texte de la justification du duc de Bourgogne par Jean Petit (Bibl. de l'Ecole de chartes), 1911, p. 57. For a draft of a second justification in which Petit refutes the testimony that Abbot Thomas von Cerisi had given on Sept 11, 1408; see O. Cartellieri, Beiträge zur Geschichte der Herzöge von Burgund, V, Sitzungsbericht der Heidelberger Akademie der Wissenschaften 1914, p. 6; further Wolfgang Seiferth, Der Tyrannenmord von 1407, Leipziger Inaugural-Dissertation, 1922.

12. Leroux de Lincy, Le proverbe français, see E. E. Langois (Bibl. de l'Ecole des chartes), LX, 1899, p. 569; J. Ulrich, Zeitschr. f. franz Sprache u. Lit. XXIV, 1902, p. 191.

13. Les Grandes chroniques de France, ed. P. Paris, IV, p. 478.

14. Alain Chartier, ed. Duchesne, p. 717.

15. Jean Molinet, Faictz et Dictz, ed. Paris, 1537, fos. 80, 119, 152, 161, 170.

16. Coquillart, Oeuvres, I, p. 6.

17. Villon, ed. Longnon, p. 134.

18. Roberti Gaguini, Epistole et orationes., ed. Thuasne, II, p. 366.

19. Gerson, Opera, IV, p. 657; ibid. I, p. 936; Carnahan, The Ad Deum vadit of Jean Gerson, pp. 61, 71; see Leroux de Lincy, Le proverbe français, I, p. lii.

20. Geoffroi de Paris, ed. de Wailly et Delisle, Bouquet, Recueil des Historiens des Gaules et de la France, XXII, p. 87, see index rerum et personarum s.v. Proverbia, p. 926.

21. Froissart, ed. Luce, XI, p. 119; ed. Kervyn, XIII, p. 41, XIV, p. 33, XV, p. 10; Le Jouvencel, I, p. 60, 62, 63, 74, 78, 93.

22. "Je l'envie" is a play on words with the meaning, I command you here, I invite. "Ic houd" is the answer thereto: I accept. "Cominus et eminus" is an allusion to the belief that the porcupine could also shoot its quills.

23. See my "Uit de voorgeschiedenis van ons nationaal besef," De Gids, 1912, I.

24. See above, p. 143.

25. A. Piaget, Le livre Messire Geoffroy de Charny, Romania XXVI, 1897, p. 396.

26. L'arbre des batailles, Paris, Michel le Noir 1515. See for Bonet, Molinier, Sources de l'histoire de France, no. 3861.

27. Chap. 25, p. 85 bis (numbers 80–90 appear in the edition of 1515 twice), pp. 124–26.

28. Chaps. 56, 60, 84, 132.

29. Chaps. 82, 89, 80 bis and ff.

30. Le Jouvencel, I, p. 222, II, p. 8, 93, 96, 133, 124.

31. Les vers de maitre Henri Baude, poete du XVe siecle, ed. Quicherat (Trésor des pieces rares ou inédites), 1856, pp. 20–25.

32. Champion, Villon, II, p. 182.

33. Still stronger is the formalism of South American tribes who demand that anyone who accidentally wounds himself must pay his clan blood money because he has spilled the blood of the clan. L. Farrand, Basis of American history, p. 198 (The American nation, A history, vol. II).

34. La Marche, II, p. 80.

35. La Marche, II, p. 168.

36. Chastellain, IV, p. 169.

37. Chron. scand., II, p. 83.

38. Petit-Dutaillis, Documents nouveaux sur les moeurs populaires etc.; see Chastellain, V, p. 399 in Jacques du Clercq, passim.

39. Du Clercq, IV, p. 264; see III, pp. 180, 184, 206, 209.

40. Monstrelet, I, p. 342, V, p. 333; Chastellain, II, p. 389; La Marche, II, pp. 284, 331; Le livre des trahisons, pp. 34, 226.

41. Quicherat, Th. Basin, I, p. xliv.

42. Chastellain, III, p. 106.

43. Sermo de nativ. domini, Gerson, Opera, III, p. 947.

44. Le pastoralet, vs. 2043.

45. Jean Jouffroy, Oratio, I, p. 188.

46. La Marche, I, p. 63.

47. Gerson, Querela nomine Universitatis etc., Opera, IV, p. 574; see Rel. de S. Denis, III, p. 185.

48. Chastellain, II, p. 375, see 307.

49. Commines, I, p. 111, 363.

50. Monstrelet, IV, p. 388.

51. Basin, I, p. 66.

52. La Marche, I pp. 60, 63, 83, 88, 91, 94, 134[1]; III p. 101.

53. Commines, I, pp. 170, 262, 391, 413, 460.

54. Basin, II, pp. 417, 419; Molinet, Faictz et Dictz f. 205. In the third line I read sa for la.

55. Deschamps, Oeuvres, t. IX.

56. Deschamps, Oeuvres, t. IX, pp. 219ff.

57. Deschamps, Oeuvres, t. IX, pp. 293ff.

58. See Marett, The threshold of religion, passim.

59. Monstrelet, IV, p. 93; Livre des trahisons, p. 157; Molinet, II, p. 129; see du Clercq, IV, pp. 203, 273; Th. Pauli, p. 278.

60. Molinet, I, p. 65.

61. Molinet, IV, p. 417; Courtaulx is a musical instrument, Mornifle is a card game.

62. Gerson, Opera, I, p. 205.

63. Le songe du vieil pelerin, in Jorga, Phil. de Mézières, p. 69[1].

64. Juvenal des Ursins, p. 425.

65. Juvenal des Ursins, p. 415.

66. Gerson, Opera, I, p. 206.

67. Gerson, Sermo coram rege Franciae, Opera, IV, p. 620; Juvenal des Ursins, pp. 415, 423.

68. Gerson, Opera, I, p. 216.

69. Chastellain, IV, pp. 324, 323, 314[1]; see du Clercq, III, p. 236.

70. Chastellain, II, p. 376; III, pp. 446, 447[1], 448; IV p. 213; V, p. 32.

71. Monstrelet, V, p. 425. [Trans.] Gilles de Rais: See above, chap. 3, note 10.

72. [Trans.] Malleus Maleficarum: See above, chapter 8, note 59.

73. Chronique de Pierre le Prêtre, in Bourquelot, La vauderie d'Arras (Bibl. de l'Ecole des chartes), 2 série, III, p. 109.

74. Jacques du Clercq, III, passim; Matthieu d'Escouchy, II, pp. 416ff.

75. Martin lefranc, Le champion des dames, in Bourquelot, La vauderie d'Arras, p. 86; in Ro. Gaguini, ed. Thuasne, II, p. 474.

76. Froissart, ed. Kervyn, XI, p. 193.

77. Gerson, Contra superstitionem praesertim Innocentum, Op. I, p. 205; De erroribus circa artem magicam, I, p. 211; De falsis prophetis I, p. 545; De passionibus animae, III, p. 142.

78. Journal d'un bourgeois, p. 236.

79. Journal d'un bourgeois, p. 220.

80. Dion. Cart., Contra vitia superstitionum quibus circa cultum veri Dei erratur, Opera, t. XXXVI, pp. 211ff.; see A. Franz, Die kirchlichen Benediktionen im Mittelalter, Freiburg 1909, 2 vols.

81. For example, Jacques du Clercq, III, pp. 104–7.

Chapter 12

1. The major parts of chapters 12 and 13 are a restructuring and expansion of the essay: De Kunst der Van Eyck's in het leven van hun tijd, De Gids, 1916, nos. 6 and 7.

2. [Trans.] Hugo's Notre Dame de Paris is best known to most Americans as The Hunchback of Notre Dame.

3. Rel. de S. Denis, II, p. 78.

4. Rel. de S. Denis, II, p. 413.

5. Rel. de S. Denis, I, p. 358.

6. Rel. de S. Denis, I, p. 600; Juvenal des Ursins, p. 379.

7. La Curne de Sainte Palaye, I, p. 388; see also Journal d'un bourgeois, p. 67.

8. Journal d'un bourgeois, p. 179 (Charles VI); 309 (Isabella of Barvaria); Chastellain, IV, p. 42 (Charles VII), I, p. 332 (Henry V); Lefèvre de S. Remy, II, p. 65; M. d'Escouchy, II, pp. 424, 432; Chron. scand., I, p. 21; Jean Chartier, p. 319 (Charles VII); Quatrebarbes, Oeuvres du roi René, I, p. 129; Gaguini compendium super Francorum gestis, ed. Paris, 1500, burial of Charles VIII, f. 164.

9. Martial d'Auvergne, Vigilles de Charles VII. Les poésies de Martial de Paris, dit d'Auvergne, Paris, 1724, 2 vols., II, p. 170.

10. For example Froissart, ed. Luce, VIII, p. 43.

11. Froissart, ed. Kervyn, XI, p. 367. A variant of the text has "proviseurs" for "peintres." The context makes the latter more probable.

12. [Trans.] *Plourants: pleurants,* mourners.

13. Betty Kurth, Die Blütezeit der Bildwirkerkunst zu Tournay und der Burgundische Hof, Jahrbuch der Kunstsammlungen des Kaiserhauses, 34, 1917, 3.

14. [Trans.] *Nicopolis:* September 25, 1396, a combined European force putatively led by John of Nevers (later John the Fearless, duke of Burgundy) met the Turkish forces of Sultan Bajazet. The Europeans fought bravely, but the disarray caused by their quarrels over precedence in the order of battle combined with the genius of Bajazet to give the battle to the Turks. Hundreds of knights were captured, stripped naked, and executed one by one in full view of their fellows. Only the most prominent were spared to be held for ransom. John of Nevers personally pled with Bajazet for the life of Boucicaut, who was allowed to live once it was understood that he, too, was wealthy. See Tuchmann, *Mirror.*

15. Pierre de Fenin, p. 624 of Bonne d'Artois: "et avec ce ne portoit point d'estate sur son chief comment autres dames à elle pareilles."[Trans.: "furthermore, she did not have a formal hairdo like other ladies who were of royal standing."]

16. Le livre des trahisons, p. 156.

17. Chastellain, III, p. 375; La Marche, II p. 340, III p. 165; d'Escouchy, II, p. 116; Laborde, II; see Moliner, Les sources de l'hist. de France, nos. 3645, 3661, 3663, 5030; Inv. des arch. du Nord, IV, p. 195.

18. La Marche, II, pp. 340ff.

19. This is a type of merchant ship; the low German form is *Kracke.*

20. Laborde, II, p. 326.

21. La Marche, III, p. 197.

22. Laborde, II, p. 375, no. 4880.

23. Laborde, II, pp. 322, 329.

24. Although on the primary references, the master's seal says "Claus Sluter," one can hardly think that the non-Dutch Claus could have been the original form of his Christian name.

25. A. Kleinclausz, Un atelier de sculpture au XVe siecle, Gazette des beaux arts, t. 29, 1903, I.

26. Exod. 12:6: "The whole assembly of the congregation of Israel shall kill it in the evening." Ps. 21:18: "They pierced my hands and my feet. I may tell all my bones." Isaiah 53:7: "He is brought as a lamb to the slaughter, and as a sheep before her shearers is dumb, so he openeth not his mouth." Lamentations 1:12: "All ye who pass by, behold and see if there is any sorrow like unto my sorrow." Daniel 9:26: "After threescore and two weeks shall Messiah be cut off." Zechariah 11:12: "They weighed for my price 30 pieces of silver."

27. The now vanished colors are known through a report composed in 1832.

28. Kleinclausz, L'art funéraire de la Bourgogne au moyen âge, Gazette des beaux arts, 1902, t. 27.

29. Chastellain, V, p. 26^2, Doutrepont, p. 156.

30. [Trans.] *The stag with the crown:* This emblem was of special significance to Charles VI, who, when he was told that such a stag had been taken, wearing

a crown around its neck inscribed *Caesar hoc mihi donavit,* ordered the emblem placed on the royal crockery. See Tuchmann, *Mirror.*

31. Juvenal des Ursins, p. 378.

32. Jacques du Clercq, II, p. 280.

33. Foulquart, in d'Hericault, Oeuvres de Coquillart, I, p. 23[1].

34. Lefèvre de S. Remy, II, p. 291.

35. London, National Gallery; Berlin, Kaiser-Friedrich-Museum.

36. W. H. J. Weale, Hubert and John van Eyck, Their life and work, London–New York, 1908, p. 70[1].

37. Froissart, ed. Kervyn, XI, p. 197.

38. P. Durrieu, Les très riches heures de Jean de France, duc de Bery (Heures de Chantilly), Paris, 1904, p. 81.

39. Moll, Kerkgesch. II[3], p. 313; see J. G. R. Acquoy, Het klooster van Windesheim en zijn invloed, Utrecht, 1875–90, 3 vols., II, p. 249.

40. Th. à Kempis, Sermones ad novitios no. 29, Opera, ed. Pohl, t. VI, p. 287.

41. Moll, Kerkgesch. II[2], p. 321; Acquoy, Het klooster van Windesheim . . ., p. 222.

42. Chastellain, IV, p. 218.

43. La Marche, II, p. 398.

44. La Marche, II, 369.

45. Chastellain, IV pp. 136, 275, 359, 361, V p. 225; du Clercq, IV, p. 7.

46. Chastellain, III, p. 332; du Clercq, III, p. 56.

47. Chastellain, V p. 44, II p. 281; La Marche, II, p. 85; du Clercq, III, p. 56.

48. Chastellain, III, p. 330.

49. du Clercq, III, p. 203.

50. See p. 206.

51. Bonaventura's editor in Quaracchi ascribes them to Johannes de Caulibus, a Frenchman of San Gimignano who died in 1370.

52. Facius, Liber de viris illustribus, ed. L. Mehus, Florenz 1745, p. 46.

53. Dion. Cart., Opera, t. XXXIV, p. 223.

54. Dion. Cart., Opera, t. XXXIV, pp. 247, 230.

55. O. Zöckler, Dionys des Kartäusers Schrift de venustate mundi, Beitrag zur Vorgeschichte der Ästhetik, Theol. Studien und Kritiken, 1881, p. 651; see E. Anitchkoff, L'esthétique au moyen âge XX, 1918, p. 221.

56. Summa theologiae, pars. 1a, q. XXXIX, art. 8.

57. Dion. Cart., Opera, t. I, Vita, p. xxxvi.

58. Dion. Cart., De vita canonicorum, art. 20, Opera, t. XXXVII, p. 197: An discantus in divino obsequio sit commendabilis; see Thomas Aquinas, Summa theologiae, IIa, IIae, q. 91, art. 2: Utrum cantus sint assumendi ad laudem divinam.

59. [Trans.] *Text painting:* The effort to make the music mirror the meaning of the words so that, for instance, in a mass, the word *ascendit* would be accompanied by a rising melodic line, *descendit,* the opposite. "Suffered, crucified and was buried" would be set in an agitated texture. This is the musical equivalent of symbolism and allegory.

60. Molinet, I, p. 73; see p. 67.

61. Petri Alliaci, De falsis prophetis, in Gerson, Opera, I, p. 538.

62. La Marche, II, p. 361.

63. De venustate etc., t. XXXIV, p. 242.

64. Froissart, ed. Luce, IV p. 90, VIII p. 43, 58, XI pp. 53, 129; ed. Kervyn, XI pp. 340, 360, XIII p. 150, XIV pp. 157, 215.

65. Deschamps, I p. 155; II p. 211, II, no. 307, p. 208; La Marche, I, p. 274.

66. Livre des trahisons, pp. 150, 156; La Marche, II pp. 12, 347, III pp. 127, 89; Chastellain, IV, p. 44; Chron. scand., I, pp. 26, 126.

67. Lefèvre de S. Remy, II, pp. 294, 296.

68. Couderc, Les comptes d'un grand couturier parisien au XVe siecle, Bulletin de la soc. de l'hist. de Paris, XXXVIII, 1911, pp. 125ff.

69. For example Monstrelet, V, p. 2; du Clercq, I, p. 348.

70. [Trans.] *Palfrey:* a knight generally had to have at least two horses; the warhorse was a stallion and the palfrey a less high-spirited animal suited for general purposes. Some palfreys were especially trained to be suitable for women and priests.

71. La Marche, II, p. 343.

72. Chastellain, VII, p. 223; La Marche, I p. 276, II pp. 11, 68, 345; du Clercq, II, p. 197; Jean Germain, Liber de virtutibus, p. 11; Jouffroy, Oratio, p. 173.

73. d'Escouchy, I, p. 234.

74. See p. 142.

75. Le miroir de mariage, XVII vs. 1650, Deschamps, Oeuvres, IX, p. 57.

76. Chansons françaises du quinzième siècle, ed. G. Paris (Soc. des anciens textes français), 1875, no. XLX, p. 50; see Deschamps, no. 415, III, p. 217, no. 419, ib. p. 223, no. 423, ib. p. 227, no. 481, ib. p. 302, no. 728, IV, p. 199; L'amant rendu cordelier, sect. 62, p. 23; Molinet, Faictz et Dictz, fol. 176.

77. Blason des couleurs of the herald Sicile (in La Curne de Sainte Palaye, Mémoires sur l'ancienne chevalerie II, p. 56). Concerning color symbolism in Italy, see Bertoni, L'Orlando furioso, pp. 221ff.

78. Cent balades d'amant et de dame, no. 92, Christine d'Pisan, Oeuvres poétiques, III, p. 299. See Deschamps, X, no. 52; L'histoire et plaisante chronicque du petit Jehan de Saintré, ed. G. Hellény, Paris, 1890, p. 415.

79. [Trans.} *Huik:* a hooded cloak. In Holland, the saying has it that one "hangs one's huik out to test the wind."

80. Le pastoralet, vs. 2054, p. 636; see Les cent nouvelles, II, p. 118: "craindroit tres fort estre du rang des bleuz vestuz qu'on appelle communement noz amis."

81. [Trans.] *The blue boat:* As in the painting by Bosch in the Louvre.

82. Chansons du XVe siecle, no. 5, p. 5; no. 87, p. 85.

83. La Marche, II, p. 207.

Chapter 13

1. Concerning this problem see my Renaissancestudiën I: Het probleem, de Gids, 1920, IV.

2. La Renaissance septentrionale et les premiers maîtres des Flandres, Bruxelles 1905.

3. Erasmus, Ratio seu Methodus compendio perveniendi ad veram theologiam, ed. Basel 1520, p. 146.

4. E. Durand-Gréville, Hubert et Jean van Eyck, Bruxelles, 1910, p. 119.

5. [Trans.] In the English translation done by F. Hopman under Huizinga's supervision this paragraph is replaced by the following:

> Are not unity and harmony lost in this aggregation of details as Michelangelo affirmed of Flemish art in general? Having recently seen the picture again, I can no longer deny it as I formerly did on the strength of recollections many years old.

If this reflects a true change of position on the issue on the part of Huizinga, it is strange that the alteration did not make it into any subsequent Dutch editions.

6. [Trans.] *Unbridled elaboration:* The Dutch is *ongebreidelde uitwerking;* German, *zügellose Detaillierung.*

7. P. 251.

8. Alain Chartier, Oeuvres, ed. Duchesne, p. 594.

9. Chastellain, I pp. 11, 12, IV pp. 21, 393, VII pp. 160; La Marche, I, p. 14; Molinet, I, p. 23.

10. [Trans.] *cothurnism:* see chap. 2, n. 65

11. Jean Robertet, in Chastellain, VII, p. 182.

12. Chastellain, VII, p. 219.

13. Chastellain, III, pp. 231ff. —Saint Anthony's day is January 17.

14. Oratory, a carpeted and secluded little corner of a chapel.

15. [Trans.] *prie-Dieu:* Dutch *bidstoel;* German, *Betstuhl.* Literally, "prayer stool." The piece of furniture is most likely similar to that on which the donor kneels in the *Madonna of Chancellor Rolin.*

16. [Trans.] *Camille Lemonnier.* A Belgian novelist who was active during the last decade of the nineteenth century. In his memoirs, Huizinga says he was strongly influenced by modern literary movements. See his *My Path of History,* page 253, where he says:

> [S]oon after we enrolled ten of us from the class of 1891 formed a club. . . . We were all enthusiastic supporters of the *Tachtigers,* a literary movement round the journal *De Nieuwe Gids* (1885), and consequently rated literature far higher than science, sought the meaning of life within our selves (which was a great blessing) and completely ignored politics and allied topics (which was a grave fault). Throughout my student years I never took a newspaper. We looked up to Van Deijssel, Kloos, Gorter *et al.* as to so many demigods. In the comfortable reading room of *Mutua Fides,* we not only followed the Kloos crisis in *De Nieuwe Gids* month by month, and dutifully denounced Van Eeden, but also devoured the *Mercure de France,* watched Pierre Louys's star rise by side of Rémy de Gourmont's, and finally hailed Alfred Jarry's *succès de scandal*—in short, we took a most one-sided view of what was happening in literature, even though Edgar Allan Poe, Robert Louis Stevenson, Dante Gabriel Rossetti and many other authors made a great impression on us as well. In later years our enthusiasm for the *Tachtigers* was jolted by the appearance of P. L. Tak's *De Kroniek,* in which our own contemporaries, among them Jan Kalf and the talented and precocious André Jolles, put forward their views. *At the time, literary ideas had begun to have a profound effect on me.* [Emphasis added.]

17. Chastellain, III, p. 46; see above p. 109; and see Chastellain, III p. 104, V p. 259.

18. Chastellain, V, pp. 273, 269, 271.

19. See the reproduction in E. Chmelarz, Jahrb. der Kunsthist. Samml. des allerh. Kaiserhauses XI, 1890; and P. Durrieu, Les belles heures du duc de Berry, Gazette des beaux arts, 1906, t. 35, p. 283.

20. Froissart, ed. Kervyn, XIII, p. 50, XI, p. 99, XIII, p. 4.

21. Unknown poet printed in Deschamps, Oeuvres, X, no. 18; see Le Débat du cuer et du corps de Villon, and Charles d'Orléans, rondel 192.

22. Ed. de 1522, fol. 101, in A. de la Borderie, Jean Meschinot etc., Bibl. de l'Ecole des chartes LVI, 1895, p. 301. See die ballads von Henri Baude, ed. Quicherat (Trésor des pieces rares ou inédites), Paris, pp. 26, 37, 55, 79.

23. Froissart, ed. Luce, I pp. 56, 66, 71, XI p. 13, ed. Kervyn, XII pp. 2, 23; see also Deschamps, III, p. 42.

24. Froissart, ed. Kervyn, XI, p. 89.

25. Durrieu, Les très-riches heures de Jean de France duc de Berry, 1904, pl. 38.

26. Oeuvres du roi René, ed. Quatrebarbes, II, p. 105.

27. Deschamps, I, nos. 61, 144; III, nos. 454, 483, 524; IV, nos. 617, 636.

28. Durrieu, Les très-riches heures de Jean de France duc de Berry, pls. 3, 9, 12.

29. Deschamps, VI, p. 191, no. 1204.

30. Froissart, ed. Luce, V p. 64, VIII pp. 5, 48, XI p. 110; ed. Kervyn, XIII pp. 14, 21, 84, 102, 264.

31. Froissart, ed. Kervyn, XV pp. 54, 109, 184; XVI pp. 23, 52; ed. Luce, I p. 394.

32. Froissart, XIII, p. 13.

33. G. de Machaut, Poésies lyriques, ed. V. Chichmaref (Zapiski ist. fil. fakulteta imp. S. Peterb. universiteta XCII, 1909) no. 60, I, p. 74.

34. La Borderie, Jean Meschinot etc., p. 618.

35. Christine de Pisan, Oeuvres poétiques, I, p. 276.

36. Ibid., I, p. 164, no. 30.

37. Ibid., I, p. 275, no. 5.

38. Froissart, Poésies, ed. Schéler, II, p. 216.

39. P. Michault, La dance aux aveugles etc., Lille, 1748.

40. Recueil de poésies françoises des XVe et XVIe siècles, ed. de Montaiglon (Bibl. elzavirienne), IX, p. 59.

41. Deschamps, VI, no. 1202, p. 188.

42. Froissart, Poésies, I, p. 91.

43. Froissart, ed. Kervyn, XIII, p. 22.

44. Deschamps, I, p. 196, no. 90; p. 192, no. 87; IV, p. 294, no. 788; V, p. 94 no. 903, p. 97 no. 905, p. 121 no. 919; VII, p. 220, no. 1375. See II, p. 86, no. 247, no. 250.

45. Durrieu, Les très-riches heures, pls. 38, 39, 60, 27, 28.

46. Deschamps, V, p. 351, no. 1060; V, p. 15, no. 844.

47. Chastellain, III, pp. 256ff.

48. Journal d'un bourgeois, p. 325[2].

49. Deschamps, nos. 1229, 1230, 1233, 1259, 1299, 1300, 1477, VI pp. 230, 232, 237, 279, VII pp. 52, 54, VIII p. 182; see Gaguin's De validorum mendicantium astucia, Thuasne, II, pp. 169ff.

50. Deschamps, no. 219, II, p. 44, no. 2, p. 71.

51. Ibid. IV, p. 291, no. 786.

52. Bibliothèque de l'école des chartes, 2ᵉ série III 1846, p. 70.

53. Proverbs 14:13.

54. [Trans.] The Hopman translation includes two fragments from Granson at this point

> Veillier ou lit et jeuner à table
> Rire plourant et en plaignant chanter.
> [Lying abed awake and fasting at the board, laughing in tears and lamenting in song.]

And:

> Je prins congiè de ce tresdoulz enfant
> Les yeulx mouilliez et la bouche riant.
> [I took leave of this most sweet child With tearful eyes and a laughing mouth.]

55. Alain Chartier, La belle dame dans mercy, pp. 503, 505,; see Le débat du reveille-matin, p. 498; Chansons du XVᵉ siècle, p. 71, no. 73; L'amant rendu cordelier à l'observance d'amours, vs. 371; Molinet, Faictz et dictz, ed. 1537, 172f.

56. Alain Chartier, Le débat des deux fortunes d'amours, p. 581.

57. Oeuvres du roi René, ed. Quatrebarbes, III, p. 194.

58. Charles d'Orléans, Poésies complètes, p. 68.

59. Charles d'Orléans, Poésies complètes, p. 88, ballade no. 19.

60. Charles d'Orléans, Poésies complètes, chanson no. 62.

61. [Trans.] Pierrot: The use of this image here is perhaps an indication of Huizinga's awareness of modern art and literature. Pierrot, the clown figure from French pantomime, figures prominently in early twentieth-century art, noticeably the paintings of Picasso and in the setting of the Pierrot Lunaire ("Moonstruck Pierrot") poems of Albert Giraud (whose work Huizinga would have known) by Arnold Schönberg in 1912. In these poems Pierrot is touchingly crushed by love.

62. Compare Alain Chartier, p. 549: "Ou se le vent une fenestre boute/Dont il cuide que sa dame l'escoute/S'en va coucher joyeulx . . ."

63. Huitains 51, 53, 57, 167, 188, 192, ed. de Montaiglon (Soc. des anc. textes français), 1881.

64. Museum of Leipzig, no. 509.

65. Journal d'un bourgeois, p. 96. Prof. D. C. Hesseling has brought to my attention that, in addition to modesty, another image is in play here; Namely, that the dead may not appear without a shroud at the last judgment, and he refers me to a Greek text of the seventh century (Johannes Moschus c. 78, Migne Patrol. graecam t. LXXXVII, p. 2933 D.), which might be a parallel to Western conceptions. On the other hand, one should not forget that in the depictions of the resurrection of the dead in miniatures and in paintings, the dead always come from the grave naked.

66. [Trans.] Bastard of Vauru: In the winter of 1421–22, the city of Meaux was

besieged by Henry V. The Bastard of Vauru was one of the city garrison who exploited the populace, demanding ransoms and hanging those who could not pay on "Vauru's tree." The woman in question was pregnant (according to the Burgher of Paris) and hung and left to die from this tree. "That cruel and evil monster, the Bastard de Vauru, hearing her saying things that annoyed him, had her beaten with sticks and then dragged off at a great rate to his elm. He had her tied to it and bound and all of her clothes cut off short so that she was naked as far as her navel, an inhuman thing to do!" *A Parisian Journal 1405–1449,* trans. Janet Shirley, Oxford: Clarendon Press, 1968.

67. Juvenal des Ursins, 1418, p. 541; Journal d'un bourgeois, pp. 92, 172.

68. J. Veth and S. Muller, A. Dürers Niederläandische Reise, Berlin-Utrecht, 1918, 2 Bde., I, p. 13.

69. Chastellain, III, p. 414.

70. Chron. scand., I, p. 27.

71. Molinet, V, p. 15.

72. Lefebvre, Theatre de Lille, p. 54, in Doutrepont, p. 354.

73. Th. Godefroy, Le ceremonial françois, 1649, p. 617.

74. J. B. Houwaert, Declaratie van die triumphante Incompst van den . . . Prince van Oraingnien etc.; t'Antwerpen, Plantijn, 1579, p. 39.

75. The thesis of Emile Mâle concerning the influence of theatrical representations on paintings may be left standing in this instance.

76. See P. Durrieu, Gazette des beaux arts, 1906, t. 35, p. 275.

77. Christine de Pisan, Epitre d'Othéa à Hector, Ms. 9392 de Jean Miélot, ed. J. van den Gheyn, Bruxelles 1913.

78. Ibid., Pls. 5, 8, 26, 24, 25.

79. Christine de Pisan, Epitre d'Othéa, pls. 1 and 3; Michel, Histoire de l'art, IV, 2, p. 603: Michel Colombe, Grabmonument aus der Kathedrale von Nantes, p. 616: figure of Temperantia on the grave monument of the Cardinal of Amboise in the Rouen Cathedral.

80. See my essay Uit de voorgeschiedenis van ons nationaal besef, De Gids, 1912, I.

81. Expositions sur vérité mal prise, Chastellain, VI, p. 249.

82. Le livre de paix, Castellain, VII, p. 375.

83. Advertissement au duc Charles, Chastellain, VII, pp. 304ff.

84. Chastellain, VII, pp. 237ff.

85. Molinet, Le miroir de la mort, fragment in Chastellain, VI, p. 460.

86. Chastellain, VII, p. 419.

87. Deschamps, I, p. 170.

88. Le pastoralet, vs. 501, 7240, 5768.

89. Compare for the mixture of pastoral and politics, Deschamps, III, p. 62, no. 344, p. 93, no. 359.

90. Molinet, Faictz et dictz, f. 1.

91. Molinet, Chronique, IV, p. 307.

92. In E. Langlois, Le roman de la rose (Soc. des anc. textes), 1914, I, p. 33.

93. Recueil de chansons etc. (Soc. des bibliophiles belges), III, p. 31.

94. La Borderie, Jean Meschinot etc., pp. 603, 632.

Chapter 14

1. Alma Le Duc, Gontier Col and the French Prerenaissance, 1919, was not available to me.

2. N. de Clémanges, Opera, ed. Lydius, Lugd. Bat., 1613; Joh. de Monasteriolo, Epistolae, Martene et Durand, Amplissima Collectio, II, col. 1310.

3. Montreuil, Epistolae 69, c. 1447, ep. 15, c. 1338.

4. Epistolae 59, c. 1426, ep. 58, c. 1423.

5. Epistolae 40, cols. 1388, 1396.

6. Epistolae 59, 67, cols. 1427, 1435.

7. Le livre du voir-dit, p. xviii.

8. See p. 76.

9. See p. 226.

10. Gerson, Opera, I, p. 922.

11. Epistolae 38, col. 1385.

12. Dion. Cart., t. XXXVII, p. 495.

13. Petrarca, Opera, ed. Basel, 1581, p. 847; Clémanges, Opera, Ep. 5, p. 24; J. de Montr., Ep. 50, col. 1428.

14. Chastellain, VII, pp. 75–143, see V, pp. 38–40, VI, p. 80; VIII, p. 358, Le livre des trahisons, p. 145.

15. Machaut, Le voir-dit, p. 230; Chastellain, VI, p. 194; La Marche, III, p. 166; Le pastoralet vs. 2806; Le Jouvencel, I, p. 16.

16. Le pastoralet, vs. 541, 4612.

17. Chastellain, III, pp. 173, 117, 359 etc.; Molinet, II, p. 207.

18. J. Germain, Liber de virtutibus Philippe ducis Burgundiae (Chron. rel. à l'hist. de Belg. sous la dom. des ducs de Bourg. III).

19. Chron. scand., II, p. 42.

20. Christine de Pisan, Oeuvres poétiques, I, no. 90, p. 90.

21. Deschamps, no. 285, II, p. 138.

22. Villon, ed. Lognon, p. 15, h. 36–38; Rabelais, Pantagruel, 1.2, chap. 6.

23. Chastellain, V, pp. 292ff.; La Marche, Parament et triumphe des dames, Prologue; Molinet, Faictz et dictz, Prologue, Molinet, Chronique, I, pp. 72, 10, 54.

24. Summaries by Kervyn de Lettenhove, Oeuvres de Chastellain, VII, 1. pp. 45–186; see P. Durrieu, Un barbier de nom français à Bruges, Académie des inscriptions et belles-lettres, Comptes rendus, 1917, pp. 542–58.

25. Chastellain, VII, p. 146.

26. Chastellain, VII, p. 180.

27. La Marche, I, pp. 15, 184–86; Molinet, I p. 14, III p. 99; Chastellain, VI: Exposition sur vérité mal prise, VII pp. 76, 29, 142, 422; Commines, I p. 3; see Doutrepont, p. 24.

28. Chastellain, VII, p. 159.

29. Ibid.

30. R. Gaguini, Ep. et Or., ed. Thuasne, I, p. 126; Allen, Erasmi Epistolae no. 43 I, p. 145.

31. R. Gaguini, ed. Thuasne, I, p. 20.

32. R. Gaguini, ed. Thuasne, I, p. 178, II, p. 509.

33. See F. von Bezold, Das Fortleben der antiker Götter im mittelalterlichen Humanismus, Bonn und Leipzig, 1922.

34. Deschamps, no. 63, I, p. 158.

35. Villon, Testament, vs. 899, ed. Longnon, p. 58.

36. Le pastoralet, vs. 2094.

37. Ibid., vs. 30, p. 574.

38. Molinet, V, p. 21.

39. Chastellain, Le dit de Vérité, VI, p. 221, see Exposition sur vérité mal prise, ibid., pp. 297, 310.

40. La Marche, II, p. 68.

41. Roman de la rose, vs. 20141.

BIBLIOGRAPHY

Achéry, Luc d', *Spicilegium,* nova ed., Paris, 1723, III, p. 730: *Statuts de l'ordre de l'Etoile.*

Acquoy, J. G. R., *Het klooster van Windesheim en zijn invloed,* 3 vols., Utrecht, 1875–80.

Acta Sanctorum, see Colette, François de Paule, Pierre de Luxembourg, Pierre Thomas, Vincent Ferrer.

Ailly Pierre d', *De falsis prophetis,* in Gerson, *Opera,* I, p. 538; *De Reformatione,* ibid., II, p. 911; *Tractatus I adversus cancellarium Parisiensem,* ibid., I, p. 723.

Alain de la Roche = Alanus de Rupe, Beatus Alanus redivivus, ed. J. A. Coppenstein, Naples, 1642.

Amant rendu cordelier à l'observance d'amours, L', poème attribué à Martial d'Auvergne, published by A. de Montaiglon (Société des anciens textes français), 1881.

Anitchkoff, E., *L'esthétique au moyen âge,* Le Moyen Age, vol. XX (1918), p. 221.

Baisieux, Jacques de, *Des trois chevaliers et del chainse,* Scheler, Trouvères belges, vol. I, 1876.

Basin, Thomas, *De rebus gestis Caroli VII et Ludovici XI historiarum libri XII,* ed. Quicherat, Société de l'histoire de France, 4 vols., 1855–59.

Baude, Les vers de maître Henri, ed. Quicherat, Trésors des pièces rares ou inédites, 1856.

Beatis, Antonio de, *Die Reise des Kardinals Luigi d'Aragona,* ed. L. von Pastor, Freiburg, 1905.

Becker, C. H., *Ubi sunt qui ante nos in mundo fuere,* Islamstudien I, 1924, p. 501.

Bertoni, G., *L'Orlando furioso e la rinacenza a Ferrara,* Modena, 1919.

Blois, Extraict de l'enqueste faite pour la canonization de Charles de, in André du Chesne, *Histoire de la maison de Chastillon sur Marne,* Paris, 1621, Preuves, p. 223.

Bonaventura, Saint, *Opera,* Paris, 1871.

Bonet, Honoré, *L'arbre des batailles,* Paris, Michel le Noir, 1515.

Boucicaut, Le livre des faicts du mareschal de, ed. Petitot, Collection de mémoires, VI.

Bourquelot, F., *Les Vaudois du quinzième siècle,* Bibliothèque de l'Ecole des chartes, 2nd series, III, p. 109.

Burckhardt, J, *Die Kultur der Renaissance in Italien,* 10th ed., Leipzig, 1908.

———, *Weltgeschichtliche Betrachtungen,* Berlin-Stuttgart, 1905.

Byvanck, W. G. C., *Spécimen d'un essai critique sur les oeuvres de Villon,* Leyde, 1882.

————, *Un poète inconnu de la société de François Villon,* Paris, 1891.

Carnahan, D. H., *The "Ad Deum vadit" of Jean Gerson,* University of Illinois studies in language and literature, 1917, III, no. 1.

Caroli ducis Burgundiæ, De laudibus, De Morte, etc., Chroniques relatives à l'histoire de la Belgique sous la domination des ducs de Bourgogne, ed. Kervyn de Lettenhove, vol. III, Brussels, 1873.

Cartellieri, O, *Geschichte der Herzöge von Burgund, I Philipp der Kühne,* Leipzig, 1910.

————, *Beiträge zur Geschichte der Herzöge von Burgund,* Sitzungsbericht der Heidelberger Akademie der Wissenschaften, 1911, etc.

Cent ballades, Le livre des, ed. G. Raynaud, Société des anciens textes français, 1905.

Cent nouvelles nouvelles, Les, ed. Th. Wright, Bibliothèque elzévirienne, 2 vols., Paris, 1857–58.

Champion, P, *Vie de Charles d'Orléans, 1394–1465,* Paris, 1911.

————, *François Villon, sa vie et son temps,* Bibliothèque du XVe siècle, 2 vols., Paris, 1912.

Chansons françaises du quinzième siècle, ed. G. Paris, Société des anciens textes français, 1875.

Charney, Geoffroy de, see Piaget.

Chartier, Les oeuvres de maistre Alain, ed. A. Du Chesne, Tourangeau, Paris, 1617.

Chartier, Jean, *Histoire de Charles VII,* ed. D. Godefroy, Paris, 1661.

Chastellain, Oeuvres de Georges, ed. Kervyn de Lettenhove, 8 vols., Brussels, 1863–66. Especially Chronique, vols. I–V; Le miroir des nobles hommes en France, Le dit de vérité, Exposition sur vérité mal prise, La mort du roy Charles VII, vol. VI; L'entré du roy Loys en nouveau règne, Advertissement au duc Charles, Le livre de la paix, Recollection des merveilles, La temple de Bocace, Le douze Dames de rhétorique, Le lyon rampant, Les hauts faits du duc de Bourgogne, La mort du duc Philippe, vol. VII.

Chesne, André du, *Histoire de la maison de Chastillon sur Marne,* Paris, 1621.

Chmelarz, E., *König René der Gute und die Handschrift seines Romanes "Cuer d'amours espris" in der K. K. Hofbibliothek,* Jahrbuch de Kunsthist. Sammlungen des allerh Kaiserhauses, XI, Vienna, 1890.

Chopinel, Jean. See *Roman de la rose.*

Chronique de Berne, ed. H. Moranvillé, Société de l'histoire de France, 3 vols. 1891–97.

Chronique scandaleuse. See Roye.

Clémanges, Nicolas de, *Opera,* ed. Lydius, Leyden, 1613.

Clercq, Jacques du, *Mémoires (1448–1467),* ed. de Reiffenberg, 4 vols. Brussels, 1823.

Clopinel, Jean. See *Roman de la rose.*

Colette, Sainte, *Acta Sanctorum Martii,* vol. I, 532–623.

Commines, Philippe de, *Mémoires,* ed. B. de Mandrot, Collection de textes pour servir à enseignement de l'histoire, 2 vols., 1901–3.

Complainte du povre commun et des povres laboureurs de France, La, in Monstrelet, *Chronique,* vol. VI, p. 176.

Coopland, G. W., *The Tree of Battles and Some of Its Sources*, Revue d'histoire du droit, V, 173, Haarlem, 1923.

Coquillart, G., *Oeuvres*, ed. Ch. d'Héricault, Bibliothèque elzévirienne, 2 vols., 1857.

Couderc, C., *Les comptes d'un grand couturier parisien au XVe siècle*, Bulletin de la société de l'histoire de Paris, vol. XXXVIII (1911), p. 118.

Coville, A, *Les premiers Valois et la guerre de cent ans, 1328–1422*, in Lavisse, *Histoire de France*, vol. IV, 1.

————, *Le véritable texte de la justification du duc de Bourgogne par Jean Petit*, Bibliothèque de l'Ecole des chartes, 1911, p. 57.

Débat des hérauts d'armes de France et d'Angleterre, Le, ed. L. Pannier and P. Meyer, Société des anciens textes français, 1887.

Denifle, H, *La désolation des églises, etc. en France*, 2 vols, Paris, 1897–99.

————, and Chatelain, Aemilio, *Chartularium universitatis Parisiensis*, 4+2 vols., Paris, 1889–97.

Déprez, E, *La Bataille de Najera, 3 avril 1367*, Revue historique, vol. CXXXVI (1921), p. 37.

Deschamps, Eustache, Oeuvres complètes, ed. De Queux de Saint Hilaire et G. Raynaud, Société des anciens textes français, 11 vols., 1878–1903.

Dionysius Cartusianus (or of Ryckel), *Opera omnia, cura et labore monachorum sacr. ord. Cart.*, 41 vols. Montreuil and Tournay, 1896–1913. Especially Dialogion de fide catholica, vol. 18; De quotidiano baptismate lacrimarum, vol. 29; De munificentia et beneficiis Dei, vol. 34; De laudibus sanctae et individuae trinitatis, de passione domini salvatoris dialogus, vol. 35; De mutua cognitione, De modo agendi processiones, Contra vitia superstitionum quibus circa cultum veri Dei erratur, vol. 36; De vita et regimine episcoporum, nobilium, etc., etc., vol. 37ff.; Inter Jesum et puerum dialogus, vol. 38; Directorium vitae nobilium, vol. 37; De vitiis et virtutibus, vol. 39; De contemplatione, De quattuor hominum novissimis, vol. 41.

Dixmude, Jan van, *Chronike*, ed. J. J. Lambin, Ypres, 1839.

Douet, d'Arcq, *Choix de pièces inédites relatives au règne de Charles VI*, Société de l'histoire de France, 2 vols., 1863.

Doutrepont, G., *La littérature française à la cour des ducs de Bourgogne*, Bibliothèque du XVe siècle, Paris, 1909.

Durand-Gréville, E., *Hubert et Jean Van Eyck*, Bruxelles, 1910.

Durrieu, P., *Les très-riches heures de Jean de France, duc de Berry*, Paris, 1904.

————, *Les belles heures du duc de Berry*, Gazette des beaux arts, 1906, vol. XXXV, p. 283.

————, *Un barbier de nom français à Bruges*, Comptes rendus de l'Académie des inscriptions et belles-lettres, 1917, p. 542.

————, *La miniature flamande au temps de la cour de Bourgogne (1450–1530)*, Brussels, 1921.

Eckhart, Meister, *Predigten*, ed. F. Pfeiffer, in *Deutsche Mystiker des XIV Jahrhunderts*, 2 vols., Leipzig, 1857.

Elisabeth, Saint of Hungary, Report on an Autopsy of the body of, by bishop Konrad of Hildesheim and abbot Hermann of Georgenthal, Historisches Jahrbuch der Görresgesellschaft, vol. XXVIII, p. 887.

Erasmus, Desiderius, *Opera omnia,* ed. J. Clericus, 10 vols., Leyden, 1703–6.

——, *Ratio seu methodus compendio perveniendi ad veram theologiam,* ed. Basileae, 1520.

——, *Opus epistolarum . . . denuo recognitum et auctum,* P. S. and H. M. Allen, 5 vols., Oxford 1906–24 (–1524).

——, *Colloquia,* ed. Elzevier, 1636.

Escouchy, Mathieu d', *Chronique,* ed. G. du Fresne de Beaucourt, Société de l'histoire de France, 3 vols., 1863–64.

Estienne, Henri, *Apologie pour Hérodote,* ed. Ristelhuber, 2 vols., 1879.

Facius, Bartolomæus, *De Viris illustribus liber,* ed. L. Mehus, Florence, 1745.

Fenin, Pierre de, *Mémoires,* Petitot, Collection de mémoires, VII.

Ferrer, see Vincent.

Fierens, Gevaert, *La renaissance septentrionale et les premiers maîtres des Flandres,* Brussels, 1905.

Fillastre, Guillaume, *Le premier et le second volume de la toison d'or,* Paris, Franc. Regnault, 1515–16.

François de Paule, Saint, *Acta sanctorum Aprilis,* vol. I, pp. 103–234.

Fredericq, P., *Codex documentorum sacratissimarum Indulgentiarum Neerlandicarum,* Rijks geschiedkundige Publicatiën (small series), no. 21, The Hague, 1922.

Fresne de Beaucourt, G. du, *Histoire de Charles VII,* 6 vols., Paris, 1881–91.

Froissart, Jean, *Chroniques,* ed. S. Luce et G. Raynaud, Société de l'histoire de France, 11 vols., 1869–99 (–1385).

——, *Chroniques,* ed. Kervyn de Lettenhove, 29 vols., Brussels, 1867–77.

——, *Poésies,* ed. A. Scheler, Académie royale de Belgique, 3 vols., 1870–72.

——, *Meliador,* ed. A Longnon, Société des anciens textes français, 3 vols., 1895–99.

Gaguin, Robert, *Epistolae et orationes,* ed. L. Thuasne, Bibliothèque littéraire de la Renaissance, 2 vols., Paris, 1903.

——, *Compendium super Francorum gestis,* Paris, 1500.

Gartia Dei, Oratio Antonii, ed. Kervyn de Lettenhove, *Chron. rel. à l'hist. de la Belgique sous la dom. des ducs de Bourgogne,* vol. III.

Geoffroi, de Paris, *Chronique,* ed. De Wailly et Delisle, Bouquet, Recueil des historiens, vol. XXII.

Germain, Jean, *Liber de virtutibus Philippi ducis Burgundiae,* ed. Kevyn de Lettenhove, *Chron. rel. à l'hist. de la Belgique sous la dom. des ducs de Bourgogne,* vol. II.

Gerson, Jean, *Opera omnia,* ed. L. Ellies du Pin, 2nd ed., Hagae Comitis, 1728, 5 vols. Especially vol. I, De examinatione doctrinarum, De probatione spirituum, De distinctione vera visionum a falsis, Epistola super librum Joh. Ruysbroeck, etc., Ep. contra libellum Joh. de Schonhavia, id. contra defensionem Joh. de Schonhavia, Contra vanam curiositatem, De libris caute legendis, De consolatione theologiae, Contra superstitionem praesertim Innocentum, De erroribus circa artem magicam, Compendium theologiae, De decem praeceptis, De praeceptis decaolgi, De susceptione humanitatis Christi, De falsis prophetis; vol. II, De nuptis Christi et ecclesiae, Expostulatio adv. eos qui publice volunt dogmatizare, etc., Contra impugnantes ordinem Carthusiensium; vol. III, Liber de vita spirituali animae, Regulae morales, De passionibus animae, Centilogium de impulsibus, Contra foedam tentationem blasphemiae, de parvulus ad Christum trahendis, Expostulatio adversus corruptionem juventutis per lascivas imagines, Discours de l'excellence de virginité, Oratio ad bonum angelum suum, De monte contemplationis, De vita imitativa, Considérations sur Saint Joseph, De triplici theologia, Considérations sur le péché de blasphème, Contra gulam sermo, Sermo contra luxuriem, Sermo de nativitate Domini, Sermo de natalitate b. Mariae Virginis, Sermones in die S. Ludovici, Sermo de Angelis, Sermones de defunctis, Sermo de S. Nicolao; vol. IV, Meditatio super VII^{mo} psalmo poenitentiali, Tractatus super Magnificat, Querela nomine Universitatis, Sermo coram rege Franciae, Oratio ad regem Franciae, Josephina.

Godefroy, Th., *Le cérémonial françois*, 2 vols., Paris, 1649.

Grandes chroniques de France, Les, ed. Paulin Paris, 6 vols., Paris, 1836–38

Hanotaux, G., *Jeanne d'Arc*, Paris, 1911.

Hefele, K., *Der heilige Bernhardin von Siena und die franziskanische Wanderpredigt in Italien*, Freiburg, 1912.

Hintzen, J. D., *De kruistochtplannen van Philips den Goede*, Rotterdam, 1918.

Histoire littéraire de la France, XIVe siècle, vol. XXIV, 1862.

Hoepffner, E., *Frage- und Antwortspiele in der französischen Literatur des 14 Jahrhunderts*, Zeitschrift für romanische Philologie, vol. XXXIII, 1909.

Hospinianus, R., *De templis, hoc est de origine, progressu, usu et abusu templorum, etc.*, 2nd ed., Zürich, 1603.

Houwaert, J. B., *Declaratie van die triumphante incompst van den Prince van Oraingnien, etc.*, Antwerp, Plantijn, 1579.

Huet, G., *Notes d'histoire littéraire III*, in Le Moyen Age, vol. XX, 1918.

Huizinga, J., *Uit de voorgeschiedenis van ons nationaal besef*, De Gids, 1912, vol. III.

———, *Renaissancestudiën I: Het probleem*, De Gids, 1920, vol. IV.

James, W., *The Varieties of Religious Experience*, London, 1903.

Jorga, N., *Philippe de Mézières et la croisade au XIVe siècle*, Bibliothèque de l'Ecole des hautes études, Fasc. CX, 1896.

Jouffroy, Jean, *De Philippo duce oratio*, ed. Kervyn de Lettenhove, *Chron. rel. à l'hist. de la Belgique sous la dom. des ducs de Bourgogne*, vol. III.

Journal d'un bourgeois de Paris, 1405–1449, ed. A. Tuetey, publications de la Société de l'histoire de Paris, doc. no. III, 1881.

Jouvencel, Le, ed. C. Favre et L. Lecestre, Société de l'histoire de France, 2 vols., 1887–92.

Juvenal des Ursins, Jean, *Chronique*, ed Michaud et Poujoulat, Nouvelle collection des mémoires, II.

Kempis, Thomas à, *Opera omnia*, ed. M. J. Pohl, 7 vols., Freiburg, 1902–10.

Kleinclauz, A., *Histoire de Bourgogne*, Paris, 1909.

———, *L'art funéraire de la Bourgogne à moyen âge*, Gazette des beaux arts, vol. XXVII, 1902.

———, *Un atelier de sculpture au XVe siécle*, Gazette des beaux arts, vol. XXIX, 1903.

Krogh-Tonning, K., *Der letzte scholastiker, Eine Apologie*, Freiburg, 1904.

Kurth, Betty, *Die Blütezeit der Bildwirkerkunst zu Tournay und der burgundische Hof*, Jahrbuch der Kunstsammlungen des Kaiserhauses, XXXIV, 1917.

Laborde, L. de, *Les ducs de Bourgogne, Etudes sur les lettres, les arts et l'industrie pendant le XVe siècle*, 3 vols., Paris, 1849–53.

La Curne de Sainte Palaye, J. B., *Mémoires sur l'ancienne chevalerie*, 1781.

Lalaing, *Le livre des faits du bon chevalier messire Jacques de*, ed. Kervyn de Lettenhove, *Oeuvres de Chastellain*, vol. VIII.

La Marche, Olivier de, *Mémoires*, ed. Beaune et d'Arbaumont, Société de l'histoire de France, 4 vols., 1883–88.

————, *Estat de la maison de duc Charles de Bourgogne*, ibid., vol. IV.

————, *Rationarium aulae et imperii Caroli Audacis ducis Burgundiae*, ed. A. Matthæus Analecta, I, pp. 357–494 (Middle Dutch translation of the preceding work).

————, *Le parement et triumphe des dames*, Paris, Michel le Noir, 1520.

Langlois, E., *Anciens proverbes français*, Bibliothèque de l'Ecole des chartes, vol. LX (1899), p. 569.

————, *Recueil d'arts de seconde rhétorique*, Documents inédites sur l'histoire de France, Paris, 1902.

Lannoy, Ghillebert de, Oeuvres, ed. Ch. Potvin, Louvain, 1878.

La Roche, see Alain.

La Salle, Antoine de la, *La Salade*, Paris, Michel le Noir, 1521.

————, *L'histoire et plaisante cronicque de Jehan de Saintree*, ed. G. Helleny, Paris, 1890.

————, *Le reconfort de Madame du Fresne*, ed. J. Nève, Paris, 1903.

La Tour Landry, *Le livre du chevalier de*, ed. A. de Montaiglon, Bibliothèque elzévirienne, Paris, 1854.

Lefèvre de Saint Remy, Jean, *Chronique*, ed. F. Morand, Société de l'histoire de France, 2 vols., 1876.

Leroux, de Lincy, A., *Le livre des proverbes français*, 2nd ed., 2 vols., Paris, 1859.

Liber Karoleidos, ed. Kervyn de Lettenhove, *Chron. rel. à l'hist. de la Belgique sous la dom. des ducs de Bourgogne,*, vol. III.

Livre des trahisons, Le, ed. id., ibid., vol. II.

Loër, Theodericus, *Vita Dionysii Cartusiani*, in Dionysii, Opera, I, p. xlii.

Lorris, Guillaume de, see *Roman de la rose*.

Louis XI, lettres de, ed. Vaesen, Charavay, de Mandrot, Société de l'histoire de France, 11 vols., 1883–1909.

Luce, S., *La France pendant la guerre de cent ans*, Paris, 1890.

Luther, Martin, *De captivate babylonica ecclesiae praeludium*, Werke, Weimar edition, vol. VI.

Luxembourg, see Pierre.

Machaut, Guillaume de, *Le livre du voir-dit*, ed. Paulin Paris, Société des bibliophiles françois, 1875.

————, *Oeuvres*, ed E. Hoepffner, Société des anciens textes français, 2 vols., 1908–11.

————, *Poésies lyriques*, ed. V. Chichmaref, Zapiski istoritcheski fil. fakulteta imp. S. Peterb. univers., vol. XCII, 1909.

Magnien, Ch., *Caxton à la cour de Charles le Téméraire*, Annuaire de la société d'archéologie de Bruxelles, vol. XXIII, 1912.

Maillard, Olivier, *Sermones dominicales, etc.*, Paris, Jean Petit, 1515.

Mâle, E., *L'art religieux du treizième siècle en France*, Paris, 1902.

——, *L'art religieux à la fin du moyen-âge en France*, Paris, 1908.

Mangeart, J., *Catalog des manuscrits de la bibliothèque de Valenciennes*, 1860.

Martial (d'Auvergne), *Les poésies de Martial de Paris dit d'Auvergne*, 2 vols, Paris, 1724. See *Amant rendu . . .*

Meschinot, Jean, *sa vie et ses œuvres*, par A. de la Borderie, Bibliothèque de l'Ecole des chartes, vol. LVI, 1895.

Meyer, P., *Les neuf preux*, Bulletin de la société des anciens textes français, 1883, p. 45.

Michault, Pierre, *La dance aux aveugles et autres poésies du XVe siécle*, Lille, 1748.

Michel, André, *Histoire de l'art*, vols. III and IV, Paris, 1907, etc.

Molinet, Jean, *Chronique*, ed. J. Buchon, Collection de chroniques nationales, 5 vols., 1827–28.

——, *Les faicts et dictz de messire Jehan*, Paris, Jehan Petit, 1537.

Molinier, A., *Les sources de l'histoire de France, des origines aux guerres d'Italie* (1494), 6 vols., Paris, 1901–6.

Moll, W. *Kerkgeschiedinis van Nederland vóór de hervorming*, 5 parts, Utrecht, 1864–69.

——, *Johannes Brugman en het godsdienstig leven onzer vaderen in de vijftien eeuw*, 2 vols., Amsterdam, 1854.

Monstrelet, Enguerrand de, *Chroniques*, ed. Douet d'Arcq, Société de l'histoire de France, 6 vols., 1857–62.

Montreuil, Jean de, *Epistolae*, ed. Martène et Durand, Amplissima collectio, II col., 1398.

Mougel, D. A., *Denys le Chartreux, sa vie, etc.*, Montreuil, 1896.

Nys, E. *Le droit de guerre et les précurseurs de Grotius*, Brussels and Leipzig, 1882.

——, *Etudes de droit international et de droit politique*, Brussels and Paris, 1896.

Ordonnances des rois de France, Paris, 1723–77.

Orléans, Charles d', *Poésies complètes*, 2 vols., Paris, 1874.

Oulmont, Ch., *Le verger, le temple et la cellule, Essai sur la sensualité dans les oeuvres de mystique religieuse*, Paris, 1912.

Pannier, L., *Les joyaux du duc de Guyenne, recherches sur les goûts artistiques et la vie privée du dauphin Louis*, Revue archéologique, 1873.

Pastoralet, Le, ed. Kervyn de Lettenhove, *Chron. rel. à l'hist. de la Belgique sous la dom. des ducs de Bourgogne*, vol. II.

Pauli, Theodericus, *De rebus actis sub ducibus Burgundiae compendium*, ed. id., ibid., vol. III.

Petit Dutaillis, Ch., *Charles VII, Louis XI et les premières années de Charles VIII (1422–1492)*, in Lavisse, *Histoire de France*, vol. IV, part 2.

——, *Documents nouveaux sur les moeurs populaires et le droit de vengeance dans les Pays-bas au XVe siècle*, Bibliothèque de XVe siècle, Paris, 1908.

Petrarca, Francesco, *Opera*, Basle edition, 1581.

Piaget, A., *Oton de Granson et ses poésies*, Romania, vol. XIX, 1890.

——, *Chronologie des épistres sur le Roman de la rose*, Etudes romanes dédiées à Gaston Paris, 1891, p. 113.

——, *La cour amoureuse dite de Charles VI*, Romania, vol. XX, 1891; XXI, 1892.

——, *Le livre messire Geoffroy de Charney*, Romania, vol. XXVI, 1897.

——, *Le chapel des fleurs de lis, par Philippe de Vitri*, Romania, vol. XXVII, 1898.

448   BIBLIOGRAPHY

Pierre de Luxembourg, the Blessed, *Acta sanctorum Julii*, vol. I, pp. 509–628.

Pierre Thomas, Carmelite Saint, *Acta sanctorum Januarii*, vol. II (his life by Philippe de Mézières).

Pirenne, H., *Histoire de Belgique*, 5 vols., Brussels, 1902–21.

Pisan, Christine de, Oeuvres poétiques, ed. M. Roy, Société des anciens textes français, 3 vols., 1886–96.

———, *Epitre d'Othéa à Hector*, Manuscrit 9392, de Jean Miélot, ed. J. van den Gheyn, Brussels, 1913.

Poésies françoises des XVe et XVIe siècles, Recueil de, ed. A. de Montaiglon, Bibliothèque elzévirienne, Paris, 1856.

Polydorus Vergilius, *Anglicae historiae libri XXVI*, Basle, 1546.

Pool, J. C., *Frederik van Heilo en zijne schriften*, Amsterdam, 1866.

Portiers, Aliénor de, *Les honneurs de la cour*, ed. La Curne de Sainte Palaye, *Mémoires sur l'ancienne chevalerie*, 1781, II.

Quinze joyes de mariage, Les, Paris, Marpon et Flammarion, no date.

Ramsay, J. H., *Lancaster and York, 1399–1485*, 2 vols., Oxford, 1892.

Raynaldus, *Annales ecclesiastici*, vol. III (= Baronius, vol. XXII).

Raynaud, G., *Rondeaux, etc., du XVe siècle*, Société des anciens textes français, 1889.

Religieux de Saint Denis, Chronique du, ed. Bellaguet, Collection des documents inédits, 6 vols., 1839–52.

Renaudet, A., *Préréforme et humanisme à Paris, 1494–1517*, Paris, 1916.

René, Oeuvres du roi, ed. Quatrebarbes, 4 vols., Angers, 1845.

Roman de la rose, Le, ed. M. Méon, 4 vols., Paris, 1814.

———, ed. F. Michel, 2 vols., Paris, 1864.

———, ed. E. Langlois, Société des anciens textes français, 1914, I.

Rousselot, P., *Pour l'histoire du problème de l'amour*, Beiträge zur Geschichte der Philosophie im Mittelalter, ed. Bäumker and von Hertling, vol. VI, 1908.

Roye, Jean de, *Journal dite Chronique scandaleuse*, ed. B. de Mandrot, Société de l'histoire de France, 2 vols., 1894–96.

Rozmital, Leo von, *Reise durch die Abendlände, 1465–1467*, ed. Schmeller, Bibliothek des literarischen Verins zu Stuttgart, vol. VII, 1844.

Ruelens, Ch., *Recueil de chansons, poèmes, etc. relatifs aux Pays-Bas*, 1878.

Ruusbroec, Johannes, *Werken*, ed. David and Snellaert, Maetschappij der Vlaemsche bibliophilen, 1860–68. Especially II, Die chierheit de gheesteleker brulocht, Spieghel de ewigher salicheit; IV, Van seven trappen in den graet der gheestelicker minnen, Boec van der hoechster waerheit, Dat boec van seven sloten, Dat boec van den rike der ghelieven.

Ruysbroeck l'Admirable, Oeuvres de, Translation from the Flemish by the Bénédictines de Saint Paul de Wisques, vols. I–III, Brussels and Paris, 1917–20.

Salmon, Pierre le Fruictier dit, *Mémoires*, ed. Buchon, Collection de chroniques nationales 3e supplément de Froissart, vol. XV.

Schäfer, D. *Mittlealterliche Brauch bei der Ueberführung von Leichen*, Sitzungsberichte der preussichen Akademie der Wissenschaften, 1920, p. 478.

Schmidt, C., *Der Prediger Olivier Maillard*, Zeitschrift für historische Theologie, 1856.

Seuse, Heinrich (Suso), *Deutsche Schriften*, ed. K. Bihlmeyer, Stuttgart, 1907.

Sicard, *Mitrale sive de officiis ecclesiasticis summa,* Migne, Patr. lat., vol. CCXIII.

Stavelot, Jean de, *Chronique,* ed. Borgnet, Collection des chroniques belges, Brussels, 1861.

Stein, H., *Etude sur Olivier de la Marche,* Mémoires couronnés de l'Academie royale de Belgique, vol. XLIX, 1888.

Tauler, Johannes, *Predigten,* in Vetter, Deutsche Texte des Mittelalters, vol. XI, Berlin, 1910.

Thomas Aquinas, Saint, *Historia transltionis corporis sanctissimi ecclesiæ doctoris divi Th. de Aq. 1368,* auct. fr. Raymundo Hugonis O. P., Acta sanctorum Martii, vol. I, p. 725.

Thomas, see Pierre.

Trahisons, see *Livre des.*

Upton, Nicolas, *De officio militari,* ed. E. Bysshe, London, 1654.

Valois, Noël, *La France et le grand schisme d'occident,* 4 vols., Paris, 1896–1902.

Varennes, Jean de, *Responsiones ad capitula accusationum, etc.,* in Gerson, Opera, I, pp. 906–43.

Vigneulles, Philippe de, *Mémoires,* ed. H. Michelant, Bibliothek des lit. Verins zu Stuttgart, vol. XXIV, 1852.

Villon, François, *Oeuvres,* ed. A. Longnon, Les classiques français du moyen âge, vol. II, Paris, 1914.

Vincent Ferrer, Saint, *Vita,* auct. Petro Ranzano O. P., 1455, Acta sanctorum Aprilis, vol. I, pp. 82–512.

——, *Sermones quadragesimales,* Cologne, 1482.

Vitri, Philippe de, *Le chapel des fleurs de lis,* ed. A. Piaget, Romania, vol. XXVII, 1898.

Voeux du héron, Les, ed. Société des bibliophiles de Mons, no. 8, 1839.

Walsingham, Thomas, *Historia Anglicana,* ed. H. T. Riley, in *Rer brit. medii aevi scriptores* (Rolls series), 3 vols., London, 1864.

Weale, W. H. J., *Hubert and John van Eyck, their Life and Work,* London and New York, 1908.

Wielant, Philippe, *Antiquites de Flandre,* ed. De Smet, Corpus chronicorum Flandriae, vol. IV.

Wright, Th., *The Anglo-Latin Satirical Poets and Epigrammatists of the Twelfth Century,* in *Rerum britannicarum medii aevi scriptores* (Rolls series), 2 vols., London, 1872.

Zöckler, O., *Dionys des Kartäusers Schrift De venustate mundi, Beitrag zur vorgeschichte der Asthetick,* Theologische Studien und Kritiken, 1881.

INDEX